Mental Health Economics

Denise Razzouk
Editor

Mental Health Economics

The Costs and Benefits of Psychiatric Care

Springer

Editor
Denise Razzouk
Centre of Economic Mental Health
Department of Psychiatry
Universidade Federal de São Paulo
São Paulo, Brazil

ISBN 978-3-319-55265-1 ISBN 978-3-319-55266-8 (eBook)
DOI 10.1007/978-3-319-55266-8

Library of Congress Control Number: 2017940271

Printed on acid-free paper

This Springer imprint is published by Springer Nature
The registered company is Springer International Publishing AG
The registered company address is: Gewerbestrasse 11, 6330 Cham, Switzerland

Foreword

Mental disorders represent a huge burden and high costs to society, affecting all aspects of a nation's development, causing intangible suffering to many people, and hindering humankind's well-being. Notwithstanding this obvious reality, investments in preventing and treating mental disorders are still scarce and disproportionate to their deleterious consequences.

Over the past decade, stakeholders from multiple international organizations such as the World Health Organization, the World Bank, the United Nations, the Organisation for Economic Co-operation and Development, and the Lancet Commission on Investing in Health have been warning about the need for efficient use of resources to tackle mental disorders, developing global policies aligned with 17 goals of sustainable development. Regarding this scenario, the discipline of Health Economics brings a valuable body of knowledge to help create mental health policies that optimize the use of scarce resources to maximize the promotion of mental health and well-being in society and to decrease negative externalities caused by mental disorders.

However, health economists are rare or nonexistent in the majority of low- and middle-income countries, which need even more optimization of scarce resources than high-income countries. Despite the growing popularity of terms such as *cost-effectiveness*, *cost-benefit*, *disability-adjusted life-year*, and *quality-adjusted life-year* in global health policy agenda, a remarkable gap exists between the need for efficient allocation of resources and the number of economic evaluations produced in academic research in such countries. A growing willingness has been observed among researchers to add an economic component to their mental health studies, though many non–economist researchers are significantly ignorant of the principles of health economics and relevant research methods. Moreover, the available literature in Health Economics is written using specific jargon and complex mathematical formulas that are not easily understood by mental health researchers and non–health economists.

In this regard, this book has the goal of reducing this gap between the Health Economics and Mental Health disciplines, allowing mental health researchers and non–health economists to acquire knowledge of the basic principles of health economics and to be able to apply this knowledge in their research in a local context or in collaboration with other research centers. It is a paramount that low- and middle-income countries produce national health economics data to guide health policies based on real scenarios and cultural values. Moreover, the spread of health economics principles may help establish partnerships with health economics centers around the world.

Therefore, our goal is not to produce yet another book of deep technical knowledge on Health Economics, but rather to invite health economists, mental health professionals, and other researchers to discuss the advantages and limits of Health Economics as they apply to mental health disciplines. We acknowledge that the basic methods and principles of health economics are similar for the health field, but mental health has additional demands and obstacles that require more discussion on specific issues.

We divided this book into four main sections. The first is related to methodological aspects and theoretical principals of Health Economics, the second focuses on studies of determining costs of mental health services, the third section provides a methodological overview of cost-effectiveness studies in Mental Health, and the last section raises the main issues related to the economic and social burdens of mental disorders to be addressed by mental health policies.

It is our great pleasure and honor to develop this book in partnership with the most outstanding health economics centers in the world and with our amazing colleagues from Psychiatry and other mental health disciplines. Therefore, this book has been written by contributors with diverse professional backgrounds and different perspectives, who are willing to show multiple views of Health Economics and discuss their application in Mental Health research.

Denise Razzouk

Acknowledgements

I express my deepest gratitude to all authors involved in the preparation of this book. The idea for this book emerged from observing my graduate students' motivation in applying concepts of health economics in mental health during the annual course I coordinate on Mental Health Economics in the Department of Psychiatry at the Universidade Federal de São Paulo in Brazil. The vast available literature is challenging for junior researchers to absorb and to understand, and this book is dedicated to all my students. I thank all my students for triggering my motivation for organizing this book.

I thank my volunteer team in the Centro de Economia em Saúde Mental (CESM) in the Department of Psychiatry for participating in all steps of the creation of this book. We have been working to disseminate health economics principles in an academic setting and among health managers and policymakers. Our ultimate goal is to see effective investments in high-quality mental health services covering access to cost-effective and evidence-based treatment for all people and families burdened by mental illness. Also, ambitiously, we dream of a more inclusive society whereby citizens' mental health is the most worthwhile value to be pursued.

As a psychiatrist, I must admit that my perspective about psychiatry and mental health policy has been completely changed by learning about health economics principles and global health policy with amazing experts—including Martin Knapp, Graham Thornicroft, Renee Romeo, Anita Patel, David McDaid, and Paul McCrone—while I was doing my postdoctoral fellowship, sponsored Brazilian Agency Funding (CAPES), at the Institute of Psychiatry in King's College, London.

Denise Razzouk

Contents

Contributors

Paula Becker Centre of Economic Mental Health (CESM), Department of Psychiatry, Universidade Federal de Sao Paulo, São Paulo, Brazil

Vladislav Berdunov Centre for Primary Care and Public Health, Blizard Institute, Queen Mary University of London, London, UK

Bernard van den Berg Faculty of Economics and Business, University of Groningen, Groningen, The Netherlands

Mary Lou Chatterton Deakin Health Economics, Centre for Population Health Research, School of Health and Social Development, Deakin University, Melbourne, VIC, Australia

Joanna Coast Health Economics at Bristol, School of Social and Community Medicine, University of Bristol, Bristol, UK

The National Institute for Health Research Collaboration for Leadership in Applied Health Research and Care West (NIHR CLAHRC West), University Hospitals Bristol NHS Foundation Trust, Bristol, UK

Michaela Coenen Department of Medical Informatics, Biometry and Epidemiology – IBE, Chair for Public Health and Health Services Research, Research Unit for Biopsychosocial Health, Ludwig-Maximilians-Universität, Munich, Germany

Mírian Cohen Institute for Health Technology Assessment (IATS/CNPq), Porto Alegre, Brazil

Health Department of Rio Grande do Sul State, Hospital Psiquiátrico São Pedro, Porto Alegre, Brazil

Luciane Cruz Hospital Moinhos de Vento, Porto Alegre, Brazil

Institute for Health Technology Assessment (IATS/CNPq), Porto Alegre, Brazil

Ana Flávia Barros da Silva Lima Institute for Health Technology Assessment (IATS/CNPq), Porto Alegre, Brazil

Sandro René Pinto de Sousa Miguel Hospital Moinhos de Vento, Porto Alegre, Brazil

Institute for Health Technology Assessment (IATS/CNPq), Porto Alegre, Brazil

Rita Faria Centre for Health Economics, University of York, York, UK

Matthew Franklin HEDS, School of Health and Related Research (ScHARR), University of Sheffield, Sheffield, UK

Ilias Goranitis Health Economics Unit, Institute of Applied Health Research, University of Birmingham, Birmingham, UK

Wolter Hassink Utrecht University School of Economics, Utrecht University, Utrecht, The Netherlands

Catherine Henderson Personal Social Services Research Unit (PSSRU), London School of Economics and Political Science, London, UK

Ivana Ivandic Institute for Public Health and Health Services Research, Department of Medical Informatics, Biometry and Epidemiology (IBE), Ludwig-Maximilians-University, Munich, Germany

Monica Kayo Centre of Economic Mental Health, Department of Psychiatry, Universidade Federal de Sao Paulo, São Paulo, Brazil

Helen Killaspy Division of Psychiatry, University College London, London, UK

Martin Knapp PSSRU, London School of Economics and Political Science, London, UK

Jeroen Luyten Department of Social Policy, London School of Economics and Political Science, London, UK

Leuven Institute for Healthcare Policy, KULeuven, Leuven, Belgium

Paul McCrone King's Health Economics, Health Service and Population Research Department, Institute of Psychiatry, Psychology & Neuroscience, King's College London, London, UK

David McDaid Personal Social Services Research Unit, London School of Economics and Political Science, London, UK

Cathrine Mihalopoulos Deakin Health Economics, Centre for Population Health Research, School of Health and Social Development, Deakin University, Melbourne, VIC, Australia

Marta Miret Department of Psychiatry, Universidad Autónoma de Madrid, Madrid, Spain

Instituto de Salud Carlos III, Centro de Investigación Biomédica en Red de Salud Mental, Madrid, Spain

Department of Psychiatry, Hospital Universitario la Princesa, Instituto de Investigación Sanitaria Princesa (IIS-Princesa], Madrid, Spain

Paul Mitchell Health Economics at Bristol, School of Social and Community Medicine, University of Bristol, Bristol, UK

The National Institute for Health Research Collaboration for Leadership in Applied Health Research and Care West (NIHR CLAHRC West), University Hospitals Bristol NHS Foundation Trust, Bristol, UK

The UK Renal Registry, Southmead Hospital, Bristol, UK

Edilaine Moraes Alcohol and Other Drugs Research Unit, Universidade Federal de São Paulo (UNIAD/UNIFESP), São Paulo, Brazil

Anita Patel Barts and The London School of Medicine and Dentistry, Blizard Institute, Centre for Primary Care and Public Health, Queen Mary University of London, London, UK

Marcelo Pinheiro Department of Social and Legal Sciences, Fundação Getulio Vargas, São Paulo, Brazil

Denise Razzouk Centre of Economic Mental Health, Department of Psychiatry, Universidade Federal de Sao Paulo, São Paulo, Brazil

Renee Romeo King's Health Economics, Health Service and Population Research Department, Institute of Psychiatry, Psychology & Neuroscience, King's College London, London, UK

Carla Sabariego Department of Medical Informatics, Biometry and Epidemiology – IBE, Chair for Public Health and Health Services Research, Research Unit for Biopsychosocial Health, Ludwig-Maximilians-Universität, Munich, Germany

Alessandra Brisola Siomi Centre of Economic Mental Health (CESM), Department of Psychiatry, Universidade Federal de Sao Paulo, São Paulo, Brazil

Aglae Sousa Centre of Economic Mental Health, Department of Psychiatry, Universidade Federal de Sao Paulo, São Paulo, Brazil

Graham Thornicroft Centre for Global Mental Health, Health Service and Population Research Department, Institute of Psychiatry, Psychology & Neuroscience, King's College London, London, UK

Dominic Trépel Global Brain Health Institute (GBHI), Trinity College Dublin, Dublin, Ireland

The Irish Longitudinal Study on Ageing (TILDA), Trinity College Dublin, Dublin, Ireland

Helen Weatherly Centre for Health Economics, University of York, York, UK

Jacques José Zimmermann Institute for Health Technology Assessment (IATS/CNPq), Porto Alegre, Brazil

Abbreviations

ABC method	Active-based costing method
ACER	Average cost-effectiveness ratio
AChEI	Acetylcholinesterase inhibitor
ACT	Assertive community treatment
ANOVA	Analysis of variance
AOT	Assisted outpatient treatment
ASCOT	Adult social care outcomes toolkit
ASI	Addiction Severity Index
AIC	Akaike's information criterion
AUC	Area under the curve
BIC	Bayesian information criterion
BRL	Real Brazilian currency
CAPS	Center of Psychosocial Care
CASUS	Child and adolescence service use schedule
CATIE	Clinical antipsychotic trials of intervention effectiveness
CBA	Cost-benefit analysis
CBT	Cognitive behavioral therapy
CCA	Cost-consequences analysis
CEA	Cost-effectiveness analysis
CEAC	Cost-effectiveness acceptability curve
CGI	Clinical global impression
CHEERS	Consolidated health economics evaluation reporting standards
CHOICE	Choosing Interventions that are Cost-Effective
CI	Confidence interval
CIDI	Composite international diagnostic interview
CMA	Cost-minimization analysis
CODA	Cost of discrimination assessment
CORE-6D	Clinical Outcomes in Routine Evaluation-Six Dimensions
CQRoL	Caregiver-related quality of life
CRA	Comparative risk assessment
CSSRI	Client Sociodemographic and Service Receipt Inventory
CUA	Cost-utility analysis
CUtLASS	Cost Utility of the Latest Antipsychotic Drugs in Schizophrenia Study
DALY	Disability-adjusted life year
DES	Discrete event simulation model

DIRUM	Database of Instruments for Resource Use Measurement
DISC	Discrimination and Stigma Scale
DRG	Diagnosis-related group
DSA	Deterministic sensitivity analysis
DSM	*Diagnostic and Statistical Manual of Mental Disorders*
EAA	Equivalent annual annuity
EAP	Employee assistance program
ECT	Electroconvulsive therapy
EE	Economic evaluation
EMA	European Medicines Agency
EMERALD	Emerging mental health systems in low- and middle-income countries
EPDS	Edinburgh Postnatal Depression Scale
EPSILON	European Psychiatric Services: Inputs Linked to Outcome Domains and Needs
EQ-5D	EuroQol–Five Dimensions
EVSI	Expected value of sample of information
FC	Fixed costs
FDA	U.S. Food and Drug Administration
FGA	First-generation antipsychotics
GAD	Generalised anxiety disorder
GBD	Global burden of diseases
GDP	Gross domestic product
GDS	Reisberg Global Deterioration Scale
GLM	Generalised linear model
GNI	Gross national income
HADS	Hospital Anxiety and Depression Scale
HAMD	Hamilton Rating Scale for Depression
HE	Health Economics
HONOS	Health of the Nation Outcome Scales
HRQoL	Health-related quality of life
HTA	Health technology assessment
ICER	Incremental cost-effectiveness ratio
ILO	International Labour Organization
ISDUCS	Brazilian version of CSSRI
ISPOR	International Society for Pharmaeconomics and Outcomes Research
ISSR	Inhibitor of selective serotonin reuptake
LAMICs	Low- and middle-income countries
LCHD	Life course health development
MADRS	Montgomery Asberg Depression Rating Scale
MAE	Mean absolute error
MANSA	Manchester Short Assessment of Quality of Life
MAR	Missing at random
MCAR	Missing completely at random
MCER	Marginal cost-effectiveness ratio
MDD	Major depressive disorder
ME	Magnitude estimation method

MHFA	Mental health first aid
MI	Motivational interviewing
MICE	Multiple imputation using chained equations
MIG	Motivational interview group
MNAR	Missing not at random
NCD	Noncommunicable diseases
NGO	Nongovernmental organization
NHS	National Health Service (Britain)
NICE	National Institute for Health and Care Excellence
NMDA	N-methyl-D-aspartate
OLS	Ordinary least squares
PANSS	Positive and Negative Syndrome Scale
PBMA	Program budgeting and marginal analsysis
PORT	Patient outcomes research team
PRIMA-EF	European Framework for Psychosocial Risk Management
PROGRES	*Progetto Residenze*, or Residential Project
PROM	Patient-reported outcome measure
PSA	Probabilistic sensitivity analysis
QALY	Quality-adjusted life year
QuIRC	Quality indicator for rehabilitative care
RESET	Ramsay regression equation specification error test
RTW	Return to work
SD	Standard deviation
SDG	Sustainable development goal
SE	Standard error
SG	Standard gamble
SGA	Second-generation antipsychotic
SLR	Supported living residences
SNRI	Serotonin-norepinephrine reuptake inhibitor
SSRI	Selective serotonin reuptake inhibitor
STM	State transition model
TAU	Treatment as usual
TC	Total cost
TCA	Tricyclic antidepressant
TTC	Time to change
TTO	Time trade-off
UN	United Nations
VAS	Visual analogue scale
VC	Variable cost
VOSL	Value of statistical life
WHO	World Health Organization
WHO-CHOICE	Choosing interventions that are cost effective
WHOQOL	World Health Organization Quality of Life Scale
WMH	World Mental Health Survey
WTA	Willingness to accept
WTP	Willingness to pay
YFC	Years of full capability equivalent
YLD	Years lost due to disability
YLL	Years of life lost

List of Figures

Part I

Introduction of Health Economics Applied to Mental Health

Introduction to Mental Health Economics

1

Denise Razzouk

Abstract

Health Economics (HE) emerged in healthcare in the 1950s but was only applied in Mental Health mainly after the 1990s. One of the reasons for such a delay was the previous approach to psychiatric care based exclusively in hospitals. With the shift from a hospital to community care model, and with the availability of new, expensive treatments and a growing demand for treatment, HE became a powerful tool to guide mental health policies and to assess the costs and benefits of mental health interventions. HE has its origins on the principles of the welfare theory, which aims to maximize welfare (well-being and happiness) underpinned by a cost-benefit analysis. Because methodologies measure health in monetary units, the health sector adapted economic principles to an extra-welfarist approach through cost-effectiveness and cost-utility analyses in order to maximize health outcomes and guide public health resource allocation. In this chapter we present the main concepts of HE and how economic principles can be applied in mental health care. Economic evaluation is the most important method to verify benefits over costs, demonstrating which of several alternatives is the best value for the money. Regarding some peculiarities of mental health care, this chapter raises some challenging issues of applying HE methods and how the social and economic burden of mental disorders exert influence on the type of economic evaluation chosen.

D. Razzouk (✉)
Centre of Economic Mental Health, Department of Psychiatry, Universidade Federal de Sao Paulo, Rua Borges Lagoa 570 1, andar Vila Clementino, São Paulo 04038-000, Brazil
e-mail: drazzouk@gmail.com

D. Razzouk (ed.), *Mental Health Economics*, DOI 10.1007/978-3-319-55266-8_1

Key Points Summary

- The birth of Health Economics
- The Welfare Theory: from Utilitarianism to the Neoclassic economics period
- Neoclassic economics and Pareto's efficiency concept
- Cost analysis and economic evaluation
- Health Economics applied to mental health

1.1 Introduction to Mental Health Economics

Mental Health encompasses multiple disciplines such as Psychiatry, Psychology, Occupational Therapy, and other related disciplines. This book focuses on the economics of the most burdensome mental disorders and some mental health problems related to social and economic risk factors. Mental disorders place a huge economic burden on society, and in this regard Health Economics (HE) offers valuable knowledge for evaluating whether scarce resources are efficiently applied to obtain the best results. Almost three decades from the Global Burden of Disease study in the 1990s [1], stakeholders, researchers, and policymakers have been discussing the need for increased investments in mental health care worldwide. There is now a consensus that mental disorders are one of the leading causes affecting well-being and productivity, ultimately hindering the potential of a nation's mental capital [2]. Mental health has recently been included as a priority in the agenda for the 17 sustainable development goals [3]. Therefore, it is time to discuss how scarce resources will be applied in mental healthcare. This book aims to present Health Economics principles for professionals involved in mental health research and mental health policy.

HE has been applied to healthcare for more than five decades; although some studies of HE and Mental Health were published between the 1960s and 1980s, the growing interest in applying HE principles in Mental Health was mostly noticed after the 1990s [4]. Among the reasons for the delay in incorporating economic components in Mental Health are seven important factors [5, 6]:

- Mental health care was delivered exclusively in psychiatric hospitals in the 1950s and 1960s, and budgets were specifically allocated for it.
- During that period, few treatments were available.
- In general, people did not have information about mental disorders or about the existence of efficacious treatment for them, leading to a low demand for treatment.
- Research in psychiatry suffered limitations until the development of standardized instruments and diagnostic systems, mainly in the 1980s.
- The growing burden of mental disorders was initially brought to light by the World Health Organization in the 1990s [7] (see Chap. 25).
- The shift of mental healthcare from a hospital-based model to a community healthcare model increased coverage and the availability of services and interventions, though the costs of services also increased [8] (see Chap. 15).
- New medications, most more expensive than older ones, emerged especially after the 1990s.

Despite the growing number of economics studies in Psychiatry and Mental Health, some peculiarities in this domain challenge the application of HE principles. In this chapter we present the main concepts of HE and discuss how these principles might be applied in Psychiatry and Mental Health. Also, we discuss the main methodological challenges and consequences of using economic analysis in these areas.

1.2 The Birth of Health Economics

The context in which HE emerged as a discipline in the 1950s was characterized by two factors, according to Selma Mushkin [9]: the first was the development of new medicines for infectious diseases, which led to lowering mortality rates; the second factor was the increased life expectancy caused by improved treatments. These two factors influenced the costs of health care because more people became eligible to benefit from the new treatments, resulting in greater demand for health services and consequently increasing the costs of health services.

Therefore, HE initially emerged in the United States as a tool to help health managers and the government deal with the growing demand for health services. Faced with this challenge, bioethics and economics domains also raised two other issues: the former focused the discussion on the moral right of people to have access to healthcare, and the latter focused on the efficiency of the allocation and distribution of resources to provide healthcare for those in need [10]. Yet, during this period, economists tried to demonstrate the importance of investing in health as one crucial factor to increase human productivity in the workplace [11] and to provide benefits to the whole of society.

After World War II, the growing development of decision-making theories led to the adoption of rational theory choice based on scientific principles to formulate health policy, allocate resources, and provide equity in healthcare [12].

In summary, the scarcity of resources to supply the growing needs and demands of the people, added to the increased life expectancy and the exponential increase in health costs, allowed HE to flourish, moving toward improving healthcare efficiency through rational resource allocation. HE is not aimed at reducing costs, but to optimizing costs and benefits to achieve the best value for money [13]. As Knapp [14] states, "The difference between economic and other evaluations is the meaning attached to the term worthwhile."

1.2.1 Economic Concepts and Principles of Health Economics

Economics is a social science aimed at analyzing societal values, preferences, and choices as they relate to the production of goods and services and, ultimately, to the best use of societal resources to maximize benefits and welfare. In other words, the economic perspective focuses on how society decides to produce, use, and distribute its resources toward meeting its goals for the greatest number of people [15, 16].

Multiple economic schools of thought exist, but it is beyond the scope of this chapter to present them all; instead, we present some concepts that originated from the classic era of economics, in the eighteenth century, because they provide some understanding on the concepts used in neoclassic economics, which mainly emerged in the twentieth century and substantially influenced the HE framework.

HE has been defined as a branch of economics, and its framework is embedded in welfare theory; that is, the resources produced by the society are always scarce and they should be used efficiently to maximize benefits [10] (see Chaps. 4 and 10).

1.2.2 Welfare Theory

Welfare economics addresses social welfare, which is sometimes understood as well-being, and this framework is the basis for some public health policies and decisions regarding how to allocate resources to produce the maximum social welfare [17]. In other words, *welfare* means adopting efficient strategies to satisfy all societal objectives [18].

The welfare theory has been affected by different influences over time since the classical period of economics [17]. Of interest in this book are two main influences: one is "old welfare economics," influenced by utilitarianism, which focused on maximizing pleasure/happiness; the second is the new welfare economics, which was influenced by neoclassical economics and focused on maximizing social welfare through efficient allocation of resources under Pareto's rules. Overall, the principle of this theory entails the following concepts: *scarcity of resources, opportunity costs, utility, maximization of welfare*, and *efficiency*.

1.2.2.1 Scarcity of Resources

From an economic perspective, resources are *always* scarce because the demand ("wishes" and "wants") to achieve a benefit (good or service) is always greater than the resources to supply it [16]. Once resources are always *scarce*, society is obliged to make a rational decision (choice) on how to use the resources to achieve the *maximum benefits*.

1.2.2.2 Opportunity Costs

Each choice implies a gain of one benefit and a loss of the forgone benefit. Therefore, every decision has an *opportunity cost*, which includes the value of the benefit not chosen and the costs associated with losing it. This term was introduced in 1914 by the economist Friedrich Freiherr von Wieser in order to affirm that the costs of one good or service would not correspond only to the production costs of goods and services, as was the dominant view at that time. Instead of cost production, the opportunity costs would be directly linked to the buyers (demand) and how they would choose to pay for one good over another according to their preferences [19].

The concept of opportunity costs is crucial for economic analysis and decision making because resource allocation has direct consequences on people's lives and health (see Chaps. 8, 9, and 10). It is important to bear in mind that, in healthcare, any resource allocation favoring one group with one specific disease would not be addressed for another group with another disease yet similarly in need. Cost is the value of a benefit, or how worthwhile it is. Hence, the cost of not treating conditions (and not promoting health gains) among the latter group corresponds to opportunity costs.

Another example of an opportunity cost is the time spent by families in caring for a family member with dementia. The family could spend its time in leisure or working instead of caring for the patient; in this case, the "value" of time spent caring for the family member (informal care) corresponds to opportunity costs (see Chap. 17).

1.2.2.3 Utility

Utility is an concept that was initially used in Jeremy Bentham's *utilitarianism theory* to define the amount of pleasure or satisfaction one individual obtains when making a rational choice between two or more alternatives (for example, buying goods or services) [20, 21] (see Box 1.1). The assumption with this choice is that individuals prefer "things" that bring them "more happiness and pleasure" over those that cause pain.

Hence, from an utilitarian perspective, consumers know which utility is best for them, and individuals' choices thereby reveal individual preferences, in that people express their preferences through their actions (choosing something in particular, for example) [22]. Consequently, it would be possible to quantify and compare utilities by verifying individual preferences and choices. In this case, *utility* was defined as a cardinal variable, and the value of pleasure given to each choice would be verified based on its intensity, duration, uncertainty, and propinquity [22, 23]. Considering the health domain, utility corresponds to an individual's preference for one desired health outcome.

Box 1.1 Utilitarianism Principles: Jeremy Bentham

- Each individual knows what is best for him/herself (*consumer sovereignty*)
- *Utility* is a cardinal measure, and to estimate the value of pleasure and pain, it is necessary to verify its intensity, duration, and uncertainty.
- The principle of utility is guided by the action increasing or reducing overall happiness/pleasure.
- Each individual chooses rationally and should make decisions about his/her own welfare.
- Society prefers maximizing pleasure and minimizing pain.
- Societal welfare is the sum of all individual utilities.
- Maximizing pleasure is to choose an action producing "the greatest pleasure for the greatest numbers" (consequentialism).

However, criticisms of the feasibility of measuring utility at a cardinal level led to a new definition of utility during the neoclassic economics period, and other levels of utility measurement were proposed: the ordinal level, probabilistic measurement, and mathematical function.

1.2.2.4 Welfare Maximization

Society decides how to achieve maximum welfare according to its values and utilities. Thus welfare maximization is related to the extent to which public policies should or should not intervene to promote global welfare. The concept of maximizing welfare has varied from maximizing the happiness of the majority—as in utilitarianism—to maximizing wealth or the amount of physical goods to more recently maximizing health, as in Health Economics [22]. The mechanisms involved in targeting welfare maximization depend on two main macroeconomic principles: the noninterventionist approach (free market) and the interventionist approach (income transfer and correcting market failures).

1.2.2.4.1 Old Welfare Economics: Classical Utilitarianism and the Maximization of Pleasure

Welfare theory has its origins during the Utilitarianism period. Jeremy Bentham (1748–1832) defined the main goal for society as the maximization of pleasure ("happiness") and the avoidance of pain. From a utilitarian perspective, an individual pursues happiness and should be able to maximize his or her happiness by making rational choices according to his or her preferences (utilities) (see Box 1.1). Then, the sum of utilities for all individuals compose the total welfare. The main classical utilitarian principle to maximize welfare was "the greatest happiness for the greatest number." Therefore, maximizing happiness was maximizing the total sum of happiness (utility) for the majority, which does not mean maximizing and distributing utility at the individual level. This perspective is consequentialist because actions and choices are driven by the outcomes; that is, actions are only evaluated according to their results. It is also a deterministic approach, in that Bentham defended that human beings were driven by pleasure and pain; that is, all human behavior is oriented toward maximizing pleasure and avoiding pain.

On the basis of classical utilitarianism, maximizing welfare would be driven by the government in an attempt to maximize the sum of utilities for the majority.

Taking the concept of *diminishing marginal utility* as defined by Daniel Bernouilli in the nineteenth century—people's net happiness (utility) diminishes as they acquire more units of the same benefit—Bentham warned that rich and poor people do not get the same satisfaction from the same amount of benefit. For instance, if we give a rich person US$1.00, he or she would be less satisfied (get less utility) than if we give US$1.00 to a poor person; in this case, a rich person would need more "dollars" to become as satisfied as the poor person. According to this rationale, it would be easier to maximize welfare if utility is improved for the poor people, distributing the resources from the rich to the poor people with a goal of egalitarian distribution of resources. However, Bentham warned about the inverse effect, whereby rich people would stop producing utilities in order to not donate to poor people. He raised a controversial concept of practical equality in which the government would be able to distribute resources to the poor without triggering rich people to stop producing utilities.

1.2.2.4.2 Neoclassic Welfare Economics: Pareto's Allocative Efficiency and Maximization of Social Welfare

The lack of clarity and possible solutions in the utilitarian view of distribution issues led neoclassical economists to abandon this issue. Instead, they focused solely on how the market works.

Free Market, Perfect Competition, and Marginal Utility

The neoclassic era emerged from a "marginalist revolution" at the end of the nineteenth century. The neoclassic scenario was influenced by capitalist principles, which emerged in the eighteen century with the notion that the market was self-regulated (free market), achieving an equilibrium through a balance between supply and demand; that is, to use the words of Adam Smith, the market was regulated by an "invisible hand" [21]. According to this principle, perfect competition through the supply-demand rule would lead to utility maximisation. Then, society's wishes (demand) and preferences would determine the value of obtaining a service or good. On the other hand, the availability of such services and goods (supply) would influence the price (value) of products and services according to the magnitude of the demand for them. Adam Smith defended the idea that all individuals act on their own self-interest, and in perfect market competition (Fig. 1.1), this self-interest is converted to a common good, emphasizing the concepts of "value in exchange" and "marginal utility." In the other words, Adam Smith's assumptions related to the concept of margin value (the cost of an additional unit) rather than the total sum of utilities. Marginal utility depends on the scarcity of resources, and each additional unit has a marginal cost corresponding to the benefit or utility gained by one additional unit. Therefore, choices and preferences give more value to scarce goods.

Utility in the Neoclassic Period

The shift from the old to the new welfare economics faced various main changes: (a) utility was defined as an ordinal variable, instead of a cardinal variable, as in classical utilitarianism; (b) individuals' utility was not comparable and was not measurable; (c) maximizing welfare becomes a product of *allocative efficiency* obtained under perfect market competition (see Box 1.2). Maximizing social welfare, then, was linked to the allocation of resources to achieve the best value for money—in other words, an *allocative efficiency* of scarce resources (see Chaps. 8 and 10).

Pareto's Efficiency

The concept of *efficiency* in the welfare theory is based on the *Pareto's efficiency* (or *Pareto's optimal*) for resource allocation, developed by Vilfredo Pareto (1848–1923). The *efficiency (E)* is achieved when it is not possible to produce any additional Pareto's improvement (Fig. 1.2). In other words, any change after achieving efficiency would make a person worse off.

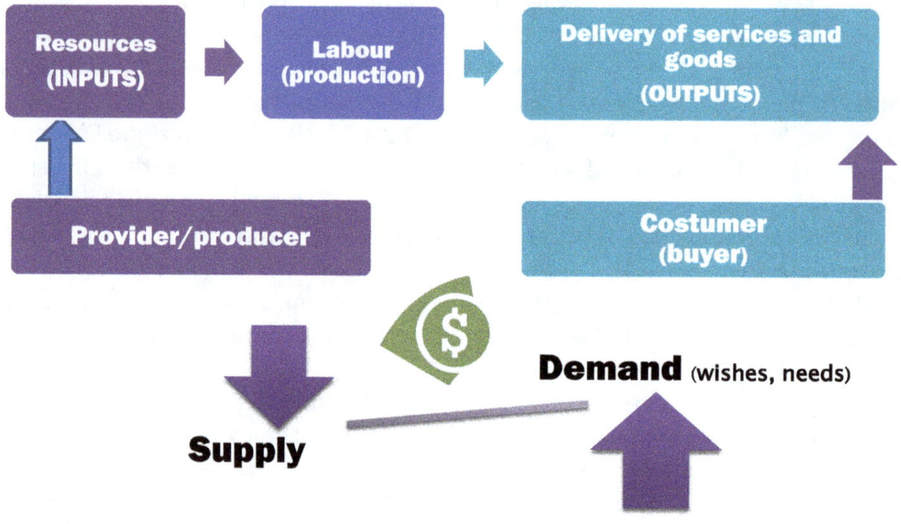

Provider and costumer get satisfaction ("exchange value") and market is self-regulated – supply/ demand

Fig. 1.1 Welfare framework in perfect market competition

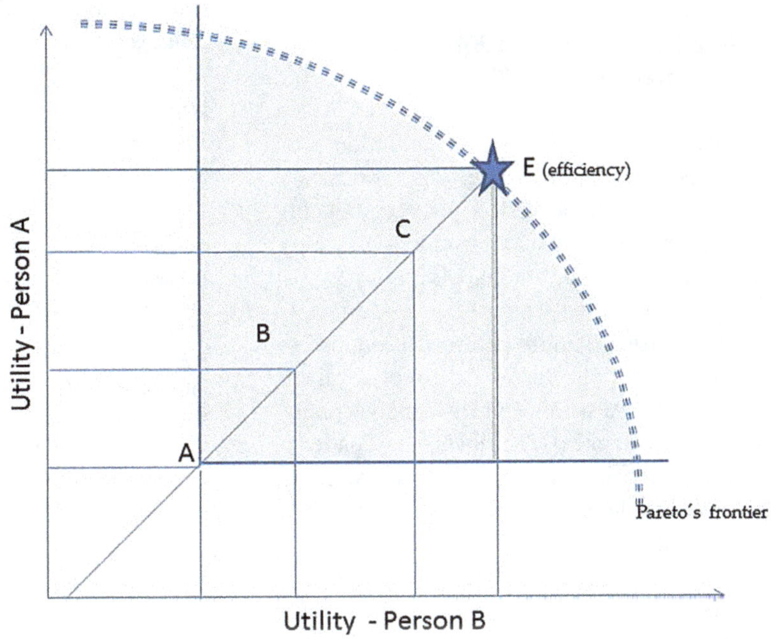

Fig. 1.2 Pareto's Pareto improvement criterion

Pareto's improvement criterion is shown in Fig. 1.2; when moving from A to B to C through to E, all these movements produce improvement (utility gain) for both peoples A and B. This means that given two or more alternatives producing benefits (exchanging goods, for instance), a choice would lead to an improvement (utility gain) if it produces gain ("better off") for one individual (A or B) without causing harm or loss ("worse off") to another individual (A or B) [24]. This concept is based on some of Pareto's assumptions [18]: (a) an individual is the best judge of his or her own well-being, (b) individuals make choices through rational decisions, (c) the best alternative is making someone better off without making another worse off (Pareto's improvement), (d) no externalities are involved. All these assumptions are not met by the market in healthcare. However, Pareto's efficiency is achieved only with perfect market competition, though that is not the case in healthcare. A modification of the Pareto's criterion was proposed in the 1930s by Nicholas Kaldor and John Hicks in their Kaldor-Hicks compensation criterion test or, alternatively, the potential Pareto's criterion, described in the Chap. 4.

1.2.2.5 Efficiency

The term *efficiency* has been used in different contexts, assuming multiple meanings according to the field of knowledge. For economists, the term *efficiency* is directly related to the idea of the best use of resources achieving optimal benefits [25]. In Health Sciences, however, especially in research, applies three different concepts, which are frequently misused in terms of semantics and as defined in the literature: efficacy, effectiveness, and efficiency [26] (Box 1.2). However, the term *efficiency* can be used in three situations: technical efficiency, productive efficiency, and allocative efficiency [25] (Box 1.3).

1.3 Application of Economic Principles to the Health Sector

In 1963, Kenneth Arrow [27], considered to be the pioneer of HE, wrote a paper entitled "Uncertainty and the Welfare Economics of Medical Care," in which he highlighted that the health sector could not be regulated exclusively by a competitive mar-

Box 1.2 Definitions of *Efficacy*, *Effectiveness*, and *Efficiency*

Efficacy means that one intervention produces effects, for example, when comparing one antipsychotic with a placebo, benefits from the antipsychotic must be significantly superior to those from the placebo.

Effectiveness means how this effect is lower than or similar to effects produced in controlled trials; that is, the effect occurs in real practice, within a heterogeneous population and contexts. For instance, if patients do not adhere appropriately to an antipsychotic in daily life, its effects will fail in practice.

Efficiency means that this effect is worthwhile and justifies its costs within a specific budget. If the same antipsychotic is efficacious and works well in practice, the next step is to evaluate whether it is affordable and if the cost is justifiable given a specific budget and conditions.

Box 1.3 Classification of Efficiency [25]

Technical efficiency is used to optimize resources (inputs) to obtain the same outcome using fewer resources. This is a way of avoiding resource waste.

Productive efficiency is related to cost-effectiveness, that is, comparing the costs and outcomes of available alternatives and choosing the one producing similar outcomes with lower costs or producing better outcomes that justify the costs. The goal in this case is to maximize (health) outcomes.

Allocative efficiency is a concept related to welfare and resource allocation within the broader context of decision making. The goal is to maximize benefits for the whole society.

Table 1.1 Differences between perfect and imperfect market competition

Perfect competition principles	Imperfect market competition
Free market, self-regulated	Market failures (e.g., healthcare) Need for external regulation (e.g., government)
Individual spontaneous demand for services or goods in order to get "satisfaction"	Individual does not pursue satisfaction; demand is irregular, unpredictable, and represents risk to individual life
Symmetry of information about goods and services	Asymmetry of information: the nature of health services implies complex and technical decision making and procedures, and patients are not able to judge the quality of physicians' actions; recovery from a disease is unpredictable
No restriction on entry into the market	Licensing required to enter the market
Choices are rational	Choices are emotional and enforces a trust relationship between a patient and physician

ket, as is usually applied to other goods and services, because of the high degree of uncertainty of disease outcomes and treatments, and because of the lack of customer information on healthcare (information asymmetry).

Arrow argued that health was not a commodity and, consequently, healthcare maximization was not compatible with the principles of perfect market competition (Table 1.1) because there was market failure in the healthcare field, leading to imperfect competition and externalities. He defended that because of "market failures" and "imperfect competition" in healthcare, non–market institutions would be able to correct these market inefficiencies, or in other words, the state should regulate them.

At the beginnings of HE, this welfarist approach dominated, and cost-benefit analysis (CBA) was the main focus of this theory. However, because of methodological difficulties in measuring health outcomes in monetary units, as required in CBA, the extra-welfarist approach emerged exclusively in healthcare, allowing methods such as cost-effectiveness and cost-utility analysis to become dominant over CBA (see Chaps. 4, 5, 6, 9, and 10).

HE is still in progress with regard to conceptualizing how to assess health preferences or other measures requiring equity, and in terms of how to promote the maximization of health and the distribution of healthcare services to all people in need. Also, each society adopts a different economic model for healthcare, and this has ethical and distributive implications, and ultimately affects the efficiency of the entire health system [28]. While the United States has traditionally used CBA, the United Kingdom adopted cost-utility and cost-effectiveness analyses for guiding resource allocation, though some welfarist approaches are also accepted according to some conditions (see Chap. 10) (Table 1.2).

1.4 Economic Evaluation and Cost Analysis

The main goal of applying economic principles in healthcare is to guide decision making in how to choose among available treatments and health services in order to achieve the best value for the money and respond to people's health needs. Two levels of economic studies exist: (a) those based exclusively on costs (called "cost-analysis studies") and (b) those based on costs and outcomes (called economic evaluations).

1.4.1 Cost-Analysis Studies

Cost-analysis studies are based exclusively on the costs of treatment and services; they do not take outcomes into account. These studies are common in the literature and they are frequently misinterpreted as being similar to cost-effectiveness studies. Terminology in HE is used and "misused" in a heterogeneous format, misleading readers who are not familiar with such concepts. These studies have limitations because they are addressed toward cost-savings goals without assessing the consequences of choosing each alternative; that is, they do not take into account the opportunity costs nor the benefits and harms to patients.

On the other hand, cost-saving studies have been used to show the "benefits" of cutting costs because they might help to decrease hospitalization rates or health services use. Policymakers are particularly interested in these studies because they might allow costs-savings with regard to budget allocation. Such studies might seem similar to economic evaluations, giving the idea of an outcome (service use), but in fact these "outcomes" are not directly related to patient health, nor with welfare or health maximization.

Moreover, decisions based exclusively on costs might lead to negative externalities or eventually might increase costs for other sectors (the "spillover effect") [14]. Negative externalities are adverse consequences of an action affecting one person or group not involved in the market transaction. For example, if no adequate treatment for depression is offered in mental health care, then people with depressive disorders might be less productive in the workplace, leading to absenteeism, to the use of more sick leave, or even to unemployment. This affects not only the patient but also families and production in the workplace. Actually, costs-analysis studies do not allow decisions to achieve efficient allocative resources.

In summary, costs-analysis studies are designed to measure costs of illnesses, interventions, and health services, and they provide an overview of how a financial budget is allocated or how expenditures are distributed among different levels of care. Also, they are useful for estimating the economic burden of mental disorders, that is, the costs of the impact of a disease on society, such as costs associated with productivity losses, suicide, and healthcare use (see Chap. 25).

1.4.2 Economic Evaluation

Economic evaluations (EEs) compare the costs and outcomes (or consequences) between two or more competitive alternatives [13, 24, 29, 30]. In terms of public health policies, EE is a powerful tool to verify the consequences and costs of choosing one treatment over another.

EE is always a *comparative analysis*, and it involves *choice* (decision) with a goal of getting the *maximum of benefits* at *the minimum costs*; that is, EE is a tool to enhance the *efficiency* of the use of scarce resources.

For instance, if a new antipsychotic drug for treating treatment-resistant schizophrenia is available in the market, EE can provide information about the extent to which this new drug can add benefits (outcome) over the available drug(s), and how much those additional benefits would costs compared with the current treatment. Decision making, though, is not straightforward; the budget might be too small to buy new technology or the additional benefit might be not really relevant (see Chap. 10).

1.4.2.1 Types of Economic Evaluation

CBA is an EE method whose main principle is based on the assumption that benefits should be greater than costs; that is, benefits are worthwhile, justifying their costs and maximizing welfare [18, 24, 31] (see Chap. 4). In CBA, all benefits are captured, eliciting people´s preferences for different health statuses and how much they would be willing to pay for that status. CBA is not easily applied in healthcare because of difficulties with and limitations on the methods for assessing benefits in monetary terms.

Instead of CBA, alternative methods have been applied in healthcare, under assumptions similar to those in CBA, but with the main goal of maximizing health. The most used economic methods in healthcare are cost-effectiveness analysis (CEA) [32] and cost-utilities analysis (CUA) [33].These two methods are able to determine which intervention produces more health at the best costs (see Chaps. 5 and 6).

CEA is usually used with clinical trials or pragmatic trials [34, 35]. There is one single primary outcome, and it is most often a clinical outcome, though it is possible to choose other outcomes such as quality of life. Results are expressed as a ratio of costs and benefits, the incremental cost-effectiveness ratio (ICER) (see Chap. 5).

CUA uses multiple outcomes converted in one outcome, from estimating utility and life expectancy. For instance, indicators such as quality-adjusted life years (QALYs) combine estimating gains in morbidity and in mortality, or the product between utility and life expectancy. One QALY equals 1 year living with good health, and estimated costs per QALY correspond to the costs to be paid to gain health. Methods for estimating utility and other indicators are discussed in the Chaps. 3 and 6.

Cost-consequences analysis (CCA) and cost-minimization analysis (CMA) are two other methods of EE. CCA measures multiple outcomes through multiple specific scales (e.g. quality of life, psychiatric symptoms, social participation) [36]. The method applied for measuring outcome is similar to that used in CEA. However, results are not straightforward enough to be interpreted because this method shows the differences and similarities between two or more alternatives for improving different outcomes, and it also shows the total costs for each alternative, though the decision regarding the best alternative is subjective and not expressed as any ratio or numerical data. However, CCA is very useful to complement CEA because of the need for measuring multiple outcomes.

CMA is based on the assumption that two treatments produce the same outcome; for this reason, there is no need to measure it again, meaning only the costs of each are compared, allowing the least costly option to be chosen. However, it is unlikely that two medications produce exactly the same results.

These methods of EE differ especially on how their outcomes are measured and how results are presented [24] (Table 1.2).

1.4.3 Components of Economic Studies

Whatever the goal of studies of cost analysis or EE, some methodologic steps are necessary

Table 1.2 Methods of economic evaluation

Methods of economic evaluation	Outcome	Measurement	Results
CEA	Single	Specific rating scale	ICER = ΔCosts/ΔOutcomes
CUA	Multiple	Utility Methods (preferences)	Cost per QALY gained, cost per DALY avoided
CCA	Multiple	Multiple scales	Comparison of outcomes Comparison of costs
CMA	Single		Comparison of costs
CBA	Multiple (converted to monetary units)	Willingness to pay approach	Net benefit = ΔBenefits – ΔCosts (>0)

CBA cost-benefit analysis, *CCA* cost-consequences analysis, *CEA* cost-effectiveness analysis, *CMA* cost-minimization analysis, *CUA* cost-utility analysis, *DALY* disability-adjusted life year, *ICER* incremental cost-effectiveness ratio, *QALY* quality-adjusted life year

before assessing cost. Detailed methodology to assess costs is discussed in detail in Chap. 2. The second component is related to the choice of outcome and is discussed in detail in Chap. 3.

1.4.3.1 Cost Measurement and Perspective

The first step in economic analysis is to define which costs should be included in the study, and these depend on the perspective of the study. Perspective means that costs are measured for different levels of interest, varying from a narrow to a comprehensive view: an individual, a public health provider, private or insurance companies, employers, government, society.

When adopting a comprehensive perspective such as a societal viewpoint, all relevant costs related to the illness should be collected, including costs related to other nonhealth sectors. Taking the example of depressive disorders, it is known that depressive disorder is highly related to absenteeism, presenteeism, early retirement, sick leave, and suicide. Therefore, it is important to collect data not only on direct costs (health-care costs), but also from other sectors involved, such as the workplace (see Chaps. 28 and 29). If adopting a narrower perspective, such as a public health provider, only direct costs would be included in the study. Yet, the costs of depression for families and patients (see Chap. 17) might be dismissed, depending on the perspective adopted. Hence, the choice of study perspective has implications not only in decision making but also in producing social welfare [37].

1.4.3.2 What Is a Benefit?

Outcomes, from an economic perspective, represent a relevant benefit for the user (consumer) [25]. Outcomes are grouped into three main categories: (a) those focused on single measure (e.g., a clinical symptom), (b) health indicators obtained by estimating utilities (QALYs, disability-adjusted life years), and (c) monetary units (the benefit is expressed through monetary values). This topic will be detailed in Chap. 3.

1.5 Economic Principles Applied to Mental Health

Applying HE principles to Mental Health is challenging, especially in terms of measurement [38], the high degree of uncertainty and variability of treatments [39], and the large social and economic burden and many externalities related to mental illness. We highlight these challenges through five main questions, which are discussed in detail throughout the book. Although not all relevant economic concepts are presented in this introductory chapter, we invite readers to keep in mind these five questions as they moving from one chapter to another, in order to understand the pitfalls in conducting research in this field and what might be relevant and applicable to mental health care.

1.5.1 What Does "Maximization of Mental Health" Mean?

Defining mental health has never been an easy task, and it is even harder to establish the amount of mental health a person needs and where lie the borders of mental health maximization. While health maximization due to mortality reduction or a significant improvement in clinical symptoms (e.g., pain, mobility) is relatively easier to measure in other medical specialties, maximization of mental health is not easily captured by assessing only health indicators.

World Health Organization defines mental health as being a sort of balance of all human dimensions of well-being, including physical, social, and psychological spheres [7]; this definition approaches utilitarianism's goals of pursuing happiness and pleasure.

On the other hand, mental disorders cause a remarkable portion of the global burden of disease (see Chap. 25). Burden caused by mental disorders affects all sectors of society, and consequently, it not only increases healthcare costs but also affects the costs of productivity (absenteeism), education (missed schooling), early mortality, and impoverishment, among others (see Chaps. 24 and 25). Therefore, maximizing mental health means improving outcomes and reducing costs in all of these spheres. The benefits of intervention and the relative reduction of costs might not be captured in a narrow perspective, such as a health provider's viewpoint, if the intervention effects are related to reducing global burden [38, 40] (see Chap. 10). Accepting this assumption raises an issue that a broader perspective, such as a societal viewpoint, would be preferable in economic studies in mental healthcare.

1.5.2 How to Measure Mental Health Gain

From an economic perspective, mental health gain means generating utility and ultimately welfare using the welfarist approach. As presented in this chapter, utility is a concept related to the consumer (patient or general public), under the assumption that individuals make rational choices based on their own preferences and on opportunity costs. From public policymaker's view, maximizing welfare in the mental health field is elusive because the "production" of mental health (utility) is not easily measurable or visible when compared with the "production" of physical health [41, 42]. The majority of techniques to assess utilities and preferences are not appropriate to capture patients' preferences about mental health outcomes because mental disorders affect judgment and the ability to choose and to express preferences (see Chap. 3), though in CUA, preferences of the general public are measured (see Chap. 6). Yet, these measurements are not sensitive enough to capture all mental health gains, especially for more severe disorders. Moreover, there is a perverse stigma against mental disorders (see Chap. 27), and decision makers might not acknowledge the relevance of mental health effectiveness within scenarios mixing physical and mental diseases [10] (see Chap. 11).

1.5.3 Which Costs Are Relevant in Mental Health?

The cost-effectiveness of mental health care and psychiatric interventions vary widely depending on the perspective adopted in CEA studies and, ultimately, on which costs are included in the analysis. Because mental disorders mainly cause costs in nonhealthcare sectors, conducting a CEA or CUA study that only takes into account healthcare costs might not capture the reduction of indirect costs, in that mental healthcare costs represent only a tiny part of the total costs of mental disorders. Therefore, conducting EE using a comprehensive approach for measuring costs is preferable in mental healthcare [43].

1.5.4 How to Measure Benefits from Mental Health Interventions

The fourth issue is the complex nature of mental health interventions and outcomes [32, 44]. Mental disorders impair mental functions and hinder different spheres of people's lives globally, even when clinical improvement is achieved. Therefore, there is not one unique intervention able to promote total mental recovery [45]. A recovery model has been adopted in global policy agenda that refers to recovery of not only mental health symptoms but also social roles and participation, as well as access to opportunities in social spheres and in the workplace. For instance, less than half of people with bipolar disorders return to work within 1 year after having one mood disorder episode. Instead, a complex combination of mental health interventions from different fields of knowledge (not necessarily health related) is used to help patients recovering partially or totally their mental and psychosocial functions (see Chap. 28).

Hence, defining the relevant outcome in terms of mental health functions is tricky because the ultimate goal of mental health treatment is to restore, when possible, all the previous mental abilities that patient had to live fully before becoming ill, and to empower people with permanent impairment to experiment a full life and citizenship [38, 40, 41, 43, 45]. Yet, because of the complexity of the nature of mental health interventions, it is difficult to identify many embedded components and measure their costs and effects, and usually it is necessary to adapt the economic study design [32].

1.5.5 Is Health Economics Really Helpful in the Mental Health Field?

Among multiple possible arguments to affirm that HE is useful in the Mental Health field, we highlight one argument here: HE is a strong ally to be used toward reducing the global burden of mental disorders [38]. While mental health research verifies the effects of mental health interventions on clinical and global functional status, HE focuses on the worth of those interventions; in other words, it measures how relevant the interventions are to justify their costs [38]. HE provides information on the magnitude of costs and the mental health burden affecting different sectors of society, and allows simultaneous verification of mental health interventions in terms of effects and costs. Hence, it is possible to reduce the mental health burden with cost-effective interventions and to plan a budget for improving the efficiency and quality of mental healthcare.

Key Messages

- Health resources are always scarce and, for this reason, rational choices on how to use them efficiently are necessary.
- Every choice implies acquiring and distributing one benefit for one person or group and not acquiring and distributing the forgone benefit to another person or group. Opportunity cost is the cost of the unchosen benefit. Each choice has gains, losses, and costs.
- The healthcare domain is not a good or service regulated exclusively by the free market under perfect competition. On the contrary, because of market failures and the negative externalities of mental disorders and other health conditions, government regulation is needed.
- HE evaluates which alternatives are the best value for the money, that is, which treatments in mental health are valuable in terms of producing more benefits than costs.
- Mental disorders are burdensome and costly to society as a whole; for this reason, economic studies should be comprehensive, adopting a societal perspective, including indirect costs.
- Maximizing mental health gains improves patient and family lives, and it contributes to reducing externality costs affecting multiple sectors of society.

References

1. Murray CJL, Lopez AD. The global burden of disease: a comprehensive assessment of mortality and disability from diseases, injutries, and risk factors in 1990 and projected to 2020. Boston: Harvard School of Public Health; 1996.

2. Weehuizen R. Mental capital: the economic significance of mental health. Maastricht: University of Maastrich; 2008. Available: https://www.merit.unu.edu/training/theses/Thesis_Weehuizen_final.pdf.
3. United Nations. Transforming our world: the 2030 Agenda for sustainable development. United Nations; 2015. Report No.: A/RES/70/1.
4. Knapp M. Economic evaluation and mental health: sparse past. Fertile future? J Ment Health Policy Econ. 1999;2(4):163–7.
5. Singh B. The role of economic evaluation in mental health care. Aust N Z J Psychiatry. 2001;35:104–17.
6. Shearer J, Byford S. The basics of economic evaluation in mental healthcare. Brit J Psych Advances. 2015;21:345–53.
7. World Health Organization. The World Health Report. Mental health: new understanding. Geneve: New Hope; 2001.
8. Knapp M, Beecham J, McDaid D, Matosevic T, Smith M. The economic consequences of deinstitutionalisation of mental health services: lessons from a systematic review of European experience. Health Soc Care Community. 2011;19(2):113–25.
9. Mushkin SJ. Toward a definition of health economics. Public Health Rep. 1958;73(9):785–93.
10. Chisholm D, Stweart A. Economics and ethics in mental health care: traditions and trade-offs. J Ment Health Policy Econ. 1998;1:55–62.
11. Acemoglou D, Autor D. Lectures in labour economics: the basic theory of human capital. Lectures in labour economics. Cambridge: Massachusetts Institute of Technology Department of Economics; 2011. Available: http://economics. mit. edu/files/4689
12. Rebelo LP. The origins and the evolution of health economics: a discipline by itself? Led by economist, practitioners or politics? 2007.
13. Chisholm D, Evans D. Economic evaluation in health: saving money or improving care? J Med Econ. 2007;10:325–37.
14. Knapp M. The economic evaluation of mental health care. 1st ed. Aldershot: Ashgate Publishing Limited; 1995.
15. Begg D, Fischer S, Dornbusch R. Economics. 8th ed. Berkshire: McGraw-Hill; 2005.
16. Parkin D. Health economics. http://www.healthknowledge.org.uk/public-health-textbook/medical-sociology-policy-economics/4d-health-economics [4]. 2009. London: Health knowedge. 28 Jan 2016.
17. Baujard A. Welfare economics. Working paper GATE −33.2013.<halshs-00906907>. 2013. 28 Jan 2016.
18. Slothuus U. Economic evaluation: theory, methods and application. Health economics paper. University Southern od Denmark; 20052 Feb 2016.
19. Hazlitt H. Understanding "Austrian" economists. Fondation for Economic Evaluation; 1981. 28 Jan 2016.
20. Kahneman D, Wakker P, Sari R. Back to bentham? Explorations of experienced utility. Q J Econ. 1997;112(2):375–405.
21. Stigler G. The development of utility theory. J Polit Econ. 1950;58(4):307–27.
22. Rothbard M. Toward a reconstruction of utility and welfare economics. The logic of action one. Edward Elgar Publishing Limited; 1997. p. 211–54. https://mises.org/library/toward-reconstruction-utility-and-welfare-economics-1/html.
23. Read D. Utility theory from Jeremy Bentham to Daniel Kahneman. Working paper No: LSEOR 04–64. London: London School of Economics and Political Science; 2004. 28 Jan 2016.
24. Drummond MF, Sculpher MJ, Torrance GW, O'Brien BJ, Stoddart GL. Methods for the economic evaluation of health care programmes. 3rd ed. Oxford: Oxford University Press; 2007.
25. Palmer S, Togerson D. Definitions of efficiency. Br Med J. 1999;318:1136.
26. Andrews G. Efficacy, effectiveness and efficiency in mental health service delivery. Aust N Z J Psychiatry. 1999;33:316–22.
27. Arrow K. Uncertainty and the welfare economics of medical care. Am J Econ Rev. 1963;LIII(5):941–73.
28. Ferraz MB. Health economics, equity, and efficiency: are we almost there? ClinicoEcon Outcome Res. 2015;7:119–22.
29. Drummond M, McGuire A. Economic evaluation in health care: merging theroy with practice. 2nd ed. New York: Oxford University Press; 2004.
30. Byford S, McDaid D, Sefton T. Because it's worth it: a practical guide to conducting economic evaluations in the social welfare field. 2003. London, York Publishing Services Ltd.
31. McIntosh E, Clarke P, Frew EJ, Louviere JJ. Applied methods of cost-benefit analysis in health care. New York: Oxford University Press Inc; 2011.
32. Byford S, Sefton T. Economic evaluation of complex health and social care interventions. Natl Inst Econ Rev. 2003;186:98–108.
33. Luyten J, Naci H, Knapp M. Economic evaluation of mental health interventions: an introduction to cost-utility analysis. Evid Based Ment Health. 2016;19(2):49–53.
34. Gray A, Clarke P, Wolstenholme J, Worsworth S. Applied methods of cost-effectiveness analysis in health care. 1st ed. Oxford: Oxford University Press; 2011.
35. Gray AM. Cost-effectiveness analyses alongside randomised clinical trials. Clin Trials. 2006;3(6):538–42.
36. Mauskopf JA, Paul JE, Grant DM, Stergachis A. The role of cost-consequence analysis in healthcare decision-making. PharmacoEconomics. 1998;13(3):277–88.
37. Jönsson B. Ten arguments for a societal perspective in the economic evaluation of medical innovations. Eur J Health Econ. 2009;10:357–9.
38. Knapp M. Economic outcomes and levers: impacts for individuals and society. Int Psychogeriatr. 2007;19(3):483–95.
39. Frank G, McGuire TG. Economics and mental health. In: Culyer A, Newhouse J, editors. Handbook of

health economics volume 1B. Oxford: Elsevier; 2000. p. 894–945.
40. McCrone P. Mental health economics: current methodological issues. Epidemiol Psychiatr Sci. 2011;20(3):239–43.
41. Brazier J. Measuring and valuing mental health for use in economic evaluation. J Health Serv Res Policy. 2008;13(Suppl3):70–5.
42. Chisholm D, Healey A, Knapp M. QALYs and mental health care. Soc Psychiatry Psychiatr Epidemiol. 1997;32(2):68–75.
43. Beecham J, Knapp M. Costing psychiatric interventions. In: Thornicroft G, editor. Measuring mental health needs. London: Gaskell; 2001. p. 200–24.
44. Stant AD, Buskens E, Jenner JA, Wiersma D, TenVergert EM. Cost-effectiveness analysis in severe mental illness: outcome measures selection. J Ment Health Policy Econ. 2007;10(2):101–8.
45. Bonney S, Stickley T. Recovery and mental health: a review of the British literature. J Psychiatr Ment Health Nurs. 2008;15(2):140–53.

2 Methods for Measuring and Estimating Costs

Denise Razzouk

Abstract

This chapter focuses on costing methods usually applied in cost analysis and health-related economic evaluations. The quality of an economic evaluation depends on the quality and precision of data collection and on transparency and comprehensiveness of costing resources. Costs, from an economic perspective, are related to opportunity costs; this economic conceptualization is different from a financial perspective. Costs are classified as direct, indirect, intangible, and total costs. In this chapter I focus exclusively on the measurement of direct costs. Costing involves multiple steps: choosing the perspective of the study; identifying the component of costs, collecting data on costs and services use, estimating the unit cost for each resource, and estimating costs. Although the majority of economic evaluations includes only direct costs, indirect costs correspond to the major parcel of diseases costs. Mental disorders, for instance, cause innumerable negative externalities and indirect costs, and the benefits of psychiatric and psychosocial interventions go beyond clinical improvement, leading to systematic recommendations for measuring costs in a comprehensive way, such as using societal perspective. There is a debate among health economists regarding the inclusion of indirect costs in the economic evaluation, though, thieir exclusion in assessing cost-effectiveness, for instance, might understimate the economic impact of psychiatric intervention. Costing methods for indirect costs are discussed in another chapter in this book.

D. Razzouk (✉)
Centre of Economic Mental Health, Department of Psychiatry, Universidade Federal de Sao Paulo, Rua Borges Lagoa 570 1, andar Vila Clementino, São Paulo 04038-000, Brazil
e-mail: drazzouk@gmail.com

D. Razzouk (ed.), *Mental Health Economics*, DOI 10.1007/978-3-319-55266-8_2

Key Points Summary

- Definition and classification of costs
- Identification of costs components
- Measurement of direct costs
- Top-down and bottom-up approaches
- Unit costs
- Cost analysis and bias of cost estimation

2.1 What Is Cost?

The term *cost* is used in the literature in a heterogeneous way, with multiple meanings, hindering clear understanding by readers who are not familiar with the Economics field. In general, cost is the value of resources used to produce a good or a service. However, defining cost imposes the need to distinguish between "accounting costs" and "economic costs" [1].

Accounting costs are directly related to the monetary costs of all inputs used for producing a good or service. Usually, the price of acquiring a product is used for accounting costs. In the case of healthcare, accounting costs are equivalent to the costs of all resources for producing and delivering healthcare [1]. Accountants focus exclusively on financial costs in order to plan and to manage expenditures and the consumption of resources. Moreover, accounting databases usually do not provide detailed information of costs for one specific patient and all costs incurred by patients and families, such as out-of-pocket expenditures [2].

On the other hand, economic costs are related to opportunity costs; that is, when facing a choice between two alternatives, opportunity costs refer to the costs of losing the forgone benefits that would be gained if another alternative was chosen. In other words, to obtain a health gain, there are always opportunity costs when choosing to invest on a new medical technology or health services rather than in a current treatment [3, 4]. The main implication, then, from an economic perspective, is that costs are the value of opportunity costs; for this reason, decision makers and health economists focus on the value of allocating resources efficiently, that is, maximizing benefits for patients. If a considerable investment is allocated for a treatment that is able to benefit 100 persons with depressive disorder instead of being allocated for another treatment that benefits 10 persons with schizophrenia, then the opportunity costs represent the benefits of those latter 10 people.

Therefore, these costs should be estimated taking into account whether "this investment" (opportunity costs) is more valuable in terms of producing more benefits than costs. Health gain is often expressed as increasing life expectancy and decreasing morbidity (see Chap. 3), but it also leads to the consumption of fewer health services and promotes increased productivity in the workplace. For instance, investing in research and development for a new drug and trading it into a market should not only allow profits for the pharmaceutical industry but also improve health and individual quality of life, ultimately maximizing utility and welfare [4] (see Chap. 1).

Once healthcare is not driven through free-market competition (see Chap. 1), costs are not similar to the prices of product or services [5]. The price of a service usually represents the average costs. In health economic analysis guiding decision-making for healthcare resources allocation, however, costs should be estimated using marginal analysis rather than the average costs used by accountants [1, 6]. Marginal analysis computes the costs of one additional unit; providing the intervention for 10 people is much more costly than providing it for more than 10 people because it maximizes use and the benefits provided by the intervention (e.g., lab test, program, group intervention), reducing the marginal costs [3, 4, 7]. While average costs cover fixed costs (FCs) and variable costs (VCs), marginal costs are estimated based exclusively on VCs, excluding all FCs [1, 5]. VCs vary according to the consumption of services (for instance, food, water, disposables, clothes, electricity, telephone). These costs are particularly addressed in economic evaluations comparing interventions in the same setting using a similar infrastructure. However, when comparing two interventions or programs under a different infrastructure, it is recommended to estimate the average costs, which also include FCs [5]. FCs are regular costs not related to consumption, and they do not vary over the short term (<1 year), such as human resources.

In summary, the differences between both approaches (accounting and economic) imply different costing methods. Accounting costing is not accurate for the majority of economic evaluations because nonmonetary costs are not included in accounting costs, as they are in economic evaluations using a societal perspective (for instance, informal care costs, productivity costs; see Chaps. 17 and 29). Also, accountant costing does not take into account the impact of a new technology on resource consumption [8]. In this book, we use the term *costs* always from an economic perspective (economic costs).

2.2 Classification of Costs

Again, the classification of costs varies, and the same term often has different meanings. In terms of components of costs, costs are traditionally divided in the following categories [7]: (a) direct costs, (b) indirect costs, (c) intangible costs, and (d) total costs. This classification of costs is often criticized, and many authors have adopted and developed other terminologies for this purpose [5], but we still use this classification because the majority of research articles use it, and for this reason, it is helpful for easy understanding by beginner readers.

Direct costs are costs that are closely related to healthcare and to any type of care because of sickness (nonhealth sectors) (see Box 2.1). Some authors divide direct costs into health direct costs and nonhealth direct costs (see Chaps. 14, 15, and 16). Mental healthcare encompasses multiple sectors and nonhealth interventions [6, 9–11], for example, costs for accommodation such as residential facilities (housing for mental disabled people who have no social or family support) (see Chap. 16), costs of criminal justice (in the case of offenders or drug misuse), and costs for educational interventions (in the case of attention-deficit/hyperactivity disorder and autism).

Box 2.1 Direct Costs
Capital costs – land and buildings (or rent);

Capital costs – equipment and medical devices

Capital costs Building maintenance and repairs

Capital costs Maintenance, depreciation and repairs costs – equipment

Furniture – renewal and maintenance

Human resources

Clinical staff (psychiatrists, psychologists, social workers, occupational therapists, nurses, psychiatric nurses, nonpsychiatric doctors, physiotherapists, music therapists, art therapists, counselors, health visitors, other therapists)

Nonclinical staff (nonhealth sectors)

Overhead (general management and administrative costs)

Nonhealth services (cleaning, diet, security, electricity, water, telephone, waste)

Medication and interventions (surgery)

Lab tests and imaging

Consumables (materials, clothes, disposables)

Transportation (ambulance)

Accommodation (residential facilities)

Criminal justice (in some cases)

Educational interventions or services specific for people with mental illness (e.g., autism)

*Patient and family expenditures for treatment and travel, including informal caregivers (depending on the perspective)

Future medical costs related to a current intervention (e.g., clozapine use requires blood tests controls)

Voluntary services

Training and supervising mental health professionals

Depending on the perspective of the study (e.g., a societal or patient viewpoint), costs incurred by families and patients can also be included in direct costs; these include costs for transportation (travel to a health service), of medication and disposables, for hiring a caregiver, or for refurbishing a house to adapt to specific health needs) [7]. Informal care by family represents a sacrifice of benefit (this time spent caring could be spent in leisure activities or working) – that is, opportunity costs – and should be measured, though some studies consider them to be indirect costs [7]. For example, mothers with children with autism disorders frequently quit their jobs to caring the child (see Chap. 17). Future medical costs related to a current treatment should be also considered [12] in an economic evaluation; for instance, in the case of clozapine, it requires weekly blood tests control. However, there is still a debate over the inclusion or exclusion of future costs incurred in prolonging life and that are not related to a current treatment [13].

Most economic studies do not include transfer payments in their cost analysis. Transfer payments such as social and disability benefits, work compensation, and taxes are not considered costs because they are not resources available for consumption and they are not "produced" like a good or service; they are considered by economists as income redistributions [7, 11, 14]. However, these "costs" could be included in economic evaluation for those studies using Governement perspective.

Indirect costs are related to social and economic costs such as a decrease in workplace production, suicide rate, early retirement, accidents, income losses, and loss of years of education [15]. Indirect costs are usually called "productivity costs" because the majority of studies covering indirect costs focus on productivity losses (see Chap. 29). Intangible costs are "invisible" costs that are not directly measured, such as the pain of losing a son or the pain of watching a son's suffering because of a treatment or disease. Total costs are the sum of all above-mentioned costs.

2.3 Costs Measurement

The quality of economic evaluations and cost analysis studies depends on the quality of the measurement of costs and outcomes [16]. The level of detail and accuracy vary from one study and purpose to another. "Gross costing" is used in cost analysis to provide an overview of the effects of costs, but it is not appropriate for economic evaluation because it lacks accuracy and detail [12], though it is easier and less time consuming. Some examples are available using diagnosis-related groups (DRG), in which national tariffs are used as the units costs in order to estimate costs of resources consumed by a diagnostic group, ignoring cost variation among individuals and opportunity costs. These estimates are calculated using the mean of accounting costs among patients with the same diagnosis; these estimates are proxies for reimbursement [17]. Some countries have national tariffs for reimbursement, and the method for estimating them varies by country. However, these national reimbursement tariffs might not represent good estimates of real costs, depending on the country and on the financial public health system. Some reports show cost estimate discrepancies between diagnosis-related groups and micro-costing, ranging between 9% and 66% [17].

Beecham and Knapp [10] recommend as a general rule that costs be measured in a comprehensive manner to avoid bias in economic evaluations. According to this rule, the broader and the most accurate approach is collecting individual data through a micro-costing bottom-up method (see item 2.3.3). Costs vary among individuals, and this variation should be analyzed carefully when guiding public policies [10]. Moreover, these authors emphasize the necessity of comparing costs in "like-to-with-like basis", that is, comparing similar services and with the same infrastructure and public profile [10]. Likewise, medication costs and effects should be compared head-to-head.

Several costing guidelines have emerged [1, 4, 6, 11, 18], but detailed methodology on costing is still lacking. The International Society for Pharmacoeconomics and Outcomes Research has published a series of task force reports on methodological issues in costing methods to be used in economic evaluation, because many studies were flawed in this regard [18–20]. However, guidelines vary in terms of recommended methods, and costing variations among economic evaluations affect the validity, comparability, and transferability of results, as well as decision-making [21, 22].

Of note, multiple factors affect cost estimation, and for this reason, the description of methods used to measure and estimate costs should be transparent, detailed, and accurate, with a well-defined costing time frame, justifications for the exclusion or inclusion of components of costs, and explicit demonstration of how uncertainty and variation of data are handled [16, 19, 20] (see Chap. 7). Last but not least, the unique rationale to measure costs must be put it into a context aligned with outcomes, because isolated numbers are useless and meaningless for allocating resources and guiding health policies[10, 23, 24] (see Chaps. 10 and 11).

In this chapter, I focus on methods for measuring direct costs; indirect costs and informal care costs are discussed in Chaps. 17 and 29. Some basic steps must be taken into account before starting to measure costs [6, 7, 9–13, 25]. The first step is to define the study perspective, because it defines which costs should or should not be included in the cost analysis. The second step is to identify all components of costs related to a program, service, or group of services. The third step is to collect data regarding the frequency and the amount of services consumed. The fourth step is to define and estimate the unit cost for each component of costs. The fifth step is to estimate and analyze the costs.

2.3.1 Study Perspective and Costs

The first step when conducting an economic evaluation is to define the study perspective and, consequently, to determine which costs should be included in the study [7, 8]. When adopting a comprehensive perspective, such as a societal viewpoint, all relevant costs related to the illness should be collected, including costs related to production sectors [7]. A societal viewpoint includes time costs, opportunity costs, and community preferences [4]. Although public health systems in different countries do not adopt this perspective, some health economists strongly recommend using a societal viewpoint for economic evaluation when possible [7, 10, 26, 27]. In general, a societal perspective is adopted as a rule in cost-benefit analysis (see Chap. 4) and rarely in cost-effectiveness analysis; instead, cost-effectiveness analysis and especially cost-utility analysis use mainly health provider viewpoint.

The implication of choosing one perspective [4, 26, 28] therefore not only affects the components of costs to be included in the analysis; it mainly influences decision-making under misleading conclusions [4, 9–12, 25, 26, 28]. Take depressive disorder as an example . It is known that depression causes high costs to society and to the healthcare system because it is strongly related to productivity losses (absenteeism, presenteeism, early retirement, sick leave), suicide, lost school years, and greater use of the healthcare system when compared with people with no mental illness (see Chaps. 25 and 26). Therefore, it is important to collect data not only on direct costs but also in other sectors involved, such as the workplace (see Chap. 28), and to measure absenteeism and productivity losses (see Chap. 29). For instance, if one intervention is superior to another in reducing absenteeism due to depression, then it may be the most cost-effective alternative. Conversely, if adopting a narrower perspective, such as a public health provider viewpoint, only direct costs would be included in the study; supposing that the new intervention is not superior to the current alternative in improving clinical outcome, even though it is superior for reducing absenteeism, it might be not considered a cost-effective option. Moreover, adopting a narrow perspective does not take into account intangible suffering and societal preferences for treating depression (see Chap. 3), though these are matters of extensive debate. For instance, a study using cost-benefit analysis found that people with depressive disorders were willing to pay 10% of their household income [29], representing greater monetary value for the benefits of treating depression than the real costs of treatment (see Chap. 4).

Yet, a heath provider perspective does not take into account patient or family expenditures (out-of-pocket) for treatment and other related negative externalities. Out-of pocket payments may represent catastrophic health costs [30] because they can represent a substantial amount of income, leading to impoverishment (see Chaps. 24 and 25). If one intervention is supposed to

Table 2.1 Components of costs according to perspective

Costs	Society	Public health provider	Private health provider/health insurance company	Patient and family	Employer
Direct costs					
Capital equipment	x	x	x		
Health services use, human resources, interventions	x	x	x	Out-of-pocket	?
Medication and lab tests	x	x	x	Out-of-pocket	
Transportation	x	x	x		
Travel expenses (patients)	x			x	
Informal care	x			x	
Paid caregivers	x			x	
Criminal justice services	x				
Accommodation	x	x			
House refurbishment because of illness (place adapted)				x	
Social benefits		x			
Patient/family time	x			x	
Voluntary services	x			x	
Indirect costs					
Work losses (absenteeism, presenteeism, worker replacement costs) [32])	x			x	x
Accidents	x			x	x
Sick leave	x				x
Early retirement	x				
Early death (suicide)	x				
Expenditures on drugs and alcohol	x			x	
Education losses	x			x	
Impoverishment (job losses, homeless, income)				x	

decrease healthcare consumption under a public health provider perspective, it might also increase out-of-pocket costs paid by individuals and families. On the other hand, a patient and family perspective would lead to the inclusion of costs due to illness, such as costs for caregivers, drugs, transportation, work and income losses, and time spent caring (see Chap. 17). Although interest in studies using a patient and family perspective has been growing, a systematic review showed that all costs relevant to patients and families were not included satisfactorily [31]. Other costs such as productivity losses are estimated (see Chap. 29) mostly when studies use an employer viewpoint or, ultimately, in broader studies adopting a societal perspective (see Table 2.1).

2.3.2 Identification of Components of Costs

Each scenario involves different components of costs because each entails a different level of care and services. Before collecting data, it is important to know which services are available, how the services work, and which components of costs are incurred upon delivery of the services (see Chaps. 13, 14, 15, and 16). It is useful to map all process involved in services delivery and interventions in order to identify all relevant costs.

Unlike other medical specialties, few expensive health medical technologies are available for treating mental disorders. Despite some expensive medications (such as antipsychotics), the great parcel of direct mental healthcare costs is due to human resources from multiple sectors (health, social care, education, criminal justice). Therefore, costing mental healthcare is not easy because the identification of such components it is not always straightforward [10, 24, 25, 33]. For instance, treatment for schizophrenia disorders is not based only on administering medication to ameliorate symptoms, but on providing psychosocial interventions and all sorts of services and supports to include these patients in society and to boost their autonomy and skills for better performance in social and personal roles (see Chaps. 20 and 25). Also, families need support for expenditures and caring for patients; in the case of patients without family support, public health and social sectors also have to provide them accommodation (see Chap. 16). Psychosocial rehabilitation process, then, requires use of both health and nonhealth sectors, and this may generate costs to families and other sectors, the so-called spillover effect [34]. A study of costs of schizophrenia in England by Mangalore and Knapp [35] included, for example, the following costs: health services, social care, other public expenditures, private expenditures, informal care costs, costs of productivity losses, costs of premature mortality, and criminal justice system costs.

Autism is another disorder that requires multiple services such as support for families, accommodation, special educational interventions (educational psychologists), and healthcare. It is a high-cost disease not only for services but also for families [36] (see Chap. 23), and for this reason an economic evaluation of autism should include all these costs [37, 38]. For instance, a study of the costs of autism in England included costs for education, accommodation, medication, healthcare, community and social sectors, out-of-pocket expenditures, and productivity losses [37]. Costs for education are not always easy to measure and depend on the country's educational system. An instrument is available for this purpose, the Child and Adolescence Service Use Schedule, and includes educational costs [6].

Similarly, economic evaluations of alcohol and drug use disorders should consider that criminal costs account for almost two-thirds of costs for alcohol use disorder in the United Kingdom [6], for 42% of homicides in the United States [39], for one-fifth of accidents in the workplace, and for an annual 1.2 million deaths in traffic accidents in Brazil (see Chap. 26). Including such components of costs is worthwhile for guiding health policies in terms of reducing violence, accidents, and other negative externalities. Criminal justice costs related to alcohol and drug use should be included in economic evaluations as nonhealth direct costs. Moreover, criminal justice costs are extremely relevant when estimating costs among people with challenging behavior [38]. On the other hand, some extremely debilitating disorders such as dementia may need full-time informal care or require a paid caregiver, which are not usually provided by public health systems (see Chaps. 17 and 22). Health economists have been warned for the need of conducting economic evaluation taking into account costs with informal care and productivity losses, addressing studies targeting vulnerable population (mental disorders in children and the elderly), and adopting broader perspective enabling to include relevant components of cost in the analysis. Also, there is need of studies verifying how the narrow measurement of costs affects resource allocation and equity [10, 24–26, 33, 40–42] (see Chap. 10). In the case of mental disorders, because a large proportion of total costs are due to indirect costs and nonhealth direct costs [23–25, 38, 43], effects of interventions might be underestimated, misleading decisions on resource allocation and favoring inequality [44] (see Chaps. 8, 9, 10, and 11). It is not possible to measure all costs incurred, but the most relevant costs should not be omitted in a costing analysis. The main question is, "What is a relevant cost?" In this regard, Knapp and Beecham [33] noted that it was possible to determine the core services predicting the major proportion of total costs among mental health services, allowing a smaller list of services to be costed. Byford et al. [11] noted that two patterns of services inclusion usually occur: one linked with the inclusion of all possible services and programs involved, some of which are not relevant, and the other linked with the exclusion of important services and programs leading to cost underestimation. The recommendation, in this case, is to ask experts which programs and services are relevant to the topic of research (See examples in chaps. 14–16).

2.3.2.1 Classifying Components of Costs

After choosing the components of costs to be included in the study, it is necessary to classify them as direct or indirect costs in order to choose the method and the instrument with which to measure them. Direct costs compose three major types of components of costs: capital costs (land, buildings, equipment), treatment costs (interventions, clinical staff, medications), and revenue costs (support services, overhead, utilities, and other nonhealth costs). Treatment costs and some nonhealth costs are the core of an individual's costs variation, whereas capital costs, support services, and overhead are usually not closely related to an individual's variation of costs. Therefore, these costs can be classified into VCs and FCs, allowing for the use of different methods suitable for estimating them.

However, the classification of costs as VCs and FCs is not straightforward, depending on the characteristics of the services and the costing system, and on the presence of physical comorbidities. For example, we could consider the use of a transportation service as a VC because it is used according to the need of patients, and needs vary from one patient to another. Conversely, if a hospital and a third party (for instance, a rental car company) agree on monthly FCs, then these costs would be the same even if the service is not used, and therefore they could be classified as FCs (see Chap. 14).

Of note, classifying costs implies focusing on variation by individual, that is, is a cost variable or fixed according to the individual's consumption pattern. Sometimes it is necessary a pilot study to verify the relevance of this variation.

2.3.2.2 Time Horizon: Long-run Versus Short-run costs

In economic evaluation it is important to set a follow-up long enough to observe costs variations and effects, that is, time horizon. Then, costs can be measured over the short-run term or the long-run term. Costing measurement according to Economic principles should be based on long-run marginal opportunity costs [10]. A long-run term basis is appropriate for identifying an individual's variation and for marginal costs, which are especially important in economic evaluation and in planning service expansions. For instance, Hallam and Trieman [45] evaluated outcomes of and costs for patients with persistent challenging behaviors who were discharged from a psychiatric hospital in London to community services; they found an important reduction on the costs 5 years afterward, though no remarkable difference in psychiatric outcomes occurred during this period. Also, while implementing a new intervention, a learning period may be required, and costs are usually higher in the beginning of the new intervention implementation than some period afterwards. Therefore, the choice of time horizon can substantially affect costs and the estimation of the cost-effectiveness of an intervention, especially if the follow-up is not long enough to allow outcomes and benefits to occur [5].

Short-run marginal costs usually includes only revenue costs and for this reason, it is not reccomended for costing services where targets are expanding or creating new services. However, it is acceptable to use short-run average costs when including revenue and capital costs as proxies of long-run marginal costs. Therefore, in the long run, average costs are close to marginal costs. Usually, it is recommended costing services and programs for at least 3–6 months, though a longer time might be required [24]. However, the majority of economic evaluations running with clinical trials collect short-run costs. Then, they should include average revenue costs, overhead, and capital costs to be approximately equivalent to long-run marginal costs [9, 10].

2.3.3 Data Collection and Costs Measurement

Once all services and supplies are identified, it is important to verify the nature of each item and its payment process in order to choose the costing method and the unit cost.

In general, two main approaches are used to measure healthcare costs: the top-down and the bottom-up approach [13, 46, 47]. The top-down approach (or gross costing) starts from the total costs of resources consumed, which are obtained retrospectively from administrative databases, and it estimates the average costs of consumption per person. The bottom-up approach (or micro-costing approach) is based on collecting all individual data of consumption of resources and then aggregating all individual costs, summing them to achieve the total costs. The latter method is more accurate, though also more time-consuming, than the former because it takes into account cost variability among individuals.

Economic studies usually combine the two methods (top-down and bottom-up approaches), creating a mixed approach, depending on data availability and the feasibility of estimating costs.

2.3.3.1 Top-Down Approach

A top-down approach is useful and easier for estimating FCs, such as human resources, over the short term. Estimating costs on the consumption of variable items is much more complex.

However, depending on the degree of the difficulty in estimating costs, it is important to bear in mind that consuming too much time for measuring irrelevant costs is useless [7]. For example, if the electricity costs of an entire hospital are paid in one bill, it is difficult to determine what amount of electricity was consumed by each unit of the hospital. And it is not possible to determine the amount of electricity consumed by each patient in the psychiatric unit, for example. Different methods are available to estimate these costs, but the direct allocation method is commonly applied in hospital costing studies, in which the total costs are estimated, after which it may be possible to estimate the average costs when not considering variation among units; if considering such variations, the proportional ratio per unit may be used (see Chap. 14). Once costs per unit are estimated, it is possible to estimate the average costs per patient. When information on the occupation rate of a hospital unit is not available, it is usually arbitrated with a value of 80% of the total occupancy rate [7].

On the other hand, items such as medications vary too much from one patient to another; for this reason the average costs are not accurate. In this case, using a micro-costing approach for estimating individual costs is more appropriate [7].

2.3.3.2 Bottom-Up Approach

Micro-costing involves collecting data on the frequency of consumption of services directly from the patient, family, health professionals, or medical records. No gold standard exists, and each source of data has advantages and disadvantages.

Collecting data from patients and families is useful, especially for reporting the use of several services (outpatient, emergency care, primary care), because each health service is not able to provide information on the consumption of services outside its unit [48]. The main disadvantage is recall bias (see Chap. 13). In this regard, diaries are more accurate and minimize recall bias [11].

On the other hand, health services, health professionals, and medical records are able to provide more accurate data on the frequency of visits to services and about the type and the number of procedures and interventions delivered. However, health professionals and medical records are less reliable in a hospital context because missing information is common [48].

A few questionnaires and inventories address the measurement of mental health services utilization (see Chap. 13). One of the most used questionnaires to collect data on direct costs, including mental healthcare, is the Client Sociodemographic and Services Receipt Inventory, developed by Knapp and colleagues [10, 49] in the United Kingdom. This tool is designed to collect data on sociodemographics, benefits, occupational and work statuses, work days lost because of a mental disorder, healthcare utilization (including mental healthcare), medication, intervention by mental health professionals, accommodation, emergency unit use, hospital use, primary and outpatient care, and criminal justice use. These tools are discussed in detail in Chap. 13. The Database of Instruments for Resource Use Measurement is an open database to support health economists and researchers in this field to find questionnaires and resources in order to collect data on costs and health services utilization (available at http://www.dirum.org).

2.3.4 Estimation of Unit Costs

Overall, the estimation of costs is the product between the frequency of resources consumed and the unit costs. In micro-costing, data collection is addressed to measure the frequency of resource utilization, such as the number of visits to a psychiatrist in the past month or the number of days spent in a hospital. However, it is necessary to estimate the unit costs, that is, the cost of one visit to a psychiatrist or the daily costs per person in a hospital.

Different methods, perspectives, and purposes are used to estimate the unit costs, and each leads to different results [1, 7, 50]. Some countries deliver national unit costs with the average costs for each unit cost, like the United Kingdom (Unit Costs of Health and Social Care; http://www.pssru.ac.uk/project-pages/unit-costs/2015/), the Netherlands (the Dutch Manual for Costing in Economic Evaluation) [18], and Austria (http://healtheconomics.meduniwien.ac.at/science-research/dhe-unit-cost-online-database).

In the absence of national data, it is obligatory to estimate the unit cost of each relevant resource. The World Health Organization provides a database (http://www.who.int/choice/country/countryspecific/en/) of the average values of unit costs for 191 countries, which is useful when there are no national data, but micro-costing and accurate estimation of unit costs are preferred in cost-effectiveness analyses.

Some detailed guides are available to estimate unit costs, but a lack of consensus exists about the methods to estimate them [21]. In this chapter we present a global overview of how to estimate unit costs of the main resources consumed in healthcare. Detailed methods are described elsewhere [10, 51–53].

2.3.4.1 Capital Costs

Capital costs compose land, buildings, and equipment, and methods for costing them are based on measuring the opportunity costs, lifetime use, and interest rate (see Table 2.2). Building Rent can be considered a proxy of capital costs in some cases. Repair and maintenance of buildings and equipment are included in this item.

Multiple methods can be used to estimate capital costs, but one of the methods most recommended by Drummond et al. [7] is equivalent annual costs (or equivalent annual annuity). This method considers the current price, the discount rate, and the period of time related with lifetime use. The discount rate (interest rate) is a concept related to the value of a benefit over the time, that is, the so-called time preference. Usually, people prefer getting a benefit now rather than in the future, and for this reason, its value decreases over time. The costs of one good or service now are, for instance, much higher than they would be within 5 or 10 years, not considering depreciation (for equipment). Therefore, the costs of a new health program in the first year are higher than in the fifth year. When estimating costs of goods and services over the long term (>1 year), it is a paramount to apply a discount rate from 3% to 5% of the current cost.

Moreover, costs of buildings and equipment depreciate because their lifetime use decrease over time. A useful life for buildings varies from 8 to 40 years; the average number used in the majority of economic studies is 20 years. For equipment, useful life can vary from 3 to 8 years, with an average of 5 years. In the case of rent, it is possible to use its value as a proxy for capital costs.

Table 2.2 Estimation of unit costs and costing methods

	Item	Method to estimate unit costs
Capital costs	Land	Opportunity costs (interest) Interest rate (discount) Nondepreciable
	Buildings	rateEEA= r (NPV)/(1+r)$^{-n}$ EAA= Equivalent annual annuity, r= discount rate, n = lifetime use in years NPV=net present value Depreciation rate = (1 + discount rate)$^{n \text{ years}}$
	Equipment	Current price and depreciation or Cost of acquisition and EAA
Human resources	Health and nonhealth professionals	Professional time (by hour or by minute) Total costs (wages + charges and taxes) divided by working time For professionals not directly assisting the patient, the average cost per patient can be used. When the same professional serves two units or departments, it is important to determine the ratio of time spent in each one to derive the unit of cost
Overhead	Administrative management Sharable services/Support services (laundry cleaning, laboratory, etc.)	Direct allocation (does not consider simultaneous use of resources or use of resources external to the unit) Step-down allocation (hierarchical costs centers) Multiple allocation (proportional use of resources by unit of service)
Medication	Variable costs	Micro-costing per patient: the unit costs depend on whether the service is public or private
Interventions, vaccines, and lab tests	Variable costs	Micro-costing per patient

For more details consult references [1, 6, 7]

2.3.4.2 Human Resources

In healthcare, human resources can be divided in two main categories: those linked directly to assisting patients (e.g., psychiatrists, psychologists, nurses, occupational therapists) and those linked to supporting professionals and services (e.g., administrative functions, cleaning, cooking, security). Work agreements vary widely, and costing methods vary accordingly. Moreover, the costing method depends on the healthcare setting– for instance, whether a hospital or outpatient care.

Roughly speaking, costs with no direct health-related professional may not vary too much among mental health patients from the same unit or with the same condition; for this reason, a top-down approach using average costs per patient is far more useful and less time-consuming than bottom-up approach. Costs are estimating based on the salaries and fees of each category, on the job time scale, and on the number of patients assisted. The main problem is estimating costs of professionals working in two or more units in a hospital (shared costs), or perhaps for professionals working on laboratory tests for the entire hospital.

However, situations in which micro-costing is preferred depend on the purpose of the study and on the patient profile. Some patients consume services from multiple service units in a hospital, such as surgery rooms, emergency department, intensive care unit, whereas others remain in one unit, consuming only local interventions and professionals. In psychiatric wards, especially wards caring for patients with chronic mental illness, lower use of other units and interventions is expected than in clinical or surgical wards. If the consumption of services from other units of a hospital is low, it may be better to estimate the costs for a procedure, costing the entire process to deliver the intervention alone (professional plus material and equipment plus time required for the intervention) (active-based costing method). On the other hand, costs for health-related professionals vary depending on the need and profile of each patient.

2.3.4.3 Overhead (Administration Costs)

This term addresses those costs related to administrative services covering multiple units of a hospital or other health services. Drummond et al. [7] emphasize that there is not only one right way to estimate overhead costs, and it is not clear whether one method is better than another. The items included in the overhead costs can vary from institution to another; the usage of services and the method of cost allocation can vary as well. Overhead can be broken into two categories: (a) overhead related exclusively to management and administrative services, (b) overhead not directly related to health intervention or "hotel costs" (catering, cleaning, laboratory, dietary, security, gas, water, and so on).

2.3.4.4 Nontreatment Services (Supportive Services)

In this category of costs is included all necessary services for running and maintaining health services, such as diet, clothing, laundry, cleaning, security, administration services, informatics, pharmacy, and repair. These services can be subdivided as human resources, catering, transportation, external or third-party services (repairing services), utilities (e.g., electricity, telephone, internet, water, gas), and administrative services (overhead) (see Chaps. 14, 15, and 16).

2.3.4.5 Disposables and Suppliers

Disposable costs cover the consumption of all materials, and they can be estimated using a top-town approach considering the same unit with the same routine for interventions and similar diagnoses. If consumption varies extensively among patients, then micro-costing would be preferable. In psychiatric hospitals with patients who have few clinical comorbidities, low variation in the consumption of such suppliers is expected. However, the consumption of suppliers may be different in psychiatric units in a general hospital because the profiles of patients may be different with regard to the degree of psychiatric severity and on presenting clinical comorbidities; then, micro-costing would be more appropriate. For instance, patients with delirium tremens may need multiple clinical interventions and might consume more suppliers than patients in an acute psychotic episode who have no clinical comorbidities.

2.3.4.6 Medications

Medication costs vary substantially, adding substantial difficulties in estimating their costs in economic evaluation studies [4, 54, 55]. Three different types of drug costs may be used, according to the perspective of the study [4, 54, 55]: (a) production costs (costs for companies), (b) market costs (consumers), and (c) costs for public health sector (government). In addition, issues related to drug patents and investments in the research and development of new drugs affect how these costs are estimated.

Regarding a government and public health perspective, drug costs usually are lower than costs for consumers in a free market; in some countries, such as Brazil, the government pays drugs up to 24.38% (price adjustment coefficient) less than factory prices [56]. However, drug costs vary among public services, as can be observed in the Brazilian public medication price database, and it might be difficult to obtain accurate values of drug acquisition [57]. In some countries, consumers have to pay for medications at their market price (out-of-pocket costs) or are partially subsided (copayment). Excess profit from drug costs may also be a factor in overestimating costs in cost-effectiveness studies. Depending on the study perspective, such as health managed care, a dispensing fee should be included and copayments by patients should be excluded [55]. However, drugs often have multiple manufacturers, hindering costing exercises. More details are described in the International Society for Pharmacoeconomics and Outcomes Research Task Force guidelines [4].)

2.4 Costs Analysis and Cost Estimation Bias

The aggregation and estimation of total costs involve some common obstacles that might result in biased cost estimations: the nature of cost data, the accuracy of cost data, and the variability of unit costs. Bias should be adjusted in statistical analysis (see Chap. 7). Cost data are always skewed, that is, they have a non-normal distribution. This has some implications in terms of the low power of a study, and the use of nonparametric tests and regression models with bootstrapping. Accuracy is another important problem related to data validity. Several biases exist regarding the validity and reliability of questionnaires assessing services use and in the methods used for estimating unit costs (see Chap. 13). Item costs vary from one setting to another, and the range of this variability should be taken into account through sensitivity analysis. Data uncertainty should be addressed in statistical analysis, which is discussed in detail in Chap. 7. In epidemiological studies, randomized controlled trials are the gold standard, in particular because baseline differences are avoided by randomization. However, randomization does not work for cost data. Other statistical strategies are available to deal with these limitations.

Cost data are not generalizable because they depend on the setting and region; in terms of comparability among countries, costs should be converted to purchase power parity (see Chap. 11). Drummond and Sculpher [19] described in detail the main methodological flaws in reporting costs analysis in economic evaluations. All these issues are discussed in the following chapters, especially Chap. 7.

Key Messages

- Methods for defining, classifying, and estimating direct costs vary across guidelines, hindering data validity and accuracy.
- Costing depends on the perspective and goal of the study, on the identification and measurement of components of costs, on the costing approach for estimating unit costs, and on costs analysis.
- Costing in mental health should encompass costs from other sectors such as criminal justice, social care, education, and informal care, and include them in the economic evaluation. Not considering these costs might underestimate mental health intervention effects.
- A bottom-up approach, long-run marginal costs, a broader perspective, and comprehensive data collection are key elements recommended for costing in economic evaluation.
- Methodological flaws are common in costing studies, and transparency and a detailed description of the methods used to estimate costs are paramount to avoid misleading decisions on resource allocation.

Reference

1. Mogyorosy Z, Smith P. The main methodological issues in costing health care services. Centre for Health Economics, University of York; 2005. 12 Feb 2016.
2. Barnett PG. Review of methods to determine VA health care costs. Med Care. 1999;37(4 Suppl Va):AS9–17.
3. Luce BR, Elixhauser A. Estimating costs in the economic evaluation of medical technologies. Int J Technol Assess Health Care. 1990;6(1):57–75.
4. Garrison Jr LP, Mansley E, Abbott T, Bresnahan B, Hay J, Smeedin J. Good research practices for measuring drug costs in cost-effectiveness analyses: a societal Perpective the ISPOR drug costs task force report – part II. Value Health. 2010;13(1):8–13.
5. Drummond M, McGuire A. Economic evaluation in health care: merging theroy with practice. 2nd ed. New York: Oxford University Press; 2004.
6. Shearer J, McCrone P, Romeo R. Economic evaluation of mental health interventions: a guide to costing approaches. PharmacoEconomics. 2016;34(7):651–64.
7. Drummond MF, Sculpher MJ, Torrance GW, O\` Brien BJ, Stoddart GL. Methods for the economic evaluation of health care programmes. 3rd ed. Oxford: Oxford University Press; 2007.
8. Smith MW, Barnett PG. Direct measurement of health care costs. Med Care Res Rev. 2003;60(3 Suppl):74S–91S.
9. Beecham J. Collecting and estimating costs. In: Knapp M, editor. The economic evaluation of mental health care. 1st ed. Aldershot: Arena; 1995. p. 61–82.

10. Beecham J, Knapp M. Costing psychiatric interventions. In: Thornicroft G, editor. Measuring mental health needs. London: Gaskell; 2001. p. 200–24.
11. Byford S, McDaid D, Sefton T. Because it's worth it: a practical guide to conducting economic evaluations in the social welfare field. 2003. London, York Publishing Services Ltd.
12. Brouwer W, Rutten F, Koopmanschap M. Costing in economic evaluation. In: Drummond M, McGuire A, editors. Economic evaluation in health care: merging theory with practice. 2nd ed. Oxford: Oxford University Press; 2004. p. 68–93.
13. Slothuus U. An evaluation of selected literature on the measurement of costs in health economic evaluations. Odense: Syddansk Universitets Trykkeri. Health Economics Papers, 3. 2000. http://www.sdu.dk/-/media/files/om_sdu/centre/cohere/working+papers/20005.pdf
14. Institute for Quality and Efficiency in Health Care (IQWiG). Working paper: cost estimation. Cologne; 2009.
15. Jacobs P, Fassbender K. The measurement of indirect costs in the health economics evaluation literature. A review. Int J Technol Assess Health Care. 1998;14(4):799–808.
16. Barnett PG. An improved set of standards for finding cost for cost-effectiveness analysis. Med Care. 2009;47(7 Suppl 1):S82–8.
17. Heerey A, McGowan B, Ryan M, Barry M. Microcosting versus DRGs in the provision of cost estimates for use in pharmacoeconomic evaluation. Expert Rev Pharmacoecon Outcomes Res. 2002;2(1):29–33.
18. Oostenbrink JB, oopmanschap MA, Rutten FF. Standardisation of costs: the Dutch manual for costing in economic evaluations. PharmacoEconomics. 2002;20(7):443–54.
19. Drummond M, Sculpher MJ. Common methodological flaws in economic evaluations. Med Care. 2005;43(suppl7):II5–II14.
20. Husereau D, Drummond M, Petrou S, Carswell C, Moher D, Greenberg D, et al. Consolidated health economic evaluation reporting standards (CHEERS) statement. Value Health. 2013;16(2):e1–5.
21. Adam T, Evans D. Cost-effectiveness analysis: can we reduce variability in costing methods? Int J Technol Assess Health Care. 2003;19(2):407–20.
22. Edwards RT, Charles JM, Lloyd-Williams H. Public health economics: a systematic review of guidance for the economic evaluation of public health interventions and discussion of key methodological issues. BMC Public Health. 2013;13:1001.
23. McCrone P. Mental health economics: current methodological issues. Epidemiol Psychiatr Sci. 2011;20(3):239–43.
24. McCrone P, Weich S. Mental health care costs: paucity of measurement. Soc Psychiatry Psychiatr Epidemiol. 1996;31(2):70–7.
25. Knapp M. The economic evaluation of mental health care. 1st ed. Ashgate Publishing Limited; 1995.
26. Jönsson B. Ten arguments for a societal perspective in the economic evaluation of medical innovations. Eur J Health Econ. 2009;10:357–9.
27. Neumann PJ. Costing and perspective in published cost-effectiveness analysis. Med Care. 2009;47(7 Suppl 1):S28–32.
28. Hu TW. Perspectives: an international review of the national cost estimates of mental illness, 1990–2003. J Ment Health Policy Econ. 2006;9(1):3–13.
29. Unutzer J, Katon WJ, Russo J, Simon G, Von KM, Lin E, et al. Willingness to pay for depression treatment in primary care. Psychiatr Serv. 2003;54(3):340–5.
30. Xu K, Evans DB, Kawabata K, Zeramdini R, Murray C. Household catastrophic health expenditure: a multicountry analysis. Lancet. 2003;362:111–7.
31. Tai B, Bae Y, Le Q. A systematic review of health economic evaluation studies using the patient's perspective. Value Health. 2016;19(6):903–8.
32. Koopmanschap MA, Rutten FF, van Ineveld BM, van Roijen L. The friction cost method for measuring indirect costs of disease. J Health Econ. 1995;14(2):171–89.
33. Knapp M, Beecham J. Reduced list costings: examination of an informed short cut in mental health research. Health Econ. 1993;2(4):313–22.
34. Knapp M, Razzouk D. Costs of schizophrenia. Psychatry. 2008;7(11):491–4.
35. Mangalore R, Knapp M. Cost of schizophrenia in England. J Ment Health Policy Econ. 2007;10(1):23–41.
36. Cidav Z, Marcus SC, Mandell DS. Implications of childhood autism for parental employment and earnings. Pediatrics. 2012;129(4):617–23.
37. Barrett B, Byford S, Sharac J, udry K, Leadbitter K, emple K, et al. Service and wider societal costs of very young children with autism in the UK. J Autism Dev Disord. 2012;42:797–804.
38. Knapp M. Hidden costs of mental illness. Br J Psychiatry. 2003;183:477–8.
39. Miller T, Levy D, Cohen M, Cox KL. Costs of alcohol and drug-involved crime. Prev Sci. 2006;7(4):333–42.
40. Chisholm D, Evans D. Economic evaluation in health: saving money or improving care? J Med Econ. 2007;10:325–37.
41. Jones PB, Barnes TR, Davies L, Dunn G, Lloyd H, Hayhurst KP, et al. Randomized controlled trial of the effect on quality of life of second- vs first-generation antipsychotic drugs in schizophrenia: cost utility of the latest antipsychotic drugs in schizophrenia study (CUtLASS 1). Arch Gen Psychiatry. 2006;63(10):1079–87.
42. Trautmann S, Rehm J, Wittchen HU. The economic costs of mental disorders: do our societies react appropriately to the burden of mental disorders? EMBO Rep. 2016;17(9):1245–9.
43. McDaid D, Knapp M, Medeiros H. MHEEN group. Employment and mental health: assessing the economic impact and the case for intervention. London: London School of Economics & Political Science; 2008.

44. Weatherly H, Drummond M, Claxton K, Cookson R, Ferguson B, Godfrey C, et al. Methods for assessing the cost-effectiveness of public health interventions: key challenges and recommendations. Health Policy. 2009;93(2–3):85–92.
45. Hallam A, Trieman N. The cost effectiveness of specialised facilities for service users with persistent challenging behaviours. Health Soc Care Community. 2001;9(6):429–35.
46. Slothuus U. An evaluation of selected literature on the measurement of costs in health economic evaluations. Odense: Syddansk Universitets Trykkeri. (Health economics papers, 3); 2000.
47. Gray A, Clarke P, Wolstenholme J, Worsworth S. Applied methods of cost-effectiveness analysis in health care. 1st ed. Oxford: Oxford University Press; 2011.
48. Byford S, Leese M, Knapp M, Seivewright H, Cameron S, Jones V, et al. Comparison of alternative methods of collection of service use data for the economic evaluation of health care interventions. Health Econ. 2007;16(5):531–6.
49. Chisholm D, Knapp MKH, Amaddeo F, Gaite L, Winjgaarden B. Client socio-demographic service receipt inventory European version: development of one intrument for international research. Br J Psychiatry. 2000;177(39):s28–33.
50. Riewpaiboon A, Malaroje S, Kongsawatt S. Effect of costing methods on unit cost of hospital medical services. Tropical Med Int Health. 2007;12(4):554–63.
51. Oostenbrink JB, Buijs-Van der Woude T, van Agthoven M, Koopmanschap MA, Rutten FF. Unit costs of inpatient hospital days. PharmacoEconomics. 2003;21(4):263–71.
52. McFarkand B, Smith J, Bigelow D, Mofidi A. Unit of costs of community mental health services. Admin Pol Ment Health. 1995;23(1):27–42.
53. Curtis L, Burn A. Unit of costs of health & social care 2015. Personal Social Services Research Unit; 2015.
54. Mullins C, Seal B, Seoane-Vasquez E, Sankaranarayanan J, Asche C, Jayadevappa R, et al. Good research practices for measuring drug costs in cost-effectiveness analyses: medicare, medicaid and other US government payers perspectives: the ISPOR drug cost task force report—part IV. Value Health. 2010;13(1):18–24.
55. Mansley E, Carroll N, Chen K, Shah N. Good research practices for measuring drug costs in cost-effectiveness analyses: a managed care perspeective: the ISPOR drug cost task force report-part III. Value Health. 2010;13(1):14–7.
56. South American Institute of Government in Health, Giovanella L, Feo O, Faria M, Tobar K. Health systems in South America: challenges to universality, integrality and equity. Rio de Janeiro: ISAGS; 2012.
57. Razzouk D, Kayo M, Sousa A, Gregorio G, Cogo-Moreira H, Cardoso AA, et al. The impact of antipsychotic polytherapy costs in the public health care in Sao Paulo, Brazil. PLoS One. 2015;10(4):e0124791.

3 Outcomes Measurement for Economic Evaluation

Denise Razzouk

Abstract

Benefits or outcomes are used in economic evaluation to assess welfare maximization or health gain, depending on theoretical view – whether its a welfarist or extra-welfarist perspective. On the other hand, the measurement of health outcomes are usually related to clinical symptoms, physical functioning, and quality of life. In the Mental Health field, using exclusively clinical outcomes is not appropriate to capture all benefits obtained from treatments. Social and psychological dimensions are also crucial components to evaluate mental health gains. In economic evaluation, the choice of outcome should be based on the relevance to the patient's health and quality of life. Therefore, several challenges exist in defining the best mental health outcome in economic evaluation. In an extra-welfarist approach, outcomes in economic evaluation are classified into two main groups: one *not* based on client preferences (so-called measures), and a second *based* on client preferences (so-called values). Methods for assessing measures are scales based on specific and nonspecific disease symptoms. Methods for assessing outcome values are standard gamble, time trade-off, rating scales, and ratio scales. Only standard gamble assesses utility because it involves preferences based on uncertainty. The person trade-off method and multiattribute tools use expert panels and indirect methods, respectively, to assess outcome values. The capability approach has recently emerged as a new alternative to welfarist approach, focusing in broader measurement of outcomes related to individual's capability and quality of life. This concept was operationalized into a multidimensional instrument for the Mental Health field: ICECAP-MH. In the welfarist approach, outcomes are expressed in mon-

D. Razzouk (✉)
Centre of Economic Mental Health (CESM),
Department of Psychiatry, Universidade Federal de Sao Paulo, Rua Borges Lagoa 570, 1° andar, São Paulo, Brazil, 04038-000
e-mail: drazzouk@gmail.com

D. Razzouk (ed.), *Mental Health Economics*, DOI 10.1007/978-3-319-55266-8_3

etary units and assessed mainly by contingent valuation (CV; willingness-to-pay method) and discrete experiment choice. This chapter describes these methods and discusses their advantages and disadvantages for economic evaluation in the Mental Health field.

Key Points Summary

- Definition of *outcome* in mental health, mental health services, and in economic evaluation
- Outcomes measures and valuation
- Preference, utilities, and values
- Methods for utility/values estimation (rating scaling, standard gamble, time trade-off, magnitude estimation, person trade-off)
- Multiattribute methods
- Capability approach tools
- Willingness-to-pay methods and discrete experiment choice for monetary outcomes

3.1 What Is an Outcome for Economic Evaluation?

Outcomes in Health Economics are usually called outputs or benefits. Benefits, from an economic perspective, have their origins in the economic principles of the welfare theory (see Chap. 1). In this sense, benefits are based on individuals' preferences and values. A benefit, then, is not solely the amount of an output produced, but rather the value of an output attributed by an individual (a patient or the general public). According to the welfarist viewpoint, the goal in public policy is to maximize welfare. For this purpose, cost-benefit analysis (CBA) is the mainstream economic evaluation analysis in terms of the comprehensiveness of measuring all benefits and costs, that is, computing the overall welfare produced by a certain costs (see Chap. 4). In this regard, maximization of welfare includes gains on health and nonhealth outcomes, such as reducing productivity costs (see Chap. 29).

Despite some criticisms about its validity, the framework beyond the concept of welfare maximization was adapted in the healthcare domain within the extra-welfarist approach, in which the goal of maximization of health replaced maximization of welfare [1, 2] (see Chaps. 4 and 6). The allocation of resources in health policies has thereby been addressed for the maximization of health gain. While maximization of welfare is related to CBA, maximization of health is mainly related to cost-utility analysis (CUA) and cost-effectiveness analysis (CEA) (See Chaps. 5 and 6). However, this distinction is far from being simple and free of divergent views and conceptualizations among health economists [2–10] (See Chap 4, 10 and 11).

The main divergence between these two approaches is related to resource allocation [6–9]. While in CBA all relevant (health- and non–health-related) outcomes to society are included to verify potential benefits and to what extent they are worthwhile, in CUA and in the majority of CEA studies, only some dimensions of well-being and health outcomes are supposed to be included. Moreover, the former is based on individuals' preferences elicited through their ability to pay for the benefit, whereas in the latter approach, decision-making is usually based on an arbitrated threshold acceptable to be paid for each unit of health gain, or it is hierarchically based on the best intervention in terms of producing more health gains (See Chap. 6). Preferences, in this case, are based on the wishes of the general public rather than those of patients.

While determining the efficacy and safety of a treatment is the crucial step for receiving approval to be available on the market, this is not the case for resource allocation. Yet, once the effect of a treatment is well established, it is necessary to verify how affordable and valuable the treatment is in terms of public health policies [7]. Hence, health economic evaluation compares two or more alternatives in order to verify which one produces more benefits with optimal costs, that is, which has dominant cost-effectiveness. Then, health managers and policymakers are willing to pay and to allocate resources for that alternative, allowing greater health gain with the best value for the money. These theoretical conflicts among economic approaches for measuring and evaluating outcomes and costs raise equity and ethical considerations [11], although these are not discussed in this chapter (See Chaps. 5, 8–11).

Notwithstanding a lack of consensus about which outcome should be maximized and how outcomes should be measured, the majority of methods for measuring economics outcomes are not completely satisfactory for economic evaluation in mental health, especially those for severe mental disorders.

This chapter presents the main methods available for measuring outcomes in economic evaluation and discusses to what extent these measures are appropriate for assessing mental health and well-being among people suffering from mental disorders and other mental health problems.

3.2 What Is a Health Outcome?

In the health domain, an outcome is linked to two major concepts: mortality and morbidity. Health gain is expressed when mortality rates decrease and when it is possible to decrease morbidity and disability and, ultimately, increase quality of life and well-being. Outcomes are measured through scales assessing symptoms related to specific diseases and the degree of symptom severity. Benefits for health science focus on health status rather than on welfare, though there might be a relationship between them, because healthy states produce more satisfaction and well-being than sickness.

In addition, health outcomes have three main characteristics: uncertainty regarding response to treatment (partial and total remission or no remission of symptoms and eventually death), uncertainty of the duration of the health state, and uncertainty regarding the health outcome (cure, disability, death) [12]. In the case of chronic diseases, a fourth characteristic is related to unpredictable disease recurrence. And, in the case of poor prognosis or in those with more severe symptoms, a fifth characteristic is due to permanent complications or injuries such as blindness due to diabetes, even after controlling glucose levels. In this sense, if health gain is assessed by effective glycemic control and general health index, it should be considered that the permanent disability (blindness) also causes social, psychological, and economic losses.

On the other hand, in mental health, outcomes are not solely focused on diseases symptoms, because mental disorders hinder the social and global functioning of subjects in society, including the ability for work, leisure, and relationships (see Chap. 25). The nature of mental health outcomes is complex because a lack of consensus exists on the clear definition and consistency of the most relevant outcome, and sometimes, relevant outcomes are intangible and difficult to measure, or they comprise multiple components [13].

Also, mental disorders produce negative externalities that are not related with health, such as absenteeism from work, education failures, more need for social benefits, and a higher frequency of stigmatizing behaviors. All these externalities hinder not only the quality of life of patients, but block them from having a normal life and engaging in societal activities as a citizen, acting toward the development of and innovation in society, and producing wealth. Yet, improving from a mental disorder is a complex process, and no clear consensus exists on the criteria to ascertain recovery and participation in society (See Chap 12) [4, 13]. Therefore, in mental health, benefits are not only health gains, but also welfare gains, opportunity gains, citizenship gains and productivity gains, though measuring these presents challenges [14].

3.3 What Is a Mental Health Outcome in Economic Evaluation?

The measurement of health gain and welfare maximization is still an open question in the healthcare domain. Welfarist health economists defend the societal perspective and the measurement of utilities based on individuals' preferences, expressed in monetary terms (see Chap. 4). On the other hand, extra-welfarist health economists focus on health indicators combining the quality and quantity of life, such as quality-adjusted life years (QALYs), using methods to assess utility, estimated on the basis of the general public's preferences and experts' opinions (See Chap 6). They focus, rather, on health gain and on the distribution of health gain in order to guide resource allocation in health policies by prioritizing resources for some health states or vulnerable groups, that is, taking into account equity issues, though debate on that is still in progress. Moreover, mental health challenges both approaches in terms of defining "mental health gain" and regarding the validity of methods available to measure outcomes.

Therefore, at least two major concerns relate to mental health outcomes in economic evaluation. First, the choice of outcome for economic evaluation is complex and tricky, because the outcome chosen should be relevant in terms of changing individuals' mental health and quality of life. All diagnostic criteria for mental disorders are based on the presence of psychiatric symptoms and on the global impact of psychiatric symptoms on individuals' lives and on their global functioning. For example, if we compare two antipsychotics for individuals with schizophrenia disorder using the Positive and Negative Syndrome Scale (PANSS) to assess changes in clinical outcome, a statistically significant difference between two drugs might be not detectable; that is, symptoms (e.g., delusions and hallucinations) may remain unchanged. However, if one group retains psychotic symptoms but exhibits less violent behavior when taking one of the drugs, then this is not exact the "benefit" because it decreased the psychotic state (no health gain measured by PANSS), but rather because the patients are enabled to establish more friendly and less violent relationships; therefore, the drug affects patients' lives and their family's lives. It is likely that a patient's family would prefer the decrease in violent behavior, whereas policymakers would choose the cheaper drug because no relevant differences are shown in the PANSS. If someone breaks a leg and recovers from it after orthopedic treatment, patients and policymakers do not really disagree about what is relevant in terms of health gain. However, in terms of mental health, which outcome is more relevant when a mental disorder cannot yet be cured?

Therefore, mental health interventions aims more to address reducing disability and overcoming global losses rather than just gaining "health" in clinical terms. If a treatment enables a patient with schizophrenia to work or to live with some level of autonomy and quality of life, the impact or benefit for him and his family might be higher than solely improving some digits in the PANSS. Of course, both clinical and social outcomes may usually improve, but gains might be not proportional in terms of benefits and relevance. Therefore, outcome relevance and importance is closely linked to individuals' preferences, and in this regard, welfarists and extra-welfarists have divergent views on how to consider this question [8] (see Chaps. 4–6 and 8–10).

The second issue is about outcome measurement. Using CEA, it is only possible to choose one outcome representing the impact of interventions, and this outcome is usually clinical because CEA is mainly carried out in clinical trials. However, it is not possible to analyze simultaneously other relevant outcomes, unless cost-consequence analysis (CCA) is added to CEA. On the other hand, CUA uses a generic health index (e.g., QALYs) based on utility measures. However, methods to estimate utility are not sensitive enough to capture changes in many dimensions of mental health, and it is therefore also difficult to affirm mental health gains (see Chaps. 6, 9, and 10).

3.4 Methods for Outcome Measurement in the Economic Evaluation

There are different levels for the measurement and valuation of outcomes in economic evaluation. The distinction between measurement and valuation is important because it involves different conceptions of outcomes [15]. Measurement is traditionally related to the measurement of symptoms through scales based on a specific disease or on generic health status. For instance, psychotic symptoms are usually assessed by scales such as PANSS, and quality of life is assessed using a multidimensional scale such as the World Health Organization Quality of Life Scale. These instruments do not involve individuals` preferences about the value of health states. Therefore, the measurement of psychiatric symptoms is limited to the interpretation of the improvement or worsening of the amount of these symptoms and does not consider the value of such improvement or worsening to individuals.

On the other hand, the valuation of outcomes refers to the value given by a subject to one particular health state in comparison with others health states; that is, it represents a preference for one health state over another [9, 15]. In addition, preferences can be related to the duration of health states and with nonhealth outcomes as well. The method used to elicit preferences and to estimate the value of outcomes varies according to theoretical approach: welfarist or extra-welfarist. Extra-welfarist assesses the value of preferences in terms of utility (ordinal level according to preference strength), whereas welfarists assess the value of preferences in monetary terms. Both use preference measures with the goal of outcome (health or welfare) maximization. However, both approaches have been criticized in terms of which societal values and preferences are being maximized and which people would benefit from these goals (see Chaps. 8 and 9). In this regard, the capability approach is a new alternative to the welfarist approache because it is not based on the preference for one or more specific outcome. Instead, it proposes to estimate multiple health and nonhealth dimensions in order to verify an indicator of the minimum level of life living with "decency"; that is, this approach is oriented toward equity issues, rather than maximization of health or welfare. This theory was introduced by Amartya Sen on the 1990s in order to re-define outcomes embedded in welfare assessment [6, 16–18]. According to this theory, capabilities should be added as an outcome to redefine the welfare concept in opposition to the welfare economics theory from neoclassical economics (see Chaps. 1, 6, and 9). In this regard, capabilities are related to individual objectives, choices, freedom, and equity [19]. In other words, capabilities are not related exclusively to the functionality or the health gain, but to individuals' well-being according to principles of autonomy, freedom, and access to opportunities [6, 16–18] (see Chap. 9).

Multiple classifications exist for the measurement and valuation of outcomes; here they are divided into four parts: (a) health outcome measurement, (b) methods for outcome valuation in utility using the extra-welfare approach, (c) outcomes based on the capability approach, and (d) methods for valuation of monetary outcome using the welfarist approach (see Box 3.1).

3.4.1 Health Outcome Measures

These measures are used mainly in CEA (see Chap. 5) when comparing two drugs or treatments in terms of effects and costs; they are also used in CCA when comparing health programs or complex health packages. The main limitations of such measures is the difficulty in comparing the treatment effects and benefits, because multiple instruments are assessing different domains [15]. This means that one treatment for depression might show improvement if it was chosen by one specific instrument covering a certain group of domains and no improvement if it was chosen by another instrument covering other domains. Also, they not allow comparability between different diseases and outcomes, as in outcomes valuation in estimating QALYs (CUA). Some recent efforts have used algorithms for converting such measures into QALYs [20] (see Chap. 6).

Moreover, issues exist on how each subitem or subdomain is equally weighted (or not) to be summed in overall scores. In CEA, it is only possible to use numerical outcomes such as total scores to estimate cost-effectiveness ratios (see Chap. 5). However, overall scores might not

Box 3.1 Methods for the Measurement and Valuation of Outcomes in Health Economics

1. **Health outcome measurement (mainly CEA and CCA)**
   Disease and specific symptoms scale (e.g., PANSS)
   Non-disease-specific and generic global functioning or quality-of-life scale (e.g., World Health Organization Quality of Life scale)

2. **Methods for outcome valuation in terms of utility (extra-welfare approach, CUA)**
   Standard gamble
   Time trade-off
   Rating scaling method
   Ratio scaling or magnitude estimation
   Person trade-off* (panel experts)
   Multiattribute tools: SF-6D, EQ-5D (indirect method) (see Chap. 6)

3. **Outcomes based on the capability approach**
   ICECAP-MH (Chap. 9)

4. **Method for the valuation of monetary outcome (welfarist approach, CBA)**
   (see Chap. 4)
   Willingness-to-pay method
   Discrete experiment choice

reflect improvement and worsening in subdomains in terms of relevance and preferences, as described in the example mentioned earlier in this chapter about improving violent behavior in PANSS without changing psychotic symptoms scores (see item 3.4).

3.4.1.1 Disease and Specific Symptom Scale

The majority of instruments measuring psychiatric symptoms uses dichotomous categorial outputs (present/absent) and ordinal measurement like the severity and frequency of symptoms (e.g., Clinical Global Impression scale).

Fewer scales provide total scores with a *cutoff* distinguishing normal and abnormal mental health status. The Hamilton Rating Scale for Depression scale, for instance, combines an assessment of the presence and severity of symptoms, resulting in scores and a cutoff for the presence and the severity of depression states. However, improvements in terms of decreasing suicidal thoughts are different from improvements in terms of eating and sleeping better; different patients might have the same total score, but the relevance of such improvement might be different.

Moreover, some scales combine within the same instrument clinical symptoms with the ability to work and to perform social roles, whereas others focus on specific clinical symptoms. However, the majority of such scales are not sensitive or comprehensive enough to capture all relevant mental health and social outcomes improved by interventions. It is a commonplace in psychiatric clinical trials to assess multiple outcomes (e.g., social behavior, daily life skills, recovery, social skills) using different instruments or using multidimensional tools in mental health, but these data are difficult to interpret in terms of economic evaluation.

3.4.1.2 Non-Disease-Specific and Generic Global Functioning Scales

Usually, tools assessing multidimensional aspects of quality of life and global daily functioning are used as generic measures and are not disease specific. The 36-item Short Form is used as a measure of global health and quality of life, but this scale is not sensitive to many improvements in mental health status.

Scales based specifically on psychiatric symptoms are not appropriate to assess global improvements among people with long-term disease and chronic psychiatric symptoms, as in schizophrenia disorders. In that case, psychiatric symptoms might remain unchanged but social and daily skill performance might improve over time. This is important because in terms of preferences, patients and families gives equal values to other nonhealth dimensions, and these instruments are not appropriate for distinguishing them [13].

Equally important, the measurement of quality of life in mental health involves assessment of health and nonhealth areas such as psychiatric status, well-being, family burden, functional status, access to resources and opportunities (stigma), social and occupational roles, community safety, social inclusion, social network, personal relationships, and criminal and justice domains (see Chaps. 24–29). However, the overall score estimated through tools assessing multidimensional areas does not reflect improvements and worsening by subdomains, as mentioned earlier in this section.

3.4.2 Methods for Outcome Valuation in Utility Terms According to the Extra-Welfarist Approach

3.4.2.1 The Concept of Preference and the Valuation of Outcome

Outcome valuation refers to those methods that estimate the value to and the preference of an individual for an outcome. Health outcomes are unpredictable; that is, they are embedded with some level of risk and uncertainty. Therefore, value is also linked with the notion of choice (preferences) under an uncertain outcome (risk and probability). Some authors, such as Drummond et al. [9] and others, distinguish the concept of value from the concept of utility. Value represents the amount of preference under a no-risk condition, whereas utility is a weight representing the worth of a preference under uncertain outcomes. However, the term *utility* is used in practice to express the worth of elicited preferences.

Despite the indistinguishable use within the literature of terms such as *utility*, *values*, *preferences*, and *outcome*, there are relevant differences among health economics theoretical conceptualizations (see Box 3.2). The welfarist approach focuses on the maximization of the sum of all individuals' preferences. In this case, individuals express their preference and desire for the outcome that produces more pleasure and satisfaction according to their own judgement.

Box 3.2 Outcome Valuation, Preferences, and Utility

- Outcome valuation is related to individuals' preferences.
- The concept of preference is closely related to the concept of utility.
- In general, utility is the value, generally expressed on an interval scale, given to one preferable state over another under uncertain outcomes.
- For extra-welfarists, utility represents the value of a health gain according to the general public preferences.
- For welfarists, utility is the amount of satisfaction or well-being according to individuals' preferences and is expressed in monetary terms.

On the other hand, the extra-welfarist approach applies multiple and heterogeneous methods to elicit preferences from the general public, patients, and experts. In this case, preferences are not always linked to an individual's choice for a more desirable alternative for his or her own satisfaction. Instead, in the extra-welfarist approach the focus is to inform policymakers on general public preferences about resource allocation, rather than on maximizing welfare [9, 21, 22] (Chap. 6).

Preferences regarding health states fall into two main categories: expected preferences ("decision utilities") and experienced preferences ("experienced utilities") [21]. Expected preferences are usually elicited from healthy people among the general public. In this case, an individual should express a preference for one health state that may occur to them in the future or to somebody else. For instance, an individual should choose between a psychotic state or depressive state, even without any knowledge of or familiarity with these states, only based on descriptive scenarios. On the other hand, "experienced preferences" refer to those of people who suffered from one particular disease or who currently present active symptoms of disease. Then, the choice is based on the individual's own experience of being sick.

Despite preferences being predominantly elicited from among samples of the general public in the extra-welfarist approach, an open debate still exists on how preference should be captured and whether it is more appropriate to capture preferences of patients or the general public. Some authors argue that, in the case of psychiatric symptoms, the general public would not be able to express preferences appropriately because of their lower sensitivity to and familiarity with the nature of psychopathology. Conversely, other authors warned that people with schizophrenia disorders and other cognitive impairments or lack of insight would underestimate utilities preferences in comparison with the general public. In this regard, Versteegh and Brouwer [23] acknowledge that balancing preferences from mixed sources – both the general public and patients – might be preferable in the decision-making process.

3.4.2.2 Methods for Outcome Valuation in the Extra-Welfare Approach

Definition of Utility

Although *utility* has been given multiple definitions according to different theories since its welfarist origin (see Chap. 1), the term *utility* has been used – especially in the extra-welfarist approach – according to decision theory in order to support policymakers in resource allocation [24]. In this regard, the concept of utility derives from John von Neumann and Oscar Morgenstern's [25] utility theory described in 1944 as part of game theory. According to this theory, utility represents the value of individual preferences when choosing benefits (health status) under conditions of an uncertain outcome [9]. This theory relies on the fact that individuals make rational choices, and their preferences express what is best for them, that is, they maximize utility [24]. When one health state is preferable to another, we may conclude that the former health state has greater utility than the latter. The measurement of utility, then, represents the value an individual gives to his or her own health state [26]. The utility value is used to estimate generic outcomes, such as QALY, used in CUA (see Chap. 6).

This concept is innovative for the health field because it is not based on the measurement of one sole outcome or on symptom-based criteria. Instead, it captures multiple outcomes converted to an interval of values between 0 (death) and 1(normal health), according to a health preference scale. For instance, consider two individuals with the same severity of depressive symptoms, but one lives in a rural area and the other in an urban area. They may not present the same preference for therapeutic alternatives and for outcomes [27]. The concept of utility is very interesting for decision makers with regard to public policies because it allows the value of benefits to be measured from a societal viewpoint and under an uncertain outcome. Also, utility captures opportunity costs in that it encompasses individuals' choices. Individuals would choose those alternatives that would supposedly improve their lives as a whole (multiple outcomes) and not those that would ameliorate one specific symptom.

However, individuals' choices are not always rational and straightforward, so economists rely on normative assumptions of decision theory. Multiple factors interfere with behavior, like risk aversion or risk-seeking profiles. For instance, Daniel Bernouilli demonstrated that, given a gamble condition, people in general are risk-averse regarding uncertain gains and behave to maintaining the status quo, whereas they exhibit risk-seeking behavior in order to avoid uncertain losses [28]. Other factors, such as context, may influence an individual's preferences. When eliciting preferences, two descriptions or scenarios of the same health state should elicit the same preference, but this principle ("invariance principle") is not observed in practice [28]. Several studies have shown that the amount of details in a description of health states affects utility weights. Moreover, cognitive deficits may affect the ability of people to express preferences in terms of risks and probabilities, such as in schizophrenia and dementia disorders.

Methods for Eliciting Preferences

Multiple methods are available to estimate utility, and there is no gold standard well established in the literature, though standard gamble (SG) has been recommended by some authors as being preferable to other methods because it takes into account choices under uncertain and risky outcomes [9, 24, 29, 30]. However, because of difficulties in eliciting preferences from some respondents using SG methods, the time-trade off (TTO) method seems to be easier and more feasible than SG, especially among people with mental disorders, and for this reason it has is preferred by other authors [31].

Two main groups of methods are used to assess the value of preferences (utilities): direct and indirect methods. The difference between them is that the direct method is used to elicit individuals' preferences to health states, whereas the indirect method does not assess individual preferences because it verifies the current health state through multiattribute scales. Each multiattribute scale comprises a different number of health states embedded with utility values. These tools use utility values estimated from previous studies using different methods (e.g., SG and TTO). However, some authors consider indirect methods as being tools to assess values, rather than utilities [9] (see Chap. 6). Person trade-off (PTO) is an exception among all methods because it elicits preferences among experts using Delphi consensus to estimate final values for "utility," that some authors do not consider as utility but rather as a disability weight, used for estimating the disability-adjusted life year (see Chap. 6).

In this chapter we describe the following direct methods for eliciting preferences [32]: (a) rating scales (categorical, numerical, visual analog), (b) magnitude estimation (ME), (c) SG, and (d) TTO. Indirect methods for eliciting preferences are PTO (based on expert panel preferences) and multiattribute systems (e.g., EQ-5D).

Rating Scales

RSs allow individuals to express their preferences for different health states by ranking them from the worst to the best health states on an interval basis [32] (Fig. 3.1). The difference in the preferences among health states correspond to intervals between them [24]. For instance, moving from 10 to 20 would be interpreted as being the same as moving from 30 to 40 in terms of difference between preference strength. The Visual Analog Scale (VAS) is commonly used to allow people to express their perceptions of subjective symptoms, and it has been applied in Health Economics with

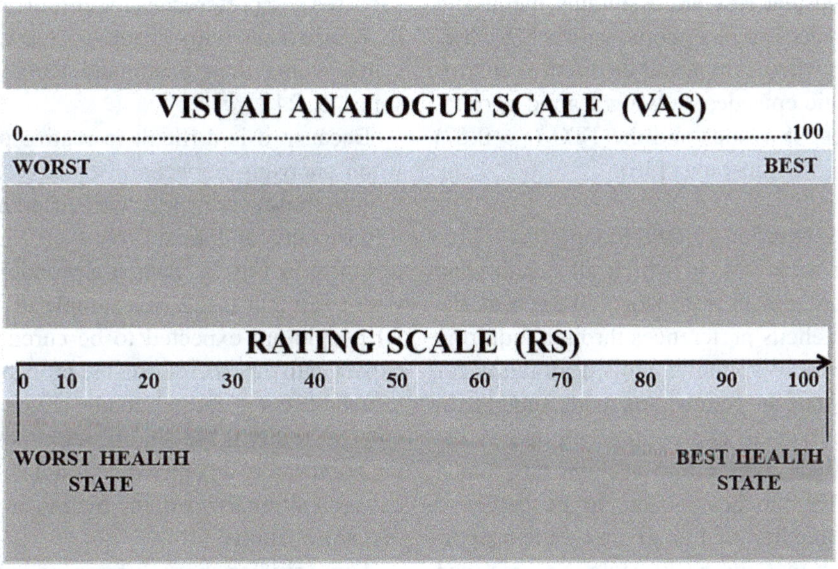

Fig. 3.1 Visual analog scale and rating scale

the purpose of eliciting preferences about health states. This method does not take into account uncertainty and risk in measuring preferences, and for this reason, preferences are expressed in values and then converted into utility (0 to 1), usually through power curve calculation [33, 34]. This methods varies in the use of numerical sequences (rating scales) or categories, or just a line between two values (VAS) [9].

The accuracy of this method is lower than the SG and TTO methods, and it should not be used along; the values obtained using this method should be corrected by comparing with the SG or TTO methods [24]. Two main measurement biases exist regarding VAS: one related to the number of health states (better or worse) to be ranked (context bias), and the other related to end-aversion behavior exhibited by some respondents who are resistant to use the extreme points of the scale [34]. In the first case, if the majority of health states are much better than one particular health state, then its attributed value would be decreased. Conversely, if the majority of health states are worse than a particular health state, that its value would be increased. For this reason, it is necessary to adjust these effects. Usually, the values from preferences elicited by the VAS are lower than the values elicited by SG and by TTO.

Despite these limitations, some studies have demonstrated that RSs are a suitable method to elicit preferences among people with schizophrenia disorder when comparing different scenarios of a psychotic episode, showing a good correlation between RS results and the TTO ($r = 0.67$) and SG ($r = 0.74$) methods [35].

Magnitude Estimation or Ratio Scaling

Contrasting with RSs, in which all health state categories are ranked from worse to the best, the ME method elicits preferences through inquiring about the level of an individual's desirability for one health state in comparison with another. In this case, individuals express their preference for one health state, taking into account how much they consider one health state to be better or worse than another, that is, given by the proportion at which that one health state is worse than another (e.g., 4 times worse, 10 times better) [30, 32]. The limitation of this method is how the standard health state is chosen to be comparable with other health states. For instance, choosing as standard a health state with mild or minor symptoms would allow different results than if the chosen standard was a health state with moderate or severe symptoms. In practice, this method is deemed a difficult task among respondents [30], resulting in low reliability values, especially among people with mental disorders such as schizophrenia and depression disorders [35].

Standard Gamble

The SG method, rooted in decision theory based on the von Newman–Morgenstern theory, elicits preferences under a scenario of uncertainty and involves probabilistic reasoning. It has been reported as being the most accurate method to assess utility because it takes into account the uncertainty of the outcome, and it involves individual risk behavior [24, 29]. Hence, individuals choose either "no treatment," leading them to remain in their current sick health state, or they choose the alternative "treatment," with different probabilities of cure or immediate death [9, 24, 29, 30]. Then, different probabilities of death are offered and the individual decides how much risk of dying he/she is willing to accept in order to achieve perfect health. This method is suitable for assessing preferences for chronic health states in comparison with death, or for those health states worse than death and temporary health states [9, 24].

Because it is difficult to realize probabilities when choosing between alternatives, it is common to show score cards with different probabilities of cure and death [9] (see Fig. 3.2) For instance, in Fig. 3.2, when a probability of cure with treatment is 0.2 in a sample of 100 people, 20 people are expected to be cured and 80 are expected to die. Increasing the probability of cure to 0.4, 40 cures and 60 deaths are expected. The value of utility is the "indifference point," that is, the point where an individual is not able to choose between alternatives in the treatment arm for one given probability.

Some studies show differences in the weights of assessing utilities between SG and TTO meth-

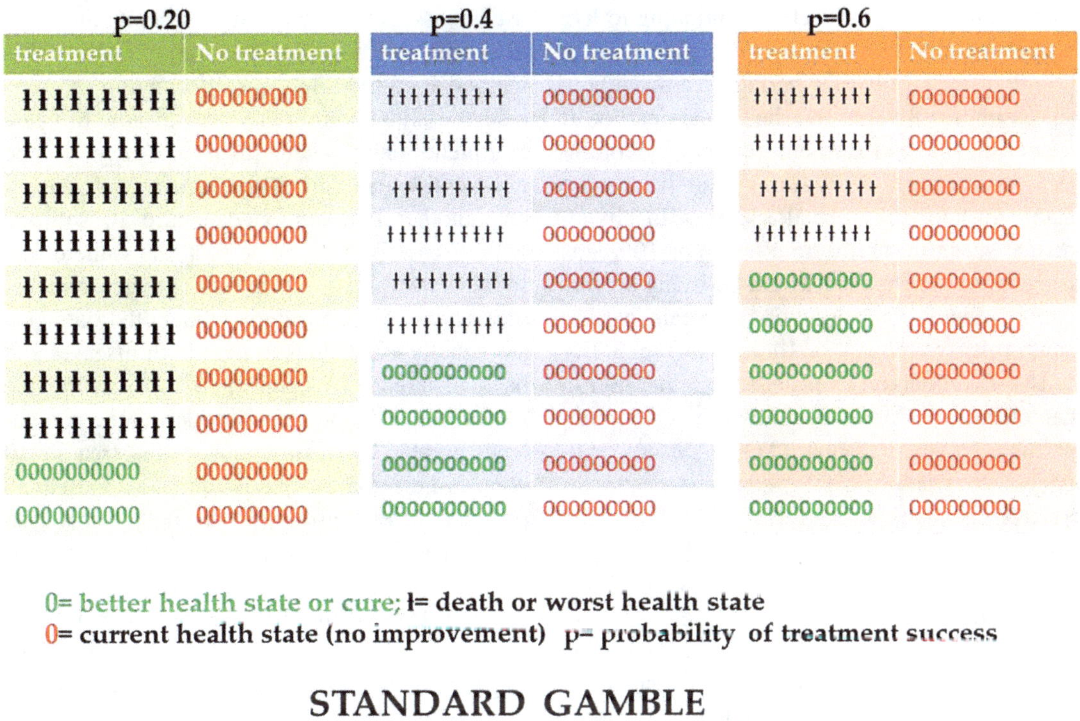

Fig. 3.2 Standard gamble using score cards

ods, resulting in higher weights using SG than TTO [30, 35]. It may be a challenging task to use SG among people with greater cognitive impairment, as in some cases of schizophrenia disorder, in part because of difficulties with probabilistic reasoning and in part because of the significant presence of risk-averse behavior among them [35]. Despite this, people with schizophrenia expressed similar utility (U) weights ($U = 0.19$) for the worst psychotic states using SG (described by the patients) in comparison with people with depressive disorders ($U = 0.18$) [35]. In one study using SG to assesses utilities among a sample of general public found weights of 0.47 and 0.88 for severe and mild schizophrenia, respectively [36].

Another study used SG to elicit preferences among a small sample of people with depressive disorder regarding 11 different depression-related health states according to depressive symptom severity and treatment received [37]. According to this study, the utility weights for severe untreated depression were, on average, 0.30, but 25% of the sample reported utilities equal to or worse than death. Greater utility weights were attributed to mild or moderate depression using antidepressant drugs (between 0.55 and 0.74). Utility weights were lowered by the presence of side effects of drugs by 0.1, on average.

Time Trade-Off

This method was created by Torrance [24] and was validated taking SG as the gold standard. Like the SG method, the TTO method has a similar principle, offering two alternatives to elicit preferences. In this case, however, TTO does not take into account outcome uncertainty; that is, individuals should decide whether they are willing to achieve a good health outcome in exchange for years of life. For this reason, this method assesses value rather than utility.

The utility weight is the point of indifference achieved when individuals are not able to choose between a health outcome and how many years of life they would be willing to lose in order to live with a better quality of life. For instance, considering a depressive state, we might want to know whether the individual prefers continuing to live in this state for 10 years or would prefer to accept the treatment and live in perfect health without depression for 8 years and die 2 years earlier. If he/she accepts the treatment, the inquiry continues, varying time (life years) until he/she are unable to choose between alternatives. In a hypothetical scenario with a time frame of 10 years, the point of indifference would be living 4 years without depression and dying 6 years earlier; then, utility would be 4 of 10, or 0.4. (Fig. 3.3).

The TTO method is easier to use than SG in mental health samples. People with schizophrenia disorder reported that TTO, VAS, and willingness to pay (WTP) easier to express preferences than SG and EM [35]. However, Konig et al. [31] assessed utility (U) weights using TTO in a sample of subjects with schizophrenia ($U = 0.75$), bipolar ($U = 66$), and alcohol-related ($U = 0.61$) disorders in an inpatient setting. They found a "ceiling effect," especially among the group with schizophrenia disorders, in which 43% of respondents were not willing to trade any time of life to perfect life, probably related to a lack of insight and greater severity in PANSS. In this regard, another study compared utility weights using the TTO method between a sample of laypersons and a sample of people with stable schizophrenia disorder [38]. On average, utility weights were 0.077 higher in the patient group than in the layperson group, showing the greater reluctance of patients for trading life years. Conversely, SG and multiattribute instruments were considered suitable when applied among people with bipolar disorder, showing similar lower values for a depressive state and a hypomanic state [39]. In summary, no consensus yet exists on the best method to elicit preferences among people with mental disorders. While some studies show some degree of evidence of the suitability of TTO to derive utilities among people with stabilized schizophrenia, SG and ME are still a cognitive hurdle [35].

Person Trade-Off

While the previously described methods are focused on the measurement of individuals' preferences, PTO, or the equivalence of numbers, is used to assess the social value of health interventions and programs [26, 40]. The rationale of this method is to provide clear information to guide resource allocation on the basis of how to value treatments and how to distribute them. If one intervention can cure 50 subjects with disease A and another intervention can cure 10 subjects with disease B at the same cost, the value of the former intervention is five times greater than that of the latter. Yet, considering that both treatments are equally efficacious to treat both diseases and have different costs, the goal is to define the social value of treatment considering the equivalence number between groups, that is, treating 10 people of disease group A is equivalent to treat 30 people of disease group B. This method was used to estimate disability-adjusted life years, an indicator of the burden of disease [41] (see Chaps. 6, 24, and 25). In this case, an expert panel was asked to ascertain the value of extending the lives of people without disabilities in comparison with those of people with disabilities, supposing that this latter group would have less "social value," and PTO was used to estimate disability weight (which is not a real utility, though it is not preference-based). For instance, if 100 people with a disability were equivalent to 800 people without a disability, then the disability weight (dw) would be estimated as:

$$dw = 1 - \left(\frac{100}{800}\right) = 0.875$$

This method was repeated to establish the value for curing each chronic condition in comparison with healthy people.

Multiattribute Method

This method is an effort to join multidimensional clinical scales and the estimation of utilities. Unlike direct methods, the multiattribute method is a system of generic health quality measurement that uses a multidimensional questionnaire inquiring about an individual's current health state. This method is not based on individual preferences, but rather assigns weights (derived from preferences assessed in population studies) to each health state defined in dimensions in each system [9, 42]. Each dimension has levels of

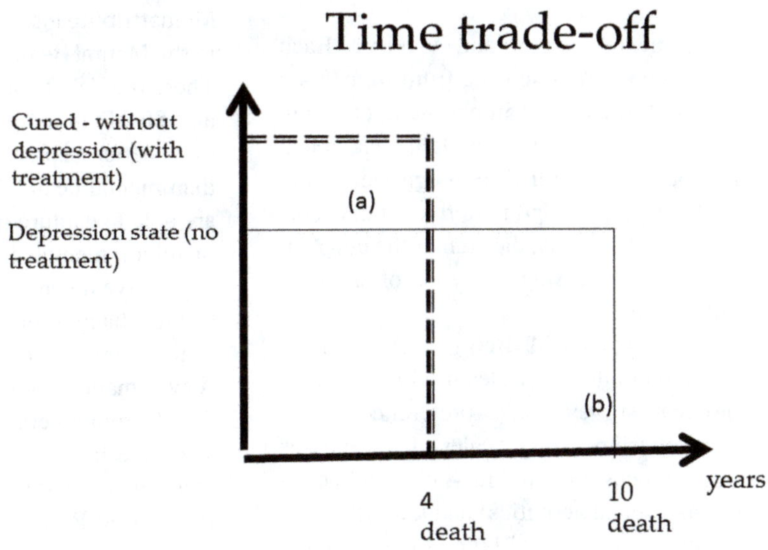

Fig. 3.3 Time trade-off

health and function impairments attached to one value based on the mean of general population preferences (utilities). Ultimately, it estimates a "health index utility" based on the values obtained from a scoring formula. This health index is, in practice, used in cost-utility studies as an equivalent of utility (though in fact, it is a value and not a real utility), with 0 meaning death and 1 meaning perfect health [42] (see Chap. 6).

This method has the advantages of being less time-consuming and easier to apply than direct methods for eliciting preferences. However, it challenges conceptual and methodological issues in Health Economics and in health domains, especially mental health. Many systems are available, but the most widely used are the five-dimension EuroQol (EQ-5D), the Health Utilities Index (HUI) Mark 2 and Mark 3, the six-dimension Short Form (SF-6D), and the Quality of Well-Being scale, among others [9, 42, 43] (see Box 3.3 and Chap. 6).

Differences Among Multiattribute Instruments

These instruments differ in their composition, methods used to estimate weights for a health state, and number of health states covered [42]. As consequence, these instruments might allow different estimations of "utility" for the same health state. For instance, some studies have shown that the SF-6D is more sensitive among healthy indi-

Box 3.3 Multiattribute Tools

EQ-5D: This was developed by the Centre for Health Economic in York (U.K.). It comprises five dimensions (mobility, self-care, usual activities, pain/discomfort, and anxiety/depression) covering 243 health states [44]. Each dimension has three levels of intensity: no problem, some problems, and extreme problems.

A survey of the British general public used the TTO method to measure preferences [45]. Multivariate regression analysis was used to assign weights to those preferences and to obtain a final scoring formula, that is, the sum of the constant coefficient and the weight of each of the five attributes, plus 1 [42]. Other variations of this tool exist (see Chap. 6).

SF-6D: This was developed by Brazier et al. [46] based on 11 items from the 36-item Short Form, an instrument commonly used to assess quality of life in health domains. Preferences of a general public sample in the United Kingdom were obtained using the SG method. The SF-6D comprises six dimensions (physical functioning, role limitations, social functioning,

(continued)

pain, mental health, and vitality). Each dimension allows scoring from four to six levels of intensity of impairment, covering 18,000 health states. A modeling statistical approach was applied to assign weights to each health state and to derive a final scoring formula, that is, the sum of the constant coefficient, the weight of each of six attributes, plus 1.

Quality of Well-Being scale: This is based on multiples scales used in epidemiological surveys, and preferences were derived from rating scales. It comprises three dimensions (mobility, physical activity, and social activities) and a fourth component with "21symptoms/complex problems" (dichotomic variable).

HUI Mark 2 and HUI Mark 3: Each version of the HUI was developed with a different purpose, and they comprise different dimensions, each with five or six levels, covering 972,000 health states. The latest version, the HUI3, has eight attributes: hearing, vision, speech, ambulation, emotion, cognition, pain, and dexterity [42].

viduals and it produces higher values for "utilities" than the EQ-5D and HUI3. Conversely, these latter two instruments are better able to capture severe impairment than the former.

Moreover, comparability among them is questionable, since utility values for the same health state might vary enormously [42, 47]. For instance, an individual with severe depressive symptoms might receive utility scores ranging from 0.26 to 0.8 [42].

Therefore, the choice between these methods leads to different values of utility to be used in the estimation of QALY in cost-utility studies, and it might mislead those involved in the decision-making process for health resource allocation [48] (see Chap. 6). In comparison with the HUI3, the EQ-5D is supposed to produce larger changes in scores favoring cost-effectiveness ratios of interventions, whereas the SF-6D has produced smaller cost-effectiveness ratios [48].

Multiattribute Instruments Applied in the Mental Health Domain

There is a debate on the usefulness of the EQ-5D and SF-6D in the mental health domain because they better capture changes in physical rather than mental health. In general, these instruments are able to capture improvements in health states in minor mental disorders such as anxiety and depressive disorders, but are not effective in capturing changes in psychotic disorders, such as schizophrenia and bipolar disorder [14, 49, 50]. A systematic review of the use of the EQ-5D and SF-36 among people with schizophrenia emphasized the low correlations between such instruments and specific symptom scales, such as Brief Psychiatric Rating Scale in people with schizophrenia, failing to capture therapeutic improvements in this group [51].

Moreover, the EQ-5D and SF-6D do not perform similar to estimated utility for anxiety and depression states, according to symptom severity. The EQ-5D results in a better cost-utility ratio, whereas the SF-6D performs worst in capturing changes in severe mental health states. Some evidence shows that utilities derived using the SG method have higher values than those derived using the TTO method, which might be an explanation for the differences between these two instruments [46].

A research team from the University of Sheffield recently developed a multiattribute system called the six-dimensional Clinical Outcomes in Routine Evaluation (based on the Clinical Outcomes in Routine Evaluation–Outcome Measure), with five items in an emotional component and a physical item, enabling cost-effectiveness and cost-utilities studies for minor mental disorders [52] (see Chap. 6).

3.4.3 Outcomes Based on the Capability Approach

The capability approach advocates the replacement of health maximization with "capability maximization" (see Chap. 9). The outcome is an individual's capability well-being, allowing the impact of complex health and social interventions to be evaluated [17]. In this regard, this approach would be aligned with the complexities of mental health outcomes, though research in this field is just beginning [6, 16] (see Chap. 9). The ICECAP-MH is a multidimensional instrument developed to assess the capabilities of people with severe mental disorders. It comprises aspects relevant to the Mental Health field, such as issues related to stigma, social participation, daily activities, freedom and ability to make decisions, and quality of relationships, among others [19] (see Chap. 9).

3.4.4 Methods for Valuating Monetary Outcomes Using the Welfarist Approach

In the welfarist approach, the cornerstone of economic evaluation studies is the CBA [9, 53]. Different from cost-effectiveness and cost-utility studies, CBA uses only monetary outcomes [53]. The WTP method is used to estimate outcomes in monetary terms based on two principles: one based on expressed individual preferences for one product or service, and the other on the individual's behavior in the real market [54]. The CV method is a direct survey–based approach used in the WTP method to elicit monetary values for treatments and health states [55]. There are four techniques used in CV [56] (see Box 3.4).

Face-to-face interviews to elicit preferences using the WTP method are preferable to self-response questionnaires or virtual contacts (e.g., telephone, Internet, mail; see Chap. 4). However, CV techniques vary in terms of respondents' acceptance, ability to pay, and understanding, and on welfare estimation. Another alternative to the WTP approach is Discrete choice experiments [56]. This technique is used to elicit WTP for a program or health service in which multiple attributes of healthcare are included, and it enables respondents to put a value on each of these attributes. Usually, a set of scenarios are presented and respondents choose one of their preferences and determine the intensity of that preference according to a hierarchical preference ordering (see Chap. 4). The

Box 3.4 Contingent Valuation Techniques with the WTP Method

Open-ended technique: This method allows consumers to give the maximum monetary value they would pay for a benefit or which proportion of their budget they would willing to sacrifice to get the benefit produced by a health treatment [9, 57]. Usually, a hypothetical scenario describing the new intervention or health program and the potential benefit for a health state are presented to individuals, and they judge the benefit's monetary value based on the assumption that treatment is available in the real market.

Bidding game: This method is used through an interview asking an individual whether he/she would accept paying a certain amount for one specific treatment. If he/she agree, then the interviewer continues to ask about higher values until the interviewee rejects the value, at which point the interviewer reduces the value until the identify the amount the interviewee would be willing to pay.

Payment card: The participant should choose the alternative with the higher amount he/she is willing to pay for one treatment; the value the participant is willing to pay is considered between the alternative chosen and the next highest one.

Close-end: This is a variation of the bidding game. If the respondent accepts paying the amount defined by the interviewer, then the highest amount is offered; if that amount is rejected, the amount the respondent is willing to pay lies between this two offers.

WTP approach has some advantages when compared with utility (QALY) and other approaches: it is aligned with economic principles of the welfare theory, it is more comprehensive in terms of capturing nonhealth and health outcomes (welfare gain), and it is more easily interpreted in policy decisions because it is expressed in monetary terms [12].

Despite some growing interest in the WTP method, few studies in healthcare use this approach, especially in the Mental Health field. This method has limitations, such as the influence of individuals' income and ability to pay on the monetary value assessed by WTP. However, some evidence from studies using WTP have shown that preferences were not affected by individual income [58].

Criticisms about the WTP method also refer to ethical issues related to assigning monetary values to human suffering and intangible costs. Yet, it is not clear-cut what should be asked (to patients or the general public), which level of outcome uncertainty and detail should be described in the scenario, and which individuals should be interviewed. Moreover, mental health challenges the general public's preferences in investing in mental healthcare because of stigmatizing behavior. For instance, Smith et al. [59] used WTP with a representative North American sample of 710 individuals to verify preferences to pay for physical and mental health treatments. Despite the fact participants of this study acknowledged the greater burden of mental disorders when compared with physical diseases, they were willing to pay 40% less for treatment for mental disorders than for care for physical diseases [59].

3.5 Economic Outcomes and Mental Health Services

Interest in assessing the efficiency, quality of care, and costs of mental health services has been growing. Indicators for measuring the quality of mental health care are still under development (see Chap. 12). However, deciding about quality of care is debatable according to different viewpoints, such as those of mental health professionals, policymakers, and patients and families. While some are preferably oriented toward improving processes (logistics) and costs (management), others are oriented toward patient outcomes. The shift of a hospital-based model of care to community-based mental health care has brought about several obstacles in terms of defining the promotion of mental health care and how to measure it. However, the majority of economic studies are oriented almost exclusively toward measuring costs with a goal of reducing costs, using "process measures" as the main outcome (duration of hospitalization), regardless of health outcome or patient gain. This can be useful for health managers and accountants, but Health Economics is driven to improve people's health and well-being, an in this regard, outcomes linked to patients and families (satisfaction, health, burden) are the cornerstone of economic evaluation. Few economic evaluations have been conducted on this topic (see Chaps. 15 and 16). CEA is not the best method to evaluate services in this regard, and other economic outcome measures should be developed and tested for this purpose.

3.6 Conclusion

In summary, the process to assess outcomes in economic evaluation is far from simple. Theoretical frameworks in Health Economics are based on promoting the best use of available health resources to maximize health and well-being in accordance with equity principles. There are relevant differences among conceptualizations of gain in well-being (e.g., welfare, health, utility, capability) and on the methods used to measure it. This heterogeneity in Health Economics methods leads to divergent results in terms of recommendations and guidance on resource allocation. The choice of theoretical approach is related to societal values, the nature of the health system (public or private), and the particular country's political and economic systems. On the other hand, the Mental Health field faces some peculiarities and challenges in assessing mental health improvements, especially because part of this "mental health gain" is the result of "social gain" rather than exclusively health gain. Moreover, methods available to assess outcomes in mental health are not comprehensive or sensitive enough to verify overall gains from interventions. In this regard, the capability approach promises a method aligned with mental health maximization (see Chaps. 9, 24,

Table 3.1 Comparison among health economic methods to assess outcomes

Approach	Economic Evaluation	Methods	Outcome	Limitations
Welfarist	CBA	WTP	Monetary	Difficult and time-consuming
Extra-welfarist	CEA	Health scales	Symptoms and functioning	Narrowness of measurement
	CCA	Multiple health and nonhealth scales	Multiple health and social measures	Difficult to decide on resource allocation
	CUA	SG, TTO, VAS, ME, PTO	Utility (QALY, DALY)	Low sensitivity to capture mental health dimensions
Extra-welfarist/Decision theory	CUA	Multiattribute tools: EQ-5D, SF-6D, CORE-6M	Health states (QALY)	Not appropriate for all mental disorders
Capability approach*	*	ICECAP-MH	Capability	To be tested

*Some authors classify capability as being extra-welfarist and close to the quality-adjusted life years (QALYs) model despite not measuring utility [60], whereas others see the capability approach as an alternative to extra-welfarism and welfarism [18] (see Chaps. 6 and 9)

CBA cost-benefit analysis, *CCA* cost-consequences analysis, *CEA* cost-effectiveness analysis, *CUA* cost-utility analysis, *DALY* disability-adjusted life year, *ME* magnitude estimation, *PTO* person trade-off, *SG* standard gamble, *TTO* time trade-off, *VAS* visual analog scale, *WTP* willingness to pay

and 25), though it is still in progress, and further research will ascertain these assumptions. Therefore, all methods available to for economic evaluation in mental health have relevant limitations (Table 3.1). However, Health Economics offers a valuable measure of the evaluation of mental health interventions: the economic worth of benefits for promoting mental health gain.

Key Messages

- Outcome in Health Economics is mainly expressed in terms of individuals' preferences (utility) for a particular health state in comparison with others, whereas health outcomes are traditionally measured to assess morbidity and mortality parameters.
- Mental health outcomes involve health and nonhealth attributes, and both are relevant in terms of patients' and families' preferences.
- Preferences are elicited to estimate utilities weights falling within an interval between 0 and 1, where 0 corresponds to death and 1 corresponds to perfect health.
- Standard gamble is aligned with decision theory and takes into account choices under uncertainty and according to risk-seeking/aversion profiles, though it is a challenging method to elicit preferences among people with mental disorders, especially in schizophrenia disorders.
- Time trade-off is an easier and more feasible method than SG for use among people with mental disorders, though some patients are reluctant to trade life years.
- Multiattribute methods such as the EQ-5D, SF-6D, and CORE-6D are feasible for use to capture health gains among people with minor mental disorders, but they fail among people suffering from psychotic disorders.
- The capability approach has emerged as a new alternative to be explored and tested in the Mental Health domain.

(continued)

References

1. Birch S, Donaldson C. Valuing the benefits and costs of health care programmes: where's the 'extra' in extra-welfarism? Soc Sci Med. 2003;56(5):1121–33.
2. Brouwer WB, Culyer AJ, van Exel NJ, Rutten FF. Welfarism vs. extra-welfarism. J Health Econ. 2008;27(2):325–38.
3. Brazier JE, Dixon S, Ratcliffe J. The role of patient preferences in cost-effectiveness analysis: a conflict of values? PharmacoEconomics. 2009;27(9):705–12.
4. Byford S, Sefton T. Economic evaluation of complex health and social care interventions. Natl Inst Econ Rev. 2003;186:98–108.
5. Coast J. Is economic evaluation in touch with society's health values? BMJ. 2004;329(7476):1233–6.
6. Coast J. Maximisation in extra-welfarism: a critique of the current position in health economics. Soc Sci Med. 2009;69(5):786–92.
7. Knapp M. Economic outcomes and levers: impacts for individuals and society. Int Psychogeriatr. 2007;19(3):483–95.
8. Drummond M, McGuire A. Economic evaluation in health care: merging theory with practice. 2nd ed. New York: Oxford University Press; 2004.
9. Drummond MF, Sculpher MJ, Torrance GW, O'Brien BJ, Stoddart GL. Methods for the economic evaluation of health care programmes. 3rd ed. Oxford: Oxford University Press; 2007.
10. Dolan P. Utilitarianism and the measurement and aggregation of quality – adjusted life years. Health Care Anal. 2001;9(1):65–76.
11. Dolan PA, Olsen JA. Equity in health: the importance of different health streams. J Health Econ. 2001;20(5):823–34.
12. Olsen JA, Smith RD. Theory versus practice: a review of 'willingness-to-pay' in health and health care. Health Econ. 2001;10(1):39–52.
13. Thornicroft G, Tansella M. Mental health outcomes measures. 3rd ed. Glasgow: RC Psych Publications; 2010.
14. Brazier J. Measuring and valuing mental health for use in economic evaluation. J Health Serv Res Policy. 2008;13(Suppl3):70–5.
15. Gray A, Clarke P, Wolstenholme J, Worsworth S. Applied methods of cost-effectiveness analysis in health care. 1st ed. Oxford: Oxford University Press; 2011.
16. Coast J, Kinghorn P, Mitchell P. The development of capability measures in health economics: opportunities, challenges and progress. Patient. 2015;8(2):119–26.
17. Mitchell PM, Al-Janabi H, Richardson J, Iezzi A, Coast J. The relative impacts of disease on health status and capability wellbeing: a multi-country study. PLoS One. 2015;10(12):e0143590.
18. Mitchell PM, Roberts TE, Barton PM, Coast J. Assessing sufficient capability: a new approach to economic evaluation. Soc Sci Med. 2015;139:71–9.
19. Simon J, Anand P, Gray A, Rugkasa J, Yeeles K, Burns T. Operationalising the capability approach for outcome measurement in mental health research. Soc Sci Med. 2013;98:187–96.
20. Mortimer D, Segal L. Comparing the incomparable? A systematic review of competing techniques for converting descriptive measures of health status into QALY-weights. Med Decis Mak. 2008;28:66–89.
21. Dolan P, Kahneman D. Interpretations of utility and their implications for the valuation of health. Econ J. 2008;118:215–34.
22. Dolan P, Metcalfe R. Valuing health: a brief report on subjective well-being versus preferences. Med Decis Mak. 2012;32(4):578–82.
23. Versteegh MM, Brouwer WB. Patient and general public preferences for health states: a call to reconsider current guidelines. Soc Sci Med. 2016;165:66–74.
24. Torrance GW. Utility approach to measuring health-related quality of life. J Chronic Dis. 1987;40(6):593–603.
25. Von Neuman J, Morgenstein O. Theory of games and economic behavior. Princeton: Princeton University Press; 1944.
26. Prades J. Is the person trade off a valid method for allocating health care resources? Health Econ. 1997;6:71–81.
27. Bennett KJ. Development and testing of a utility measure for major, unipolar depression (McSad). 2000
28. Kahneman D, Tversky A. Choices, values and frames. Am Psychol. 1984;39(4):341–50.
29. Bleichrodt H, Johannesson M. Standard gamble, time trade-off and rating scale: experimental results on the ranking properties of QALYs. J Health Econ. 1997;16(2):155–75.
30. Froberg DG, Kane RL. Methodology for measuring health-state preferences–II: scaling methods. J Clin Epidemiol. 1989;42(5):459–71.
31. Konig H, Gunther O, Angrmeyer M, Roick C. Utility assessment in patient with mental disorders: validity and discriminative ability of the time trade off method. PharmacoEconomics. 2009; 27(5):405–19.
32. Brazier J, Deverill M, Green C. A review of the use of health status measures in economic evaluation. J Health Serv Res Policy. 1999;4(3):174–84.
33. Bennett KJ, Torrance GW, Boyle MH, Guscott R. Cost-utility analysis in depression: the McSad utility measure for depression health states. Psychiatr Serv. 2000;51(9):1171–6.
34. Torrance GW, Feeny D, Furlong W. Visual analog scales: do they have a role in the measurement of preferences for health states? Med Decis Mak. 2001;21(4):329–34.
35. Voruganti LN, Awad AG, Oyewumi LK, Cortese L, Zirul S, Dhawan R. Assessing health utilities in schizophrenia. A feasibility study. PharmacoEconomics. 2000;17(3):273–86.
36. Lenert LA, Sturley AP, Rapaport MH, Chavez S, Mohr PE, Rupnow M. Public preferences for health states with schizophrenia and a mapping function to

estimate utilities from positive and negative symptom scale scores. Schizophr Res. 2004;71(1):155–65.

37. Revicki DA, Wood M. Patient-assigned health state utilities for depression-related outcomes: differences by depression severity and antidepressant medications. J Affect Disord. 1998;48(1):25–36.
38. Briggs A, Wild D, Lees M, Reaney M, Dursun S, Parry D, et al. Impact of schizophrenia and schizophrenia treatment-related adverse events on quality of life: direct utility elicitation. Health Qual Life Outcomes. 2008;6:105.
39. Revicki DA, Hanlon J, Martin S, Gyulai L, Nassir GS, Lynch F, et al. Patient-based utilities for bipolar disorder-related health states. J Affect Disord. 2005;87(2–3):203–10.
40. Nord E. The person trade-off approaching to valuing health care programs. Med Decis Mak. 1995;15(3):201–8.
41. Arnesen T, Nord E. The value of DALY life: problems with ethics and validity of disability adjusted life years. BMJ. 1999;319(7222):1423–5.
42. Kopec JA, Willison KD. A comparative review of four preference-weighted measures of health-related quality of life. J Clin Epidemiol. 2003;56(4):317–25.
43. Richardson J, Khan MA, Iezzi A, Maxwell A. Comparing and explaining differences in the magnitude, content, and sensitivity of utilities predicted by the EQ-5D, SF-6D, HUI 3, 15D, QWB, and AQoL-8D multiattribute utility instruments. Med Decis Mak. 2015;35(3):276–91.
44. The EuroQol Group. EuroQol: a new facility for the measurement of health-related quality of life. Health Policy. 1990;16:199–208.
45. Lamers LM, Bouwmans CA, van Straten A, Donker MC, Hakkaart L. Comparison of EQ-5D and SF-6D utilities in mental health patients. Health Econ. 2006;15(11):1229–36.
46. Brazier J, Roberts J, Deverill M. The estimation of a preference-based measure of health from the SF-36. J Health Econ. 2002;21(2):271–92.
47. Walters SJ, Brazier JE. Comparison of the minimally important difference for two health state utility measures: EQ-5D and SF-6D. Qual Life Res. 2005;14(6):1523–32.
48. McDonough CM, Tosteson AN. Measuring preferences for cost-utility analysis: how choice of method may influence decision-making. PharmacoEconomics. 2007;25(2):93–106.
49. Brazier J. Is the EQ-5D fit for purpose in mental health? Br J Psychiatry. 2010;197(5):348–9.
50. Brazier J, Connell J, Papaioannou D, Mukuria C, Mulhern B, Peasgood T, et al. A systematic review, psychometric analysis and qualitative assessment of generic preference-based measures of health in mental health populations and the estimation of mapping functions from widely used specific measures. Health Technol Assess. 2014;18(34):vii–xxv.
51. Papaioannou D, Brazier J, Parry G. How valid and responsive are generic health status measures, such as EQ-5D and SF-36, in schizophrenia? A systematic review. Value Health. 2011;14(6):907–20.
52. Mavranezouli I, Brazier JE, Rowen D, Barkham M. Estimating a preference-based index from the clinical outcomes in routine evaluation-outcome measure (CORE-OM): valuation of CORE-6D. Med Decis Mak. 2013;33(3):381–95.
53. Gafni A. Willingness to pay in the context of an economic evaluation of healthcare programs: theory and practice. Am J Manag Care. 1997;3(Suppl):S21–32.
54. Klose T. The contingent valuation method in health care. Health Policy. 1999;47(2):97–123.
55. Diener A, O'Brien B, Gafni A. Health care contingent valuation studies: a review and classification of the literature. Health Econ. 1998;7(4):313–26.
56. Ryan M, Watson V, Amaya-Amaya M. Methodological issues in the monetary valuation of benefits in healthcare. Expert Rev Pharmacoecon Outcomes Res. 2003;3(6):717–27.
57. Quevedo J, Contreras Hernández I, Espinosa JG, scuderoII G. The willingness-to-pay concept in question. Rev Saude Publica. 2009:43(2).
58. McIntosh E, Donaldson C, Ryan M. Recent advances in the methods of cost-benefit analysis in healthcare. Matching the art to the science. PharmacoEconomics. 1999;15(4):352–58.
59. Smith DM, Damschroder LJ, Kim SY, Ubel PA. What's it worth? Public willingness to pay to avoid mental illnesses compared with general medical illnesses. Psychiatr Serv. 2012;63(4):319–24.
60. Franklin M. The role of utility, health, and capabilities in economic evaluation: a case study in frail older people. Nottingham: The University of Nottingham; 2016.

4 Cost-Benefit Analysis

Denise Razzouk

Abstract

Cost-benefit analysis (CBA) is the root of Health Economics and is based on the welfare theory. CBA is the broadest economic evaluation (EE) method that assesses all benefits and costs in monetary units; the production of welfare is expressed in terms of net benefit (the difference between benefits and costs). The main goal in the welfarist approach is to maximize welfare according to individuals' preferences. The application of CBA principles faces multiple obstacles, mainly because valuing health in terms of monetary units is challenging and raises ethical and methodological constraints. In the health sector, CBA has received relevant criticism, leading to the emergence and adoption of other methods of EE, such as cost-effectiveness analysis (CEA) and cost-utility analysis (CUA). However, attempts to apply welfarist principles to CEA were far of being accepted, and consensus among health economists in this regard still does not exist. The extra-welfarist approach encompassing CEA and CUA has progressed toward maximizing health outcomes and focusing on equity and fairness issues. The most common technique used in CBA to elicit preferences is the contingent valuation (willingness to pay). Despite the challenging task of valuing mental health outcomes, some studies demonstrate the feasibility of this technique in people with mental disorders, though some level of inconsistency and inaccuracy in respondents' answers was reported. Despite methodological limitations among all EE methods applied to health, there is a growing interest in CBA and, more specifically, in discrete choice experiment, especially for health services and public health policies, and in exploring patients' treatment preferences. The Mental Health field adds challenges to CBA regarding the complexity of defining and measuring outcomes representing mental health maximization.

D. Razzouk (✉)
Centre of Economic Mental Health (CESM),
Department of Psychiatry, Universidade Federal de Sao Paulo, Rua Borges Lagoa 570, 1° andar, São Paulo, Brazil, 04038-000
e-mail: drazzouk@gmail.com

D. Razzouk (ed.), *Mental Health Economics*, DOI 10.1007/978-3-319-55266-8_4

Key Points Summary

- Origins of cost-benefit analysis
- Cost-benefit analysis in health care
- Relationship between cost-benefit and cost-effectiveness analyses
- Revealed preferences and stated preferences (willingness to pay, willingness to accept, discrete choice experiment)
- Cost-benefit analysis in mental health

4.1 What Is Cost-Benefit Analysis?

In general, cost-benefit analysis (CBA) applied to the health field addresses the monetary efficiency of the utilization of resources applied to produce and maximize societal welfare. In economic terms, CBA is the broadest economic evaluation method, based on the welfare economics theory, and it evaluates whether benefits converted to monetary values outweigh the costs of resources used to produce them (net benefits). In addition to the production of welfare, CBA is linked to the concept of allocative efficiency (see Chap. 8), that is, whether resources are used and distributed efficiently [1–3]. The production of a welfare framework, based on the work of Knapp [4] (Fig. 4.1), comprises input (resources), resource allocation, and output (goods and services producing welfare) [4, 5]. The use of resources is based on efficient allocation of resources (see Chap. 10), that is, the choice of how to allocate resources while taking into account opportunity costs. To be considered worthwhile, a health program should be able to provide relevant health improvement. However, the societal perspective adopted in CBA highlights the need for a health program to be good for the entire society and not only individuals. In this sense, investments in health programs mean that society agree to sacrifice in order to maximize social welfare and agrees to give up of other benefits (opportunity costs) [6]. On the other hand, health is not a good or service regulated exclusively by the market, and because of uncertain outcomes and market failure [7], governmental regulations are created to allow people with low incomes to have access to healthcare (equity issues) and to maximize social welfare. The production of welfare in the health field should therefore consider private and public resources, and its distribution is linked to social welfare.

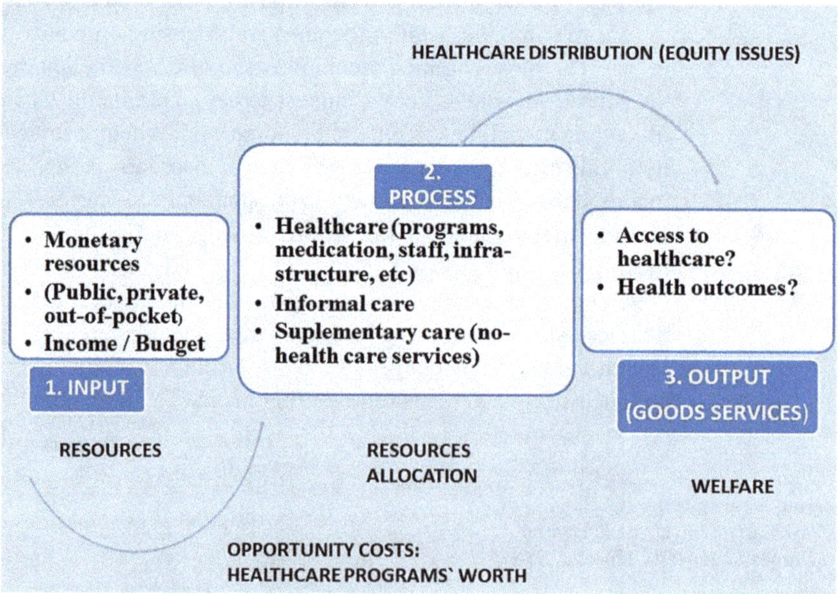

Fig. 4.1 Welfare framework

In CBA applied to the health field, all benefits and costs (direct and indirect costs) originating from health technologies and programs should be estimated and aggregated into monetary measures [3]. CBA also includes the values of benefits from goods and services that do not have market prices, because CBA focuses costs estimation taking into account opportunity costs (see Chap. 1), that is the sacrifice of one benefit in order to obtain another benefit, presumably to generate greater welfare. In perfect competition, market prices correspond to opportunity costs, but in market failure, opportunity costs do not correspond to market prices [8]. In that case, "shadow prices" are imputed for those nonmarket goods and services in order to reflect the opportunity costs [3, 8]. Therefore, the difference between costs and all benefits with their shadow prices allows policymakers to realize the "worth" (the social value for the money) of healthcare programs and services and how to improve the efficiency of resources allocation.

4.1.1 The Origins of CBA

The theoretical framework underlined in CBA originated from the welfare theory and utilitarian principles in the nineteenth century. However, scholars reacted to this initial view, developing two different principles in the twentieth century: the Pareto improvement criterion and the Kaldor-Hicks compensation test [9, 10].

The principle of the welfare theory in the Utilitarian period was based on the maximization of people's welfare or satisfaction ("maximization of the utility for the greatest number of people"), summing up all individual preferences for a desired outcome [2] (see Chap. 1). Preferences were expressed in utility units, which are the value a consumer gives to one outcome (product or service) in terms of satisfaction or desirability. One of the earliest assumptions beyond preference measurement was based on the fact that consumers expressed their preferences for a product or service by trading it in the free market, which it was supposed to be self-regulated. Therefore, under such an assumption, consumers were the best judges to choose a product or service that gives more utility and ultimately contributes to the overall social welfare. However, in terms of decision-making and public policy–making, this perspective has received criticism because of methodological constraints in terms of utility estimation, comparability among individuals, and utility aggregation into the overall welfare measure. Moreover, criticisms to utilitarianism welfare theory emerged regarding distributive issues and inequity. In terms of public policies and fairness (see Chaps. 8 and 9), studies have shown that individuals express their preferences toward their self-interests and ignore healthcare allocation for covering people in need [11].

The modern era of welfare economics, in the twentieth century, emerged with the economist Vilfred Pareto, who proposed that preferences should be considered in terms of ranking and ordinal scale rather than cardinal values subject to individual variations. According to Pareto's improvement criterion (see Chap. 1), efficient resource allocation would allow welfare improvement only if someone could gain utility (become better off) without making someone else lose utility (become worse off). In other words, it means that someone gains and nobody loses. In practice, though, allowing someone to gain pushes someone else toward a "worse off" state because he/she loses the potential gain or would indirectly pay for the other's gain. Pareto's criterion could be met whether "the loser" could be compensated by the "winner." In terms of policy regulation, however, compensation does not occur.

A modification of Pareto criterion was proposed in the 1930s by Nicholas Kaldor and John Hicks, in the Kaldor-Hicks compensation criterion test, also called the potential Pareto criterion [12]. The core of this criterion was that compensation would be hypothetical; that is, it should not occur necessarily. Instead, policy regulations and decisions to improve overall social welfare would be justifiable if making one group better off would allow this group to "compensate" losers by giving up something else. These principles were the basis for the emergence of the willingness-to-pay (WTP) and willingness-to-accept (WTA) concepts used in CBA. In other words, the assumption beyond these concepts was that social welfare was improved according to the preferences of people in obtaining benefits and the sacrifices people were willing to make in giving up benefits. However, criticisms of the Kaldor-Hicks criterion have arisen because it implies an unequal distribution of resources and ethical considerations.

Despite methodological constraints and conflicts among scholars, CBA has been guiding policy regulation in countries like the United States since the 1930s, and it became a predominant technique of resource allocation in the majority of areas after Reagan's mandate in the 1980s [13]. In this regard, Frank [14] emphasizes that scarcity is a reality of the human condition and that a trade-off between competing values is unavoidable. In simple words, Frank synthesized the core principle of CBA with this quote: "To have more one thing, we must settle for less of another."

4.1.2 Preferences, Market, and Welfare Change

The concept of welfare is closely related to individuals' preferences in the market. Economic principles evaluate how consumer preferences apply values to goods and services according to the welfare they produce. Although economic principles based on rational consumer behavior in the market have been currently questioned, the main rationale according to these principles states that consumers supposedly know which goods or services produce more welfare for them, and in this sense, they rationally seek that alternative in maximizing welfare. Consumers give values to good and services and are compelled to pay an amount of money to enhance their welfare. Prices in the market are regulated by supply-and-demand transactions (perfect market competition; see Chap. 1), and consumer preferences influence the prices of goods and services, as well as the amount of goods and services available in the market. One classical way to estimate welfare changes is based on price changes.

Welfare changes have been measured in economics through three main methodologies: consumer surplus, compensating variation, and equivalent variation [3, 8]. Consumer surplus, defined by Alfred Marshall, is the difference between value and price, in other words, the difference of the maximum value a consumer is willing to pay for a good or service and its price on the market [15]. Therefore, consumer surplus corresponds to the excess satisfaction a consumer obtains after acquiring a good or service. One limitation of this method is that this "satisfaction" (utility) depends on the price variation; that is, if the price of the product increases, then satisfaction would be lower, and if the price of the product decreases, then, consumer surplus would be greater. Another limitation is that only observing consumer behavior does not allow the measurement of welfare changes; that is, it is necessary to assess the value (utility) consumers give to goods and services. Yet, consumer surplus is also affected by income and prices (price elasticity of demand). If someone has a low income, he/she is not able to pay for one good or service if its price is unmanageable within a restricted budget. Inelastic demand represents that consumers are not willing to pay for a good or service, even when the price increase is very small.

The method of compensating variation, defined by Hicks, considers a scenario in which consumer utility changes because price changes. For instance, if the price of a good or services increases, then this increase affects a consumer's utility, because he/she should pay an extra amount of money to achieve the same utility he/she had before the price changed. In this sense, compensating variation corresponds to the extra amount of money a consumer would need pay to return to the same level of utility (welfare gain), or to the amount of compensation a consumer would like to receive to accept the loss of his/her ability to pay for it (welfare loss). The method of equivalent variation is the maximum amount of money a consumer would be willing to pay to avoid price changes.

Health is not a commodity per se, but to achieve healthy "output," it is necessary to use health services (input). In this sense, health services have some characteristics similar to other commodities. For instance, when buying one commodity, consumer knows what satisfaction he/she would acquire; it is the same for some parts of health service delivery, especially in terms of choosing more comfortable hospitals or more expensive technologies, which would reduce waiting times or other discomfort. However, all these components do not provide "health," and it is not possible to buy a "quantifiable amount of health" because the outcome is uncertain, independent of the "amount" of healthcare received [6]. In addition, sick people do not choose treatment rationally as they would choose any other commodity. People are not able to discriminate what is good (or not) in terms of enhancing utility in the realm of health because of information asymmetry. Moreover, a sick person would have no choice between living and dying; a survival principle makes the person want to receive treatment, whether it may increase or decrease utility (health).

4.1.3 Problems in CBA

Despite the growing interest in and application of CBA in diverse contexts, including healthcare, CBA has faced a myriad of resistance and criticism from deontologists, philosophers, decision-makers, and health policymakers, among others [6, 16–20]. One of the most controversial aspects of CBA is imputing a monetary value for some "incommensurable" or "priceless" things, such as human life and other non-market goods. Regardless of the innumerable claims against the unethical aspect of the principle, Mooney [19] argued that if the value of human life was infinite, nobody would put their life at risk, even for daily activities such as leaving the house, walking in the street, playing sports, or getting a job. There is an intrinsic risk of death in all human activities, but despite this, people are willing to take these risks every day to gain satisfaction and to obtain other benefits. There is a trade-off in the amount of risk of death we are willing to take to satisfy our desires; in other words, the value of human life is finite, and we give it value without awareness. In this sense, Mooney defended the ethics of the application of CBA as a tool to guarantee efficient resource allocation in healthcare, that is, to avoid decisions such as investing too many resources to save one life when those same resources could save many lives: "The price of inefficiency, inexplicitness and irrationality in health care is paid in death and sickness. Is that ethical?" [19, p. 179].

The second controversial aspect of CBA has been extensively debated: the contingent valuation (CV) method used to elicit people's preferences – applying the WTP and the WTA techniques – has methodological and philosophical limitations. In this regard, Hasson [17] highlighted the incomparability between categories or consequences. For instance, if reducing all consequences into one category – that is, converting and aggregating all values of diseases, suffering, climate change, and safety into monetary terms – it would be impossible to compare them and to ascertain priorities. In addition, several factors contribute to biased responses when reporting preferences, such as how questions are formulated, the level of detail in a scenario description, respondents' income, and context, among others. These can inflate the value of some interventions over others [14, 20]. Yet, preferences elicited by such methods are driven by self-interest, leading to social distribution issues because the method could favor some groups (usually wealthy people) over others [11, 14, 17]. Hasson enumerated 10 key problems in CBA, emphasizing that the topic framing, perspective, and components included in CBA would vary according to policymaker interests, leading to biased results.

4.1.4 CBA in Healthcare

As described above, CBA has been hindered in healthcare, especially because of existing conflicts between ethical views and economic principles. For a long time, scarcity was not acknowledged as an obstacle for healthcare [21] because few treatments were available and ethical principles in the medicine-patient relationship ruled out any economic component regarding the value of health and human life. As pointed out by Donovan [22], "Medicine involves doctors and patients, not providers and consumers, not insured lives."

However, the growing expenditures with the public health sector after the 1950s contributed to the emergence of Health Economics and to the need to seek for efficiency in health resource allocation (see Chap. 1). In this regard, CBA influenced Health Economics for decades, but because of constraints on the measurement of health outcomes in monetary units, the health sector, detached from other sectors, has pursued other methods, such as CEA and CUA (see Chaps. 1, 5, 6, and 9).

There is extensive debate among health economists on the equivalence of CBA and CEA [5, 14, 18, 20, 23–28]. Welfare theory is the theoretical basis for CBA, and in this sense, studies of CBA should adopt a societal perspective, consider all costs and consequences (health and nonhealth outcomes) in the analysis, and focus on the opportunity costs and on the return to society as a whole. The goal is to efficiently allocate resources to the best alternative in terms of net benefit, or in other words, to choose the alternative that will produce more welfare, regardless of who would have their welfare enhanced. With regard to the goal of bringing greater return and satisfaction to society, CBA is useful in deciding about investments among available alternatives and in allocating resources efficiently among different sectors of society (e.g., education, transportation, healthcare) (see Chaps. 10 and 11).

Because all benefits and consequences are expressed in monetary units, ethical and methodological constraints, as mentioned above, pushed the healthcare sector to "modify" CBA using principles that seem similar at first glance – CEA and CUA – leading to some authors considering CEA equivalent to CBA in the health sector [28]. In this regard, CEA is a comparative method of economic evaluation that assesses which of available alternatives offers the best outcome (usually a health outcome) for the lowest (or optimal) cost. The idea is to maximize health, rather than welfare, though there are some variations in the extent to which CEA and CUA include nonhealth outcomes in the analysis. In contrast to CBA, CEA considers only one outcome for treating one group of patients with the same disease. In addition, nonclinical dimensions are not considered together in the analysis, even if a societal perspective is adopted. User and public preferences are not taken into account in CEA, although CUA assesses preferences using methods different from those used in CBA (see Chaps. 3 and 6). Moreover, there is no consensus on how CEA should be carried out in terms of inclusion of components of costs, study perspective, and incremental cost-effectiveness ratio use in resource allocation [27].

However, authors disagree on the application of CBA and CEA in resource allocation in the healthcare sector. Donaldson [28] disagrees with classifying economic evaluation only in terms of outcome measurement, warning that it is a fallacy to consider CEA as equivalent to CBA. In his view, differences between CBA and CEA do not lie solely in measuring outcomes in monetary and health/quality-of-life outcomes, but rather which question each method is able to address (see Chap. 10). Others authors reject CEA and CUA because these methods do not take into account society's preferences and values in terms of all benefits, consequences, and opportunity costs; in other words, these techniques would not be in accordance with "real" economics [18, 25, 29]. On the other hand, extra-welfarists criticize the rationale of an individual being the best judge of his or her own health, because this can restrict resource allocation in terms of social welfare, maximization of health, and fairness [30] (see Chaps. 6, 8, 9, 10).

It is not within the scope of this chapter to discuss details of authors' views on CBA and other economic evaluation methods in the healthcare sector. The marriage between Health and Economics has been far from harmonic and uncontroversial. While the Health discipline focuses on evidence for treatment extracted from experimental research in order to offer better health outcomes to patients, Economics brings theoretical knowledge of how to enhance efficiency of resource use and of the consequences of resource use to society. Policymakers are in the middle of both pleas for resource use, and the decision-making process needs to be transparent, fair, and efficient, regardless of small budgets [27] (see Chap. 10). Franken and Koolman [31] pointed out that health system policies underpin their goals for improving social welfare using at least three relevant outcomes: health maximization, healthcare process improvement, and fair distribution of financial resources. This debate is not merely academic; it affects how society demands would be met (see Chaps. 8 –11). In a review of the choice of economic evaluation and adoption decision recommended, Buchanan [32] found that at least 22% of studies led to different decisions according to the economic evaluation method used. As Buchanan and Wordsworth [32] well pointed out, Health Economics advances have a long way to go moving this debate forward in order to achieve standardized, transparent, reliable, and valid methods and measures to be widely accepted among researchers, health professionals, and decision makers:

> "...health economists are increasingly conducting economic evaluations of interventions that may not necessarily be a good match for standard methods. The reference cases detailed within methods guidelines issued by HTA [health technology assessment] agencies are currently quite narrowly defined, providing little scope to apply alternative economic evaluation approaches.
>
> In part, this is because the evidence base to justify alternative approaches is limited. To move this debate forward over the next decade, health economists should concentrate on widening this evidence base by conducting comparative studies, and more readily applying existing welfarist methods where there is a sound theoretical basis to do so. [32, p. 578]"

4.2 Monetary Outcomes in Cost-Benefit Analysis

4.2.1 What Is an Economic Value of Health?

The concept of economic value is related to the production of welfare, that is, the sum of all benefits an individual is able to acquire through consumption of goods or services in the market, plus benefits obtained from unpaid goods and services, plus those benefits experienced indirectly [33]. However, economic value comprises all values an individual gives to benefits to himself or to other people, in the present or in the future (with or without consumption). In this sense a person gives a value to health as whole (healthy and nonhealthy status) based on the idea that, for instance, the individual is able to acquire more benefits in life (work, leisure, achievement of desires, consumption of goods) when healthy than when unhealthy. Also, he/she can give value to peoples' health for altruistic reasons or for indirect benefits, for instance, providing vaccines for infectious diseases can save lives on a large scale, but the individual decreases his or her own current or future risk of contracting the disease (a positive externality). Moreover, healthcare can be provided by the public health system, in which the individual does not pay for it, or it can be provided in the private market through the health insurance system, whereby individuals pay for it. There is a value for health and for healthcare independent of whether the individual knows his risk of becoming sick. In summary, health per se has an intrinsic value, healthcare has an economic value in the market, and healthcare has a social value (access and coverage of treatment). In Economics, values are expressed directly or indirectly by preferences; that is, the stronger the preference, the greater the value. Preferences can be measured in utility values (see Chaps. 3 and 5) and in monetary values. From a Health Economics perspective, preferences should be assessed in a representative sample of society that includes people who are currently sick, those at risk of becoming sick, and those who are healthy. Health per se cannot be "distributed" among individuals, but health*care* can be distributed, and in this sense, efficient resource allocation is the core of how to prioritize healthcare access and health interventions.

4.2.2 How to Measure the Economic Value of Health?

In CBA, all outcomes and consequences are valued in monetary terms, according to peoples' preferences (consumer). The main approaches used in CBA for this purpose are revealed preferences, contingent valuation, and human capital approach [3, 8, 33]. The human capital approach is a particular method that is not in accordance

Table 4.1 Methods used in cost-benefit analysis to elicit preferences on health and nonhealth improvements (welfare changes)

	Direct and indirect methods for eliciting consumer preferences	
	Revealed preferences	Stated preferences
Methods	Competitive market price Travel costs method Hedonic pricing method (wage-risk trade-off)	Contingent valuation (WTP and WTA) Discrete choice experiment
Preferences	Are based on observations of individual behavior choices in the real market (perfect competition)	Are based on an individual expressing preferences according to hypothetical scenarios and multiple attributes (nonmarket goods)
Welfare change	Consumer surplus	Compensating and equivalent variation
Use in CBA in health field	Very limited use	Contingent valuation (WTP) is the most used method. DCE has been used more recently

CBA cost-benefit analysis, *DCE* discrete choice experiment, *WTA* willingness to accept, *WTP* willingness to pay

with welfare economics principles [33, 34] and is discussed in Chap. 29.

Table 4.1 outlines the main differences between revealed and stated preferences, though the latter are more used in Health Economics than the former because CV addresses nonmarketed goods [33]. The major difference between revealed and stated preferences is that the former is based on market demand rules (consumer surplus) closely dependent on income elasticity, and the latter is based on Kaldor-Hicks' compensation principles (compensation and equivalent variation) more appropriate for nonmarket goods and services. In this chapter, we focus on CV (WTP methods) because it is largely the most common method applied in CBA in healthcare.

4.2.2.1 Revealed Preferences

The value of one good or service in the competitive market can be observed through consumers' behavior. For instance, if a consumer desires or needs one good or service and pays for it, it is because the benefit acquired from this trade is greater than the price paid by the consumer. Then, if the consumer chooses to buy one product over another, it is supposed that he/she prefers that product; this is called a "revealed preference." In other words, the value of a benefit is related to its consumption, and valuation is focused on the outcome produced ("welfare change"). However, for nonmarket goods and services, especially in health, this valuation is neither straightforward nor obvious. The revealed preference approach (indirect method) was developed to address monetary valuation of nonmarket goods. In the health field, this method was used with a focus on the amount of money people are willing to pay for a product or service that is able to reduce the risk of becoming sick or dying. For instance, if 1000 people would be willing to pay US$500 for a vaccine not provided by a public health service in order to avoid a lethal disease (the disease causes 1 death among every 10,000 people per year), then in this case the value of statistical life would be U$5 million for each of these people accepting an opportunity cost of U$500 to save their lives.

However, there is no linear relationship between the consumption of healthcare (service) and health improvement (output). Health outcomes are always uncertain and multidimensional (multiple outputs) [8]. Moreover, the process of expressing preferences and valuing all outcomes generated by the provision of healthcare is not an easy and straightforward task for the majority of people. In the mental health field, this approach would be much more of a challenge because of negative attitudes and stigma against mental disorders (see Chap. 27); people would prefer physical rather than mental interventions, leading to lower values for mental health treatments [35].

4.2.2.2 Stated Preferences

Two main methods are used in the stated preferences approach: CV and discrete choice experiment (DCE). CV focuses on the WTP technique to elicit preferences for products and services as a whole; that is, with this technique it is not possible to infer which attributes of goods and services are in fact related to preferences. On the other hand, DCE focuses on assessing preferences for each of the main attributes of goods and services, followed by the aggregation of all attributes values.

Contingent Valuation: The Willingness-to-Pay Technique

The CV approach was developed in the 1960s in the United States to assess the monetary value of nonmarket goods [33]. In the case of market failure, the consumption of a good or service does not achieve equilibrium through supply/demand regulation. This is the case for health, in which demand for treatment is uncertain, the effects of treatment on health outcomes are uncertain, and externalities lay down in a third-part in a negative or positive way (the spillover effect). Therefore, in CBA, all people directly or indirectly affected by a treatment should be included in order to express their preferences in terms of costs and consequences.

CV is therefore a direct method and the main approach used to ascribe monetary valuation to stated preferences in health outcomes and services through WTP in CBA. The WTP method verifies the maximum amount of money a person would be willing to pay for healthcare services (welfare gain) in a hypothetical scenario simulating a market for nonmarket goods. Also, it is possible to use the willingness-to-accept (WTA) method to verify the minimum amount someone would accept to not receive a healthcare service (welfare loss). At least three components are used to measure the monetary value of health components of welfare using WTP [3]: the value of a certain health outcome, the value of a treatment or program with uncertain outcomes, and the value of having access to a treatment for uncertain future use.

CV is used to ask the general public and patients to assign a monetary value to health and to healthcare, considering a free market scenario from two distinct perspectives: the *ex post user approach* and the *ex ante insurance-based approach* [3, 8]. The ex post user approach is addressed to people seeking/using/eligible for treatment to know how much they would be willing to pay for a treatment or health service (current or new) considering an uncertain health outcome. The ex ante insurance-based approach is addressed to the general public to explore how much they would be willing to pay to insurance (or taxation) for future access to a treatment or healthcare program if they become sick in the future. Currie et al. [24] noted that CV in public health ("restricted WTP valuation") does not take into account individuals' preferences but rather decision makers' choices on the monetary valuation of specific benefits produced by public health programs. Therefore, the sum of the valuations of benefits in CBA based on individual preferences would be different from the sum of the valuations of benefits in CBA based on a decision maker's perspective. The cause of this difference between these approaches is the result of market failure. In the presence of market failure, individual preferences would be not appropriate for health resource allocation because social benefits and externalities would not usually be considered.

Although WTP based on individuals' preferences is considered a benchmark in CBA, the majority of health studies using CBA vary considerably in terms of broadness and preference assessment, leading to discrepant values of healthcare programs. Currie et al. [24] pointed out that one solution would be to combine WTP using a decision makers' approach (for intangible costs, externalities, and health outcomes related to programs) with WTP based on individual preferences for those components for which a market exists (productivity costs). Also, the broadness of the valuation of nonhealth outcomes in CBA vary. It is possible to include health cost savings and return-to-work and productivity gains in WTP valuation, though it is elusive whether respondents regarding WTP taking into account nonhealth outcomes when expressing their preferences. There is always a risk of double counting if it is summed with monetary values defined using other techniques, such as the human capital approach in CBA.

One important issue regarding the comprehensiveness of CBA using the WTP method is that focusing only on health outcomes and on patients with diseases or who are at high risk of diseases is that it is not completely in accordance with the economic theory underpinning CBA. In this regard, O'Brien and Gafni [36] noted that the way that a health program is available may affect both currently sick and currently healthy people, and for this reason, CBA using WTP should be conducted with a representative sample encompassing all people affected directly or indirectly by the availability of a health program.

The Willingness-to-Pay Technique

Although surveys can be done over the telephone, by mail, and on the Internet, face-to-face interviews are more accurate and are a recommendable gold-standard method [3]. However, these interviews vary in the way WTP is queried and in the description of the hypothetical scenario.

The description of the hypothetical scenario for a health treatment or program should detail all relevant aspects, be easy to understand, and be realistic [8]. Hoyos and Mariel [37] pointed out that the valuation of health is ultimately the valuation of the scenario and for this reason, it should contain accurate information in order to allow respondents to know what is really being evaluated in unambiguous way. In this regard, Smith [38] compared five scenarios to describe the same health improvement among a sample of 104 members of the general public in Australia. The values of WTP were much lower when narratives were longer and detailed than when brief and moderate. Another factor influencing WTP values was the presence of the "label of disease" in the narrative, such as cancer or stroke, leading respondents to focus on previous knowledge of these diseases than on the narrative of the health condition per se. This is relevant because some misconceptions and negative attitudes toward some diseases may influence WTP values. For instance, Smith et al. [39] compared WTP values among three physical diseases and two mental disorders assigned by a representative sample of the general population in the United States. In addition to eliciting WTP values, the authors assessed the perceptions of the burden of these diseases. Although this sample recognized the greater burden of mental disorders in comparison with physical diseases, they were willing to pay 40% less money for mental disorders.

Another methodological component influencing respondents' answers is that the question about WTP should be clear in terms of type of payment – that is, the particular "payment vehicle" (because values could be different if payment occurs through additional taxes or monthly payments) – and information on payment duration [8].

Once the scenario description is well detailed, the literature details at least six ways that WTP can be elicited [8]: (a) open-ended questions, (b) the iterative bidding technique, (c) a payment card, (d) dichotomous choice, (e) a closed-ended item with a follow-up question, and (f) the marginal approach. These techniques vary in terms of giving the respondent an opportunity to choose among a range of monetary values, or asking them to assign potential values in stepwise progression (bargain method), or even in a test format with a set of alternatives to choose from (see Chap. 3).

Bias in Contingent Valuation

Diverse factors influence the type of answer and the amount of money respondents would be willing to pay [3, 8, 40] (Table 4.2). Biases are common during processes in how respondents receive information, the way questions are asked, the context where interview occurs, and the relationship established between respondent and interviewer (perception of the desired answer) [40]. One particular issue of interest in the Mental Health field is attitudes toward mental disorders. As mentioned earlier, one study showed that even considering the huge burden and the importance of mental disorders, people expressing their preferences using WTP do not acknowledge that they

Table 4.2 Bias in contingent valuation

Bias	Description
Anchoring bias [8]	Using algorithms from iterative bidding techniques allows variability on the starting point to elicit WTP. If the first question starts by asking the respondent whether he/she would be willing to pay $10 or $50, it may influence respondents as defining the amount for the next options. For instance, if the starting point is $10, in the case of acceptance to pay it, the next question is accepting to pay $50, and so on. Instead, if the starting point is $50 and in the case of acceptance it goes to $100, then respondents may react differently in terms of the amount of money to pay. Randomization of the starting point is a possible solution to minimize this type of bias
Range bias [8]	Using the technique payment card, a range of monetary values usually are presented to respondents. However, variations in the range of these values may affect answers regarding WTP. A possible solution is to randomly present different ranges of values to respondents
Strategic bias [8]	Respondents may be influenced by external factors that are not related to interventions ascertaining much higher or lower values. For instance, a study by Sevy et al [41] found this bias among patients with schizophrenia who would not be willing to pay much more for a treatment decreasing side effects because they were afraid of losing social benefits if they present improvement in this respect
Embedding bias and warm glow effect [42].	Respondents do not discriminate among different alternatives, giving the same value to all together or separately. This is linked to "moral satisfaction" and the "warm glow effect," rather than to real preferences
Sequence-ordering bias [40]	Respondents ascertain different values depending on the order of questions
Social desirability bas [40]	Respondents answer what they imagine people expect from them
Cognitive bias	Some people have difficulties reasoning using probabilities, and this is a commonplace in people with schizophrenia. Although some studies have shown the feasibility of WTP in a sample of people with schizophrenia disorders, some evidence shows that expressing WTP using probabilities is a difficult cognitive task for them [47]
Protest zero bias [40] and emotional bias	Respondents do not accept the WTP method and refuse to give any value. Answers can be influenced by emotions and beliefs. For instance, a study using WTP with families of people with mental disorders demonstrated that families expressed anger at paying too much already, and the WTP question was seen as a suggestion to pay more, or the WTP would be lower because they do not believe in the cure for the mental disorder [47]
Hypothesis bias [40]	Respondents assign greater values than they would really pay in practice

would be at risk of having a mental disorder or that valuable efficient treatments are able to "cure" mental disorders [41].

Validity and Reliability of Contingent Valuation

Bayoumi [38] summarized some consensus in the literature about CV: direct interviews are the benchmark; WTP is preferred to WTA because people have an aversion to losses and assign much larger unrealistic values in WTA than WTP; respondents' understanding should be systematically checked (answer accuracy), and visual aids are good supports for respondents.

However, questions related to the validity and reliability of WTP remain unanswered because there is no gold standard and a lack of empirical studies assessing these issues. Although answer validity is not easily comparable to market prices (because they do not exist), one solution in checking answer consistency is to verify whether the amount of money reported through WTP is greater than an individual's budget or income. In this sense, face and construct validity of questions in WTP interviews could be explored based on the assumption that it is expected that people with a higher income would be willing to pay larger amounts than people with lower incomes.

Of interest, some attempts have been made to validate WTP compared with studies measuring utilities through standard gamble and time trade-off, though differences are expected because of their different theoretical backgrounds.

Although CBA is not common in mental health, few studies in the literature report the application of WTP techniques in samples with mental disorders (Box 4.1).

Box 4.1 Example of Willingness to Pay in Mental Health

Study: "Contingency Valuation and Preferences of Health States Associated with Side Effects of Antipsychotic Medications in Schizophrenia" (Sevy et al. [43]).

Sevy et al. interviewed 96 patients with schizophrenia, using WTP and standard gamble methods, to ask them about the value of eliminating the side effects of antipsychotics for a 1-year. First, they listed all side effects patients had experienced while using antipsychotics and asked the patients about the level of discomfort associated with each side effect using an ordinal Likert scale ("it doesn't bother me" to "it bothers me greatly") in order to obtain a ranking of the severity of symptoms. Following this, patients classified the side effects in the list according to the level of severity. Then, they used the WTP method with an open-ended question asking how much these patients would be willing to pay for a medication that made them free of side effects for 1 year with 100% certainty. In the second phase, they presented a scenario in which inpatients would benefit from one medication for side effects, but at the same time have some level of risk of becoming worse. Level of uncertainty was expressed using drawing cards showing different probabilities in terms of chance for side effects to improve or get worse. Then, they asked patients whether they thought doctors should prescribe this medication for inpatients, and if yes, whether the patient would be willing to take this medication under such conditions. Then they asked how much the patient would be willing to pay for this medication under this uncertain scenario and considering their income. In this experiment, patients were willing to pay 6% of their income in the certain scenario and 3% of their income in the uncertain scenario.

Discrete Choice Experiment

DCE is a disaggregated method used to elicit preferences based on components (attributes) of goods and services, rather than in a "package," as in CV. According to the theory of Lancaster, [44] the utility extracted from goods and services is the result of some characteristics (attributes) of them, and for this reason, identifying such attributes allows preferences for them to be measured. Multiple alternatives are presented, but individuals should choose only one. This technique is based on random utility theory, a probabilistic choice theory that states that each alternative has a probability of being chosen, and the higher the probability for choosing an alternative, the larger its utility in comparison with another alternative. Preferences of multiple dimensions of goods are elicited, and a model of preferences are estimated through modeling techniques and econometrics methods [33, 45] (Chap. 7). Using this method, it is possible to verify which attribute or component of goods and services most influences the WTP response. There is a growing interest in this technique in healthcare, with a trend to include more attributes (seven or eight) in DCE than before (four attributes, on average), and methods have been refined and their accuracy increased [42].

Table 4.3 outlines an example of DCE, eliciting preferences for three antidepressants among a sample of subjects with depressive disorder, considering six attributes of antidepressants and the same efficacy. If a subject chooses antidepressant C, than the estimation of utility of each attribute can be estimated through modeling techniques. Attributes have positive (efficacy) or negative (side effects) utilities. Moreover, it is possible to include the cost attribute (price of antidepres-

Table 4.3 Example of DCE

	Antidepressant A	Antidepressant B	Antidepressant C
Frequency (pills per day)	Once	Twice	Once
Side effects			
Nausea	Yes	No	No
Libido impairment	Yes	No	Yes
Weight gain	No	Yes	No
Average price (US$) for 1 month of treatment	100.00	30.00	50.00
Preferred option			x

Box 4.2 Example of the Discrete Choice Technique in Mental Health

Study: "Patient Preferences for Depression Treatment Programs and Willingness to Pay for Treatment," Morey et al. [46]

Morey et al. carried out a survey of 104 subjects with a diagnosis of major depressive disorder (MDD) in order to determine whether they were willing to pay for eliminating MDD and to know how much they were willing to accept to continue in a depressive state. The authors elaborated a survey in which subjects were invited to choose between two alternatives related to treatment programs, whereby depression would be reduced or abolished for a period of 12 months. They displayed the alternatives of treatment in a table format and listed seven attributes related to treatment for depression: effectiveness, hours of psychotherapy per month, use of antidepressants, monthly costs to patients with treatment, and side effects (weight gain, decrease on libido, and anorgasmia). Then, respondents expressed their preferences between the two alternatives. The authors found remarkable differences in the estimates of willingness to pay according to individuals' demographic characteristics.

sants), whereby WTP is derived indirectly [33]. Some examples of DCE in the Mental Health field are available in the literature (Box 4.2).

4.3 Cost-Benefit Analysis in Mental Health

The use of CBA in health has been controversial, and in this sense, this was similar in the Mental Health field because there were few attempts to apply this method, especially regarding economic evaluation of public policies and services [41, 47–51]. Using broad economic evaluation as CBA in mental health has the advantage of exploring externalities, indirect costs, the economic burden of mental disorders in other non-health sectors, and economic return to society when adopting policies to treat and prevent mental disorders. Recent economic evaluations reported economic return to society in treating depression, anxiety disorders, and other mental disorders [52, 53]. However, methodological limitations and disagreements on theoretical frameworks in Health Economics are common obstacles in conducting economic evaluation, especially CBA, in mental health.

Economic evaluation in the health domain is dominated by CEA and CUA methods, though some economists argue that these methods are not in accordance with economic principles [18]. Based on the theoretical framework, there are two major views in Health Economics [10, 23, 30, 32, 36, 54]: the welfarist and extra-welfarist approaches (see Chaps. 1, 6, 9, and 10). The former focuses on the individual's welfare and on the sum of all individuals' welfare, with the main goal to maximize society's welfare and well-being. On the other hand, extra-welfarists criticize welfarists in terms of favoring wealthy groups in society in disfavoring people in need, and also because public policies need to address issues regarding equity, fairness, and prioritizing neglected diseases. Extra-welfarists focus on "distributing health" equally to all, considering similar needs among individuals and maximizing the main dimensions related to health. Individuals' preferences are not the guiding principle underpinning the extra-welfarist approach, and not all benefits produced by treatment are captured in it.

Notwithstanding this conflict between the two approaches, mental health imposes additional challenges in comparison to other medical specialties:

(a) Interventions in mental health address multidimensional benefits (health and nonhealth) that cannot be totally captured in CEA (one outcome) and CUA (low sensitivity to measure mental health changes) (see Chaps. 3–, 4, 5 and 6)
(b) Outcomes in mental health encompass health and nonhealth outputs. The most challenging issue is to define *outcome* in mental health (in terms of promoting "mental health"; see Chap. 3). The definition of mental health is very close to the concept of well-being, since well-being has been recently connected with mental state [55] (see Chap. 25). Moreover, mental disorders cause disutility as well as negative externalities in nonhealth sectors, and allow people to be permanently worse off in society if not treated. Therefore, rather than discussing the appropriate method for measuring mental health promotion (or utility originating from interventions), it is important to establish objectively the quantifiable meaning of producing mental health (utility).
(c) Methods available to estimate preferences in mental health are biased, disfavoring estimates using WTP techniques (because of stigmatizing societal attitudes toward mental illness (see Chap. 27) and a scarcity of information about the effectiveness of interventions from the public and policymakers). Also, mental disorders affect preferences (different estimates in WTP among subjects with depression) and impair cognition, hindering the use of techniques using probabilities (WTP) and SG. The principle that states a consumer chooses rationally what is the best for him- or herself in terms of maximization of utility (sovereignty) is not always the case among people suffering from mental disorders because of the lack of insight regarding the mental disorder and their impaired critical thinking.
(d) Mental disorders produce high indirect costs in comparison with direct costs; only adopting a broad perspective and measuring all dimensions of the benefits and costs involved allow a conclusion of whether mental interventions and policies are worth the money [6, 52]. In this sense, people with mental disorders are at a disadvantage in terms of demonstrating utility improvement when compared with people with physical diseases when using CEA and CUA, and using CBA would allow all relevant costs and benefits to be included.

In summary, CBA has some advantages in comparison with other economic evaluation methods in terms of analyzing all relevant gains and losses of healthcare programs from a broad perspective, and it is a useful tool to support decision makers regarding resource allocation in macro scenarios of public policies. The main goal of CBA is to maximize social welfare, and in this regard, the concept of welfare has been closely redefined to the concept of mental health; therefore, maximizing mental health is much more than maximizing one health dimension. However, methodological constraints limit the achievement of welfare principles in mental health care because the general public is less willing to invest in mental health problems, leading to inequitable resource allocation for mental health programs. DCE techniques open promising opportunities to explore preferences for treatment and adherence to treatment issues in mental health policies. To date, no appropriate and feasible economic evaluation method is able to capture all effects of mental health programs and simultaneously allow allocative choices of resources using fair and equitable distribution. In this regard, the capability approach, an emergent extra-welfarist method, promises to take into account these particularities in the Mental Health field, though it is too early to draw conclusions about this method.

Key Messages

- CBA is the broadest economic evaluation method, allowing all relevant costs and benefits, including externalities and opportunity costs, to be mapped.
- The maximization of welfare principle underpinning CBA is not equivalent to the maximization of health in the extra-welfarist approach. The maximization of mental health falls between health and welfare concepts.
- The distributional issues in CBA that lead to inequity are the key component of the debate over public health policies.
- Economic evaluation methods in the Mental Health field face diverse constraints and biases that should be addressed in future empirical studies. Individuals are not always the best judges to maximize mental health, and in this regard, policymakers relying in extra-welfarist studies do not have appropriate data in order to analyze the worth of mental health programs and the needs of people with mental disorders.
- DCE could be a useful technique to explore adherence to mental health treatment and to enhance the effectiveness of mental health programs.

Reference

1. Palmer S, Togerson D. Definitions of efficiency. Br Med J. 1999;318:1136.
2. Bentham J. An Introduction to the Principles of Morals and Legislation. Library of Economics and Liberty. Retrieved April 6, 2017 from the World Wide Web: http://www.econlib.org/library/Bentham/bnthPML.html
3. Drummond MF, Sculpher MJ, Torrance GW, O'Brien BJ, Stoddart GL. Methods for the economic evaluation of health care programmes. 3rd ed. Oxford: Oxford University Press; 2007.
4. Knapp M. The economic evaluation of mental health care. 1st ed. Brookfield: Ashgate Publishing Limited; 1995.
5. Knapp M. Economic outcomes and levers: impacts for individuals and society. Int Psychogeriatr. 2007 Jun;19(3):483–95.
6. Byford S, Barrett B. Ethics and economics: the case for mental healthcare. Adv Psychiatr Treat. 2010;16:468–73.
7. Arrow K. Uncertainty and the welfare economics of medical care. Am J Econ Rev. 1963;LIII(5):941–73.
8. McIntosh E, Clarke P, Frew EJ, Louviere JJ. Applied methods of cost-benefit analysis in health care. New York: Oxford University Press Inc; 2011.
9. Adler MD, Posner EA. New foundations of cost-benefit analysis. Cambridge: Harvard University Press; 2006.
10. Baujard A. Welfare economics. Working paper GATE-33.2013.<halshs-00906907>. 2013. 28 Jan 2016.
11. O'Shea E, Nui G, Stewart J, Donaldson C, Shackley P. Eliciting preferences for resource allocation in health care. Econ Soc Rev. 2001;32(3):217–38.
12. Hicks JR. The foundation of welfare economics. Econ J. 1939;49(196):696–712.
13. Adler MD, Posner EA. Rethinking cost-benefit analysis. 1999. University of Chicago Law School, John M. Olin Law & Economics Working Paper No. 72.
14. Frank RH. Why is cost-benefit analysis so controversial? J Leg Issues. 2000;29:913–30.
15. Johannesson M, Jonsson B. Economic evaluation in health care: is there a role for cost-benefit analysis? Health Policy. 1991;17:1–23.
16. Adler M, Posner EA. New foundations of cost-benefit analysis. Regul Gov. 2009;3:72–83.
17. Hasson S. Philosophical problems in cost-benefit analysis. Econ Philos. 2007;23:163–83.
18. Johnson FR. Why not real economics? PharmacoEconomics. 2012;30(2):127–31.
19. Mooney GH. Cost-benefit analysis and medical ethics. J Med Ethics. 1980;6:177–9.
20. Cookson R. Willingness to pay method in health care: a sceptical view. Health Econ. 2003;12:891–4.
21. Knapp M. Economic evaluation and mental health: sparse past … fertile future? J Ment Health Policy Econ. 1999;2:163–7.
22. Donovan GK. Doctors, documentation, and the professional obligation: has everything changed? Linacre Q. 2015;82(3):197–202.
23. Coast J, Smith RD, Lorgelly P. Welfarism, extra-welfarism and capability: the spread of ideas in health economics. Soc Sci Med. 2008 Oct;67(7):1190–8.
24. Currie GR, Donaldson C, O'Bbrien BJ, Stoddart GL, Torrance GW, Drummond MF. Willingness to pay for what? A note on alternative definitions of health care program benefits for contingent valuation studies. Med Decis Mak. 2002 Nov;22(6):493–7.

25. Gafni A. Economic evaluation of health-care programmes: is CEA better than CBA? Env Res Econ. 2006;34:407–18.
26. McIntosh E, Donaldson C, Ryan M. Recent advances in the methods of cost-benefit analysis in healthcare. Matching the art to the science. PharmacoEconomics. 1999 Apr;15(4):357–67.
27. Williams I, Bryan S. Understanding the limited impact of economic evaluation in health care resource allocation: a conceptual framework. Health Policy. 2007;80:135–43.
28. Donaldson C, Currie G, Mitton C. Cost effectiveness analysis in health care: contraindications. BMJ. 2002 Oct 19;325(7369):891–4.
29. Johannesson M. The relationship between cost-effectivenness analysis and cost-benefit analysis. Soc Sci Med. 1995;41(4):483–9.
30. Birch S, Donaldson C. Valuing the benefits and costs of health care programmes: where's the 'extra' in extra-welfarism? Soc Sci Med. 2003 Mar;56(5):1121–33.
31. Franken M, Koolman X. Health system goals: a discrete choice experiment to obtain societal valuations. Health Policy. 2013 Sep;112(1–2):28–34.
32. Buchanan J, Wordsworth S. Welfarism versus extra-welfarism: can the choice of economic evaluation approach impact on the adoption decisions recommended by economic evaluation studies? PharmacoEconomics. 2015 Jun;33(6):571–9.
33. Kjær T. A review of the discrete choice experiment with emphasis on its application in health care. 2005. Report No.: 1.
34. Slothuus U. Economic evaluation: theory, methods and application. Health Economics Paper. 2005. University Southern od Denmark. 2 Feb 2016.
35. Healey A, Chisholm D. Willing to pay as a measure of benefits of mental health care. J Ment Health Policy Econ. 1999;2:55–8.
36. O'Brien B, Gafni A. When do dollars make sense? Towards a conceptual framework to contingent valuation studies in health care. Med Decis Mak. 1996;16:288–99.
37. Hoyos D, Mariel P. Contingent valuation: past, present and future. Prague Econ Pap. 2010;4:329–43.
38. Smith R. Contingent valuation in healthcare: does it matter how the good is described? Health Econ. 2008;17:607–17.
39. Smith DM, Damschroder LJ, Kim SY, Ubel PA. What's it worth? Public willingness to pay to avoid mental illnesses compared with general medical illnesses. Psychiatr Serv. 2012 Apr;63(4):319–24.
40. Bayoumi AM. The measurement of contingent valuation for health economics. PharmacoEconomics. 2004;22(11):691–700.
41. Mulvaney-Day NE. Using willingness to pay to measure family Members' preferences in mental health. J Ment Health Policy Econ. 2005;8:71–81.
42. O'Shea E, Gannon B, Kennelly B. Eliciting preferences for resource allocation in mental health care in Ireland. Health Policy. 2008 Dec;88(2–3):359–70.
43. Sevy S, Nathanson K, Schechter C, Fulop G. Contingency valuation and preferences of health states associated with side effects of antipsychotic medications in schizophrenia. Schizophr Bull. 2001;27(4):643–52.
44. Lancaster KJ. A new approach to consumer theory. J Polit Econ. 1966;74(2):132–57.
45. Clark MD, Determann D, Petrou S, Moro D, de Bekker-Grob EW. Discrete choice experiments in health economics: a review of the literature. PharmacoEconomics. 2014 Sep;32(9):883–902.
46. Morey E, Thacher JA, Craighead WE. Patient preferences for depression treatment programs and willing to pay for treatment. J Ment Health Policy Econ. 2007;10:87–99.
47. Nunes PALD, Schokkaertd E. Identifying the warm glow effect in contingent valuation. J Environ Econ Manag. 2003;45:231–45.
48. Murphy JD, Dattel W. A cost-benefit analysis of community versus institutional living. Hosp Community Psychiatry. 1976;27(3):165–70.
49. O'Brien B, Novosel S, Torrance G, Streiner D. Assessing the economic value of a new antidepressant a willingness-to-pay approach. PharmacoEconomics. 1995;8(1):34–45.
50. Popova S, Mohapatra S, Patra J, Duhig A, Rehm J. A literature review of cost-benefit analyses for the treatment of alcohol dependence. Int J Environ Res Public Health. 2011 Aug;8(8):3351–64.
51. Unutzer J, Katon WJ, Russo J, Simon G, Von KM, Lin E, et al. Willingness to pay for depression treatment in primary care. Psychiatr Serv. 2003 Mar;54(3):340–5.
52. Layard R, Knapp M, Mayraz G. Cost-benefit analysis of psychological therapy. Natl Inst Econ Rev. 2007;202:90–8.
53. Roberts G, Grimes K. Return in investment: mental health promotion and mental illness prevention. Canadian Policy Network at the University of Western Ontario; 2011.
54. Chisholm D, Sweeny K, Sheehan P, Rasmussen B, Smit F, Cuijpers P, et al. Scaling-up treatment of depression and anxiety: a global return on investment analysis. Lancet Psychiatry. 2016 May;3(5):415–24.
55. Brouwer WB, Culyer AJ, van Exel NJ, Rutten FF. Welfarism vs. extra-welfarism. J Health Econ. 2008 Mar;27(2):325–38.
56. Donaldson C. The (near) equivalence of cost-effectiveness and cost-benefit analyses. Fact or fallacy? PharmacoEconomics. 1998 Apr;13(4):389–96.
57. Angner E. Current trends in welfare measurement. In: Davis JB, editor. The Elgar companion to recent economic methodology. Glos: Edward Elgar Publishing; 2011. p. 121–54.

Cost-Effectiveness Analysis

5

Jeroen Luyten and Catherine Henderson

Abstract

Economic evaluation of healthcare programs seeks to compare treatments and preventive measures in terms of their efficiency, that is, their ability to generate health and well being relative to the costs incurred. This chapter provides an introduction to one particular but widely used evaluation technique: cost-effectiveness analysis (CEA). We present the main conceptual elements of a CEA, measurement techniques that are used, and the challenges and limitations, and we discuss the final interpretation of results within the context of the mental health field.

Key Points Summary

- Costs
- Outcomes
- Discounting
- Cost-effectiveness ratios
- Net benefits
- Uncertainty

5.1 Introduction

Purchasers and planners of mental health services need to make investments that achieve the best results for their patients using available resources. Some guidance for deciding how to make these investment choices is required. For instance, how should a decision maker determine how to divide funds between different treatments for depression (such as cognitive-behavioral therapy, antidepressant medication, and psychotherapy)? The decision-maker will naturally want to choose among the most effective treatments, but there is also an unavoidable economic aspect to this choice (see Chap. 10). The resources necessary to make treatments available are, by definition, finite, in terms of not only funding but also health personnel, treatment spaces, and infrastructure. A central concern for decision makers who have to manage these resources is

J. Luyten (✉)
Department of Social Policy, London School of Economics and Political Science, London, UK

Leuven Institute for Healthcare Policy, KULeuven, Kapucijnenvoer 35, 3000 Leuven, Belgium
e-mail: J.Luyten@lse.ac.uk; Jeroen.luyten@kuleuven.be

C. Henderson
Personal Social Services Research Unit (PSSRU), London School of Economics and Political Science, London, UK
e-mail: C.Henderson@lse.ac.uk

D. Razzouk (ed.), *Mental Health Economics*, DOI 10.1007/978-3-319-55266-8_5

therefore to provide a mix of treatments that maximize desired mental health outcomes for patients. Or, in economic terms, to allocate resources in a way that minimizes opportunity costs (see Chap. 1), the value of the "next best alternative use" of a resource that is not chosen and is consequently lost forever. The opportunity cost of providing one treatment for depression is the loss of another treatment that could have been provided instead, at the expense of the potential benefits to patients of that other treatment.

Allocating resources based on minimizing opportunity costs is complex and requires extensive counterfactual information. Economic evaluation has been developed as a standardized and evidence-based technique to facilitate decision making based on opportunity costs [1–3]. It has become increasingly influential in health policy making [4, 5], often with a formal role in many policy contexts, most notably in health insurance coverage decisions (e.g., in the United Kingdom, France, Germany, Belgium – but not in the United States). An economic evaluation compares the costs and outcomes that are linked to at least two interventions, one of which is often the current practice of usual care. Different forms of economic evaluation exist (see Box 5.1). They all have a common approach to costs (see Sect. 5.2) but differ in their assessment of consequences. Depending on the level at which resources need to be allocated and opportunity costs need to be assessed – broad or narrow – one particular type of analysis will be more appropriate than the others. Cost-benefit analysis (CBA) (see Chap. 4) is the broadest form. It assesses consequences in monetary terms so that the return on investment from spending a sum of money in one program can be compared with investing that same sum in any other program – within the health sphere but also beyond, for example, by investing these resources in public infrastructure. Cost-utility analysis (CUA) is limited to comparisons within the health domain [6]. Consequences are expressed in generic health units that compose the effects of a condition on both mortality and morbidity, such as quality-adjusted life years (QALYs), disability-adjusted life years, or healthy year equivalents. This enables opportunity costs of health programs to be assessed in terms of the health units forgone by not investing these resources in competing health programs. Cost-effectiveness analysis (CEA) is a narrower form of assessing opportunity costs in which the assessed consequences are more specific and limited to a particular field of healthcare, mostly one specific disease area. In this chapter, we outline the main elements of cost-effectiveness studies and their interpretation.

5.2 Main Elements of Cost-Effectiveness Studies

5.2.1 Costs

Costs are a function of the volume of the resources consumed when making an intervention available, multiplied by their respective unit cost (see Chaps. 2 and 11). Distinguishing quantities from unit costs is important because it allows the reliability and relevance of the valuations made to be assessed. It also allows assessment of the transferability of results from the original study to other contexts (e.g., countries or times).

5.2.1.1 Resource Use

Typical resources that are used by providing a program are consumables (e.g., pharmaceuticals), labor (e.g., nursing, caregiving), capital (buildings, devices, equipment), and overhead costs (e.g. electricity, management) (see Chaps. 2 and 11). In the domain of mental health, resources consumed outside of the health sector could also be relevant: costs associated with criminal justice, provision of special housing, social care, and additional costs falling on schools because of special educational needs [7] (see Chap. 2). Box 5.2 gives a possible classification of different types of costs that should be considered in a CEA (see Chap. 2).

Overhead costs, such as those of common equipment, personnel, or facilities, can be attributed to individual interventions by relating the proportion of resources used by the intervention relative to the total potential use of the resources, for instance, the number of hours a facility can be

Box 5.1 Different Types of Full Economic Evaluations

- *Cost-minimization analysis* compares the costs of different programs that broadly lead to the same result. Because uncertainty always exists around costs and expected outcomes, in reality, the effectiveness of two programs can rarely be assumed as being equal.
- *Cost-effectiveness analysis* compares the costs and health effects of two or more interventions. Health outcomes in a cost-effectiveness analysis are expressed in terms of specific clinical or other "natural" end points that are measurable and that can be considered important within a particular health domain.
- *Cost-utility analysis* is a broader form of economic evaluation in which health outcomes are both measured and valued. Outcomes are translated into a generic measure of overall health. Several generic outcome measures are available, but the most widely used are the QALY (a measure of health) and the disability-adjusted life year (a measure of illness, mostly used in low- and middle-income contexts).
- *Cost-benefit analysis* is the broadest form of economic evaluation. It assesses health consequences in the most common metric used to assess value: money. Expressing the health effects of an intervention in monetary terms and comparing them with the costs associated with that intervention allows decision makers to judge the return on investment of a program, that is, how much net value an intervention offers. This estimate can consequently be compared with other interventions for which the benefits can also be expressed in monetary terms, both within healthcare and beyond.

(continued)

(continued)

- *Cost-consequences analysis* presents a range of outcomes (measured in natural units) alongside the costs of alternative programs, without defining any one outcome as primary.

Box 5.2 Types of Costs

- **Direct costs** often represent the healthcare resources used by providing a program: doctors' hours, medications, hospital beds, overhead costs of running facilities, capital costs of buildings, training, or equipment. In mental health the costs of other forms of care (e.g., social care) also could be considered direct costs.
- **Indirect costs** are the opportunity costs of patients and caregivers in terms of time lost through ill health, undergoing treatment, or providing unpaid care. These costs mainly represent productivity losses due to an inability to work because of illness, but they could also include disrupted domestic, educational, social, and leisure activities.
- **Patient costs** are those costs borne by patients and their families, such as transport costs, user charges, and time lost. They can be substantial but are often not considered in analyses from a payer perspective.
- **Future costs** are often split between future costs that are directly related to the disease or the intervention (e.g., a mental health problem that gives a higher risk of developing diabetes), and those costs that are unrelated (e.g., increased life expectancy leading to higher pension costs).
- **Intangible costs** are the psychological "costs" of pain and suffering that patients experience during an episode of illness or while undergoing the treatment. These are obviously difficult to quantify.

used to provide a treatment as a proportion of the total hours the facility is available for medical use.

Which cost categories should be considered in a CEA depends on the perspective from which the analysis is undertaken (see Chaps. 1 and 2): that of the patient, the employer, the hospital, the healthcare payer, or society. If a healthcare payer perspective (e.g., national health insurance) is adopted, only those costs that are incurred by the payer should be considered. These primarily include the direct costs of providing the program (other costs predominantly falling on other parties). Analogously, from a patient, employer, or hospital perspective, only the costs borne by those groups are relevant. If a societal perspective is adopted, however, all costs borne by the whole of society should be considered. The benefit of the societal perspective is that it does not neglect any economically relevant costs. A disadvantage is that it does not consider how these costs are distributed among the various affected parties.

The choice of costing perspective can have a substantial effect on the estimated costs of an intervention. This is especially true in the field of mental health. For instance, prevention of depression is much more cost-effective from a societal perspective than from a payer perspective, as the bulk of the cost burden is indirect, attributable to an inability to work rather than to costs associated with healthcare treatment (see Chap. 25). For instance, an English study estimated that 90% of the societal cost of depression was due to unemployment and absenteeism from work [8]. From a patient or employer perspective, it is possible for the (tangible) costs of depression to be lower than the costs for society or the healthcare payer. For instance, if disability payments (state benefits or social insurance payments) sufficiently compensate patients for loss of income, or if employers quickly find replacement employees, then the cost to patients and employers could be minimal (see Chap. 29). Consequently, from a financial perspective, prevention of depression is more or less attractive depending on whose costs are considered.

5.2.1.2 Unit Costs

The resources consumed as part of a treatment program must be valued. Unit costs are mainly understood as prices or charges and can be accessed via national price lists or data on purchasing prices from institutions (e.g., hospitals). The level of detail required depends on the importance of the particular item, the scope of the study, and the time and resources available for the analysis. We can illustrate this point by considering the unit cost of hospital stays. It is less precise but more convenient to use a general per-day cost calculated on the basis of the total cost of the hospital or one of its departments. More precise estimates take into account the particular characteristics of the admission and the treatment, down to the specific resource use of an individual patient (micro-costing) (see Chaps. 2 and 11).

However, some resources (e.g., volunteer time from caregivers) do not have market prices. This obviously does not mean that they are without value, and a costing method that does not account for this use of nontradeable resources would underestimate the opportunity cost of a program. In those cases, a value may be imputed to approximate the value of the resource should there be a market in which the resource could be bought (see Chap. 15). For instance, caregiver time can be valued at average market wage or at hourly wages for overtime (see Chap. 17). Several valuing techniques exist to put a monetary figure on nonmarket resources, most notably contingent valuation (willingness-to-pay or willingness-to-accept studies) (see Chap. 4).

The unit cost that should be used also depends on the costing perspective that is adopted. From a payer, patient, or employer perspective, the market price is often the price actually paid, and it consequently reflects the actual economic loss incurred by the payer, patient, or employer. From a societal point of view, arriving at a valuation can be more complex. What matters here is the change (i.e., the loss) in available economic resources within a country. Market prices of used resources can be misleading in terms of reflecting the true social cost of using these resources.

Hospital charges may reflect cross-subsidization across departments and could artificially inflate or deflate the economic loss incurred by providing one type of treatment. Drug prices often reflect monopoly profits and, depending on the recipient and usage of these profits (e.g., domestic or foreign pharmaceutical companies that either reinvest profits or not), the social loss will be larger or smaller. Moreover – and this is also relevant to payer or patient perspectives – unit costs can become variable (see also Sect. 5.2.5 on marginal cost-effectiveness ratios). Being subject to supply-and-demand dynamics, the prices (and opportunity costs) of particular resources can increase or decrease as a function of the quantity needed. For instance, the value of one unit of nursing time depends on alternative deployment possibilities, and this value will likely be higher when more time is needed. As an example, in the initial stages of an epidemic, spare capacity in a nursing service can be used, but gradually higher opportunity costs will be incurred as more nursing time is taken from other, more productive activities [9]. A fixed unit cost (e.g., an hourly wage) does not reflect such dynamics. These issues of finding appropriate unit costs highlight difficulties in assessing the "true" societal cost of diseases. Obviously, social opportunity costs cannot be a requirement for every single CEA, and the label "societal perspective" is often used for an analysis that just uses indirect costs in addition to direct costs, all valued at listed prices. But it is important to highlight that the value attributed to resources must in some cases be treated with caution, especially for resources that are used in large quantities and for which there are reasons to believe that official prices do not reflect the value of alternative deployments.

5.2.2 Outcomes

A focus on costs only (a cost analysis) might indicate that mental health programs can lead to cost savings (when a sufficiently long time horizon is considered). If a decision maker's only concern is to contain or reduce costs, this information may be sufficient to identify the preferred program. Full economic evaluations, aiming to inform the decision maker of the value received per amount invested in an intervention, also take into account the benefits received for the costs incurred. Estimating the net health effect of an intervention – the denominator of cost-effectiveness – consists of two separate tasks: defining relevant outcomes and measuring them.

5.2.2.1 Defining Outcomes

Ideally, a single and unambiguous outcome (an event, a biological marker, a disease stage, reduction of a specified risk factor) needs to be achieved so that the alternatives being evaluated can be compared in terms of their achievement. This outcome measure needs to be observable, relatively easy to measure, and meaningful in the particular disease context. A "final" outcome, such as depression-free days, might be useful in some study contexts; in others, however, a measure that can be linked to a final outcome (an "intermediate" outcome) may be more relevant or feasible. For example, detecting suicidal ideation could lead to the prevention of death by suicide (the final outcome). Drummond et al. [2] recommend that analysts should explain why the intermediate end point has value or clinical relevance in its own right, be confident that the link between the intermediate and final health outcomes has been adequately established by previous research, or ensure that any uncertainty surrounding that link is adequately characterized in the study.

CEA has a narrower range of applications than a CUA. Nonetheless, CEA may be the natural choice in certain circumstances. It may be that clinicians are very interested in the effect of a treatment on a particular clinical outcome; a CEA based on that outcome might produce evidence that clinicians see as more relevant than a CUA. Clinicians' perceptions of the relevance of the outcome could influence their decision to implement that treatment. In addition, generic preference-based measures (from which utilities are derived) may not perform equally well across all mental health conditions when measuring clinically relevant change. For instance, the evidence is mixed on the validity and responsiveness of the

EuroQol five-dimension questionnaire and SF-6D in measuring the effects of schizophrenia and psychotic disorders [10–13] (see Chaps. 3 and 6). Thus limitations may exist in assessing utility on the basis of these measures in these populations. A CEA based on condition-specific measures of quality of life or symptom rating scales might be considered here in order to adequately capture changes brought about by the intervention [12, 14]. One approach in this circumstance would be to carry out both a CEA and a CUA within one study [compare with refs. 15, 16].

Table 5.1 provides an overview of outcome measures that have been used in economic evaluations within some clinical areas of mental health.

It needs to be said, however, that pinning down the most relevant end point can be complex for many diseases, and there will often be disagreement on the best measure to judge the effectiveness of an intervention. Mental health conditions are often multidimensional. A solution to this issue – at least for researchers – is to expand a CEA into a *cost-consequences analysis*. This is a variant of CEA whereby, instead of defining one single outcome, a range of output measures is presented to decision makers, without judging which measure is the more relevant one.

5.2.2.2 Study Designs

The effects of treatments (and also costs) are likely to differ between individuals. Moreover, different individuals may undergo different treatment regimens, experience the course of a disease differently, and respond differently to treatment. The quality of a CEA is often judged based on the quality of its underlying effectiveness assessment and the extent to which it manages to account for patient heterogeneity. Different study designs have different weaknesses.

In a randomized controlled trial (RCT) with adequate power and appropriate follow-up

Table 5.1 Examples of outcome measures used in cost-effectiveness analyses in mental health

Clinical area	Outcome measure	Studies using the measure
Schizophrenia	Clinical Global Impressions scale (CGI) [17]	King et al. [18]
	Positive and Negative Syndrome Scale for Schizophrenia (PANSS) [19]	Priebe et al. [20]
	Investigators Assessment Questionnaire (IAQ) [21]	King et al. [18]
	Global Assessment of Functioning [22]	Hastrup et al. [23]
Depression	Beck Depression Inventory [24, 25]	Hollinghurst et al. [16]; Kuyken et al. [26]; Maljanen et al. [27]
	Hospital Anxiety Depression Scale (HADS) [28]	Romeo et al. [29]
	Cornell Scale for Depression in Dementia (CSDD) [30]	Banerjee et al. [31]
	General Health Questionnaire, 28-item version (GHQ-28) [32]	Woods et al. [33]
	Time to relapse (using the Structured Clinical Interview for DSM Disorders) [34]	Kuyken et al. [26]; Kuyken et al. [35]
Dementia	The Neuropsychiatric Inventory (NPI) [36]	D'Amico et al. [37]
	Cohen-Mansfield Agitation Inventory (CMAI) [38]	Chenoweth et al. [39]
	Quality of Life in Alzheimer's Disease measure (QOL-AD) [40]	Woods et al. [33]; D'Amico et al. [41]; Orgeta et al. [42]
	The Alzheimer's Disease Assessment Scale – Cognition (ADAS-Cog) [43]	D'Amico et al. [41]; Orgeta et al. [42]
Substance abuse	Addiction Severity Index (ASI) [44]	McLellan et al. [45]
	Days of abstinence (using the Global Appraisal of Individual Needs [GAIN]) [46]	McCollister et al. [47]; McLellan et al. [45]
	Longest duration of abstinence (based on laboratory sampling)	Olmstead et al. [48]
Suicide	Beck Scale for Suicide Ideation [49]	van Spijker et al. [50]

duration, health effects can be recorded on an individual patient basis and can later be causally attributed to the treatment. Adequate randomization across treatment and control groups ensures that other characteristics that might cause differences in effectiveness (confounders) are equally prevalent in both groups. An RCT can also record resource use by individual patients, after which average costs and effects can be calculated [51]. However, RCTs can be costly to carry out and take a long time to complete. Further, depending on the nature of the trial, the outcomes are the products of treatment regimens conducted in ideal circumstances to assess whether the treatment *can* work. Such trials are unlikely to be fully representative of the costs and outcomes of day-to-day clinical practice. This difference between efficacy and effectiveness needs to be considered carefully when relying on RCTs for CEA. More pragmatic RCT designs test the effectiveness of a treatment within routine clinical practice settings [52], for instance, by avoiding the imposition of rigid inclusion and exclusion criteria to reflect the real-world patient population who would receive the treatment. An example of a pragmatic trial in the mental health field is a pharmacological trial comparing classes of antipsychotic medications for people with chronic schizophrenia [53–55]. It is also important to make sure that the control group actually represents the "do nothing" option that is implemented in a particular setting, and that the additional benefit of a program is not overestimated or underestimated by comparing it to an irrelevant alternative (see also Sect. 5.2.4). Alternative study designs such as observational cohort studies have been advocated on the grounds that they can be carried out without the strictures imposed by randomization that may limit the generalizability of findings [56]. Observational studies provide information on the effectiveness of interventions and are important bases for CEAs. Attributing the outcomes of controlled but not randomized studies to the intervention of interest can, however, be affected by confounding due to a lack of random assignment of patients to treatment and control groups. Selection bias has traditionally been a weakness of these designs, but alternative approaches involving statistical methods for creating "synthetic control groups" are coming into use [56].

When experimental studies are not feasible because of financial, practical, or sometimes even ethical concerns, modeling can be an alternative basis for economic evaluation analyses [57] ((see Chap. 7). Models can be used to project the evolution of a condition in a population, based on a combination of available insights obtained from published estimates. A model allows a simplified depiction of possible consequences resulting from different treatment choices or events. Two popular techniques are decision trees [58], generally used for acute events, and Markov models [59], mostly used to synthesize events that require a longer time frame, as is often the case in mental health.

5.2.3 Discounting

It is important that the time frame considered in an evaluation is long enough so that it captures all relevant aspects of the alternatives under evaluation. But costs and outcomes may occur on separate time scales. In economic evaluation, it is standard practice to revalue costs and effects, depending on whether they occur at more distant or more proximate moments in time. The "present value" (PV) represents the contemporary value of a cost or outcome X occurring n years from now, depreciating at a yearly discount rate of r:

$$PV(X) = \frac{X}{(1+r)^n}$$

Discounting can be contentious, especially when applied to health outcomes [60]. When it comes to costs, there are convincing reasons to account for time preference. First, the future is uncertain; various catastrophic events might occur that would invalidate projected future costs. Second, a sum of money at our disposal now can be invested and generate a larger amount later. If we were to pay a cost in the future but need to account for it now, we would only need to pay a fraction of it. Third, if people are wealthier in the future than they are now, a sum of money at current prices would represent a smaller proportion of the funds available later. Fourth, as additional units of income will at some point lead to decreasing marginal levels of utility, the relative sacrifice of that cost (its opportunity cost in terms of consumption of the forgone alternative) will likely be lower in the future. And fifth, people tend to have an innate pure time preference (or bias) for the present over the future. We prefer to enjoy life now and to pay later.

Whether these arguments for discounting costs also hold for discounting health outcomes is less clear. Health seems to be a normal (or even luxury) good, rather than one of necessity: as our income grows, we are likely to attribute higher values to extra health gains. Moreover, we cannot invest health over time like we can with money. And a pure time preference may be less pronounced for health than for costs (becoming sick now or in 10 years vs. paying a cost now or in 10 years). On the other hand, health, as with money, arguably has decreasing marginal utility over time: an 85th year may be less valuable than a 65th one. Whether the extra gains from years lived in more prosperous times outweigh the decreased marginal utility of greater longevity is an open question. Also, not applying a discount rate for health gains while discounting costs can create problems of inconsistency and could lead to counterintuitive results. Every program seems better the longer it is postponed into the future (as costs would be discounted but health effects would not). And some interventions (e.g., disease eradication programs) have benefits that last indefinitely. Refraining from discounting these benefits would lead us to overinvest scarce resources in such programs. Last, plenty of empirical evidence shows that people de facto discount health gains in practice, for example, smokers who prefer short-term pleasure to long-term health.

Discounting can have a substantial effect when interventions aim to generate lasting and long-term effects, which is often the case in mental health programs. Most guidelines propose using a well-defined discount rate for costs and often a smaller one for health effects, but recommend presenting results with different rates as well [e.g., 61, 62].

5.2.4 Analytical Methods

5.2.4.1 Cost-Effectiveness Ratios

Combining (discounted) costs and effects, we can derive an *average* cost-effectiveness ratio (ACER), a *marginal* cost-effectiveness ratio (MCER), and – most often reported – an *incremental* cost-effectiveness ratio (ICER).

The ACER expresses the total costs of an intervention per achieved health outcome, as compared with a baseline situation, which in many cases would be the current situation (usual care):

$$ACER_A = \frac{\text{Cost intervention } A}{\text{Effects intervention } A}$$

The MCER expresses the changes in cost and effect within one program when it is expanded in scale (e.g., an education program that is rolled out in two regions instead of one). If the size of program is flexible, the MCER can give a useful indication of the economies of scale that can occur, which is informative in finding the optimal level of program provision:[1]

$$MCER_{A_Q} = \frac{\text{Cost intervention } A \textit{ at} \text{ scale } Q + 1 - \text{Cost intervention } A \textit{ at} \text{ scale } Q}{\text{Effect intervention } A \textit{ at} \text{ scale } Q + 1 - \text{Effect intervention } A \textit{ at} \text{ scale } Q}$$

The most common form of expressing the results of an economic evaluation is the ICER, comparing the costs and effects of the two most relevant interventions under evaluation. The ICER gives an indication of the extra (or incremental) cost of one program for the extra effect it generates over another:[2]

$$ICER_{A \text{ vs } B} = \frac{\text{Costs intervention } A - \text{Costs intervention } B}{\text{Effects intervention } A - \text{Effects intervention } B}$$

[1] Strictly speaking, the "marginal" value of a variable is its rate of change (first derivative) with respect to quantity. This is equivalent to the formula provided if Q is sufficiently large.

[2] Note that when we are evaluating only one intervention and the comparator intervention is the "do nothing" scenario, the ICER is the same as the ACER.

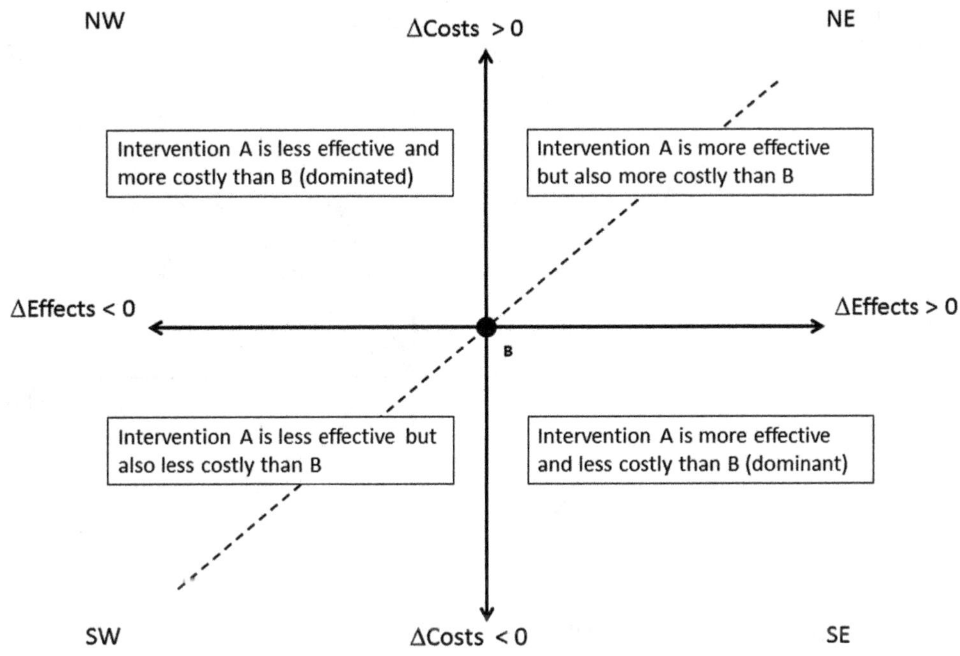

Fig. 5.1 The cost-effectiveness plane

ACERs, MCERs, and ICERs can be represented on a "cost-effectiveness plane," represented in Fig. 5.1. The plane has four quadrants, corresponding to the four main possible outcomes of CEA. An intervention can be more costly and lead to fewer health gains than another one (quadrant NW); in this case the "do nothing" strategy is represented in the origin O. If so, the new intervention is said to be "dominated" by the other one (so we should do nothing). Conversely, if the new intervention is less expensive but leads to better outcomes, it is said to be "dominant" over the other strategy (quadrant SE). More difficult questions arise when one intervention is both more expensive and more effective than the other (quadrant NE). In that case we need to judge whether paying more for better outcomes is "worth it." Similarly, if an intervention is less costly but also less effective than the alternative, are the cost-savings worth the health losses (quadrant SW)? The question "is it worth it?" can only be answered when we have an estimate of the maximum monetary value of the health effect in question, for example, a societal willingness to pay per health effect (represented in Fig. 5.1 by the dashed line through the origin; see also Sect. 5.3).

Analysts need to be cautious when interpreting cost-effectiveness ratios (CERs) with regard to whether the ratio represents the most relevant information. Several implementable strategies may be available, and not all ICERs are ultimately meaningful. Figure 5.2 illustrates the different types of CERs and how to exclude irrelevant ones. The slopes of all lines connecting the points are all CERs. The slopes of the lines starting from the origin (the "do nothing" strategy) represent the ACER of each strategy, indicating how much the average gain in effect would cost in each strategy. A′ is intervention A scaled up by one unit. The dotted line connecting intervention A and A′ represents the MCER of A′ versus A, and doing this for the entire range of possible output levels provides information about the optimal level of program provision for A. In this case, the slope between A and A′ is smaller than the one between O and A, indicating economies of scale: the same health effect can be offered at a lower unit cost, for instance, because of the fixed costs of starting up the program. When several programs are available (A, A′, B, C, D, and X), the analyst must plot the costs and outcomes on the cost-effectiveness plane and

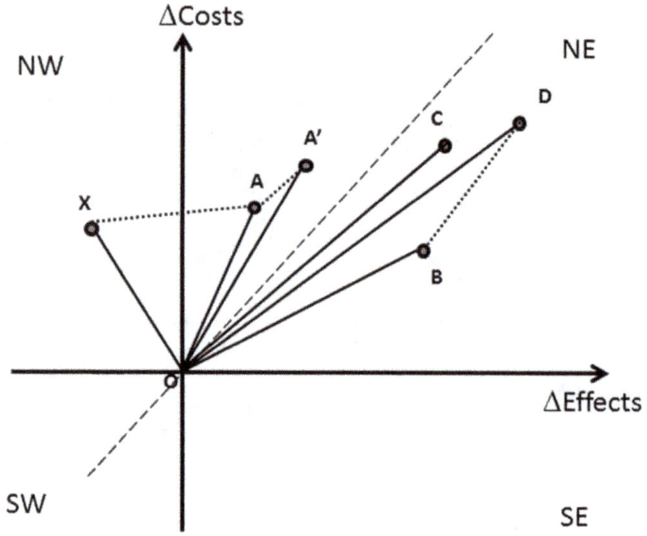

Fig. 5.2 Cost-effectiveness ratios of different strategies

eliminate those strategies that are dominated. In this example, interventions A, A′, X, and C are all dominated by B and D. A, A′, and X are "strictly dominated" by intervention B (i.e., B leads to better health outcomes at a lower cost). C is dominated by extension ("extended dominance") because the combination of strategies B and D is more cost-effective than C and leads to better health outcomes. The rationale for extended dominance is that a decision maker who is willing to pay the dominated CER of C can better pay the lower CER of implementing B combined with D, which leads to more health effects. The figure also illustrates how easy it can be to misrepresent the efficiency of a program by comparing it with the wrong comparator. An ICER that compares a new intervention A to an obsolete and irrelevant comparator X may make A *appear* favorable (the slope of the dotted line connecting both points is lower than the slope of the dashed cost-effectiveness threshold line through the origin), but in fact both strategies A and X are dominated. In Figure 5.2, the relevant ICERs to be reported and considered by the decision maker are B versus O and D versus B. Compared with the threshold, B versus O is clearly cost-effective, whereas D versus B is not. In general, the intervention with the smallest slope is the most cost-effective one and should be implemented first, followed by the one with the smallest slope starting from that intervention onward, and so on.

Note: The slope of the lines in Fig. 5.2 are all CERs. Average CERs represent the cost per health effect achieved by a program (e.g., the slope of OA). Marginal CERs represent the change in cost-effectiveness when the scale of a program is varied (e.g., AA′). Incremental CERs represent the extra cost per extra health effect of one program versus another (e.g., OB or DB). An ACER is a particular case of an ICER (i.e., a comparison with the "do nothing" scenario)

5.2.4.2 Net Benefits

Some studies prefer to express cost-effectiveness results as "net benefits" rather than as ICERs because the latter is a ratio instead of a single number, which has a number of analytical disadvantages and is more difficult to interpret. For instance, as a ratio, the ICER does not give an indication of the scale of the programs being considered. Also, ICERs falling in the southeast and northwest quadrants of the CE plane (Fig. 5.1) will have the same (negative) sign, although we would want to adopt the former (more effective/less costly) intervention but not the latter (less effective/more costly). Moreover, for statistical analyses, net benefits can be easier to work with than ICERs. Net benefits incorporate the threshold willingness-to-pay value for a gain in health outcome (to which CERs otherwise need to be compared in order to assess whether they are too expensive). Net benefit is calculated by subtracting the incremental costs of the programme (ΔC) from the monetary equivalent (WTP[E]) of the achieved incremental health gain (ΔE) it would generate. A value above zero indicates a net gain, and a negative value indicates a net loss.

$$Net\ \text{benefit} = WTP(E) * \Delta E - \Delta C$$

The net benefit approach resembles CBA, which also expresses both costs and effects in monetary values. CBA (see Chap. 4), however, typically allows the patient to do the valuing of the health effects, whereas net benefits usually represent a valuation of health gains by the general public (welfarism vs. extra-welfarism; see Chap. 9). If so, CBA implies an overall valuation of all the specific consequences of the program (including highly particular effects on individual patients' quality of life, such as improved social life; ability to work, parent, participate in sports; and the degree to which these particular aspects matter to a patient), whereas net benefits based on social valuations only provide generic values for the particular health consequence that was measured.

5.2.5 Uncertainty

A combination of inputs on costs, outcomes, and probabilities leads to a point estimate of the incremental cost per outcome of one intervention versus another (as illustrated in Fig. 5.1). But the accuracy of this estimate depends on the degree of uncertainty that is embodied in the underlying observations and calculations, and it would be misleading not to report this uncertainty in the final results.

Three sources of uncertainty can be distinguished [61]. The first is parameter uncertainty: uncertainty in the input variables that are used. This is mainly the result of sampling and measurement error, in that the observed estimates are at best only an approximation of the "real" value of a parameter. Second, there will be *structural* uncertainty, related to uncertainty in the modeling approach or the trial design. For instance, are any disease outcomes ignored in the model or the trial? Are disease outcomes or treatment outcomes really independent, as is assumed in the analysis, or do different arms of the trial or branches of the decision tree in reality interact? And finally, there is *methodological* uncertainty. Are the methods used in the CEA sufficient to measure the costs and outcomes of an intervention? For instance, is the outcome chosen the most relevant for measuring health gain in a particular area? Is it sensitive enough to reflect meaningful changes in outcomes? Do discount rates represent social time preferences? Should indirect costs be considered and, if so, how? This more general type of uncertainty about how to measure the efficiency of an intervention cannot easily be solved and is most relevant to the correct interpretation of the results (see Sect. 5.3).

The effect of parameter and structural uncertainty can mostly be analyzed via "sensitivity analysis" (see Chap. 7), exploring the impact on the estimated CER of making different assumptions in terms of models and parameters. Structural uncertainty can be addressed by exploring the effect of different model structures. Parameter uncertainty can be dealt with by changing the value of particular inputs. In univariate, deterministic sensitivity analysis, alternative values are used for an individual key model parameter (e.g., the price of a drug). In multivariate, deterministic sensitivity analysis, the effect of changing many assumptions at the same time is explored (also called a "scenario analysis"). These alternative values are still determined by the analyst.

In probabilistic sensitivity analysis, statistical distributions are added to variables from which random values are drawn (e.g., 10,000 random picks). These iterations lead to a "cloud" of cost-effectiveness estimates (10,000 estimates) across the four quadrants of the CEA plane, which gives a general indication of the location of the "real" ICER, given the statistical distributions of the variables used. The magnitude of this cloud indicates the extent of the uncertainty that is embodied in the ICER. It also shows whether mainly outcomes or costs are uncertain, or both. Figure 5.3 illustrates

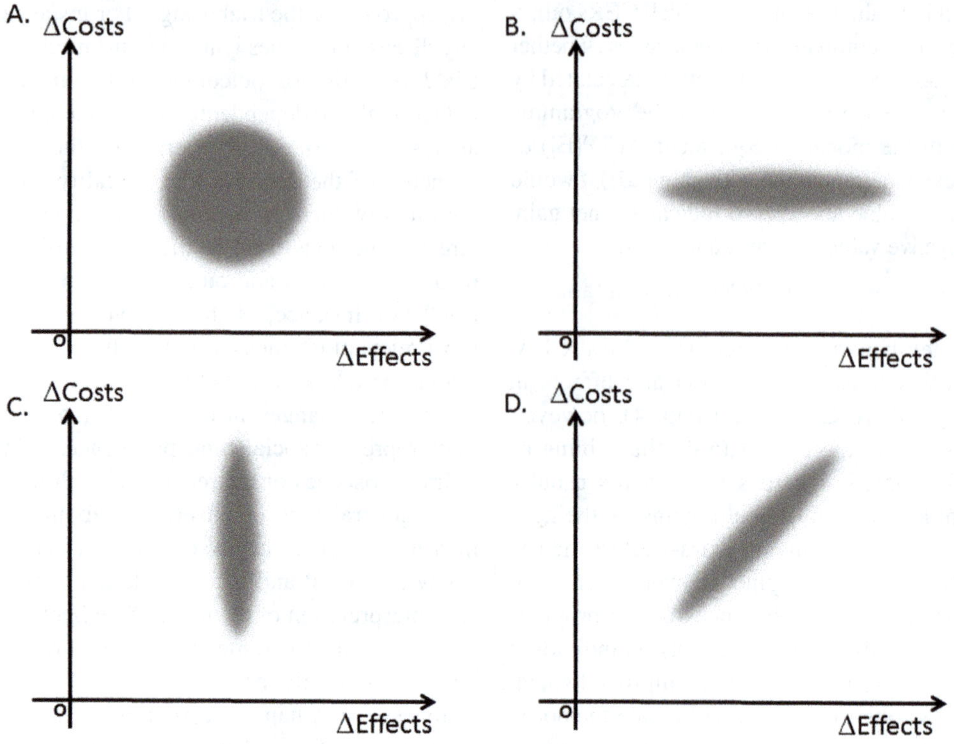

Fig. 5.3 Cost-effectiveness clouds

this. In panel A, costs and effects are equally uncertain. A cloud resembling a horizontal ellipse (panel B) indicates that the variation in outcomes is greater than the variation in cost estimates. In panel C, effects are more certain than costs. Costs and effects can also be correlated. Panel D represents a situation where costs and effects are equally uncertain but positively correlated.

Sensitivity analysis can be used to identify the main drivers of the results and the inputs for which further research can reduce uncertainty. For instance, it can demonstrate that the most influential variable in the cost-effectiveness of an antidepressant is the effectiveness of the drug in the patient group younger than 60 years of age. Consequently, those who interpret the CEA need to judge the certainty of the particular value of that parameter that was used in the study. If there is substantial uncertainty about this estimate, an additional "value of information analysis" (VOI) can be performed to establish the monetary value of acquiring additional information (i.e., certainty) on that specific parameter, which can consequently be compared with the extra research cost of obtaining it [62, 63] (see Chap. 7). VOI can be used to aid decision makers by demonstrating how much it would cost to reduce the uncertainty surrounding the resource allocation decision (e.g., by increasing the sample size), and whether the cost is worth incurring, versus making that decision on the basis of the presently available information [64]. For an example of the use of VOI in the mental health field, see the work by McCollister and colleagues [47].

A convenient way to graphically represent the uncertainty involved in an ICER is the "cost-effectiveness acceptability curve" (CEAC), which is illustrated in Fig. 5.4. CEACs are a different way of representing cost-effectiveness clouds and visualize, for every willingness-to-pay threshold per outcome gained, the proportion of ICER estimates that would fall below that threshold; put another way, CEACs show the probability that the net monetary benefit is greater than zero at each of a range of potential willingness-to-pay values. This point is illustrated in Fig. 5.4, where 50% of the estimated ICERs of one intervention over another lies below the threshold willingness-to-pay

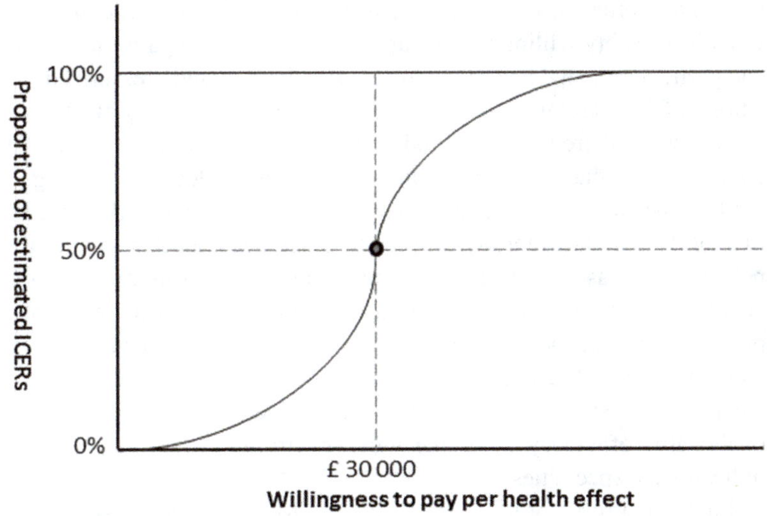

Fig. 5.4 Cost-effectiveness acceptability curve

value of £30,000. This means that a decision maker has a 50% chance that the intervention will offer good value for the money and a 50% chance that it will be too expensive, relative to that specific threshold value.

To conclude this section, most countries have developed practical guidelines for analysts on how to handle the technical assumptions and controversies related to quantifying costs, effects, uncertainty, and results [65, 66].

5.3 Interpretation

Once presented with the results of a CEA, a decision maker is faced with the task of assessing and interpreting the evidence at hand. The decision maker must assess the quality and also the usefulness of the evidence. We address these issues in turn.

First, what is the quality of the study in assessing the real "value for money" of the intervention? Is uncertainty properly accounted for? Are the options under evaluation clearly defined and described? Are differences in reported costs and effects between interventions fully attributable to the interventions or also to unreliable or invalid methodologies, which is less desirable? Are important categories of costs neglected? As mentioned, economic evaluations of mental health interventions may be particularly sensitive to the perspective adopted in the analysis, and an atypical cost profile often occurs in mental health. Such broader costs can be estimated, but often with a degree of uncertainty. Are all relevant outcomes captured? CEA uses specific effect measures that may focus on only one aspect of an illness and neglect other important outcomes. It may also fail to capture the adverse effects of a treatment.

Second, assessing whether an intervention is cost-effective (i.e., it is "worth it") requires a benchmark – a cost-per-effect threshold – that distinguishes health benefits that come at a "reasonable" cost from those that are excessively costly. Benchmarks or threshold values for a life year in full health (a QALY) exist in several countries, but typically not for condition-specific health outcomes. This immediately brings us back to the main weakness of CEA in providing information on efficient resource allocation. CEA allows assessments of efficiency at a local level, within the budget available for a condition or to achieve a particular outcome. But ultimately, a more general idea of the value of one particular type of effect (e.g., one depressive episode) in the overall picture of health and well-being is still required to assess whether costs are acceptable.

How many other health gains, products, or services is a society willing to give up for a gain in one particular mental health outcome? This limitation of CEA is relevant in the context of mental health, where there remains a major challenge to obtain funding that is proportionate to the disease burden associated with mental health disorders. Mental health interventions are often seen by policymakers as less important than physical health interventions, as the prevailing conception of health and sickness is still predominantly a biomedical one. CEA, constrained to particular mental health specialties, cannot address issues of allocative efficiency across the wider spectrum of healthcare specialties.

Last but surely not least, an efficient allocation of the available resources will maximize achievable health effects under budget constraints. But this outcome is not necessarily the most desirable one from a social or an ethical perspective. It does not acknowledge the relation of health programs with other important objectives of healthcare, including tackling health inequities; promoting respect for individual autonomy, dignity, and patient preferences; personal responsibility; solidarity with the worst-off groups in society; or even bioethical considerations about the moral desirability of particular technologies [67]. There may be good reasons why a less efficient program still deserves funding, or why an efficient strategy is not desirable. However, CEA would indicate that accommodating and upholding other ethical values would come at a higher opportunity cost. This point is discussed in further detail in Chap. 10.

5.4 Conclusion

CEA is of most use in situations where (a) a budget holder needs to make allocation decisions among a number of options within a particular clinical field (or has "ring-fenced" money to spend), and (b) there is a clear measure of success. It is increasingly used to complement evidence of the efficacy and effectiveness of interventions in order to demonstrate that the costs of an intervention are also proportionate to the gains achieved. In the context of mostly fixed and pressurized healthcare budgets, these considerations of efficiency become increasingly relevant. Given its increasing effect on decision-making, it is important that individuals who work in the field of mental health policy are familiar with the primary components and assumptions of CEA, the complexities inherent to the methodology, and the particular challenges that occur when it is applied to the context of mental health.

Key Messages

- CEA compares the costs of implementing a mental health program with its achieved outcome. In contrast to CBA or CUA, this outcome is defined in terms of natural units that are specifically relevant to a particular disease area.
- CERs provide an indication of the efficiency of resource allocation within a particular disease area. What do competing programs cost per health effect achieved? Or, vice versa, per amount invested in a program, how much improvement in health effects can be "bought"?
- Results are sensitive to the costing perspective that is adopted and to whether all relevant costs are considered. As atypical cost patterns may emerge in mental healthcare, this is an important point to highlight.
- Cost-effectiveness estimates embody large uncertainties, but methods exists to account for these. The quality of a study can often be judged by the extent to which this uncertainty is dealt with.
- Cost-effectiveness estimates provide useful but nonetheless complex information to an already difficult decision-making process, and they do not "make decisions." To avoid oversimplification, attention must be paid to the correct normative interpretation of study results.

References

1. Gold M, Siegel JE, Russell LB, Weinstein MC. Cost-effectiveness in health and medicine. New York: Oxford University Press; 1996.
2. Drummond M, Sculpher M, Torrance GW, O'Brien B, Stoddard G. Methods for the economic evaluation of health care programmes. Oxford: Oxford University Press; 2005.
3. Edejer T, Baltussen R, Adam T, Hutubessy R, Acharya A, Evans D, et al. WHO guide to cost-effectiveness analysis. Geneva: World Health Organization; 2003.
4. Clement FM, Harris A, Li JJ, Yong K, Lee KM, Manns BJ. Using effectiveness and cost-effectiveness to make drug coverage decisions: a comparison of Britain, Australia, and Canada. JAMA. 2009;302(13): 1437–43.
5. Dakin H, Devlin N, Feng Y, Rice N, O'Neill P, Parkin D. The influence of cost-effectiveness and other factors on nice decisions. Health Econ. 2014; 24(10): 1256–71.
6. Luyten J, Naci H, Knapp M. Economic evaluation of mental health interventions: an introduction to cost-utility analysis. Evidence-based mental health. 2016;19(2).
7. Shearer J, McCrone P, Romeo R. Economic evaluation of mental health interventions: a guide to costing approaches. PharmacoEconomics. 2016;34(7):651–64.
8. Thomas CM, Morris S. Cost of depression among adults in England in 2000. Br J Psychiatry J Ment Sci. 2003;183:514–9.
9. Luyten J, Beutels P. Costing infectious disease outbreaks for economic evaluation: a review for hepatitis A. PharmacoEconomics. 2009;27(5):379–89.
10. Mulhern B, Mukuria C, Barkham M, Knapp M, Byford S, Soeteman D, et al. Using generic preference-based measures in mental health: psychometric validity of the EQ-5D and SF-6D. Br J Psychiatry. 2014;205(3):236–43.
11. Brazier J. Is the EQ–5D fit for purpose in mental health? Br J Psychiatry. 2010;197(5):348–9.
12. Saarni SI, Viertiö S, Perälä J, Koskinen S, Lönnqvist J, Suvisaari J. Quality of life of people with schizophrenia, bipolar disorder and other psychotic disorders. Br J Psychiatry. 2010;197(5):386–94.
13. Papaioannou D, Brazier J, Parry G. How valid and responsive are generic health status measures, such as EQ-5D and SF-36, in schizophrenia? A systematic review. Value Health. 2011;14(6):907–20.
14. Hastrup LH, Nordentoft M, Hjortheøj C, Gyrd-Hansen D. Does the EQ-5D measure quality of life in schizophrenia? J Ment Health Policy Econ. 2011;14(4):187–96.
15. Priebe S, Savill M, Wykes T, Bentall RP, Reininghaus U, Lauber C, et al. Effectiveness of group body psychotherapy for negative symptoms of schizophrenia: multicentre randomised controlled trial. Br J Psychiatry. 2016;209(1):54–61.
16. Hollinghurst S, Peters TJ, Kaur S, Wiles N, Lewis G, Kessler D. Cost-effectiveness of therapist-delivered online cognitive-behavioural therapy for depression: randomised controlled trial. Br J Psychiatry. 2010;197(4):297–304.
17. Guy W. Clinical Global Impressions Scale (CGI). In: Rush AJ, editor. Handbook of psychiatric measures. Washington, DC: American Psychiatric Association; 2000.
18. King D, Knapp M, Thomas P, Razzouk D, Loze JY, Kan HJ, et al. Cost-effectiveness analysis of aripiprazole vs standard-of-care in the management of community-treated patients with schizophrenia: STAR study. Curr Med Res Opin. 2011;27(2):365–74. 10p.
19. Kay SR, Fiszbein A, Opler LA. The Positive and Negative Syndrome Scale (PANSS) for schizophrenia. Schizophr Bull. 1987;13(2):261–76.
20. Priebe S, Savill M, Wykes T, Bentall R, Lauber C, Reininghaus U, et al. Clinical effectiveness and cost-effectiveness of body psychotherapy in the treatment of negative symptoms of schizophrenia: a multicentre randomised controlled trial. Health Technol Assess. 2016;20(11):1 100.
21. Tandon R, Devellis RF, Han J, Li H, Frangou S, Dursun S, et al. Validation of the Investigator's Assessment Questionnaire, a new clinical tool for relative assessment of response to antipsychotics in patients with schizophrenia and schizoaffective disorder. Psychiatry Res. 2005;136(2–3):211–21.
22. American Psychiatric Association. Diagnostic and statistical manual of mental disorders. 4th ed. Washington, DC: American Psychiatric Association; 1994.
23. Hastrup LH, Kronborg C, Bertelsen M, Jeppesen P, Jorgensen P, Petersen L, et al. Cost-effectiveness of early intervention in first-episode psychosis: economic evaluation of a randomised controlled trial (the OPUS study). Br J Psychiatry. 2013;202(1):35–41.
24. Beck A, Steer R, Brown G. Manual for the beck depression inventory: the psychological corporation. 1987;19(2).
25. Beck AT, Erbaugh J, Ward CH, Mock J, Mendelsohn M. An inventory for measuring depression. Arch Gen Psychiatry. 1961;4(6):561.
26. Kuyken W, Byford S, Taylor RS, Watkins E, Holden E, White K, et al. Mindfulness-based cognitive therapy to prevent relapse in recurrent depression. J Consult Clin Psychol. 2008;76(6):966–78.
27. Maljanen T, Knekt P, Lindfors O, Virtala E, Tillman P, Harkanen T, et al. The cost-effectiveness of short-term and long-term psychotherapy in the treatment of depressive and anxiety disorders during a 5-year follow-up. J Affect Disord. 2016;190:254–63.
28. Zigmond AS, Snaith RP. The hospital anxiety and depression scale. Acta Psychiatr Scand. 1983;67(6): 361–70.
29. Romeo R, Knapp M, Banerjee S, Morris J, Baldwin R, Tarrier N, et al. Treatment and prevention of depression after surgery for hip fracture in older people: cost-effectiveness analysis. J Affect Disord. 2011;128(3):211–9.

30. Alexopoulos GS, Abrams RC, Young RC, Shamoian CA. Cornell scale for depression in dementia. Biol Psychiatry. 1988;23(3):271–84.
31. Banerjee S, Hellier J, Romeo R, Dewey M, Knapp M, Ballard C, et al. Study of the use of antidepressants for depression in dementia: the HTA-SADD trial – a multicentre, randomised, double-blind, placebo-controlled trial of the clinical effectiveness and cost-effectiveness of sertraline and mirtazapine. Health Technol Asses. 2013;17(32):1–166.
32. Goldberg DP, Hillier VF. A scaled version of the General Health Questionnaire. Psychol Med. 1979;9(1):139–45.
33. Woods R, Bruce E, Edwards R, Elvish R, Hoare Z, Hounsome B, et al. REMCARE: reminiscence groups for people with dementia and their family caregivers – effectiveness and cost-effectiveness pragmatic multicentre randomised trial. Health Technol Asses. 2012;16(50):1–121.
34. First MB, Spitzer RL, Gibbon M, Williams JBW. The structured clinical interview for DSM-IV Axis I disorder with psychotic screen. New York: New York Psychiatric Institute; 1995.
35. Kuyken W, Hayes R, Barrett B, Byng R, Dalgleish T, Kessler D, et al. Effectiveness and cost-effectiveness of mindfulness-based cognitive therapy compared with maintenance antidepressant treatment in the prevention of depressive relapse or recurrence (PREVENT): a randomised controlled trial. Lancet. 2015;386(9988):63–73.
36. Cummings JL, Mega M, Gray K, Rosenberg-Thompson S, Carusi DA, Gornbein J. The neuropsychiatric inventory: comprehensive assessment of psychopathology in dementia. Neurology. 1994;44(12):2308.
37. D'Amico F, Rehill A, Knapp M, Lowery D, Cerga-Pashoja A, Griffin M, et al. Cost-effectiveness of exercise as a therapy for behavioural and psychological symptoms of dementia within the EVIDEM-E randomised controlled trial. Int J Geriatr Psychiatry. 2016;31(6):656–65. 10p.
38. Cohen-Mansfield J. Measurement of inappropriate behavior associated with dementia. J Gerontol Nurs. 1999;25(2):42–51.
39. Chenoweth L, King MT, Jeon YH, Brodaty H, Stein-Parbury J, Norman R, et al. Caring for Aged Dementia Care Resident Study (CADRES) of person-centred care, dementia-care mapping, and usual care in dementia: a cluster-randomised trial. Lancet Neurol. 2009;8(4):317–25.
40. Logsdon RG, Gibbons LE, McCurry SM, Teri L. Assessing quality of life in older adults with cognitive impairment. Psychosom Med. 2002;64(3): 510–9.
41. D'Amico F, Rehill A, Knapp M, Aguirre E, Donovan H, Hoare Z, et al. Maintenance cognitive stimulation therapy: an economic evaluation within a randomized controlled trial. J Am Med Dir Assoc. 2015;16(1):63–70.
42. Orgeta V, Leung P, Yates L, Kang S, Hoare Z, Henderson C, et al. Individual cognitive stimulation therapy for dementia: a clinical effectiveness and cost-effectiveness pragmatic, multicentre, randomised controlled trial. Health Technol Asses. 2015;19(42):1–108.
43. Rosen WG, Mohs RC, Davis KL. A new rating-scale for Alzheimers-disease. Am J Psychiatry. 1984;141(11):1356–64.
44. Patel A, Knapp M, Romeo R, Reeder C, Matthiasson P, Everitt B, et al. Cognitive remediation therapy in schizophrenia: cost-effectiveness analysis. Schizophr Res. 2010;120(1–3):217–24. 8p.
45. McLellan AT, Luborsky L, Woody GE, O'Brien CP. An improved diagnostic evaluation instrument for substance abuse patients. The Addiction Severity Index. J Nerv Ment Dis. 1980;168(1):26–33.
46. Dennis ML, Titus JC, White M, Unsicker J, Hodgkins D. Global Appraisal of Individual Needs (GAIN): administration guide for the GAIN and related measures. Bloomington: Chestnut Health Systems; 2003.
47. McCollister KE, French MT, Freitas DM, Dennis ML, Scott CK, Funk RR. Cost-effectiveness analysis of Recovery Management Checkups (RMC) for adults with chronic substance use disorders: evidence from a 4-year randomized trial. Addiction. 2013;108(12):2166–74.
48. Olmstead TA, Sindelar JL, Easton CJ, Carroll KM. The cost-effectiveness of four treatments for marijuana dependence. Addiction. 2007;102(9):1443–53.
49. Beck AT, Steer RA. Manual for the Beck scale for suicide ideation. San Antonio: The Psychological Corporation; 1991.
50. van Spijker BA, Majo MC, Smit F, van Straten A, Kerkhof AJ. Reducing suicidal ideation: cost-effectiveness analysis of a randomized controlled trial of unguided web-based self-help. J Med Internet Res. 2012;14(5):e141.
51. Petrou S, Gray A. Economic evaluation alongside randomised controlled trials: design, conduct, analysis, and reporting. BMJ. 2011;342:d1548.
52. Zwarenstein M, Treweek S, Gagnier JJ, Altman DG, Tunis S, Haynes B, et al. Improving the reporting of pragmatic trials: an extension of the CONSORT statement. BMJ. 2008;337:a2390.
53. Jones PB, Barnes TR, Davies L, Dunn G, Lloyd H, Hayhurst KP, et al. Randomized controlled trial of the effect on quality of life of second- vs first-generation antipsychotic drugs in schizophrenia: Cost Utility of the Latest Antipsychotic Drugs in Schizophrenia Study (CUtLASS 1). Arch Gen Psychiatry. 2006;63(10):1079–87.
54. Stroup TS, McEvoy JP, Swartz MS, Byerly MJ, Glick ID, Canive JM, et al. The National Institute of Mental Health Clinical Antipsychotic Trials of Intervention Effectiveness (CATIE) project: schizophrenia trial design and protocol development. Schizophr Bull. 2003;29(1):15–31.
55. Lewis S, Lieberman J. CATIE and CUtLASS: can we handle the truth? Br J Psychiatry. 2008;192(3):161–3.
56. Gillies C, Freemantle N, Grieve R, Sekhon J, Forder J. Advancing quantitative methods for the evaluation of complex interventions. In Raine, R., Fitzpatrick, R.,

Barratt, H., Bevan, G., Black, N., Boaden, R. et al. Challenges, solutions and future directions in the evaluation of service innovations in health care and public health. Health Serv Deliv Res. 2016;4(16):37–54.
57. Briggs A, Claxton C, Sculpher M. Decision modelling for health economic evaluation. Oxford: Oxford University Press; 2006.
58. Detsky AS, Naglie G, Krahn MD, Naimark D, Redelmeier DA. Primer on medical decision analysis: part 1 – getting started. Med Decis Making Int J Soc Med Decis Making. 1997;17(2):123–5.
59. Sonnenberg FA, Beck JR. Markov models in medical decision making: a practical guide. Med Decis Making. 1993;13:322–38.
60. Oliver A. A normative perspective on discounting health outcomes. J Health Serv Res Policy. 2013;18(3):186–9.
61. Bilcke J, Beutels P, Brisson M, Jit M. Accounting for methodological, structural, and parameter uncertainty in decision-analytic models: a practical guide. Med Decis Making Int J Soc Med Decis Making. 2011;31(4):675–92.
62. Drummond M, Sculpher MJ, Torrance GW, O'Brien B, Stoddart GL. Methods for the economic evaluation of health care programmes. 3rd ed. Oxford: Oxford University Press; 2005.
63. Ades AE, Lu G, Claxton K. Expected value of sample information calculations in medical decision modeling. Med Decis Making. 2004;24(2):207–27.
64. Wilson EC. A practical guide to value of information analysis. PharmacoEconomics. 2015;33(2):105–21.
65. KCE. Guidelines for pharmacoeconomic evaluations in Belgium In: Centre BHCK, editor. KCE reports 78C. Brussels. 2008.
66. National Institute for Health and Care Excellence. Guide to the methods of technology appraisal. London: National Institute for Health and Clinical Excellence; 2013. June. 2008. Report No.
67. Schokkaert E. How to introduce more (or better) ethical arguments in Hta? Int J Technol Assess Health Care. 2015;31(3):111–2.

Cost Utility Analysis

6

Matthew Franklin

Abstract

Cost-utility analysis (CUA) has become widely used, particularly in the United Kingdom, compared with other techniques within cost-effectiveness analysis. CUA uses metrics such as the quality-adjusted life year (QALY) to assess the effectiveness of an intervention compared with an alternative. The QALY accounts for mortality (life years) and morbidity (severity of a state) in a single metric; the quality adjustment is based on stated preferences (also referred to as utility weights) that can be obtained from patients or the general public using preference elicitation techniques. For trial-based evaluations, preference-based measures have been developed to assess effectiveness and to elicit QALYs. Once the costs and QALYs for a study have been established, incremental cost-effectiveness ratios (ICERs) can be used as part of a decision rule whereby an ICER threshold (or league table) is set to inform decision makers about the potential comparative cost-effectiveness of an intervention. Within this chapter, extra-welfarism as the conceptual basis for CUA and reasons for the use of stated preference to represent utility weights are described. Preference-based outcome measures and how they are used as part of cost-per-QALY analysis are also described; disability-adjusted life years are also considered. How ICERs, thresholds, and league tables can be used to inform decision-making is also introduced. Throughout this chapter, examples within the context of mental health are used. A final section is dedicated to specific implications of using CUA for evaluating mental health interventions and aspects to consider as CUA evolves.

M. Franklin (✉)
HEDS, School of Health and Related Research (ScHARR), University of Sheffield,
West Court, 1 Mappin Street, Sheffield S1 4DT, UK
e-mail: matt.franklin@sheffield.ac.uk

D. Razzouk (ed.), *Mental Health Economics*, DOI 10.1007/978-3-319-55266-8_6

Key Points Summary

- CUA for economic evaluation is evolving within the remit of extra-welfarism. These methods have practical and conceptual implications.
- This chapter describes relevant evaluative outcomes, methods for interpersonal comparability, sources of valuing outcomes, and weighting outcomes.
- Conceptual issues include who should value the severity of a condition (the patient or the general public) and implications of using the quality-adjusted life year or disability-adjusted life year.
- Practical issues include using preference-based measures and how decision-making could be informed by a central threshold amount or league tables.
- Examples will be given in a mental health context, and a final section is dedicated to specific implications of using CUA in the context of mental health.
- Topics maybe simplified for descriptive purposes; however, references are provided and are recommended for further reading around complex topics.

6.1 Introduction and Overview of Cost-Utility Analysis

Economic evaluation techniques such as cost-utility analysis (CUA) have become widely used, particularly in the United Kingdom, compared with other techniques within cost-effectiveness analysis (CEA; see also Chap. 5). CUA is regarded as a subtechnique of CEA whereby the outcome is still measured in natural units (such as health benefits); however, these natural units are utility-weighted to provide a "quality adjustment" to the natural outcome of interest.

Cost-utility studies have relied largely on a single metric of these natural outcomes while accounting for a utility-weighted quality adjustment, referred to as the quality-adjusted life year (QALY). The QALY acts as a single end point to assess the "effectiveness" of a new intervention compared with an alternative, for cross-comparison across different interventions. Alternatives such as the disability-adjusted life year (DALY) have been promoted in situations where the QALY may not be deemed suitable for the relevant outcome being assessed, it is not possible to elicit the QALY, or it is not the outcome of interest for the decision makers or commissioning group. The DALY is briefly described later in comparison to the QALY, but "cost-per-QALY" analysis dominates the focus of this chapter.

CUA and CEA are identical when accounting for costs, and it is mainly the metric of effectiveness that differs between the two approaches for economic evaluation. In general, CEA is deemed a more sensitive method for evaluating health outcomes because the outcome of interest is usually associated with the primary outcome of the study (e.g., cost per life years saved, cost per disability day avoided, cost per adverse event avoided). CUA has gained popularity because the outcome can be single or multidimensional, is usually generic rather than condition or program specific for comparability between evaluations, and can account for a quality adjustment of the relevant outcomes rather than assuming equal weight between outcomes [1, 2]. This has led to the debate that a "QALY is a QALY is a QALY—or is it?" [3], which is a discussion about whether the QALY can used to compare effectiveness across multiple studies focused on different health conditions or technologies. The cross-comparability aspect of the QALY is what has made the QALY useful when informing decision makers about resource allocation (i.e., which new interventions to finance) across the whole healthcare setting. However, the use of the QALY for assessing the effectiveness of interventions has its conceptual and practical advantages and disadvantages, which are discussed within this chapter in the context of mental healthcare. It is worth noting that utility weights are required for the practical implementation of the QALY. These utility weights for a trial have traditionally been obtained from the EQ-5D-3L [4], although in theory any preference-based measure could be used. Utility values could also be obtained directly using a preference elicitation task (see Chap. 3) or even from the empirical literature (this aspect is described in Chap. 7 as part of economic modeling).

As an overview of the content of this chapter, first a distinction will be made about the conceptual basis of what "utility" is in the context of CUA and how it relates to other interchangeably used terms of *preference* and *value*. Once the reader is familiar with preference and utility as concepts, an overview of extra-welfarism is described as a conceptual framework that underpins the use of CUA. This chapter then focuses on the conceptual basis of using utility weights for allocative decision-making, how these weights can be sourced (such as from patients or the general public), and how this has implications for economic evaluation in the context of mental health. This chapter then focuses on the practical aspects of CUA. This includes the use of preference-based measures for assessing health-related quality of life, how preference weights are used in the quality adjustment of the QALY, how the QALY and DALY compare (the DALY as a metric and its calculation are also described), and how CUA is used for informing decision-making through the use of decision rules (such as thresholds and league tables). A final section features a more specific discussion about the use of CUA in the context of mental health and some key aspects the reader may want to be aware of as CUA evolves. For descriptive purposes, some aspects may be oversimplified, but references are provided to allow the reader to explore these aspects in more detail as required.

6.2 Preference, Utility, and Value

Utility has a number of distinct meanings, and as part of classical utilitarianism(see Chap. 1) has been described as a metric that represents "happiness" [5–8] and fulfillment of desires [9–12] (see Chap. 1). In the case of the extra-welfarist perspective of welfare economics, which dominates current healthcare decision-making, a more prominent description of utility could be "satisfaction of preference." The terms *utility*, *preference*, and *value* have been used interchangeably by authors in the past and have therefore caused some confusion. These terms do have specific meanings, as described in Box 6.1, whereby "uncertainty within decision-making" is a key difference between utility and value.

Box 6.1 Quick Definitions of Preference, Utility, and Value

- "Preference is an umbrella term that describes the overall concept; utilities and values are different types of preference" ([2] p. 143).
- *Utility* is associated with "expected utility" theory, whereby people take into account the uncertainty of the option(s) in the decision-making process. Uncertainty can be introduced into a situation when the individual making the decision does not have perfect information about all options presented to them.
- By contrast, *values* are certain options, and therefore uncertainty is removed from the decision-making process.

The healthcare market is typically characterised by imperfect information, and so uncertainty exists around decision-making. For example, a patient may be diagnosed with a mental health condition such as schizophrenia or depression, but the choice of healthcare and/or medication is recommended by a clinician, and future prognosis can, to a certain extent, be uncertain both for the patient and clinician.

In this context, it is Von Neumann–Morgenstern (vNM) utility theory (the axioms of which have been described by Torrance and Feeny [13]) that is of interest in healthcare decision-making; this theory captures behavior under conditions of uncertainty and is different to other theories of utility [2, 13]. The vNM utility theory is better described as an economic theory of rational decision-making under conditions of uncertainty, rather than neoclassical theories of utilitarianism that focus on happiness or fulfillment of desires. The axioms that form the basis of vNM utility theory provide a normative model by which people *ought to* make decisions in the face of uncertainty as a rational decision maker, and it is therefore used as a conceptual basis for describing decision-making under conditions of uncertainty, rather than representing real-life decision-making within the market for healthcare. *Preference* is extensively used in reference to vNM utility (Von Neumann and Morgenstern referred to the preference measures associated with their utility theory as "utility," resulting in the interchangeable use in terms) and provides a description that fits in well with concepts, methods, and techniques used in the extra-welfarist framework and healthcare decision-making. For example, measures that include a "quality adjustment" in their scoring algorithm that are designed specifically for the purpose of CUA are referred to as "preference-based" or "utility-weighted" measures, indicating the interchangeable use of terms between utility and preference when describing CUA.

Methods to elicit preferences have already been described in Chap. 3. If these methods elicit what could be defined as utility or a value depends on whether an uncertain option has been made certain (thus eliciting a value for a state) or whether the option remains uncertain when the preference is elicited for the state (thus eliciting a utility for the state). In reality, only the standard gamble (SG) method elicits a preference under conditions of uncertainty and so elicits what could be described as utility. Methods that require a scale (such as a rating scale or visual analogue scale) or require a choice to be made (such as the time-trade off [TTO] method, discrete choice experiments, or best-worst scaling) all make an uncertain option certain in their design and so elicit a value, not utility. For the purpose of progressing through this chapter, it is important to note that among modern methods used in the overall design of CUA, *utility* refers mainly to a metric of a preference for a particular state in the case of QALY analysis (the DALY is not preference-based), and does not adhere to its actual definition of *utility* as would be classified within utilitarianism, welfarism, or even vNM utility theory. For this purpose, utility weights are also referred to as preference weights within this chapter, although preference weight is perhaps the more accurate description, even if utility weights are still often referred to in the empirical literature. The term *utility* is also used for name's sake when referring to CUA as a different method of economic evaluation compared with CEA, as described in Chap. 5.

6.3 Extra-Welfarism: A Framework for Healthcare Decision-Making and CUA

Welfare economics uses microeconomic techniques to evaluate well-being in order to measure various aspects of efficiency within an economy. The welfarist approach to welfare economics is an important concept underpinned by economic theories about how resources are allocated across members of society (see Chaps. 1 and 4). However, as neoclassical theories of welfare economics and the market have progressed, so has the conceptual basis about how resources should be allocated, how decision-making should occur, and how data to inform these decisions should be generated practically. The extra-welfarist framework was developed in response to the limitations of welfarism when making allocative decisions alongside policy objectives, when an efficient outcome is not always the socially desired outcome [14].

The framework of extra-welfarism has been the dominant conceptual basis of welfare economics in modern healthcare decision-making and for informing the design of CUA [1, 2]. Extra-welfarism as a conceptual framework has historically been misinterpreted, perhaps because of a lack of a single definitive definition of the extra-welfarist framework, but more recently the framework has been described by Brouwer et al. [15] based on four key aspects for assessing and informing resource allocation. Extra-welfarism is best described when compared with welfarism, as it is key aspects of welfarism that extra-welfarism wishes to transcend in order to aid decision makers (although some have described extra-welfarism as "non-welfarsim" because it is suggested to lack a solid basis within economic theory to support its framework). Extra-welfarism in comparison to welfarism is therefore described within Table 6.1.

Table 6.1 A simplified overview of welfare economics, welfarism, and extra-welfarism

Welfare economics and welfarism*	Extra-welfarism
Utility maximization – individuals are able to comprehensively rank their set of options and choose that option that gives them the highest level of utility.	Relevant outcome(s) – extra-welfarism allows for the use of outcomes other than overall utility to be the objective goal for policymakers; for example, focusing on specific outcomes such as health, well-being, or capability.
Consumer sovereignty – individuals are the best and only judge of what is in their best interest.	Interpersonal comparability of relevant outcomes – it is possible to compare characteristics of individuals against those of other individuals, for example, health, disability, and ability to function.
Consequentialism – all judgements should be based entirely and exclusively on resulting effects (outcome), and behavior and process should be ignored.	Source of valuation of relevant outcomes – the use of different sources of valuation other than the individual, such as proxies or expert opinion.
Social welfare – resources should be reviewed only on the basis of the utility levels reached by an individual, the aggregation of which represents social welfare.	Weighting of relevant outcomes – it is possible to weight different outcomes to account for a variety of equity considerations, such as age or productivity.

*Note: This restriction on the source and nature of valuation has been labeled as "welfarism" [15], also referred to as the welfarist approach to welfare economics (see Chaps. 1, 4, and 9)

The four key points used to define extra-welfarism in Table 6.1 compose a relatively simplistic view of the extra-welfarist framework; however, these four aspects do form much of the conceptual basis for CUA, and the first key aspect ("relevant outcome[s]") is important for both CUA and CEA: both rely on the conceptual basis that the "effectiveness" of an intervention should be judged based on the relevant outcome from the intervention. This had predominately been based on health outcomes within CEA and CUA, although well-being and capability (see Chap. 9) have both started developing as other potential relevant outcomes for assessment [14, 16–18]. The other three key aspects set out the connection between the extra-welfarist framework and the development of CUA, as well as some key differences between CUA and CEA.

The second key aspect, "interpersonal comparability of relevant outcomes," suggests that it is a necessity that relevant outcomes can be compared between individuals. This is important for resource allocation because it may not always be transparent to whom or within what healthcare sector funds should be allocated, but this decision needs to be made within a finite fixed healthcare budget. These decisions often affect people at an individual level (i.e., an opportunity cost exists between individuals receiving a new treatment compared with keeping current care or funding an alternative intervention when any treatment option cannot benefit all individuals in a society). Individuals should be compared based on the relevant outcome from a healthcare intervention (although other equity considerations can be accounted for within the extra-welfarist framework; see key point 4 in Table 6.1, "weighting of relevant outcomes"), but this needs to account for marginal benefit and be transparent for all levels of illness severity or health-related quality of life, not just based on who lives and who dies – the reality of the matter is that for many health conditions the outcome from an intervention is not a matter of immediate life or death, but rather a change in feeling "bad" to feeling "good," or even feeling "bad" to feeling "less bad," and this needs to be accounted for transparently in the decision-making process. Preference weights have become the basis for such decision-making within CUA. These weights could be elicited from the general public or from patients (or even expert opinion) per the basis of the third key point listed in Table 6.1: "source of valuation of relevant outcomes."

The fourth key point, "weighting relevant outcomes" other than preference weights for health states, such as weights to account for equity considerations like age or productivity, are described briefly within this chapter (mainly in reference to DALYs). A discussion about equity considerations is included in Chap. 8.

6.4 Source of Preference Elicitation for Outcome Assessment

Metrics of effectiveness for use with CUA need to be preference-based, such as within the quality adjustment of the QALY [1, 2] (the QALY is described in more detail in Sect. 6.6). These preferences can be elicited using various techniques such as SG or TTO. However, note that not all elicitation techniques have been described as eliciting preferences (such as the person trade-off (PTO) technique used for the DALY) (see Chap. 3). The elicited preferences can be included in the tariff score of outcome measures (also described as multiattributed tools in Chap. 3), and these measures are then referred to as preference-based outcome measures. Some preference-based outcome measures are described in Sect. 6.5.

Anthony Culyer [19], a modern father of Health Economics, suggests that two simultaneous demands exist for healthcare: that of the individual and that of the rest of society. Two potential sources for preference elicitation are available when valuing outcomes: the *patient* or the *general public* (expert opinion could also be used, but for descriptive purposes this option is not discussed here). How outcomes are valued directly affects the information provided to decision makers via CUA. For example, consider that preferences are measured on a score of 0 to 1, where 0 is a state equivalent to dead and 1 is perfect health (this is the anchoring used within the QALY). A low preference weight (e.g., 0.6) applied to a health state suggests that this state is considered to be more severe than a state with a higher preference weight (e.g., 0.8). It may be the case that the general public may not perceive a state of health to be as severe as a patient might, and this could lead to different estimations of effectiveness when assessing marginal benefit when moving between preference-weighted states of being. For example, an intervention moving a patient back to perfect health (a score value of 1) has a larger marginal benefit if the depressive state was initially valued as 0.6 (incremental benefit of 0.4) instead of 0.8 (incremental benefit of 0.2).

The patient as the source of valuation in this case refers to patients with a particular condition. For example, in the case of depression, if a patient perspective is taken, then only patients with depression should value the states associated with being clinically depressed. This perspective is directly linked with the welfarist perspective of consumer sovereignty – individuals are the best and only judge of what is in their best interest (see Chaps. 1 and 4).

If the general public is the source of valuation, then a representative group of people are asked to value the relevant outcome of interest, and this group may include the patient. *Representative* in this context means that all sociodemographic groups should be present in the valuation process, such as people from different genders, age groups, and ethnicities, as examples. In reality, it is difficult to recruit enough people for valuation studies to be truly representative of society, although studies still attempt to recruit large samples of people in order to elicit preferences (see Sect. 6.5). Compared with the welfarist perspective, the extra-welfarist perspective suggests that the general public can be used for these types of valuation tasks. However, the source of valuation that should be used is of substantial debate within the field of health economics.

6.4.1 General Public as the Source of Valuation

The use of general public values for health states has support from the Washington Panel on Cost-Effectiveness in Health and Medicine [20], and this has been reflected in economic guidelines produced in the United Kingdom [21], as an example. The debate among economists has generally been in favor of the general public as the source of valuation, but health economists have extensively described and discussed the implications of using either source [22–25]. A key reason for this support of using the general public has generally been based on the idea that general public preferences are linked to the "societal perspective" and therefore include a generalization of the preference of "everyone" who could be affected by the allocation of healthcare resources. This debate has recently been revisited by Versteegh and Brouwer [25], and it is recommended that readers refer to that article and the references cited therein and in this section to get a better understanding of this rationalization for using the general public as the source of valuation.

General public valuations are elicited by asking respondents to value a set of formulated, generic states that are typically defined in negative terms (such as "full health is the absence of ill health"). The elicitation task involves asking the respondents to imagine themselves in a particular state (such as poor health), and then asking them either (a) the gamble they would be willing to take to move to the optimum level of that state (such as full health), such as with the SG method; or (b) the reduction in the length of life they would be willing to take to reach the same optimum state, such as with the TTO technique. The framing of the question generally involves asking respondents for their ex ante valuation of a state as the patient. That is, although they have not yet experienced the state, how they would value that state if they themselves were to experience it, rather than valuing that state as an outsider looking in. This question framing is meant to make the general public value the outcome as if they were the patient. As described in the next section, however, discrepancies can occur between patient and general public values.

6.4.2 Discrepancies Between Patient and General Public Preferences

The patient as the source of valuation is relatively simple compared with using the general public; the patient is asked to complete the preference elicitation technique based on their own experience of the state. This has practical implications for mental health conditions whereby the patient may lack the cognitive ability to complete such tasks, or because these tasks are based on subjective valuations, the patient's state of being at the point of valuation may cause bias (see also Sect. 6.5.6).

Considerable evidence suggests that, when patients are able to perform the preference elicitation task, they give a higher valuation to a particular physical state than the general public, and so patients believe they are in a better state of health than the general public would suggest [26–29]. In this regard, population groups such as the physically disabled have argued that, because of the discrepancies between patient and public health state valuation, individuals should value their own health state [24]. It could be argued that a patient is able to value their whole state of being in a particular state (for example, being confined to a wheelchair), whereas society is valuing the horror or trauma of a state (for example, losing the ability to walk). However, the results seem to change when the focus is on depression [30–32] or dementia [33], with the general public giving a higher valuation to these states than patients. This suggests than the general public does not perceive depression to be as severe as the patient would perceive, which has implications for resource allocation. For example, if the general public valuation gives a higher weight to mental health conditions (assuming this result maybe generalizable to mental health conditions other than just depression and dementia) and a lower weight to physical health than patients would value these states, more resources may be allocated to physical than mental health interventions. This could occur because a smaller change in physical health is perceived to be of greater aggregate benefit than an improvement in mental health to the general public compared to the patient because of the valuation of these relative states of being compared with perfect health. Related to this discussion, a recent article by Versteegh and Brouwer [25] suggested that economic guidelines should consider requiring that the analysis of benefits (such as in terms of QALYs) should be based on *both* patient and public preferences; this idea requires further assessment and discussion, but is an interesting idea to note.

6.5 Preference-Based Outcome Measures Used Within CUA

As described in Sect. 6.3 focused on extra-welfarism, there is a conceptual basis which suggests that the relevant outcomes from healthcare interventions can and should be assessed as part of an economic evaluation. To assess these relevant outcomes, a variety of outcome measures have been designed. Theoretically, effectiveness can be assessed using clinical outcomes, although patient-reported outcome measures have often been used as subjective ways to assess the outcome from an intervention. For mental health, these measures could include the Hospital Anxiety and Depression Scale [34, 35], Positive and Negative Syndrome Scale [36, 37], or Schizophrenia Quality of Life Scale [38], to name just a few developed specifically to assess aspects of mental health. These measures would certainly allow interpersonal comparisons in a quantifiable manner; however, for CUA as underpinned by the extra-welfarist framework, the outcome also needs to be preference-weighted. Outcomes are usually weighted based on a tariff score, which is representative of preference. A measure has to be preference-based to elicit the QALY.

One of the most widely used preference-based measures is the five-dimension EuroQoL (EQ-5D) instrument three-level version [4] (although a newer five-level version exists [39]). Although this measure has been criticizd as not being valid or responsive enough for certain mental health conditions such as schizophrenia [40], studies have suggested that the EQ-5D can be used for the economic evaluation of depression with "some confidence" [41], but there is less convincing evidence for anxiety disorder [41–45] (see Chap. 3). A number of condition-specific measures exist for mental health, but if these are not preference-based they cannot (in their current format) be used to elicit the QALY. Assigning preference-based weights to condition-specific measures will allow these measures to be a part of economic evaluation [46, 47]. Preference weights have been assigned to already established condition-specific measures [48–50] after a health state classification system (HCS) was devised that can be used for valuation [51–56]. Two particular examples of existing measures (condition-specific or generic in terms of common mental health disorders) that have been developed into preference-based measures are (1) the Clinical Outcomes in Routine Evaluation – Outcome Measure's (CORE-OM's) [57] shorter, preference-based measure called the Clinical Outcomes in Routine Evaluation – Six Dimensions (CORE-6D) [48] for the economic evaluation of people with common mental health disorders; and (2) the DEMQOL and DEMQOL-Proxy [58, 59] developed into the DEMQOL-U and DEMQOL-U-Proxy [49] for the economic evaluation of dementia interventions (see Chap. 22). The EQ-5D (three-level and five-level), CORE-6D, and DEMQOL-U(-Proxy) are now described as examples of generic health status, generic mental health (in terms of common mental health conditions), and condition-specific preference-based measures, respectively. Other preference-based measures are described in Sect. 6.5.4; a short overview of the implications of using condition-specific versus generic measures is described in Sect. 6.5.5; and practical aspects for consideration when using these measures in mental health studies is described in Sect. 6.5.6.

6.5.1 Five-Dimension EuroQoL (EQ-5D)

The EQ-5D is a generic health status measure that consists of five domains of health: mobility, self-care, usual activities, pain/discomfort, and anxiety/depression. There are currently two versions of the EQ-5D for adults (aged 18+ years): the EQ-5D-3L, which consists of three severity levels, and the EQ-5D-5L, which consists of five severity levels. The EQ-5D-3L is the older of the two EQ-5D measures and has therefore been used the most widely and will be used as the focus of examples within this chapter; the EQ-5D-5L was developed in part because of criticisms about the sensitivity of the three-level version [39, 60]. The EQ-5D uses preference- weights from the general public which are country specific. For example, for the EQ-5D-3L for use in the United Kingdom, a sample of 3395 members of the general public were interviewed using the TTO technique in 1993 [61]. Linear regression was used to predict the value of all states except for full health and a state equivalent to dead (valued at 1 and 0, respectively) [61]. The scoring algorithm used in the United Kingdom allows for a person's health state to be valued from a minimum of −0.594 (health state 33333) to a maximum of 1.0 (health state 11111). All positive values are states better than dead, and all values

Table 6.2 Example of calculating total utility for HCS code 12321 for EQ-5D-3L (U.K. tariff)

1	– 0.081	– 0	– 0.104	– 0.094	– 0.123	– 0	– 0.269	=	0.329
Baseline	Constant	Mobility	Self-care	Usual activities	Pain/ discomfort	Anxiety/ depression	N3		Total utility

HCS health state classification system. The utility decrements are for the U.K. tariff

HCS code 12321 represents the following health states (utility decrement [UD]): no problem with mobility (level 1; UD = 0); some problem with self-care (level 2; UD = 0.104); extreme problems with usual care (level 3; UD = 0.094); some problem with pain/discomfort (level 2; UD = 0.123); no problem with anxiety/depression (level 1; UD = 0)

below zero are states worse than dead. For a list of countries that have a preference-based value set for the EQ-5D-3L and -5L see: http://www.euroqol.org/about-eq-5d.html.

Overall, 243 health states can be described by the EQ-5D-3L's HCS, which has been considered a simple approach to describing health. These states can be described using a five-digit code, where each of the five digits can be one of three values (1, 2, or 3). Each of the figures represents a severity score as part of the HCS. For example, consider the three levels of perceived problems as level 1, no problem; level 2, some problems; and level 3, extreme problems. An HCS code of 12321 would mean no problem with mobility (level 1); some problem with self-care (level 2); extreme problems with usual care (level 3); some problem with pain/discomfort (level 2); no problem with anxiety/depression (level 1). In this example, a health state defined with HCS code 12321 would be associated with an overall utility value of 0.329 when using the U.K. tariff score [61]; Table 6.2 shows how this is calculated.

When calculating a utility score from EQ-5D-3L, the scoring algorithm starts off with a baseline score of 1; that is, everyone starts off in perfect health, represented by a value of 1. If anyone is classified in a health state other than perfect health (HCS = 11111), then a *constant term* is used as a utility decrement to define leaving this state of perfect health (this utility decrement is a value of 0.081 for the U.K. tariff). If anyone obtains a level 3 severity score for any health domain, then an *N3* term is also added as a utility decrement to represent having this severe level of health (this utility decrement is a value of 0.269 for the U.K. tariff). The total utility score is then obtained by accounting for the utility decrements of each of the five domains of health, depending on the level of severity within each domain, and then calculated as previously described (see Table 6.2). Note that each preference-based score is a utility decrement (rather than a utility gain) because of an assumption that everyone starts off in perfect health (a value of 1) until a problem reduces their health, which is represented by a utility decrement (a negative utility value). Therefore, the utility decrement of having "no problem" in any domain is a value of 0, because having no problem does not reduce the overall utility.

6.5.2 Clinical Outcomes in Routine Evaluation-Six Dimension (CORE-6D)

The CORE-6D [48, 52] was developed from the CORE-OM [57] in order to produce a preference-based measure for the assessment of common mental health problems within CUA. The CORE-6D offers a preference-based measure with a more specific focus on mental health than currently offered by the EQ-5D or other generic preference-based measures, without being focused on one specific mental health condition (such as the DEMQOL-U for dementia). Unlike the EQ-5D measures, the CORE-6D is not a standalone measure and is elicited directly from the CORE-OM (this is a similar design as the SF-6D as elicited from the SF-12 or SF-36; see Sect. 6.5.4).

Mavranezouli et al. [52] described in detail the development of the HCS system for the CORE-6D from the unweighted versions of the questionnaire (CORE-OM). The CORE-6D consists of six dimensions, five of which are emotional components and the other a physical item; all six consist of three severity levels (coded as three numerical values: 0, 1, or 2, where 2 is the most severe state within each item). For the emotional components this generates 243 possible health states (729 when accounting for the physical item); however, it is noted that this component has shown to be unidimensional, which means that some response combinations are implausible and thereby restricts the number of health states that can be generated [52]. Rasch analysis was used to identify 11 emotional health states from the CORE-6D that were frequently observed in the study population and are thus, plausible [52]. When accounting for the three response levels of the physical item, this generates 33 plausible health states, 18 of which were selected for valuation. A valuation survey of 220 members of the public in South Yorkshire, United Kingdom, was undertaken using the TTO method and subsequent multivariate regression analysis, then a cubic model was used to predict values for all 729 CORE-6D health states [48]. The preference-based scoring algorithm allows a score range from 0.10 (health state 222222) to 0.95 (health state 000000). These preference-based scores for health states are based on the total score of the emotional component of the state (e.g., 0 to 10) and the response level of the physical item (e.g., 0 to 2).

6.5.3 Utility-Weighted Dementia Quality of Life (DEMQOL-U) and DEMQOL-U-Proxy Measures

The utility-weighted Dementia Quality of Life (DEMQOL-U) and DEMQOL-U-Proxy [49] are elicited from particular questions within the Dementia Quality of Life (DEMQOL) and DEMQOL-Proxy instruments [58, 59] (see Chap. 22). Dementia can cause severe and irreversible decline in physical and mental health and functioning, and can have a detrimental impact on personal, social, health, and economic well-being for those with dementia – it is these aspects of quality of life that these dementia-specific measures try to account for in their design. The DEMQOL-U and DEMQOL-U-Proxy are much shorter than the DEMQOL and DEMQOL-Proxy, with only 5 and 4 items compared with 28 and 31 items, respectively, each with four levels. The DEMQOL-U and DEMQOL-U-Proxy represent the first measures designed to represent dementia-related quality of life that can be used in an economic evaluation.

Mulhern et al. [49] describes in detail the development of an HCS for the DEMQOL-U and DEMQOL-U-Proxy from the unweighted versions of the questionnaires. The final HCS for the DEMQOL-U(-Proxy) generates 1024 (256) possible health states. Mulhern et al. [49] conducted a valuation study of 593 members from the general public in the United Kingdom (306 for the DEMQOL-U, 287 for the DEMQOL-U-Proxy) using the TTO technique. A range of mean and individual-level multivariate regression models were then used to derive preference weights for each measure. The scoring algorithm allows for a person's self-reported dementia-related quality of life (DEMQOL-U) to be valued from a minimum of 0.243 (health state 44444) to a maximum of 0.986 (health state 11111). A standard utility decrement of 0.014 is used in the scoring algorithm for the DEMQOL-U to account for loss in quality of life in general for those people with dementia (or related condition), so perfect health – as represented by the value 1 for the EQ-5D (for example) – can never be reached using this measure. The scoring algorithm for the DEMQOL-U-Proxy allows a valuation from a minimum of 0.363 (health state 4444) to a maximum of 0.937 (health state 1111), and a standard utility decrement of 0.063 is used by the scoring algorithm for the proxy measure.

6.5.4 Other Preference-Based Measures for Mental Health

This section briefly describes eight other examples of preference-based measures that might be of interest to the reader. However, measures are dropped from use or refined, or new measures are developed, so listing all possible preference-based measures has limited benefit in the long term for the relevance of this section. Therefore, Table 6.3 is just a short list of generic and condition-specific measures, as well as measures for assessing mental well-being, capability-based well-being, and carer-related quality of life (rather than assessing only the patient's quality of life). This list is also an example of how CUA is evolving to measure more aspects than just health benefits to the patient for the purpose of economic evaluation – the references provided should be consulted to further understand the constructs of these measures and their purpose for economic evaluation.

All these measures are (or will be) preference-based and so could logically be used to elicit the QALY; however, a debate currently exists regarding whether this is the practical or conceptual end point for capability-based measures [14, 70, 73, 74]. For the ICECAP capability measures, researchers should consult the University of Birmingham development team if they have questions about the use of these measures for economic evaluation [75] (see Chap. 9). The reader should also be aware that an alternative form of economic evaluation has been suggested as a possible end point for capability-based measures focused on assessing years of sufficient capability [76].

Table 6.3 Examples of alternative preference-based measures

Measure	No. of states	Domains (levels)	Domain construct	Comments/references
Generic health status and HRQoL				
SF-6D	7,500	6 (3–5)	Physical functioning, role limitations, bodily pain, vitality, mental health, social functioning	Elicited from the SF-12 [62] or the SF-36 [63]
HUI2	24,000	7 (3–5)	Sensation, mobility, emotion, cognition, self-care, pain, fertility	A HUI exists, but the HUI2 and HUI3 have been mainly used for research [64, 65]
HUI3	972,000	8 (5–6)	Vision, hearing, speech, ambulation, dexterity, emotion, cognition, pain	A HUI exists, but the HUI2 and HUI3 have been mainly used for research [64, 65]
Depression-specific				
McSad	4,096	6 (4)	Emotion, self-appraisal, cognition, physiology, behavior, role function	Designed for major unipolar depression [66]
Mental well-being				
ReQoL-10	9,765,625	10 (5)	Five examples: everyday tasks, ability to trust others, feeling happy, loneliness, self-confidence	A 20-item version also exists. Not yet preference-based – consult ReQoL website [67]
Capability-based well-being[a]				
ICECAP-A[a]	1,024	5 (4)	Attachment, security, role, enjoyment, control	For adults (18–64 years) [68, 69]
ICECAP-O[a]	1,024	5 (4)	Attachment, stability, achievement, enjoyment, autonomy	For older people (≥65 years) [70, 71]
Carer-related QoL				
CES	729	6 (3)	Activities, support, assistance, fulfillment, control and getting on	For completion by caregivers, not the patient [72]

[a] There is a currently a debate whether capability-based measures can or should be used to elicit QALYs [14, 70, 73, 74]. Researchers should consult the University of Birmingham development team if they have questions about the use of this measure for economic evaluation [75].

HR(QoL) health-related (quality of life), *SF-6D* Short from 6 dimension, *HUI(2;3)* Health Utilities Index (mark 2; mark 3), *ReQoL-10* Recovering Quality of life 10 item, *ICECAP-A(-O)* ICEpop CAPability measure for adults (older people), *CES* Carer Experience Scale

6.5.5 Use of Generic Versus Condition-Specific Measures

Outcomes were discussed to a certain extent in Chap. 3. Here is presented a specific discussion of the implications of generic versus condition-specific measures for eliciting QALYs, the examples of which are based on the EQ-5D-3L and DEMQOL-U.

Although multiple preference-based outcome measures could be used for the purpose of CUA (as previously described within Sect. 6.5), two general groupings of these types of preference-based measures are described in Box 6.2.

The change in focus of the EQ-5D as a generic measure compared with the DEMQOL-U as a condition-specific measure is clear based on their domains (i.e., moving from generic aspects such as mobility and pain/discomfort to dementia-specific aspects such as cognition and loneliness) (Box 6.2). Both sets of measures can be used to elicit QALYs as long as they are preference-based; however, a debate still exists around the implications this may have as part of CUA and for the outcome assessment of mental health conditions in general.

Sensitivity to the relevant outcome of interest is one major aspect that suggests that condition-specific measures may be more appropriate than generic measures for outcome assessment. Sensitivity in this context can be defined simply as the ability of a measure to detect a change in a person's state of being (e.g. health state) in response to some direct or indirect effect of a change in the person's actual state of being. Therefore, if a generic measure is used it may (a) not be assessing the relevant outcome of interest that is important to the person with the condition, or (b) not be designed to pick up any minimal change that could be important to the person. For this reason, the U.S. Food and Drug Administration has recommended the use of condition-specific measures to support drug labeling claims [77]. This also has implications for resource allocation. For example, if the quality adjustment of the QALY is not sensitive to the outcome of interest, then the effectiveness of the intervention may not be appropriately reflected within a "cost per QALY" analysis. This could lead to clinically effective interventions not being funded because the economic evaluation could be deemed to have not appropriately assessed the relevant outcome of interest, suggesting an intervention is not cost-effective because the outcome of interest was not captured by a generic measure but could have been identified by a condition-specific measure.

Generic measures, however, may be able to more appropriately capture aspects of comorbidity and allow easier comparison between conditions. The recommendation of generic measures by governing bodies such as the National Institute for Health and Care Excellence (NICE) in the United Kingdom has focused mainly on the latter reason [21]. The recommendation by NICE states that for trial-based cost-per-QALY analysis, the quality adjustment should be derived using the EQ-5D; although this assessment can be supplemented by other data, including outcome assess-

Box 6.2 A Simple Description of Generic and Condition-Specific Measures

1. *Generic measures* – these measures are described as generic because they are designed to include domains that cover broad aspects of physical and/or mental health. *Example*: EQ-5D – includes five domains focused on mobility, self-care, usual activities, anxiety/depression, and pain/discomfort.
2. *Condition-specific measures* – compared with generic measures, these measures are designed with a particular condition as their focus. *Example*: DEMQOL-U – focused on measuring aspects of quality of life that are perceived to be important to people with dementia. Includes five domains focused on positive emotion, cognition, relationships, negative emotion, and loneliness.

ment using condition-specific measures [21]. This has led to the EQ-5D being used as the gold standard measure for the economic evaluation of both physical and mental health interventions in the United Kingdom. However, there is still a valid point that although this may make the information more transparent for cross-condition and cross-service decision-making, it may not be the most appropriate method for assessing the outcome of interest as part of an economic evaluation. This has led to a discussion about the use of generic or condition-specific measures and the QALY for cross-comparability [78] (see also Sect. 6.6.2).

Using the EQ-5D-3L and DEMQOL-U as examples, empirical analysis has attempted to understand which of these measures may be more appropriate for the purpose of CUA in the case of interventions for dementia. The results from Mulhern et al. [49] suggest the DEMQOL-U (and DEMQOL-U-Proxy) would provide a substantially different preference-based tariff score compared with the EQ-5D – this means that the QALY value could be different when elicited using the different measures. Therefore, the two measures may never produce the same tariff scores and QALY values when assessing the same patients and conditions, although it should be noted that because the two measures include different domains, then they probably would not produce the same scores anyway because they are assessing different relevant outcomes.

6.5.6 Practical Implications of Using Outcome Measures for Patients with Mental Health Conditions

As well as the conceptual issues of CUA associated with mental health conditions, there are practical implications for CUA when using preference-based outcome measures. Various issues might limit the ability to collect preference-based outcome measure data from patients with mental health conditions for the purpose of CUA. For the purpose of this discussion, the focus here is on two key aspects for consideration: (1) the ability or appropriateness to self-complete the measure; and (2) the subjective response depending on the timing of the response.

First, for self-reported outcome measurement, the patient's cognitive ability should be assessed, or the appropriateness of self-completion if there is a perceived issue in the ability to do so. The ability to self-complete is a subjective decision and depends on circumstance; for example, if the patient is in a manic or depressed state, then it may not always be appropriate to ask them to self-complete a questionnaire if it is not considered ethical. This aspect also has implications for subjective assessment, which is discussed later in this section. The assessment of a patient's cognitive ability can be assessed using measures such as the Mini Mental State Examination [79, 80], where a certain score pertaining to a particular level of cognitive ability could be used as a cutoff for when a patient should be allowed to self-complete. Whatever the reason for a patient not being able to self-complete, a decision has to be made whether to administer the measure or to use a proxy response. The implication with the use of a proxy compared with a self-reported measure is this: the proxy response should match how the patient would have responded had he or she been able to respond. It is the patient's quality of life which is of interest during the assessment, and so if the proxy cannot accurately infer the patient's quality of life, then this can result in an inaccurate measurement and could mean the benefit of an intervention is overestimated or underestimated, depending on the proxy response relative to the patient's unknown true response. In the case of the DEMQOL-U-Proxy, this measure was specifically designed for when the self-reported DEMQOL-U cannot be used. For patients with dementia who often have declined cognitive ability because of their condition, the design of the proxy measure seems to be a logical choice for the practical use of the measure. However, the two measures (self-reported and proxy DEMQOL-U) do have different designs and preference-based scoring tariffs, which means that a proxy-based score may never naturally be the same as if the patient had self-reported (the rationale for this design is described by Mulhern et al. [49]); this has implications for how the preference-based scores should be used as part of economic evaluation, which warrants further consideration and empirical analysis to inform researchers wishing to use these measures. Measures such as the EQ-5D do not have a specifically designed proxy measure, and it is not always the case that measures are designed specifically for proxy response. Using the EQ-5D as an example, there is mixed evidence of whether proxies give the same response as a patient, had the patient been asked to complete the same questionnaire [81, 82]. The use of proxies (or maybe even expert opinion) may currently be the best practical way to elicit a preference score for use as part of CUA when the patient cannot self-report, but it is worth noting that there may be discrepancies with the self-reported scores.

Second, subjective measurement is an issue for patients with mental health conditions because of the often erratic effects of the condition. Following the work by Parfit [83], three main aspects of well-being could be assessed: (1) objective lists, (2) preference satisfaction, and (3) mental states that are strongly related to subjective well-being. Given the association between mental state and a person's subjective well-being, subjective measurement is dependent on the person's mental state. Typically, preference-based measures are interested in capturing some aspect of well-being or quality of life to which a preference-based score is attached, but when a patient's quality of life may change from manic to depressive over a short or long time period, then this subjective assessment becomes very time dependent. It is important to consider what the purpose of the intervention is to know when and how often to get a response from the patient in order to understand the impacts of the condition on the patient' quality of life over a certain time period; however, it could be argued that with large enough sample sizes and systematic data collection for outcome measures (i.e., assessing a patient at baseline and then following up once/three times a month over the time horizon of the study), a range of quality-of-life states could be captured, the mean and distribution of which could be considered appropriate enough for assessment. Again, this is perhaps patient and project dependent, and practical issues exist for collecting outcome measure data for large samples of people at multiple time points, but this is the trade-off between attempting accurate measurement of the severity of a state and the practical implications of research that need to be considered.

6.6 Metrics of Effectiveness Within CUA

Cost-utility studies have relied largely on a single metric to assess the "effectiveness" of a new intervention compared with an alternative. Within this section is described an overview of the QALY as a metric of effectiveness that combines quality and quantity of life into a single end point. Implications of the QALY are described, one positive aspect of which has been described as its generalizability for enabling cross-comparative evaluations of healthcare interventions, bringing about an idea that "a QALY is a QALY is a QALY." Many have debated this idea, and it is a key focus of this section. Alternatives to the QALY, such as the DALY, and their design and purpose in economic evaluation are also described within this section.

6.6.1 The QALY: An Overview of Its Design and Concept

The QALY is designed to capture both a change in morbidity (quality of life) and potential mortality (quantity of life), combining both aspects into a single metric. The "quality adjustment" is based on preference weights. The use of the QALY can be represented in a simple diagram (see Fig. 6.1), and a simple decision-making example is provided in Box 6.3, using the values presented in Table 6.4. In this example the utility values could have been obtained from any preference-based measure (such as the EQ-5D) and the life years gained estimated from a trial or from the empirical literature. This is a simple example, but one that gives a clear indication about how the QALY can be used in the decision-making process.

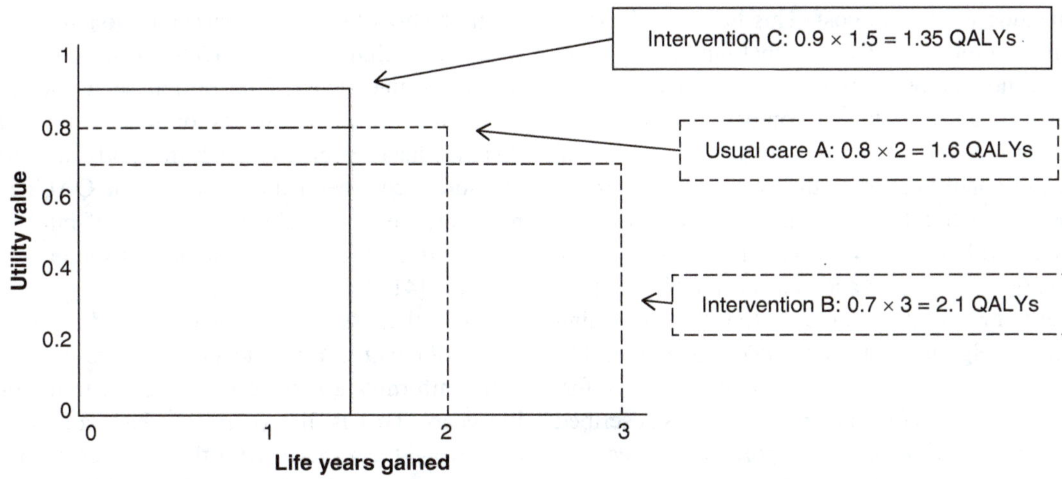

Fig. 6.1 Diagrammatic presentation of calculating quality-adjusted life years

Box 6.3 Example – Calculating QALYs Gained and Simple Decision-Making

This example describes how a decision can be made between three options (intervention B or C compared with usual care [intervention A]) when the choice is based on only QALYs gained (i.e., the trade-off between life years gained and a health-related quality-of-life state). Data for this example are presented in Table 6.4.

Question: Three options of care have been assessed. Usual care (option A) provides a constant state of health-related quality of life defined by a utility value of 0.8 over 2 life years gained before the patient dies (state of death equivalent, utility value = 0). Interventions B and C provide a constant state of health-related quality of life defined by a utility value of 0.7 or 0.9 over 2 or 1.5 life years gained, respectively, before the patient dies. Based on effectiveness only, is there rationale to change care from option A (usual care)?

Answer: Intervention B would be the preferred option to usual care (and to intervention C) because of its relative QALY gain (0.5), assuming that the choice is based on effectiveness measured in QALYs only. Intervention C would be rejected compared with usual care (and intervention B) because of its relative QALY loss (0.25).

Table 6.4 Calculation of incremental QALYs based on potential HRQoL and extra life years

Option	HRQoL (utility value)	Life years gained (before death)	QALYs (utility × life years)	Inc. QALYs (vs. option A)
A	0.8	2	1.6	–
B	0.7	3	2.1	0.5 (gain)
C	0.9	1.5	1.35	−0.25 (loss)

HRQoL health-related quality of life, *Inc.* incremental, *QALY* quality-adjusted life year

6.6.2 "A QALY Is a QALY Is a QALY": Implications of Using a Single Metric of Effectiveness

The QALY as a single metric of effectiveness has implications that have been discussed extensively in the empirical literature – one article even used the phrase "A QALY is a QALY is a QALY – or is it?" as its title[3]; this has become a popular phrase for describing the QALY (often ignoring the "or is it?" part of the phrase). This section summarizes some of these issues.

The QALY as a single metric that enables cross-comparability of health interventions, irrespective of condition or disease, can be considered one of its strengths for informing resource allocation decision-making. All outcomes are assessed based on the same criteria: QALY maximization relative to cost. This has clear benefits when informing decision-making and budget allocation across different conditions and diseases, even providing a comparison of relative cost-effectiveness across physical and mental health conditions (e.g., the cost-effectiveness of an intervention for cancer treatment can be compared with an intervention for dementia care). The QALY can also account for a quality adjustment of relevant outcomes, rather than assuming equal weighting between outcomes, the quality adjustment of which is based on stated preferences (the basis for using preferences is described in Sect. 6.4). This has important implications because certain aspects of health may have a higher value to a person or have a different effect on a person's quality of life, which should be accounted for in the decision-making process; that is, if depression is perceived as being more detrimental to a person's quality of life than mobility, for example, then this should be taken into account when allocating resources to mental or physical health interventions.

It seems unfortunate, then, that the benefits of the QALY for allocative decision-making are also related to its criticisms. For example, the QALY may not be considered a sensitive metric for assessing effectiveness across all condition- and disease-specific areas, particularly when the quality adjustment is based on a single measure such as the EQ-5D. A person's mental health has many aspects that may or may not be adequately captured by the EQ-5D (when the EQ-5D is the "gold standard" recommended measure for eliciting QALYs), and this has led to some suggestions that the QALY is not sensitive, particularly in the case of mental health. There is a case that preference-based condition-specific measures could be used to elicit the QALY, which could make it more sensitive to the relative outcome of interest. Evidence from the DEMQOL-U and EQ-5D-3L already shows that condition-specific and generic measures can have quite different score tariffs [49], which could translate into producing different QALYs during assessment. The implications for cross-comparability when using condition-specific measures has been discussed by Brazier and Tsuchiya [78]. Similar to the discussion about the use of generic versus condition-specific measures included in Sect. 6.5.5, the same issues occur for the QALY. The option seems to be between cross-comparability or sensitivity, and this may have specific issues if the gold-standard measure recommended for eliciting the QALY is not sensitive to the relevant outcome of interest (as could be the case for anxiety disorder, for example [41–45]).

As well as issues with the quality adjustment aspect of the QALY, implications exist associated with uniformly assessing outcomes in terms of life years. That is, life years may have a preference weight associated with them, either from a patient or general public perspective. This discussion has often focused on the use of QALYs to value outcomes for older people compared with younger people [84], where shorter periods of time may be more valuable to older people with little time left compared with the young, but life-saving interventions may also be valued as a higher priority for children than for older people (the latter could be considered to have had a "fair inning") [84]. Patients with mental health conditions may or may not value time differently from other people receiving healthcare; however, to account for this aspect within the QALY, other equity weights would have to be considered, such as weighting outcomes based on age. This aspect is not explicitly discussed here in reference to the QALY, but is instead included in the discussion of the DALY given that age weights are an option to be used in its calculation.

6.6.3 Disability-Adjusted Life Year: Calculation, History, and Evolution

The focus of this chapter so far has been on the QALY as the sole metric of effectiveness within CUA. The QALY has a number of limitations, and alternatives could be used based on the conceptual or practical limitations of the QALY. The most commonly used alternative to the QALY in international decision-making is the DALY.

DALYs were initially developed by the World Health Organization (WHO) for their Global

Burden of Disease (GBD) Study in 1990 [85] and was launched into the international development community as part of the 1993 *World Development Report* (WDR) [86]. However, a number of GBD studies have occurred since 1990 that have further developed the DALY. The WHO promotes the use of the DALY as part of generalized CEA, and the DALY is most likely to be used if international agencies, such as the WHO, are commissioning the study or if preference weights are not available for a particular country (for example, for the EQ-5D measures). An example of the use of the DALY in a country where the QALY is dominant (England in this example) can be seen using data from the GDB 2013 study, in which DALYs were compared between England and 18 other countries to assess and then describe the potential for reducing the burden of preventable diseases in England [87].

The calculation of the DALY has been described by the WHO [88] as the calculated sum of years of life lost (YLL) due to premature mortality in the population multiplied by years lost due to disability (YLD) for people living with the health condition or its consequences. It follows that the DALY is calculated as:

$$DALY = YLL + YLD$$

where

$$YLL = N \times L$$

and,

$$YLD = (I \times L) \times DW$$

For the YLL calculation, N is the number of deaths and L is the standard life expectancy at the age at which death occurs (in years). For YLD, for a particular cause in a particular time period, I is the number of incident cases in that period, L is the average duration of the disease until death occurs, and DW is a disability weight (calculated using the PTO method) that reflects the severity of the disease on a scale from 0 (no disability) to 1 (full disability, equivalent to death).

At this point these basic formulas do not include other social preferences (discussed below) and are the standard calculations for YLLs or YLDs for a given cause, age, and sex. Although these formulas seem basic and therefore a simple example could be provided here to aid the reader, in fact neither YLLs nor YLDs can be calculated directly, and the various types of DALYs estimated for a population may be different depending on the assumptions used by the researchers when calculating DALYs. Useful references for understanding and calculating DALYs are provided in Box 6.4.

In the recent 2010 GBD study, an updated life expectancy standard was used to calculate YLLs based on a global standard of the lowest observed death rate for each age group in countries from around the world, rather than being focused on Japan [89]; this was calculated to 86 years from the point of birth for both men and women [90]. The calculation of YLDs has also recently changed: an incidence perspective was taken in the original GBD study (1990) and in subsequent WHO updates for years 2000 to 2004; this

Box 6.4 Useful References for Understanding and Calculating DALYs

As described within Sects. 6.6.3 and 6.6.4, multiple ways to calculate DALYs now exist. It is difficult to provide here an example of how to calculate DALYs when they can be based on quite complex mathematical models.

However, WHO provides tools to aid GBD studies; these include an instruction manual, a spreadsheet for calculating DALYs, a table of disability weights, and other useful material that should be consulted before calculating DALYs. These useful resources can be obtained from the WHO website (http://www.who.int/healthinfo/global_burden_disease/tools_national/en/).

The methodological evolution of the DALY has also been described by Chen et al. [91]; they describe the complexities of calculating DALYs. This is a useful reference for anyone wanting to understand the evolution of the DALY and its different designs from 1990 to 2010.

changed to a focus on prevalence in the subsequent 2010 study for the calculation of YLDs. The focus on incidence means that for the calculation of DALYs, YLDs account for the incidence of the disease, which is of interest (incidence describes the risk of a disease occurring; i.e., 5000 new cases of disease A occur per year) rather than the prevalence of the disease, which is accounted for in the 2010 GBD study (prevalence indicates how many cases are apparent at a particular time; i.e., 50,000 people have disease A). This altered the YLD calculation to:

$YLD = P \times DW$ where P is the number of prevalent cases and DW is the disability weight based on this updated calculation for the time period of interest (be it 1 year or a lifetime horizon).

As well as accounting for disability weights in the calculation of DALYs, other "social value weights" have been included, such as time discounting and age weights. These were developed as part of the original GBD study and the updates in 2000 to 2004. As part of the original GBD study, a 3% time discount and nonuniform age weight were used, giving less weight to years lived at younger and older ages. Based on the age-weight curve for the 1993 WDR, uniform weighting for age occurs at around ages 10 and 55 years, with a peak at the age of 25 [86, 91, 92]; that is, in the 1993 WDR it was assumed that productivity peaked at 25 years, and so a higher weight was given to this age group than any other.

DALYs have evolved since the original GBD study. Based on the 2004 GBD study, standard DALYs included a 3% time discount and were weighted by age, but "no frills" DALYs (no time discounting or age weights) and discounted DALYs (3% time discount but no age weights) were also available. The purpose of these other DALY options was to allow for alternative DALY calculations depending on the preferred assumptions of the researcher; the implications related to cross-comparison of DALYs has been described by Chen et al. [91]. The key implication to mention here is that because of the different methods for calculating DALYs and the ever-changing design of the DALY, cross-comparison is very difficult – if not impossible – and it is not always transparent how DALYs have been calculated. The move from incidence toward prevalence, the omission of age weights, and the reestimation of life expectancy as part of the 2010 GBD study marked the biggest changes to the DALY since the original 1990 study; however, its ever-changing design has led to a wide range of discussions about the types of implications the DALY may have, particularly for informing resource allocation.

6.6.4 The DALY: Overview of How It Differs from the QALY

The DALY has been heavily debated since it was originally developed; the criticisms led to a reestimation of the DALY as part of the WHO's GBD study in 2010 [93]. Some of these original and new developments are conceptually or practically different from the QALY. Table 6.5 describes five key aspects about how the QALY differs from the DALY as it was original developed (1990) and its most recent estimations as part of the 2010 GBD study. The evolution of the DALY is described in more detail by Chen et al. [91].

6.6.5 Implications of the DALY: An Ongoing Debate

In general, the DALY was designed to explicitly account for certain egalitarian principles (e.g., people are believed to be equal and deserve equal rights and opportunities) such that the same disability weights are used for everyone; the only things accounted for in the calculation of the DALY are a specified health state, age, and sex [97]. However, the DALY is not always perceived to be egalitarian; in fact, the design of the DALY has implications for certain patient groups that have changed as the DALY has evolved. Two aspects can be focused on here as sources of general concern or criticism of the DALY in particular: age weights (omitted after the 2010 GBD study but worth discussing here) and the use of the disability weights themselves in an international context.

Table 6.5 Five key differences between the QALY and DALY (1990 and 2010)

Key difference	QALY	Original DALY (1990)	DALY reestimation (2010)
Source and method of outcome weighting	Preference weights Variety of elicitation methods (e.g., TTO, SG; see Chap. 3) General public or patient valuations	Not preference based PTO method (see Chap. 3) Expert opinion (healthcare workers who met in Geneva in 1995) [85]	Not preference based PTO method (see Chap. 3) General public (household panel surveys from different world regions, e.g., Bangladesh, Indonesia, Peru, and Tanzania [93])
Life expectancy assumption	Depends on the time period of interest (i.e., time horizon of trial [e.g., 3 months] or economic model [e.g., 50 years])	Set constant Set at greatest national life expectancy of any country Japan: 82.5 years for women, 80 years for men [86, 91, 92]	Set constant Lowest globally observed death rate for different age groups [93] 86 years from birth for both men and women [89, 90]
Anchoring and number of weighted states	Anchored between 0 (equivalent to death) and 1 (perfect health) Number of states depends on underlying preference-based measure (e.g., EQ-5D, 243 states; DEMQOL-U, 1024 states)	Anchored between 0 (no disability) and 1 (full disability; equivalent to death) Weights were assigned to 22 indictor conditions that served as a basis for assigning weight to other health states [85]	Anchored between 0 (no disability) and 1 (full disability; equivalent to death) Weights were assigned to 220 unique health states [93]
Age-weights	Not age-weighted Implications discussed by Tsuchiya [84]	Lower weights to life years of younger and older people based on productivity (productivity was perceived to peak at age 25; uniform at ages 10 and 55) [86]	Omitted from the DALY as part of the 2010 GBD study [90, 94] Implications of age weights discussed in more detail elsewhere [95, 96]
Incidence/prevalence of the disease used directly in calculation	Not directly included in calculation Could be used to estimate aggregate benefit (e.g., estimated mean QALY gain of 0.1 from intervention; prevalence, 500 people; aggregated benefit = 50 QALYs)	Incidence included directly in YLD calculation of the DALY [88] Incidence = risk of new cases occurring over a defined time period (e.g., 1 year)	Prevalence (rather than incidence) included directly in YLD calculation of the DALY [88] Prevalence = total number of cases at any given time point

DALY disability-adjusted life year, *GBD* Global Burden of Disease study, *PTO* person trade-off, *QALY* quality-adjusted life year, *SG* standard gamble, *TTO* time trade-off, *YLD* year lost due to disability

Age weights have been a concern for many when using the DALY, which has led to some major studies choosing not to use this aspect of the calculation [98, 99], and it was eventually omitted from the DALY after the 2010 GBD study [90, 94]. Debate about the use of age weights and ageism occurred not only for the DALY [100] but also for the QALY [84]. Various aspects of ageism could be debated here, but for the purpose of discussion let us focus on economic productivity and why this may be used as a basis for informing resource allocation, then what implications exist for certain age groups, such as older people, with a focus on mental health. First, age weighting has been discussed as a specific aspect of the DALY, which made it unique from other metrics such as the QALY back in 2006 [101]. The idea of weighting resource allocation based on productivity is not, however, a unique idea; it is underpinned by economic theories such as rationalization of the human capital model and the demand for health proposed by Grossman [102]. Implications for certain patient groups have led to discussions about whether the specific age weights focused on productivity are appropriate for informing resource allocation as part of the DALY. For example, when age weighting is applied, the YLDs assigned to a disabled person aged 30 years are almost twice the YLDs assigned to a 70-year-old person with the same condition [91]. Consider two interventions for depression: one for an adult population and the other for older adults; in this example, consider that the intervention for older people is more effective in terms of reducing YLDs than the intervention for the adult population when age is given equal weighting. After age weights are applied, assume the effectiveness of the intervention for the adult population as more "effective" in terms of YLD estimates than that for older people. This could mean that although an intervention may be more effective in terms of relieving the effects of a disability for older people, because they are perceived as being less productive, as a result of the application of age weights the intervention may not receive funding despite its actual benefit in terms of YLDs. More resources could be allocated to healthcare interventions for the adult population, taking away from the finite budget and reducing the ability to fund healthcare resources for older people, who are naturally high users of healthcare resources because of aspects such as frailty and multiple morbidities, which can include facets such as depression and cognitive impairment. These types of equity weights are controversial, and so although they may have conceptual or theory-based foundations, they are often criticized when used in practical decision-making approaches.

Disability weights themselves have been criticized in an international context, particularly when the disability weights might have some social context and the "ability to achieve" with a condition might also depend on resources currently available within a country or region. For example, depression-free days may be more valuable in lower-income, rural communities where ability to work is given a much higher value than within higher-income, developed countries where existing welfare and care programs (e.g., benefit programs and care groups) already exist. Although studies have shown that disability weights from country-specific general public valuation exercises have remained reasonably consistent across different countries [93, 103–106], there is still an argument that the values are not universally generalizable [107–110], and so there is a case for developing region-specific values [111].

Another implication exist based on the ability to attribute multiple morbidities into the DALY calculation [91]. Whereas logically, one person should not be able to contribute more than 1 DALY to a model for any year assessed, people with multiple morbidities could end up being double counted if disability weights are merely added together for each condition. For example, using hypothetical weights, an older person has cognitive impairment (weighted as 0.6), depression (weighted as 0.7), and anxiety (weighted as 0.8); the sum of these weights is 2.1, whereas the total disability weight should be no more than 1. People can have multiple morbidities related to both their physical and mental health, which should be accounted for in the evaluation process; however, the ability to do this as part of the DALY calculation is an area for future research, although some possible methods based on apportioning the disability weights have been described briefly by Chen et al. [91].

6.7 Cost-Utility Analysis for Decision-Making

The main purpose of CUA is to provide to decision makers information about the potential cost-effectiveness of an intervention compared with an alternative (normally usual care). To make this information transparent for decision makers, methods have been developed for summarizing this information when it is obtained from multiple different interventions. Some of the methods are not specific for CUA. This section summarizes the incremental cost-effectiveness ratio (ICER) and how the ICER can be used alongside specific decision rules for aiding allocative decisions (such as thresholds and league tables).

Box 6.5 Incremental Cost-Effectiveness Ratios

The ICER are calculated as shown below:

$$ICER = \frac{Cost_B - Cost_A}{QALY_B - QALY_A}$$

where $Cost_B$ is the cost for intervention B, $Cost_A$ is cost for usual care (option A), $QALY_B$ is the QALYs gained from intervention B, and $QALY_A$ is the QALYs gained from usual care (option A). If the DALY was to be used for the ICER, the QALY would simply be replaced by the DALY in this calculation.

6.7.1 Incremental Cost-Effectiveness Ratios for Cost-Utility Analysis

ICERs are not specific to CUA and are also covered in Chap. 5 as part of CEA. The difference between an ICER in CEA and in CUA is that the denominator is constant between interventions for CUA; so, for the cost-per-QALY technique, the denominator is the QALY (rather than, for example, cost per errors avoided compared with cost per life year lost as part of CEA). The calculation of the ICER for CUA is shown in Box 6.5.

If we return to an earlier example from Box 6.3, we can show how ICERs can be used in a simple decision-making approach. The example in Box 6.6 shows a clear case when an intervention (intervention C) would not be funded because, based on the ICER, the intervention was shown to be less effective and more costly than usual care; in this case, the negative ICER is simply described as representing a dominated intervention. However, in the case of intervention B, the intervention was shown to be more costly but more effective, producing an ICER of £20,000. In this case there is an explicit question for decision makers: Is gaining one QALY worth £20,000? This information alone is not sufficient to be able to answer this question, and therefore the decision is generally aided using decision rules. Two examples of potential decision rules are threshold ICER values (Sect. 7.2) and league tables (Sect. 7.3).

6.7.2 Informing Decision Makers Based on Thresholds

The concept of a willingness to pay threshold is simple, and we can explain a hypothetical threshold using the example from Box 6.6. Note that this example assumes that the threshold is a strict decision rule, whereas in reality it is used more as guidance for decision makers. In that example, intervention B produced an ICER of £20,000 (per QALY). If we state that a top threshold amount of £10,000 per QALY is set for funding new interventions, then intervention B would not be eligible for funding because it is above our threshold (£20,000 > £10,000). However, if the threshold was £30,000 per QALY, then the intervention would be eligible for funding because the ICER for intervention B is lower than the threshold (£20,000 < £30,000). Thresholds are simply used to give general guidance and rationale to decision makers about which new interventions should or should not be funded based on their relative cost-effectiveness compared with usual care. In reality, these decisions are not usually based only on cost-effectiveness in this manner, but this is the logic behind the use of thresholds.

In the United Kingdom, NICE used a threshold of £20,000 to £30,000 per QALY for the purpose of informing decisions around funding new interventions [21]. This threshold lacks any sort of empirical basis and has been criticized, particularly by those who have tried to design a single central threshold based on empirical evidence [112, 113]. Recent studies have suggested that the central threshold used by NICE should be £18,317 [112], and another more recent study reestimated an even lower central threshold at £12,936 per QALY [113], but at the time of writing these thresholds have not been used for decision-making in any explicitly meaningful way. The logic for the estimation of these thresholds is based on two ideas of what a threshold should represent [112]: (a) a measure of opportunity

Box 6.6 Example – ICERs and Simple Decision-Making

This example describes how a decision can be made between three options (intervention B or C compared with usual care [option A]) when the choice is based on the ICER for cost-per-QALY analysis (the trade-off between the cost and QALY benefit of a new intervention compared with usual care). Data for this example are presented in Table 6.6.

Question: Three options of care have been assessed. Usual care (option A) provides a gain of 1.6 QALYs at a cost of £5,000. Intervention B provides a gain of 1.6 QALYs at a cost of £15,000, and intervention C provides a gain of 1.35 QALYs at a cost of £10,000. Based on the ICERs, is there a rationale to change care from usual care (option A)?

Answer for intervention C: There is no rationale to move away from usual care (option A) because intervention C has been *dominated* by usual care. In this case, an ICER is not calculated because intervention B costs more (by £5000) and is not as effective (QALY loss of 0.25). Note that if this intervention had saved costs and been more effective than usual care, then it would be referred to as being dominant compared with usual care.

Answer for intervention B: This intervention is more effective than usual care (option A) (QALY gain of 0.5) but costs more (by £10,000); this produces an ICER of £20,000 (that is, it will cost £20,000 per QALY gained using intervention B compared with usual care). Here, the decision to choose usual care or intervention B is not too clear and therefore requires a *decision rule* to help inform which option to choose. Two possibilities for imposing a decision rule (one current and one outdated) are described in Sects. 7.2 and 7.3.

cost between alternatives when funded by a fixed finite budget, and (b) the rate at which individuals are willing to forgo other forms of consumption to achieve health improvement (i.e., a value of health consumption). If a threshold amount is not designed to represent these aspects of healthcare consumption between alternatives, then the threshold might not be fit for purpose. This suggests that even the lower £20,000 threshold proposed by NICE might be inefficient for informing resource allocation if this amount if higher than that which can or should be spent on healthcare resources for an intervention; this has domestic and international implications for how thresholds are currently set.

Threshold values external to the United Kingdom differ and depend on a country's own particular perspective of how a threshold amount should be set. In low- and middle-income countries (LAMICs), there has been some debate and research into how a threshold value should be set. This debate about the threshold for LAMICs has historically mainly arisen from the WHO's Choosing Interventions That Are Cost Effective (WHO-CHOICE) initiative: "This initiative aimed to build global and regional databases of the relative costs and effects of interventions for a wide range of diseases and risk factors, to identify the optimal mix of interventions to address issues of allocative efficiency in health" [114].

The WHO-CHOICE initiative designed league tables (see Sect. 7.3) for the purpose of decision-making, but thresholds were also developed within their initiative. Therefore, the cost-effectiveness of an intervention could be ranked against that of other interventions, but these interventions also had to be cost-effective based on the defined threshold. It was decided that a threshold of three times the gross domestic product (GDP) per capita could act as a country-specific threshold. The decision to base the threshold on GDP per capita was chosen based on criteria set out by the WHO Commission on Macroeconomics and Health [115]. In economic terms, a country's GDP per capita has traditionally been perceived as a (perhaps imperfect) measure of well-being or utility

Table 6.6 Calculation of ICERs for cost-per-QALY analysis

Option	Cost	Incremental cost (vs. option A)[a]	QALYs gained	Incremental QALYs (vs. option A)[a]	ICER (vs. option A)[a]
A	£5,000	–	1.6	–	–
B	£15,000	£10,000	2.1	0.5 (gain)	£20,000
C	£10,000	£5000	1.35	−0.25 (loss)	Dominated

ICER incremental cost-effectiveness ratio, *QALY* quality-adjusted life year
[a] Incremental difference (cost, QALY, and ICER) is compared with usual care (option A)

[116]; it takes into account the total output of a country (the GDP) and divides it by the number of people in the country. The WHO report suggested that a life year saved or a DALY prevented should be at least equal to the per capita income or extra market income created as a result of the intervention's outcome, but also that the real benefit may be much higher (e.g., up to three times higher) than the per capita figure because of other non-income-based benefits (e.g., equitable outcomes such as a change in pain and suffering). Therefore, in the absence of any other defined threshold, up to three times the GDP per capita of a country could be used as a defined threshold.

The WHO-CHOICE threshold has been widely adapted internationally by researchers to help inform resource allocation within a country's decision-making process when an alternative threshold does not exist. However, this frequently adopted threshold for international cost-effectiveness has been argued to not be fit for the purpose; this argument can be summed up within the work by Revill et al. [117], who have assessed the use of these thresholds for LAMICs:

> Consequently current judgements [in particular with regard to the cost-effectiveness thresholds recommended by WHO] about which interventions and programmes are cost-effective are often aspirational and do not reflect the reality of resource constraints. As a consequence their use is likely to reduce overall population health and exacerbate healthcare inequalities. They also fail to identify the real (and greater) value of devoting more resources to these efforts. By obscuring the true implications of current arrangements they do not contribute to greater understanding of and accountability for global and local decisions made on behalf of populations in low and middle as well as in high income countries. (p. i)

To simplify the above quote: if the threshold by which an intervention is judged to be cost-effective (and therefore whether it should be funded) is not appropriately set, this could lead to inappropriate allocation of funds. For example, if the threshold is too high, then cost-effective interventions that could be funded do not get funded within a budget that *could* fund such interventions, and the potential benefit to patients is lost. On the other hand, if the threshold is too low, then relatively cost-ineffective interventions may get funded, which could drain the finite budget, meaning that more cost-effective interventions cannot be funded at a later date. The threshold needs to be appropriate for the finite budget that will fund the interventions in order to ensure that the correct cost-effective interventions are funded at the right time, which consequently enables benefits for patients without draining the finite budget too early to enable benefit in the future. In this instance, the suggestion is that basing a threshold on GDP per capita is not an appropriate basis for a threshold and may not take into account the actual health needs and inequalities of a country's population. The paper by Revill et al. [117] uses examples from HIV/AIDS to illustrate their point, but one of the key messages was that thresholds based on GDP per capita conflict with the central principle of resource allocation, which is to enable the appropriate allocation of funds within a finite budget system. They suggest that there needs to be a threshold that more appropriately accounts for the resource constraints of the country within which the allocation decision needs to be made. Work to develop thresholds for LAMICs is ongoing; however, Woods et al. [118] have developed initial estimates for some LAMICs (Malawi, Cambodia, El Salvador, and Kazakhstan).

6.7.3 QALY League Tables

The concept and design of QALY league tables are only briefly mentioned here because the idea of allocating resources based on league tables has become outdated since the introduction of thresholds (discussed in Sect. 7.2), which have become the dominant option for informing decision makers.

The concept of league tables is relatively simple: interventions (any intervention, be it hip replacements, breast cancer screening, or medication for depression) are ranked based on their cost-per-QALY ICER, and the lowest amount is ranked the highest (e.g., option A is £220 per QALY) and the highest amount is ranked the lowest (e.g., option Z is £100,000 per QALY); therefore, option A would be funded and option Z would not be funded, assuming enough options were available between options A and Z to equal the amount of the budget used for funding them.

There were two main motivations for these tables before the introduction of thresholds. First, to put the results of a study into a broader context: researchers could say whether the ICER produced by their study was similar to those of other funded treatments. Second, for direct use in resource allocation: authors argued that switching resources from programs near the bottom to those near the top of the league table would result in health gains.

The main problem with QALY league tables was in their construction. There was no guarantee that the studies used to generate the ICERs were of high quality, and even if they were, they could have been undertaken using different methods because of a lack of guidance about how these tables could have been used appropriately. For example, studies could have used different perspectives, discount rates, or utilities. An even more problematic issue is the choice of comparators. Simply taking an ICER from an isolated study without considering other comparators can be deeply misleading. Although logically, league tables are how decision-making could be approached when using the cost-per-QALY method, their practical use requires caution. The most famous example of the use of league tables arose in Oregon, where the purpose was to produce a QALY league table for services provided under the state of Oregon's Medicaid program. In the first stages the league tables produced a list of interventions that would be funded by Medicaid based largely on how the intervention was ranked based on its cost per QALY. The list produced some peculiarities: funding may cover tooth caps, but would not cover surgery for emergent appendicitis [119].

Without quality assurance of all studies, standardized methods, and full incremental analyses, QALY league tables are problematic. Some of these problems have been overcome by the Center for the Evaluation of Value and Risk in Health at Tufts Medical Center in Boston [120], which maintains a database of quality-assured studies, but each study does not need to include a full incremental analysis of all relevant alternatives; users must construct these from multiple studies within the database (if they exist).The database can be viewed online (http://healtheconomics.tuftsmedicalcenter.org/cear4/Resources/LeagueTable.aspx). Users of the database also need to consider how generalizable the studies are to their own decision-making context. QALY league tables and other decision rules are also covered in the report by Malek [121]. However, it is also worth noting that although thresholds do not solve many of the issues associated with league tables (such as the ability to use different methods that could change the ICER, which would be assessed against the set thresholds), guidance about how to perform economic evaluations alongside thresholds has governing bodies such as NICE in the United Kingdom to prefer this method.

6.8 CUA for Mental Health Studies: Concluding Comments

This chapter has described some practical and conceptual considerations with regard to the use of CUA, often using examples in a mental health context. As described within the chapter, some aspects of mental health need to be considered for the purpose of performing an economic evaluation, although these aspects are not always specific to CUA. For example, the issue around cognitive ability to self-report preference-based outcome measures is not specific to CUA. Also, non-preference-based measures or other self-reported data could be used as part of CEA, which would be affected by the mental state of the person reporting the data. The collection of subjective self-reported data is an issue for mental health research in general, although it is important to recognize this limitation for CUA, which has largely relied on self-reported data [122].

Specific issues for CUA in the context of mental health are mainly related to two key factors that have been described within this chapter: (a) weighting relevant outcomes using a general public (QALY and modern DALY) or expert opinion (original DALY) perspective compared with a patient perspective, and (b) using a single metric of effectiveness for the purpose of CUA (e.g., the QALY or DALY). Two other aspects that have not been explicitly described within this chapter but are areas for further consideration as CUA evolves are also described in this section; these aspects are specific to CUA and mental health: (a) implications of resource allocation focused on health benefits when the patients' preference may be to not receive treatment even when there is a health benefit (for example, when healthcare is enforced or strongly encouraged against the patient's own preference), and (b) moving away from only health as the relevant outcome of interest as part of an economic evaluation (such as within CEA and CUA) toward broader aspects focused on well-being or capability, as examples.

First, weighting outcomes has been a major source of controversy and debate, mainly because of the source of the valuation process. The source of valuation has implications for both patients with physical conditions and those with mental health conditions if for the purpose of discussion we assume that health is binary in this way; however, the issue could be considered more problematic for mental health than physical health because of the way resources could be allocated when relying on general public compared with patient values. When the general public places lower weights on physical health states, and therefore potential for higher incremental benefit, then more resources could be allocated to patients with physical health conditions compared with if a patient had valued the state (see also Sect. 4.2), but the opposite seems apparent for mental health conditions, where the higher general public values could move resources away from mental health interventions than if patients had been the source of the valuation exercise. The extent to which receiving more resources than are perceived necessary based on patients' valuation of the state is an issue for those with physical health conditions is debatable (for example, patients with physical health conditions may be altruistic about the healthcare they receive and perceive it as an injustice they receive more resources than they would if patient values had been used), but from a patient perspective it is certainly an issue for patients with mental health conditions, from whom resources are moved away because of these higher weights. Again, this issue is debatable, and the use of the general public or patients as the source of valuation has many implications. The extent to which these issues will be solved by using both patients and the general public as two sources of valuation simultaneously in an economic evaluation is also debatable, but this is a suggested option by at least two authors [25].

Second, the use of a single metric of effectiveness is considered a more transparent method for decision makers to make judgements about which interventions to fund when focused on the comparative cost-effectiveness of multiple interventions across different health conditions and care services. However, the multidimensional and often changing impact of mental health suggests that a single metric of effectiveness – even when based on a multiattribute tool (such as a preference-based outcome measure) – may not be a sufficient and sensitive method of evaluating the cost-effectiveness of all mental health interventions. The extent to which CUA is transparent when a single metric of effectiveness, such as the QALY, is elicited from various generic or condition-specific preference-based measures in order to improve sensitivity as necessary is also debatable. The trade-off between the practical and conceptual basis of performing CUA is complicated and not necessarily specific to mental health, but given the complicated nature of mental health, the shortcomings of CUA using a single metric may seem more transparent. This issue is a general one with an economic evaluation and is not necessarily solved by using an alternative method (such as CEA or CBA), but it still needs to be considered as methods for economic evaluation evolve.

In general, the focus for CUA has been based on evaluating health benefits, including aspects of mental health, compared with any other relevant outcome. There are instances in mental health when the patient may wish to refuse or not adhere to treatment that may improve their health; they may have a preference for some other outcome that outweighs their preference for improved health. In more extreme cases, this could relate to the need for monitored care in the form of being admitted to a mental health hospital, where the patient may prefer not to reside. A less extreme example would be nonadherence to medication for mental health conditions. Either way, when the relevant outcome for CUA is focused only on health benefits, then these other nonhealth aspects may be ignored. The extent to which patient preference should be chosen over potential health benefits is debatable. There may be instances where the perceived benefit to the patient goes against the patient's own perceived benefit from an intervention, and in this case it becomes a moral and ethical dilemma whether to adhere to the patient's own preference. In terms of resource allocation, it becomes an ethical issue whether to fund interventions that the patient would prefer not to receive, despite the health benefit associated with the intervention. How resources should be allocated in these instances is worthy of further discussion, but an issue to note here is that these other relevant outcomes could be assessed using methods associated with CUA, such as preference elicitation techniques to trade-off health and nonhealth benefits [123] and the use of alternative preference-based outcome measures not focused on health [68, 72].

There is a growing body of literature regarding the evaluation of aspects other than health as part of CUA. Two examples focus on well-being and capability. The Recovering Quality of Life measure is a preference-based measure for assessing well-being associated with mental health, and the ICECAP measures are focused on capability-based well-being. Although whether the latter should be used to elicit the QALY as part of CUA is debatable (see Sect. 5.4), these represent a conceptual and practical move away from evaluating only health outcomes as part of an economic evaluation and CUA. I have just described some cases when health benefits may not be the preferred outcome from an intervention, which indicates only some cases when something other than health may need to be assessed for the purpose of an economic evaluation. We can generalize the examples to suggest that a health benefit may not always be the primary relevant outcome for mental health patients, and in some cases they may be more interested in being able to perform everyday tasks (an item within the 10-item Recovering Quality of Life measure) or the ability to be independent (an item within the ICECAP-A). The inclusion of these other relevant outcomes in an economic evaluation may result in more social- and community-based interventions (such as support groups) being financed because they could be identified as "cost-effective" when effectiveness in based on outcomes that are not relevant to only health. An aspect for future discussion is how to trade off between health and nonhealth benefits when making resource allocation decisions, but these aspects are part of current debates in the field of Health Economics in general and CUA in particular [14, 16–18, 74].

Key Messages

- The use of CUA has grown in popularity, though the methods and measures associated with CUA are still evolving – this includes movement from measuring health only to measuring other aspects such as well-being and capability. The design of CUA has both practical and conceptual implications for the evaluation of mental health interventions.

(continued)

(continued)

- The use of preference weights when sourced from patients or the general public has implications for how the severity of a condition is quantified, and therefore may affect how resources are allocated when informed by CUA. This has particular implications for the funding of mental health interventions using a fixed, finite healthcare budget.
- The QALY as a single metric of effectiveness enables cross-comparability of potential benefits among different interventions for all conditions. The extent to which the QALY is sensitive to the relevant outcome of interest for evaluation depends on the underlying preference-based measure used for the quality adjustment of the QALY. However, the use of different measures for eliciting QALYs also questions to what extent a "QALY is a QALY is a QALY."
- The DALY has evolved since 1990 until its recent developments as part of the 2010 GBD study. The use of incidence or prevalence, a life expectancy assumed to be constant, age weights, and the PTO technique for assigning disability weights rather than preferences have all been areas of debate in relation to the DALY. These aspects are different from those related to the design of the QALY.
- The growing use of thresholds compared with league tables for informing decision makers about comparative cost-effectiveness (based on ICERs) between interventions when there is a finite, fixed budget has led to new evidence-based methods for calculating central threshold amounts. These methods have been developed for calculating thresholds in high-income countries as well as LAMICs, and these methods are still developing to help inform international decision-making.

References

1. Drummond MF, Sculpher MJ, Claxton K, Stoddart GL, Torrance GW. Methods for the economic evaluation of health care programmes. New York: Oxford University Press; 2015.
2. Drummond MF, Sculpher MJ, Torrance GW, O'Brien BJ, Stoddart GL. Methods for the economic evaluation of health care programmes. New York: Oxford University Press; 2005.
3. Weinstein MC. A QALY is a QALY is a QALY—or is it? J Health Econ. 1988;7(3):289–90.
4. The EuroQol Group. EuroQol-a new facility for the measurement of health-related quality of life. Health Policy. 1990;16(3):199–208.
5. Bentham J. An introduction to the principles of morals and legislation. Oxford: Clarendon Press; 1879.
6. Edgeworth FY. Mathematical psychics: an essay on the application of mathematics to the moral sciences. London: Kegan Paul C. Kegan Paul and Co; 1881.
7. Marshall A. Principles of economics. London: Macmillian; 1890.
8. Pigou AC. The economics of welfare. London: Macmillan; 1920.
9. Hare RM. Moral thinking: its levels, method, and point. Oxford: Carendon Press; 1981.
10. Harsanyi JC. Essays on ethics, social behaviour, and scientific explanation. New York: Springer; 1976.
11. Mirrlees JA. The economic uses of utilitarianism. 1982.
12. Sidgwick H. The economics of welfare. London: Macmillian; 1874.
13. Torrance GW, Feeny D. Utilities and quality-adjusted life years. Int J Technol Assess Health Care. 1989;5(04):559–75.
14. Coast J, Smith RD, Lorgelly P. Welfarism, extra-welfarism and capability: the spread of ideas in health economics. Soc Sci Med. 2008b;67(7):1190–8.
15. Brouwer WB, Culyer AJ, van Exel NJA, Rutten FF. Welfarism vs. extra-welfarism. J Health Econ. 2008;27(2):325–38.
16. Coast J. Is economic evaluation in touch with society's health values? BMJ. 2004;329(7476):1233–6.
17. Coast J. Maximisation in extra-welfarism: a critique of the current position in health economics. Soc Sci Med. 2009;69(5):786–92.
18. Coast J, Smith R, Lorgelly P. Should the capability approach be applied in health economics? Health Econ. 2008a;17(6):667–70.
19. Culyer AJ. Health, health expenditures and equity. University of York, Centre for Health Economics; 1991.
20. Gold M, Siegel J, Russell L, Weinstein M. Cost-effectiveness in health and medicine. New York: Oxford University Press; 1996.
21. NICE. Guide to the methods of technology appraisal. London: National Institute for Health and Care

Excellence; 2013. https://www.nice.org.uk/process/pmg9/chapter/foreword
22. Brazier J, Akehurst R, Brennan A, Dolan P, Claxton K, McCabe C, et al. Should patients have a greater role in valuing health states? Appl Health Econ Health Policy. 2005;4(4):201–8.
23. Fryback DG. Whose quality of life? or Whose decision? Qual Life Res. 2003;12(6):609.
24. Ubel PA, Loewenstein G, Jepson C. Whose quality of life? A commentary exploring discrepancies between health state evaluations of patients and the general public. Qual Life Res. 2003;12(6):599–607.
25. Versteegh M, Brouwer W. Patient and general public preferences for health states: a call to reconsider current guidelines. Soc Sci Med. 2016;165:66–74.
26. Boyd NF, Sutherland HJ, Heasman KZ, Tritchler DL, Cummings BJ. Whose utilities for decision analysis? Med Decis Mak. 1990;10(1):58–67.
27. Froberg DG, Kane RL. Methodology for measuring health-state preferences—II: scaling methods. J Clin Epidemiol. 1989;42(5):459–71.
28. Hurst N, Jobanputra P, Hunter M, Lambert M, Lochhead A, Brown H. Validity of EuroQoL—a generic health status instrument—in patients with rheumatoid arthritis. Rheumatology. 1994;33(7):655–62.
29. Sackett DL, Torrance GW. The utility of different health states as perceived by the general public. J Chronic Dis. 1978;31(11):697–704.
30. Gerhards SA, Evers SM, Sabel PW, Huibers MJ. Discrepancy in rating health-related quality of life of depression between patient and general population. Qual Life Res. 2011;20(2):273–9.
31. Papageorgiou K, Vermeulen KM, Schroevers MJ, Stiggelbout AM, Buskens E, Krabbe PF, et al. Do individuals with and without depression value depression differently? And if so, why? Qual Life Res. 2015;24(11):2565–75.
32. Pyne JM, Fortney JC, Tripathi S, Feeny D, Ubel P, Brazier J. How bad is depression? Preference score estimates from depressed patients and the general population. Health Serv Res. 2009;44(4):1406–23.
33. Rowen D, Mulhern B, Banerjee S, Tait R, Watchurst C, Smith SC, et al. Comparison of general population, patient, and carer utility values for dementia health States. Med Decis Making. 2014;35(1):68–80. doi:10.1177/0272989X14557178.
34. Bjelland I, Dahl AA, Haug TT, Neckelmann D. The validity of the hospital anxiety and depression scale: an updated literature review. J Psychosom Res. 2002;52(2):69–77.
35. Zigmond AS, Snaith RP. The hospital anxiety and depression scale. Acta Psychiatr Scand. 1983;67(6):361–70.
36. Kay SR, Flszbein A, Opfer LA. The positive and negative syndrome scale (PANSS) for schizophrenia. Schizophr Bull. 1987;13(2):261.
37. Kay SR, Opler LA, Lindenmayer J-P. Reliability and validity of the positive and negative syndrome scale for schizophrenics. Psychiatry Res. 1988;23(1):99–110.
38. Wilkinson G, Hesdon B, Wild D, Cookson R, Farina C, Sharma V, et al. Self-report quality of life measure for people with schizophrenia: the SQLS. Br J Psychiatry. 2000;177(1):42–6.
39. Herdman M, Gudex C, Lloyd A, Janssen M, Kind P, Parkin D, et al. Development and preliminary testing of the new five-level version of EQ-5D (EQ-5D-5L). Qual Life Res. 2011;20(10):1727–36.
40. Papaioannou D, Brazier J, Parry G. How valid and responsive are generic health status measures, such as EQ-5D and SF-36, in schizophrenia? A systematic review. Value Health. 2011;14(6):907–20.
41. Mulhern B, Mukuria C, Barkham M, Knapp M, Byford S, Soeteman D, et al. Using generic preference-based measures in mental health: psychometric validity of the EQ-5D and SF-6D. Br J Psychiatry. 2014;205(3):236–43. doi:10.1192/bjp.bp.112.122283.
42. Brazier J. Measuring and valuing mental health for use in economic evaluation. J Health Serv Res Policy. 2008;13(suppl 3):70–5.
43. Brazier J. Is the EQ–5D fit for purpose in mental health? Br J Psychiatry. 2010;197(5):348–9.
44. Lamers L, Bouwmans C, van Straten A, Donker M, Hakkaart L. Comparison of EQ-5D and SF-6D utilities in mental health patients. Health Econ. 2006;15(11):1229–36.
45. Peasgood T, Brazier J, Papaioannou D. A systematic review of the validity and responsiveness of EQ-5D and SF-6D for depression and anxiety. HEDS Discussion paper 12/15.2012; 2012.
46. Brazier J, Dixon S. The use of condition specific outcome measures in economic appraisal. Health Econ. 1995;4(4):255–64.
47. Brazier J, Rowen D, Mavranezouli I, Tsuchiya A, Young T, Yang Y, et al. Developing and testing methods for deriving preference-based measures of health from condition-specific measures (and other patient-based measures of outcome). Health Technol Assess. 2012;16(32):1–114.
48. Mavranezouli I, Brazier JE, Rowen D, Barkham M. Estimating a preference-based index from the Clinical Outcomes in Routine Evaluation–Outcome Measure (CORE-OM) valuation of CORE-6D. Med Decis Making. 2012;33(3):381–95. doi:10.1177/0272989X12464431.
49. Mulhern B, Rowen D, Brazier J, Smith S, Romeo R, Tait R, et al. Development of DEMQOL-U and DEMQOL-PROXY-U: generation of preference-based indices from DEMQOL and DEMQOL-PROXY for use in economic evaluation. Health Technol Assess. 2013;17(5):v–xv.
50. Yang Y, Brazier J, Tsuchiya A, Coyne K. Estimating a preference-based single index from the overactive bladder questionnaire. Value Health. 2009;12(1):159–66.
51. Brazier J, Czoski-Murray C, Roberts J, Brown M, Symonds T, Kelleher C. Estimation of a preference-

based index from a condition specific measure: the kingə s health questionnaire. Med Decis Making. 2007.
52. Mavranezouli I, Brazier JE, Young TA, Barkham M. Using Rasch analysis to form plausible health states amenable to valuation: the development of CORE-6D from a measure of common mental health problems (CORE-OM). Qual Life Res. 2011;20(3): 321–33.
53. Mulhern B, Smith SC, Rowen D, Brazier JE, Knapp M, Lamping DL, et al. Improving the measurement of QALYs in dementia: developing patient-and carer-reported health state classification systems using Rasch analysis. Value Health. 2012;15(2): 323–33.
54. Rowen D, Brazier J, Young T, Gaugris S, Craig BM, King MT, et al. Deriving a preference-based measure for cancer using the EORTC QLQ-C30. Value Health. 2011;14(5):721–31.
55. Young TA, Rowen D, Norquist J, Brazier JE. Developing preference-based health measures: using Rasch analysis to generate health state values. Qual Life Res. 2010;19(6):907–17.
56. Young TA, Yang Y, Brazier JE, Tsuchiya A. The use of Rasch analysis in reducing a large condition-specific instrument for preference valuation the case of moving from AQLQ to AQL-5D. Med Decis Making. 2011;31(1):195–210.
57. Evans JM-C. Frank Margison, Michael Barkham, Kerry Audin, Janice Connell, Graeme McGrath, Chris. CORE: clinical outcomes in routine evaluation. J Ment Health. 2000;9(3):247–55.
58. Smith S, Lamping D, Banerjee S, Harwood R, Foley B, Smith P, et al. Measurement of health-related quality of life for people with dementia: development of a new instrument (DEMQOL) and an evaluation of current methodology. Health Technol Assess (Winch Eng). 2005;9(10):1–93.
59. Smith S, Lamping D, Banerjee S, Harwood R, Foley B, Smith P, et al. Development of a new measure of health-related quality of life for people with dementia: DEMQOL. Psychol Med. 2007;37(05):737–46.
60. Devlin NJ, Krabbe PF. The development of new research methods for the valuation of EQ-5D-5L. Eur J Health Econ. 2013;14(Suppl 1):1.
61. Dolan P. Modeling valuations for EuroQol health states. Med Care. 1997;35(11):1095–108.
62. Brazier JE, Roberts J. The estimation of a preference-based measure of health from the SF-12. Med Care. 2004;42(9):851–9.
63. Brazier J, Roberts J, Deverill M. The estimation of a preference-based measure of health from the SF-36. J Health Econ. 2002;21(2):271–92.
64. Horsman J, Furlong W, Feeny D, Torrance G. The health utilities index (HUI®): concepts, measurement properties and applications. Health Qual Life Outcomes. 2003;1(1):1.
65. HUInc. Health Utilities Inc: health-related quality of life. HUInc; 2016. http://www.healthutilities.com/
66. Bennett KJ, Torrance GW, Boyle MH, Guscott R. Cost-utility analysis in depression: the McSad utility measure for depression health states. Psychiatr Serv. 2000;51(9):1171–6.
67. ReQoL Website. ReQoL: recovering quality of life. University of Sheffield; 2016. http://www.reqol.org.uk/
68. Coast J, Flynn TN, Natarajan L, Sproston K, Lewis J, Louviere JJ, et al. Valuing the ICECAP capability index for older people. Soc Sci Med. 2008;67(5): 874–82.
69. Coast J, Peters TJ, Natarajan L, Sproston K, Flynn T. An assessment of the construct validity of the descriptive system for the ICECAP capability measure for older people. Qual Life Res. 2008;17(7): 967–76.
70. Flynn TN, Huynh E, Peters TJ, Al-Janabi H, Clemens S, Moody A, et al. Scoring the ICECAP-A capability instrument. Estimation of a UK general population tariff. Health Econ. 2015;24(3):258–69.
71. Al-Janabi H, Flynn TN, Coast J. Development of a self-report measure of capability wellbeing for adults: the ICECAP-A. Qual Life Res. 2012;21(1): 167–76.
72. Al-Janabi H, Flynn TN, Coast J. Estimation of a preference-based carer experience scale. Med Decis Making. 2011;31(3):458–68.
73. Cookson R. QALYs and the capability approach. Health Econ. 2005;14(8):817–29.
74. Lorgelly PK. Choice of outcome measure in an economic evaluation: a potential role for the capability approach. PharmacoEconomics. 2015;33(8): 849–55.
75. ICECAP website. ICECAP capability measures. University of Birmingham; 2016. http://www.birmingham.ac.uk/research/activity/mds/projects/HaPS/HE/ICECAP/index.aspx
76. Mitchell PM, Roberts TE, Barton PM, Coast J. Assessing sufficient capability: a new approach to economic evaluation. Soc Sci Med. 2015;139:71–9.
77. FDA. Food and Drug Administration. Guidance for industry: patient-reported outcome measures: use in medical product development to support labeling claims. Fed Regist. 2009;74(235):65132–3.
78. Brazier J, Tsuchiya A. Preference-based condition-specific measures of health: what happens to cross programme comparability? Health Econ. 2010;19(2): 125–9.
79. Cockrell JR, Folstein MF. Mini-mental state examination. In: Principles and practice of geriatric psychiatry; 2002. p. 140–1.
80. Folstein MF, Folstein SE, McHugh PR. "Mini-mental state": a practical method for grading the cognitive state of patients for the clinician. J Psychiatr Res. 1975;12(3):189–98.
81. Devine A, Taylor SJ, Spencer A, Diaz-Ordaz K, Eldridge S, Underwood M. The agreement between proxy and self-completed EQ-5D for care home residents was better for index scores than individual domains. J Clin Epidemiol. 2014;67(9):1035–43.
82. Orgeta V, Edwards RT, Hounsome B, Orrell M, Woods B. The use of the EQ-5D as a measure of

health-related quality of life in people with dementia and their carers. Qual Life Res. 2015;24(2):315–24.
83. Parfit D. Reasons and persons. Oxford: Oxford University Press; 1984.
84. Tsuchiya A. QALYs and ageism: philosophical theories and age weighting. Health Econ. 2000;9(1): 57–68.
85. Murray CJ, Lopez AD. The global burden of disease: a comprehensive assessment of mortality and disability from diseases, injuries, and risk factors in 1990 and projected to 2020. Cambridge, MA: Harvard School of Public Health; 1996.
86. World Bank. World development report: investing in health. New York: Oxford University Press; 1993.
87. Newton JN, Briggs AD, Murray CJ, Dicker D, Foreman KJ, Wang H, et al. Changes in health in England, with analysis by English regions and areas of deprivation, 1990–2013: a systematic analysis for the Global Burden of Disease Study 2013. Lancet. 2015;386(10010):2257–74.
88. WHO. Metrics: Disability-Adjusted Life Year (DALY). Geneva: World Health Organization; 2016a. http://www.who.int/healthinfo/global_burden_disease/metrics_daly/en/.
89. Murray CJ, Ezzati M, Flaxman AD, Lim S, Lozano R, Michaud C, et al. GBD 2010: design, definitions, and metrics. Lancet. 2012;380(9859):2063–6.
90. Murray CJ, Vos T, Lozano R, Naghavi M, Flaxman AD, Michaud C, et al. Disability-adjusted life years (DALYs) for 291 diseases and injuries in 21 regions, 1990–2010: a systematic analysis for the Global Burden of Disease Study 2010. Lancet. 2013; 380(9859):2197–223.
91. Chen A, Jacobsen KH, Deshmukh AA, Cantor SB. The evolution of the disability-adjusted life year (DALY). Socio Econ Plan Sci. 2015;49:10–5.
92. Murray CJ. Quantifying the burden of disease: the technical basis for disability-adjusted life years. Bull World Health Organ. 1994;72(3):429.
93. Salomon JA, Vos T, Hogan DR, Gagnon M, Naghavi M, Mokdad A, et al. Common values in assessing health outcomes from disease and injury: disability weights measurement study for the Global Burden of Disease Study 2010. Lancet. 2013;380(9859): 2129–43.
94. WHO. WHO methods and data sources for global burden of disease estimates 2000–2011; 2013.
95. Barendregt JJ, Bonneux L, Van der Maas P. DALYs: the age-weights on balance. Bull World Health Organ. 1996;74(4):439.
96. Murray CJ, Lopez AD. The incremental effect of age-weighting on YLLs, YLDs, and DALYs: a response. Bull World Health Organ. 1996;74(4):445.
97. WHO. Disability weights, discounting and age weighting of DALYs. World Health Organization; 2016b. http://www.who.int/healthinfo/global_burden_disease/daly_disability_weight/en/
98. Essink-Bot M-L, Pereira J, Packer C, Schwarzinger M, Burström K. Cross-national comparability of burden of disease estimates: the European disability weights project. Bull World Health Organ. 2002; 80(8):644–52.
99. Melse JM, Essink-Bot M-L, Kramers P, Hoeymans N. A national burden of disease calculation: Dutch disability-adjusted life-years. Dutch Burden of Disease Group. Am J Public Health. 2000; 90(8):1241.
100. Murray CJ, Acharya A. Age weights and discounting in health gaps reconsidered. In: CJL M, Salomon JA, Mathers CD, Lopez AD, editors. Summary measures of population health: concepts, ethics, measurement and applications. Geneva: World Health Organization; 2002.
101. Sassi F. Calculating QALYs, comparing QALY and DALY calculations. Health Policy Plan. 2006;21(5): 402–8.
102. Grossman M. On the concept of health capital and the demand for health. J Polit Econ. 1972;80(2): 223–55.
103. Nord E. Disability weights in the Global Burden of Disease 2010: unclear meaning and overstatement of international agreement. Health Policy. 2013;111(1): 99–104.
104. Schwarzinger M, Stouthard ME, Burström K, Nord E. Cross-national agreement on disability weights: the European disability weights project. Popul Health Metrics. 2003;1(1):1.
105. Üstün TB, Rehm J, Chatterji S, Saxena S, Trotter R, Room R, et al. Multiple-informant ranking of the disabling effects of different health conditions in 14 countries. Lancet. 1999;354(9173):111–5.
106. Ütün TB, Saxena S, Rehm J, Bickenbach J, Group WNJPCS. Are disability weights universal? Lancet. 1999;354(9186):1306.
107. James KC, Foster SD. Weighing up disability. Lancet. 1999;354(9173):87–8.
108. Jelsma J, Chivaura VG, Mhundwa K, De Weerdt W, De Cock P. The global burden of disease disability weights. Lancet. 2000;355(9220):2079–80.
109. Mathers CD, Vos T, Lopez AD, Salomon J, Ezzati M. National burden of disease studies: a practical guide. Geneva: World Health Organization; 2001.
110. Stoudhard M. Disability weights for diseases: a modified protocol and results for a Western European region. Eur J Pub Health. 2000;10:24–30.
111. WHO. Making choices in health: WHO guide to cost-effectiveness analysis; 2003.
112. Claxton K, Martin S, Soares M, Rice N, Spackman E, Hinde S, et al. Methods for the estimation of the NICE cost effectiveness threshold. York: University of York, Centre for Health Economics; 2013.
113. Claxton K, Martin S, Soares M, Rice N, Spackman E, Hinde S, et al. Methods for the estimation of the National Institute for Health and Care Excellence cost-effectiveness threshold. Health Technol Assess. 2015;19(14):1–542.
114. Newall A, Jit M, Hutubessy R. Are current cost-effectiveness thresholds for low-and middle-income

countries useful? Examples from the world of vaccines. PharmacoEconomics. 2014;32(6):525–31.
115. WHO. Investing in health for economic development. Report of the Commission on Macroeconomics and Health Geneva (Switzerland). Geneva: World Health Organization; 2001.
116. Fleurbaey M. Beyond GDP: the quest for a measure of social welfare. J Econ Lit. 2009;47(4):1029–75.
117. Revill P, Walker S, Madan J, Ciaranello A, Mwase T, Gibb DM, et al. Using cost-effectiveness thresholds to determine value for money in low-and middle-income country healthcare systems: are current international norms fit for purpose? York: Center For Health Economics; 2014.
118. Woods B, Revill P, Sculpher M, Claxton K. Country-level cost-effectiveness thresholds: initial estimates and the need for further research. York: University of York, Centre for Health Economics; 2015.
119. Jacobs L, Marmor T, Oberlander J. The Oregon health plan and the political paradox of rationing: what advocates and critics have claimed and what Oregon did. J Health Polit Policy Law. 1999;24(1):161–80.
120. Chapman RH, Stone PW, Sandberg EA, Bell C, Neumann PJ. A comprehensive league table of cost-utility ratios and a sub-table of "panel-worthy" studies. Med Decis Mak. 2000;20(4):451–8.
121. Malek MH. Implementing QALYs. Hayward Medical Communications; 2000.
122. Sonntag M, König H-H, Konnopka A. The estimation of utility weights in cost-utility analysis for mental disorders: a systematic review. Pharmaco Economics. 2013;31(12):1131–54.
123. Morton RL, Snelling P, Webster AC, Rose J, Masterson R, Johnson DW, et al. Factors influencing patient choice of dialysis versus conservative care to treat end-stage kidney disease. Can Med Assoc J. 2012;184(5):E277–E83.

7 Introduction to Statistics and Modeling Methods Applied in Health Economics

Vladislav Berdunov and Matthew Franklin

Abstract

The increasing complexity of health economics methodology has raised the need for technical methods to systematically use patient-level data and characterize uncertainty around the decision problem for decision makers. This chapter provides an introduction to these methods, focusing on trial-based statistical techniques and economic modeling methods for the purpose of health economic analysis. This chapter describes some differences between the more commonly used frequentist approach for clinical analysis and the developing use of Bayesian methods for health economic analysis. Statistical methods described include the use of power calculations, hypothesis testing, and regression analysis, and their relevance for economic analysis. More advanced statistical methods are also introduced, such as the area under the curve method for assessing incremental benefit, controlling for missing data and baseline characteristics, and using mapping algorithms for eliciting preference-based tariff scores when a preference-based measure has not been collected within a study. The second part of the chapter focuses on modeling methods designed to synthesize data from multiple sources when the economic analysis needs to go beyond a single source of primary data or for a longer time horizon. Multiple types of economic models are described, including decision trees, state transition models (including Markov chain models), microsimulation, and discrete event simulation. The chapter breaks down key elements of model design and offers recommendations on possible sources

V. Berdunov (✉)
Centre for Primary Care and Public Health, Blizard Institute, Queen Mary University of London, E1 2AB London, UK
e-mail: v.berdunov@qmul.ac.uk

M. Franklin
HEDS, School of Health and Related Research (ScHARR), University of Sheffield, S1 4DT Sheffield, UK
e-mail: matt.franklin@sheffield.ac.uk

D. Razzouk (ed.), *Mental Health Economics*, DOI 10.1007/978-3-319-55266-8_7

of data that may be used to derive parameter estimates. The conclusion of the chapter includes recommendations for appropriately reporting results of the statistical and modeling analyses carried out as part of an economic evaluation.

Key Points Summary

- Characteristics of data used in economic analysis, including different types of data (e.g., continuous, categorical, bounded) and distributions of data (normal, skewed), and how these affect statistical methods in economic evaluation
- The role of regression analysis in the context of economic evaluation
- More advanced statistical methods, which include nonparametric bootstrapping, area under the curve analysis, mapping, and methods to account for missing data
- Steps involved in designing a decision-analytic model for an economic evaluation and the key elements of the model
- Different types of decision-analytic models used for economic evaluation
- The concept of uncertainty in decision-analytic models, different types of uncertainty that need to be addressed as part of a modeling analysis, and appropriate methods for reporting uncertainty in the results of a modeling analysis

7.1 Introduction

The development of complex healthcare systems has increased demand for economic evaluation as a method for informing decisions in healthcare. The increasing complexity of evaluation methods has raised the need for technical methods to systematically use evidence and characterize uncertainty around the decision problem when informing decision makers. Health economists often use sampled patient-level data on the costs and effects of an intervention to populate an economic evaluation. This approach poses a number of analytical challenges for investigators, such as skewed data, missing data, and censored data. The primary source of costs and outcomes may be subject to bias, such as confounding from differences in patient characteristics and nonrepresentative samples. Statistical methods are used as tools to draw inferences regarding the economic effect of a healthcare intervention based on a sample of data collected alongside a clinical study. In instances when data from a clinical study do not exist or do not provide sufficient information upon which a decision can be informed, economic modeling can be used to extrapolate results from current or previous studies, include data from the empirical literature, and evaluate the decision problem over a longer time horizon. This chapter outlines various ways in which statistical tools and modeling methods could be used in both deterministic and stochastic economic analyses.

This chapter aims to provide guidance to introductory statistical and economic modeling methods for health economic analysis, but it is not a technical guide on how to perform these methods. Within this chapter, methods are introduced and described, guidance is given about when these methods may be useful, and references are provided to studies which have used these methods in practice; we also make the reader aware of more complex methods that may be useful in the future. However, it is up to the reader to use the references provided to learn more about the technical aspects of these methods. It should also be noted that, as an introductory guide, methods may be over simplified for descriptive purposes, and it is again the reader's duty to use the references provided to understand the more complex aspects of these methods for statistical and modeling analyses for health economics.

The purpose of this chapter is to provide a general introduction to concepts in statistical and modeling analysis methods that is not setting or country-specific. Certain examples from the

United Kingdom are used within this chapter to illustrate concepts, particularly in terms of sources of data, in order to inform decision-analytic models and applications of methods to real studies.

7.2 Introductory Statistics for Health Economics and Economic Evaluation

7.2.1 Overview of Introductory Statistical Methods for Economic Evaluation

Health economics requires statistical methods to enable inferences of results from data sets of interest for descriptive purposes. Although Health Economics as a discipline is not limited to just economic evaluations, the introductory statistical methods described within this chapter focus on those methods that are most commonly associated with economic evaluations, as well as the assessment of costs and outcome data obtained from clinical studies. This includes describing basic methods for determining statistically significant results, descriptive statistics when reporting results, and then an overview of basic linear regression models such as ordinary least squares (OLS). Other slightly more advanced methods that are commonly used for the purpose of economic evaluation are also described, such as performing regression analyses using generalized linear models (GLMs), and the use of bootstrapping methods for nonparametric assessments and resampling; bootstrapping for the generation of cost-effectiveness acceptability curves (CEACs) is also described within this chapter. More advanced or generally useful methods are also acknowledged; however, this is only to make the reader aware of these methods for potential use in the future while providing references for further reading. These advanced methods include: (a) area under the curve (AUC) analysis for calculating incremental benefit; (b) controlling for baseline factors, including patient characteristics, utility scores, and cost differences between trial arms; (c) multiple imputation for missing data; and (d) "mapping" (cross-walking) and the potential use of mapping algorithms for specific use in cost-utility studies when a preference-based measure has not been included in the study design [see also Chap. 6 with regard to cost-utility analysis (CUA)].

7.2.2 A Note on the Distribution of Data for Health Economic Analysis

It is important to note immediately that data for economic analysis are different from clinical data. The data for economic analyses are not necessarily unique or even complex, but methods have been developed to analyze the data appropriately. Key aspects about the data used for economic analysis mostly stem from the distribution of the data and the type of data being analyzed. A normal distribution is a desirable trait for data, and statistical methods rely on this assumption for appropriate use; however, a normal distribution is rarely observed within the data used for economic analysis. The data can be *continuous* or *categorical* (or *binary*) (Box 7.1), and often the data are *skewed* (Box 7.2), *bounded*

Box 7.1 Types of Data for Health Economic Analysis: Categorical Data

It may be necessary to generate categorical (or binary) data from continuous data for the purpose of analysis (such as generating age groups), or the data may be naturally categorical (for example, the three item levels of the EQ-5D-3 L domains). Categorical data need to be analyzed and presented for descriptive purposes in specific ways, such as using logistic regression models or using frequency-based plots for descriptive statistics. Often, the data used for economic analysis are continuous (such as cost data), and so the main focus of this chapter is based on continuous data, but the reader should be aware that if the data are not continuous (categorical or binary, for example), then certain statistical methods may not be appropriate.

Box 7.2 Types of Data for Health Economic Analysis: Skewed Data

Positively skewed data are most often observed with cost data. Costs have a finite upper bound but can be bound at zero (logically, there is no negative price for goods or services). Often there is a small number of patients with very high costs, and depending on whether the analysis is specific to a whole service or a care service (e.g., inpatient care), people can have zero costs associated with a service. When presented with skewed data, it might seem rational to just report the median, but the median is not always appropriate for economic analysis. Alternative methods such as bootstrapping have been developed for dealing with skewed data (see Sect. 7.2.7).

Box 7.3 Types of Data for Health Economic Analysis: Bounded Data

Bounded data are most commonly observed with outcome measure data or cost data (see also "skewed data" in Box 7.2), whereby the data are bounded by the scoring algorithm of the measure, or simply a lower bound at a value of zero (i.e., no cost) for cost data. For preference-based measures such as the EQ-5D-3 L (see Chap. 6), the preference-based algorithm is bounded by a value of −0.594 (states worse than death) to 1 (perfect health). The bounded nature of the data should be accounted for in an economic analysis. For example, during mapping exercises (see Sect. 7.2.8.4), estimating values outside of the measures score range is a real issue that can be accounted for using various regression-based methods.

(Box 7.3), *missing* (Box 7.4), or *censored* (Box 7.5). A simplistic explanation of what these aspects mean for data analysis and when they may

Box 7.4 Types of Data for Health Economic Analysis: Missing Data

Missing data are common with patient-level data. Missing data can occur because of poor response rates, incomplete responses, or loss to follow-up (due to patients dropping out of a study or their inability to complete a study, for example). Missing data can be particularly problematic for economic analysis, where arithmetic mean values are of great importance and where not accounting for missing data may lead to biased results. For example, patient dropout because of an inability to complete the study may remove particular patient groups (for example, those with very poor health or cognitive impairment) from the assessment process, which means their potential benefit from an intervention is not accounted for in the economic analysis. Imputing data is useful in this instance (see Sect. 7.2.8.3).

occur are provided in the descriptions in the respective boxes. Simplistic methods for dealing with these data traits are described within this chapter, but for a more comprehensive overview of these statistical methods, please refer to Jones et al. [1].

7.2.3 Descriptive Statistics: Use and Interpretation

Descriptive statistics are important for any study when it is necessary to describe the distribution of the data and subsequent results. Mean point estimates are one of the most commonly reported descriptive statistics, but it is "arithmetic means" (compared with other means such as "geometric" or "harmonic" means) that need to be reported for health economic analysis. These mean values are reported to describe the central tendencies of a probability distribution, but they are not robust statistics for describing the data distribution; within health economics we are just as concerned with the

Box 7.5 Types of Data for Health Economic Analysis: Censored Data
Censored data are a specific type of missing data (and can be dealt with using similar methods; see "missing data" in Box 7.4), whereby the data are not collected or not used for analysis. For example, this may be the result of administrative censoring, whereby patients can drop into or out of databases, but analysis is carried out for a specific period for which data are available for all/most of the desired patient group. A key assumption when using this type of data is that the uncensored data are the same as the censored data (i.e., the censored data is "uninformative"); however, cost and event data can occur and accumulate over time (that is, future events are often response on past events), and therefore this assumption is not valid, and censored data can lead to bias within economic analyses.

Box 7.6 Simple Descriptive Statistics and Potential Use: Point Estimates

- *Mean (average)*: The arithmetic mean is the sum of a collection of observed values divided by the number of observations. The arithmetic mean value should *always* be described for economic data. To say "always reported" may not be restrictively true, but it is recommended to report this statistic in the vast majority of cases.
- *Median*: The median, in essence, describes the middle value. Consider presenting the median when the data are skewed; however, still describe the arithmetic mean along with this value.
- *Mode*: The mode is the most commonly reported value in a collection of values. This statistic is rarely reported alongside economic data, but it might be useful for frequency data, where knowing the mode might be useful.

uncertainty around estimates (i.e., the distribution of the data) as we are with the mean point value.

A basic overview of some simple descriptive statistics is provided in Box 7.6 (point estimates) and Box 7.7 (interval estimates); note that these descriptive statistics, their use, and their interpretation depend on the distribution of the data. Normally distributed data sets rarely exist for the purpose of health economic analysis, but for the purpose of describing descriptive statistics, we now assume that the data are normally distributed and compare how these statistics alter when the data is non-normally distributed (in this instance, positivity skewed for descriptive purposes). These descriptive statistics will be reintroduced and then expanded upon to deal with different data distributions later within this chapter.

Figures 7.1 and 7.2 describe how the values of central tendency, such as mean and the median point estimates, can vary according to the underlying empirical distribution. Figure 7.1 includes a normal distribution and Fig. 7.2 a positively (right) skewed distribution. The latter is common with cost data. (Note that cost data often follow a gamma distribution rather than a positively skewed normal distribution, but the example is still useful in this instance).

As can be observed, the mean, median, and mode are the same value for a normal distribution, but these values are different when the data are skewed. When the data are right-skewed, the mode is a lower value than the median, and the median a lower value than the mean (mode < median < mean). The general distribution of the data around these point estimates is observably quite different as well, indicating the need to use interval estimates to describe the distribution of the data as appropriate.

Box 7.7 Simple Descriptive Statistics and Potential Use: Interval Estimates

- *Interquartile range (IQR; p50, p25, p75)*: The IQR is a measure of variability based on dividing the observed data into quartiles (p50, p25, p75). In this instance, p50 is the same as the median; p25 and p75 represent the observed value at the 25th and 75th percentile of the data spread, respectively. The value of the difference between these is the IQR (IQR = p75 – p25). Present the IQR when the data are heavily skewed; however, consider using methods to account for the skew to report adjusted (standard errors or confidence intervals; adjusted estimates are common when using bootstrapped estimates) instead of the IQR.
- *Standard deviation (SD)*: The SD is a measure of data set value variation around the mean. A lower value indicates that data set values are closer to the mean and vice versa for higher values. The SD of the sample is the degree to which individuals within the sample differ from the sample mean; therefore present the SD when the size of variation in the entire observed data sample is the main statistic of interest (see also *SE* for comparative use).
- *Standard Error (SE)*: The SE is the SD of the sampling distribution of a statistic, which is commonly the mean. For the SE of the mean, the SD is divided by the square root of the sample size. The SE of the sample mean is an estimate of how far the sample mean is likely to be from the population mean; therefore, present the SE when potential error around the mean is of interest.
- *Confidence interval (CI)*: The CI is a frequentist statistic that describes a range within which the "true value" might exist given a particular confidence level (normally 95%, but could be 99% or 90%). For a 95% CI, the interval suggests that the true parameter value of interest for a patient population may lie with the value range, with 95% confidence.
- *Credible intervals*: Credible intervals are similar to CIs but are a Bayesian rather than a frequentist statistic. For credible intervals, the bounds are regarded as fixed and the estimated parameter is a random variable, whereas for CIs, their bounds are considered random variables and the parameter is a fixed value; however, their use is analogous.

7.2.4 Sample Size and Power Calculations: Relevance for Economic Evaluations

Power calculations are used to establish an appropriate sample size in order to identify a statistically significant treatment effect (if one exists) from a clinical trial. Clear implications exist for methods to indicate appropriate sample sizes if the primary focus of a trial is the economic analysis; however, because the primary focus is usually a clinical outcome (health economic analysis is dominantly a secondary outcome), the sample size of clinical trials is of little relevance to health economists and their desired analysis (which is often focused on more generalized health benefits and costs). It is worth noting that methods have been developed to inform sample sizes if the primary focus of a trial was to "power" the economic analysis (for example, expected value of sample of information [2, 3]), although these methods can be applied post hoc, provided an economic model is designed alongside the trial.

7.2.5 Hypothesis Testing and Statistical Significance

The standard method for statistical inference in healthcare research from a clinical perspective involves a frequentist approach. This involves

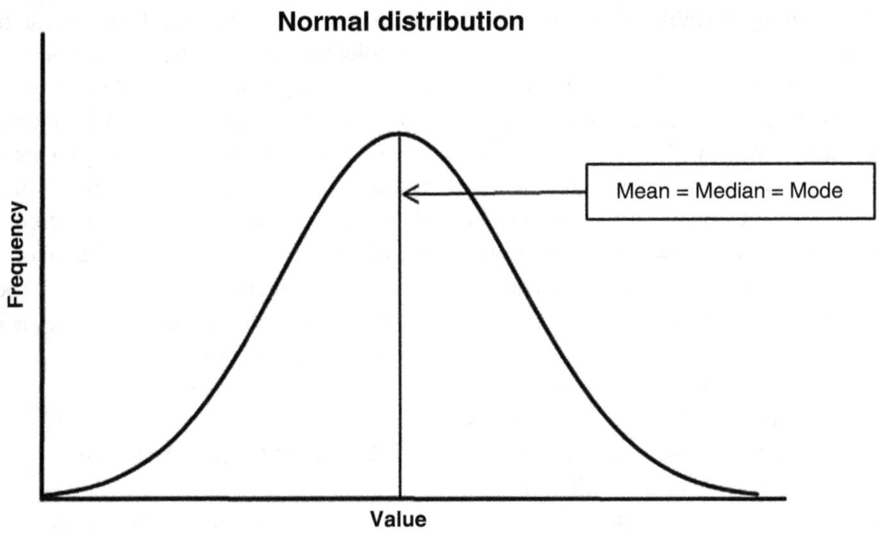

Fig. 7.1 Normal distribution

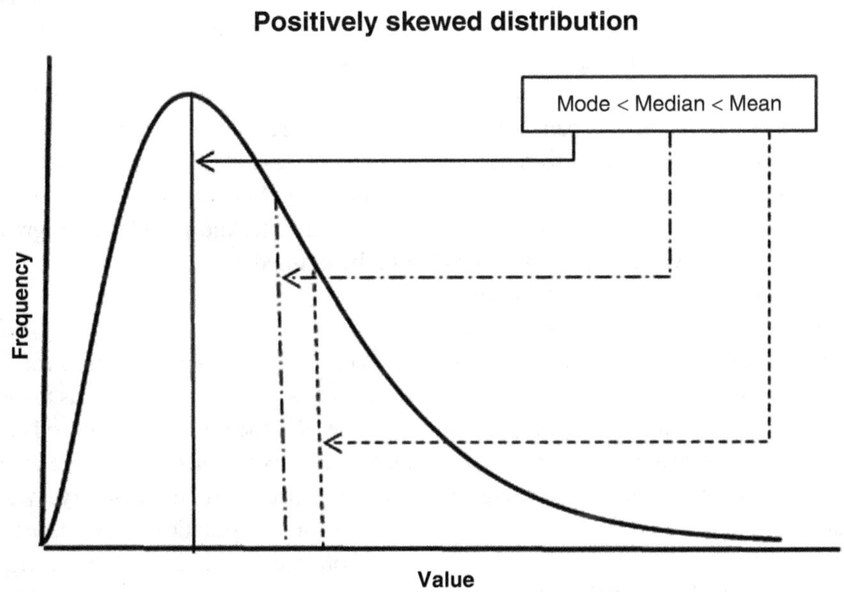

Fig. 7.2 Right-skewed distribution

testing specific hypotheses relating to relationships between variables by drawing conclusions from the observed frequency of a particular event. Within health economics analysis, hypothesis testing is not generally used to establish cost-effectiveness. Health economic analyses generally uses a Bayesian framework for statistical inference, which assumes a posterior probability distribution for the relationship of interest based on observed data; however, frequentist methods can still be used to describe potentially statistically significant differences in costs and outcomes between trial arms or patient groups.

As three examples and their potential use, hypothesis testing can be based on:

t Test: Consider using the *t* test when there are two groups for comparison, data are normally distributed, and the variable for assessment is continuous.

Chi-squared test: Consider using the chi-squared test when there are two groups for comparison, data are normally distributed, and the variable for assessment is categorical.

Analysis of variance: Consider using analysis of variance when there are two or more groups for comparison, data are normally distributed, and the variable for assessment is continuous.

Each of the aforementioned tests are parametric tests (i.e., they rely on an assumption about the distribution of the data) and often assume the data assessed have a normal distribution, which is a limited assumption when applied to cost and outcome data used for economic analyses. Nonparametric tests that might be of interest include:

- *Wilcoxon rank-sum test* (also known as *Mann-Whitney U test*): Consider using when there are two explanatory groups for comparison and the data are continuous or can have an ordinal ranking (i.e., there is way to rank the variables to know which is greatest).
- *Wilcoxon signed-rank test*: Consider using when there are two matched or paired groups (i.e., from the same population) for comparison and the data are continuous or can have an ordinal ranking (the *sign test* could also be used in a similar manner).
- *Kruskal-Wallis test*: Consider using when there are two or more groups for comparison and the data are continuous or can have an ordinal ranking.

Note that these examples describe when these tests might be considered useful, but they are by no means a comprehensive list of times when these tests could or should be used.

These tests and their results (i.e., *P* values) still have a place as descriptive statistics within economic analysis, rather than a definitive result when used for the purpose of clinical assessments (treatment A is statistically significantly more clinically effective that treatment B, for example). For example, validity testing (in terms of construct, convergent, and discriminant validity) of outcome measures can be based on hypothesis testing using these types of tests [4–6]. *P* values can be used as an indication of a statistically significant result at a predefined significance threshold (e.g., a *P* value <0.05 indicates statistical significance), but they should be treated as an indicator of a potential relationship for descriptive purposes rather than a definitive relationship that may be used to support the adoption of an intervention based on its impact on costs or outcomes (guidance on reporting the results of cost-effectiveness analyses is described in more detail in Sect. 7.4).

7.2.6 Regression Analysis

7.2.6.1 Simple Linear Regression and Continuous Variables

Regression analysis is a statistical method often used for inferring relationships between variables. An example of a simple regression model is the OLS model. For this model, it is important that the response variable be continuous; however, if the response variable is categorical, then logistic regression analysis is a simple alternative (described in Sect. 7.2.6.2). As an example of the OLS model, let the population regression equation be defined as:

$$y_i = \alpha + \beta x_i + \varepsilon_i \tag{7.1}$$

Within this simple regression model, y_i is the response variable of interest, x_i is the explanatory variable, β is the OLS estimator, α is the constant term, and ε_i is the error term. The error term and the response and explanatory variables are defined for a population of N and each observation from the population of $i = 1, \ldots, N$. These models are typically used when one wants to understand the relationship between y and x, which is described by the coefficient β, while accounting for the constant term (α) and potential "noise" (ε) around the estimation. These models often involve the use of multiple explanatory variables in an effort to control for "confounding" factors; these regression models can be defined as:

$$\begin{aligned} y_i &= \alpha + \beta_1 x_{i1} + \ldots + \beta_p x_{ip} + \varepsilon_i \\ &= \alpha + \beta x_i^{'} + \varepsilon_i \end{aligned} \tag{7.2}$$

Multiple explanatory variables (up to p in this example) can be included within a regression model, and their relationship with y_i is defined by the coefficient β_p. In Eq. 7.2, $'$ denotes the matrix transpose, so that $\beta x_i'$ is the scalar resulting from the inner product of vectors x_i and β; that is, $\beta x_i'$ represents the multiple possible explanatory variables and their potential possible relationships with the response variable y_i.

The purpose of running a simple regression model such as OLS is to assess the relationship between the response variable (e.g., health-related quality of life) and the explanatory variable (e.g., mental health status) while controlling for other factors that may have an relationship with the response variable (factors such as age and sex, for example, can be included as additional explanatory variables in the regression equation). Practical examples are presented in Sect. 7.2.6.5.

7.2.6.2 Logistic Regression and Categorical Variables

Logistic regression is used when the response variable is categorical. Categorical variables might include age, sex, or ethnicity; however, rarely would these variables be included as the response variable within a regression model. Types of logistic regression models might sometimes be useful because the response variable is categorical, such as for assessing diagnostic interventions where the outcome is either "positive" or "negative" (true or false; an outcome has occurred or has not). Practical examples are presented in Sect. 7.2.6.5.

7.2.6.3 Generalized Linear Models

A GLM is a flexible version of the OLS model – it is flexible in relation to the ability to make parametric assumptions about how the explanatory variable(s) are related to the response variable. The assumed relationship between the linear estimator (β) and the mean of the distribution function can be explicitly fitted to the model using a link function; this allows response variables that have error distributions other than a normal distribution to be included in the regression model. It is also possible to make assumptions around the family of the error distribution of the response variable. The ability to fit family distributions and link functions (common examples of which are presented in Table 7.1) to the GLM regression model has made this type of model popular for the purpose of health economic analysis when the response variable cannot be assumed to be normally distributed. For example, when exploring what aspects are driving costs as the response variable, a GLM model could be fitted to a data set with a chosen distribution to account for the skewed and bounded nature of costs (e.g., gamma distribution) and a defined link function (e.g., identity or log), and then explanatory variables could include aspects such as age, sex, and/or score from a clinical or

Table 7.1 Common family distributions and links for generalized linear models

Family name	Distribution support	Typical uses	Link name	Link function
Gaussian (normal)	Continuous $(-\infty, +\infty)$	Linear-response relationship	Identity	$\beta x' = \mu$
Gamma	Continuous $(0, +\infty)$	Exponential-response relationship; scale parameter	Inverse	$\beta x' = \mu^{-1}$
Inverse Gaussian	Continuous $(0, +\infty)$	–	Log	$\beta x' = 1n(\mu)$
Bernoulli	Integer	Binary outcome	Logit	$\beta x' = \ln\left(\frac{\mu}{1-\mu}\right)$
Binomial	Integer 0, 1, …, N	Number of successes in a sequence of N binary (yes/no) experiments	Log-log	$\beta x' = -1n\{-1n(\mu)\}$
Poisson	Integer 0, 1, 2, …	Probability of N events in a fixed time interval	Power #	$\beta x' = \mu^{\#}$

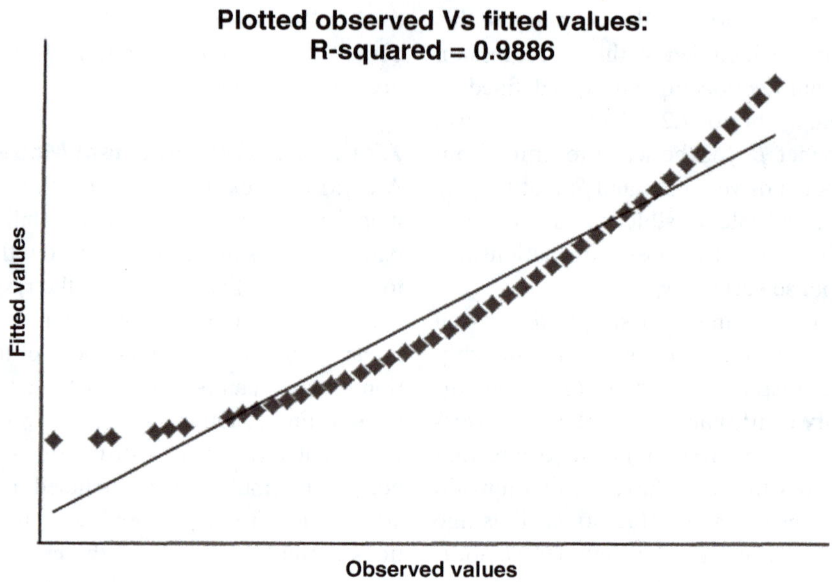

Fig. 7.3 Judging goodness of fit using R^2: example of good model fit

subjective patient-reported outcome measure to assess mental health [7–9].

Some link functions are more commonly used with particular family distributions (for example, a Gaussian distribution with an identify link; this is the same structure as an ordinary least squares regression model). Mixing link functions with distributions is possible within software packages, but the conceptual basis of doing so should be assessed before using link functions with distributions for practical analysis.

7.2.6.4 Judging Goodness of Fit and Specification for Regression Models

The goodness of fit of a regression model describes the extent to which the model will be able to fit predicted values compared with observed values. Goodness of fit can be assessed in various ways, including by assessing the statistical significance, sign, and size of coefficients from the model; R^2 and adjusted R^2; the Akaike's information criterion (AIC) [10] and the Bayesian information criterion (BIC) [11]; tests of model fit such as the Ramsey regression equation specification error test (RESET) [12], the Park test [13], and the Jarque-Bera test [14]; and using plots to examine whether model assumptions are valid. These methods are described within this section.

7.2.6.4.1 Statistical Significance, Sign, and Size of Coefficients

Two subjective ways of assessing goodness of fit are first to judge the statistical significance, sign, and size of coefficients from the model against a priori assumptions about whether explanatory variables should have a certain relationship with the response variable. This relationship can also be assessed using visual plots (such as scatter plots or kernel density plots), whereby the plotted regression line and the observed data points can be assessed; this kind of subjective judgement is described in relation to the R^2 statistic.

7.2.6.4.2 R^2 and Adjusted R^2

Measures of explanatory power (such as the R^2 and adjusted R^2 statistics) describe how well a model explains the variation in the observed data set. This can be visually observed using a scatter plot, whereby statistics like R^2 describe how well the observed data match the fitted regression line (see Fig. 7.3 for an example of good fit and Fig. 7.4 for an example of poor fit). The R^2 statistic lies between a value of 0 (0%) and 1 (100%):

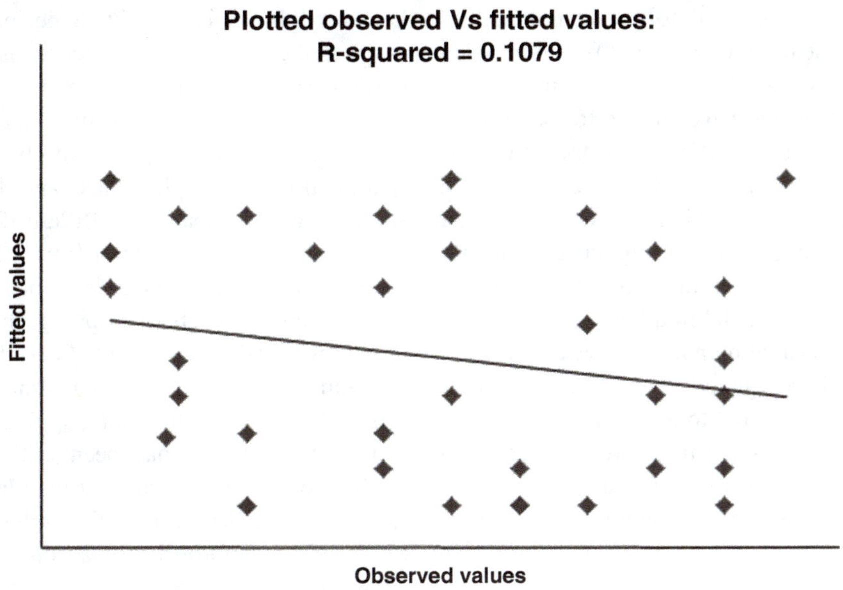

Fig. 7.4 Judging goodness of fit using R^2: example of poor model fit

0 indicates that the regression model explains none (0%) of the variability of the response variable data around its mean, whereas 1 indicates that the regression model explains all (100%) of the variability of the response variable data around its mean. Within Figs. 7.3 and 7.4, a linear regression line has been fitted to the plotted relationship between the observed and fitted values from the linear regression model. As can be observed, when the plotted relationship is close to the fitted linear regression line (Fig. 7.3), the R^2 statistic is high ($R^2 = 0.9886$) and suggests the model may have a good fit because it has high explanatory power. However, when the plotted relationship is not close (scattered around) the fitted linear regression line (Fig. 7.4), the R^2 statistic is low ($R^2 = 0.1079$) and suggests the model may not have a good fit because it has low explanatory power.

7.2.6.4.3 Akaike's and Bayesian Information Criteria

AIC [10, 15] and BIC [11] provide statistics on relative model performance and so can be used for model selection when two or more model options are available. AIC and BIC offer a statistic of information lost when the model is fitted to a set of observed data – the lower the AIC and BIC figures, the less information is lost when fitting one model compared with another model. For a relative choice between models, the larger the difference in the AIC and BIC statistics (the one with a lower statistic is the preferred model), the larger the "preference" for one model compared with another model. The AIC and BIC statistics offer a balance between goodness of fit and model complexity, which is a concern when overfitting models is possible. It should be recognized that AIC and BIC do not have the same criterion for model selection, and so the two may disagree about which model is preferred; in this situation it is debatable which criterion should be used for choosing a model [16].

7.2.6.4.4 Tests of Model Fit

Tests of model fit can also be used, such as the Ramsey Regression Equation Specification Error Test (RESET) test for omitted variables [12], the Park test for heteroscedasticity [13], and the Jarque-Bera test for assessing the normality of regression errors [14]. Each of these tests can be used to test different aspects of model fit. Here I explain in more detail (but still in a simplified manner) how the Ramsey RESET test can be used.

The Ramsey RESET for omitted variables within linear least-squares (e.g., OLS) regression models assesses whether nonlinear combinations of the fitted values have power to explain the response variable [12]; if this is true, then the model could be misspecified in its current form. Note that the RESET test is only a test of whether the model is linear in the original explanatory variables; that is, by adding certain explanatory variables into the model in a higher order power if these nonlinear combinations have explanatory power (e.g. in a squared or cubic form; this is why the test is referred to as an omitted variable test, the RESET tests if there are any neglected nonlinearities in the model) – the RESET test cannot be used to pick up the influence of other variables.

7.2.6.5 Practical Examples of Regression Models for Health Economic Analysis

Regression models have multiple applications when used for the purpose of health economics, and the OLS model is often used first, before more complicated models are applied to a data set. Three types of commonly used and relatively simple regression models have been described. The choice of model often depends on the research question and the data set used for analysis.

Examples of when these regression models have been used include identifying the relationship between quality-of-life aspects and mental health [17–19], mapping exercises where a relationship is defined between two outcome measures and their constructs, such as the five-dimension EuroQoL (EQ-5D) and a clinical measure (for example, the Hospital Anxiety and Depression Scale [HADS]) [20] (see also Sect. 7.2.8.4), and identifying aspects that drive increased healthcare and associated costs [7–9].

7.2.7 Bootstrap Analysis

Bootstrapping has gained popularity in Health Economics as a method of nonparametric assessment through random resampling with replacement. Although a parametric bootstrap is possible, what made this method attractive within health economics is its ability to perform analysis without the need for parametric assumptions, particularly when such assumptions are difficult to fit to the data. Readers with an interest in the more complicated aspects of bootstrapping (parametric use, applications, and limitations) should refer to Lepage and Billard [21] and the extensive work by Bradley Efron [22–25]. This section focuses on nonparametric bootstrapping.

Nonparametric bootstrapping has gained popularity for the assessment of cost data and is a recommended method for economic evaluation [26, 27]. Although the bootstrapping method is technically valid, it has been criticized when applied to cost data because it may lead to inefficient and perhaps misleading inferences as a result of not appropriately accounting for the skew of the data [28]; for the purposes of the discussion here, however, it is important to note that nonparametric bootstrapping is a popular method for health economic analysis despite this criticism. To provide a relatively simple understanding of the process of nonparametric bootstrapping, four stages of the process are described in Box 7.8, with reference to hypothetical cost data.

As described, the nonparametric bootstrap method allows the sampling distribution to be estimated without the need to make a parametric assumption. In doing so, alternative statistics are required for reporting the distribution of the bootstrapped (replacement) data set. This includes reporting the bootstrapped standard errors (SEs) and bias-corrected and accelerated 95% confidence intervals (CIs) [23] rather than the normal SE and 95% CI. Although it is possible to report these statistics that rely on an assumed normal distribution of the residuals (i.e., normal CIs and SEs as described in Box 7.7), these alternative statistics account for the skew of the data and the subsequent effect of the bootstrap. The benefits of using these statistics alongside bootstrapped analysis are described by Efron [23].

Bootstrapping is the most commonly used trial-based technique (compared with modeling methods) for (a) obtaining the CIs around an incremental cost-effectiveness ratio (ICER; see Chaps. 5 and 6) and (b) deriving the CEAC for assessing the probability of cost-effectiveness at

Box 7.8 Summary Stages of a Nonparametric Bootstrapping Method When Applied to Cost Data

1. A sample of cost data is elicited from a patient sample of *N* patients; these are described as the *observed cost data set*.
2. The bootstrapping method pulls a sample from (and of equal size to) the observations of the observed costs data set using *simple random sampling and replacement*.
3. A simple random sample is pulled from the observed data and a *replacement data set* is populated based on this random sample; with the improvement of speed and processing ability of statistical software, *≥1000 iterations* (with more rather than less) are preferred, which will generate ≥1000 replacement data points.
4. Because of the nature of the nonparametric bootstrap, it is recommend that *bootstrapped SEs* and *bias-corrected and accelerated 95% CIs* be provided when reporting the distribution [23].

various willingness-to-pay (WTP) thresholds. In the example of the ICER for an analysis of cost per quality-adjusted life year (QALY), the bootstrap is applied to the costs and effects (QALYs) from the study of interest. Note that probability sensitivity analysis (PSA) could be used in place of bootstrapping when the economic evaluation is performed within a model; therefore, the use of CEACs and WTP thresholds are described within Sect. 7.3.7.5 alongside a description of economic modeling, rather than repeating these aspect here.

7.2.8 An Acknowledgement of Other Advanced and Useful Statistical Methods

Statistical methods for health economic analysis are constantly advancing. It is difficult to make the reader aware of all new and developing methods; however, at the basic level, some advanced statistical methods often rely on aspects that have already been described in this chapter, such as regression-based methods. This section acknowledges four statistical methods that are commonly used for the purpose of health economic analysis (particularly for economic evaluation) and their importance: (1) AUC analysis, which is more commonly used for calculating incremental benefit, particularly for QALYs within CUA; (2) controlling for baseline differences such as patient characteristics, utility, and costs; (3) controlling for missing data using multiple imputation; and (4) mapping from a non-preference-based measure to a preference-based measure when data have not yet been collected using a preference-based measure (specifically for use with CUA).

7.2.8.1 Area Under the Curve Analysis

AUC analysis is not really an advanced statistical method, but it is useful for calculating incremental benefit over a particular time period, is often used in CUA for calculating QALYs gained, and has been used for modeling purposes. It is therefore worth noting this method in this section. The logic behind the method is that the incremental benefit of an intervention is calculated as the difference between the overall benefit of two interventions using linear approximation rather than simple extrapolation, when benefit (e.g., utility value) is recorded at multiple (at least two) time points. For the purpose of demonstrating the difference between linear approximation using AUC and simple extrapolation, consider that a person's utility (as a value of a person's health-related quality of life, for example) is captured at five time points (this example is presented in Fig. 7.5). If a utility value is assumed to be constant between time points (simple extrapolation), then the area representing the person's utility would be captured by the area under the black lines; using linear approximation through the AUC method, however, the area of utility representing the person's utility is represented by the area under the blue lines. The "area of difference" represents the difference in the amount of utility calculated using simple extrapolation compared with using the AUC method. The AUC method does not assume that a person's health-related quality of life is constant between time points (rather, there is a linear change in a person's utility between time points), and so is considered a more accurate measure of calculating utility, incremental benefit, and QALYs over time.

In general, QALYs could be calculated using the AUC method in two ways: (1) at the group level using the mean utility value, and (2) at the patient level using patient-level utility values. It is generally recommended that the patient level be used rather than the group level, if possible [29]. The AUC method for calculating QALYs using patient-level data can be expressed using Eqs. 7.3 and 7.4:

$$q_{jti} = \frac{\left(u_{j(t-1)i} + U_{jti}\right)}{2}\delta_t \tag{7.3}$$

where u is the utility score, i denotes an individual, and t is time, so that at baseline, $t = 0$. For each group j (where j represent the two groups being assessed [e.g., intervention and control]), the consecutive time measures can be added, averaged, and then rescaled (δ) for the percentage of a year that t and $t - 1$ cover. The total QALYs (Q) for the whole estimation period (T) is then the sum of the utility values across all time points starting at $t = 1$, such that

$$Q_{ji} = \sum_{T}^{t=1} q_{jti} \tag{7.4}$$

In this example, total QALYs can be calculated for both groups (j), and the incremental benefit is the difference between the two total QALY (Q) values. Practical examples of using the AUC method and its importance for calculating incremental benefit when using the QALY has been described by Hunter et al. [29].

7.2.8.2 Controlling for Baseline Differences Between Groups

The need to control for baseline differences when making comparisons between at least two groups has become the norm within health economic analysis, particularly when dealing with observational data. Often, studies such as randomized controlled trials (RCTs) involve a process of randomization (random allocation of patients to the intervention or control arm, for example) and stratification (specific allocation of certain patient groups or characteristics so they are equal in both arms) in order to try and achieve balanced characteristics between the two groups, when these certain characteristics may have a relationship with the outcome of interest (health state, utility, or cost of care, for example). Baseline adjustments can also be used to control for these group differences, but it should be noted that adjusting for baseline differences does come with some caveats, and some guidelines or recommendations for adjusting for baseline covariates have been published [30]. Although patient characteristics such as age and sex could be controlled for in the baseline adjustment, the examples here focus on utility and cost differences because these aspects are not usually directly controlled for, even in a randomization or stratification process. The recommended method for baseline adjustment is a regression-based method, whereby the outcome of interest is the response variable and explanatory variables could include a binary dummy variable of the two groups (e.g., 0 = control group; 1 = intervention group) for comparison and baseline utility or costs. An educational review about dealing with utility data including baseline adjustments (and missing data; also briefly explained in the next section) has been provided by Hunter et al. [29]; for costs these adjustments have been described by van Asselt et al. [31].

7.2.8.3 Controlling for Missing Data

Missing data – where the data for analysis obtained from self-reported methods or even healthcare systems are often incomplete – are a problem for economic analysis. Reasons for incomplete data could be poor response rates and inadequate or untrustworthy data collection or recording, among others. Issues with missing data may be the result of a study design flaw, but for the purpose of this section the focus is on how to deal with missing data using statistical methods while assuming that repeat or further data collection is not an option. First, it is up to the analyst to determine the "level of missingness"; for example, are the data:

(a) *Missing completely at random*: no relationship exists between the data that are missing and any values in the data set, missing or observed.

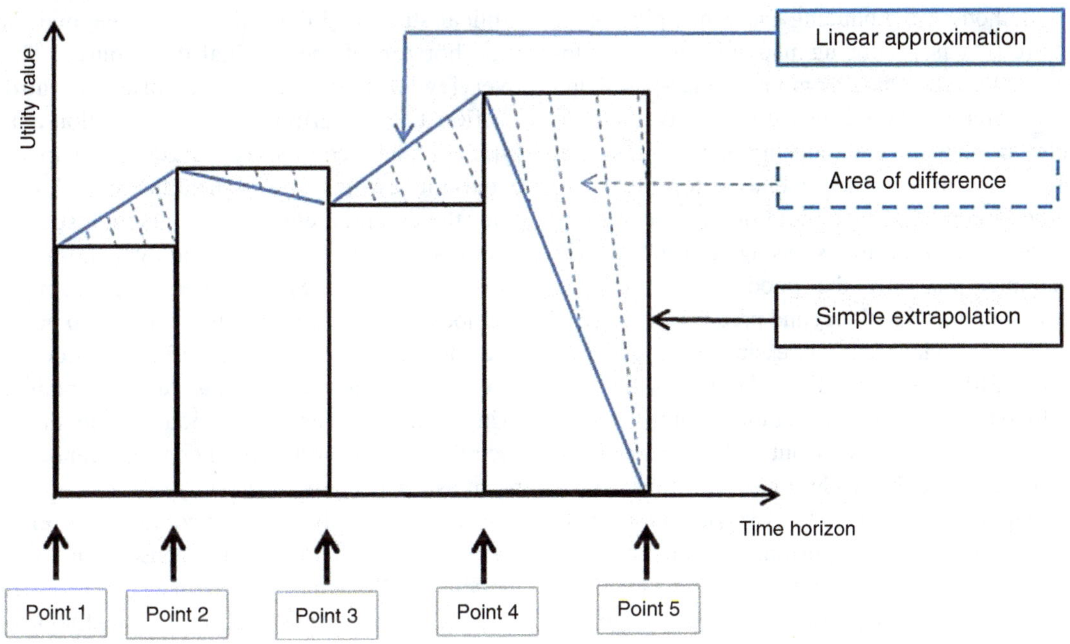

Fig. 7.5 Calculating utility over time using simple extrapolation or area under the curve

(b) *Missing at random*: no relationship exists between the missing data and the mechanism of their missingness, but this mechanism may be related to the observed data.
(c) *Missing not at random*: a relationship exists between the missing data and mechanism of their missingness

Dealing with missing data is explored and described in more detail by Little and Rubin [32]; note that if the data are missing completely at random, then little can be done statistically at this point, but when the data are determined to be missing at random, then imputation can be used to predict the missing data. Multiple univariate or multivariate methods are available for imputation: various linear and logistic regressions [33], predictive mean matching [34], and multiple imputation using chained equations [35]. Statistical software packages often include built-in code to perform these types of multiple data imputations, making what used to be quite complicated methods relatively simple when used appropriately. Multiple imputation using chained equations has become particularly popular over the past decade; guidance on using this method with an example focused on mental health data is described by White et al. [35].

7.2.8.4 Mapping (Cross-Walking) for Cost-Utility Analysis

Statistical mapping has become popular for health economic analysis as a method for enabling the ability to perform CUA when a preference-based measure (e.g., the EQ-5D) was not administered within a trial but a non-preference-based measure (e.g., HADS) was administered and for which a mapping algorithm exists. The mapping algorithm defines the statistical relationship between the two measures, so that if you know the score for one measure (e.g., HADS), you can use the algorithm to calculate the (preference-based) score of the other measure (e.g., EQ-5D). Brazier et al. [20] describe a few examples of this process of mapping from a mental health condition-specific measure (e.g., HADS) to a generic preference-based measure (e.g., EQ-5D) in order to elicit a mapping algorithm to be used in the future when the non-preference-based measure has been administered but a preference-based measure has not (i.e., in this example, the HADS was administered but the EQ-5D was not).

Methods for producing these mapping algorithms (that is, producing mapping algorithms for future use when data from preference-based and non-preference-based measures are available to infer the statistical relationship) have well set out guidelines that include methods for their use, regression models that could or have been used, as well as methods for assessing performance, for example, assessing the goodness of fit (e.g., assessing the R^2 statistic) and predictive ability of the fitted models (e.g., assessing mean absolute error) [36]. These guidelines should be consulted if there is an interest in or requirement to perform cost-per-QALY analysis but a preference-based measure has not been administered within a study –a mapping algorithm may exist and could enable this analysis; if an algorithm is not available, these guidelines describe how to elicit a mapping algorithm if the appropriate data are available from a which a mapping algorithm could be elicited (i.e., an existing data set with a preference-based and non-preference-based measure included and from which a statistical relationship could be inferred). Caveats to using these algorithms also exist and are described within the guidance [36]. As of September 2013, a database of mapping studies was published by the Health Economic Research Centre (http://www.herc.ox.ac.uk/downloads/mappingdatabase) [37].

7.3 Modeling Methods for Health Economics and Economic Evaluation

7.3.1 Overview of Economic Modeling

The design of an economic evaluation requires good-quality data on patient outcomes, the costs of an intervention, and its comparators. Investigators are frequently limited in the quantity and quality of data obtained from a clinical study, which does not allow an adequate assessment of the economic effect of a healthcare intervention. This has given rise to mathematical modeling methods that combine multiple sources of data in order to assess economic end points that may not be available from a single clinical study and that might occur beyond the time horizon of the original data source. This overview of modeling methods offers an introduction to the various types of decision-analytic model commonly used to support economic evaluations in healthcare and outlines the essential elements of a model, such as nodes, states, time horizon, and cycle duration. This section includes a comment on appropriate methods used for sourcing information to populate model parameters and offers a guide for reporting economic analysis results obtained using both trial-based and modeling methods, including appropriate methods for reporting point estimates and uncertainty.

A decision-analytic model combines information on the likelihood of each consequence with the values of outcomes to estimate the expected value of each alternative option. The likelihood of occurrence of each event built into the model is determined by probabilities, which are derived either from primary data collected as part of a clinical study or secondary data obtained from external sources, including previous epidemiological studies, systematic reviews, or meta-analyses. The values of consequences are evaluated in a way similar to CEA (see Chap. 5) or CUA (see Chap. 6), and they typically include the total cost per participant accumulated over the model horizon and a measure of outcome, such as QALYs, life years gained, or a clinical outcome.

One important function of decision-analytic models is the possibility of incorporating the uncertainty of consequences over a defined time horizon. Decision-making in healthcare inevitably has to deal with uncertainty around the likelihood of the success or failure of interventions, as well as variability around the impact of the chosen intervention on the cost of treatment and patient outcomes. This chapter discusses two types of uncertainty: one that deals with the variation of costs and outcomes among individuals, known as first-order or stochastic uncertainty, and variation of the expected value of an outcome among multiple trials or samples, which is known as second-order uncertainty. An appropriately designed decision-analytic model needs to characterize both types of uncertainty. The issue of uncertainty within decision-analytic modeling in healthcare is explored in more depth in Sect. 7.3.7.

Decision-analytic models are often used by healthcare authorities to provide evidence on whether to reimburse for new health technologies [38]. In the context of healthcare in the United Kingdom, the National Institute for Health and Care Excellence requires that appraisal for candidate technologies for reimbursement by the National Health Service (NHS) involve an explicitly defined decision problem, a synthesis of the evidence, and characterization of uncertainty around economic end points using a probabilistic analysis. Therefore, all three of these aspects are vital for a model-based analysis, which aims to inform a health technology assessment (HTA).

This section offers an overview of the modeling designs most frequently used in economic evaluation, rather than an exhaustive list of all types of model used, of which there is a large number within a rapidly growing field. This text is designed as an introduction to the key concepts in modeling and the principal decisions involved in the design of a model, with reference to advanced texts for a more in-depth exploration of the subject. Definitions of the concepts addressed in this chapter can be found in Box 7.9.

Modeling is applicable to decision problems in the context of mental health. This section uses an example of a model-based economic evaluation of a mental health intervention from the empirical literature to illustrate the main issues in the design, conduct, and interpretation of decision-analytic models for the purpose of economic evaluation.

Box 7.9 Definition of Key Terms Used in Decision-Analytic Modeling

- *Decision tree*: A graphical method of representing every consequence of a decision using branches and nodes
- *Node*: An element of a decision-tree model corresponding to a change in the pathway, such as a decision, stochastic event, or end of the pathway
- *Transition probability*: Probability of an individual patient progressing to a particular pathway or state in a model
- *Time horizon*: The time interval over which the consequences of treatment are evaluated
- *State transition model* (*STM*): A model that represents a decision problem in terms of a set of discrete health states and transition probabilities between health states
- *Markov model*: An STM that assumes that the probability of progression for an individual is explanatory of past health states
- *Microsimulation*: An STM that simulates the progression of individuals, rather than the entire cohort, at predetermined time intervals
- *Discrete event simulation*: A decision-analytic model that simulates the time to progression to one of a discrete set of events
- *Expected value of information analysis*: An approach for quantifying the expected monetary value of reducing uncertainty around a decision problem by obtaining additional or better-quality information through research

7.3.2 Designing a Model: Conceptualizing and Illustrating the Decision Problem

7.3.2.1 Defining the Relevant Decision Problem, Population, Setting, and Comparators

Designing a decision-analytic model requires a number of necessary steps. Examine each of these is examined here in the context of a study by Stevenson and colleagues from the University of Sheffield (in the United Kingdom), who aimed to estimate the cost-effectiveness of group cognitive behavioral therapy (CBT) in the treatment of postnatal depression (PND; also called postpartum depression) as an example of a model-based

Box 7.10 Example Study: Cost-Effectiveness of Group CBT for PND: Stevenson et al. [39]

Background: The authors aimed to evaluate the cost-effectiveness of group CBT compared with usual care in women with PND up to 1 year after birth.

Methods: A modeling analysis simulated the comparative effect of CBT compared with usual care for improving symptoms of PND and utility, which were estimated by mapping the Edinburgh Postnatal Depression Scale (EPDS) to a preference-based outcome measure (the six-dimension Short Form [SF-6D]). An incremental CEA was conducted by estimating the mean difference in the cost of delivery of group CBT and usual care per QALY gained as a result of the intervention. Model parameters were populated through data synthesis from published studies and expert opinion.

https://www.journalslibrary.nihr.ac.uk/hta/hta14440#/abstract

economic analysis of a mental health intervention [39]. The details of the study are described in Box 7.10.

1. The first step involves formulating a clear research question. It must be set in the form of a decision problem presented to a decision maker with a limited set of options. In our example, the authors used a decision-analytic model to examine whether group CBT is a cost-effective treatment option in women with PND.
2. The next step involves identifying relevant treatments to be included as comparators in order to place the proposed treatment in the context of existing modes of care offered to patients. Current practice for PND was identified as individual CBT and usual primary care. The authors thus compared group CBT with these two alterative options.
3. The authors specified that the cost-effectiveness analysis (CEA) included all healthcare settings and the model population included women with a diagnosis of PND or who had been identified as being at high risk of developing PND.
4. After defining the question and the relevant options, the investigators stated which end points were used to evaluate each option. The study used QALYs as a measure of utility-weighted health gain to compare the intervention with the control treatments over a 1-year time horizon.

Before proceeding with the model design and analysis, the authors explicitly stated the alternatives to the intervention currently available to the decision maker, the end points used to evaluate the proposed intervention against these alternatives, the setting in which it is planned for delivery, and the target population.

In the context of healthcare decision-making, economic evaluation typically includes measures of cost and treatment outcome. Economic analyses commonly include those measures of cost and outcome which are strategically relevant to the party in charge of funding the proposed intervention in the context of a healthcare system (such as an insurance company or state).

7.3.2.2 Model Time Horizons and Cycles

The time scale across which treatment consequences are evaluated influences model design decisions. Models that evaluate the impact of an intervention over the time horizon of a clinical trial with limited follow-up may involve a relatively simple design, with most evidence sourced from primary data for costs and outcomes. However, modeling is more commonly used to evaluate the economic consequences of an intervention beyond the follow-up period of the original clinical study. A major advantage of modeling is that it may be used to synthesize evidence on treatment efficacy, cost, and patient outcomes from multiple secondary sources.

In our example evaluation of group CBT in women with PND, different data sources may be used to populate each component of the model. For instance, the efficacy of PND relative to the two comparison treatments may be estimated from the results of a systematic review of published studies. The short-term effect in terms of QALYs gained as a result of each treatment may be sourced using self-reported outcomes collected from patients with PND. The impact of treatment on QALYs generated later in life can be extrapolated by combining data collection during the follow-up period of the clinical study with knowledge of the progression of disease obtained from the published literature, then applying QALY weights using an AUC approach (the AUC method is described in Sect. 7.2.8.1. In certain cases a modeler may wish to incorporate the impact of treatment on the probability of events occurring in the future after treatment, including recurrence, complications, and death. This likely requires a considerably more complex design, with a longer pathway and a larger number of branches. A more complex design would often be required to adequately model such a scenario, such as ones featuring Markov chain processes or individual-level simulation. These model types are defined and examined in Sect. 7.3.4.

Similarly, the timing of disease progression is a key consideration for model design. The rate at which patients move through a model nodes needs to reflect the amount of time that typically elapses between the different stages of the disease or therapy represented in the model.

7.3.3 Decision-Tree Model: A Basic Model Structure

The structure of the model reflects both the nature of the decision problem and the natural history of the disease or other process in question. In our example in Sect. 7.3.2.1, the model would involve the typical therapeutic pathway for PND and would include the possible future consequences and subsequent treatment involved under different scenarios. Evaluating the decision problem involves breaking it down into components. First, split the model into separate mutually exclusive pathways corresponding to each option: group CBT, individual CBT, and usual primary care. The initial part of the model contains information on the estimated efficacy of each treatment and the cost of delivery. This is followed by the short-term consequences of each treatment option: in our example this involves estimated improvement in quality of life based on the EPDS score determined 6 months after treatment. Some decision problems require the evaluation of long-term outcomes, which would require additional model components to reflect the effect of alternative treatments on life expectancy and QALY gain over a lifetime time horizon. The structure of the model and the elements included should reflect the research question and the nature of the disease or therapeutic process under investigation.

A basic way of breaking down a decision problem into its component parts is to represent it using a decision tree, which is a visual representation of the available options and the consequences corresponding to each choice. A decision-tree diagram includes all transitions occurring in the model and nodes representing decisions and chance events. Figure 7.6 presents an example of a decision-tree diagram for the problem outlined in Sect. 7.3.2.1, and Fig. 7.7 defines each node used in the diagram. A standard way of illustrating nodes in a decision tree is from left to right, reflecting the logical sequence of decisions and events that are expected to feature in the pathway.

A decision-tree model contains various elements. The initial decision node in Fig. 7.6 represents the choices for treatment of women with PND presented to the decision maker. From this initial decision node, several branches lead to circular symbols, which represent chance nodes corresponding to the three therapy options: group CBT, individual CBT, and standard primary care.

Chance nodes indicate points in the model at which two or more possible paths of progression exist, and movement of a patient through a node is governed by transition probabilities. In our example, chance nodes represent the probability of success or failure of a therapy and each consequence from these therapy outcomes in terms of disease progression. Each chance node must contain at least two subsequent paths of progression,

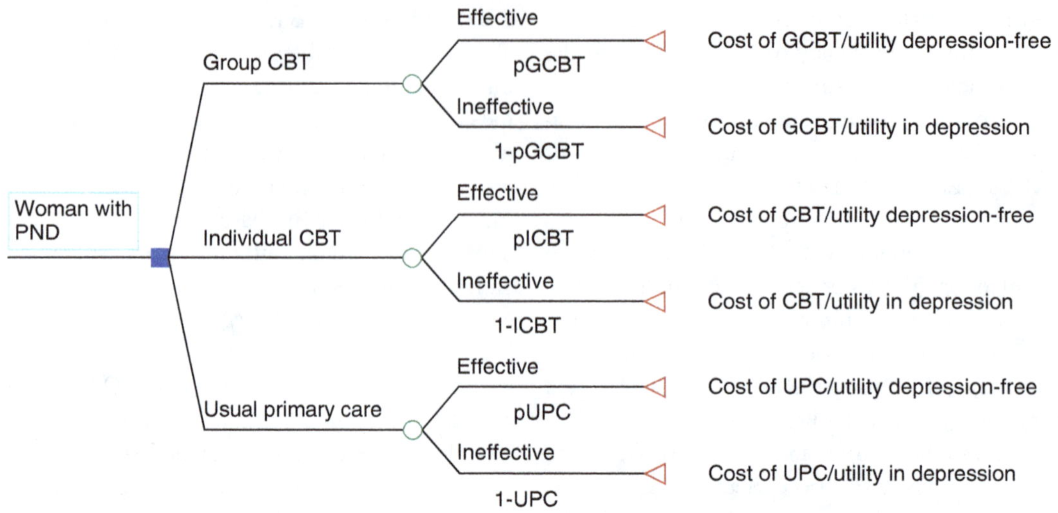

Fig. 7.6 Simple decision-tree model

and transition probabilities of each consequence necessarily sum to 1 (100%); this is known as probability coherence. The consequences that follow the decision and the initial response to therapy are entirely response on the nature of the disease being modeled and the aims of the analysis. The model may end at this point if the investigator aims to examine only the proportion of patients responding to each treatment. However, health economists are typically interested in final patient end points, such as cost and QALY gain per patient, rather than process outcomes such as dose response or clinical markers. Therefore, pathways represented in health economic models tend to include all events up to the final patient outcome for a defined time horizon. The final nodes in the model, known as terminal nodes, represent the point at which the expected values of consequences of each treatment option are evaluated.

Figure 7.6 represents the decision-tree structure for the model by Stevenson et al. [39] used as the example in this section. The chance nodes, which follow the square decision node on the far left, each include two options: the treatment is either effective or ineffective. The progression of patients through the pathway is governed by the transition probabilities corresponding to the treatment effect of each option: *pGCBT* for group CBT, *pICBT* for individual CBT, and *pUPC* for usual primary care. The values of end points are ascertained at the terminal nodes represented on the right side of the diagram.

Figure 7.7 represents the definitions of the different node types used in a decision-tree model.

7.3.4 More Complex Model Designs

7.3.4.1 State Transition Models

In certain cases, the consequences of therapy may be conceptualized in terms of discrete health states. For instance, in our example evaluation of group CBT described in Sect. 7.3.2.1, treatment may result in one of three outcomes: recovery (no depression), no change (depression), and death. Each of these outcomes has consequences in terms of healthcare services use and individual utility in the future. A state transition model (STM) can be used to represent a decision problem in terms of mutually exclusive discrete health states that form part of a known disease or treatment pathway [40]. The movement of individuals through the cohort is determined by the likelihood of each outcome (transition probabilities), and the consequences of the model are determined by state values (costs and outcomes associated with each health state). The disease or treatment pathway incorporates the natural history of the disease and the effect(s) of treatment.

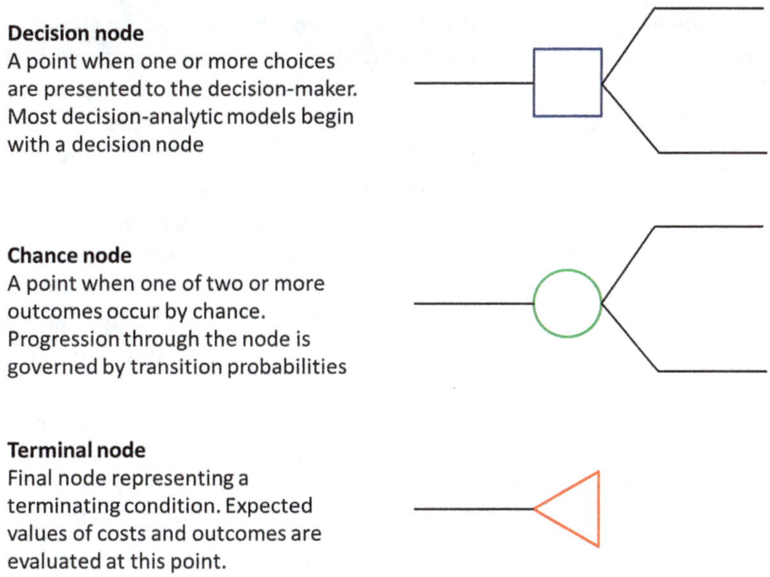

Fig. 7.7 Definitions of nodes used in a decision-tree diagram

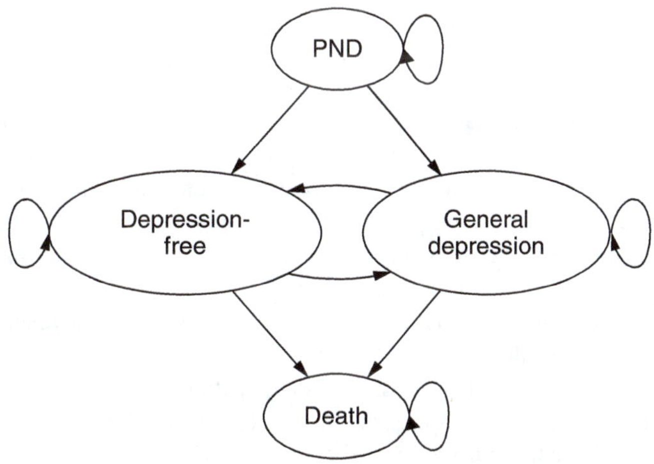

Fig. 7.8 Example of a state transition model

STMs are useful when an investigator wishes to reflect the timing of events or repeated events in a model. For instance, the amount of time spent in a depressed state as a result of PND varies from patient to patient. Some patients may remain depressed for the remainder of their lives, whereas others may become depressed for a second time following recovery from PND. These features may be incorporated into a classic decision tree using nodes. However, incorporating multidirectional movement and timing of events results in an exponential growth of the number of nodes in a model, increasing the likelihood of error in its design. An STM may be a more appropriate option for more complex decision problems, such as the one illustrated in Fig. 7.8. All patients start in the PND state. Treatment results in one of three outcomes: remain in PND, recovery (move to a depression-free state), and deterioration (move to a general depression state). In future life years, patients may transition back and forth between depression-free and general depression states until death, when they move to the absorbing state "Dead."

STMs have structural similarities to decision-tree models and may be conceptualized using a Markov tree. The model starts with a decision node representing the alternative options in the decision problem, with branches leading to multiple Markov nodes, which represent the modeled health states. Three types of STMs are described below: cohort simulation models, Markov models, and microsimulations.

7.3.4.1.1 Cohort Simulation Model

The most basic type of STM is a cohort simulation model, which involves the progression of an entire cohort through the model pathway at the end of each cycle. An STM is a way of representing a continuous process, such as disease progression, in discrete terms whereby individual health states correspond to stages of disease and the corresponding costs of treatment. Once the model has reached a terminating condition set within the model (maximum number of cycles elapsed, all patients reaching the absorbing state, or other, depending on the objectives of the analysis), the costs and outcomes are summed for each patient in order to estimate the mean cost and outcome per patient for the purpose of a cost-effectiveness, cost-utility, or cost-benefit analysis.

In a cohort simulation design, the consequences of decisions are modeled as transitions between health states, rather than as a sequence of chance nodes. This design allows patients to remain in a particular state for a longer time period or to return to an earlier part of the pathway and experience an event more than once. A cohort simulation model design is appropriate if the timing of events is consistent, in which case the decision problem can be modeled as a sequence of cycles with equal durations. The chosen cycle duration necessarily needs to reflect the natural history of the modeled disease process.

Markov Cohort Models

Cohort simulation models are commonly referred to as Markov models if they assume the Markovian condition, which stipulates that the progression of an individual from each state is explanatory of the individual's history. As a result, Markov models are often referred to as "memory-less" models, in the sense that they do not retain information about events that previously occurred within the model. This may be a limitation for certain applications, as patient outcomes are often response on past events. This is particularly relevant in a situation where the probability of an event is a condition of its occurrence in the past, such as the probability of a repeat stroke or myocardial infarction. Memory can be built into cohort models by creating additional health states, which may result in excessive complexity if the initial model is large.

Patients in a Markov model accumulate costs and outcomes according to the number of cycles spent in each health state within the model. The aggregate cost and outcome for each individual patient in the model is estimated once they reach a final state from which no transitions may occur, which is known as an absorbing state, or the model time horizon is reached. The most commonly used absorbing state in health economic Markov models is "dead."

However, cohort simulation models do not take into account heterogeneity among patients. They make the assumption that all patients in the same state have an equal probability of progressing from the state, which allows the entire cohort to be simulated at once.

Microsimulation

Individual-level simulation, also known as microsimulation, is an extension of the basic cohort simulation design. It involves simulating the progress of each patient, rather than the entire cohort, through the pathway. It is less restrictive than cohort simulation design in that it acquires memory on past events by updating patient characteristics and reflects patient heterogeneity by sampling baseline patient characteristics from random distributions, which affects the progression of a patient through the model. Individual-level simulation is computationally intensive, requiring a considerably longer amount of time to reach stable estimates of the means and SEs of the cost and outcome.

7.3.4.2 Design of State Transition Models

Designing an STM involves a set of decisions similar to those in a decision-tree model.

An STM is only applicable if the disease pathway can be conceptualized in the form of individual health states reflecting the natural history of the disease and the expected treatment processes.

Similar to decision-tree models, in STMs probability parameters may be populated from data collected as part of a previous clinical study, a literature review, or expert opinion. In the presence of collected data on the timing of events, it may be possible to derive transition probabilities from hazard functions estimated using parametric time-to-event models, as described by Briggs et al. [41]. The effects of the intervention treatment, such as risk ratios, odds ratios, and hazard ratios for specific outcomes from clinical studies, may be incorporated into the model by modifying the transition probabilities for the corresponding health states in the intervention pathway. In addition, the treatment effect may be reflected by changes in outcomes attached to health states. Similarly, cost and utility effects for each comparator may be incorporated using state cost values using self-reported methods (e.g., the EQ-5D and resource use questionnaires) or the literature. Given that most clinical studies collecting self-reported outcomes have a limited follow-up duration, investigators need to consider carefully how cost and utility effects may evolve beyond the time horizon of the original study.

7.3.4.3 Discrete Event Simulation

A different type of individual-level simulation known as discrete event simulation (DES) models the progression of patients through a pathway using the amount of time spent in a particular state, rather than probabilities of progression. A DES samples the "length of stay" for each individual in any particular state as a function of the characteristics of that particular individual. Just as in a standard microsimulation, DES builds previous events into a memory that affects future progression. Thus a DES may be used to build both heterogeneity (progression response on patient characteristics) and memory into a model. For a more comprehensive overview of DES models, refer to Karnon et al. [42].

7.3.5 Methods to Measure Consequences

Each consequence of a modeled decision has a corresponding end point, depending on the research question. One of the end points in a health economic model typically reflects the resource use or the cost of the initial treatment and its consequences. The other end point typically measures the outcome of treatment. This may be an intermediate outcome, such as days of illness avoided or improvement in symptoms. The expected value of each endpoint is calculated for each pathway to compare the consequences of each alternative. These end points are then used for the purpose of an economic evaluation, such as CUA or cost-benefit analysis. Well-designed models should incorporate features that allow each option to be placed in the context of the budget constraint or WTP threshold relevant to the healthcare system in question.

Public bodies that issue guidance based on evidence from economic evaluations assign greater importance to final patient outcomes, such as QALYs gained (see also Chap. 6), compared with intermediate or surrogate clinical outcomes. However, preference-based scores that are used to compute QALYs may not always be available. In this case mapping, which is a method of converting a condition-specific clinical measure into a preference-based one, may be used to derive QALY estimates using a clinical outcome (see Sect. 7.2.8.4 for a description of mapping).

This was the approach taken by Stevenson et al. [39] in our example. PND affects health and quality of life only in the first 12 months following birth, after which any cases are reclassified as general depression and would thus be beyond the scope of PND care. To handle this issue, the authors decided to use an under-the-curve approach to estimate the incremental QALY gains of the intervention, rather than a standard approach that would assume proportional QALY gains in patients with and without the disease. Data on the improvement of PND symptoms at 6 months were used to estimate the incremental gain in utility, which linearly approached zero 12 months after treatment initiation.

In some cases it may not be possible to map a non-preference-based measure to one that is determined by patient preferences for use in an economic evaluation because of an absence of prior studies that collected both outcome measures simultaneously. In this case, an investigator may opt to use a clinical or surrogate outcome as the denominator in the ICER. This is a common approach in evaluations of mental health interventions because of uncertainty in the effect of mental health conditions of patient quality of life. For instance, Peveler et al. [43], in an RCT of tricyclic antidepressants, selective serotonin reuptake inhibitors, and lofepramine for the treatment of depression in primary care, used depression-free weeks as the outcome of choice in their economic evaluation, which was justified by the fact that the effect of depression on patient utility was unknown. The end point of the economic evaluation was thus the mean cost per depression-free week gained. The authors used CEA, rather than CUA (see Chaps. 5 and 6).

7.3.6 Sourcing Values for Model Parameters

In Sect. 7.3.1, we noted that modeling is applicable in situations when data from multiple sources need to be combined in order to conduct an economic evaluation. Lack of data on the costs and outcomes of treatments is a frequent issue in under-researched areas of healthcare, which nonetheless require economic evaluations to inform decisions about resource allocation. Health economists frequently work with patient-level study data, which have a short follow-up (i.e., <1 year) or missing cost and outcome variables, which are required to carry out an economic evaluation. One of the solutions in this case is to complement study data with information from external published sources, which may include previously published peer-reviewed articles or HTA reports. In the absence of estimates from published sources that are representative of the study population, expert opinion may be sought to form a more complete picture of the economic impact of an intervention.

In our example outlined in Sect. 7.3.2.1, the authors found little evidence on the clinical and economic effectiveness of CBT for the treatment of PND. They constructed a model that used estimates of clinical effectiveness from an RCT. The chosen outcome measure for the analysis was the number of QALYs gained. However, as the RCT used as the primary source of effectiveness data used a condition-specific measure (EPDS), the authors had to find a way to estimate a utility score. This was done by mapping the EPDS (a condition-specific measure) to the SF-6D (a preference-based measure; the measure is described in Chap. 6) using data from another RCT that collected data for both measures. A regression model with Monte Carlo simulation was used to estimate the relationship between the EPDS and SF-6D scores among study patients and construct a CI for incremental utility gain. Finally, the authors estimated the cost of delivering the intervention and comparators by combining resource use assumptions made in previously published studies with those obtained from expert opinion.

Our example illustrates how decision-analytic modeling may be used to combine information from published sources to inform an economic evaluation. A similar approach is appropriate when populating parameters for other types of models, including STMs and DESs. More complex designs incorporate a large number of components, which determine the probability of transition and how cost and outcomes are accumulated over a model's pathways. Such models frequently combine data from many primary and secondary sources.

It is important for investigators to have a consistent search strategy in order to obtain literature-based estimates for a model. Modelers may begin by conducting a search of large databases of the medical literature, such as MEDLINE and EMBASE, using terms from the Medical Subject Headings terminology. Systematic reviews may be searched using the Cochrane Library. These databases contain both clinical and health economic studies. For a more targeted search of previously published economic evaluations, one may additionally search the NHS Economic

Evaluation Database or HTA reports, which are all available from the Centre for Reviews and Dissemination at the University of York [44]. As in any review of scientific evidence, investigators must consider studies in the context of the hierarchy of evidence. Priority should be given to meta-analyses and systematic reviews of RCTs, followed by individual RCTs, which are generally considered to have better internal validity than other study designs. In the absence of evidence from these types of studies, a model may incorporate the results from other types of studies, including observational and case-control studies with adequate control for nonrandom treatment assignment, followed by cross-sectional studies and case series.

Modelers may sometimes make use of databases that specifically focus on the measurement of health economic end points. These include the Health Utility Database developed by the School of Health and Related Research at the University of Sheffield [45], which holds a library of studies reporting health state utility values for economic evaluations. Another example is the Database of Instruments for Resource Use Measurement [46], developed by Bangor University in collaboration with institutions in the United Kingdom; this database contains a comprehensive list of resource use questionnaires (see Chap. 13) for use in economic evaluations, with links to specific studies that have used these instruments in practice.

The choice of data source to inform cost parameters in a model depends on the cost perspective and healthcare setting in which the proposed intervention has been set. This aspect of a search for evidence is country-specific and often depends on the availability of cost estimates specific to the healthcare system in question. In the context of economic evaluation in England, investigators often use published sources of unit costs to derive cost parameters, which are subsequently attached to resource use items. These include the NHS Reference Costs (Department of Health) [47], which provides unit costs for hospital inpatient and outpatient care in a dictionary of unit costs for primary, specialized, and social care issued by the Personal Social Services Research Unit [48]. The British National Formulary [49] is used to obtain unit costs of medications. Alternatives to these data sources include unit costs obtained from previously published studies and reimbursement costs for packages of care or equipment obtained directly from the finance department of a clinic or hospital.

One of the aims of a modeling analysis is to characterize uncertainty around the consequences of each option in a decision problem. To this end, a modeler needs to obtain estimates of the dispersion, as well as point estimates for the value of model parameters. One must therefore pay attention to CIs or SEs reported in studies. This applies to all parameters, including clinical effectiveness (95% CIs for risk, odds, and hazard ratios), cost and utility estimates (a range of 95% CIs). Where applicable, investigators should derive distribution parameters for variables, if such information is available – for example, from a previously conducted probabilistic sensitivity analysis. Accurate estimates of dispersion and parametric assumptions that may be reused in the model may save considerable time for the modeler, who may then focus their effort on other parts of the model.

7.3.7 Characterizing Uncertainty

7.3.7.1 Introduction to Uncertainty in Economic Evaluation

Economic modeling involves the estimation of the consequences of a healthcare intervention, which are often uncertain. Several factors may contribute to this uncertainty: the treatment effect of the intervention compared with the control, resource use during the model time horizon, and individual utility scores in response to treatment. In addition, the mean values of parameters estimated empirically are likely to vary from sample to sample.

A model that simulates a disease process with the aim of informing a healthcare decision needs to examine how uncertainty in the values of inputs translate into uncertainty around its outputs and the decision in question. Addressing uncertainty in decision analysis is of importance to healthcare policymakers for three reasons. First, resource allocation decisions should be based on the expected values of model outputs, rather than model inputs. It is thus necessary to obtain the distribution of an output by making distributional assumptions regarding model inputs, particularly in the presence of nonlinear relationships (which is the case with cohort simulation or more complex models) [50]. Second, it is of interest to decision makers in a publically funded healthcare system to know the probability of making a suboptimal decision, as reversing it may entail significant costs. Third, identifying which parameters contribute most to decision uncertainty is useful for highlighting areas for further research.

When considering uncertainty in the context of decision-analytic modeling, a distinction must be made between the different types of uncertainty that need to be considered. These include variability (first-order uncertainty), parametric (second-order uncertainty), and structural uncertainty [51]. The key terms used to describe uncertainty in decision-analytic models are defined in Box 7.11.

Box 7.11 Definitions of Key Terms Used to Describe Uncertainty in Decision-Analytic Models

- *First-order uncertainty*: Random variability around a parameter value among individuals in a data sample
- *Second-order uncertainty*: Variability around the mean value among data samples
- *Heterogeneity*: Variability around a parameter value attributed to the characteristics of individuals
- *Structural uncertainty*: Uncertainty in model results attributable to the structure and assumptions of the model
- *Deterministic sensitivity analysis*: An uncertainty analysis designed to measure the effect of varying the values of individual parameters over a preassigned range of model outputs
- *Monte Carlo error*: Variability around output values between simulated samples generated using DES
- *Probabilistic sensitivity analysis (PSA)*: An uncertainty analysis that measures the aggregate impact on model output of varying the values in all model parameters simultaneously by assigning probability distributions to each model parameter
- *Incremental cost-effectiveness plane*: A plot of mean incremental cost (x-axis) and mean incremental outcome (y-axis) of an intervention versus control treatment generated using a PSA
- *Willingness-to-pay*: The maximum amount a third-party funder is willing to invest per unit of outcome, typically per QALY gained
- *Cost-effectiveness acceptability curve*: A plot of the probability of the cost-effectiveness of one or more interventions (based on the results of a PSA) as a function of the ceiling WTP per unit of outcome set by the decision maker

7.3.7.2 First- and Second-Order Uncertainty

At the most basic level, values of inputs vary from patient to patient, which is known as variability, or first-order uncertainty. The level of resource use over a model's time horizon or the number of adverse effects from therapy will vary among individuals by chance. These differences may be driven by patient factors (heterogeneity) or random variation. *Heterogeneity* refers to systematic variability in outcomes between individuals that may be explained by characteristics such as age, sex, or the presence of known risk factors. The design of the studies used as sources of patient data play an important role in limiting the confounding effects of patient or other characteristics on the model outputs. If the distribution of patient characteristics is assumed to be no different among comparison groups, any interpatient variation may be attributed to first-order uncertainty.

Second-order, or parametric, uncertainty characterizes the variation in the mean value of a parameter, which is analogous to the SE of a coefficient estimate in a linear regression model.

7.3.7.3 Structural Uncertainty

In the context of decision-analytic modeling, *structural uncertainty* refers to the aggregate impact of the chosen design and parametric assumptions in a model on the values of its outputs. The choice of a particular design to model the consequences of a healthcare intervention invariably affects the results of the analysis as a result of the impacts of individual design features and constraints imposed by the modeler. For instance, a Markov model with a fixed cycle duration will produce results different from those of a DES, as the Markov model estimates the distribution of patients in a cohort across a discrete set of health states, rather than amount of time individual patients take to progress through a pathway. Although it is not explicitly quantified as part of an assessment of uncertainty in a decision-analytic model, investigators need to consider the impact of structural assumptions on the internal validity of a study.

7.3.7.4 Addressing Different Types of Uncertainty in Economic Models

An important role of a modeling exercise is to derive the distribution of the outcome based on defined distributions of input parameters. As such, uncertainty surrounding parameter values is generally of more interest to modelers that is variability among individuals. First-order uncertainty is a major issue in models that simulate individual patients, such as microsimulations and DESs. In the case of these models, differences in outcomes among individuals who pass through the model are likely to influence the final model outcome, which is known as Monte Carlo error. The standard approach for minimizing error in individual-level models is to carry out a large number of Monte Carlo simulations until expected values and SEs become stable. This approach is computationally intensive and may be require additional computer processing power to execute.

Analysis of point estimates derived from a modeling analysis should ideally be accompanied by an adequate analysis of uncertainty. This allows a modeler to test the robustness of the model output against changes in its inputs and assumptions. A deterministic sensitivity analysis can identify the key areas of uncertainty within a model by estimating the model's sensitivity to a change in one or more input parameters. Before running a deterministic sensitivity analysis, the modeler needs to set a defensible range around the point estimate from observed data (a 95% CI based on the SE) or prior knowledge regarding the variability of the point estimate based on expert opinion.

The effect of parametric uncertainty in a model may be assessed using a PSA. This involves estimation of the uncertainty around expected values of the model end points through repeated sampling of parameter values from probability distributions assumed a priori.

Structural uncertainty cannot be examined as part of a formal uncertainty analysis of a model because of an absence of standard methods of measuring the effects of structural assumptions on model output. Appropriate handling of structural uncertainty involves taking a number of steps to improve model credibility: (a) ensuring the transparency of the model design by allowing access to technical documentation such as model diagrams, structural equations, and parameter values while ensuring that the model assumptions are described in language that is accessible to readers who may have less technical training than the modeler; (b) providing sufficient information to allow the replication of the model results by a third party; and (c) validation of the model results by comparing those results with data obtained from an alternate source.

7.3.7.5 Reporting Uncertainty in a Model

Correct and transparent presentation of uncertainty is an important part of good modeling practice. Typically, a CEA presents the value of an intervention relative to alternative treatments in the form of ICERs, which represent the additional cost incurred per additional unit of outcome gained (e.g., life year or QALY). Other analyses may present the costs and outcomes in a disaggregated format (cost-consequence analysis) or examine the net benefit of an intervention

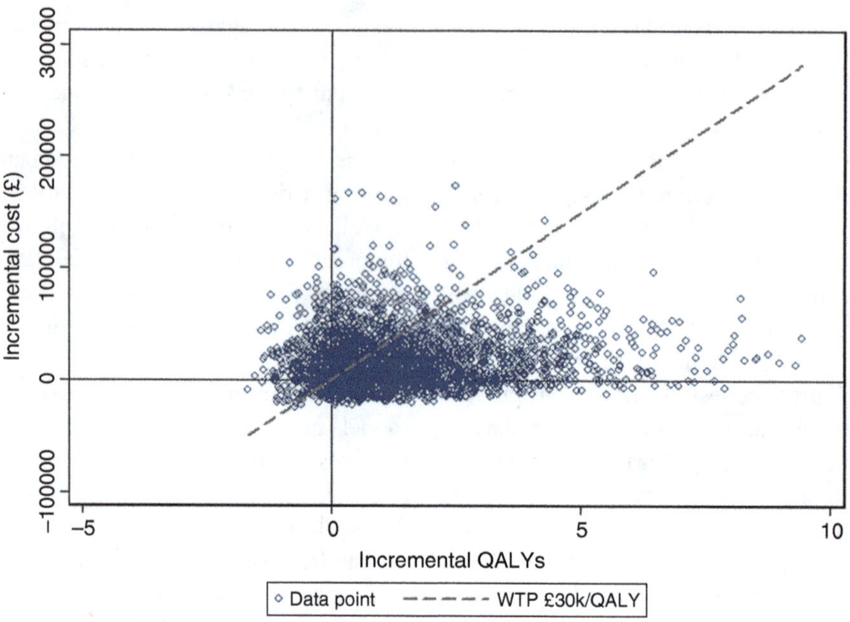

Fig. 7.9 Probability sensitivity analysis results represented on a cost-effectiveness plane

by evaluating both costs and outcomes in monetary terms (cost-benefit analysis; see Chap. 4). In each case the modeler needs to ensure that uncertainty around each end point included in the results is adequately described. Specifically, the base case results of a CEA should include the expected value of the ICER and a CI between two extreme points (typically 2.5% and 97.5%) of the distribution of the ICER obtained from a PSA. Frequently, decisions based on the results of a PSA are supported using a graphical distribution of the ICER mapped on a cost-effectiveness plane. This involves plotting each observation from a PSA on a graph, with incremental costs of the intervention represented along the *y*-axis and incremental outcomes along the *x*-axis (see the example in Fig. 7.9). The four corners of the plot, known as quartiles, represent different cost-effectiveness scenarios. Points falling in the northeast and southwest quadrants on a plot have both positive incremental costs and outcomes and both negative incremental costs and outcomes, respectively, resulting in a positive ICER. The northwest and southeast quadrants involve scenarios where either the numerator or denominator of the ICER is negative. The cost-effectiveness plane is particularly useful to interpret where both *x*-axis and *y*-axis values produce a negative ICER, which may signify that an intervention is dominant (a negative incremental cost and a positive outcome) or dominated (a positive incremental cost and a negative outcome). It is difficult to distinguish which of these is the case based on the ICER alone.

The aggregate effect of uncertainty around the values of outputs of an economic evaluation can be estimated using a PSA, the exact form of which depends on the type of analysis being carried out. In a CEA or CUA, where data on both the costs and effects of treatment are collected from patients, nonparametric bootstrapping can be carried out to replicate a large number of samples of incremental costs and effects based on the distribution of the observed data. This allows the investigator to construct a distribution and 95% CI of the ICER without the need for distributional assumptions. In the case of an economic evaluation based on a decision-analytic model, values of inputs are drawn repeatedly from prior distributions and fed into the model, producing an implicit distribution of the ICER. In both cases, the results can be presented graphically

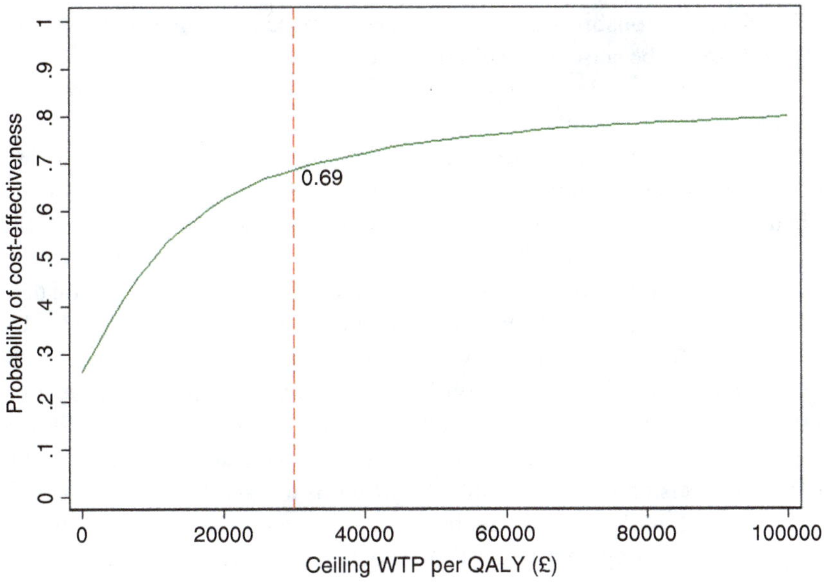

Fig. 7.10 Cost-effectiveness acceptability curve

using an incremental cost-effectiveness plane, as shown in Fig. 7.9. The distribution of points in the cost-effectiveness plan can be used to gauge the probability of the optimality of each alternative option among a range of ceiling WTP values using a CEAC, as shown in Fig. 7.10.

Figure 7.9 graphically represents incremental cost and outcome points generated by a PSA of a hypothetical CEA. Most points lie in the north-east quadrant, meaning that the decision about whether the intervention is cost-effective is response on the WTP per unit of outcome by the third-party funder. Some of the points lie in the other three quadrants, which means there is a probability that the intervention could both save costs and be more effective (dominant), or be more costly and less effective (dominated), compared with standard care. The ceiling WTP threshold is represented by the slope of the dashed line in Fig. 7.9. An increase in the slope (and the amount of money the decision maker is willing to invest per QALY) results in a larger proportion of points falling below the line, which corresponds to a larger probability that the true value of the cost per QALY falls below the WTP threshold. The relationship between the slope of the WTP threshold and the probability of cost-effectiveness can be estimated directly from the cost-effectiveness plane by changing the slope of the line across a predefined range. Figure 7.10 illustrates a CEAC of the probability of cost-effectiveness of the intervention derived from Fig. 7.9 across a range of WTP values per QALY (£0–100,000). The probability that the intervention is deemed to be cost-effective at a particular WTP value can be read directly from the CEAC. For instance, if the decision maker is willing to allocate a maximum of £30,000 per additional QALY gained, the intervention has a 69% probability of being cost-effective. The larger this probability, the more confidence a decision maker will have of making a correct choice to allocate scarce healthcare resources, and the higher the chance of the new intervention being adopted.

7.3.8 Expected Value of Information

The purpose of economic evaluation is to inform decisions regarding resource allocation toward new healthcare interventions. A decision model provides an estimate of the economic end points under evaluation based on currently available information. Inevitably, a probability of making an incorrect decision exists because of the different types of uncertainty in a model, which were described in Sect. 7.3.7; this is known as "decision uncertainty." Incorrect allocative decisions represent an opportunity cost in terms of foregone health benefits elsewhere in the system. Assessment of decision uncertainty through a PSA creates an opportunity to inform research priorities through analysis of the expected value of information (EVI). EVI analysis allows investigators to quantify the expected gain in terms of reduced uncertainty in a decision resulting from the availability of new information. A decision maker may delay the decision until better information is available, which will reduce the probability of an incorrect decision, given the cost of additional research required to obtain more accurate parameter estimates.

7.4 Reporting Results from Statistical and Modeling Analyses

This chapter provides an overview of introductory methods for statistical and modeling analysis in the context of economic evaluation of healthcare interventions. It describes methods commonly used by health economists when analyzing data collected alongside clinical studies that are aimed at eliciting the explanatory effect(s) of a healthcare intervention on economic end points of interest, such as the cost of treatment or patient utility. In the absence of sufficient data collected alongside a trial to adequately measure these end points, a variety of modeling methods may be used to combine multiple sources of information in order to evaluate the costs and effects of an intervention. The choice of which specific statistical and modeling techniques to use is response on several factors, such as the research question, the type of economic end point(s) considered, the study population, and the time horizon. There is often more than one appropriate way of conducting an economic evaluation. Although the choice of method ultimately lies with the investigator, when reporting the results of an evaluation it is important to state clearly which statistical and/or modeling methods were applied and why.

In Sect. 7.2.6 we described the use of regression analysis to gauge the effects of an intervention on the economic end points in an economic analysis, which allows investigators to control for factors that may influence this relationship. When reporting the results from a regression model, it is important to mention the rationale for using the particular type of regression and to comment on the selection of covariates used within the analysis. It is standard practice to report measures of goodness of fit, such as those described in Sect. 7.2.6.4. The same applies to other statistical methods that may be used as part of an analysis, such as adjusting for bias within SEs from bootstrap-generated data. Any specific methods used to account for missing data must be addressed, including statistical imputation, as these are a potential source of bias. Accurate reporting of the statistical analysis methods along with the results adds transparency to the reported analysis, which allows the reader to judge the quality of the specific methods used and the reliability of the study's conclusions.

A study that requires multiple sources of data or aims to extrapolate the results of an economic evaluation over a longer time horizon may use modeling methods. The starting point in a modeling exercise is to state a clearly defined decision problem; alternative options to be evaluated; and the population, setting, and the time horizon across which the economic end points will be evaluated. The investigator needs to explain how the chosen model design will facilitate a comparison between the alternative strategies. In addition, the choice of outcome and the perspective of analysis need to be stated. The sources of data used to populate model parameters, such as transition probabilities, resource use assumptions, unit costs, and utility weights, need to be stated and referenced in order to allow the quality of underlying data used as a basis for the model to be scrutinized. Methods used to quantify uncertainty in the economic analysis need to be clearly stated, taking into account the different types of uncertainty present in the economic data (explained in Sect. 7.3.7). Ideally, any reported point estimates for the economic end points need to include a measure of spread, such as an SE or a 95% CI, to allow a reader to acknowledge not just the expected cost or outcome, but the range of values across which it could vary.

The consistent application of good practices when conducting and reporting statistical and modeling analyses as part of economic evaluations will improve the quality of evidence on the relative cost-effectiveness of competing health-care interventions, leading to better informed decision-making.

Key Messages

- Statistical analyses carried out as part of economic evaluations deal with different types of data: continuous, categorical, and dichotomous. Economic data are often non-normally distributed, such as right-skewed costs or bounded utility scores.
- Regression models are used to infer relationships between explanatory variables (such as treatment assignment) and a response variable (such as cost or patient outcome), while controlling for other factors that may influence the response variable (e.g., age, sex, health status). Different types of regression models exist: OLS is used when the response variable is continuous, and logistic regression is used when it is categorical/dichotomous. A GLM allows a parametric distribution to be prespecified for the response variable, such as a right-skewed distribution of the mean cost.
- More advanced statistical methods are used in economic evaluation to deal with complex economic data. Examples include nonparametric bootstrapping when it is difficult to fit a parametric distribution to the data, AUC analysis to compute QALYs, baseline adjustments to control for differences among groups in an RCT, and mapping to derive preference-based outcomes in CUA.
- Modeling is used to combine multiple sources of information in an economic evaluation when data collected alongside a single study are insufficient to adequately measure the health economic end points, or when a study aims to extrapolate the results of an economic evaluation beyond the time horizon of the study data collected.
- Several types of decision-analytic model are commonly used for economic evaluation: decision trees, state transitions, Markov chains, microsimulations, and DES. The choice of model depends on the research question, model population, model horizon, cycle duration, and the end points used in the analysis.
- A modeler needs to adequately account for both first- and second-order uncertainty and report model uncertainty using accepted methods, including cost-effectiveness planes and CEACs generated using a PSA.

References

1. Jones AM, Rice N, d'Uva TB, Balia S. Applied health economics. Abingdon: Routledge; 2013.
2. Ades A, Lu G, Claxton K. Expected value of sample information calculations in medical decision modeling. Med Decis Mak. 2004;24(2):207–27.
3. Eckermann S, Willan AR. Expected value of information and decision making in HTA. Health Econ. 2007;16(2):195–209.
4. Al-Janabi H, Peters TJ, Brazier J, Bryan S, Flynn TN, Clemens S, et al. An investigation of the construct validity of the ICECAP-A capability measure. Qual Life Res. 2013;22(7):1831–40.
5. Coast J, Peters TJ, Natarajan L, Sproston K, Flynn T. An assessment of the construct validity of the descriptive system for the ICECAP capability measure for older people. Qual Life Res. 2008;17(7):967–76.
6. Malley JN, Towers A-M, Netten AP, Brazier JE, Forder JE, Flynn T. An assessment of the construct validity of the ASCOT measure of social care-related quality of life with older people. Health Qual Life Outcomes. 2012;10(1):1.

7. Barber J, Thompson S. Multiple regression of cost data: use of generalised linear models. J Health Serv Res Policy. 2004;9(4):197–204.
8. Buntin MB, Zaslavsky AM. Too much ado about two-part models and transformation?: comparing methods of modeling Medicare expenditures. J Health Econ. 2004;23(3):525–42.
9. Moran JL, Solomon PJ, Peisach AR, Martin J. New models for old questions: generalized linear models for cost prediction. J Eval Clin Pract. 2007;13(3):381–9.
10. Akaike H. Information theory and an extension of the maximum likelihood principle. In: Kotz, Samuel, Johnson, Norman L, editors. Breakthroughs in statistics. New York: Springer; 1992. p. 610–24.
11. Schwarz G. Estimating the dimension of a model. Ann Stat. 1978;6(2):461–4.
12. Ramsey JB. Tests for specification errors in classical linear least-squares regression analysis. J R Stat Soc Ser B Methodol. 1969:350–71.
13. Park RE. Estimation with heteroscedastic error terms. Econometrica. 1966;34(4):888.
14. Jarque CM, Bera AK. A test for normality of observations and regression residuals. Int Stat Rev/Revue Internationale de Statistique. 1987;55:163–72.
15. Bozdogan H. Model selection and Akaike's information criterion (AIC): the general theory and its analytical extensions. Psychometrika. 1987;52(3):345–70.
16. Burnham KP, Anderson DR. Multimodel inference understanding AIC and BIC in model selection. Sociol Methods Res. 2004;33(2):261–304.
17. Ciarrochi J, Deane FP, Anderson S. Emotional intelligence moderates the relationship between stress and mental health. Personal Individ Differ. 2002;32(2):197–209.
18. Meltzer H, Bebbington P, Brugha T, Farrell M, Jenkins R. The relationship between personal debt and specific common mental disorders. Eur J Public Health. 2013;23(1):108–13.
19. Miller CJ, Grogan-Kaylor A, Perron BE, Kilbourne AM, Woltmann E, Bauer MS. Collaborative chronic care models for mental health conditions: cumulative meta-analysis and meta-regression to guide future research and implementation. Med Care. 2013;51(10):922.
20. Brazier J, Connell J, Papaioannou D, Mukuria C, Mulhern B, Peasgood T, et al. A systematic review, psychometric analysis and qualitative assessment of generic preference-based measures of health in mental health populations and the estimation of mapping functions from widely used specific measures. Health Technol Assess. 2014;18(34).
21. Lepage R, Billard L. Exploring the limits of bootstrap. New York: John Wiley & Sons; 1992.
22. Efron B. The jackknife, the bootstrap and other resampling plans: society for industrial and applied mathematics (SIAM). Philadelphia: Society for Industrial and Applied Mathematics; 1982.
23. Efron B. Better bootstrap confidence intervals. J Am Stat Assoc. 1987;82(397):171–85.
24. Efron B. Bayesian inference and the parametric bootstrap. Ann Appl Stat. 2012;6(4):1971.
25. Efron B, Tibshirani RJ. An introduction to the bootstrap. Boca Raton: CRC Press; 1994.
26. Briggs AH, Wonderling DE, Mooney CZ. Pulling cost-effectiveness analysis up by its bootstraps: a non-parametric approach to confidence interval estimation. Health Econ. 1997;6(4):327–40.
27. Gomes M, Grieve R, Nixon R, Edmunds W. Statistical methods for cost-effectiveness analyses that use data from cluster randomized trials a systematic review and checklist for critical appraisal. Med Decis Mak. 2012;32(1):209–20.
28. O'Hagan A, Stevens JW. Assessing and comparing costs: how robust are the bootstrap and methods based on asymptotic normality? Health Econ. 2003;12(1):33–49.
29. Hunter RM, Baio G, Butt T, Morris S, Round J, Freemantle N. An educational review of the statistical issues in analysing utility data for cost-utility analysis. PharmacoEconomics. 2015;33(4):355–66.
30. Committee for Medicinal Products for Human Use (CHMP) Guideline on adjustment for baseline covariates. European Medicines Agency. 2013. Available from: http://www.ema.europa.eu/docs/en_GB/document_library/Scientific_guideline/2013/06/WC500144946.pdf. Accessed 4 Oct 2016.
31. van Asselt AD, van Mastrigt GA, Dirksen CD, Arntz A, Severens JL, Kessels AG. How to deal with cost differences at baseline. PharmacoEconomics. 2009;27(6):519–28.
32. Little RJ, Rubin DB. Statistical analysis with missing data. New York: Wiley; 2002.
33. Raghunathan TE, Lepkowski JM, Van Hoewyk J, Solenberger P. A multivariate technique for multiply imputing missing values using a sequence of regression models. Surv Methodol. 2001;27(1):85–96.
34. Landerman LR, Land KC, Pieper CF. An empirical evaluation of the predictive mean matching method for imputing missing values. Sociol Methods Res. 1997;26(1):3–33.
35. White IR, Royston P, Wood AM. Multiple imputation using chained equations: issues and guidance for practice. Stat Med. 2011;30(4):377–99.
36. Longworth L, Rowen D. NICE DSU technical support document 10: the use of mapping methods to estimate health state utility values. Sheffield: Decision Support Unit, ScHARR, University of Sheffield; 2011. p. b4.
37. Dakin H. Review of studies mapping from quality of life or clinical measures to EQ-5D: an online database. Health Qual Life Outcomes. 2013;11(1):1.
38. Claxton K, Sculpher M, Drummond M. A rational framework for decision making by the National Institute for Clinical Excellence (NICE). Lancet. 2002;360(9334):711–5.

39. Stevenson MD, Scope A, Sutcliffe PA, Booth A, Slade P, Parry G, et al. Group cognitive behavioural therapy for postnatal depression: a systematic review of clinical effectiveness, cost-effectiveness and value of information analyses. Health Technol Assess. 2010;14(44):1–107. iii–iv
40. Siebert U, Alagoz O, Bayoumi AM, Jahn B, Owens DK, Cohen DJ, et al. State-transition modeling: a report of the ISPOR-SMDM modeling good research practices task force-3. Med Decis Mak. 2012;32(5):690–700.
41. Briggs A, Campbell H, Clarke P. Parametric survival models and decision models: relating continuous hazards to discrete-time transition probabilities. Glasgow: Health Economists' Study Group; 2004.
42. Karnon J, Stahl J, Brennan A, Caro JJ, Mar J, Moller J. Modeling using discrete event simulation: a report of the ISPOR-SMDM modeling good research practices task force-4. Med Decis Mak. 2012;32(5):701–11.
43. Peveler R, Kendrick T, Buxton M, Longworth L, Baldwin D, Moore M, et al. A randomised controlled trial to compare the cost-effectiveness of tricyclic antidepressants, selective serotonin reuptake inhibitors and lofepramine. Health Technol Assess. 2005;9(16):1–134. iii
44. Centre for Reviews and Dissemination. Available from: http://www.crd.york.ac.uk/CRDWeb/. Accessed 6 Oct 2016.
45. School of Health and Related Research. Health utility database. Available from: http://www.scharrhud.org/. Accessed 06 Oct 2016.
46. Bangor University. Database of instruments for resource use measurement. Available from: http://www.dirum.org/. Accessed 06 Oct 2016.
47. Department of Health. NHS reference costs 2014 to 2015. Available from: https://www.gov.uk/government/publications/nhs-reference-costs-2014-to-2015. Accessed 16 Feb 2016.
48. Personal Social Services Research Unit. Unit costs of health and social care 2015. Available from: http://www.pssru.ac.uk/project-pages/unit-costs/2015/index.php. Accessed 16 Feb 2016.
49. British National Formulary. BNF 70. London: British Medical Association & The Royal Pharmaceutical Society; 2015.
50. Claxton K. Exploring uncertainty in cost-effectiveness analysis. PharmacoEconomics. 2008; 26(9):781–98.
51. Briggs AH, Weinstein MC, Fenwick EA, Karnon J, Sculpher MJ, Paltiel AD, et al. Model parameter estimation and uncertainty analysis: a report of the ISPOR-SMDM modeling good research practices task force working group-6. Med Decis Mak. 2012;32(5):722–32.

Equity and Efficiency

8

Anita Patel

Abstract

There are insufficient resources to meet all health care needs, and some form of prioritization is needed to ensure that these limited resources are used to their best effects. Resource allocation decisions need to account for the goals of a health care system, which can be numerous, diverse, and possibly in conflict with each other. Two such goals, central in many health care systems worldwide, are to provide health care both efficiently and equitably. Efficiency is usually considered in terms of the relationship between resource inputs and outputs, with the aim being to maximize "value" from the given resources. While the acceptability of including efficiency considerations in resource allocation decisions, the methods of doing so, and subsequent successes vary, seeking efficiency is a relatively noncontroversial aim for any health care system. *Equity* refers to the fair allocation of resources and involves subjective and moral judgement. It differs from *equality*, which refers to an objectively equal distribution of inputs or outcomes across a population. Definitions of equity are characterized by variations in underlying principles of access and need. While many governments consider equity alongside efficiency in policymaking, methods for doing so are not as explicit as those for efficiency considerations, and there is a belief that the two criteria of efficiency and equity are not fully compatible.

Key Points Summary

- Definition of *efficiency*
- Technical, productive, allocative efficiency
- Definition of *equity*
- Horizontal and vertical equity
- Efficiency and equity, or equity versus efficiency?

A. Patel (✉)
Barts and The London School of Medicine and Dentistry, Blizard Institute, Centre for Primary Care and Public Health, Queen Mary University of London, Yvonne Carter Building, 58 Turner Street, London E1 2AB, UK
e-mail: anita.patel@qmul.ac.uk

D. Razzouk (ed.), *Mental Health Economics*, DOI 10.1007/978-3-319-55266-8_8

8.1 Introduction

Previous chapters and this book emphasize more generally the disparity between the resources that are available for healthcare and the demands placed on those resources. Furthermore, resources are becoming ever scarcer in many health systems, while demand continues to rise. Tackling this growing gap is a fundamental concern worldwide, especially for low- and middle-income countries [1].

Balancing supply and demand in healthcare is a challenge even in flourishing economies. The economic theory of competitive markets suggests that, in a perfectly competitive market, supply and demand will reach an equilibrium whereby no supply is wasted and no demand is unmet. This is reached through demand, supply, prices and profits guiding both suppliers' and buyers' decisions about investment. If we consider the theoretical conditions that define a perfectly competitive market, however, it becomes clear why this equilibrium cannot be achieved in healthcare markets: fully informed consumers, numerous sellers, largely homogeneous products, and freedom of entry into and exit from the market (see Chap. 1). Further, many health systems (and related sectors, such as social care) are publicly funded to varying degrees, and goods and services are often provided free at the point of delivery or for less than their production costs. Therefore, prices charged to healthcare consumers do not reflect the full costs of providing that care. This absence of perfect competition conditions and an adequately functional price mechanism in healthcare prevents equilibrium between supply and demand – a situation termed *market failure*, which triggers a requirement for government intervention/regulation to help achieve an efficient allocation of resources and address the usually negative consequences of an imperfect market.

A major issue related to public-sector healthcare provision is that of limited budgets, certainly in relation to the costs of meeting all healthcare needs. At a broad level, some form of prioritization is needed to ensure the limited resources that are available for healthcare are used to their best effects. Resource allocation is arguably more contentious in low- and middle-income countries (see Chap. 11), where there are often less resources for health care, significant socioeconomic inequality, and larger gaps between the number of people with mental health problems and the number receiving treatment for such problems [1, 2].

Resourcing aside, a key complexity here is that the goals of a healthcare system can be many in number, diverse in nature, and possibly in conflict with each other, particularly when the healthcare economy cuts across both public and private sectors, as is the case in virtually all countries worldwide. Two such goals central to many healthcare systems are to provide healthcare both efficiently and to provide it in an equitable, socially acceptable way. So, the growing gap between the supply of and demand for healthcare represents not only a significant funding challenge to many governments and other agencies, but also a complex allocation challenge. This chapter thus examines these central concepts of efficiency and equity in turn and discusses some complex interactions between them.

8.2 Efficiency

Efficiency is usually considered in terms of the relationship between resource "inputs" and "outputs" (see Knapp [3], page 16, for an example of a production of welfare diagram), and is thus a measure of the extent to which a particular resource configuration achieves outcomes. In the case of healthcare, inputs could be staff time, equipment, and buildings, whereas outputs of interest could be any number of either intermediate/final health outcomes (such as correct diagnosis, cure, death, quality of life, quality-adjusted life years (QALYs), alleviation of symptoms) or measures of the process of care (e.g., time spent waiting for treatment). Economists refer to several types of efficiency [4], three of which are commonly discussed in relation to health:

Technical Efficiency Technical efficiency relates to quantities of *physical resources*, for example, staff hours or the number of specific pieces of equipment. It concerns finding a way of producing a given output using the smallest amount of these resources, such as which of two treatment approaches use the least staff time to achieve a desired health outcome, or which of two treatment approaches maximizes a desired outcome for an available level of staff time? Technical *in*efficiency implies that the maximum amount of output is not being achieved from a given combination of inputs. Examples of leading causes of technical inefficiency in health systems include inappropriate or costly staff mix, substandard or counterfeit drugs, and inappropriate hospital admissions [5].

Productive Efficiency Where treatment comparisons involve different, and thus incomparable, sets of physical resources (e.g., consultations with hospital staff versus self-monitoring equipment), it is more convenient to consider and compare the total *costs*, rather than physical quantities, of these resources. Therefore, production efficiency concerns maximizing outcomes for a given cost or minimizing costs to achieve a specific outcome. Note that although this may be a more useful concept than technical efficiency for the evaluation of healthcare interventions, given the diversity of resources used even within a single clinical condition (e.g., psychological therapy versus medication for depression), it nevertheless carries a requirement for a common outcome of interest to enable a comparison of two or more alternatives. This presents a very real challenge or constraint for those who want to use efficiency assessments in their decision-making, as discussed in Chap. 5.

Allocative Efficiency Technical and productive efficiency have an implicit focus on maximizing aggregate outcomes or minimizing aggregate resources/costs, without considering distributional implications. Therefore, it is possible that a productively optimal approach to healthcare isn't the "right" mix. For example, centralizing specialist mental health services in one location may create productive efficiency but may also prevent access for particular subsets of patients (e.g., those without their own transportation), thus providing better health outcomes for some at the expense of negative health consequences for others. Such allocative concerns tend to be considered within a broader, population-level context because they naturally relate to the overall goals of health systems, which in turn may relate to wider goals concerning societal welfare or social justice.

These economic definitions clearly illustrate that seeking efficiency is a relatively uncontroversial aim for any healthcare system – hence the earlier chapters outlining the main economic evaluation methods available to assess the relative efficiency of different healthcare interventions. The explicit examination of the efficiency of alternative treatments is therefore an activity undertaken by many healthcare systems, although the methods, successes, and acceptability of the approaches taken vary extensively [6], and much is yet to be done given the large-scale inefficiencies that continue to exist even in better-resourced healthcare systems [5]. A well-known example of efficiency considerations in national policy-making – one being emulated by many countries – is that of the National Institute for Health and Care Excellence in England, which produces guidelines for the management of specific health conditions/treatments, with an explicit consideration of cost-effectiveness. In a completely different context, Brazil's evolving priority-setting process has been documented by Cruz et al. [7], who describe the country initiating over a decade ago, a process to define its prioritization criteria, develop methodology for assessing healthcare interventions, commission new research, and produce mechanisms for disseminating assessment findings. At the core of this is an explicit consideration of efficiency. Other key healthcare prioritization attempts that explicitly consider efficiency and are specifically in the area of mental health care have been usefully described by Mihalopoulos et al. [8]. These include the use of a program budgeting and marginal analysis approach to appraise community mental health services in South Australia, whereby stakeholders were asked to select options to appraise and define what constitutes a benefit. Three dimensions of benefit were identified in this respect:

health gain, equity, and empowerment. Another example, also from Australia but subsequently applied in several other countries, is the assessing cost-effectiveness approach. This entails a stepped approach that starts with a relevant research/policy question and then proceeds, with stakeholder involvement, to select interventions and methods, assess their cost-effectiveness, and agree on and disseminate findings.

However, some mistrust of economic considerations in health care remains [9, 10]. Reasons are many, ranging from misconceptions of economics/efficiency entailing only monetary rationing to concerns about the methods that are used to operationalize underlying economic theory to unease about specific decisions that incorporated efficiency considerations. A well-documented example of this comes from the priority-setting system implemented in Oregon in the United States in 1990 [11]. To try to extend health insurance coverage to a larger proportion of its population, Oregon prioritized interventions using an explicit ranking of condition-treatment pairs based on cost-effectiveness; this covered both physical and mental health, with effectiveness/cost-effectiveness assessment based on the Quality of Well-Being Scale. Both the methodology used to generate the list and the treatment decisions it implied proved highly unpopular. While a form of the process remains in place, the emphasis now is on broader criteria, although methodological refinement is ongoing. This example illustrates that the palatability of efficiency considerations is very dependent on the robustness with and context through which efficiency is assessed. Context becomes particularly relevant in relation to mental health because it carries many specific challenges for assessing both outcomes and costs [2], as discussed in earlier chapters.

It is thus clear that efficiency considerations must necessarily account for other goals of a healthcare system. Healthcare is merely one contributor to health, and health itself is one contributor to broader welfare. The outcome goals of healthcare systems can thus extend beyond health improvements toward broader societal goals such as welfare maximization. As mentioned earlier, equity remains a major criterion against which healthcare systems are judged – if not by governments, then certainly by those who observe, monitor, and compare healthcare system performance, such as the World Health Organization or the European Observatory on Health Systems and Policies [12].

8.3 Equity

From the outset, it is important to note that we are discussing here the concept of equity, rather than equality. *Equality* refers to an objectively equal distribution of inputs or outputs across a population, whereas *equity* refers to a more subjective, or moral, judgement of what is fair [13]. Given the subjectivity surrounding notions of equity, the principles of equity in the context of healthcare can vary [14, 15]. Oliver and Mossialos [15] describe three:

- Equal access to healthcare for those in equal need of healthcare
- Equal utilization of healthcare for those in equal need of healthcare
- Equal/equitable health outcomes

Despite much consideration in the literature, no consensus yet exists regarding what the central concepts within these principles – access and need – even mean [15], and health outcome can be conceived and assessed using one of many ways. Oliver and Mossialos [15] discuss the significant implications of this conceptual uncertainty for policymakers internationally.

More generally, equity in the area of healthcare refers to the fair or just allocation of inputs (healthcare/funding) or outputs (outcomes). This may mean that resources may be distributed unequally with the aim of, for example, creating a more equal *opportunity* to benefit from healthcare, regardless of factors such as age and income. As mentioned earlier, this may result in a situation whereby total health benefits across a population are lower than if such social justice criteria were ignored. This tension between equity and egalitarianism is evident in relation to universal health coverage schemes [16], which may, for example, equalize access to healthcare but not necessarily provide an equitable distribution of health outcome.

Per the distinctions between different types of efficiency, two main types of equity are discussed in relation to healthcare:

Horizontal Equity Equal treatment of those who share similar circumstances. For example, two people diagnosed with the same condition with the same severity would receive the same healthcare package regardless of other circumstances such as income.

Vertical Equity Unequal treatment of those with unequal circumstances. An example of this may be offering priority access to a healthcare service to those from lower-income groups because they have a reduced overall capacity to achieve the same health status as those from higher-income groups.

Many governments explicitly consider equity in their policy-making (e.g., progressive income taxation systems address issues of vertical equity). Examples specifically related to mental health care exist: the 2015 Mental Health Act 1983: Code of Practice in England [17] refers to both efficiency and equity in its "guiding principles." However, equity in the distribution of health and healthcare remains elusive for many countries, including high-income ones [18, 19]. Moreover, while social justice is an important dimension of health, it is often perceived to be a dimension that competes with efficiency, requiring some level of trade-off between the two [20]; this trade-off suggests a tension between different stakeholders (e.g., healthcare funders versus healthcare recipients) (see Chaps. 9, 10, and 11).

8.4 Efficiency and Equity, or Equity Versus Efficiency?

While it is clear that both efficiency and equity broadly refer to optimal balances between outcomes and costs, it is also evident that conceptual and practical definitions have many nuances, and that a perception exists that the two goals conflict with each other.

A clear example relates to the common use of the QALY as a metric for outcome measurement in economic evaluations (i.e., assessments of productive efficiency). As discussed in Chap. 6, this outcome has several advantages for decision-making: it has a generic (rather than condition-specific) nature, it is based on preferences, and it is able to provide a combined measurement of two keys aspects of health – duration and quality of life. However, the equity implications of the bias of QALY values raise concerns since they favor people who are less disabled or who are more likely to have a longer life expectancy [21], with the implication that such groups of individuals somehow carry greater social value [22] simply because they have greater opportunities to generate more QALYs. Various solutions to the QALY equity issue have been discussed; the most common is the use of equity/distributional weights, that is, allocating a greater weight to the QALYs of those with greater disability (or other disadvantage). However, the operationalization of this remains a challenge because it is unclear what the basis of such weights should be (see Chap. 9). More generally, it suggests that some level of compromise in total health gain (and thus in productive efficiency) is required so that a fairer distribution of health can be achieved, and it requires prior knowledge of the potential for individual-level health gain [22]. Franklin [22] proposes an alternative approach of recalibrating QALY values such that the zero-to-one scale represents an individual-level *capacity to benefit*. The theory of capability and functioning [23] was developed as an alternative to welfarist economics and is now developing quickly in the field of outcome measurement for economic evaluation, including in the mental health area (see Chap. 9). While Franklin [22] concedes conceptual and practical challenges associated with rescaling QALY values still exist, it offers a start in avoiding "implicit discrimination" (p. 1) against some subgroups in the population. Developing an alternative approach that is not similarly characterized by inconsistencies is a challenge, perhaps reflecting the paradoxes that exist in individual and societal attitudes and practices related to social justice.

Chisholm and Stewart [20] helpfully describe some specific competing economic incentives and ethical trade-offs that occur at three key levels of the mental health system – government and society, care purchasers and providers, and users and carers – and in doing so summarize a long-accepted paradigm that "equity must come at a price" (p. 61). Two commonly experienced and discussed examples illustrate such potential trade-offs. First, resource pressures can prevent the adoption of newer and more cost-effective interventions, especially if they might benefit a smaller proportion of the population than adopting a less cost-effective intervention that can be delivered more cheaply overall and/or reach more people. Examples of this can be found in many contexts, but particularly in low- and middle-income countries, where resource pressures can be exceptionally acute in both monetary and physical terms. Second, the implications that may arise from the use of hard cutoffs for cost-effectiveness thresholds. In England, the unpopularity of some decisions made on this basis has led to the less than equitable outcomes of exceptions to the rule (in relation to access to expensive cancer drugs) and geographic variations in access to healthcare within the country (since local decision makers can nevertheless offer treatments that are not recommended at a national level).

However, Anthony Culyer, a British economist who has long written about matters of efficiency, equity, and ethics, asserts that nuances exist in the traditional definitions of efficiency and in the relationship between efficiency and equity, which mean that trade-offs between the two are not necessarily required. He illustrated this recently using a health frontier – a chart showing the health allocation between two groups of people – to represent a classic heath allocation scenario whereby the average health of one group can only be improved at the expense of less health for the other group [24]. This situation is termed *Pareto efficiency* (see Chaps. 1 and 4) and describes a resource allocation in which one person's health cannot be further improved without reducing at least one other person's health. Culyer then goes on to illustrate alternative health allocations on the health frontier in which both efficiency and equity can be preserved but depend on what criteria are being used regarding equity (e.g., equal health gain versus equal marginal value). He therefore concludes that the important question "equity of what?" is the source of trade-offs and requires greater explicit consideration than it is currently given.

Equity is a key societal concern with policy relevance; however, proper consideration of equity issues are perceived by many to trail behind efficiency issues. It has also been noted that when equity is given its due consideration, it may involve an element of waste, for example, in relation to the large costs associated with administering a publicly funded health system [25] – which again suggests some level of unavoidable trade-off.

8.5 Conclusion

This chapter has described how the situation of a lack of equilibrium or of market failure in the area of healthcare necessitates intervention, and that a common pursuit of many healthcare funders is the achievement of greater efficiency (see Chap. 1). Efficiency is simply about the optimal production and distribution of resources or, more simply, achieving the best value. However, for a "commodity" as complex and emotive as healthcare (and health), this raises important questions about what efficiency/inefficiency actually mean and whether an efficient allocation of resources would be considered desirable based on other important criteria such as equity (see Chaps. 4, 9, and 10). Complex issues exist in terms of both definition and measurement. And complexities abound given the numerous social and physical determinants of health (see Chap. 24) beyond the healthcare system (e.g., housing, income, education), particularly for the area of mental health, which is characterized not only by many determinants but also comorbidity, multi-sectoral care inputs, broad impacts beyond health, and multiple outcomes of relevance.

Despite a dominant belief in the incompatibility of efficiency and equity, it is clear that any possible trade-off is not a direct one, and that that the balance between the two is influenced by definitions and societal goals related to equity [24]. It is worth noting that while we have focused our attention on efficiency and equity, given their particular relevance and importance in health systems, these are nevertheless just two of many criteria (see Sabik and Lie [6] for others) upon which healthcare provision is allocated and judged (see Chaps. 9, 10, and 11).

Key Messages

- Limited resources in healthcare systems worldwide necessitate prioritization of what can be offered to populations.
- Efficiency and equity are two important considerations in resource allocation decisions.
- Both efficiency and equity have several definitions, and the latter is particularly nuanced because of the greater subjectivity involved.
- Efficiency and equity goals are often seen to be in contention with each other.

References

1. Lancet Global Mental Health Group. Scale up services for mental disorders: a call for action. Lancet. 2007;370(9594):1241–52.
2. Patel A. The inevitable pursuit of efficiency. J Ment Health. 2013;22(2):89–92.
3. Knapp M. The economic perspective: framework and principles. In: Knapp M, editor. The economic evaluation of mental health care. Aldershot: Arena; 1995.
4. Palmer S, Torgerson D. Definitions of efficiency. BMJ. 1999;318(7191):1136.
5. Chisholm D, Evans DB. Improving health system efficiency as a means of moving towards universal coverage. World Health Report, Background Paper, Number 28. Geneva: World Health Organisation; 2010.
6. Sabik LM, Lie RK. Priority setting in health care: lessons from the experiences of eight countries. Int J Equity Health. 2008;7(4):1–13.
7. Cruz LN, da Silva Lima AF, Graeff-Martins AS, Maia CR, Ziegelmann PK, Polanczyk CA. Mental health economics: insights from Brazil. J Ment Health. 2013;22(2):111–21.
8. Mihalopoulos C, Carter R, Pirkis J, Vos T. Priority-setting for mental health services. J Ment Health. 2013;22(2):122–34.
9. Parkin D, Appleby J, Maynard A. Economics: the biggest fraud ever perpetrated on the world? Lancet. 2013;382:e11–5.
10. Horton R. What have economists ever done for global health? Lancet. 2014;383:1024.
11. Tengs TO. An evaluation of Oregon's Medicaid rationing algorithms. Health Econ. 1996;5:171–81.
12. Papanicolas I, Smith PC, editors. Health system performance comparison. An agenda for policy, information and research. Berkshire: Open University Press McGraw-Hill Education; 2013.
13. Rawls J. Justice as fairness: political not metaphysical. Philos Public Aff. 1985;14:223–51.
14. Oliver A. Why care about health inequality? London: Office of Health Economics; 2001.
15. Oliver A, Mossialos E. Equity of access to health care: outlining the foundations for action. J Epidemiol Community Health. 2004;58:655–8.
16. World Health Organization. The world health report. Health systems financing: the path to universal coverage. Geneva: WHO; 2010.
17. Department of Health. Mental health act 1983: code of practice 2015. London: Department of Health; 2015.
18. Department of Health. Inequalities in health: report of an independent inquiry chaired by Sir Donald Acheson. London: The Stationery Office; 1998.
19. Sassi F, Le Grand J, Archand L. Equity versus efficiency: a dilemma for the NHS. BMJ. 2001;323:762–3.
20. Chisholm D, Stewart A. Economic and ethics in mental health care: traditions and trade-offs. J Ment Health Policy Econ. 1998;1:55–62.
21. Johannesson M. Should we aggregate relative or absolute changes in QALYs? Health Econ. 2001;10:573–7.
22. Franklin D. Calibrating QALYs to respect equality of persons. Utilitas; 2016. (FirstView Article June 2016, p. 1–23).
23. Sen A. Commodities and capabilities. Amsterdam: North-Holland; 1985.
24. Culyer AJ. Efficiency, equity and equality in health and health care. CHE Research Paper 120. York: University of York; 2015.
25. Woolhandler S, Campbell T, Himmelstein DU. Costs of health care administration in the United States and Canada. N Engl J Med. 2003;349:768–75.

Ethics and Values in Welfarism and Extra-Welfarism

9

Joanna Coast, Paul Mitchell, and Ilias Goranitis

Abstract

This chapter focuses on the ethical values that underpin different types of economic evaluation. Welfarism, the standard health maximization approach to extra-welfarism, and a capability approach to extra-welfarism are all discussed in terms of the different values incorporated. Alternative decision rules around maximization and sufficiency are also examined. These theoretical discussions are then supplemented by two case studies related to mental health. The first considers the relative priority that might be given to depression treatment relative to a variety of physical health conditions, using both forms of extra-welfarism. The second explores the use of health and capability measures in interventions for drug addiction. The evidence presented indicates that interventions for mental health conditions will receive different priorities where different value judgements form the basis for the economic evaluation. This underlines the importance of these ethical decisions.

J. Coast (✉)
Health Economics at Bristol, School of Social and Community Medicine, University of Bristol, Canynge Hall, 39 Whatley Road, Bristol, BS8 2PS, UK

The National Institute for Health Research Collaboration for Leadership in Applied Health Research and Care West (NIHR CLAHRC West), University Hospitals Bristol NHS Foundation Trust, Bristol, UK
e-mail: jo.coast@bristol.ac.uk

P. Mitchell
Health Economics at Bristol, School of Social and Community Medicine, University of Bristol, Canynge Hall, 39 Whatley Road, Bristol, BS8 2PS, UK

The National Institute for Health Research Collaboration for Leadership in Applied Health Research and Care West (NIHR CLAHRC West), University Hospitals Bristol NHS Foundation Trust, Bristol, UK

The UK Renal Registry, Southmead Hospital, Bristol, UK
e-mail: paul.mitchell@bristol.ac.uk

I. Goranitis
Health Economics Unit, Institute of Applied Health Research, University of Birmingham, Birmingham, UK
e-mail: i.goranitis@bham.ac.uk

D. Razzouk (ed.), *Mental Health Economics*, DOI 10.1007/978-3-319-55266-8_9

Key Points Summary

- All economic evaluations are based on particular ethical positions; the value judgements that result from these ethical positions drive how an economic evaluation is conducted, influencing both the evaluative space and the decision rule used.
- Welfarism, the traditional economic approach, is associated with an evaluative space of utility and uses a maximization rule based on Pareto optimality.
- Extra-welfarism as usually practiced in health economic evaluation is associated with an evaluative space of health and uses a maximization rule based on maximizing cardinal health-related utility.
- An emerging alternative application of extra-welfarism associated with the capability approach uses an evaluative space of capability well-being and may use decision rules based on maximization or sufficiency.
- Sufficiency is an alternative decision rule to maximization and aims to bring all members of society to a sufficient level of what is being measured, rather than to maximize the total level of this within society.
- Two mental health case studies are examined in relation to the priorities and choices that would result from application of extra-welfarism in both its health and capability variants.
- Both case studies suggest that different funding priorities would result from making different value judgements about the evaluative space; the capability approach seems to favor interventions for mental health conditions relative to those for other conditions.

9.1 Introduction

This chapter focuses on the value judgements that underlie the economic analysis of healthcare interventions. These value judgements are numerous, ranging from broad judgements, such as the perspective from which an economic evaluation should be conducted, to more specific judgements, such as who should provide the tariff scores we use in assessing benefit. One value judgement that is common to all such evaluative attempts, however, is a population focus, rather than the more common ethical focus of clinicians on an individual patient. In this chapter, this population focus is assumed as a given for economic analysis and is not discussed further; rather, the focus is on the value judgements made within population-based economic evaluations.

This chapter focuses specifically on two areas of value judgement: the evaluative space within which the economic evaluation is conducted, and the decision or combining rule used to make a judgement about the appropriate course of action.

Here, the evaluative space is concerned with what we are interested in assessing. This may at first seem self-evident: surely we are just concerned about getting the best outcomes we can? Yet, it is considerably more complex than this. Traditionally, economists have been concerned with utility (see Chaps. 1 and 6), which is essentially an ordering of preferences but can be seen as somehow representing pleasure or satisfaction (See Chap. 4) [1]. Mainstream health economists, on the other hand, are focused on health, where health is often measured as concern with such factors as mobility, pain and anxiety, or depression, as well as the ability to complete functional activities [2].

While these two outcomes often align, they may not always do so: a good example relates to physical activity and obesity – my preferences (utility) might be maximized by eating a bar of chocolate and lazing on the sofa watching television, whereas my health might be maximized by going for a walk and eating a carrot or a stick of celery. A choice to focus on health or utility here would lead to different recommendations about the optimal course of action. An alternative to both of these approaches, the use of capability well-being (the well-being that arises from what a person is able to do or be in their life), is currently also being explored by health economists because of its potential to consider a broader set of outcomes that relate to what is valuable to people in their lives [3–5].

Decision, or combining, rules are concerned with how we aggregate information about costs and benefits and how that feeds through into our decision-making processes. Approaches within economic evaluation are almost exclusively focused on maximizing outcomes, that is, achieving the most total utility or total health gain from the resources available [6]. This focus on maximization derives from the economist's concern with an efficiency objective, yet other objectives may be considered in resource allocation (see Chaps. 8 and 10). These have been acknowledged by health economists in efforts to establish equity concerns (see Chap. 8) within a population and determine ways of incorporating these into economic evaluation while still retaining an overall focus on maximization [7–9]. Unfortunately, while these efforts have resulted in much being learned about what objectives are important within a population, such equity concerns have not made it into the day-to-day practice of economic evaluation.

It is important to note that the value judgements we make about what to measure, and how to use those measures in decision-making, determine in part which (mental health) interventions seem (most) cost-effective. Indeed, there is no escaping ethical issues when conducting economic analysis, and implications for both efficiency and equity certainly stem from the choices made (see Chap. 8). These issues are explored further in the sections below, both in theoretical terms and empirically, using two case studies from within mental health.

9.2 Ethical Value Judgements in Welfarism and Extra-Welfarism

9.2.1 Choice of Evaluative Space

Normative debates on the appropriateness of welfarism and extra-welfarism for the economic evaluation of healthcare interventions continue to remain central in the health economics literature (see Chaps. 1, 4, 5, and 6). At the heart of these debates lie, primarily, opposing value judgements about the choice of utility or health as the appropriate evaluative space [3, 10]. Welfarism evaluates healthcare interventions on the basis of their indirect effects on individual expected utility (see Chap. 4), whereby health is accounted for only insofar as utility is derived from the consumption of healthcare. Extra-welfarism evaluates healthcare interventions on the basis of their direct effects on health status, irrespective of the level of utility that a person then derives from that healthcare consumption (see Chaps. 5 and 6).

Welfarism has robust theoretical foundations in neoclassical welfare economics (see Chaps. 1 and 4), but ethical and methodological limitations associated with the source and method of utility valuation have limited its use in healthcare decision-making. All national health technology assessment agencies [11] that use economic evaluation or cost-effectiveness information as the basis for decision-making (for example, the National Institute for Health and Care Excellence in the United Kingdom, the Zorginstituut Nederland in the Netherlands, the Canadian Agency for Drugs and Technologies in Health, and the Pharmaceutical Benefits Advisory Committee in Australia) base reimbursement and coverage decisions on the extra-welfarist framework. Even though supplementary welfarist approaches may sometimes be permitted, these have been found to influence health technology assessment decisions only rarely [12].

Welfarism, having as a source of valuation the expected utility of "affected" individuals, can suffer from the problem of adaptation, whereby individuals may adjust their expectations to meet the adversities they experience in life as well as their objective circumstances or personal characteristics. Amartya Sen [13] (pp. 21–22) argued that "mental reactions to what we actually get and what we can sensibly expect to get may frequently involve compromises with a harsh reality."

According to Sen, utility as an evaluative space is dependent on a person's mental attitudes and, as a result of these compromises and realistic adaptations, utility may overlook the person's physical health state (physical condition neglect) or personal values (valuation neglect). For this reason, utility has been judged by some as an "unsuitable" evaluative space on which to base resource allocation decisions in healthcare [14].

The welfarist contingent valuation method (see Chaps. 3 and 4) for estimating expected utility has also been criticized within the healthcare decision-making context [15, 16]. One issue is that contingent valuation is dependent on the distribution of economic resources such as income and wealth, which potentially biases resource allocation decisions against more deprived individuals. Another issue is that a key underpinning of welfare economics, that of individual sovereignty, may not hold in all circumstances, such as in mental health conditions [2], which could prohibit the application of exercises to determine monetary valuations in this population group [17] (see Chap. 4). Other concerns with a welfarist approach in healthcare that have limited its use in practice are the consistency and reliability of results [17, 18], individuals' willingness to participate in such valuation exercises [18], and the tendency of the method to overestimate the value of interventions offering small clinical benefits [19]. A move from expected utility to experienced utility [20, 21] (see Chap. 4) within the welfarist framework may overcome problems with the source and method of utility valuation, but still leaves the focus on utility alone, without accounting for nonutility characteristics such as health and capabilities [22].

Is health, however, a more appropriate evaluative space for economic evaluations? Extra-welfarism emerged from the need to directly account for people's characteristics in healthcare decision-making [2], but its narrow focus on an individual's health is increasingly criticized [23–27] on the grounds that healthcare interventions may affect outcomes other than health. In the case of mental health, for example, outcomes such as personal autonomy, social involvement, sense of achievement, and self-perception may determine patient well-being but may not be perceived as directly tapping into the health domain [28, 29] (see Chaps. 1, 3, 4, and 25). Interventions may also cross health and other domains, affecting a variety of outcomes through integrated packages of care. The recovery model that is pursued in the United Kingdom for mental health, for example, involves collaboration between health and social care services with aims that go beyond treating and managing health-related symptoms to also focus on helping individuals regain control, on supporting recovery, and, ultimately, on helping these individuals to lead meaningful lives [30]. Finally, health and social care interventions may have external nonhealth effects on groups other than the patient, such as informal caregivers (see Chaps. 17 and 27), close family, and friends [24, 31]; this may be a particular issue for mental health conditions. Since the current narrow application of extra-welfarism using patient health status as the evaluative space cannot appropriately capture these effects, it can be argued that some interventions and population groups, such as those with severe conditions like schizophrenia, Alzheimer's disease, or other forms of dementia, are disadvantaged using the current orthodoxy in decision-making regarding resource allocation (see Chap. 10).

9.2.2 Choice of Maximization as the Appropriate Combining Rule

The normative focus on maximizing total utility within economics, and latterly health economics, derives from Paretian welfare economics [32] (see Chaps. 1 and 4). The focus on maximization is justified through the possibility that those who lose utility as the result of an intervention can theoretically be compensated in utility terms by those who gain. Where this situation arises, it is known as a "potential Pareto improvement," and the notion of theoretical compensation was justified by Hicks [33, 34] and Kaldor [35] (see Chap. 4), with the most convincing argument being that decisions could theoretically be split into an "efficiency" decision (in the economist's domain and focusing on whether the total gain from a policy intervention leads to an increase in utility) and a separate "distributive" decision (in the domain of politicians and focusing on judgement about how gains and losses should be distributed) [35].

For example, within a utility evaluative space, evaluation of a proposed policy change might suggest that large utility gains will be obtained from developing a new facility to treat mental health problems, but in doing so an existing parking lot will be lost, causing a loss in utility for those who will now have to use public transport alternatives or walk farther to arrive at their place of employment. If the gain in utility from the facility is greater than the loss in utility to those using the parking lot, then the parking lot users could be compensated with anything that replaces their utility loss – a free bus pass, an annual health checkup, or even champagne and chocolate bars. Of course, this utility replacement does not need to actually happen; to meet the efficiency criterion and thus allow economists to focus on maximization, it is enough that it could happen *theoretically*. This focus on efficiency in terms of achieving the greatest amount of utility from the resources available is intrinsic to welfarism and is based on this sound theoretical base. It should be noted that this theoretical basis arises from a relatively small number of value judgements that are often seen as being relatively weak and therefore uncontroversial [6].

The shift within health economics to an extra-welfarist health evaluative space has not altered the maximization rule (see Chaps. 4–6), despite the fundamentally different nature of the evaluative space. Indeed, this "drift" [6], largely unacknowledged, occurred at the same time as the much more openly justified shift in the evaluative space [36] from welfarism to extra-welfarism. This drift toward the maximization of health within extra-welfarism cannot, however, be justified using the same theoretical mechanisms as for the potential Pareto improvement and hypothetical compensation [6]. The production of health gain is inextricably linked to an individual, and thus the decision to provide health gain through one intervention is also, and inevitably, a decision to provide healthcare to some persons and not others. (Although, in a small number of instances – for example, infectious disease or jointly produced health gain such as for a mother and baby or, potentially, a patient and their caregiver – the issue becomes production of health gain that is inextricably linked to a dyad or group of individuals at the expense of other individuals.) It is not possible to compensate such others within a health evaluative space, and so the choice to pursue a maximization rule is much closer to the idea of Bentham's "felicific calculus," or achieving the greatest good [37]. Extra-welfarists who choose not to make any equity adjustments within their analyses are "endorsing the ethical position that the total sum of health produced within the health care system is what matters, no matter how that health is distributed" (Coast [6], p. 789); this is the usual position taken within the vast number of published health economic evaluations in mental health and elsewhere in the healthcare system.

Of course, in the realities of decision-making through health technology agencies, this maximization position is not completely upheld. In the United Kingdom, for example, an element of deliberation enables decision makers to go beyond a pure focus on maximization of health [38], and in the Netherlands there is an explicit focus on considering equity through the mechanism of "proportional shortfall" [39]. Nevertheless, there may be other alternatives to a pure maximization rule that enable focusing on those with the most severe problems; this possibility is considered later in this chapter.

9.3 Alternative Ethical Value Judgements

9.3.1 Capability as an Alternative Evaluative Space

Recent years have seen the major growth of an approach that uses an evaluative space that is an alternative to both that of utility and the standard interpretation of extra-welfarism as health gain. This is evaluation within a capability well-being space, where the evaluation considers gains in what a person is able to do or be within his or her life [40]. The approach is thus broader than a single focus on utility or a single focus on health [41], instead providing a multidimensional approach to the measurement of well-being.

The notion of capability well-being as an evaluative space arises from the work of Amartya Sen [40], who generated the concept in response to the adaptation problem outlined above; much of Sen's work has been conducted in the context of human development, where the possibility of adaptation becomes particularly acute. This led Sen to focus on what he refers to as "functionings" and "capabilities" as the appropriate focus of evaluation [40]. Here, functionings refer to those things that a person does or is in his/her life, whereas capability shifts the focus to a person's ability to do or be those things, whether or not they choose to do so. Sen's preferred focus for evaluation is capability, rather than functioning, because it allows for the freedom to choose. In the mental health context, for example, a person may be able to have a role (for example, a job), even if they choose not to do so; it would be the ability to pursue a role that is considered important from a capability well-being perspective, rather than actually having a job at the current time. Of course, capability well-being may be affected by many factors, not just health.

Within the recent health economics literature, there has been a variety of attempts to generate measures of capability well-being for use in economic evaluation. These include the ICECAP measures, which are based on a life-course approach and, to date, include measures for the adult population [42], older people [43], and those at the end of life [44]; the Oxford Capability (OxCAP) measures, which derive from a 64-item inventory and have specific measures for public health (the OCAP-18) [45] and mental health [46]; and more specific measures of capability well-being for patients with chronic pain [47], for social care (Adult Social Care Outcomes Toolkit, or ASCOT) [48], and for women in rural Malawi [49].

These measures contain a variety of attributes developed either through participatory methods [42, 44, 47, 49, 50] or by drawing on philosophically generated lists of capabilities [45, 46]. The two most relevant from a mental health perspective are probably the generic ICECAP-A measure for all adults, which contains attributes relating to stability, autonomy, achievement, attachment, and enjoyment [42], and the OxCAP mental health measure, which contains questions relating to life expectancy, daily activities, suitable accommodation, neighborhood safety, potential for assault, freedom of expression, imagination and creativity, love and support, losing sleep, planning one's life, respect and appreciation, social networks, discrimination, appreciate nature, enjoy recreation, influence local decisions, property ownership, and access [46].

The ICECAP and ASCOT measures have both generated value sets [48, 51] that allow meaningful comparison among items within the measure and across interventions using best/worst scaling [52] as the method of valuation. By contrast, for the OxCAP mental health measure, Simon et al. [46] argue for the multidimensional nature of the capability approach as a basis for not generating a single value representing trade-offs between items. Again, this is an example of the different value judgements that can go into different approaches, even when the measures fall into the same broad evaluative space.

9.3.2 Sufficiency as an Alternative Decision Rule

Standard welfare economics is primarily concerned with the efficient allocation of resources to produce their maximum benefit. In many ways, this relates to the notion of an ideal economically efficient world in which perfect competition (in healthcare) theoretically leads to the optimum benefit for suppliers and consumers. Market failure (see Chaps. 1, 4, 8, and 10) in healthcare, however, is the reason why national governments usually provide at least some form of public healthcare.

With the move away from healthcare markets toward public provision, the focus of evaluations has changed, with space being created to focus on health-related aspects of quality of life as the primary evaluative space. The rejection of healthcare provision on the basis of ability to pay and in favor of access based on needs also provides a reason for considering objectives other than the maximization of output; if meeting needs is important, then maximizing total benefit, no matter to whom it accrues, may not be considered appropriate as the sole objective of healthcare.

One alternative approach is to set the objective of healthcare resource allocation in a way that focuses on whether people reach a sufficiently high level of attainment [53–56]. Sufficiency as an objective would aim to get all members of a population to a sufficient or "decent" level as a priority. Therefore, it is distinct from a maximization approach in two ways. First, all gains in attainment of capability well-being are not treated equally. Priority is given to those who have not reached a sufficient level [56]. Second, any gains above the sufficient level are treated the same as no change in levels below the sufficient level [56].

It is clear that a shift from maximization to this sort of sufficiency objective would be likely to make a difference in how healthcare resources are prioritized. For example, consider two patient groups, both of which could be treated for their conditions; the available healthcare budget, however, provides only enough resource to treat one group. The available evidence suggests that patient group A would receive the greatest absolute benefit of 30 units from treatment, moving from 60 to 90 on a 0–100 outcome scale. Patient group B would only benefit by 20 units, moving from 40 to 60 on the same scale. With a maximization rule, group A would be treated because this would lead to a greater total benefit overall. If, however, a sufficiency rule was in place, the results could be viewed differently. For example, if the particular sufficiency rule aimed to achieve a minimum level of 70 on the outcomes scale for all members of the population, priority would instead be given to patient group B, whose 20-unit benefits are all below the sufficiency level, whereas for patient group A only 10 of the 30 units of benefit would be below the sufficiency level and thus would "count" in terms of the sufficiency decision-making rule. Essentially, resources are focused on improving the lot of those with greater poverty in terms of capability well-being, whereby capability well-being could be measured using the sorts of index measures outlined above.

Notions of sufficiency have not been extensively explored within health economics, but the capability approach, with its greater focus on equity [57], has been more open to different approaches and is leading the way in this respect [55], with some work specifically on shortfalls in health capability [53]. A recent review of the capability literature, for example, found that a focus on sufficiency occurred more often than a focus on maximization in studies looking to identify objectives when measuring people's capabilities [54]. Practical methods have also been developed to apply a sufficiency objective in relation to the ICECAP measures [56]. In relation to the latter, years of full capability (YFCs) (equivalent) have been proposed to measure capability gains in a similar way to how health-focused quality adjusted life years (QALYs) are estimated [51], albeit they are based on differing anchors for the ICECAP measures: 1 for full capability, and 0 for no capability [43]. A year of full capability is equivalent to having full capability, that is, being at the highest capability level on all ICECAP items and remaining in full capability for a year. Years of sufficient capability (YSCs) have been proposed as an outcome in line with the majority of capability applications in practice [54]. A year of sufficient capability is equivalent to having sufficient capability on all ICECAP items, however defined, and remaining at or above sufficient capability for a year [56]. The key distinction with YSCs is that changes above the sufficient level are not valued; only gains below the sufficient level are valued.

While there has been more concern within health economic evaluation about the value judgements associated with the evaluative space than the decision rule, both are important in determining how resources are allocated. A sufficiency rule may provide an alternative to maximization that enables a greater focus of resources on those most in need.

9.4 Potential Impact of Differing Ethical Value Judgments on Priorities

Much of the argument for shifting the evaluative space to capability well-being has been based on the sorts of academic debates surrounding the theory underpinning economic approaches to assessing welfare that are outlined above. However, real-life evidence is beginning to emerge that shows that the use of different evaluative spaces could also have potentially important implications for how resources are allocated in practice. This section outlines two case studies in which we had a role, and both consider these important questions in the context of mental health conditions.

9.4.1 Priorities for Depression Compared with Other Health Conditions

A recent research study attempted to determine what impact a shift in evaluative space from health status to capability might have on treating and preventing a number of common health conditions (for full details, see Mitchell et al. [58]). A multi-instrument comparison data set collected self-reported information for individuals from six countries (Australia, Canada, Germany, Norway, the United Kingdom, and the United States). Individuals were categorized into eight different population groupings: a healthy population and seven other groups comprising individuals reporting a primary health condition of arthritis, asthma, cancer, depression, diabetes, hearing loss, or heart disease. Individuals who were classified as healthy reported no health condition and scored 70 or higher on a 0–100 visual analogue scale measuring overall health.

All eight population groups completed questions about their health status, subjective well-being, and capability well-being [58]. The seven health condition populations also completed condition-specific measures; those with a primary condition of depression completed two related measures: the 21-item Depression, Anxiety and Stress Scale [59] and the Kessler 10-item Psychological Distress Scale [60]. The measures focused on in this study were the EQ-5D-5L (a health-related quality-of-life measure used to generate QALYs) [61], the ICECAP-A [42], and the condition-specific questionnaires. Both the EQ-5D-5L and ICECAP-A ask five questions, but the content of each measure varies, as demonstrated in Table 9.1. U.K. population values were attached to both the health and capability states recorded by respondents in order to generate overall scores for health utility and capability [51, 62].

Two types of analysis were conducted in this comparison of the relative effects on health status and capability well-being. The first analysis looked at how preventing the primary health con-

Table 9.1 Dimensions on measures of overall health status (EQ-5D-5L) and capability well-being (ICECAP-A)

EQ-5D-5L dimensions	ICECAP-A	
	Dimensions	Expression
Mobility	Stability	Feeling settled and secure
Self-care	Attachment	Love, friendship, and support
Usual activities	Autonomy	Independence
Pain/discomfort	Achievement	Achievement and progress
Anxiety/depression	Enjoyment	Enjoyment and pleasure

ditions prevalent in this data set would be prioritized based on reductions in the health utility and capability of the groups with health conditions relative to the healthy population. The second analysis looked at the potential effects of treating those with differing severities of their condition. Those with health conditions were grouped as having mild, moderate, or severe conditions based on their responses to the particular condition-specific questionnaires.

The results of the first analysis showed that although both health utility and capability reductions are highest for those with depression, differences exist in the relative effects across health conditions; for example, individuals who have a primary condition of arthritis have a mean health utility score close to that of those with depression, but their capability score is closer to that of the healthy population. The much greater reduction in capability well-being for those with depression suggests that, were capability well-being the basis for setting priorities, those with depression would receive higher priority than they would under a health evaluative space. Figure 9.1 shows the loss in both capability and health for those in each of the health condition groups relative to the healthy population.

For the second analysis the findings are summarized in Fig. 9.2. Differences in both capability and health scores exist between those categorized as severe and moderate, and between those categorized as moderate and mild. It is interesting to note, however, that when comparing overall health and capability scores for individuals with a mild health condition with those of the healthy population, only those with depression record a statistically meaningful difference in mean capability score (or "effect size," to be precise). However, all health conditions record meaningful differences in mean health utility in this comparison between the mild health conditions and the healthy population. Therefore, across mild conditions, priority would only be given to people with depression if the focus was on capability.

There are a number of limitations to these research findings. The study was cross-sectional, so it is not known how capability and health utility change as diseases progress with or without treatment. The effect of mortality in these health conditions could also not be incorporated into the analysis because of the study design, and this clearly would also affect priorities. From the perspective of this chapter, this study also does not provide evidence of the potential for differing priorities between these two evaluative spaces and that of utility. Nonetheless, some interesting findings do emerge. In particular, the effect of depression on capability seems to be far greater than that of any of the other (physical) health conditions studied here. Indeed, the only mild health condition for which capability differed in any meaningful way from the healthy population was depression.

Reporting this study in this chapter is not intended to advocate for health or capability as the appropriate evaluative space in mental health economic evaluations, but it is intended to highlight the importance of this value judgement at the outset of any evaluation. This work suggests that there is potential for differing implications for depression treatments if these different evaluative spaces are used. As yet, it is unclear whether

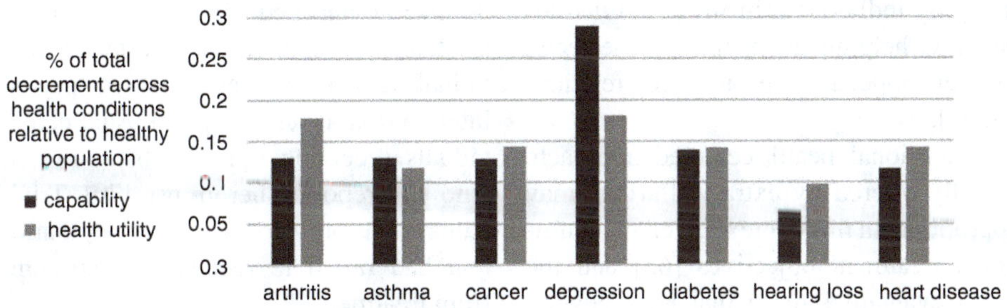

Fig. 9.1 Reductions in capability and overall health among those with health conditions compared with the healthy population (Data based on Table 3 from Mitchell et al. [58])

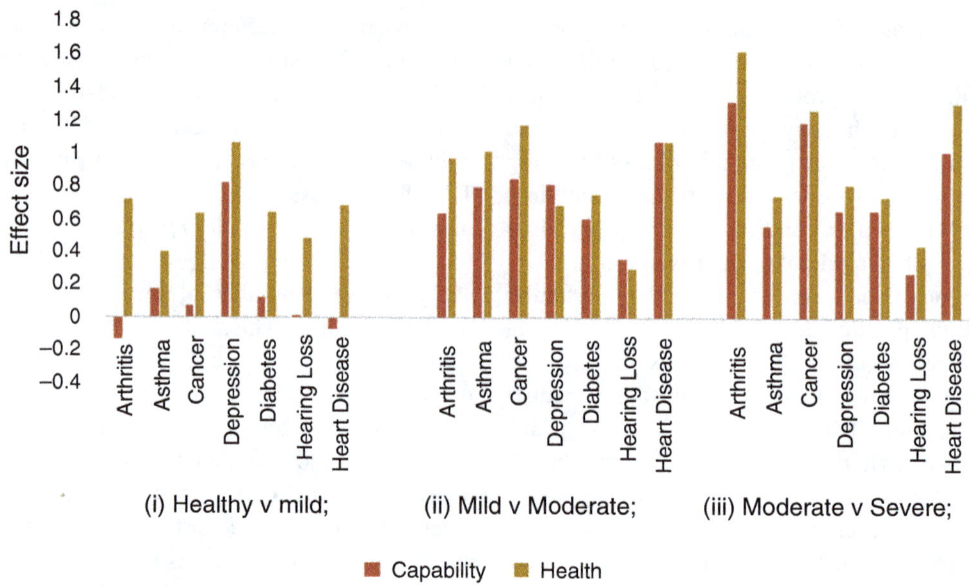

Fig. 9.2 Comparing condition severity by effect size differences in overall health and capability (Data based on Table 3 from Mitchell et al. [58])

similar results would be obtained for other mental health conditions.

9.4.2 Economic Evaluation and Evaluative Spaces in Drug Dependence

The recovery model in psychiatric care requires clinicians and policymakers to look beyond clinical recovery to the wider impact of interventions on valuable goals and outcomes for service users and their families. Clinical and policy objectives in drug dependence have been extended to incorporate not just control over drug use, but also the management of physical and mental health problems, engaging individuals in meaningful roles within society; helping them build self-esteem, aspirations and hope; and reestablishing relationships [63, 64].

A unidimensional health-centered approach, as empirically offered by extra-welfarism, may not be appropriate in this context given the multidimensional treatment objectives [65] and the need for an evaluative space that goes beyond health-related quality of life and the functional status of individuals [66]. In an influential book titled *Power, Powerlessness and Addiction*, Jim Orford uses the capability approach developed by Sen [40] and the central human capabilities outlined by Nussbaum [67] to illustrate the personal and interpersonal effects of addiction from a clinical perspective [68]. From a health economics perspective, the use of the capability evaluative space and sufficient capability as a decision rule also offer an appealing evaluative framework for assessing interventions for substance use disorders.

A recently published study explored whether capability well-being offers a more suitable evaluative space than health in the context of opiate dependence (for full details, see Goranitis et al. [69]). The study relied on data from a pilot randomized controlled trial designed to investigate the feasibility and efficacy of delivering an individual and social-based active psychological intervention as an adjunct to usual care for individuals receiving opiate substitution treatment who still reported heroin use [70]. Trial participants therefore represented a population group that had failed to receive a maximum benefit from treatment.

For the evaluation of health and capability well-being, participants completed the EQ-5D-5L

[61] (see Chap. 6) and ICECAP-A [42] at baseline and at the 3- and 12-months follow-ups. A health and capability score was assigned to individual responses to the two measures using scoring algorithms developed based on preferences elicited from a representative sample of the English [71] and U.K. population [51], respectively. A number of condition-specific measures were also completed: the Treatment Outcomes Profile [72], the Clinical Outcomes in Routine Evaluation – Outcome Measure [73], the Interpersonal Support Evaluation List [74], the Leeds Dependence Questionnaire [75], and the Social Satisfaction Questionnaire [76].

The analysis looked at the ability of the EQ-5D-5L and ICECAP-A to identify statistically significant differences between participants being better off and participants being worse off in the dimensions of each condition-specific measure. The results showed that the ICECAP-A was able to capture not only those significant differences detected by the EQ-5D-5L but also significant differences in broader well-being indicators that were not detected by the EQ-5D-5L, such as the capacity to benefit from having close people with whom to discuss personal issues and socialize, having personal self-esteem, and being socially satisfied. The analysis also looked at whether capability well-being would be more affected by changes in clinical indicators related to mental health, substance dependence, social support, and social satisfaction. As shown in Fig. 9.3, the ICECAP-A was found to be at least as sensitive as the EQ-5D-5L in capturing effects on health-related clinical indicators and significantly more sensitive for clinical indicators of broader well-being for both follow-up periods [69].

Using the same trial information, a methodological case study was subsequently undertaken to explore within an economic evaluation whether the change of evaluative space from health to capability well being, and the change of decision rule from health maximization to the maximization of sufficient capability, could affect policy recommendations (for full details, see Goranitis et al. [77]). For the purposes of the study, an incremental cost-effectiveness analysis was carried out from both a health and personal social services perspective and a government perspective, based on the outcomes of (a) cost per QALY, estimated using the EQ-5D-5L; (b) cost per YFCs equivalent, estimated using the ICECAP-A; and (c) cost per YSC equivalent [56], also estimated using the ICECAP-A. QALYs, YFCs, and YSCs were all estimated using the standard area under the curve approach [78].

The authors found that, with the standard extra-welfarist (cost per QALY gained) approach, incorporating health as the evaluative space and maximization as the combining rule, the individual-based intervention was the recommended treatment option, producing a greater health benefit at a lower cost than the other two treatment interventions [77]. The treatment recommendation, however, differed when the evaluative space was broadened from health to capability well-being. At this point, usual care became the optimal strategy from both perspectives of the analysis. Similarly, usual care was found to be the recommended intervention when the decision rule was altered from health maximization to capability sufficiency. The results differed not only because usual care seemed to offer more value for the money at potentially acceptable thresholds of willingness to pay per additional YFC or YSC, but also because the uncertainty associated with the decision to fund any intervention other than usual care was prohibitive for rational decision makers. Despite the limitations of this study, the findings highlight that incorporating differing value judgements into an economic evaluation has the potential to lead to different priorities and treatment recommendations (see Chap. 10).

9.5 Discussion

This chapter has outlined the importance of ethical values in economic evaluation and has emphasized their role in determining important aspects of the evaluation and, indeed, the results obtained. For this reason, it is important to be clear on these value judgements and the reasons for them in any evaluation.

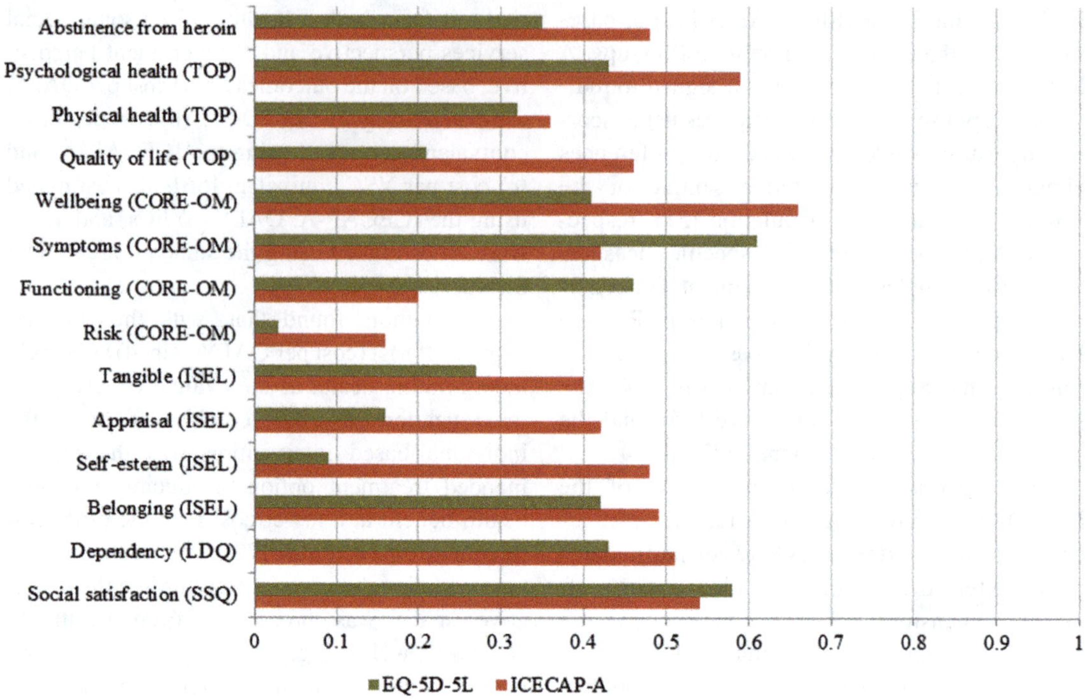

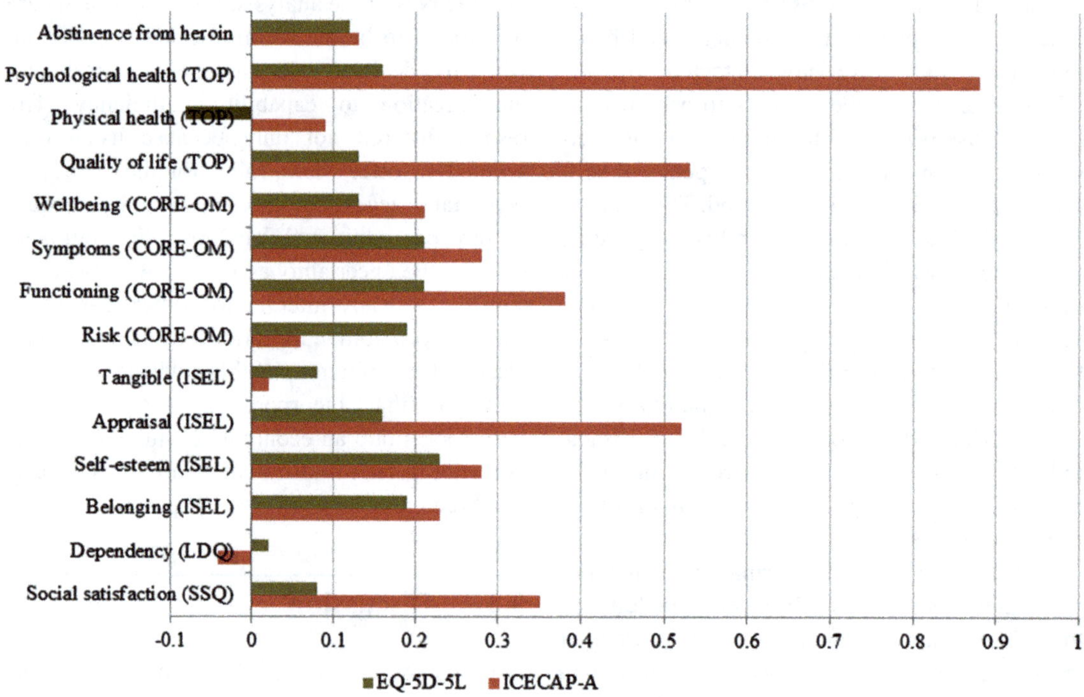

Fig. 9.3 Sensitivity to change of capability well-being (ICECAP-A) and health (EQ-5D-5L) for those participants reporting improvements in clinical indicators at 3 (**a**) and 12 (**b**) months of follow-up

The chapter focused on standard versions of welfarism (utility) and extra-welfarism (health), but also described a new approach to extra-welfarism based on the capability approach described by Sen. This capability approach is clearly defined by a different set of ethical principles, in that what matters goes beyond health or utility to focus on what is important to people in their lives.

The chapter also considered efficiency as the "automatic" goal of economic analysis, rehearsing arguments that the ethical judgements around use of maximization in health are different from those in welfarism, and that the use of maximization (without any equity adjustment) in the health context implies an acceptance that distribution of health is unimportant. The possibility of using the concept of sufficiency to temper such arguments in favor of those with lower health/capability was also discussed, although this approach has made greater inroads in the capability literature to date.

The two case studies both emphasized the different results that are obtained when the evaluative space is altered. Although both studies have limitations, it would be helpful to repeat this approach in other studies to determine the contexts in which results tend to change across the different evaluative spaces. It would also be helpful to include the welfarist approach in such studies.

The main implication of the chapter is the importance of understanding the value judgements enshrined in the chosen approach to economic evaluation, and shifting the approach if these value judgements are considered to be unsatisfactory. For many readers of this text, however, these value judgements will have been made, at least in part, by the regulatory authorities in the context in which they are working. This does not mean, however, that these value judgements cannot be challenged, either within the regulatory process itself or via the presentation of analyses from more than one ethical perspective, as in the second case study described above.

Key Messages

- All forms of economic evaluation rely on ethical value judgements.
- These value judgements determine the important outcomes to include in the economic evaluation.
- They also establish how cost and outcome data are combined to aid decision-making.
- The evidence presented here suggests that interventions for mental health conditions are prioritized differently when different evaluative spaces are used.

For health economics applied to mental health, to truly help optimize resource allocation and make better decisions, the ethics of the value judgements incorporated in an analysis must be both understood and accepted in the context in which the evaluation is being conducted.

Acknowledgments Joanna Coast and Paul Mitchell are partly funded by the National Institute for Health Research Collaboration for Leadership in Applied Health Research and Care West (NIHR CLAHRC West). Paul Mitchell is also cofunded by the UK Renal Registry. The views expressed are those of the authors and not necessarily those of the National Health Service, the National Institute for Health Research, the Department of Health, or the UK Renal Registry.

References

1. Hargreaves Heap S, Hollis M, Lyons B, Sugden R, Weale A. The theory of choice. A critical guide. Oxford: Blackwell; 1992.
2. Culyer AJ. The normative economics of health care finance and provision. Oxf Rev Econ Policy. 1989;5(1):34–56.
3. Coast J, Smith RD, Lorgelly P. Welfarism, extra-welfarism and capability: the spread of ideas in health economics. Soc Sci Med. 2008;67:1190–8.
4. Coast J, Smith RD, Lorgelly P. Should the capability approach be applied in health economics? Health Econ. 2008;17:667–70.

5. Anand P. Capabilities and health. J Med Ethics. 2005;31:299–303.
6. Coast J. Maximisation in extra-welfarism: a critique of the current position in health economics. Soc Sci Med. 2009;69:786–92.
7. Dolan P, Shaw R, Tsuchiya A, Williams A. QALY maximisation and people's preferences: a methodological review of the literature. Health Econ. 2005;14:197–208.
8. Rowen D, Brazier J, Mukuria C, Keetharuth A, Hole AR, Tsuchiya A, et al. Eliciting societal preferences for weighting QALYs for burden of illness and end of life. Med Decis Mak. 2016;36:210–22.
9. Van de Wetering EJ, Van Exel NJA, Rose JM, Hoefman RJ, Brouwer WBF. Are some QALYs more equal than others? Eur J Health Econ. 2016;17:117–27.
10. Brouwer WBF, Culyer AJ, van Exel NJA, Rutten FFH. Welfarism vs. extra-welfarism. J Health Econ. 2008;27:325–38.
11. Mathes T, Jacobs E, Morfield JC, Pieper D. Methods of international health technology agencies for economic evaluations – a comparative analysis. BMC Health Serv Res. 2013;13(1).
12. Buchanan J, Wordsworth S. Welfarism versus extra-welfarism: can the choice of economic evaluation approach impact on the adoption decisions recommended by economic evaluation studies? PharamacoEconomics. 2015;33(6):571–9.
13. Sen A. Commodities and capabilities. New Delhi: Oxford University Press; 1999.
14. Cohen GA. Equality of what? On welfare, good and capabilities. In: Nussbaum MC, Sen AK, editors. The quality of life. Oxford: Clarendon Press; 1993. p. 9–29.
15. Gold MR, Siegel JE, Russell LB, Weinstein MC. Cost-effectiveness in health and medicine. New York: Oxford University Press; 1996.
16. Kenkel D. On valuing morbidity, cost-effectiveness analysis, and being rude. J Health Econ. 1997;16(6): 749–57.
17. O'Brien B, Viramontes JL. Willingness to pay. A valid and reliable measure of health state preference? Med Decis Mak. 1994;14(3):288.
18. Diamond PA, Hausman JA. Contingent valuation: is some number better than no number? J Econ Perspect. 1994;8(4):45–64.
19. Cookson R. Willingness to pay methods in health care: a sceptical view. Health Econ. 2003;12(11):891–4.
20. Kahneman D, Wakker PP, Sarin R. Back to Bentham? Explorations of experienced utility. Q J Econ. 1997;112:375–405.
21. Kahneman D, Sugden R. Experienced utility as a standard of policy evaluation. Environ Resour Econ. 2005;32(1):161–81.
22. Sen A. Personal utilities and public judgements: or what's wrong with welfare economics? Econ J. 1979;89:537–58.
23. Birch S, Donaldson C. Valuing the benefits and costs of health care programmes: where's the 'extra' in extra-welfarism? Soc Sci Med. 2003;56:1121–33.
24. Coast J, Flynn N, Sutton E, Al-Janabi H, Vosper J, Lavender S, et al. Investigating choice experiments for perferences of older people (ICEPOP): evaluative spaces in health economics. J Health Serv Res Policy. 2008;13(Suppl 3):31–7.
25. Lorgelly PK, Lawson KD, Fenwick EAL, Briggs AH. Outcome measurement in economic evaluation of public health interventions: a role for the capability approach? Int J Environ Res Public Health. 2010;7:2274–89.
26. Chalkidou K, Culyer A, Naidoo B, Littlejohns P. Cost-effective public health guidance: asking questions from the decision-maker's viewpoint. Health Econ. 2008;17:441–8.
27. Coast J. Strategies for the economic evaluation of end-of-life care: making a case for the capability approach. Expert Rev Pharmacoecon Outcomes Res. 2014;14(4):473–82.
28. Chisholm D, Healey A, Knapp M. QALYs and mental healthcare. Soc Psychiatry Psychiatr Epidemiol. 1997;32:68–75.
29. Brazier J, Connell J, Papaioannou D, Mukuria C, Mulhern B, Peasgood T, et al. A systematic review, psychometric analysis and qualitative assessment of generic preference-based measures of health in mental health populations and the estimation of mapping functions from widely used specific measures. Health Technol Assess. 2014;18(34):1–188.
30. Department of Health. Closing the gap: priorities for essential change in mental health. London: Department of Health; 2014.
31. Al-Janabi H, Flynn TN, Coast J. QALYs and carers. PharmacoEconomics. 2011;29(12):1015–23.
32. Boadway RW, Bruce N. Welfare economics. Oxford: Blackwell; 1993.
33. Hicks JR. The foundations of welfare economics. Econ J. 1939;49:696–712.
34. Hicks JR. The rehabilitation of consumers' surplus. Rev Econ Stud. 1941;8:108–16.
35. Kaldor N. Welfare propositions of economics and interpersonal comparisons of utility. Econ J. 1939;49: 549–52.
36. Culyer AJ. Inequality of health services is, in general, desirable. In: Green DG, editor. Acceptable inequalities? Essays on the pursuit of equality in health care. London: The IEA Health Unit; 1988. p. 31–47.
37. Roncaglia A. The wealth of ideas. A history of economic thought. New York: Cambridge University Press; 2005.
38. Rawlins M, Barnett D, Stevens A. Pharmacoeconomics: NICE's approach to decision-making. Br J Clin Pharmacol. 2010;70(3):346–9.
39. Van de Wetering EJ, Stolk EA, Van Exel NJA, Brouwer WBF. Balancing equity and efficiency in the Dutch basic benefits package using the principle of proportional shortfall. Eur J Health Econ. 2013;14:107–15.
40. Sen A. Capability and well-being. In: Nussbaum MC, editor. The quality of life. Oxford: Clarendon Press; 1993.

41. Coast J, Kinghorn P, Mitchell P. The development of capability measures in health economics: opportunities, challenges and progress. The Patient. 2015;8:119–26.
42. Al-Janabi H, Flynn TN, Coast J. Development of a self-report measure of capability wellbeing for adults: the ICECAP-A. Qual Life Res. 2012;21: 167–76.
43. Coast J, Flynn TN, Natarajan L, Sproston K, Lewis J, Louviere JJ, et al. Valuing the ICECAP capability index for older people. Soc Sci Med. 2008;67:874–82.
44. Sutton E, Coast J. Development of a supportive care measure for economic evaluation of end-of-life care, using qualitative methods. Palliat Med. 2014;28: 151–7.
45. Lorgelly PK, Lorimer K, Fenwick EAL, Briggs AH, Anand P. Operationalising the capability approach as an outcome measure in public health: the development of the OCAP-18. Soc Sci Med. 2015;142: 68–81.
46. Simon J, Anand P, Gray A, Rugkasa J, Yeeles K, Burns T. Operationalising the capability approach for outcome measurement in mental health research. Soc Sci Med. 2013;98:187–96.
47. Kinghorn P, Robinson A, Smith RD. Developing a capability-based questionnaire for assessing wellbeing in patients with chronic pain. Soc Indic Res. 2014;120:897–916.
48. Netten A, Burge P, Malley J, Potoglou D, Towers A-M, Brazier J, et al. Outcomes of social care for adults: developing a preference-weighted measure. Health Technol Assess. 2012;16(16):1–166.
49. Greco G, Skordis-Worrall J, Mkandawire B, Mills A. What is a good life? Selecting capabilities to assess women's quality of life in rural Malawi. Soc Sci Med. 2015;130:69–78.
50. Grewal I, Lewis J, Flynn TN, Brown J, Bond J, Coast J. Developing attributes for a generic quality of life measure for older people: preferences or capabilities? Soc Sci Med. 2006;62:1891–901.
51. Flynn TN, Huynh E, Peters TJ, Al-Janabi H, Clemens S, Moody A, et al. Scoring the ICECAP-A capability instrument. Estimation of a UK general population tariff. Health Econ. 2015;24(3):258–69.
52. Louviere JJ, Flynn TN, Marley AAJ. Best-worst scaling: theory, methods and applications. Cambridge: Cambridge University Press; 2015.
53. Ruger JP. Health and social justice. Lancet. 2004;364:1075–80.
54. Mitchell P, Roberts TE, Barton PM, Coast J. Applications of the capability approach in health: a literature review. Soc Indic Res. 2016; doi: 10.1007/s11205-016-1356-8.
55. Fourie C, Rid A. What is enough? Sufficiency, justice and health. Oxford: Oxford University Press; 2016.
56. Mitchell PM, Roberts TE, Barton PM, Coast J. Assessing sufficient capability: a new approach to economic evaluation. Soc Sci Med. 2015;139:71–9.
57. Sen A. Inequality reexamined. New York: Russell Sage Foundation; 1992.
58. Mitchell P, Al-Janabi H, Iezzi A, Richardson J, Coast J. The relative impacts of disease on health status and capability wellbeing: a multi-country study. PLoS ONE. 2015;10(12).
59. Lovibond SH, Lovibond PF. Manual for the depression anxiety stress scales. Sydney: Psychology Foundation; 1995.
60. Kessler RC, Barker PR, Colpe LJ, Epstein JF, Gfroerer JC, Hiripi E, et al. Screening for serious mental illness in the general population. Arch Gen Psychiatry. 2003;60(2):184–9.
61. Herdman M, Gudex C, Lloyd A, Janssen MF, Kind P, Parkin D, et al. Development and preliminary testing of the new five-level version of EQ-D (EQ-5D-5L). Qual Life Res. 2011;20:1727–36.
62. Van Hout B, Janssen MF, Feng Y-S, Kohlmann T, Busschbach J, Golicki D, et al. Interim scoring for the EQ-5D-5L: mapping the EQ-5D-5L to EQ-5D-3L value sets. Value Health. 2012;15:708–15.
63. Department of Health. Drug strategy 2010. Reducing demand, restricting supply, building recovery: supporting people to live a drug free life. London: Department of Health; 2010.
64. UK Drug Policy Commission. The UK drug policy commission recovery consensus group: a vision of recovery. London: UKDPC; 2008.
65. Sindelar JL, Jofre-Bonet M, French MT, McLellan AT. Cost-effectiveness analysis of addiction treatment: paradoxes of multiple outcomes. Drug Alcohol Depend. 2004;73(1):41–50.
66. De Maeyer J, Vanderplasschen W, Broekaert E. Quality of life among opiate-dependent individuals: a review of the literature. Int J Drug Policy. 2010;21(5):364–80.
67. Nussbaum MC. Creating capabilities: the human development approach. Cambridge, MA: Harvard University Press; 2011.
68. Orford J. Power, powerlessness and addiction. Cambridge: Cambridge University Press; 2013.
69. Goranitis I, Coast J, Day E, Copello A, Freemantle N, Seddon J, et al. Measuring health and broader wellbeing benefits in the context of opiate dependence: the psychometric performance of the ICECAP-A and EQ-5D-5L. Value Health. 2016;19:820–8.
70. Day E, Copello A, Seddon JL, Christie M, Bamber D, Powell C, et al. Pilot study of a social network intervention for heroin users in opiate substitution treatment: study protocol for a randomized controlled trial. Trials. 2013;14(1):264.
71. Devlin N, Shah K, Feng Y, Mulhern B, Van Hout B. Valuing health-related quality of life. An EQ-5D-5L value set for England. London: Office of Health Economics; 2016.
72. Marsden J, Farell M, Bradbury C, Dale-Perera A, Eastwood B, Roxburgh M, et al. Development of the treatment outcomes profile. Addiction. 2008;103(9):1450–60.
73. Evans J-C, Margison F, Barkham M, Audin K, Connell J, McGrath G. CORE: clinical outcomes in routine evaluation. J Ment Health. 2000;9(3):247–55.

74. Cohen S, Hoberman HM. Positive events and social supports as buffers of life change stress. J Appl Soc Psychol. 1983;13(2):99–125.
75. Raistrick D, Bradshaw J, Tober G, Weiner J, Allison J, Healey C. Development of the leeds dependence questionnaire (LDQ): a questionnaire to measure alcohol and opiate dependence in the context of a treatment evaluation package. Addiction. 1994;89(5):563–72.
76. Tober G, Brearley R, Kenyon R, Raistrick D, Morley S. Measuring outcomes in a health service addiction clinic. Addict Res Theory. 2000;8(2):169–82.
77. Goranitis I, Coast J, Day E, Copello A, Freemantle N, Frew E. Maximizing health or sufficient capability in economic evaluation? A methodological experiment of treatment for drug addiction. Med Decis Making. 2016; doi:10.1177/0272989X16678844.
78. Drummond MF, Sculpher MJ, Claxton K, Stoddart GL, Torrance GW. Methods for the economic evaluation of health care programmes. Oxford: Oxford University Press; 2015.

Health Economics as a Tool for Decision-Making in Mental Health Care

10

Martin Knapp

Abstract

Economic analysis aims to help decision makers make better decisions. It is primarily concerned with efficiency: using available resources to maximize achievements in terms of better health and well-being. Cost-effectiveness, cost utility, and cost-benefit analyses are the main tools used by economists for this purpose. Equity is another criterion increasingly recognized as important; equity ensures that access to services and payments for them are distributed fairly across different population groups, with the hope that treatment outcomes might also be more fairly experienced. In this chapter I discuss what decision makers want from economic evaluation and consider some of the uses to which such empirical evidence could be put in the mental health field. These uses – by decision-makers and by others – include lobbying, marketing, comparison, commissioning, health technology appraisal and guidance, policy development, and personalization and empowerment. Each use is illustrated with brief examples.

M. Knapp (✉)
PSSRU, London School of Economics and Political Science, Houghton Street, WC2A2AE London, UK
e-mail: M.Knapp@lse.ac.uk

D. Razzouk (ed.), *Mental Health Economics*, DOI 10.1007/978-3-319-55266-8_10

Key Points Summary

- What decision makers want
- Efficiency and equity
- Types of policy and practice questions, and how economic analysis can respond
- Why economic evidence is helpful to support policy discussions and inform practice decisions
- Illustrations of the uses of economic evaluations
- Barriers to the use of economic evaluative evidence

10.1 Why Is Economics Evidence Needed?

When considering whether a treatment or care service should be provided, the core "clinical" question is whether it reduces symptoms, improves functioning, or has a positive effect on quality of life. The equivalent for preventive strategies would be whether the risk of developing the target illness is reduced or its effects reduced. If one adopts a recovery focus to mental health, the equivalent question would be the degree to which an individual can achieve goals that they have set personally, whether in terms of objective indicators of social roles (such as having paid employment or being in a relationship) or more subjective indicators of personal goals [1]. But because resources are scarce – and of course they are *always* scarce – individuals who are responsible for deciding how to allocate resources not only want to consider these questions but also the *economic* question: Are the resources that are required in order to deliver the treatment (or the preventive strategy or recovery-focused approach) justified by the achievements made in terms of better outcomes?

Scarcity of resources means that choices have to be made (see Chap. 1). They are not likely to be easy choices. For example, to what extent should services for people experiencing episodes of severe psychotic symptoms be delivered in inpatient hospital settings or by specialist community teams? If those psychosis services are stretched too far, with more individuals needing treatment than the services can support, which patients should be prioritized? How much treatment time (e.g., how many psychotherapy sessions, or how many home visits) should be allocated to each patient? What proportion of the budget should be diverted from treating mental health problems identified today in order instead to uncover previously unrecognized needs or to invest in a broader health promotion strategy that might prevent similar needs emerging in the future? When is it reasonable to stop treatment for one particular patient and instead use therapist time to start treatment for another patient? Should healthcare professionals focus only on alleviating symptoms rather than on wider issues such as whether their patients are employed or claiming welfare benefits to which they are entitled?

First and foremost, these are all clinical- or service-focused questions. In searching for answers, however, decision makers would do well to recognize that they are also *economic* questions. Answering each of these questions entails a tough choice for the people who control, manage, or allocate resources, because they will almost never have all the resources they would like in order to uncover or respond to every need, treat every patient, invest in prevention, or help individuals to achieve their broad life goals.

Those decision makers include government ministers, elected politicians, chief executives and boards of major corporations and nonprofit organizations, owners of small enterprises, health insurance fund managers, and almost every purchaser, provider, and professional in health, social care, housing, education, and other systems. People with lived experience of mental illness and their families are also decision makers in that they must choose how to use their own resources of income and time. For each of these people – for each of us – scarcity is an everyday reality.

If we assume that these individuals and organizations aim to be reasonably rational in their decision-making, they will allocate their resources so as to do the best they can in terms of one or more patient-related consequences. These consequences are likely to include how well needs are met or symptoms are alleviated, how much pain can be reduced, whether normal functioning at work or in relationships can be restored, what improvements can be made to overall quality of life, and the extent to which future risks of disorders are reduced. The aim of economic analysis is to help decision makers make their decisions: to use their available resources so as to maximize achievements in terms of relevant consequences. As other chapters in this book describe, cost-effectiveness, cost-utility, and cost-benefit analyses are tools economists use to provide decision makers with what is hoped to be helpful evaluative evidence (see Chaps. 4, 5, and 6). In this chapter I discuss what decision makers want from economic evaluation, then illustrate the potential uses of such empirical evidence in the mental health field.

10.2 What Do Decision Makers Want?

As noted earlier, any mental health system contains many decision makers, from those who control the budgets to those who actually deliver and use the services. Each of them is likely to be acutely aware that the resources available to them are limited. In choosing one option over another, they might have access to a number of resource-related criteria to guide their decisions. They are likely to want to maximize what they can achieve (in terms of the impact of treatment or care) from the resources they control. They might want to broaden access to evidence-based therapies, remove barriers to services, improve social and economic integration of people experiencing mental health issues, tackle unfair inequalities in what individuals or families are expected to pay for their treatment, or better target available services so they reach people with the greatest or most urgent needs. Many of these criteria fall into two groups: efficiency and equity.

10.2.1 Equity

Equity refers to the extent to which treatment outcomes, access to services, and payment for them are distributed fairly across the population (see Chap. 8). For instance, are these outcomes, services, and costs distributed unequally by sex, age, ethnicity, language, religion, political beliefs, sexual orientation, socioeconomic position, or place of residence? If so, is this inequality considered to be appropriate and fair? This obviously begs the question of what is meant by "fair." Equity (or fairness) is clearly not the same as *equality* in the provision of services, as all people do not have exactly the same needs or circumstances. Most people are likely to agree that it would be more equitable to allocate resources so that more treatment and access to care are provided to people with greater or more urgent needs. Similarly, many people might agree that it would be more equitable to ask individuals with less ability to pay for their treatment – probably those people with lower incomes or fewer assets – to pay smaller amounts to be able to receive those treatments compared with individuals with greater ability to pay.

A frequently discussed equity issue faced by mental health decision makers today relates to the links between incidence and prevalence, on the one hand, and socioeconomic status, ethnicity, age, and other personal characteristics, on the other hand. There is also a link between access to evidence-based care and treatment, and the type and level of need, as well as to other personal characteristics. How mental health care is financed and whether and how ability to pay is taken into account are widely discussed. In each respect, plenty of evidence of inequities exists. Work from my own research group, for example, has shown that income-related inequality in relation to prevalence in the United Kingdom is markedly worse for mental illness than for general ill health [2], and it varies, again markedly, by ethnicity [3]. We have also shown that income-related inequalities in relation to depression and suicide worsen considerably during periods of economic recession, as during the sustained economic difficulties experienced in South Korea during the 1990s [4]. Questions about inequities also need to be asked in relation to the receipt of healthcare; a very useful, recent review article by Cookson et al. [5] summarizes what is known about the distribution of healthcare in general in England.

10.2.2 Efficiency

Efficiency can be defined in a number of ways, but at the heart of this criterion is the relationship between effectiveness and cost: How many services or how much health gain is achieved from a specified volume of resources? An efficient allocation of resources is one that delivers a particular set of services at minimum cost, or achieves the greatest population health gain from a given budget. It is also important that the services delivered or the health gains achieved from those resources are those that society actually views as most desirable (a concept often described as "allocative efficiency").

Economic evaluation is primarily concerned with addressing questions of efficiency, although health economists are gradually paying more attention to equity issues in their evaluations [6]. The essence of an economic evaluation is to calculate the costs associated with an intervention – such as a medication, psychotherapy, or service arrangement – factor in any downstream monetary savings that might flow from using that intervention, and compare those costs with costs of some alternative intervention. The outcomes from each of the two (or more) interventions would also be measured, perhaps in terms of reduced symptoms, improved functioning (e.g., in relation to employment or personal relationships), and better well-being. The costs and outcomes would then need to be considered together: Is one intervention both cheaper and more effective than the other? If so, then it clearly represents a more efficient use of available resources. Does one intervention achieve better outcomes, but only at the expense of higher net costs (costs minus savings)? If so, it may not be immediately clear whether the intervention with the better outcomes is the more efficient choice. The quandary is whether the better outcomes *justify* the higher cost, and the decision maker needs to consider the trade-off between the better outcomes and the higher costs. This is a value judgement and is not reducible to a scientific algorithm.

10.3 Types of Questions and Evaluations

Economists can support decision makers to make these difficult value judgements in a number of ways, in particular through different types of economic evaluation. These evaluations share many common features but because they address different questions, they differ mainly in terms of how they define and measure outcomes. It is worth noting immediately that these evaluation types are not mutually exclusive: a single research study often addresses more than one question, and therefore involves more than one type of analysis; in this way the study offers answers to more than one decision-relevant question.

When evaluating an intervention targeted to a particular condition (such as severe depression) and comparing it with another intervention with the same purpose, the most relevant outcomes to use would be specific to the condition (such as alleviating core depressive symptoms, in this case). As other chapters in this book have described, the most appropriate type of evaluation for this task is a *cost-effectiveness analysis* (see Chap. 5), and this evaluative type is used most often in health economics research. It looks at disorder-specific outcomes and the costs needed to avoid them (for a preventive intervention) or to improve them (for a treatment intervention).

But the context for the decision could be broader. For example, the question could be whether to invest in preventing anxiety or preventing coronary heart disease. In this case, a disease-specific measure – such as one that assesses anxiety symptoms or one that assesses the degree of atherosclerosis – is not going to be very helpful because it is relevant to only one of the two diseases, and comparisons between them are meaningless. Health economists often turn to a generic outcome measure for this purpose, for example, health-related quality of life or disability, which lead to measures of quality-adjusted life years (QALYs) or disability-adjusted life years, respectively. When using QALYs to indicate the outcomes of treatment or prevention, this form of evaluation is referred to either as a *cost-utility analysis* (see Chap. 6) or, slightly confusingly, a cost-effectiveness analysis, albeit one that uses a generic outcome measure. A cost-utility analysis can tell the strategic decision maker where among a range of potentially quite different intervention options and disease areas they are likely to achieve the biggest effect from their resources[7].

The broadest of economic evaluations is *cost-benefit analysis* (see Chap. 4). This type of evaluation is helpful if a decision maker must choose how to allocate resources across diverse areas such as healthcare, education, and housing. In this case, the only feasible outcome to consider is either monetary valuations of what is achieved or perhaps a high-level hedonic well-being measure such as life satisfaction [8]. It is not easy to calculate the monetary values of mental health outcomes, and the use of life satisfaction as an overarching indicator of an outcome such as well-being has not been explored much to date. Consequently, cost-benefit analyses are rare in mental health contexts (indeed, they are rare across the whole health spectrum). Occasionally, it makes sense to use as the primary outcome in an evaluation something such as whether individuals are able to gain or retain employment; in this case, the evaluation could potentially attach a monetary value to the productivity gains that result, since those gains usually have market value (i.e., a price). We were able to do this in our evaluation of individual placement and support in a six-country European study. Employment gain was the main purpose of the intervention, and so we were able to conduct a cost-benefit analysis as well as other analyses [9]. Interestingly, one of the very first economic evaluations in the mental health field – a randomized controlled trial of the Training in Community Living model in Wisconsin (an assertive outreach service) – focused exclusively on patient earnings as monetized benefits of care [10]. Although the economic evaluation was therefore somewhat narrowly conceptualized, it was published in tandem with an article reporting the clinical outcomes measured more conventionally. Our own evaluation of the London equivalent – the Maudsley Daily Living Programme – did not include a cost-benefit calculation because gaining employment (hence achieving earnings) was not an objective of the service; we instead performed a cost-effectiveness analysis [11].

10.4 Uses of Economic Evidence

It should be clear from what has already been discussed that the evidence from an economic evaluation could have a number of potential uses; therefore it is possible to find many ways in which economic evaluation is blended with other evidence to inform and support the actions of decision makers. I have organized this discussion under a number of headings, distinguishing the following inter-connected uses: lobbying, marketing, comparison, commissioning, health technology appraisal and guidance, policy development, and personalization and empowerment. Each of these uses is illustrated by some brief examples.

10.4.1 Lobbying

Although not strictly a form of economic evaluation, cost-of-illness calculations have often been used to argue the case for more resources to be devoted to a particular field or to address a specific disorder. Cost-of-illness studies identify, measure, and then aggregate the economic effects of a disorder. The best such studies include all or most of those effects, particularly direct costs associated with treatment and care, as well as indirect costs linked to reduced productivity that might arise because of disrupted employment or to the unpaid care provided by a family member or friend. These calculated cost aggregates are not *evaluative* because they do not compare two or more treatment options and therefore do not provide any information to a decision maker about what should be done to meet mental health needs or to invest in prevention. But they can still be useful for highlighting the scale of an issue.

Cost-of-illness studies are popular with advocacy groups and patient organizations because the calculations usually conclude that the disorder being studied generates high, wide-ranging, and long-lasting costs. These figures can then be used to grab the attention of the media and also, it is hoped, the budget holders within strategic decision-making bodies. People usually propound the argument that a disorder that generates high costs deserves high investment in terms of funded treatment and care. In turn, this would lead to better health and quality of life for people living with the condition and for their families. Pharmaceutical, medical device, and other companies also often commission and use cost-of-illness results to draw attention to what they might argue is an under-resourced treatment area, thereby hopefully increasing demand for their products. It does need to be emphasized, however, that the scale of economic impact alone is insufficient grounds for the efficient allocation of resources; for that purpose we need to know what outcomes would flow from the investment and from the best alternative way(s) to use that same amount of resources.

I and my colleagues have conducted a few cost-of-illness studies in the mental health field. These include two dementia studies commissioned by the Alzheimer's Society, the leading charity for dementia support and research in England, Wales, and Northern Ireland [12, 13]. The 2014 dementia study had a simple structure: we first divided the older population into subgroups by age, sex, and severity of dementia, then we assigned people to different care settings (in the community, care homes, or a hospital) on the basis of national statistics. We then estimated spending on care by attaching an average weekly cost to each type of care and each severity category (including an imputed cost for unpaid support). The 2007 study included prevalence and cost projections, as well as evidence on care variations across the country, and argued the case for improving service quality; these findings have been credited [14] as leading directly to England's first national dementia strategy [15].

Another of our studies calculated the overall cost of Alzheimer disease in the United Kingdom, and compared it with similar calculations for stroke, heart disease, and cancer. Then it compared research expenditures in each of those same disease areas [16]. This study was funded by Alzheimer's Research UK, another leading charity.

We also completed two calculations of the overall costs of autism in the United Kingdom [17], and a third that compared costs between the United Kingdom and United States [18]. All were commissioned by autism charities, and the findings were extensively used to argue that autism is relatively neglected with regard to diagnosis, treatment, care, and research see Chap. 23).

Lobbying for more and better mental healthcare can of course also build on cost-effectiveness and other evaluations. For example, a membership organization of psychologists and other counselors might want to use evidence of both effectiveness and cost-effectiveness to argue for a greater proportion of treatment resources to be allocated to psychosocial interventions. Or a provider of services might use economic evaluation evidence to demonstrate how its activities are saving costs elsewhere or promoting better health and well-being for patients.

10.4.2 Marketing

This then takes us to a second broad use of economic evidence: for the purposes of marketing. Although pharmaceutical companies and other manufacturers can make good use of cost-of-illness studies, they might be able to garner stronger interest in their products if they demonstrate cost-effectiveness. Therefore, these companies often commission a cost-effectiveness study or other economic evaluation in the hope that it helps to influence local or national patterns of treatment. In fact, some countries now formally require manufacturers (particularly of new pharmaceutical products) to submit evidence of cost-effectiveness to regulatory or health technology assessment (HTA) bodies. Subsequently, these HTA or other bodies might commission their own "independent" economic evaluations, or build simulation models (see Chap. 7) that pool evidence from commercially supported and other studies.

Some of the earliest economic evaluations in the mental health field were funded by pharmaceutical companies. The first economic study of the new class of selective serotonin reuptake inhibitors for treating depression focused on fluoxetine and was commissioned by Eli Lilly, its manufacturer [19]. The first economic study of so-called atypical antipsychotics for treating schizophrenia was a retrospective database evaluation of risperidone and was funded by Janssen, the drug's manufacturer [20].

Of course, no manufacturers can commercialize interventions such as psychosocial therapies or particular service configurations (such as case management), and hence there are no "product champions." Evidence of their effectiveness or cost-effectiveness therefore needs to be generated elsewhere, for example, by a professional body, a government department, or a research charity.

10.4.3 Comparisons

Evaluations are, by definition, comparisons: in the context of treatment for a particular condition, a clinical evaluation compares the outcomes of two or more medications or other interventions, and an economic evaluation compares their relative cost-effectiveness. Beyond that, evidence from economic evaluations or other studies can be used for wider comparisons. For example, the international charity Alzheimer's Disease International commissioned research that calculated and used estimates of the global cost of dementia to support its case for earlier diagnosis, better care and treatment, and more research on causes [21]. In its subsequent annual World Alzheimer Report, the focus turned to the cost-effectiveness of shifting tasks and providing better treatment for dementia (see Chap. 22), and included detailed economic modeling of a range of evidence-based interventions in some sample countries (Canada, China, Indonesia, Mexico, South Africa, South Korea, and Switzerland). One purpose was to demonstrate how resources could be used efficiently to achieve better outcomes for people living with dementia and their families, and to stimulate local discussion in part through international comparison [13].

Other examples can be given. One of the autism cost-of-illness studies mentioned earlier integrated data from a number of previous studies of accommodation, medical services, nonmedical services, and out-of-pocket payments by families in both the United Kingdom and the United States, then combined these data with estimates of prevalence [18]. One interesting result was that the lifetime cost for an individual with autism and intellectual disability was very similar in the two countries. In general, descriptive evidence of patterns of service use, employment difficulties, costs, and other economic dimensions can provide helpful platforms for a discussion of policy frameworks and practice-level implementation. A more recent study compared the workplace-related absenteeism and presenteeism costs associated with depression across eight diverse countries (Brazil, Canada, China, Japan, South Korea, Mexico, South Africa, and the United States). A number of individual, workplace, and societal factors were found to be associated with lower productivity [22].

Heterogeneity is the norm – not the exception – between and within countries and regions, and between different service providers and funding bodies. Most obvious are the marked differences between patients with respect to their needs, strengths, characteristics, family circumstances, community contexts, preferences, and so on. These individual-level differences probably work to affect the outcomes and costs of treatment and support. Understanding what those cost and outcome variations are and the extent to which they are systematically associated with the characteristics of individual patients will help decision makers plan the funding, delivery, and targeting of treatments.

In our own work, we often seek to describe and then "explain" statistically patterns of cost variation and association. We did this, for example, at a time when national and local decisions were being taken to close long-stay psychiatric hospitals in England, and so plans were needed to allow long-term residents to move toward new lives in the community. A number of our studies looked at the economic considerations [23], including an examination of whether one provider sector is more costly than another in achieving good outcomes [24]. We subsequently reviewed the economic evidence on deinstitutionalization [25].

In another study, we used a large, nationally representative epidemiological survey to show how service utilization and cost differences for children and adolescents with mental health problems were significantly associated with the child's age, sex, ethnicity, type of disorder, severity of symptoms, and reading attainment; maternal age; parental anxiety and depression; social class; and family size and functioning [26].

10.4.4 Commissioning

Healthcare financing can take many different forms, from public-sector arrangements such as taxation (local or national, direct or indirect, general or earmarked) and social health insurance to private-sector arrangements such as voluntary health insurance, medical savings accounts, and user charges (out-of-pocket expenditures or copayments). The funds traverse a number of channels to reach the treatment and care providers, including block budgets, a capitation system, prices linked to diagnosis-related groups and other case-based arrangements, and fee-for-service transfers [27]. Attention is increasingly focused on pay-for-performance initiatives within some of these mechanisms, with the aim being not simply to pay for activity, but instead to reward achievement.

Each of these various payment mechanisms represents a form of commissioning, the aim of which is to improve quality, effectiveness, and efficiency. Commissioners need to know what it costs to provide a particular type of treatment for a particular type of patient, and how those costs relate to the outcomes that are achieved. The diagnosis-related groups system is especially dependent on high-quality economic evidence of this kind. A payment schedule might then be designed to encourage treatments to be targeted at individuals who are thought to be especially vulnerable or deemed to be priority cases because of urgent need or other factors. The studies I described earlier that explored the extent and sources of cost variations could certainly greatly help in this regard.

10.4.5 Health Technology Appraisal and Guideline Development

Many countries now have formal mechanisms to consider effectiveness and cost-effectiveness evidence on new technologies (such as new medications and medical devices) to feed into decisions about reimbursement and coverage [28] and to develop guidance. The work of the National Institute of Health and Care Excellence (NICE) in England and Wales is internationally well known for its thorough technology appraisals and its subsequent development of clinical guidelines. NICE conducts literature reviews, meta-analyses, and expert appraisals; synthesizes information on clinical effectiveness and cost-effectiveness; and then develops guidelines to help individual clinicians and other professionals choose the best treatment in the sense that it is known to be effective and is considered to be cost-effective in the context of National Health Service structures and funding levels in England and Wales. NICE uses a cost-per-QALY threshold to guide its decisions: effective interventions found to have a cost per QALY gained less than £20,000 are likely to be recommended for use within the National Health Service, whereas a cost per QALY that exceeds £30,000 is unlikely to be recommended, unless powerful other considerations exist (such as being an "orphan" technology).

HTA mechanisms vary from country to country, as do decisions about health technology use. For example, a comparison of HTA processes in England, Scotland, France, and the Netherlands revealed that a range of factors were associated with decisions – some linked to evidence of effectiveness and cost-effectiveness, and some other considerations – although a large proportion of variance remained unexplained [29].

10.4.6 Policy Development

Today, it is common to see economic evidence being used to inform policy-making at local, regional, and national levels. Strategic planning and development of mental health systems increasingly rely on such evidence, which then cascades down to influence ground-level service delivery. Government bodies might also deploy economic methods to monitor the consequences of policy change.

An early example from my own experience is how economic analysis helped to inform both broad policy discussion and local implementation plans in relation to the closure of psychiatric and other long-stay hospitals in England. My group's later systematic review of the economic evidence concluded that community-based models of care are not inherently more costly than the institutions they are intended to replace, once individuals' needs and the quality of care are taken into account [25]. But neither are they cheaper, and any policy predicated on the expectation that hospital closure will save money risks failure in the sense that many vulnerable people could be left with dangerously inadequate support in the community. Our review found that even if community-based care arrangements are more expensive than long-term hospital care, they could still be more cost-effective because they have the potential to deliver better outcomes.

Another example of direct influence on policy development is modeling of the economic consequences of common mental disorders and their treatment through psychological therapies, particularly cognitive behavioral therapy. The modeling study was published by Layard et al. [8]. This analysis influenced the U.K. Labour Party's decision to make access to psychological therapy a manifesto commitment in its national election campaign in 2005, and this subsequently became a major plank of health policy in the form of the Improving Access to Psychological Therapies (IAPT) program. IAPT has greatly improved access to evidence-based psychotherapy for people with mental health needs, thereby improving their quality of life and reducing workplace absenteeism, unemployment, and long-term National Health Service costs. The effectiveness of cognitive behavioral therapy was fundamental to the decision to invest in IAPT, but it was the economic evidence that tipped the balance and made sure that the policy idea became a service reality.

Numerous other examples can be given. The Department of Health in England commissioned a collection of small modeling studies from my research center, PSSRU at the London School of Economics, to examine the economic case for mental health promotion and mental illness prevention [30]. Among the studies included in our report were economic models of services or programs delivered in schools, workplaces, communities, and healthcare settings, and those targeted at groups including pregnant women, families with young children, school students, socially isolated older people, individuals with medically unexplained symptoms, and people who might be considered at risk for suicide. Well-established evidence of effectiveness already existed for each of the 15 interventions that were modeled, and our aim was to examine whether economic payoffs were achieved from these interventions in terms of direct (immediate or longer-term) cash savings to the public sector, to employers, or to the wider society (for example, through crimes averted). The findings fed directly into national policy discussions and local commissioning decisions.

A final example is the impressive program of cost-effectiveness work conducted by the World Health Organization in its Choosing Interventions that are Cost Effective (CHOICE) program. This international endeavor has collated information on the costs, effect on population health, and cost-effectiveness of a range of different mental health interventions for each of the 17 World Health Organization subregions [31].

10.4.7 Personalization and Empowerment

A final use for economic evidence links to the relatively recent drive in some countries to help empower people with disabilities, long-term conditions, and mental health problems. Some health and social care systems now have various forms of a consumer-directed payment scheme, whereby individual patients or service users decide for themselves how to spend public resources allocated to them in order to best meet their needs. This is in response to growing recognition that individuals want more control of their lives by participating in decisions about their treatment and care. It is also consistent with a wider change in policy and practice over recent decades to shift the balance of risk and responsibility – slowly but inexorably – from the state to the individual. This can be seen in attempts to widen choice in relation to provider, type, and time of treatment within publicly funded care systems. It has been central to the introduction of direct payments and personal budgets, which seem to be effective and cost-effective for, and popular with, people with mental health problems [32, 33]. It represents a core premise of case management arrangements that seek to tailor care and support to meet individual needs, circumstances, and preferences. Public health campaigns that emphasize *personal* responsibility to reduce future risk of poor health should also be mentioned. Most recent is the rapid growth of interest in what is now referred to as "precision medicine": using diagnostic testing to "steer patients to the right drug at the right dose at the right time" [34]. The more that responsibility shifts to the individual, the more funding bodies will need to know what resources are needed and how to transfer them, and the more individuals will need and want to know what consequences (economic and otherwise) they might expect from their actions.

10.5 Conclusions

Even if good economic evidence is available, it does not immediately follow that policy will be reoriented or that treatment practice will change. Among barriers to these goals are, for example, resource shortages (underfunding or a lack of staff with the appropriate skills) or their poor distribution (perhaps concentrated in major conurbations and unavailable in rural areas). The services available might be inappropriate in that they do not match individual needs or preferences, or they could be appropriate but poorly coordinated across health, social care, housing, and other systems [35].

These barriers obviously need to be overcome. The parlous macroeconomic state of some high-income countries has led to cuts in spending on healthcare and related services, but also a realization – even though it should have been recognized much earlier – that economic evidence is needed to guide decision-making.

Most economic analyses revolve around the question, "Is it worth it?" That is, are the resources expended to deliver an intervention justified by the outcomes that are achieved? I have emphasized that cost-effectiveness (or efficiency, to use a more general label) is only one criterion among many that decision makers must use to allocate resources. I have also argued – and illustrated through a series of examples – that it is a criterion that needs to be taken very seriously.

Key Messages

- Most economic evaluations in the mental health field are concerned with the question, Is it worth it?
- Determining whether resources are used to their best effect in delivering a particular intervention is not the only concern of decision makers, but it is one that they would be foolish to ignore.
- Equity is an important consideration for decision makers – that is, whether available resources are distributed and deployed fairly.
- Evidence provided by economic evaluations has many potential uses in informing and supporting different decision makers, especially when blended with other kinds of evidence.
- Cost-effectiveness and related studies have long been used to support the mar-

keting strategies of pharmaceutical companies and other manufacturers.
- Economic evidence is increasingly being used in appraising health technologies and developing clinical guidance, in commissioning (or purchasing) interventions, and in developing strategic policies.
- New uses are beginning to emerge, such as to support personalized approaches to decision making, giving more responsibility and power to people who use mental health services and their families.

References

1. Slade M. Measuring recovery in mental health services. Isr J Psychiatry Relat Sci. 2010;47(3):206–12.
2. Mangalore R, Knapp M, Jenkins R. Income-related inequality in mental health in Britain: the concentration index approach. Psychol Med. 2007;37(7):1037–45.
3. Mangalore R, Knapp M. Income-related inequalities in common mental disorders among ethnic minorities in England. Soc Psychiatry Psychiatr Epidemiol. 2012;47(3):351–9.
4. Hong J, Knapp M, McGuire A. Income-related inequalities in the prevalence of depression and suicidal behaviour: a 10-year trend following economic crisis. World Psychiatry. 2011;10(1):40–4.
5. Cookson R, Propper C, Asaria M, Raine R. Socio-economic inequalities in health Care in England. Fisc Stud: J Appl Public Econ. 2016;37(3):371–403.
6. Cookson R, Mirelman A, Asaria MDB, Griffin S. Fairer decisions, better health for all: health equity and cost-effectiveness analysis. York: Centre for Health Economics, University of York; 2016.
7. Luyten J, Naci H, Knapp M. Economic evaluation of mental health interventions: an introduction to cost-utility analysis. Evid Based Ment Health. 2016;19(2):49–53.
8. Layard R, Knapp M, Mayraz G. Cost-benefit analysis of psychological therapy. Natl Inst Econ Rev. 2007;202:90–8.
9. Knapp M, Patel A, Curran C, Latimer E, Catty J, Becker T, et al. Supported employment: cost-effectiveness across six European sites. World Psychiatry. 2013;12(1):60–8.
10. Weisbrod BA, Test MA, Stein LI. Alternative to mental hospital treatment. II. Economic benefit-cost analysis. Arch Gen Psychiatry. 1980;37(4):400–5.
11. Knapp M, Beecham J, Koutsogeorgopoulou V, Hallam A, Fenyo A, Marks IM, et al. Service use and costs of home-based versus hospital-based care for people with serious mental illness. Br J Psychiatry. 1994;165(2):195–203.
12. Knapp M, Prince M, Albanese E, Baneerjee S, et al. Dementia UK. London: Alzheimer Society; 2007.
13. Prince M, Comas-Herrera A, Knapp M, et al. Improving healthcare for people living with dementia: coverage, quality and costs now and in the future: world Alzheimer report. London: Alzheimer's Disease International; 2016.
14. Banerjee S. The macroeconomics of dementia – will the world economy get Alzheimer's disease? Arch Med Res. 2012;43:705–9.
15. Department of Health. Living well with dementia: a National Dementia Strategy. London: Department of Health; 2009.
16. Lowin A, McCrone P, Knapp M. Alzheimer's disease in the UK: comparative evidence on cost-of-illness and of health services research funding. Int J Geriatr Psychiatry. 2001;16:1143–8.
17. Knapp M, Romeo R, Beecham J. Economic cost of autism in the UK. Autism. 2009;13(3):317–36.
18. Buescher AV, Cidav Z, Knapp M, Mandell DS. Costs of autism spectrum disorders in the United Kingdom and the United States. JAMA Pediatr. 2014;168(8):721–8.
19. Simon GE, VonKorff M, Heiligenstein JH, Revicki DA, Grothaus L, Katon W, et al. Initial antidepressant choice in primary care. Effectiveness and cost of fluoxetine vs tricyclic antidepressants. JAMA. 1996;275(24):1897–902.
20. Addington DE, Jones B, Bloom D, Chouinard G, Remington G, Albright P. Reduction of hospital days in chronic schizophrenic patients treated with risperidone: a retrospective study. Clin Ther. 1993;15(5):917–26.
21. Prince M, Wimo A, Guerchet M, et al. The global impact of dementia: world Alzheimer report 2015. London: Alzheimer's Disease International; 2015.
22. Evans-Lacko S, Knapp M. Global patterns of workplace productivity for people with depression: absenteeism and presenteeism costs across eight diverse countries. Soc Psychiatry Psychiatr Epidemiol. 2016;51(11):1525–37.
23. Knapp M, Chisholm D, Astin J, Lelliott P, Audini B. The cost consequences of changing the hospital-community balance: the mental health residential care study. Psychol Med. 1997;27(3):681–92.
24. Knapp M, Chisholm D, Astin J, Lelliott P, Audini B. Public, private and voluntary residential mental health care: is there a cost difference? J Health Serv Res Policy. 1998;3(3):141–8.
25. Knapp M, Beecham J, McDaid D, Matosevic T, Smith M. The economic consequences of deinstitutionalisation of mental health services: lessons from a systematic review of European experience. Health Soc Care Community. 2011;19(2):113–25.
26. Knapp M, Snell T, Healey A, et al. How do child and adolescent mental health problems influence public

sector costs? Interindividual variations in a nationally representative British sample. J Child Psychol Psychiatry. 2015;56:667–76.
27. World Health Organization. The world health report 2000: health systems – improving performance. Geneva: World Health Organization; 2000.
28. McDaid D, Cookson R. Evaluating health care interventions in the European Union. Health Policy. 2003;63(2):133–9.
29. Cerri K, Knapp M, Fernandez J. Untangling the complexity of funding recommendations: a comparative analysis of health technology assessment outcomes in four European countries. Pharm Med. 2015;29:341–59.
30. Knapp M, McDaid D, Parsonage M. Mental health promotion and prevention: the economic case. London: Personal Social Services Research Unit, London School of Economics and Political Science; 2011.
31. Chisholm D, Sanderson K, Ayuso-Mateos J, Saxena S. Reducing the global burden of depression: population-level analysis of intervention cost effectiveness in 14 world regions. Br J Psychiatry. 2004;184:393–403.
32. Stevens M, Glendenning C, Jacobs S, et al. Assessing the role of increasing choice in UK social care services. J Soc Policy. 2011;40:257–74.
33. Forder J, Jones K, Glendenning C, et al. Evaluation of the personal health budget pilot programme. Canterbury: PSSRU; 2012.
34. Collins FS, Varmus H. A new initiative on precision medicine. N Engl J Med. 2015;372(9):793–5.
35. Knapp M, Funk M, Curran C, et al. Mental health in low- and middle-income countries: economic barriers to better practice and policy. Health Policy Plan. 2006;21:157–70.

Part II

Health Economics Applied to the Evaluation of the Quality and Costs of Mental Health Services

11 Financing Mental Health in Low- and Middle-Income Countries: Making an Economic Case to Support Investment

David McDaid

Abstract

This chapter provides a brief overview of the current level of funding for mental health within low- and middle-income countries. It then looks at the principal financing mechanisms used for funding in low- and middle-income countries and their implications for equity, efficiency, and sustainability at a time when a common goal is universal access to healthcare across the globe. The chapter provides some examples of approaches to funding mental health in different contexts and considers the role that can be played by aid from international donors in supporting the development of mental health services and supports. In making the case for investment, it also is important to look beyond mental health outcomes. Health policymakers and service providers may be more interested in the impacts on physical rather than mental health, whereas in other cases it will be valuable to identify non-health benefits and, if possible, attach a plausible value to these benefits.

Key Points Summary

- Many low- and middle-income countries have severely inadequate levels of funding for mental health relative to population needs.
- It does not automatically follow that achieving universal healthcare coverage will mean universal coverage of mental healthcare.
- Historically, supporting mental health has been a low priority. Country-specific economic evidence can help strengthen the case for investment.

(continued)

D. McDaid (✉)
Personal Social Services Research Unit, London School of Economics and Political Science, Houghton Street, London WC2A2AE, UK
e-mail: d.mcdaid@lse.ac.uk

D. Razzouk (ed.), *Mental Health Economics*, DOI 10.1007/978-3-319-55266-8_11

(continued)

- As economies grow there will be more opportunities for internally sustainable healthcare financing.
- Only 1% of development aid from international donors is currently allocated to mental health. More can be done to work with donors to change this.
- An intersectoral approach to funding is required for implementation of mental health promotion and disorder prevention strategies.

Box 11.1 Defining Low-, Middle-, and High-Income Countries
For the 2017 fiscal year, low-income economies are defined as those with a gross national income (GNI) per capita (in international dollars) of $1025 or less in 2015; lower-middle-income economies are those with a GNI per capita between $1026 and $4035; upper-middle-income economies are those with a GNI per capita between $4036 and $12,475; and high-income economies are those with a GNI per capita of $12,476 or more.
Source: [1].

11.1 Introduction

Many chapters in this volume have highlighted the profound effects of poor mental health both within and outside healthcare systems. These challenges are particularly acute in low- and middle-income countries (LAMICs) (see Box 11.1 for definitions), where resources for healthcare in general, let alone for mental health, typically are very limited.

This chapter provides a brief overview of the current level of funding for mental health within LAMICs. It then looks at the principal financing mechanisms used for funding in LAMICs and their implications for equity, efficiency, and sustainability at time when a common goal is universal access to healthcare across the globe. As the chapter highlights, in many countries, inadequate levels of funding are provided for mental health relative to need within publicly funded healthcare systems. It considers how this situation can be remedied, including the key role of evidence-based information in the economic case for investment in mental health, both within and outside healthcare systems. In doing this, the chapter provides some examples of approaches to funding mental health in different contexts and considers the role that can be played by aid from international donors in supporting the development of mental health services and supports. This chapter does not seek to explore the situation in all LAMICs, but rather to provide an idea of some of the key issues and concerns in differing contexts around the globe.

11.2 Living on the Edge: Funding for Mental Health in Low- and Middle-Income Countries

It remains difficult to obtain accurate information on the level of funding for mental health in almost any country. Funding may come from multiple health or insurance funds at national, regional, and local levels, as well as through out-of-pocket payments. Responsibility for services may also be fragmented so that sectors other than health may have responsibility to fund/provide some services; for example, in some countries support for child mental health may be part of the responsibilities of ministries of education and development.

Nonetheless, it is abundantly clear that many LAMICs spend very little on publicly funded health care. Only a very small fraction of healthcare budgets tend to be allocated to mental health. The World Health Organization's (WHO's) 2014 Mental Health Atlas was only able to obtain sufficient data on 23 middle-income countries to estimate that they spent, on average, around 1% of their health budgets – or less than $2 per person – on mental health in 2013 [2]. Seven lower-middle- and 16 upper-middle-income countries in that study allocated 80% and 50% of funds, respectively, to psychiatric hospitals, thus limiting reach, compared with just over 30% in 17 high-income countries. Substantive variation exists between some countries; for instance, government expenditures on mental health as a percentage of total government health budgets in seven Arab countries ranged from 2% in Syria and Egypt to 7% in Algeria [3]. In Georgia, a recent situational analysis, while not specifying the level of funding, indicated insufficient resources to adequately cover basic costs of staffing and premises, let alone to reform and modernize mental healthcare [4].

Turning to Africa and Asia, detailed analysis of three low-income countries revealed that resources invested in tackling psychosis and depression range between $0.11 and $0.33 per capita per annum in Ethiopia, Nepal, and Uganda [5]. Another recent estimate for all 31 World Bank–defined low-income countries suggests that the per-capita investment for mental health in 2014 was just $0.20 per person per annum, or just half of 1% of their total health expenditure [6].

So, there is a common pattern of low investment in many LAMICs. This low level of investment is insufficient to meet the costs of delivering a basic core package of mental health services (as defined by the WHO), which in low-income countries requires up to $2.60 per person, and as much as $6.25 in lower-middle-income countries [7]. This current level of investment translates into meeting only 11% of the desired investment in mental health necessary for an essential package of mental health services in low-income countries and between 14% and 19% of the necessary investment in lower-middle-income countries [8].

The lack of investment is compounded by political uncertainty and in some cases conflict, high disease burden, and a limited mental healthcare workforce. Healthcare systems, especially in low-income settings, have traditionally prioritized health problems that have high mortality rates. Such mortality data ignore comorbidities and do not account for the fact that poor mental health is a trigger for premature mortality from physical health disorders. Going forward, it is essential that the effects of poor mental health on multimorbidity, including effects on the management of conditions such as diabetes, heart disease, HIV/AIDs, tuberculosis, and malaria, are fully factored into estimates of the impacts of poor mental health.

A lack of investment in publicly funded mental health services potentially has far-reaching consequences. Failure to intervene early when mental health is at risk may mean more health problems that have to be addressed later. There will also be adverse consequences for physical health: poor mental health is associated with poorer management of physical health, which in turn contributes to the much higher rate of mortality among individuals with mental health needs compared with the general population [9].

But it is not just about effects within healthcare systems. There will also be economic strain and other consequences for family members, including children and young people who may have to take on caring responsibilities or engage in work (thus losing time from education) as a result of the poor mental health of their parents or siblings. At a societal level, poor mental health may also be associated with avoidable externalities related to social exclusion and stigmatization (see Chap. 27), including contacts with the criminal justice system, as well as lost opportunities in the labor market (see Chaps. 25 and 28). Understanding these wider impacts is valuable because it helps to raise the importance of mental health when looking at different Sustainable Development Goals (SDGs), for instance, the objective to "protect labour rights and promote safe and secure working environments for all workers, including migrant workers, in particular women migrants, and those in precarious employment" [10]. Opportunities may arise to consider, for example, how to seize a chance to achieve inclusive, quality, and lifelong education for all in order to promote and protect mental health, as well as to consider how better mental health may help countries attain their educational goals.

11.3 How Is Mental Health Financed in LAMICs?

Sustaining publicly funded healthcare systems in LAMICs is challenging because of the difficulties in making use of tax and/or social health insurance mechanisms, the mainstays of health system financing in high-income countries. Income-related taxation in particular tends to be a progressive and equitable way of supporting health, including mental health, but raising sufficient funds through income tax is not feasible in many LAMICs. It has been argued that "the combination of an informal economic structure, income from natural resources or specific commodities, and the availability of aid (for some countries) pushes many low-income countries into a situation of a low tax/GDP (Gross Domestic Product) ratio (around 20% of GDP compared to 40% in high income countries) levied on a narrow tax base and a narrow set of individuals" [11].

Social health insurance schemes, which usually set insurance premiums on the basis of community rather than individual risk, may ensure, to a greater extent than taxation, the availability of a defined pool of resources/benefits for mental health needs. Individuals who cannot afford to pay into these insurance schemes would have their costs met by the public purse, meaning that schemes should cover the population. There are, of course, some success stories where insurance works, as in Costa Rica, but insurance schemes can be administratively complex, and some LAMICs may find it difficult to raise sufficient revenue through social health insurance schemes because of low levels of participation in the formal economy [12].

One key challenge for access to healthcare in general, therefore, is how to increase the level of financial protection and reduce the risk of catastrophic healthcare costs, particularly in low-income countries. Employees can be enrolled in social health insurance or, alternatively, revenues generated through payroll taxes can be used to fund healthcare. Some governments will expand the use of these financing mechanisms as the economy grows, but in general there are questions of whether low-income countries will be able to raise sufficient revenue from any type of taxation to ensure access to healthcare for the majority of the population, or even whether it might be possible to voluntarily or mandatorily enroll more of the population, including those in the informal economy, into a social health insurance scheme. Even when countries have been successful in rolling out tax- or insurance-based schemes (e.g., in Rwanda), the level of general healthcare services covered can be very limited [13]. The case for mental health coverage still needs to be made, even in Rwanda, where an officially approved mental health policy exists.

In Ghana, although the publicly funded healthcare system provides some coverage for mental health, this does not extend to physical health needs, which are funded separately through a social insurance scheme that many people with mental health needs are not eligible for [14, 15]. The lack of access to healthcare can itself also be a risk factor for poor mental health. One analysis of more than 4000 adults in China found that individuals who did not have health insurance had almost double the risk of developing severe depression over a 20-month time frame compared with insured individuals [16].

In the absence of taxation and social insurance, development aid from international donors remains a major source of funding for healthcare in many LAMICs, but crucially, very little of this funding seems to be allocated to mental health. One study used the Aid Activities Database from the Creditor Reporting System of the Organisation for Economic Co-operation and Development's Development Assistance Committee to trace development assistance for mental health from 55 donors between 2007 and 2013 [8]. It found that only 1% of the total expenditure on development assistance for health during this time period focused on mental health: an average of $136.12 million per year compared with $6.8 billion for HIV/AIDS [17]. In 2011 this equated to an average of only 0.05 per person in low-income countries, $0.02 for lower-middle-income countries, and $0.03 in upper-middle-income countries.

The uncertainties of the viability of social health insurance, a stable taxation system, and dedicated donor aid inevitably mean that out-of-pocket payments and private insurance schemes are relied on much more. This is inevitable in

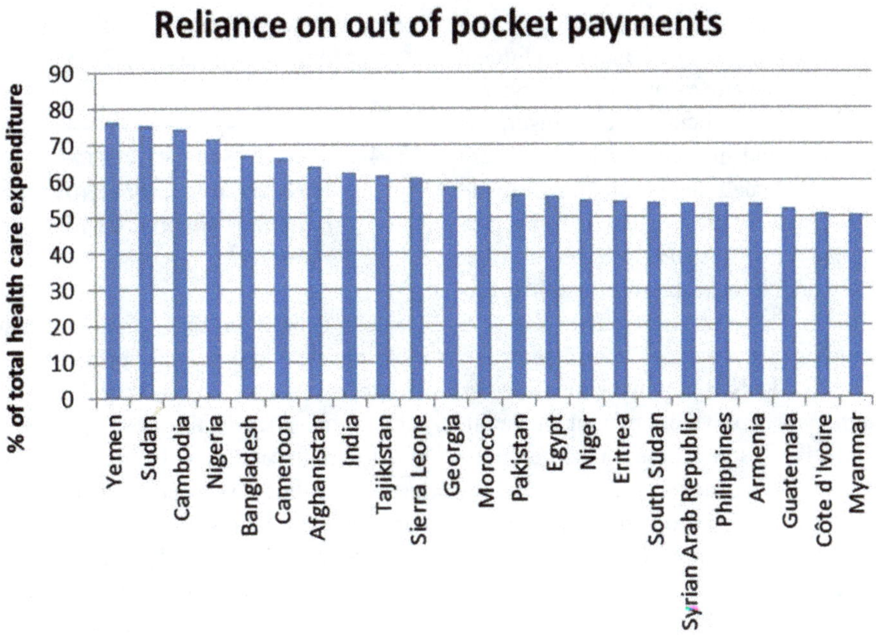

Fig. 11.1 Out-of-pocket expenditures as a share of total health expenditure in selected low- and middle-income countries (Source: [18], National Health Account Indicators 2014 data)

countries that have difficulties in developing an infrastructure and supporting a formal economy that can sustain a publicly funded healthcare system. In 2014, out-of-pocket payments accounted for at least 50% of all healthcare expenditures in 23 of 78 low- and lower-middle-income countries; the highest level of out-of-pocket payments (76% of all health care expenditures) occurred in Yemen and the Sudan (Fig. 11.1).

Relying so heavily on out-of-pocket payments in order to provide mental health services is both inequitable and inefficient [12]. In low-income countries, these out-of-pocket payments may often represent the entire costs of care; as such they are very regressive, as the costs are greatest for those who are least able to pay, heavily restricting their access to services. Given the strong correlation between mental health problems, exclusion from the labor force, and low socioeconomic status, user charges for mental health services are highly inequitable (see Chaps. 24, 25, and 28): those needing services most often are the least able to pay. The chronic nature of some mental disorders means that ongoing (possibly catastrophic) costs could potentially be incurred over many years – again discriminating against those with mental health problems, who are not often in a position to make ongoing payments.

Even in more advanced economies that have a greater fiscal space for health funding and where out-of-pocket payments are more of a supplement to revenues from tax or insurance premiums, they still almost certainly aggravate inefficiencies in the utilization of mental health services. Out-of-pocket payments in high-income countries are used to reduce unnecessary demand for services; in the case of mental health, however, this issue of excess demand is much less of an issue than might be the case for physical health concerns. Even without the financial costs of out-of-pocket payments, the stigma associated with mental illness means that individuals and their families may be reluctant to contact services (see Chap. 27). In fact, it has been estimated that at least 75% of all those who could benefit from mental health treatment in many LAMICs do not come into contact with services [19]. This increases to 89% when considering only treatment for schizophrenia in low-income countries [20]. Much of this is about the lack of services, but stigma plays a role, with some individuals preferring to pay for complementary and/or traditional healing rather than use any mental health service.

Private, rather than social, health insurance schemes can be found in many LAMICs. These schemes tend to be small, and while they provide healthcare coverage for the usually small proportion of the population that can afford to subscribe, even for these individuals, private health insurance schemes severely restrict mental health coverage, including preventing enrollment or coverage for individuals who may be identified as being at high risk of developing mental health problems; this is also the case in some high-income countries. Policymakers may wish to consider whether there is any scope for the revenues raised from private insurance to help subsidize some of the costs of essential mental health services for the majority of the population who cannot afford such insurance coverage.

In many LAMICs, mental health coverage through private insurance is, in any case, often heavily restricted, although examples of how private insurance coverage can help sustain more choice and greater access to higher quality mental health services for enrollees, including access to psychological therapies, can be seen in some countries, for example, in a hospital in Kenya [21]. In the case of this Kenyan study, however, the authors were careful to note that it was not possible to make any generalization "on the overall quality of private versus public care," adding that the example is not generalizable "because its concentration of qualified mental health care professionals would be unsustainable at scale in this low-income setting" [21].

Regardless of the funding mechanisms, it should also be stressed they will not directly influence actions that are the responsibility of other national or regional government departments. The effects of poor mental health on many different parts of the economy mean that an intersectoral approach is essential. Unfortunately, little is known about funding for mental health that does not come from health budgets in LMICs. In addition to better estimating the level of funds from these sectors, another challenge is to persuade budget holders in non-health sectors to, for example, support programs for mental health in the workplace or tackle addiction and mental health problems within the prison system.

11.4 Moving to Universal Healthcare Coverage: What Might It Mean for Mental Health?

The UN declaration on SDGs notes that "to promote physical and mental health and well-being, and to extend life expectancy for all, we must achieve universal health coverage and access to quality health care" [10]. Universal health coverage has been defined as meaning that "all people and communities can use the promotive, preventive, curative, rehabilitative and palliative health services they need, of sufficient quality to be effective, while also ensuring that the use of these services does not expose the user to financial hardship" [22]. This in turn implies greater equity in access to health services, so that this is based on need rather than ability to pay, with protection against catastrophic financial loss that might otherwise be associated with paying for healthcare services [23] .

However, while countries may now be striving to find ways to meet the welcome objective of universal healthcare coverage, what this will actually mean for mental health when implemented is far from clear. It certainly does not automatically mean that countries will achieve universal mental healthcare coverage for even the most basic package of services. Coverage of mental health has often been far from ideal, even within high-income countries that would be considered to have universal health coverage.

In many settings, securing good mental health has sometimes been perceived as a lower priority than investment in physical health, perhaps because poor mental health is sometimes (wrongly) perceived as having no impact on mortality. Mental illness is still a taboo topic in many societies; this may also have a bearing on the willingness of societies to adequately fund mental health, despite its substantive contribution to the overall global burden of disease and the importance of good mental health for economic development. As Jim Yong Kim, President of the World Bank, said, "mental health has remained in the shadows. This is not just a public health issue—it's a development issue. We need to act now because the lost productivity is something the global economy simply cannot afford" [24].

11.5 Leveraging More Funding from Governments and International Donors

The lack of funding for, and low priority given to mental health, means that there is a need not only to convey the economic case for action to national decision makers, but also to make a case to both international and national donors on the value of investing their finite resources in strengthening mental health systems. The recognition of mental health within the SDGs creates an opportunity for action, but there still is a pressing need to communicate effectively on what works, such as the integration of mental health within public health services, and the adverse effects of not taking action (see Box 11.2). There is also a case to be made for both ministries of health and donors to have protected budgets for mental health; this at least can help ensure that resources intended for mental health do indeed reach mental health services and can reduce some uncertainty about the sustainability of services.

Focused donor aid can make a difference. One example of this is the work of Basic Needs, a non-governmental organization that works to improve the lives of people with mental health problems. It invested more than $2 million for community mental health services in 11 predominantly LAMICs in 2011, benefiting almost 40,000 people [25]. Analysis in Kenya demonstrated that this multi-component mental health program was cost-effective, with a cost per disability life year averted of $727, similar to that for drug treatment for HIV/AIDs [26], while reaching the most vulnerable. Service users financially gained through an increased return to their normal economic activities, while avoiding the need to pay for some ongoing treatment costs.

While these economic benefits are strong, it is always important to remember that budgetary impacts also determine sustainability. Sustaining the Basic Needs program model without international donor assistance would be difficult, as 80% of the costs were borne by Basic Needs rather than local partners. The annual cost of $540 per year for each individual treated would be completely beyond the budget of the Kenyan government. Basic Needs itself relied on international donor aid in order to be in a position to provide these services – hence the importance of making a strong health and economic case to international donor governments and other international organizations whose objective is to promote global mental health.

Box 11.2 Facilitating Development Assistance and Governmental Support for Mental Health (Adapted from [8])

- Evidence of the effectiveness of integrating mental health services within public health services should be better documented and communicated to donors and policymakers.
- Development assistance could be used to strengthen capacity for sustainable mental health systems in the public health sector.
- Raise awareness among donors and governments of the health, developmental, and economic costs of poor mental health, benefits of treatment, and current low levels of funding relative to need.
- Donors and governments should specify a budget for mental health activities.

11.6 Strengthening the Evidence Base for the Economic Case for Investment in Mental Health

World Bank President Kim's call to action recognizes the many negative externalities of not taking action against poor mental health that were highlighted earlier in this chapter and in particular in Part 4 of this volume. Economic evidence can help persuade policymakers to invest a greater share of their health budgets in mental health. Moreover, the aim of the SDGs to achieve universal healthcare coverage should mean that policymakers in LAMICs will be interested in information that can help them determine what packages of health care might be covered.

Martin Knapp, in Chap. 10 in this volume, writes extensively about the different ways in which economic evidence can be used to inform the decision-making process. Much of that chapter draws on examples of practice from high-income countries, but the principles apply equally in LAMICs. This brief section focuses on specific issues that must be contended with more often in LAMICs.

11.6.1 Strengthening Capacity to Conduct and Interpret Economic Evaluation in LAMICs

There is a need to strengthen the capacity to conduct economic evaluations and to communicate and understand their results in policy-relevant language. One recent survey of policymakers in LAMICs suggests that local health economics capacity, for instance in universities, has only very limited contact with policymakers in many countries [27]. Thus it is important to strengthen these links, and one way to help create the conditions for effective long-term knowledge exchange between the health economics community and policymakers is through building collaborative partnerships, for instance, by involving policymakers in all aspects of health economics and health services research initiatives that may be funded through international donor aid. Example of this include the EMERALD and PRIME projects, funded by the European Union and the U.K. Department for International Development, respectively, which have brought together academics including health economists, the WHO, and senior civil servants from ministries of health in a number of LAMICs in sub-Saharan Africa, India, and Nepal to collaborate on long-term projects to promote mental health [28, 29]. These types of initiatives also allow researchers to obtain better insight into the ways in which the policy-making process works.

11.6.2 Making an Economic Case for the Prevention of Multimorbidities

Some health policymakers have little or no interest in mental health. Indeed, some may harbor negative attitudes and prejudices similar to those held by some members of the general public. These policymakers may, however, be much more interested in any actions that ultimately improve physical health outcomes. For instance, the World Mental Health Survey indicates that 36% of people with psychosis in LAMICs have two or more physical morbidities, compared with just 11% of individuals without psychosis [9]. A small but growing body of evidence looks at the benefits of better mental health as a way of avoiding diabetes, HIV, and their complications in LAMICs [30–32]. If investment in better mental health can be shown to have a positive impact on the incidence or severity of communicable or chronic diseases, then decision makers may believe the case for investment to be more compelling.

11.6.3 Making an Intersectoral Case for Investment in Mental Health

To strengthen the argument for investment in mental health going forward, it is also important to put more emphasis not only on the immediate and long-term benefits of improved mental health to the health system, but also some of the benefits of better mental health to other sectors. In high-income countries, the economic case for investing in the mental health of children and young people is increasingly focused on positive benefits to the education sector, such as improved academic performance and reduced levels of truancy [33], whereas in the criminal justice sector policymakers may be interested in reducing levels of violence.

International actors such as UNESCO, WHO, the International Labour Organisation, and the

Organisation for Economic Co-operation and Development are interested in ways in which to address health issues, including mental health promotion, through intersectoral actions. It therefore makes sense for health economists to put some focus on the outcomes of most interest to all organizations that are responsible for funding a mental health service.

For instance, in LAMICs, economists should consider how best to put an economic value on the attainment of some of the education-related objectives of the SDGs. In some countries, the education sector may fund several school-based mental health interventions, such as providing support for the victims and perpetrators of bullying or promoting emotional health literacy and resilience [33].

International donors and governments could also specify that some funding for actions to promote and protect mental health is conditional on the involvement of different sectors, so as to involve, for instance, education and health in order to provide better mental health support for children and young people. Demonstrating benefits to all participating sectors associated with these collaborations can also aid implementation [34].

11.6.4 Modeling the Costs and Benefits of Different Policy Options

Economic modeling studies can also be used to inform decision-making [35]. Essentially, models provide a mathematical framework to estimate the consequences of different policy and practice decisions. Long used in high-income countries, in resource-constrained LAMICs these models present a pragmatic way to measure the cost-effectiveness of different mental health interventions. They allow evidence of effectiveness from a local or external context to be synthesized with local information on the costs of action and the effectiveness of appropriate local comparators. Thus the results of a trial looking at the effects of an intervention in tackling perinatal depression in one specific setting, such as a state in India, might be adapted to another context, for example, in Sri Lanka. The assumptions and values used in models can be varied to give decision makers a sense of potential economic benefits, given specific factors (e.g., the level of uptake or duration of effect). This information can be particularly insightful in the absence of opportunities to conduct local randomized controlled trials.

There are many different approaches to modeling, some of which were discussed in Chap. 7 in this volume. One that can be highlighted here is the micro-simulation modeling approach that has been used by WHO as part of its CHOICE (Choosing Interventions That Are Cost Effective) program to look at the cost-effectiveness of various packages of interventions for different mental health problems in the 17 subregions, or geographic clusters of countries that are members of WHO [36]. Outcomes are expressed in terms of disability-adjusted life years, with costs (to the healthcare system only) adjusted to account for differences in purchasing power and expressed as international dollars. The relative cost-effectiveness of interventions for different mental disorders can be compared – these can, for instance, highlight that for people with schizophrenia or bipolar disorder in sub-Saharan Africa, a package of community outpatient care, older-generation psychotropics, and psychosocial care are far more cost-effective and less costly than relying on inpatient care using the latest antipsychotics [37].

While the economic information from CHOICE is powerful, it can be even more powerful if country-specific simulation models can be constructed. In Nigeria, modeling was used to determine that a package of interventions for epilepsy, schizophrenia, depression, and hazardous alcohol use was less than $320 per disability-adjusted life year avoided [38]. This would be cost-effective in a Nigerian context. Again, adapting this type of modeling to any specific local context requires collaboration between health economists and local policymakers/planners. The limits in expertise and resources for modeling in many LAMICs may act as a barrier to the development of country-specific estimates [35].

Box 11.3 Making an Economic Case for Mental Health Promotion and Disease Prevention

In England, the Department of Health commissioned research to examine the economic case for mental health promotion and mental illness prevention. Fifteen models of prevention and promotion actions were developed, including measures to tackle conduct disorder in schools, poor health in the workplace, stress arising from unmanageable debt or programs, and suicide prevention. Models provided information on economic payoffs to health and other sectors over time periods of up to 10 years. The findings fed directly into national policy documents and have been used frequently by organizations responsible for commissioning mental health services.

Source: [40].

11.7 Strengthening the Evidence Base of the Case for Investment in Mental Health Promotion

More attention is being paid to the cost-effectiveness of interventions to promote mental health and prevent mental disorders [39]. In LAMICs, where funds are tight, cost-effective prevention/promotion actions could help to reduce the level of future need for costly specialist mental health services. In high-income countries there is an evidence base pointing to significant costs that could be averted as a result of some promotion and prevention actions; economic evidence is being used in some countries (e.g., England) to inform national mental health policy (Box 11.3). This approach could be used to model the potential economic case for a group of country-relevant actions.

11.8 Conclusion

Funding for mental health in many LAMICs is precarious, only accounting for around 1% of total healthcare expenditures in some countries. Support for mental health has not been viewed as a priority, and financing mechanisms such as taxation and social health insurance premiums may not be viable ways of sustaining the public healthcare system. Yet, there will be adverse effects not only for individuals but also for society as a result of the low level of access to mental health services.

This chapter notes that many LAMICs are heavily dependent on support from international donors, but less than 1% of donor aid for health is allocated to mental health. Funds for mental health in LAMICs account for only 11% to 19% of what would be required to provide a very basic package of mental healthcare services. In some of the poorest countries in the world, up to 76% of healthcare expenditures consist of out-of-pocket payments. Individuals with severe and enduring mental health problems tend not be employed and many will not be able to afford services. Private health insurance can help to promote choice but has a limited reach within the population; one question is whether charges on health insurers could help to fund some service provision for individuals without insurance.

The SDGs explicitly include mental health, and the objective of universal healthcare coverage will potentially increase access to publicly funded mental healthcare services. However, it is far from clear that essential packages of care made available as part of universal healthcare coverage will include any mental health supports. The move toward universal healthcare coverage should, however, pique interest in economic analyses of the potential costs and benefits of different mental health interventions that could be covered within a basic package of care.

There is also an ever-increasing evidence base of actions that are cost-effective in LAMICs, but it is imperative to effectively communicate the costs and consequences of not taking action, as well as the benefits that arise from investing in mental health. These messages need to reach multiple stakeholders: ministries of health and other relevant sectors, such as education; international donors; service providers; researchers; and potentially the media and the general public.

It would also be helpful to strengthen the capacity to both conduct and interpret the results of economic analyses. Donor-supported economic evaluations of mental healthcare policy and practice could also provide opportunities for researchers and policymakers to collaborate directly to improve understanding of their respective work and develop mutual trust. This may involve evaluation of practice within any country, but it is probably going to make use of modeling techniques to give policymakers and others a sense of how likely any one intervention is to be cost-effective.

In making the case for investment, it will also be important to look beyond mental health outcomes. Health policymakers and service providers may be more interested in the impacts on physical rather than mental health, whereas in other cases it will be valuable to identify non-health benefits and, if possible, attach a plausible value to these benefits. Finally, opportunities exist to place a greater focus on the evaluation of mental health promotion and disorder prevention interventions. In high-income countries, economic arguments – particularly around the mental health of children – have been very influential in resources being allocated to mental health.

Key Messages

- In some LAMICs, as little as 1% of the total health expenditure is allocated to mental health. This is insufficient to provide even a basic package of services.
- Opportunities exist to liaise more with international donors in order to present arguments to increase the share of total donor aid going to mental health.
- The inclusion of mental health within the SDGs alongside the drive toward universal healthcare coverage provides an opportunity to convey evidence of the economic case for action to policymakers and international donors.
- It is also important to strengthen the capacity to conduct and interpret economic evaluations in LAMICs.
- Economic evaluation needs to look beyond narrow measures of the effects mental health; it should also consider effects on physical health and important outcomes that fall outside the health sector. Improving mental health will potentially contribute to the attainment of SDGs other than those focused on health.

References

1. World Bank. World Bank country and lending groups. https://datahelpdesk.worldbank.org/knowledgebase/articles/906519-world-bank-country-and-lending-groups. Washington, DC: World Bank; 2017.
2. World Health Organisation. Mental health atlas 2014. Geneva: World Health Organisation; 2014.
3. Yehia F, Nahas Z, Saleh S. A roadmap to parity in mental health financing: the case of Lebanon. J Ment Health Policy Econ. 2014;17(3):131–41. Epub 30 Dec 2014
4. Makhashvili N, van Voren R. Balancing community and hospital care: a case study of reforming mental health services in Georgia. PLoS Med. 2013;10(1):e1001366. Epub 16 Jan 2013
5. Chisholm D, Heslin M, Docrat S, Nanda S, Shidhaye R, Upadhaya N, et al. Scaling-up services for psychosis, depression and epilepsy in sub-Saharan Africa and South Asia: development and application of a mental health systems planning tool (OneHealth). Epidemiol Psychiatr Sci. 2016:1–11. Epub 30 Sept 2016
6. Caddick H, Horne B, Mackenzie J, Tilley H. Investing in mental health in low-income countries. London: Overseas Development Institute; 2016.
7. Chisholm D, Lund C, Saxena S. Cost of scaling up mental healthcare in low- and middle-income countries. B J Psychiatry J Ment Sci. 2007;191:528–35. Epub 7 Dec 2007
8. Gilbert BJ, Patel V, Farmer PE, Lu C. Assessing development assistance for mental health in developing countries: 2007–2013. PLoS Med. 2015;12(6):e1001834. Epub 4 June 2015
9. Stubbs B, Koyanagi A, Veronese N, Vancampfort D, Solmi M, Gaughran F, et al. Physical multimorbidity and psychosis: comprehensive cross sectional analysis including 242,952 people across 48 low- and middle-income countries. BMC Med. 2016;14(1):189. Epub 23 Nov 2016
10. United Nations. Transforming our world: the 2030 agenda for sustainable development. A/RES/70/1. New York: United Nations; 2015.

11. Besley T, Persson T. Why do developing countries tax so little? J Econ Perspect. 2016;28(4):99–120.
12. Dixon A, McDaid D, Knapp M, Curran C. Financing mental health services in low- and middle-income countries. Health Policy Plan. 2006;21(3):171–82. Epub 15 Mar 2006
13. Mills A. Health care systems in low- and middle-income countries. N Engl J Med. 2014;370(6):552–7. Epub 7 Feb 2014
14. Roberts M, Mogan C, Asare JB. An overview of Ghana's mental health system: results from an assessment using the World Health Organization's Assessment Instrument for Mental Health Systems (WHO-AIMS). Int J Ment Heal Syst. 2014;8:16. Epub 13 May 2014
15. Roberts M, Asare JB, Mogan C, Adjase ET, Osei A. The mental health system in Ghana. Accra: Ministry of Health, Ghana; 2013.
16. Tian D, Qu Z, Wang X, Guo J, Xu F, Zhang X, et al. The role of basic health insurance on depression: an epidemiological cohort study of a randomized community sample in Northwest China. BMC Psychiatry. 2012;12:151. Epub 22 Sept 2012
17. Mackenzie J, Kesner C. Mental health funding and the SDGs. What now and who pays? London: Overseas Development Institute; 2016.
18. World Health Organisation. Global Health Expenditure Database. Updated 17 Nov 2016. http://apps.who.int/nha/database. Geneva: World Health Organisation; 2016.
19. Dua T, Barbui C, Clark N, Fleischmann A, Poznyak V, van Ommeren M, et al. Evidence-based guidelines for mental, neurological, and substance use disorders in low- and middle-income countries: summary of WHO recommendations. PLoS Med. 2011;8(11):e1001122. Epub 24 Nov 2011
20. Lora A, Kohn R, Levav I, McBain R, Morris J, Saxena S. Service availability and utilization and treatment gap for schizophrenic disorders: a survey in 50 low- and middle-income countries. Bull World Health Organ. 2012;90(1):47–54. A–B. Epub 25 Jan 2012
21. de Menil VP, Knapp M, McDaid D, Njenga FG. Service use, charge, and access to mental healthcare in a private Kenyan inpatient setting: the effects of insurance. PLoS One. 2014;9(3):e90297. Epub 22 Mar 2014
22. World Health Organisation. What is universal coverage? http://www.who.int/health_financing/universal_coverage_definition/en/. Geneva: WHO; 2016.
23. McIntyre D, Kutzin J. Health financing country diagnostic: a foundation for national strategy development. Geneva: WHO; 2016.
24. World Bank. Investing in treatment for depression and anxiety leads to fourfold return. Press release April 12. http://www.worldbank.org/en/news/press-release/2016/04/13/investing-in-treatment-for-depression-anxiety-leads-to-fourfold-return. Washington, DC: The World Bank; 2016.
25. Raja S, Underhill C, Shrestha P, Sunder U, Mannarath S, Wood SK, et al. Integrating mental health and development: a case study of the BasicNeeds model in Nepal. PLoS Med. 2012;9(7):e1001261. Epub 18 July 2012
26. de Menil V, Knapp M, McDaid D, Raja S, Kingori J, Waruguru M, et al. Cost-effectiveness of the mental health and development model for schizophrenia-spectrum and bipolar disorders in rural Kenya. Psychol Med. 2015;45(13):2747–56. Epub 23 May 2015
27. Teerawattananon Y, Tantivess S, Yamabhai I, Tritasavit N, Walker DG, Cohen JT, et al. The influence of cost-per-DALY information in health prioritisation and desirable features for a registry: a survey of health policy experts in Vietnam, India and Bangladesh. Health Res Policy Syst. 2016;14(1):86. Epub 4 Dec 2016
28. Shidhaye R. Implementation science for closing the treatment gap for mental disorders by translating evidence base into practice: experiences from the PRIME project. Australas Psychiatry. 2015;23(6 Suppl):35–7. Epub 5 Dec 2015
29. Semrau M, Evans-Lacko S, Alem A, Ayuso-Mateos JL, Chisholm D, Gureje O, et al. Strengthening mental health systems in low- and middle-income countries: the emerald programme. BMC Med. 2015;13:79. Epub 17 Apr 2015
30. Mendenhall E, Shivashankar R, Tandon N, Ali MK, Narayan KM, Prabhakaran D. Stress and diabetes in socioeconomic context: a qualitative study of urban Indians. Soc Sci Med. 2012;75(12):2522–9. Epub 1 Nov 2012
31. Molosankwe I, Patel A, Jose Gagliardino J, Knapp M, McDaid D. Economic aspects of the association between diabetes and depression: a systematic review. J Affect Disord. 2012;142(Suppl):S42–55. Epub 25 Oct 2012
32. Sikkema KJ, Dennis AC, Watt MH, Choi KW, Yemeke TT, Joska JA. Improving mental health among people living with HIV: a review of intervention trials in low- and middle-income countries. Glob Ment Health (Camb). 2015;2. Epub 6 Oct 2015
33. McDaid D. Investing in health literacy: what do we know about the co-benefits to the education sector of actions targeted at children and young people? Copenhagen: World Health Organisation; 2016.
34. McDaid D, Park AL. Evidence on financing and budgeting mechanisms to support intersectoral actions between health, education, social welfare and labour sectors. Copenhagen: World Health Organization 2016; 2016.
35. McDaid D. Economic modelling for global mental health. In: Thornicroft G, Patel V, editors. Global mental health trials. Oxford: Oxford University Press; 2014.
36. Chisholm D. Choosing cost-effective interventions in psychiatry: results from the CHOICE programme of the World Health Organization. World Psychiatry. 2005;4(1):37–44.
37. Chisholm D, Saxena S. Cost effectiveness of strategies to combat neuropsychiatric conditions in sub-Saharan Africa and South East Asia: mathematical modelling study. BMJ (Clin Res ed). 2012;344:e609. Epub 6 Mar 2012
38. Gureje O, Chisholm D, Kola L, Lasebikan V, Saxena S. Cost-effectiveness of an essential mental health intervention package in Nigeria. World Psychiatry. 2007;6(1):42–8. Epub 8 Mar 2007
39. Mcdaid D, Hewlett E. Fast-track paper: understanding effective approaches to promoting mental health and preventing mental illness. Paris: OECD; 2017.
40. Knapp M, McDaid D, Parsonage M, editors. Mental health promotion and mental illness prevention: the economic case. London: Department of Health; 2011.

Quality Indicators for Mental Health Services

12

Helen Killaspy

Abstract

Assessing the quality of healthcare services is challenging because the concept is multidimensional and difficult to operationalize. One commonly accepted approach is to assess three main constructs: (1) clinical improvement, (2) patient safety, and (3) patient experience of treatment/care. Clinicians and healthcare providers often conflate indicators of health processes (inputs) with outcomes (outputs). For example, the percentage of people with a specific diagnosis who are offered an appropriate, evidence-based treatment is an indicator of process, whereas a measure showing improvement in symptoms is an outcome. As well as clarifying exactly which outcomes and indicators of safety and patient experience are to be assessed, additional factors have to be taken into account when choosing measures to assess service quality: the availability of relevant data; whether the psychometric properties (reliability, validity) of any standardized measure under consideration are adequate; whether staff will require training to use the measure; whether there is any cost for using the measure; how data collection will be coordinated; how data will be managed (input, cleaned, and collated); and how data will be reported, by whom, and for what purpose/audience. Most of these factors require specific resources and designated systems and individuals in order to collect and report data so that they can be interpreted meaningfully and inform further improvements to services.

H. Killaspy (✉)
Division of Psychiatry, University College London,
6th Floor, Maple House, London W1T 7NF, UK
e-mail: h.killaspy@ucl.ac.uk

D. Razzouk (ed.), *Mental Health Economics*, DOI 10.1007/978-3-319-55266-8_12

Key Points Summary

- Assessment of the quality of mental healthcare should include measures of clinical improvement, patient satisfaction with care, and patient safety.
- When choosing measures, psychometric properties and resource implications (staff training, staff burden, data management and reporting) need to be considered.
- While "universal" tools have the advantage that data can be collated across groups and services, disorder-specific tools may provide more clinically useful data.
- Few specific mental health service quality assessment tools exist, with the exception of the Quality Indicator for Rehabilitative Care.

12.1 Introduction

This chapter aims to give an overview of the use of quality indicators in mental health. To do this, it is necessary first to clarify how the concept of quality can be operationalized with regard to healthcare, including the difference between processes and outcomes. The factors that require consideration when choosing measures and outcomes that can assess the quality of mental health services are then described before specific, commonly used tools are detailed. The example of mental health rehabilitation services is used to illustrate the need to tailor the choice of measures and indicators to the main activities and aims of a service. Finally, the chapter provides a brief overview of how routinely collected data can be used to improve service performance.

12.2 What Do We Mean by "Quality"?

The term *quality* implies a degree of relativity – how well something measures up against other, similar things. It follows that we cannot assess quality without knowing what standard or standards we are judging against. When we apply this concept to health service, the problem is that what constitutes good-quality care is multidimensional, extending beyond the delivery of specific evidence-based treatments and interventions. This makes "quality" something that is potentially difficult to operationalize and measure. In the United Kingdom, the Department of Health has defined *health service quality* as the effectiveness and safety of treatment and care alongside a positive experience for those who use services [1]. This basically translates into measuring (a) clinical improvement from the perspective of both clinicians and service users (and sometimes also caregivers); (b) patient safety ("doing no harm"); and (c) patient experience (treating patients with compassion, dignity, and respect). The assessment of these different components of quality necessarily vary from one specialty to another; within a specialty, such as mental health or psychiatry, there need to be some universal measures or metrics that can be applied to all services and some that are relevant only for subspecialties.

12.2.1 Difference Between Processes and Outcomes

To have a positive impact on patients, services need to "do something," that is, perform some kind of treatment or intervention, or deliver some specific support. Another term for this is *process*. Whether the process actually leads to an improvement for patients is measured in terms of the "outcome." Measures of process often are conflated with measures of outcome. An example of a process metric is the percentage of people with a specific symptom or diagnosis who are offered an evidence-based intervention for that problem (e.g., the percentage of people diagnosed with depression in an outpatient clinic who are offered cognitive behavioral therapy [CBT]). Another important process metric in this example is the percentage of people offered CBT who engaged with it. A relevant outcome metric would then be the percentage of those who engaged with CBT who showed an improvement in their depressive symptoms within a specific time frame (assessed using a standardized measure of depressive symptoms). However, another relevant outcome indirectly related to the process might be the percentage of people who gained/regained employment within a specific time period of their CBT.

At a group or service level, it might also be relevant to report outcome metrics such as admission rates or length of admission for people with depression, whether or not they engaged with a cognitive behavioral therapist, in order to assess whether the investment in the cognitive behavioral therapist might be associated with reduced service use (and costs) elsewhere in the system. Although it is important to be clear whether the data presented are reporting on processes or outcomes, both are clearly relevant in the assessment of quality. Whether an individual is offered appropriate treatment has a bearing not just on outcome but also on the person's experience of care – both of which are key constructs contributing to the concept of service quality.

12.3 Principles When Choosing Outcome Measures and Indicators

When first considering how to assess the quality of a service, it is tempting to jump to the conclusion only an outcome tool is needed. However, a number of factors need to be taken into account before deciding which measure(s) to choose and which data are needed to complement any standardized tool(s) in order to capture best the different quality dimensions relevant to each service.

First, data have to be available. This may seem obvious, but although it might make perfect sense to, for example, assess clinical symptoms in order to monitor whether a service is having a good effect, such assessments require skilled, trained clinical staff. If a standardized tool is going to be used, all staff need to be trained to use it to ensure good interrater reliability. There need to be systems in place to coordinate when the assessments will be carried out (e.g., at the start and end of a hospital admission or other, specific episode of treatment). Busy clinicians may need to be reminded to complete the assessment at these times and provided incentive to build this into their schedules. Some services produce regular feedback to individual services, teams, or clinicians regarding completion of routinely collected data, which can act as a helpful driver. Some electronic case note systems have automated pop-ups when an assessment is overdue to remind clinicians each time they log into relevant patient case notes.

Given how busy clinical teams are, it is vital that any assessment tools that require clinicians to complete them minimize the burden on staff time. It therefore makes sense to choose brief, simple, well-validated measures – otherwise people will simply stop using them. If tools do not have good psychometric properties (e.g., internal and external validity, reliability, sensitivity to change), they will not produce meaningful results [2]. This could have negative consequences for a service; being judged by a measure that gives inconsistent results or produces data that are not relevant to the aims of the service will make impossible any interpretation of how well the service is performing. In addition, some standardized tools have copyright restrictions and require a fee for use. This also needs to be taken into account when choosing the tool, and the payment of any associated costs must be clarified before it is rolled out. As well as agreeing on any standardized measures, other relevant process and outcome metrics should be agreed on. It may be possible for data for at least some of these to be collated centrally from the organization's existing systems (e.g., the number of referrals to a service over a specific time frame, the length of stay on an inpatient unit). The more data can be collated centrally within existing systems, the less burden will be placed on frontline clinical staff.

12.3.1 Data Collation and Reporting

Data collation and reporting also require investment. Having appropriate systems in place and individuals with responsibility for data management, cleaning, and reporting are vital components in any quality monitoring system. The same data may be needed for different purposes; thus reporting needs to be tailored accordingly. For example, inpatient data (number of admissions, length of stay) might be useful across the entire organization and at the individual ward level. Different wards may have different groups of patients, some with an expected length of stay much longer than others; therefore pooling data would not be helpful. Conversely, the number of inpatients who commit suicide within a defined period is of obvious relevance across all wards in terms of addressing universal issues of safety (such as ligature points). Whoever is tasked with reporting routinely collected data needs to be given clear guidance on what the data are to be used for so they can analyze and present the data appropriately.

Those who read the report need to be able to interpret its meaning with regard to whether any changes are required to improve the quality of their service. It is disappointing how often data reports use language that is incomprehensible to the average clinician. Brief explanatory text should be included in any data report; this may require discussion between the data analyst, clinicians, and service managers to agree on the appropriate (or possible) interpretations of the results. A related issue is that service managers often want to review data at the service level, whereas clinicians might also be interested in individual patient data. Choosing measures and metrics that can deliver meaningful data for both purposes can be extremely tricky, but there are some examples of measures where this is possible. Again, the process for reporting data at the individual level needs to be established and appropriately resourced.

12.3.2 Measures and Metrics Recommended for Mental Health Services

The U.K. Royal College of Psychiatrists' publication "Outcome Measures Recommended for Use in Adult Psychiatry" [3] includes specific metrics and measures for mental health that incorporate the three main constructs of healthcare quality assessment. It was suggested that clinical effectiveness should be assessed through monitoring patient-identified goals; using a standardized clinician-reported measure of clinical and social function – the Health of the Nation Outcome Scales (HoNOS) [4], physical health measures (e.g., blood pressure, body mass index), and social outcomes (e.g., employment, accommodation, community engagement); and providing a choice of 15 symptom-specific scales and 3 service-specific scales This research recommended that patient safety be assessed through a number of metrics that would allow benchmarking and review of incident reporting, suicide and self-harm rates, harm caused to others, and in-patient safety measures. At the time, no validated patient and carer experience measures had been developed with patient and caregiver involvement. Clearly, a detailed description of all these measures is beyond the scope of this chapter (and many published compendia of specific measures already exist), but the HoNOS deserves special mention, as it is probably the most widely used routine outcome measure in mental health services.

No assessment tool is perfect, and the HoNOS has had its critics [5], but it is now established as the universal clinician-rated outcome measure for mental health services in the United Kingdom. It has also been used similarly for many years across Australia, along with the Life Skills Profile, a clinician-rated outcome measure of social function [6]. The HoNOS is also used as a mandated routine clinical outcome measure in the Netherlands and is incorporated into their national quality assessment processes for mental health services. HoNOS comprises 12 items, each rated on a scale from 0 to 4, that assess a patient's behavior, self-harm, substance misuse, cognition, physical health, psychotic symptoms, depressive symptoms, neurotic symptoms, social relationships, social function, accommodation, and occupation. In the United Kingdom, all National Health Service mental health staff are trained to use it, and this use is incentivized in that organizations are penalized financially if completion rates are low. In England it is likely that HoNOS data will be used as a mechanism to allocate resources to services according to different levels of patient need (through a so-called tariff-based system; see Chap. 6).

The current recommended universal patient-reported experience measure for mental health services in the United Kingdom is the Family and Friends Test. This is a single item extracted from the Client Satisfaction Questionnaire [7]: "How likely are you to recommend our service to friends and family if they needed similar care or treatment?" The patient is asked to rate this item on a scale from 1 (extremely unlikely) to 5 (extremely likely). Also, work is ongoing to test a brief version of the Manchester Short Assessment of Quality of Life (MANSA) [8] for potential use as the universal patient-reported outcome measure for mental health services through an interactive web-based application called DIALOG. The MANSA has 12 items that assess different aspects of life, which patients rate on a scale from 1 (couldn't be worse) to 7 (couldn't be better), and then generates a total mean score between 1 and 7. The adaption of the MANSA to DIALOG has the advantage that patients are able to review regularly, on a hand-held device, their satisfaction with different aspects of their life; together with their clinician, they discuss and agree on actions that can help them achieve their goals and improve their ratings. This approach therefore provides both a vehicle to collect routine outcome data and acts as a useful tool for care planning that encourages completion because of its clinical usefulness. The clinical effectiveness and cost-effectiveness of DIALOG are being assessed though a cluster randomized controlled trial [9].

Currently, the U.K. Department of Health is working with the Royal College of Psychiatrists to agree on additional outcome measures for each mental health specialty. In the next section, mental health rehabilitation services are used as an example.

12.4 Recommending Routine Outcome Measures and Metrics: The Example of Mental Health Rehabilitation Services

Mental health rehabilitation services focus on people with especially complex needs who struggle with managing everyday activities and whose mental health problems make them vulnerable to exploitation. These include treatment-resistant positive symptoms, severe negative symptoms (amotivation and apathy), cognitive impairment (particularly those affecting organizational skills), and other issues that further complicate recovery, such as substance misuse and challenging behaviors [10]. Their complexity means that this group tends to require lengthy hospital admissions and has high support needs upon discharge into the community. Given these issues and the vulnerability of these patients to abuse, it is imperative that appropriate processes be available to assess and monitor the quality of care provided. Although it has long been known that good leadership, adequate resources, regular supervision of staff, and avoidance of physical or organizational isolation of the service are key in preventing abuses of care [11], contemporary services need more guidance to ensure they provide good-quality, long-term mental health interventions and support.

Mental health rehabilitation services are unusual in that they have a specific, standardized quality assessment tool (the Quality Indicator for Rehabilitative Care, or QuIRC) to assist them. The QuIRC was developed between 2007 and 2010 through a research project funded by the European Commission involving 10 countries at different stages of deinstitutionalization (Bulgaria, Czech Republic, Germany, Greece, Italy, the Netherlands, Poland, Portugal, Spain, and the United Kingdom). Its content was derived from triangulating findings from three sources in order to identify the components of care that are most important for the recovery of people living in long-term mental health facilities. This included a review of the relevant care standards in each of the 10 countries, a systematic literature review [12], and an international Delphi exercise with mental health professionals, service users, caregivers, and mental health advocates from each country [13]. The QuIRC was refined through piloting and reliability testing in over 200 facilities across Europe [14], and it was cross-validated against experiences of care from 1750 service users [15]. The final version is available as a web-based application (www.quirc.eu) completed by the service manager. It comprises 145 questions that are collated to give percentage ratings of seven domains of care (living environment, therapeutic environment, treatments and interventions, self-management and autonomy, social inclusion, human rights, and recovery-based practice). These items include data on the setting (hospital or community) and size (number of beds) of the unit; the average length of stay; the gender balance of service users; the proportion of people detained involuntarily; the degree of disability of service users; the staffing of the unit; staff training in rehabilitative skills; the provision of staff supervision; staff turnover; the provision of evidence-based pharmacological and psychosocial interventions; the facilitation of community activities (education, employment, and leisure); interventions to promote physical health; the therapeutic milieu; the provision of collaborative and individualized care planning; service user involvement; the protection of human rights, including privacy, dignity, and access to advocacy and legal representation; management of challenging behaviors; and the quality of the built environment. Once completed, a printable report is produced showing the service's performance on the seven domains of care and the average performance for similar services in the same country. The report also provides further information about how the unit could improve the quality of their care.

The QuIRC is available in 10 languages and can be used for local, regional, national, or international audit and research. It has been incorporated into national quality improvement programs for long-term mental healthcare facilities in Bulgaria, Czech Republic, Germany, the Netherlands, Portugal, and the United Kingdom. It has also been used in national and international programs of research, which have identified that having an expected maximum length of stay is a predictor of the quality of the service [16] and that the degree to which the service adopts a recovery-based approach is a predictor of successful discharge [17]. The latter includes a focus on therapeutic optimism and collaboration with patients to agree on the goals of treatment and support, rather than the more traditional approach of a professional-led treatment plan, with the patient as a passive recipient.

As well as the QuIRC and the universal mental health outcome measures (HoNOS, Family and Friends Test, and possibly DIALOG), the U.K. Royal College of Psychiatrists recommends that mental health rehabilitation services also routinely assess their service users' social function and needs using clinician-rated outcome measures. Numerous measures of social function are available, but at present, the most widely used scale with the best psychometric properties is the Life Skills Profile [6]. As previously mentioned, it is recommended as a universal mental health outcome tool in Australia. It is relatively brief and simple to use. Although is comprises 39 items, each rated from 1 to 4, with high scores representing better functioning, it takes only around 5 min to complete and produces five subdomain scores and a total score. It can be used to review progress at the level of an individual service user, and data can be collated across the service. The most commonly used needs assessment is the Camberwell Assessment of Needs Short Appraisal Schedule [18], a brief version of the Camberwell Assessment of Need [19]. It comprises 22 domains (rated as "no need," "met need," or "unmet need") that are summed to give a total needs score. It can be rated by clinicians, patients, or caregivers (though ratings tend to correlate poorly). For mental health rehabilitation clinicians it is helpful for identifying the areas of need at the level of an individual service user who requires more specific care planning. In addition, given the high needs of this service user group and the time often required to facilitate recovery, data can be collated to provide evidence of the impact of the service by showing an increase in the proportion of met needs (and a corresponding reduction in the proportion of unmet needs), even when the total needs across the group may not have decreased significantly.

A number of metrics for mental health rehabilitation services are also recommended to complement these standardized measures, including patient safety data (number of serious incidents and deaths), the percentage of service users who have had their annual physical health monitored, the average length of inpatient stay in the rehabilitation ward, the number and percentage of people with complex psychosis placed in a hospital bed or care setting outside their local area (this is an indicator of inadequate provision of local rehabilitation services), the percentage of people with complex psychosis who are successfully discharged into the community per year (without readmission or community placement breakdown), and the number and percentage of people in the service who are engaged in meaningful occupation (regular leisure activities, courses, or employment).

12.4.1 The Use of Routinely Collected Data and Quality Improvement

Many countries across Europe have systems to assess and review the quality of mental healthcare (Denmark, England, France, Germany, Italy, the Netherlands, Portugal, Scotland, and Sweden).These systems are usually provided as part of the general health service mandatory quality monitoring programs, but the Netherlands has a separate system called the Foundation for Benchmarking of Mental Healthcare. All these systems gather data that are specific to mental health. In England, France, and Portugal, *universal* mental healthcare indicators are not specific to disorders, whereas in Denmark, Germany, Italy, the Netherlands, and Sweden, measures are disorder specific (e.g., in the Netherlands, those chosen for severe mental health problems are HoNOS, MANSA, and Camberwell Assessment of Needs Short Appraisal Schedule alongside some items from standardized symptom assessment measures). The advantage of "universal" indicators is that data can be collated and compared across all services, but they may not be sensitive enough to detect changes in some conditions; hence the United Kingdom's decision to add specialty-specific tools and indicators to the battery of universal measures (something France is also considering).

It is important to note that while routinely collected data are useful to assess and review service performance, they have limitations and can provide only a proxy indication of the effectiveness of complex care processes. Indeed, critics of this approach have argued that quality indicators tend to measure things that are measurable instead of the things that are most relevant to healthcare [20]. Some countries (Denmark, France, the United Kingdom) use peer-review systems that are linked to an accreditation or registration process that can complement the use of routinely collected data. Peer review takes account of the service's focus and context, and because the assessors are clinicians in the same field, the process can provide a deeper understanding of the service's performance. There is good evidence that triangulation of different methods for assessing services and feeding data back is more effective at improving quality of care than routine data collection alone [21].

Increasingly, in the United Kingdom, financial incentives are also being used to increase the quality of mental healthcare. These are often set by the local clinical commissioning groups, bodies comprising clinicians and members of the local authority who are authorized to agree on contracts with healthcare providers. The key performance indicators of specific improvements are set annually, and financial penalties are imposed when targets are not achieved. An example is the percentage of service users who receive an annual physical health check. While this approach can be very successful, the lack of nationally agreed-upon targets means that variability exists across the country in terms of which key performance indicators are prioritized.

12.5 Conclusions

Quality is a multidimensional concept. Assessment of the quality of mental healthcare should include measures of clinical improvement from the perspective of both clinicians and service users, indicators of patient safety, and assessment of patients' experiences of care. Assessment of the processes and outcomes of care should be considered but not conflated. The choice of tools and indicators should account for the psychometric properties of the measures, the resources required to train staff to use them, the burden on staff imposed by data collection, and the resources required for data management and effective reporting of results. While "universal" tools have the advantage that data can be collated across groups and services, disorder-specific tools may provide more clinically useful data. Other than the Quality Indicator for Rehabilitative Care, few tailor-made quality assessment tools exist.

Key Messages

- Assessment of the quality of mental healthcare should include measures of clinical improvement from the perspective of both the clinicians and service users, indicators of patient safety, and assessment of patients' experiences of care.
- Disorder-specific tools may provide more clinically useful data than universal tools.
- Other than the Quality Indicator for Rehabilitative Care, few tailor-made quality assessment tools exist.

References

1. Department of Health. High quality care for all: NHS next stage review final report. London: The Stationery Office; 2008.
2. Lewis G, Killaspy H. Getting the measure of outcomes in clinical practice. Adv Psychiatr Treat. 2014;20(3):165–71.
3. Hampson M, Killaspy H, Mynors-Wallis L, Meier R. Outcome measures recommended for use in adult psychiatry. Occasional paper OP78. London: Royal College of Psychiatrists; 2011.
4. Wing JK, Curtis RH, Beevor AS. HoNOS: health of the nation outcome scales: report on research and development July 1993–December 1995. London: Royal College of Psychiatrists; 1996.
5. Bebbington P, Brugha T, Hill T, Marsden L, Window S. Validation of the health of the nation outcome scales. Br J Psychiatry. 1999;174:389–94.
6. Rosen A, Hadzi-Pavlovic D, Parker G. The life skills profile: a measure assessing function and disability in schizophrenia. Schizophr Bull. 1989;15:325–37.
7. Larsen DL, Attkisson CC, Hargreaves WA, Nguyen TD. Assessment of client/patient satisfaction: development of a general scale. Eval Progam Plann. 1979;2:197–207.
8. Priebe S, Huxley P, Knight S, Evans S. Application and results of the Manchester short assessment of quality of life. Int J Soc Psychiatry. 1999;45(1): 7–12.
9. Priebe S, Kelley L, Golden E, McCrone P, Kingdon D, Rutterford C, McCabe R. Effectiveness of structured patient-clinician communication with a solution focused approach (DIALOG+) in community treatment of patients with psychosis – a cluster randomised controlled trial. BMC Psychiatry. 2013;13:173.
10. Holloway F. The forgotten need for rehabilitation in contemporary mental health services: a position statement from the Executive Committee of the Faculty of Rehabilitation and Social Psychiatry. London: Royal College of Psychiatrists; 2005.
11. Martin JP. Hospitals in trouble. Oxford: Blackwell; 1984.
12. Taylor T, Killaspy H, Wright C, Turton P, White S, Kallert T, et al. A systematic review of the international published literature relating to quality of institutional care for people with longer term mental health problems. BMC Psychiatry. 2009;9:55.
13. Turton P, Wright C, White S, Killaspy H, Taylor T, Onchev G, et al. Promoting recovery in long term mental health institutional care: an international Delphi study. Psychiatr Serv. 2010;61:293–9.
14. Killaspy H, White S, Wright C, Taylor T, Turton P, Schützwohl M. The development of the Quality Indicator for Rehabilitative Care (QuIRC): a measure of best practice for facilities for people with longer term mental health problems. BMC Psychiatry. 2011;11:35.
15. Killaspy H, White S, Wright C, Taylor T, Turton P, Schützwohl M, et al. Association between service user experiences and staff rated quality of care in European facilities for people with longer term mental health problems. PLoS One. 2012;7(6):e38070.
16. Killaspy H, Cardosa G, White S, Wright C, Caldas de Almeida JM, Turton P, et al. Quality of care and its determinants in longer term mental health facilities across Europe; a cross-sectional analysis. BMC Psychiatry. 2016a;16:31.
17. Killaspy H, Marston L, Green N, Harrison I, Lean M, Holloway F, et al. Clinical outcomes and costs for

people with complex psychosis; a naturalistic prospective cohort study of mental health rehabilitation service users in England. BMC Psychiatry. 2016b;16:95.

18. Slade M, Beck A, Bindman J, Thornicroft G, Wright S. Routine clinical outcome measures for patients with severe mental illness: CANSAS and HoNOS. Br J Psychiatry. 1999;174:404–8.
19. Phelan M, Slade M, Thornicroft G, et al. The Camberwell assessment of need: the validity and reliability of an instrument to assess the needs of people with severe mental illness. Br J Psychiatry. 1995;167:589–95.
20. Legido-Quigley H, McKee M, Walshe K, Sunol R, Nolte E, Klazinga N. How can quality of health care be safeguarded across the European Union? Br Med J. 2008;336:920–3.
21. Grol R, Grimshaw J. From best evidence to best practice: effective implementation of change in patients' care. Lancet. 2003;362:1225–30.

13 Economic Data Collection: Instruments for Measuring Health Service Use and Direct Health Costs – The Bottom-Up Approach

Aglae Sousa and Denise Razzouk

Abstract

Quality of economic data is paramount in economic evaluation. To estimate costs, it is necessary to measure consumption of resources and, in the case of direct health costs, the utilization of health services. Instruments assessing health services use rely on patient self-report, allowing bias and methodological challenges. However, the majority of health services instruments do not include mental health services. Few instruments have been developed for economic evaluation in mental health. Importantly, few instruments were validated, and in this regard, several methodological obstacles exist. The Client Sociodemographic Service Receipt Inventory is the most used instrument for estimating direct costs in economic evaluation in mental health. This chapter outlines the main methodological issues involved in developing, validating, and applying such instruments and presents the instruments available for this purpose. In this regard, an example of translating and adapting the Client Sociodemographic Service Receipt Inventory to Portuguese (ISDUCS) is described, raising the main issues related to the instrument's feasibility and applicability in a sample with moderate and severe mental disorders in a middle-income setting.

A. Sousa (✉) • D. Razzouk
Centre of Economic Mental Health, Department of Psychiatry, Universidade Federal de Sao Paulo, Rua Borges Lagoa 570, 1° andar, Vila Clementino, São Paulo, Brazil, 04038-000
e-mail: asousa8@gmail.com; drazzouk@gmail.com

D. Razzouk (ed.), *Mental Health Economics*, DOI 10.1007/978-3-319-55266-8_13

Key Points Summary

- Bottom-up approach versus top down approach
- Methods for collecting economic data and mental health service utilization data
- Instruments available for economic evaluation in mental healthcare
- Instrument bias, feasibility, validity, and reliability
- The example of Brazil's version of the Client Sociodemographic Service Receipt Inventory: translation, cultural adaptation, feasibility, and reliability

13.1 Introduction

Economic evaluations require the comprehensive and detailed measurement of outcomes and costs [1–3]. Unlike epidemiological studies using instruments for measuring a set of constructs, usually clinically related, economic studies faces several obstacles for measuring outcomes not derived from specific diseases and for estimating the costs of multiple resources [3–5]. Methodological issues about instruments for measuring outcomes are described in Chaps. 3, 4, 5, 6 and 10.

The process of measuring costs is complex and depends on many steps; it is rarely achieved using only one instrument and approach [3, 6–9]. Measuring direct health costs use two main approaches: top-down and bottom-up. The top-down approach is used to extract data from administrative databases (governments, insurance companies, and private providers). The bottom-up approach is related to empirical studies of economic evaluation and requires instruments for measuring resources consumption (treatment, health services, informal care, and other nonhealth resources) for further estimating costs per individual. The latter is more accurate and comprehensive than the former, and for this reason it is the most recommended method in economic evaluation guidelines, though it is time-consuming and expensive. Therefore, direct heath costs are closely related to health services utilization, and in this regard, methods for measuring health services are questionable because they introduce a sort of bias of relying on patient self-report [4]. In this chapter we focus on questionnaires used for measuring mental health services use and treatment.

13.2 Instruments for Collecting Economic Data

The quality and accuracy of data for estimating costs is crucial for good economic evaluation research. Notwithstanding costs, variations are expected among services and among individuals, and biased instruments and modes of data collection exert huge influences on cost-effectiveness ratios, to the extent that they might mislead conclusions and resource allocation. The most common tools used in economic evaluations for data collection on health services use are questionnaires, diaries, and medical records [10]. However, the majority of studies uses modeling approaches and extract their cost-related data from the literature or databases when available.

Despite innumerable economic evaluations, few studies have focused on methodological issues regarding the development and validity of such tools [4, 5, 10–14]. A recent systematic review [15] of validated self-reporting questionnaires for measuring health services utilization found only 15 studies; of these, five were within the mental health field [4, 10, 13, 15, 16].

One of the most challenging issues for developing and measuring health services is their heterogeneity in terms of structure and resources, quality of medical records, and user characteristics. Moreover, for each economic evaluation, one inventory is developed or modified to adapt to a health system's peculiarities and the study goals. It is extremely difficult to find an instrument with all items required for economic evaluation. Instruments are usually developed to measure specific health services and do not include mental health services. Also, social services and other service alternatives in mental healthcare are not included.

13.2.1 Cost Diary

A cost diary is used in prospective study designs in economic evaluation and provides more accurate data than questionnaires because it minimizes recall bias, though few studies have been examining its validity [17]. Cost diaries allow coverage of health and nonhealth costs and indirect costs.

13.2.2 Questionnaires

Questionnaires can be used during face-to-face interviews, during telephone contacts, in mailed and online surveys. Several publications discuss the advantages and disadvantages of each. Questionnaires are addressed to the user, and in this sense several studies show the accuracy, inconsistencies, and feasibility of self-report surveys using respondents with mental disorders. Like constraints on using different methods to elicit preferences among people with severe mental disorders (see Chap. 3), using instruments to assess economic data and services consumption are hindered by severe cognitive impairment, memory bias, illiteracy, and social desirability [4]. Also, the underreporting rate in interviews among samples with mental disorders was threefold that found in nonpsychiatric samples [4].

Although the Epidemiologic Catchment Area was among the pioneers studies of measuring mental health services use, the survey instruments designed to explore the patterns of mental health services use by people with mental disorders were not designed for gathering economic data, and a set of publications subsequently reported its feasibility and validity by comparing self-reported answers with medical records [4].

Few instruments are available in the literature for estimating mental health services use and costs and describing development, structure, and validation. Moreover, instruments for comparing them are not easily available. Among all instruments available for economic evaluation in mental health, the Client Sociodemographic Service Receipt Inventory (CSSRI), developed in the United Kingdom for this purpose, is the most used for economic evaluation in mental health and has been translated to five other languages (Box 13.1). Although modifications and adaptations of the CSSRI items were necessary because of different health system structures, the use of similar instruments facilitates economic multicenter studies such as the European Psychiatric Services: Inputs linked to Outcome Domains and Needs (EPSILON) study [12].

13.2.3 Common Bias in Methods for Collecting Economic and Health Services Use Data

Economic and healthcare use data are usually collected directly from patients or using proxies (e.g., families, caregivers), and the majority of biases are a result of relying on self-report from a unique source (the patient). Bias might lead patients to underestimate or overestimate when reporting events and resource use [4, 5, 16, 19, 29–31, 32]. Several biases occur while collecting economic and healthcare use data with self-report questionnaires [11] (see Box 13.2). Therefore, underreporting and overreporting resource use directly affects the estimation of costs and ultimately data validity.

Another sort of bias is related to the mode used to collect data. While face-to-face interviews are more time-consuming and expensive than telephone interviews and mailed questionnaires, they have a lower nonresponse rate. On the other hand, mailed questionnaires allow a longer period of time for patients to respond to and return questionnaires. A combination of methods may be useful to minimize recall bias.

13.3 Validity and Accuracy of Economic Data

The majority of instruments available for measuring economic costs and healthcare use have been never tested for validity or reliability. While the validation of questionnaires is a common and required practice in epidemiological and evidence-based studies, economic evaluation studies rarely raise such issues. In a recent review of self-report

Box 13.1 Questionnaires for Measuring Costs, Health, and Mental Health Services

Brazil

Inventario Sociodemografico de Utilização e Custos de Serviços (ISDUCS modified Brazilian version of the CSSRI) [18]: The ISDUCS was translated and adapted according to the Brazilian Health Public System (SUS), covering all available services. The instrument was initially tested in terms of feasibility and interrater reliability among a sample of people discharged from long-term psychiatric hospitalizations. (Available from http://www.pssru.ac.uk/blogs/csri/).

Canada

Self-reported mental health service use [19]: Part of the 1996/1997 National Population Health Survey in Canada, this explored all resources used and professional visits regarding mental health.

Germany

CSSRI-D: German adaption of the CSSRI [20].

Italy

Intervista Costi Assistentia Psichiatrica (ICAP; the modified Italian version of the CSSRI) [13, 21]:The ICAP was translated and adapted to the Italian health system. The instrument was compared with case registry. Good agreement was observed for items related to inpatient and residential care.

Spain

Questionnaire for Cost Evaluation in Schizophrenia (based on the CSSRI) [22].

The Netherlands

TIC-P for healthcare consumption and productivity losses for psychiatric disorders [23, 24]: This is the short version of TIC-P, aiming to assess health service use among subjects with mental disorders (available from http://www.imta.nl/questionnaires/). TIC-P has two parts: one focused on health services consumption, and another focused on productivity losses. Medication costs are not included.

United Kingdom

Client Sociodemographic and Service Receipt Inventory (CSSRI) [1, 6, 12]: See item 13.4.1.

CITRINE for psychiatric wards [25]: This was developed in the United Kingdom as a tool for assessing all activities in the previous week of interviewing involving inpatients in psychiatric ward. The instrument was tested among a sample of patients with schizophrenia and bipolar disorder. Patients' answers were compared with case notes. Patients reported more activities than were contained in the case notes. On the other hand, the case notes reported more contacts with nurses than patients did. The overall reliability coefficient was 0.79. The questionnaire is addressed to inpatients. Session duration: 5–10 min.

Annotated costs questionnaire [26, 27]: This was developed through the contributions of several British health economists to produce a standardized questionnaire for assessing costs in the United Kingdom, focusing on costs for patients and families, health and social care use, and residential care costs.

Security Facilities Service Use Schedule (SF-SUS) [28]: This was developed specifically to assess costs and resources used at the individual level among prisoners in a Dangerous and Severe Personality Disorder Program.

United States

Cornell Service Index (CSI) [29]: The CSI was developed to measure the quantity of health service use among adults with mental disorders with no cognitive impairment within the 3 months before interviewing. It was tested for reliability (interrater and test-retest) among a sample of 40 subjects seeking mental health outpatient services for the first time. It also assesses out-of-pocket expenditures by patients.

Utilization and Cost Inventory (UAC-1) [30]: This was developed to compute costs

(continued)

Box 13.1 (continued)
for individuals with mood disorders. It is a structured questionnaire covering 33 health services and assesses their usage in the previous 3 months of interviewing. The data were compared with those from provider records. Psychometric indicators showed good values for inpatient settings and por values for outpatient settings.

More instruments on mental health services utilization are cited in DIRUM (http://www.dirum.org/instruments/).

questionnaires for economic evaluation [15], only 15 studies reported some degree of questionnaire validity from among almost 2500 abstracts originating from searches developed for this purpose.

Assessment of the validity of economic data is threatened by many things (see Box 13.3). The first barrier is the heterogeneity of health services. Health services usually differ on their structure, teams, available resources, characteristics, and goals. One service is never similar to another, even if it is created for treating patients with the same diagnosis and characteristics. Therefore, external validity can be markedly compromised.

Another obstacle is deciding on the best benchmark (gold standard) against which the new questionnaire could be compared. Sources of resource use often vary in terms of accuracy from one setting to another, and it is very difficult to know which one is the most correct. The majority of studies compare patient self-report with medical records and administrative databases. However, the content of medical records can be incomplete, inaccurate, and frequently inaccessible. Questionnaires differ enormously in terms of content, the number of items, and comprehensiveness, hindering comparison among them. In addition, patient self-report is the only accurate source, though several recall biases exist regarding utilization of multiple health services in the community and in the entire health system [10]. This is particularly complex and tricky in mental health because people with mental disorders can receive multiple interventions from a multidisciplinary mental health team during one visit, and they simultaneously use other types of mental health services and community services networks with different proposals. Yet, some patients, especially those with psychosis or a low level of education, present difficulties when discriminating among mental health professionals (psychiatrists, psychologists, occupational therapists). Similarly, they may not eventually distinguish different levels of care at the community level. The use of proxies, such as a family member or caregiver, does not solve this problem. In economic evaluation, the most important data are estimated costs according to individual variation and characteristics. Some administrative databases and medical records have narrow coverage of data that is not enough for economic evaluation.

13.4 Issues with Translating and Adapting Questionnaires to Different Countries: ISDUCS, the Brazilian Version of the CSSRI

13.4.1 The Client Sociodemographic Service Receipt Inventory

The CSSRI is a semistructured questionnaire developed in the United Kingdom to assess the utilization of health services and criminal justice services [1, 6, 12] by people with severe mental disorders. It comprises six categories of assessment: sociodemographic data, usual living situation, accommodation details, employment and income, medication profile, and use of health services and criminal justice services. It has been applied in more than a 100 European studies [12]. The CSSRI was used in the EPSILON study [33], and the PROGRES study (*Progetto Residenze*, or Residential Care Project) used an Italian adaptation of the CSSRI [21]. The EPSILON study [33] described the use of this instrument to assess costs of mental healthcare provided to people with schizophrenia in five countries: Denmark, England, Italy, Spain, and the Netherlands, whereas the PROGRES study evaluated the costs of residential facilities in Italy.

Box 13.2 Bias on Reporting Resource Use (Services, Treatment)
Recall bias

- *Length of the recall period*: Patients may report events that happened before the recall period specified by an interview, or patients might underreport events occurring during a recall period determined by researchers because they wrongly judge the occurrence of the event as being before this period.
- *Intensity and relevance of the illness event/resource use*: Hospitalization, surgery, and admission to emergency departments are usually easier to report than sporadic visits to general practitioners in primary care.
- *Patient's ability to recall*: This depends on the patient's social and demographic characteristics (age, literacy, income), cognitive function (e.g., delirium episodes are not usually remembered by patients), diagnosis (e.g., psychosis affects the perception of time), and personality traits.

Social desirability bias: This depends on how an event is perceived – whether socially positive or negative. If it is a stigmatizing or not socially accepted event or behavior, individuals may underreport it (e.g., drug deals, drug use, inappropriate sexual behavior, quantity of alcohol consumed). On the other hand, overreporting may occur in the case of positive events (e.g., income).

Modes of collection that introduce bias:

- Face-to-face interviews
- Telephone interviews
- Online questionnaires
- Mailed questionnaires

Box 13.3 Types of Validity
Internal validity

Face validity and content validity: Once one concept is described, the goal is to examine whether the operationalization of the concept corresponds coherently and similarly to the description of the concept.

Criterion-related validity and concurrent validity: These refer to testing a new questionnaire against a benchmark (gold-standard) test and assessing the correlation between them. The stronger the correlation, the greater the concurrent validity.

External validity: This refers to the extent that results of, for example, using a new test are generalizable to other settings or populations.

13.4.2 Characteristics of the Brazilian Health System

The Unified Health System (SUS) is a public system comprising health services provided by the federal, state, and regional governments [34]. The private sector is regulated by ANS (the Brazilian Health Agency) and available on the market under agreement with insurance companies. Brazilian's constitution is based on egalitarian social welfare principles and universal health coverage. Therefore, all Brazilian citizens, tourists, migrants, and refugees have rights to healthcare provided by the State, free of charge, with no discrimination of any kind. Mental healthcare was included in the public health system (SUS) in 1988, and, after the Declaration of Caracas in 1990, mental healthcare has been shifting from hospital to community care. Community mental healthcare comprises psychosocial centers (CAPS), residential facilities, psychiatric emergency units, and psychiatric wards in general hospitals. Psychiatric hospitals exist within the country, but the reduction in the number of psychiatric beds over the past two decades has been substantial. Community mental health networks are linked with other community services such as clubhouses, leisure and sports centers, and shelter workshops and social activities.

13.4.3 Translation of CSSRI to Portuguese and Its Cultural Context

In 2008, after a court decision, 19 residential services were created in the city of São Paulo and two remaining public psychiatric hospitals were closed. Inpatients living in such hospitals were mostly transferred to residential facilities. The deinstitutionalization of long-term patients in Brazil fostered the need for a tool for measuring the costs of health services based on their utilization by those patients. There was extensive debate triggered by the fight among stakeholders and policymakers with differing ideological and traditional psychiatric views regarding the costs of psychiatric hospitals and community mental health services, though no accurate economic data were available. The State of São Paulo has around 50 million inhabitants and accounts for one-third of Brazil's gross domestic product. The city of São Paulo, the capital of the State of São Paulo, has approximately 12 million inhabitants (reaching 20 million if outer regions are considered) and comprises the main pool of economic, cultural, and scientific centers in the country.

In this scenario, we aimed to assess the direct costs for these patients discharged for residential facilities in the city of São Paulo. For this purpose, we decided to translate the CSSRI into Portuguese, since there was no economic instrument available for economic evaluation in mental healthcare in the country. However, Brazil's system is different from the United Kingdom's health system, and questionnaire adaptation was crucial. Moreover, it was necessary to test its feasibility among people with moderate and severe mental disorders, though it was proven to be feasible for use among people with schizophrenia in the United Kingdom.

We have made all efforts to maintain the structure of the original instrument, but some substantial changes were unavoidable. Also, an appendix was included with a list of resources for costing nonhealth costs and overhead. The so-called ISDUCS follows the structure of the CSSRI, though we made some substantial changes in the sixth category to adapt it to the type of health service in Brazil. A guide was elaborated with detailed instructions for the application of ISDUCS.

13.4.4 Feasibility, Reliability, and Challenges of ISDUCS's Application in a Sample with Mental Disorders

In 2010 we started a study with a randomly selected sample of 30 residents from 10 residential facilities in order to verify whether ISDUCS was feasible, easy, and reliable to be applied to people with moderate and severe mental disorders. All individuals were discharged from psychiatric hospitals and were placed in residential facilities. These services were addressed to people with a lower level of autonomy, who are in need of permanent care and have no family relationships. They resided in a fully staffed home, with up to eight people living there under the 24-h supervision of two caregivers taking turns working a 12-h shift daily.

Two raters simultaneously applied ISDUCS in order to measure interrater reliability. The kappa coefficient was estimated to verify interrater reliability, and the results showed good reliability for the majority of items, except the item related to occupational work.

All data collected from patients were checked with caregivers after collection. During face-to-face interviews, researchers asked patients to answer each item of the questionnaire because the majority of the sample has a low level of education and they were not able to read it themselves. The researchers also queried regarding the consumption of resources during the 30 days before the interview. Interviews lasted on average 30 min, ranging between 20 and 60 min.

A diagnosis of nonaffective psychosis corresponded to 70% of the sample, followed by alcohol and drug problems and mood disorders. Because all medications were delivered by caregivers, and because one-third of the sample had low levels of autonomy and self-care, three-fourths of residents were not able to answer questions regarding the name and dose of medication they use regularly, and almost two-thirds of the sample did not know whether they visited with a psychologist or psychiatrist in outpatient care (Centre of Psychosocial Care, CAPS).

13.4.4.1 Challenges

We faced several obstacles in conducting this research:

(a) We experienced a lack of transparency because of the great resistance from policy-makers and health management against delivering administrative data on costs.
(b) All medical records from psychiatric hospitals contained information about history and hospitalization were burnt during hospital closure.
(c) The majority of caregivers working in residential facilities did not work at psychiatric hospitals and did not know about patients' histories.
(d) Medical records of outpatient care were not available for researchers to consult.
(e) The sample had a high rate of illiteracy and low education.
(f) ISDUC has to be adapted when used for research in different settings, and new items to be included hinder validation procedures.

Notwithstanding these limitations, it was the first time in Brazil that people with moderate and severe mental disorders discharged from psychiatric hospitals were assessed for costs and community mental health services use, psychiatric and nonpsychiatric services, hospitalization, medications, and psychosocial intervention over a period of 30 days. There is a paucity of economic studies in Brazil, and the first step is to create an appropriate questionnaire for collecting individual data. Reliability was good, but determining the validity against medical records was not possible. After this initial test, ISDUCS was used in the project for estimating direct costs of 147 individuals in residential facilities in all main neighborhoods of the city of São Paulo. Obviously, this instrument should be tested in other patient samples and with other mental health services in future projects. Research using CAPS for alcohol and drug problems is ongoing, in which we are using ISDUCS to estimate the direct costs for a sample with moderate and severe alcohol and drug problems, though we had to modify some items to adjust for other interventions available in the service. It is difficult to design a universal questionnaire in terms of covering all necessary items for economic evaluation and all variations of intervention delivery. If an instrument with minimal and standardized common items among services was to be developed, the list of resources would have to be reduced, compromising cost estimation. In addition, it is important to measure healthcare utilization broadly and to include community mental health services. These methodological obstacles remain open issues that should be addressed in future research.

Key Messages

- There is no universal, standardized, and valid instrument for use in all economic evaluations in mental healthcare and health settings.
- Health systems and instruments for identifying economic data are heterogeneous, hindering the comparability of costs among services.
- Questionnaires for measuring health services use and costs rely on patient self-report, allowing several biases and methodological challenges to their validity.
- Cognitive impairment, memory recall bias, mode of interviewing, type of psychiatric diagnosis, and social desirabil-

(continued)

(continued)

ity are common biases affecting cost estimates.

- Despite limitations, people with mental disorders are able to answer self-report questionnaires on mental health services use in specific circumstances. Multiple sources of information are recommended.
- Few studies address instrument validity and the standardization of data collection.

References

1. Beecham J, Knapp M. Costing psychiatric interventions. In: Thornicroft G, editor. Measuring mental health needs. London: Gaskell; 2001. p. 200–24.
2. Drummond MF, Sculpher MJ, Torrance GW, O'Brien BJ, Stoddart GL. Methods for the economic evaluation of health care programmes. 3rd ed. Oxford: Oxford University Press; 2007.
3. McCrone P, Weich S. Mental health care costs: paucity of measurement. Soc Psychiatry Psychiatr Epidemiol. 1996;31(2):70–7.
4. Golding JM, Gongla P, Brownell A. Feasibility of validating survey self-reports of mental health service use. Am J Community Psychol. 1988;16(1):39–51.
5. van den Brink M, van den Hout WB, Stiggelbout AM, van de Velde CJ, Kievit J. Cost measurement in economic evaluations of health care: whom to ask? Med Care. 2004;42(8):740–6.
6. Beecham J. Collecting and estimating costs. In: Knapp M, editor. The economic evaluation of mental health care. 1st ed. Aldershot: Arena; 1995. p. 61–82.
7. Byford S, Sefton T. Economic evaluation of complex health and social care interventions. Natl Inst Econ Rev. 2003;186:98–108.
8. Byford S, McDaid D, Sefton T. Because it's worth it: a practical guide to conducting economic evaluations in the social welfare field. London: York Publishing Services Ltd; 2003.
9. Shearer J, McCrone P, Romeo R. Economic evaluation of mental health interventions: a guide to costing approaches. Pharmacoeconomics. 2016;34(7):651–64.
10. Byford S, Leese M, Knapp M, Seivewright H, Cameron S, Jones V, et al. Comparison of alternative methods of collection of service use data for the economic evaluation of health care interventions. Health Econ. 2007;16(5):531–6.
11. Evans C, Crawford B. Data collection methods in prospective economic evaluations: how accurate are the results? Value Health. 2000;3(4):277–86.
12. Chisholm D, Knapp MKH, Amaddeo F, Gaite L, Winjgaarden B. Client socio-demographic service receipt inventory European version: development of one instrument for international research. Br J Psychiatry. 2000;177(39):s28–33.
13. Mirandola M, Bisoffi G, Boso M, Amaddeo F. Collecting psychiatric resources utilisation to calculate costs of care: a comparison between a service receipt interview and a case register. Soc Psychiatry Psychiatr Epidemiol. 1999;34:541–7.
14. Patel A, Rendu A, Moran P, Leese M, Mann A, Knapp M. A comparison of two methods of collecting economic data in primary care. Fam Pract. 2005;22:323–7.
15. Leggett LE, Khadaroo RG, Holroyd-Leduc J, Lorenzetti DL, Hanson H, Wagg A, et al. Measuring resource utilization: a systematic review of validated self-reported questionnaires. Medicine (Baltimore). 2016;95(10):e2759.
16. Heinrich S, Deister A, Birker T, Hierholzer C, Weigelt I, Zeichner D, et al. Accuracy of self-reports of mental health care utilization and calculated costs compared to hospital records. Psychiatry Res. 2011;185(1–2):261–8.
17. Goossens M, Molken M, Vlaeyen J, Linden S. The cost diary: a method to measure direct and indirect costs in cost-effectiveness research. J Clin Epidemiol. 2000;53:688–95.
18. Sousa A, Cardoso A, Oliveira G, Mari J, Razzouk D. Standardized tool for measurement of health services costs and utilization in a sample with mental disorders: translation, cultural adaptation and interrater reliability of the client sociodemografic and service receipt inventory Brazilian version. Value Health Reg Issues. 2013;16:696.
19. Rhodes AE, Fung K. Self-reported use of mental health services versus administrative records: care to recall? Int J Methods Psychiatr Res. 2004;13(3):165–75.
20. Roick C, Kilian R, Matschinger H, Bernert S, Mory C, Angermeyer M. German adaptation of the client sociodemographic and service receipt inventory :an instrument for the cost of mental health care. Psychiatr Prax. 2001;28:S84–90.
21. Amaddeo F, Bonizzatto P, Fenyo A, Tansella KM. ICAP Un'intrevista per la raccolta dei dati necessari per la valutazione dei costi dell'assistenza psichiatrica. Epidemiol Psichiatr Soc. 1996;5:201–14.
22. Haro JM, Salvador-Carulla L, Cabases J, Madoz V, Vazquez-Barquero JL. Utilisation of mental health services and costs of patients with schizophrenia in three areas of Spain. Br J Psychiatry. 1998;173:334–40.
23. Timman R, Bouwmans C, Busschbach JJ, Hakkaart-van RL. Development of the treatment inventory of costs in psychiatric patients: TIC-P mini and midi. Value Health. 2015;18(8):994–9.
24. Bouwmans C, De JK, Timman R, Zijlstra-Vlasveld M, Feltz-Cornelis C, Tan SS, et al. Feasibility, reliability and validity of a questionnaire on healthcare consumption and productivity loss in patients with a

psychiatric disorder (TiC-P). BMC Health Serv Res. 2013;13:217.
25. Sabes-Figueira R, McCrone P, Sharac J, Csipke E, Craig T, Rose D, et al. Developing a tool for collecting and costing activity data on psychiatric inpatient wads. Epidemiol Psychiatr Sci. 2012;21:393–9.
26. Thompson S, Wordsworth S. An annotated cost questionnaire for completion by patients. HERU Discussion Paper No. [03/01]. Health Economics Research Unit, University of Aberdeen. Health Economics Research Unit, University of Aberdeen; 2017.
27. Wordsworth S, Hompson S. An annotated cost questionnaire for patients: results of piloting. HERU Dicussion paper, 2001, Discussion Paper 03/01; 2001.
28. Barrett B, Byford S. Collecting service use data for economic evaluation in DSPD populations: development of the secure facilities service use schedule. Br J Psychiatry Suppl. 2007;49:s75–8.
29. Sirey JA, Meyers BS, Teresi JA, Bruce ML, Ramirez M, Raue PJ, et al. The Cornell service index as a measure of health service use. Psychiatr Serv. 2005;56(12):1564–9.
30. Kashner TM, Stensland MD, Lind L, Wicker A, Rush AJ, Golden RM, et al. Measuring use and cost of care for patients with mood disorders: the utilization and cost inventory. Med Care. 2009;47(2):184–90.
31. Ritter PL, Stewart AL, Kaymaz H, Sobel DS, Block DA, Lorig KR. Self-reports of health care utilization compared to provider records. J Clin Epidemiol. 2001;54(2):136–41.
32. Petrou S, Murray L, Cooper P, Davidson LL. The accuracy of self-reported healthcare resource utilization in health economic studies. Int J Technol Assess Health Care. 2002;18(3):705–10.
33. Becker T, Hulsmann S, Knudsen HC, Martiny K, Amaddeo F, Herran A, et al. Provision of services for people with schizophrenia in five European regions. Soc Psychiatry Psychiatr Epidemiol. 2002;37(10):465–74.
34. Mateus MD, Mari JJ, Delgado PG, Almeida-Filho N, Barrett T, Gerolin J, et al. The mental health system in Brazil: policies and future challenges. Int J Ment Heal Syst. 2008;2(1):12.

14 Costing Psychiatric Hospitals and Psychiatric Wards in General Hospitals

Alessandra Brisola Siomi and Denise Razzouk

Abstract

Costing psychiatric hospitals was initially the main interest of accountants and hospital managers because it targets cost-saving issues. Health Economics emerged while psychiatric deinstitutionalization was in progress, shifting from hospitals to a community mental healthcare model. This triggered multiple studies comparing costs between hospitals and community services. However, methods for estimating psychiatric hospital costs have been rarely described in these studies. A top-down approach has been the method most used for estimating costs in psychiatric hospitals, because many of these costing exercises are aimed accounting goals. On the other hand, with the emergence of Health Economics, allowing the comparison of costs and benefits among multiple models of care, a bottom-up approach became the most recommended method for costing services because individual variations in costs depend on the user's profile and other factors. There are three main categories for estimating hospital costs: capital costs (including land, buildings, and equipment), "hotel" costs (support services, overhead, consumables, and human resources), and treatment costs (clinical staff, medication, laboratory tests, and imaging). The first step is to accurately describe the hospital in order to identify components of costs and to decide how data will be collected. Estimating a unit costs might be complex in some activities that share costs or in joint production costs because professionals can work in more than one ward. Double counting should be carefully avoided. This chapter ends with an example of costing psychiatric hospitals in Brazil using top-down and bottom-up approaches.

A.B. Siomi (✉) • D. Razzouk
Centre of Economic Mental Health (CESM), Department of Psychiatry, Universidade Federal de Sao Paulo, Rua Borges Lagoa 570, 1 andar, São Paulo, Brazil, 04038-000
e-mail: absiomi@gmail.com; drazzouk@gmail.com

D. Razzouk (ed.), *Mental Health Economics*, DOI 10.1007/978-3-319-55266-8_14

Key Points Summary

- Top-down and bottom-up approaches in costing psychiatric hospitals
- Steps for costing psychiatric hospitals
- Direct health costs, nonhealth costs, and capital costs
- Components of costs and estimating unit costs
- Example of costing a psychiatric hospital: the case of Complexo Hospitalar do Juquery in Brazil.

14.1 Introduction

High hospital costs and the emergence of new technologies triggered the development of Health Economics in the 1950s in the United States [1]. Health Economics methods were initially applied to help hospital managers optimize resources [2] (see Chap. 1). At that time, these methods were not driven by the welfare principles of economics, but rather were oriented towards saving costs [2]. The increase in health costs, especially in hospital settings because of their high level of complexity and the availability of new, expensive treatments, has contributed to the development of Health Economics and the use of its principles to guide resource allocation in health policies. From a historical perspective, the birth of Health Economics occurred simultaneously with the closure of psychiatric hospitals in high-income countries. After the 1950s, new treatments allowed individuals to receive care in outpatient services rather than staying in hospitals for long periods.

The shift from a hospital-based model of care to community-based care challenged public policies in terms of allocating resources for both models of care during the transition period [3, 4]. Public health budgets were allocated mainly to hospitals (50–80% of health budgets), and the majority of the health workforce was placed in hospitals [5, 6]. Similarly, psychiatric hospitals accounted for almost the entire budget (85–90%) for mental health, and after World War II, with the closure of psychiatric hospitals during deinstitutionalization in the United Kingdom, hospital costs increased fourfold. In addition, the pattern of hospital costs changed over this period, showing an extensive increase in staff costs [7]. Several costing studies have emerged comparing hospital and community care costs [2, 8–10].

However, methods for costing hospitals needed to be adapted to another model of care [11]. Notwithstanding the reduction in costs with the closure of psychiatric hospitals, other sectors incurred other costs as a result, such as higher costs for criminal justice, prison, unemployment, health benefits, and accommodation [7]. While costing methods for hospitals were mainly used for accounting purposes [11], the expansion of health services to the community raised questions of resource allocation based on heath priorities and equity issues [12, 13] (see Chap. 10).

Despite the availability of several costing manuals, costing methods in economic evaluation, mainly regarding hospitals, are rarely reported accurately [11, 14–18]. Accountants use a top-down approach, but in economic evaluations, the bottom-up approach is preferable. One method recommended for such purposes is active-based costing (ABC), in which microcosting is based on the sum of all activities necessary to deliver services to inpatients (including staff, drug, consumable, capital, equipment, and hospital infrastructure costs) [11].

The methods used in the literature for costing hospitals vary considerably, leading to different values for unit costs. For instance, Javi et al. [19] compared traditional accounting methods using a top-down approach and the ABC method for costing hospital unit costs, demonstrating that the unit costs estimated using ABC was U$50 higher than traditional accounting estimations. In this chapter we raise the main methodological issues regarding psychiatric hospital costing, and we illustrate step by step the costing process using costing for one psychiatric unit in a tertiary hospital in the State of São Paulo.

14.2 Costing Psychiatric Hospitals

At least three main types of psychiatric facilities exist: psychiatric hospitals, acute psychiatric wards in general hospitals, and specialized wards or a psychiatric building attached to tertiary hospitals. Psychiatric hospitals usually comprise one independent building, providing 100 or more beds, with the goals to treat and to provide rehabilitation interventions for patients with chronic mental disorders and a moderate or high level of disability. The majority of these inpatients are physically healthy, and psychiatrists and nurses are the main staff in the service, whereas general practitioners are called on an as-needed basis only. These institutions have been progressively closed during the deinstitutionalization process, and a remarkable proportion of inpatients remained hospitalized for a long period of time (1 year or more). An acute psychiatric unit in a general hospital comprises a few psychiatric beds given to patients with physical and mental healthcare needs and with acute episodes such as psychosis, suicide attempts, depression with psychotic symptoms, alcohol and drug dependence, severe bipolar disorders, and psychiatric episodes secondary to other medical diseases. Inpatients in this type of unit require intensive care both from mental healthcare teams and from other medical specialties, and hospitalizations are short. These inpatients consume more resources from the general hospital compared with psychiatric hospital services in terms of lab tests, imaging, and other procedures. The third type is a mix of psychiatric care between both psychiatric hospitals and general hospitals and varies in terms of user profiles, symptom severity, length of stay, and the service's goals.

The distinction among types of hospitals is important because the costs per patient or estimation of the units of costs are not equal. When using data from one hospital diary for an economic evaluation, it is important to consider which type of hospital it is because the same unit costs is not appropriate for all psychiatric hospitalizations. Complexity, quality, size, and available resources vary enormously among hospitals [20].Economic evaluations usually focus on the individual variation of costs, and depending on the goal of the study, hotel costs might not be included. However, opportunity costs are essential in economic evaluations, and in this regard, hotel costs, capital costs, and equipment costs are included. Costing psychiatric hospitals requires some particular goals, and depending on these, methods for costing may be different (Box 14.1).

In this chapter we focus on costing the main components of a psychiatric hospital and a psychiatric ward in a general hospital. We divide the costing process into five main steps: description of the hospital, identification of cost components, measurement of items consumed, choice and estimation of units costs, and estimation of total ward costs.

14.2.1 Description of the Hospital

Hospitals vary in the degree of complexity and amount of resources; for this reason, it is crucial to understand how a hospital works, what services are delivered, and which professionals are involved in providing those services [20]. Also, it is necessary to verify the quality and the level of detail of information available (databases, registers, records, billing systems, and cost centers). After defining the perspective, the goal, and the time horizon, the first step in costing is to visit the hospital in order to observe how processes are

Box 14.1 Goals for Costing Psychiatric Hospitals

- Accounting's goals
- Economic evaluation comparing interventions outside hospitals
- Economic evaluation comparing programs or packages of care exclusively in hospitals
- Comparison of unit costs using different methods
- Comparison of costs among hospitals and community services
- Comparison of hospital costs according to the type of diagnosis and patients' profiles
- Comparison of costs among different levels of hospital complexity
- Exploration of the factors influencing hospital costs

Box 14.2 Description of the Hospital

What capital and equipment are available? Building (rented?), size, land, equipment, specialties and wards, number of beds, complexity (secondary, tertiary)

How are hospitals organized? Organizational sectors: departments, cost centers, funding sources

Which interventions are delivered? (e.g., clinical, surgery, obstetric, pediatric, emergency, oncology, transplant units)

Which interventions are available? (e.g., medication, liaison team consultants, physiotherapy, occupational therapy, psychological treatment, social support, laboratory tests, imaging, surgery, electroconvulsive therapy). Are all procedures done in the hospital?

Is there any outpatient or day hospital care facilities affiliated with the hospital that provide mixed services to users?

Who is eligible for this service? Is the hospital oriented/targeted toward specific users?

Treatment staff (human resources):

- Do professionals work in one or more units?
- In which activities are professionals involved? (joint activities?) (description, length of time, eligibility)
- Are clinical staff involved in nonclinical activities (e.g., teaching)?
- Which interventions are delivered?
- Salaries and career paths

Nontreatment staff (human resources):

- Support services provided by third parties? (e.g., cleaning, laundry, nutrition, pharmacy, laboratories, trash services, security, reception)
- Which professionals are involved?
- Management and financial activities (overhead)

Utilities (telephone, electricity, water, gas)

Medication, exams, and other treatment procedures

Consumables

Transportation (ambulances)

Overhead

- Which components comprise overhead?
- How does it work?
- Which proportion of overhead costs is addressed to each unit or ward?

run and to take notes on all relevant characteristics [21] (Box 14.2). Box 14.2 outlines examples of relevant information for hospital characterizations that should be collected in order to plan which cost components should be measured in the costing process. It is important to identify more relevant activities and sectors, whether sectors share costs, and how sectors are related (joint production) and consume resources [2, 22, 23]. Two main categories of costs are usually measured: one related to health treatment and patients (medication, clinical staff, exams/tests, surgery, nursing care), and another related to hospital operation (e.g., supporting services, pharmacy, laboratories, cost centers, maintenance, management, and overhead).The former are commonly called "direct health costs" and the latter are called "nonhealth direct costs" or "indirect costs." To distinguish indirect costs in hospitals and indirect costs resulting from lost productivity, in this chapter we use direct nonhealth costs or nontreatment costs.

14.2.2 Components of Costs

Cost components vary according to the type of service, the perspective of the study, and patients' profiles. Three main cost categories exist in hospitals: direct health costs, capital costs, and direct nonhealth costs (revenue costs) [17, 23, 24] (see Box 14.3).

It is important to note that, depending on the inpatient profiles, the consumption of resources varies, and for this reason the choice of component used to measure costs should consider the relevance of resources for each group of inpatients or for a particular hospital unit. For

Box 14.3 Components of Costs of Psychiatric Hospitals and Psychiatric Units in General Hospitals

a. *Direct health costs*

Psychiatric ward

Clinical staff (doctors, nurses, occupational therapists, psychologists, nurse assistants, social workers)

Nonpsychiatric ward

Clinical staff (nonpsychiatrist doctors, nurses, physiotherapists, nurse assistants, social workers).

Procedures

Medication, lab tests, imaging, psychosocial interventions, surgical interventions and prostheses

b. *Direct nonhealth costs (revenue costs)*

Support services (pharmacy, sterilization, laboratory, laundry, housekeeping, security, nutrition, waste management, storage, archives, reception, communication, informatics)

Utilities (electricity, water, gas, telephone)

Professional training

Consumables

Overhead (management, maintenance, clerical staff)

Transportation

c. *Capital costs*

Building, land

Equipment and furniture

Vehicles, ambulances

instance, the majority of inpatients hospitalized in a psychiatric unit does not consume a large proportion of exams, surgeries, and other medical procedures. Except for some acute cases, the main resources consumed by these patients are medications, doctor visits, mental health team visits, and some exams. Therefore, compared with the other units of a general hospital, the pattern of resource consumption in the psychiatric unit is lower. Allocation methods for estimating costs of support services should take this pattern into account.

Considering inpatients with chronic psychiatric disorders and without clinical comorbidities, nonhealth costs and capital costs might not vary; in that case a top-down approach (average costs) is acceptable. Some countries implemented diagnosis-related group (DRG) systems to address inpatients with the same diagnosis and similar patterns of resource consumption; in this system, reimbursements are paid according to disease costing. Units of costs can be derived from diagnosis-related groups, especially for accounting purposes. However, some cases exist in which comorbidities occur between psychiatric and clinical diseases; then the consumption of resources might vary considerably. In economic evaluations, it is important to assess these variations among individuals and use long-term marginal opportunity costs [7]. Capital costs and informal care and out-of-pocket expenditures are examples of opportunity costs, and they should be considered depending on the study perspective.

14.2.3 Unit Costs and Service Consumption Measurement

Unit costs are estimated depending on the chosen costing method. The top-down approach is used when there is low variability in the consumption of resources among inpatients. In the case of psychiatric hospitalizations, a top-down approach can be used for estimating unit costs for fixed costs (support services, utilities, overhead). Fixed costs are described as unrelated to users' consumption; for instance, utilities would be similar with 85% or with 95% of beds occupied (see Chap. 2). For those variable costs, the bottom-up approach is recommended, as is assessing all individual variation (e.g., medication, treatment staff, interventions, exams) [14, 25] (Table 14.1). In the case of multiple comorbidities between mental and physical diseases, it may be necessary to use a bottom-up approach to cost the majority of cost components. The most expensive components of costs in a hospital are human resources (usually, over 50–60% of hospital expenses) and, in some cases, medical technologies [3].

Table 14.1 Bottom-up approach for costing variable costs (psychiatric treatment)

Cost component	Costing items	Unit costs
Medical consultation	Staff + medical equipment	Visit (minutes, hours per patient)
Psychosocial consultation	Occupational therapists/psychologists (individual/group)	Sessions per patient (hours paid per minute or per hour)
Medication	Pills	Per pill
Lab tests	Staff + medical equipment + consumables	Per test
Electroconvulsive therapy	Staff (psychiatrist, nurse assistant, anesthetist) + medication + equipment + consumables + special room use	Per session
Social worker assistance (patient and family)	Social worker (time used) + telephone use + consumables + specific room use	Per minute or hour

14.2.3.1 Measurement of Unit Costs Using a Top-Down Approach

The top-down approach is used to estimate average costs; that is, it assumes no variability in the consumption of resources among subjects. However, in a hospital setting, this is not so straightforward, because wards and units do not consume resources in the same way. For instance, emergency departments, surgery rooms, and psychiatric wards vary on the amount of cleaning required. The choice to estimate cleaning cost per square meters might not correspond to real use. On the other hand, if a third-party service is hired and the unit costs is determined by square meters in the commercial agreement, then it is better to use it. Therefore, for each support service, it is necessary to know the total consumption of a service in the hospital and to decide whether resources allocated are proportional to the size, the number of beds, and the pattern of consumption, or whether they are approximately similar. This decision depends on the data available and on the organizational complexity of the hospital, whether units have autonomy to control their expenses or whether they share financial management for the entire hospital. Once resource consumption is measured by ward and sector, the unit costs per bed or patient per day can be measured. Partial patient-day costs comprise these "fixed costs" (the "hotel" component). One of the most complex decisions is the method for apportioning joint costs and overhead [26]. Estimating these costs varies across studies in terms of definition, components, and method of allocation [26, 27]. Some studies include support services in overhead costs, whereas others consider only management and clerical sectors as overhead. Most important is to identify which services are used in a psychiatric ward and then classify each service accordingly. There is no consensus on the best allocation method for estimating nonhealth costs. Of note, it is necessary to be alert for double counting and for sharing spaces, activities, and human resources (e.g., anesthesia rooms, waiting rooms for exams, and nurses working in different sectors).

14.2.3.2 Unit Costs Using a Bottom-Up Approach

Depending on the study, the goal might focus on the marginal costs according to inpatient profiles. In this case it is crucial to use a bottom-up approach to estimate all variable costs per patient. While using top-down approach it is possible to know how much, on average, inpatients cost a hospital (provider perspective), but in economic evaluation the goal is to measure benefits from one set of interventions and programs and determine how their costs vary. For instance, an inpatient with schizophrenia refractory to treatment may require a different set of interventions and resources than a patient with non–treatment-refractory schizophrenia. To treat these patients, Clozapine, for example requires recurrent blood testing. Similarly, an inpatient with a manic episode (bipolar disorder) would require successive blood tests for measuring serum levels of lithium and anticonvulsants. Other factors can also affect the consumption of resources and costs per patient, such as age, sex, physical comorbidity, diagnosis, and duration of hospitalization.

14.2.4 Estimating Direct Costs of a Psychiatric Ward or Psychiatric Hospital

In the case of a psychiatric hospital, estimating costs is easier because there are no shared costs involved. There is a fixed cost per bed per day related to overhead and support services, and variable costs related to individual consumption of health interventions and care. Thus costs per patient are the sum of daily variable and fixed costs. On the other hand, it is possible to estimate the average costs per bed per day for accounting and reimbursement goals.

However, estimating costs of psychiatric wards in a general hospital is much more complex. For accounting goals, it is possible to estimate all costs involved in a psychiatric ward, divided by the number of beds and occupancy rate (usually 85%). However, in an economic evaluation, marginal analysis should be preferred and all efforts should be made to estimate individual variation. Moreover, capital costs and equipment should be computed in the cost analysis.

14.3 Costing a Psychiatric Hospital Attached to a Tertiary Hospital in the State of São Paulo, Brazil: Steps and Challenges for Estimating Costs

In this chapter we describe one study carried out in the city of Franco da Rocha, located in the State of São Paulo, as an example exercise for estimating costs of a psychiatric unit in a tertiary general hospital (Complexo Hospitalar do Juquery).

14.3.1 Description of Complexo Hospitalar do Juqueri

The Complexo Hospitalar do Juqueri is a public service financed by the government of the State of São Paulo and is located in the city of Franco da Rocha (population 150,000 inhabitants). This hospital has a historical background: it was created a century ago, and it has been considered a heritage site in the city. The land on which the buildings comprising the hospital sit comprises 1,500,000 m^2 and include a mental health (psychiatric) building, the general hospital and obstetrics building, and the women's healthcare outpatient service. Before the deinstitutionalization process, this hospital was an asylum for the long-term hospitalization of 18,000 inpatients with mental disorders, and currently there are 128 psychiatric beds. The human resource team comprises public servants with tenured jobs. The psychiatric building is described in Table 14.2.

14.3.2 Components of Costs

Deciding to include components of costs depends on the goal and perspective of the study. If the goal is to have average costs per bed per day, all costs incurred in services outside the hospital are not taken into account (for instance, if inpatients need to be transported to other services for imaging, outpatient care, and other procedures). However, if the goal is to verify the costs per patient, individual variation in the consumption of resources should be taken into account; in this case, imaging and outpatient care are included. Similarly, if the goal is to compare a group of inpatients or programs in the same hospital, then marginal costs should be estimated but fixed costs do not need to be considered. In economic evaluation, marginal costs are usually paramount.

Moreover, the choice of the unit costs depends on the goal of the study (e.g., cost per bed per day, cost per inpatient per ay), and methods for estimating units of costs would vary (Table 14.3).

Table 14.2 Description of the psychiatric unit

Structure	
How is the service organized?	The psychiatric unit comprises six pavilions of 795 m^2 each, with a total of 150 beds. Each module comprises 25 beds, a canteen, a nurses' room, a mental health team room, five toilets, a doctor's office, and a TV room. The total occupied area is 10,546 m^2.
What is the main service goal?	The process of closing beds is still in progress, and rehabilitation programs are offered in order to prepare inpatients for living outside the hospital in residential services.
Who is eligible for this service?	The mean duration of hospitalization is 35 years, and 128 inpatients still live there; they have a mean age of 68 years, are mostly single and illiterate; 75% have schizophrenia disorder and 20% have a mental retardation diagnosis.
Funding	It is financed by the government of the State of São Paulo.
Capital costs	
Building	It is a centenary historical building and its characteristics are different from other psychiatric hospitals existing in the state. It is located in isolated area of the city.
Equipment	It includes various items: furniture and devices (coach, beds, table, chairs, shelves, wardrobe, wheelchair, TV), and medical equipment for emergency care and physical examinations.
How does the service work?	Inpatients live in the hospital; some of them have good level of autonomy to leave alone to shop and for leisure and other activities. Others get out of the hospital with a health team (nurse assistant). There are workshops, tours outside the hospital, and leisure and cultural events (e.g., museums). All inpatients receive mental healthcare according to their needs, but there is a minimum of visits and activities with the mental health team (see next item).
Which services are delivered? (Description of intervention process, professionals involved, length of time on average)	Psychiatrist visit (30 min, weekly), medical doctor visit (30 min, monthly), individual psychological visit (30 min, two to eight monthly), social worker assistance (30 min, individual sessions, one to three monthly), individual sessions with occupational therapists (30-min sessions, zero to three monthly), nurse assistance (30 min of individual assistance, two to three sessions, monthly), nurse assistants (30-min individual procedures once a day), medication. Some inpatients leave the hospital for outpatient visits with nonpsychiatrist doctors and tests (on average, three patients per month receive outpatient care), with an average of two or three exams per month; 22% of patients use transportation into and out of the city.
Which professionals are involved?	Seven psychiatrists, 3 medical doctors, 19 nurses, 184 nurse assistant (day/night), 5 psychologists, 2 occupational therapists, 1 social worker. There are 41 Human Resources (clinical + administrative) employees.
Revenue costs (resources and expenditures)	
Which components are necessary to maintain service operation?	Agreement with third-party services: nutrition, housekeeping, laundry, security, waste. All these services and expenditures were managed directly by psychiatric unit (costs center). Consumables (clothes and hygiene supplies) are only for psychiatric inpatients. Overhead (pharmacy, transportation, supplies, communication, people management, administrative and financial sectors, maintenance) is shared with other hospital units.

Table 14.3 Components of costs of a psychiatric unit

Direct health costs	Psychiatrists
	Other medical doctors
	Psychologists
	Occupational therapists
	Social worker
	Psychiatric nurses
	Psychiatric nurses assistant
	Medication
	Labs tests and imaging (outside hospital)
	Outpatient care (outside hospital)
Direct nonhealth costs	Nutrition
	Laundry
	Housekeeping
	Waste service
	Security
	Consumables and supplies
Shared services with other units of hospital (overhead)	Management and administration
	Human resources not related directly with health treatment
	Pharmacy
	Communication, informatics
	Transportation
	Utilities
Capital and equipment	

14.3.3 Measurement of Resource Consumption and Estimation of Unit Costs

The measurement of resources depends on the goal of the study and on how unit costs are estimated. For instance, if the goal is to know average medication costs per day, data would be extracted based on the total costs of medication consumed for one period of time and divided per bed per day. In this case it is assumed that all inpatients take the same amount of medication, but that is not true. The average costs per bed per day is interesting for reimbursement goals; for instance, the national government in Brazil pays reimbursement by a tenth of the true cost for a psychiatric bed per day. Therefore, the top-down approach can be used for the majority of component of costs. However, in economic evaluation it is important to assess how inpatients vary in terms of consumption of resources. Therefore the bottom-up approach can be used mainly for direct health costs.

To use the bottom-up approach, it is necessary to describe in detail each activity and intervention available to inpatients. The first step is to observe the routine in the hospital, such as how long it takes professionals to deliver individual or group interventions (Table 14.2). For instance, if all inpatients have at least 30 min of contact with a psychiatrist each week, then the unit of cost can be estimated by calculating the psychiatrist's costs per minute multiplied by 30 min for one visit. The unit of cost for medication in this case would be the cost per pill, and through detailed individual data collection it is possible to verify the number of pills each inpatient takes per day.

We chose to describe the costs per bed per day including three categories of components of costs: direct health costs, "hotel costs" and capital costs.

14.3.3.1 Estimation of "Hotel Costs" and Overhead

These costs comprise support services (laundry, nutrition, security, waste service, housekeeping), utilities, consumables and medical supplies, overhead (financial and administrative sectors, pharmacy, storage, records, communication and informatics sectors, transport), and non–clinical professionals working exclusively for the psychiatric unit. Support services were delivered through third-party agreements, and we used the unit costs for each service to estimate the average costs per bed (Table 14.4). Overhead was estimated using proportional method allocation [2]. In this case, we considered three main categories in the structure of the entire hospital: the psychiatric unit, the general hospital, and outpatient care for women. We allocated 30% of total overhead costs to the psychiatric unit, 50% to the general hospital, and 20% to outpatient care. The total overhead for 180 days was BRL$3,274,697.40; of this, 30% (BRL$982,409.22) was allocated to the psychiatric unit. This cost was divided by 180 days and by 128 beds, resulting in overhead costs per bed (Table 14.4).

14.3.3.2 Capital Costs and Equipment

Because the Complexo Hospitalar do Juquery is a centenary institution and has heritage buildings, it was very difficult to estimate its costs. Also, it is located outside the city of Franco da Rocha, and the current price of similar land is not equivalent to its value. There is also a stigma related to the era of psychiatric institutionalization, in which this hospital functioned. Buildings used as psychiatric hospitals have been reported as having low opportunity costs because of the age of such buildings, their poor maintenance conditions, and few opportunities for alternative uses. The land on which the hospital site may be valuable if it can be used for an alternative purpose or if land prices in the neighborhood are high per square meter. However, such hospitals are usually located in isolated areas, and it might be that land in these areas is not valuable [28]. The Complexo Hospitalar do Juqueri is in the progress of closing, and it is not known whether this building will be used in the future for other purposes. Maintenance costs were not available as a separate item, and it was very challenging to estimate them; for this reason, we included them in overhead costs, though they are usually included as capital costs.

All equipment was purchased in 2013 (BRL$337,459.00), and we used the equivalent annual annuity to estimate equipment costs for 2015, using a discount rate of 5% and a lifetime use of 5 years in the following equation :

$$EAA = r\left(NPV\right)/\left(1+r\right)^{-n}$$

where *EAA* is the equivalent annual annuity, *r* is the discount rate, and *n* is the lifetime use in years, and NPV is the net present value.

The equivalent annual costs were BRL$77,944.52, that is, BRL$1.67/bed/day. Equipment costs are estimated based on the costs for acquiring the equipment (obtained from a hospital manager) or, when these data were absent, the market price of similar equipment. Equipment costs can be divided by bed, under the assumption of all patients use them equally, though this is not true. In the case of a psychiatric unit, few pieces of medical equipment were available and furniture, rooms, and offices were used similarly among patients. Because the maintenance cost for each piece of equipment was not available, we included maintenance costs in the overhead costs, though these are expected to be added to equipment capital costs.

14.3.3.3 Treatment Costs

Treatment costs vary from one patient to another, and a bottom-up approach is recommended. Treatment costs include clinical staff, medication, lab tests/exams, and all interventions related

Table 14.4 Unit costs of "hotel costs" per bed per day

Unit costs	Description	Total costs (BRL$) over 180 days in 2015	Costs per bed per day (BRL$) ($n$ = 128)
Human resources (nonclinical staff)	All nonclinical professionals working exclusively for the psychiatric unit	623,246.58	27.05
Consumables	Clothes, bed sets, personal care and hygiene products	83,298.52	3.61
Overhead	Human resources not working in the psychiatric unit: using proportional allocation, 40% of costs are allocated to the psychiatric unit	982,409.22	42.63
Nutrition	One food package (six meals per bed per day)	705,918.78	30.63
Laundry	Kilograms (6 kg per inpatient day)	349,800.00	15.16
Housekeeping	Square meters (10,546 m^2)	1,120,806.90	48.64
Security	Security checkpoint	394,300.56	17.11
Waste service	Kilograms	48,895.56	2.20
Total		4,308,676.12	187.01

directly to an individual's treatment. It is important to pay attention to double counting; some items might be counted as hotel costs and at the same time might be identified as treatment costs. For instance, transportation is included in hotel costs or in overhead costs, and if a patient uses transport for external exams that is included in the treatment costs, it should be not computed in hotel costs because it was already counted. In our study, we used both top-down and bottom-up approaches to estimate treatment costs.

Using the top-down, approach we included all clinical staff and medication to estimate costs per bed per day, that is, average costs. We used the bottom-up approach for 122 inpatients and included tests and imaging and all treatments done outside the hospital. In this case, we included transportation costs and discounted those from hotel costs to avoid double counting. Our goal was to estimate costs per patient per day, that is, marginal costs. To estimate clinical human resources costs per bed, we verified total costs per professional category (psychiatrist, psychologist, occupational therapist, social worker, nurse, nurse assistant) and the total working hours over 180 days, and then divided those by 180 days and by 128 beds, resulting unit costs per bed per day. Medication was estimated using the same approach, resulting in average costs per bed per day (see Table 14.6). These results are useful to discuss in terms of national policy, because the federal government in Brazil reimburses one-tenth of real costs per bed per day. As observed in Tables 14.4 and 14.5, treatment costs accounted for 49% of total costs of each diary.

Using the bottom-up approach, we estimated all activities and treatments delivered for each patient (n = 122). For instance, we determined that one psychiatric visit lasts, on average, 30 min; then we estimated how many psychiatrist visits each patient received during 180 days in 2015. We used the unit of cost per minute (derived by dividing the total salaries, including tax and subsides, received during the period by the total number of working hours) [25]. We repeated this estimation for each category (Table 14.2). Medication costs were estimated based on the quantity of pills used by each patient, and the unit costs for each medication was obtained from the hospital manager.

Of note, it is important to verify whether professionals share activities in different units in order to avoid overestimating costs. Similarly, some professionals perform additional nonclinical activities, such as teaching and supervising; therefore, the unit costs should be estimated based on the time spent on clinical activities when using the bottom-up approach. Costing is a time-consuming process and should be accurate, transparent, and detailed according to the study goals, study perspective, and feasibility of data collection. Last but not least, reporting costs should be detailed in terms of estimating the unit costs for each cost component.

Table 14.5 Unit costs of clinical staff per hour (top-down approach)

	Quantity	Working hours per professional over 180 days	Total working hours (180 days)	Total costs (salaries) over 180 days (BRL$)	Unit of cost (hour) BRL
Psychiatrists	7	480	3360	347,815.68	103.51
Doctors (other specialties)	3	480	1440	113,403.96	78.75
Psychologists	5	720	3600	118,215.30	32.82
Social workers	3	720	2160	67,169.88	31.09
Occupational therapists	2	720	1440	45,985.92	31.93
Nurses	19	720	13,680	534,340.80	39.06
Nurse assistants	184	720	129,600	2,968,026.72	22.90

Table 14.6 Treatment costs per bed per day (top-down approach)

	Costs over 180 days in 2005 (BRL$)	Costs per bed per day (BRL$) ($n$ = 128)
Clinical human resources	4,194,958.46	182.07
Medication	59,522.35	2.58
Total	4,254,480.85	184.65

Key Messages

- Psychiatric hospitals and wards differ in terms of structure, staff, type of interventions available, resources, and inpatient profiles. For this reason, a detailed description of the service and its resources are a crucial step in costing it.
- The bottom-up approach is recommended in economic evaluations because patients vary in terms of consumption of resources and comorbidities.
- While the top-down approach allows an overview of how resources are consumed and in what proportions, the bottom-up approach allows costs to be compared according to an individual's profile, disease severity, comorbidity, and disorder.
- Clinical human resources account for almost half of psychiatric hospitals' total costs.
- There is a lack of transparency in describing costing methods and estimating units of costs among studies in the literature, with low consensus on the best procedures for costing hospitals for economic evaluation.

References

1. Mushkin SJ. Toward a definition of health economics. Public Health Rep. 1958;73(9):785–93.
2. Newbrander W, Lewis E. Hospital costing manual: health reform and financing program & APHIA financing and sustainability project management sciences for health; 1999.
3. Knapp M, Chisholm D, Astin J, Lelliott P, Audini B. The cost consequences of changing the hospital-community balance: the mental health residential care study. Psychol Med. 1997;27(3):681–92.
4. Knapp M, Funk M, Curran C, Prince M, Grigg M, McDaid D. Economic barriers to better mental health practice and policy. Health Policy Plan. 2006;21(3):157–70.
5. Razzouk D, Gregorio G, Antunes R, Mari JD. Lessons learned in developing community mental health care in Latin American and Caribbean countries. World Psychiatry. 2012;11(3):191–5.
6. Thornicroft G, Alem A, Antunes Dos SR, Barley E, Drake RE, Gregorio G, et al. WPA guidance on steps, obstacles and mistakes to avoid in the implementation of community mental health care. World Psychiatry. 2010;9(2):67–77.
7. Knapp M. The economic evaluation of mental health care. 1st ed. Aldershot: Ashgate Publishing Limited; 1995.
8. Rothbard A, Schinnar A, Hadley T, Foley K, Kuno E. Cost comparison of state hospital and community-based care for seriously mentally ill adults. Am J Psychiatry. 1998;155:523–9.
9. Knapp M, Chisholm D, Astin J, Lelliott P, Audini B. The cost consequences of changing the hospital-community balance: the mental health residential care study. Psychol Med. 1997;27(3):681–92.
10. Mansel J, Beadle-Brown J. Deinstitutionalisation and community living: position statement of the comparative policy and practice special interest research group of the international association for the scientific study of intellectual disabilities. J Intellect Disabil Res. 2010;54(2):104–12.
11. Negrini D, Kettle A, Sheppard L, Mills GH, Edbrooke DL. The cost of a hospital ward in Europe: is there a methodology available to accurately measure the costs? J Health Organ Manag. 2004;18(2–3):195–206.
12. Chisholm D, Evans D. Economic evaluation in health: saving money or improving care? J Med Econ. 2007;10:325–37.
13. Rothbard AB, Kuno E, Schinnar AP, Hadley TR, Turk R. Service utilization and cost of community care for discharged state hospital patients: a 3-year follow-up study. Am J Psychiatry. 1999;156(6):920–7.
14. Mogyorosy Z, Smith P. The main methodological issues in costing health care services. York: Centre for Health Economics, University of York; 2005. 12-2-2016.
15. Conteh L, Walker D. Cost and unit cost calculations using step-down accounting. Health Policy Plan. 2004;19(2):127–35.
16. Oostenbrink JB, Oopmanschap MA, Rutten FF. Standardisation of costs: the Dutch manual for costing in economic evaluations. Pharmacoeconomics. 2002;20(7):443–54.
17. Oostenbrink JB, Buijs-Van der Woude T, van Agthoven M, Koopmanschap MA, Rutten FF. Unit

costs of inpatient hospital days. Pharmacoeconomics. 2003;21(4):263–71.
18. Curtis L, Burn A. Unit costs of Health & Social Care 2015. Personal Social Services Research Unit; 2015.
19. Javi M, Hadian M, Ghaderi H, Ghaffari S, Salehi M. Application of the activity-based costing method for unit-cost calculation in a hospital. Glob J Health Sci. 2016;8(1):165–72.
20. Burke L, Ryan A. The complex relationship between cost and quality in US health care. Am J Ethics. 2014;16(2):124–30.
21. Lea T. IHE summary report the state of the art in costing methods. Alberta: Institute of Health Economics; 2015.
22. Smith R. Contingent valuation in healthcare: does it matter how the good is described? Health Econ. 2008;17:607–17.
23. Luce BR, Elixhauser A. Estimating costs in the economic evaluation of medical technologies. Int J Technol Assess Health Care. 1990;6(1):57–75.
24. Beecham J, Knapp M. Costing psychiatric interventions. In: Thornicroft G, editor. Measuring mental health needs. London: Gaskell; 2001. p. 200–24.
25. Hendriks M, Kundu P, Boers A, Bolarinwa O, Pas M, Akande T, et al. Step by step guideline for disease-specific costing studies in low and middle income countries: a mixed methodology. Glob Health Action. 2014;7:23573.
26. St-Hilaire C, Crepeau PK. Hospital and unit cost allocation methods. Healthc Manage Forum. 2000;13(2):12–32.
27. Drummond MF, Sculpher MJ, Torrance GW, O'Brien BJ, Stoddart GL. Methods for the economic evaluation of health care programmes. 3rd ed. Oxford: Oxford University Press; 2007.
28. Knapp M, Beecham J, McDaid D, Matosevic T, Smith M. The economic consequences of deinstitutionalisation of mental health services: lessons from a systematic review of European experience. Health Soc Care Community. 2011;19(2):113–25.

15 Estimation of Costs for Community Mental Health Services

Paula Becker and Denise Razzouk

Abstract

This chapter briefly reviews community mental health services costs and the key methodological points regarding their costing methods. Because of the diversity in the structure of and interventions delivered among community mental health services, it is paramount to identify the components of costs for each service. Comparability across cost studies depends on at least four main issues: the study perspective, the time horizon, the type of service/subject's profile, and the data source. We present one example of costing community mental health services using data from a Brazilian study of costing a center of psychosocial care (CAPS) in the State of São Paulo.

Key Points Summary

- Types of community mental health services
- Variation in community mental health care costs
- Costing community mental health services
- Unit costs
- Example of costing one community mental health service

P. Becker (✉) • D. Razzouk
Centre of Economic Mental Health, Department of Psychiatry, Universidade Federal de Sao Paulo, Rua Borges Lagoa 570, 1° andar, 04038-000 São Paulo, Brazil
e-mail: pbecker259@gmail.com; drazzouk@gmail.com

15.1 Introduction

The implementation of community-based mental healthcare in low- and middle-income countries has begun in the past two decades [1–4], though in high-income countries it started a half century ago [5–8]. Before this reform in mental healthcare, treatments were administered exclusively in psychiatric hospitals. Progressively, mental health budgets were reoriented from hospitals to community mental health services, though extensive debate comparing costs between these two models of care has occurred to date [5, 6, 8–10]. Community mental health services comprise a network of services available in communities and are addressed to promoting the recovery of people with mental disorders [8, 11–13]. These service principles are based on a humanistic approach to care; on the efficiency and cost-effectiveness of care; on the delivery of interventions

D. Razzouk (ed.), *Mental Health Economics*, DOI 10.1007/978-3-319-55266-8_15

according to an individual's profile, needs, and context; and on combatting stigma against mental disorders [2]. Moreover, these services were designed to be placed in users' communities and outside hospital territories, and to offer a variety of specialized and multidisciplinary interventions and programs oriented toward rehabilitation and social inclusion [1].

Community mental health services vary both in options for care and in how they are defined according to the local social and political contexts [12] (see Box 15.1). However, these services aim at effectiveness and the optimal use of scarce resources [14] , especially in low- and middle-income countries. The complexity and variety of such services hinder comparability across different settings, and for this reason, systematic economic evaluations are needed. Therefore, answering the question of whether costs for community mental health services are higher or lower than those for psychiatric hospitals depends on which services and health system are being compared [5, 15, 16]. It is important to bear in mind that hospitals (see Chap. 14) deliver to patients complex and diverse services that are not available from only one community mental health service. When comparing models of care it is important to include in cost analyses all services provided in the community (outpatient care, accommodation, emergency visits, housing, informal care, and other programs) [12, 16–18].

Box 15.1 Types of Community Mental Health Care

Residential facilities

- Independent houses
- Full-time residential facilities
- Nursing homes

Outpatient care

- Ambulatory
- Community mental health centers

(continued)

Box 15.1 (continued)

- Specialized programs (e.g., addiction, autism, early intervention for psychosis, supported employment)
- Recovery and psychosocial rehabilitation centers

Outreach services

- Assertive community treatment teams

Primary care

- Community mental health teams (supervision for general practitioners)

Nonhospital emergency unit

- Crisis houses
- Acute day hospitals

Community social centers

- Sheltered workshops and social activities
- Work placement
- Clubhouses
- Leisure and sport centers

Inpatient care

- Psychiatric ward in a general hospital
- Liaison with mental health team

Self-help groups

This chapter addresses the main methodological issues regarding costing of community mental health services, focusing on outpatient care. We present the steps for costing a community mental health center oriented toward patients with alcohol and drug addiction as an example of a costing exercise. For didactic reasons, costing residential facilities is discussed in Chap. 16, though they are part of community mental health services.

15.2 How Community Mental Health Services Costs Vary in the Literature

Costing community mental health services is challenging because of the diversity of services, the complexity of interventions, the lack of transparency and availability of cost data, and other methodological constraints [19, 20]. Costing studies vary mainly in terms of goals, study perspective, time horizon, components of costs, methods for estimating unit costs, measurement approaches, and sample characteristics. Box 15.2 outlines some examples in which goals of costing mental health services vary according to different perspectives. Costing is useful to evaluate interventions, programs, services, and policies through economic evaluation and cost-analysis studies. Most importantly, the evaluation of community mental health services should not be restricted to costing one service. Instead, it is crucial to assess consumption of community mental health services throughout the entire health system because costs can decrease for one service and, as an indirect consequence, increase for another service (the spillover effect). In addition, in mental healthcare, other nonhealth services should be included in the analysis, such as criminal justice and educational and social services, depending on the relevance of such services for integrated mental healthcare and users' diagnoses, because the spillover effect also occurs in nonhealth services [16, 21, 22]. Health economists have not reached a consensus regarding the inclusion of productive costs, informal care, and patients' out-of-pocket expenditures in economic evaluations, though adopting and implementing new mental health polices or programs contributes to cost variation in health and nonhealth sectors [18, 22, 23].

Box 15.2 Costing Study Goals According to Different Perspectives

Payer/health provider perspective (only one service)

- Accounting goals (financial health management)
- Planning service expansion
- Comparison of health service consumption costs among users
- Cost-saving studies

National or regional public health perspective

- Comparison of healthcare consumption costs according to users' profiles and diagnoses
- Cost-effectiveness studies (costs for interventions, programs, and packages of care)
- Comparison of mental health service costs according to modality of care (e.g., different types of residential facilities; hospital versus community mental health services)
- Comparison of unit costs by service and region
- Cost analysis studies exploring factors affecting health services costs

Societal perspective

- Cost-benefit studies analyzing the effects of mental health policies (inclusion of informal care, productivity, and opportunity costs)

Community mental health services and psychiatric hospitals have been compared [10, 24–32]; these comparisons look at different types of the same service (such as a residential service) [24, 25] and different packages of care (for instance, current treatment versus assertive community treatment for psychosis) [31, 33] (see Box 15.2). The former are usually reported in the literature through cost analysis and cost-consequences studies, whereas packages of care has been compared in clinical trials and cost-effectiveness studies [31, 33–35]. However, the description of costing methods and the estimation of units of costs are rarely detailed in publications [14, 36, 37].

15.2.1 Variation of Unit Costs

One of the most important factors related to cost variations when comparing similar services is the estimation of units of costs. A study in Australia compared the unit costs for treatment per hour among six child and adolescent mental health services in different regions of the country and found that the unit costs varied from $156 to $273 [38]. Similarly, the cost per episode varied significantly among the six services, from $338 to $7076, though the severity of mental symptoms explained 6% of the cost variance. Despite these data, user differences were not the most relevant factor in these cost variations; rather, service delivery factors seemed to be more relevant in this regard.

15.2.2 Variation of Treatment Costs According to Different Packages of Care and Services

One the biggest challenges in community mental healthcare is to evaluate integrated care. Few studies exist of the effectiveness of community mental health services [8, 39] and few studies take into account costs [14, 14, 22, 33, 40–44] and cost-effectiveness [5, 14, 16, 25, 39, 44–48].

One study in the United Kingdom evaluated costs of 260 mental health service users receiving different sets of integrated mental health services and interventions in four centers in the north of England [22]. In that study, all modalities of care were included (inpatient, outpatient, community care, social care, primary care, accommodation, day occupation, user expenditures). In this case higher costs were associated with services targeting users with more severe symptoms, and lower costs were associated with integrated services. Note that this study showed a result opposite that of the Australian study because the goals, methods, and components of costs were completely different. Costs cannot be interpreted if isolated from the purpose of the experiment and from their methodological limitations. Another study in Spain compared the costs of services used by 81 subjects with schizophrenia disorders in two regions with different levels of care over a 3-year follow-up period: one with optimum services provision, and another with minimum services provision [40]. In that study, only direct health costs were taken into account. The authors found that direct costs in the former were 35% lower than those in the latter.

The most common studies regarding cost-effectiveness in mental health evaluate a set of interventions or specific programs, rather than services. Hastrup and Aagaard [33] compared assertive community treatment (ACT) with treatment as usual through a cost-effectiveness clinical trial, using a national public health provider perspective in Denmark. ACT is delivered in community mental health centers and encompasses a set of services such as outpatient services, home visits, crisis houses, 24-h hotline telephone services, supported employment programs, and day hospital treatments, offering multiple interventions (multi-family groups, social skills training groups). Using a top-down approach for costing treatment per person, they found ACT costs were lower (DDK493,442) than control group costs (DDK671,500). The mean total ACT costs were DDK178,058 lower over 4 years than were control group costs, including costs for supportive housing over 2 years, though when excluding accommodation costs there was no significant difference between the two groups. Costs in the ACT group were higher for psychiatric outpatient care and lower for inpatient care when compared with the control group, showing a high probability of ACT being cost-effective compared with treatment as usual.

Despite some attempts by economic evaluations to compare mental health programs and packages of care, cost-saving studies are predominant and focus on reducing costs rather than evaluating outcome improvements. In this regard, a study conducted in New York used a payer perspective to compare costs between intensive community-based treatment and assisted outpatient treatment among 255 volunteer users with severe mental illness, with a 3-year follow-up period [31]. Assisted outpatient treatment is a court-ordered program of community-based mental health services designed to improve outcomes for persons with serious mental illness and a history of repeated hospitalizations attributable to nonadherence to treatment. This is an example of including legal and criminal justice costs and health direct costs. In this case, however, the outcome was hospitalization rate, and it is not necessarily related to better user outcomes. Health managers are usually interested in saving costs, but an "outcome" in economic evaluation should express users' improvements in mental health. Decreasing costs with inpatient care does not necessarily mean saving costs from a broader perspective if costs increase in other health and nonhealth sectors, or even for patients and families.

One particularly important issue for estimating the cost-effectiveness of mental health services (or programs) is related to the time horizon and follow-up. Improvement in mental disorders outcomes can last years, and in this regard the balance between costs and effects can be unfavorable if better outcomes do not occur over the short term. One interesting example is one study of the TAPS Project regarding costs of patients with severe mental disorders who were discharged from hospitals and placed in residential facilities [49]. The authors evaluated outcomes and costs during a 5-year follow-up period. No relevant clinical changes occurred in terms of outcomes during 1 year of follow-up. However, important improvements in social behavior were observed after 5 years, resulting in costs being reduced by 14%. Therefore, costs should be measured taking into account the long-term time horizon.

It is not the scope of this chapter to present a systematic review of all studies on this topic, but rather to alert the reader to methodological issues related to methods of costing community mental health services. In this regard, the examples mentioned above show variations in terms of goals, time horizon, cost components, costing approaches, service characteristics, and user profiles, among others.

Box 15.3 Five Steps in Costing Mental Health Services

1. Detailed description of service(s) or program(s)
    - Identification of component of costs
2. Choice of unit cost for each component of costs and definition of its measurement approach (top-down × bottom-up approaches)
3. Measurement of the consumption for each component of costs
    - Prospective × retrospective
    - Short-run versus long-run marginal costs
    - Inventories (bottom up) versus database (top down)
    - Sample eligibility and characteristics
    - Reliable sources of information
4. Estimation of unit costs for each component of costs
5. Cost analysis
    - Estimation of capital costs and opportunity costs
    - Estimation of revenue costs (average costs)
    - Estimation of overhead costs
    - Estimation of health services consumption (marginal costs)
    - Estimation of users' costs for treatments (depending on perspective)
    - Discount factor, interest rate, equivalent annual costs
    - Sum of direct, indirect (support services, capital) and overhead costs
    - Costs analysis and sensitivity analyses

15.3 Costing Community Mental Health Services

In addition to the issues raised in the previous section, the process of estimating costs requires at least five steps (see Box 15.3). After defining the goal of the study and its perspective, the first step before collecting data for costs related to one service is to identify all relevant components of costs related to the service and according to perspective of the study (see Table 15.1). In other words, it is paramount to know the service and how it works in terms of structure, resources, and delivery of processes of care and interventions [16, 19, 20, 50].

Table 15.1 Description of service, program, or package of care

Infrastructure	What is the service? (type, size, location, number of rooms, pharmacy, reception, nurses' room, emergency room, kitchen)
	What is the main goal of the service? (outpatient care, residential facility, program for specific disease)
	Who is eligible for this service? (users' characteristics)
	Funding sources (public, private, charity, donations, insurance companies)
	Capital costs (building and land costs). Rent can be used by a proxy for capital costs (then it is not included in revenue costs)
	Capital costs: equipment, vehicles
How does the service work?	Coverage, operation schedule, with/without emergency beds, links with other services; number of visits per month
	How is care delivered? (screening interviews, screening tests, individual visits, group visits, domiciliary visits)
Which services are delivered? (description of intervention process, professionals involved, length of time on average)	Psychiatrist visits, medication, psychotherapy, occupational therapy, laboratory tests, nurse assistance, social worker assistance, educational activities, emergency assistance, social activities, workshops, domiciliary visits, telephone call assistance, diet, transport tickets, other treatment programs Description of each intervention in terms of duration and staff involved
Which professionals are involved?	Treatment staff (psychiatrists, psychologists, occupational therapists, nurses, social workers, educators, others) Management staff Third-party workers Voluntary workers
Revenue costs(resources and expenditures) Which components are necessary to maintain service operation?	Consumables, medication, human resources (salaries), utilities, support services, taxes, training, informatics system and maintenance, overhead

The second step is to determine how costs will be measured (e.g., per day, per visit, per hour) and which approach will be used to measure the (a top-down or bottom-up approach) (see Table 15.2). Direct health costs are more accurate if measured using a bottom-up approach; that is, data are collected taking into account variations among individuals [16, 23]. The unit of costs for each intervention is estimated according to its nature (a single patient or a group) and length of time (minutes, hours, days). However, some interventions have mixed components of costs, and in some cases cts can be aggregated in one package of intervention, such as home visits. The unit costs can be estimated by visit, but the estimation of one visit requires all components of costs for one visit (staff, supplies, length of time of visit, distance from service to home, driver's time, gas, car maintenance or travel costs) to be computed. When using composite measures in one unit cost, it is important to consider shared costs, joint costs, and double counting. The estimation of unit costs for direct nonhealth costs is complicated by the complexity of service and shared activities (see Chap. 2). The top-down approach is used most often; more detailed information can be found in costing guidelines [50].

The third step is to define the period of data collection (retrospectiveor or prospective), data sources, and instruments [16, 23]. It is recommended to collect cost data over the long run, rather than in the short term. Data collection through inventories focuses on the consumption of interventions and resources by each individual, whereas a top-down approach uses total data on the consumption of service resources, usually from a database or managerial information. One of the most used inventories for collecting data on the use of mental health, criminal justice, and other health services is the Client Sociodemographic and Service Receipt Inventory [16, 23, 51] (all versions are available from http://www.pssru.

Table 15.2 Definition of unit costs for each component of costs for community mental health services

Components of costs	Unit costs
Direct health costs	
Treatment staff (single visit): psychiatrists, medical doctors, psychologists, social workers, occupational therapists, nurses, and others	Per minute, per hour, or per visit
Treatment staff (group assistance): psychologists, occupational therapists, nurses, others	Per user per session
Medication	Per day/week/month
Domiciliary visit	Per visit (staff time per minute or hour + travel costs)
Case management	Per minute, per visit (includes staff, supplies, telephone calls, etc); use caution with joint and double counting costs
Ambulance	Per visit (staff time + gas + supplies + maintenance + driver's time)
Emergency room	Per visit (staff + medical supplies + capital costs + administrative)
Day hospital	Per day (staff + medical supplies + capital costs + administrative + diet + transportation)
Nonhealth direct costs and capital costs	
Capital costs: buildings and equipment	Estimated on a yearly basis (equivalent annual annuity)
Support and utilities services and consumables (supplies)	Top-down approach (it depends on the item, type of health service, and whether use is shared) (see Chap. 2)
Overhead costs	Administrative staff + management costs (see Chap. 2)

ac.uk/blogs/csri/). This inventory was recently translated to Brazilian Portuguese by our team [52] (see Chap. 13).

The fourth step is estimating the unit costs for each component of costs [20, 50, 53] or using some reference value, when available, such as Unit Costs of Health and Social Care in the United Kingdom (available from http://www.pssru.ac.uk/project-pages/unit-costs/2015/) and the Dutch manual for costing in economic evaluation [54].

The final step is the cost analysis, combining consumption and units costs and aggregating all costs: direct health costs, direct nonhealth costs (revenue costs), and capital costs. Marginal costs (see Chap. 2) are used in the majority of economic evaluations when comparing interventions among individuals from the same service or comparing costs of health system use among individuals with a specific profile or disease. Marginal costs are related to extra costs for each additional unit (e.g., an additional bed, additional intervention, additional patient coverage, and additional unit of service). Average costs are commonly used for accounting goals and for items that vary little among subjects (support services) (see Chap. 14). However, according to economics principles, opportunity costs should be included in cost analyses, and in this sense, capital costs are summed with revenue costs [16]. Because units costs and the costs of services and interventions vary, it is crucial to perform a sensitivity analysis (see Chap. 7).

15.4 Costing Community-Based Mental Health Services: The Case of the Center of Psychosocial Care Targeting Urban Alcohol and Drug Users in the State of São Paulo, Brazil

15.4.1 Definition of the Main Question and Perspective of the Study

This study was designed to answer the following items regarding one community mental health center (Center of Psychosocial Care [CAPS], Centro de Atenção Psicossocial para Álcool e Drogas [CAPSAD]) with a specific program for users with alcohol and drug addiction in the State of São Paulo:

a. To estimate direct costs (health, nonhealth, capital, and revenue costs and overhead) of CAPS according to a public health provider perspective
b. To estimate direct and indirect costs among a sample of users with alcohol and drug addiction according to a societal perspective
c. To verify the relationship between psychiatric and psychosocial users' profiles and total costs

In this chapter we focused on the first goal, that is, costing health services. We adopted the perspective of the public health provider because there are no national or regional data published on the units of costs and components of costs of this type of community mental health service in Brazil. This study was a retrospective study, covering data on costs extracted from the service's database for a 180-day period, from March 1 to August 30, 2015.

15.4.2 Description of the Structure and Function of the Center of Psychosocial Care (CAPS-AD)

The CAPS-AD is located in one small city (192,442 mi^2) with 186,000 inhabitants in the State of São Paulo, in the southeast region of Brazil. The mental healthcare in this city encompasses three CAPs (one addressing all mental disorders, one addressing children and adolescents with mental problems, and one targeting alcohol and drug addiction), and two outpatient services (adults and children), all funded by public resources from the mayor, the Ministry of Health, and the government of the State of São Paulo (responsible for funding high-cost medications).

The identification of components of costs for one service requires knowledge about its structure and all processes involving treatment, service maintenance, and management. Two types of CAPS-AD in Brazil offering treatment to alcohol and drug users: one offers full-day care from Monday to Friday and has no crisis support structure (called CAPS-II); the other, called CAPS III, offers 24-h assistance, including on weekends, and has a crisis support structure with few psychiatric beds. These two services have several differences, especially regarding the composition of the treatment team and the therapeutic actions delivered, which might influence cost variations among services. Table 15.3 outlines the description of CASP-AD and its cost components.

15.4.3 Definition of Unit costs and Measurement Approach for Components of Costs

The estimation of a unit of costs depends on how data are used. Table 15.4 presents the total costs for each component of costs related to a 180-day period and their units costs in Brazilian currency (R$) for 2015. For instance, considering the duration of one visit to a psychiatrist lasts an average of 30 min, then the unit cost per hour in Table 15.4 should be adjusted accordingly. Because the study is in progress, some costs have not yet been computed (such as medications), and the estimation of direct health costs by patient is forthcoming. Rent was used a proxy for capital costs in order to approximate opportunity costs. Equipment costs were estimated using market prices for 2015 as a reference, and a 5% discount factor was applied (standard in Brazil; see Chap. 2). Life of use was estimated as 5 years for all equipment, and capital costs per year was estimated by using equivalent annual annuity. As can be observed in Table 15.4, treatment staff costs are almost four times greater than the sum of nonhealth costs and capital costs.

15.5 Concluding Remarks

Costing community mental health services is challenging because they are heterogeneous at all levels. For this reason, use caution when using a standard reference for unit costs, because it may not represent the real costs of a service, when compared to reference service. Human resources are the main component of costs in community

Table 15.3 Description and components of costs of CAPS-AD

Infrastructure	The CAPS-AD is delivered in a rented house located in the downtown area of the city, close to a neighborhood in which homeless people and drug users (especially crack and alcohol users) live. The service comprises a reception hall, waiting area (for 10 patients), financial and administrative room, two health offices (one for individual assistance and one for group therapy), one room with two beds, one nurses' room, one kitchen, and three toilets. There is a garden with a space allowed for workshops and another space for gardening
What is the main service goal?	It is an outpatient care center available to the public, with spontaneous and referenced demand, open from 8:00 am to 6:00 pm. It provides three modalities of care: intensive, semi-intensive, and nonintensive. Users are allocated to one of these modalities of care according to the clinical severity and psychosocial disability of their daily activities and social roles. The purpose is to offer an integrated modality of care according to patient's needs
User eligibility	Adults older than 17 years of age with alcohol or drug problems and addiction living in the city and in neighboring cities
Funding sources	Public (mayor, state and national governments)
Capital and equipment	Rented house Equipment: four desktop computers, one printer, one refrigerator, one oven, and two televisions
How does the service work?	At the first contact with the service, a patient is welcomed by a mental health professional who conducts a brief evaluation in order to plan a therapeutic project
How is care delivered?	*Intensive care* offers support from Monday to Friday, during a period from 8:00 am to 4:00 pm. During this period, the users can attend therapeutic sessions, either in groups or individually, with nurses, psychologists, occupational therapists, or social workers; they can also attend to external activities, such as informal activities to generate income, placement assistance in the formal labor market, or cultural and sporting activities, always assisted by the mental health team In *semi-intensive care*, treatment is delivered 2 or 3 days a week, according to the user's demands and individual therapeutic plan, participating in the same activities described above *Nonintensive care* is a form of gradual detachment of the patient from the service, encompassing one monthly visit with a psychiatrist and one weekly session with others on the mental health team until final discharge In all modalities of care, users receive at least one monthly consultation with a general practitioner and a psychiatrist Every day, patients attend the service; they receive breakfast, lunch, and an afternoon snack; and undergo nursing procedures such as blood preasure measurement and assisted medication (if there is a prescription)
Which services are delivered?	Psychiatrist visits (monthly) General practitioner visits (monthly) Individual and group psychotherapy (weekly) Group sessions with occupational therapists (weekly) Nursing assistance Medication Social worker assistance Emergency assistance (two beds) Social activities Workshops and work placement Diet and transportation tickets Telephone call assistance
Which professionals are involved? Human resources	*Clinical staff* 2 psychiatrists (20 h/week) 1 general practitioner (20 h/week) 1 nurse (40 h/week) 2 nursing technician (40 h/week) 2 psychologists (40 h/week) 2 occupational therapists (30 h/week) 1 social worker (40 h/week) *Management and nonhealth staff* 1 health manager (40 h/week) 1 secretary (40 h/week) 1 general service assistant (40 h/week) 1 receptionist (40 h/week) 1 professional cleaner (40 h/week) 1 guard security (40 h/week)

(continued)

Table 15.3 (continued)

Revenue costs	Consumables: kitchen and cleaning supplies, office stationery (printer cartridges, pens, pencil, staplers, envelopes, and paper), medical supplies (syringes, pills dispensing containers, cotton, sterilizers material) Support services: cleaning, security (nighttime), maintenance and repair services Utilities: electricity, telephone, water, gas
Overhead	In this case overhead costs are those costs related to service management. Only two staff members were involved with administrative issues: the health manager and the secretary. The secretary is a staff member who helps with accounting issues. The health manager has an administrative role and coordinates service and health staff actions

Table 15.4 Unit of costs for each cost component of CAPS-AD, using a top-down approach

Components of costs	Description	Quantity	Total costs over180 days in 2015 (R$)	Unit of cost	Cost per unit of costs (R$)
Treatment staff					
Psychiatrists	20 h/week	2	54,069.48	Hour	56.32
General practitioner	20 h/week	1	27,034.74	Hour	56.32
Occupational therapists	30 h/week	2	76,160.00	Hour	26.44
Psychologists	40 h/week	2	76,160.00	Hour	19.83
Social worker	30 h/week	1	19,040.00	Hour	26.44
Nurse	40 h/week	1	19,040.00	Hour	19.83
Nursing assistants	40 h/week	2	51,568.00	Hour	13.42
Total human resources			323,072.22		
Support services					
Diet	Individual package: breakfast, lunch, snacks, gas		23,756.67	Day	197. 97
Maintenance/repair			125.50	Day	0.70
Security guard	40 h/week		2,454.36	Day	13.63
General service assistant	40 h/week		7,121.04	Hour	7.41
Utility services					
Water consumption	Not available	–	0	–	–
Electricity	Service operates 10 h/ day		1,420.94	Day	7.89
Telephone	Land lines and mobile phones		1,977.44	Day	24.72
Consumables	Medical supplies, kitchen supplies, stationery supplies, cleaning supplies		5,019.59	Day	27.89
Total support services			*41,875.54*		
Capital costs					
Rent	House is rented for a fixed price for 1 year; then it is renewable with an interest rate based on the inflation rate		6,826.68	Year	13,653.36
Equipment	4 desktop computers, 1 refrigerator, 1 oven, 1 printer	5% discount factor, 5 years	Equivalent annual annuity Total invested: R$6,500.00	Year	1524.00
Overhead					
Health manager	40 h/week	1	29,489.00	Hour	30.71
Secretary	40 h/week	1	8,556.00	Hour	8.91
Total overhead			38,045.00	Hour	39.62

mental healthcare, and the accuracy when costing this component is crucial for achieving accurate estimates of service costs. Salaries and subsides vary within the same professional category, significantly affecting service costs. Other factors affecting service costs are related to geographic region where service is located, team size, and interventions available [55]. Although some studies have emphasized that individual factors related to service costs vary [55], other studies have shown a minimal effect of individual characteristics on service cost variation [56]. The bottom-up approach is preferable when costing community mental health services for economic evaluation. Similarly, the long-term time horizon is an important component to verify cost variation across time, particularly in mental health, where outcomes or improvements can occur late. It is crucial to measure costs in a broad manner because costs can migrate from one service to another and, more worrisome, to patients and their families.

Key Messages

- Community mental health services vary in structure, intervention(s) delivered, and costs.
- The bottom-up approach and long-term time horizon are preferable when measuring costs and outcome in economic evaluation.
- Clinical staff is the main component of community mental health costs.
- Informal care and out-of-pocket expenditures can spill over to patient and families, and they should be taken into account when analyzing the costs and benefits of programs, interventions, and health policies, although these are usually not included in analysis when adopting a health provider perspective.

References

1. Alarcon RD, Aguilar-Gaxiola SA. Mental health policy developments in Latin America. Bull World Health Organ. 2000;78(4):483–90.
2. Mateus MD, Mari JJ, Delgado PG, Almeida-Filho N, Barrett T, Gerolin J, et al. The mental health system in Brazil: policies and future challenges. Int J Ment Health Syst. 2008;2(1):12.
3. Razzouk D, Sharan P, Gallo C, Gureje O, Lamberte EE, de Jesus MJ, et al. Scarcity and inequity of mental health research resources in low-and-middle income countries: a global survey. Health Policy. 2010;94(3):211–20.
4. Razzouk D, Gregorio G, Antunes R, Mari JD. Lessons learned in developing community mental health care in Latin American and Caribbean countries. World Psychiatry. 2012;11(3):191–5.
5. Knapp M, Beecham J, McDaid D, Matosevic T, Smith M. The economic consequences of deinstitutionalisation of mental health services: lessons from a systematic review of European experience. Health Soc Care Community. 2011;19(2):113–25.
6. Mansell J, Knapp M, Beadle-Brown J, Beecham J. Deinstitutionalization and community living outcomes and costs: reports of European study. Volume 2: main report. Report No. 2. Canterbury: Tizard Centre, University of Kent; 2007.
7. Thornicroft G, Bebbington P. Deinstitutionalisation–from hospital closure to service development. Br J Psychiatry. 1989;155:739–53.
8. Thornicroft G, Deb T, Henderson C. Community mental health care worldwide: current status and further developments. World Psychiatry. 2016;15(3):276–86.
9. Rothbard A, Schinnar A, Hadley T, Foley K, Kuno E. Cost comparison of state hospital and community-based care for seriously mentally ill adults. Am J Psychiatry. 1998;155:523–9.
10. Knapp M, Chisholm D, Astin J, Lelliott P, Audini B. The cost consequences of changing the hospital-community balance: the mental health residential care study. Psychol Med. 1997;27(3):681–92.
11. Thornicroft G, Tansella M. Better mental health care. Cambridge, UK: Cambridge University Press; 2009.
12. Thornicroft G, Tansella M. What are the arguments for community-based mental health care? width1. Copenhagn: WHO Regional Office for Europe; 2003.
13. Davidson L, Mezzina R, Rowe M, Thompson K. A life in the community: Italian mental health reform and recovery. J Ment Health. 2010;19(5):436–43.
14. Roberts E, Cumming J, Nelson K. A review of economic evaluations of community mental health care. Med Care Res Rev. 2005;62(5):503–43.
15. Knapp M, Beecham J, Koutsogeorgopoulou V, Hallam A, Fenyo A, Marks IM, et al. Service use and costs of home-based versus hospital-based care for people with serious mental illness. Br J Psychiatry. 1994;165(2):195–203.

16. Knapp M. The economic evaluation of mental health care. 1st ed. Brookfield: Ashgate Publishing Limited; 1995.
17. Beecham J. Collecting and estimating costs. In: Knapp M, editor. The economic evaluation of mental health care. 1st ed. Aldershot: Arena; 1995. p. 61–82.
18. Beecham J, Ramsay A, Gordon K, Maltby S, Walshe K, Shaw I, et al. Cost and impact of a quality improvement programme in mental health services. J Health Serv Res Policy. 2010;15(2):69–75.
19. Byford S, Sefton T. Economic evaluation of complex health and social care interventions. Natl Inst Econ Rev. 2003;186:98–108.
20. Shearer J, McCrone P, Romeo R. Economic evaluation of mental health interventions: a guide to costing approaches. Pharmacoeconomics. 2016;34(7):651–64.
21. Knapp M. Hidden costs of mental illness. Br J Psychiatry. 2003;183:477–8.
22. Schneider J, Wooff D, Carpenter J, Brandon T, McNiven F. Service organisation, service use and costs of community mental health care. J Ment Health Policy Econ. 2002;5:79–87.
23. Beecham J, Knapp M. Costing psychiatric interventions. In: Thornicroft G, editor. Measuring mental health needs. London: Gaskell; 2001. p. 200–24.
24. Felce D, Perry J, Romeo R, Robertson J, Meek A, Emerson E, et al. Outcomes and costs of community living: semi-independent living and fully staffed group homes. Am J Ment Retard. 2008;113(2):87–101.
25. Lapsley HM, Tribe K, Tennant C, Rosen A, Hobbs C, Newton L. Deinstitutionalisation for long-term mental illness: cost differences in hospital and community care. Aust N Z J Psychiatry. 2000;34(3):491–5.
26. Glennerster H. The costs of hospital closure: reproviding services for the residents of Darenth Park Hospital. Psychiatr Bull. 2011;14:140–3.
27. Bonizzato P, Bisoffi G, Amaddeo F, Chisholm D, Tansella M. Community-based mental health care: to what extent are service costs associated with clinical, social and service history variables? Psychol Med. 2000;30(5):1205–15.
28. Knapp M, Beecham J, Fenyo A, Hallam A. Community mental health care for former hospital in-patients. predicting costs from needs and diagnoses. Br J Psychiatry Suppl. 1995;27:10–8.
29. Reinharz D, Lesage AD, Contandriopoulos AP. Cost-effectiveness analysis of psychiatric deinstitutionalization. Can J Psychiatr. 2000;45(6):533–8.
30. Negrini D, Kettle A, Sheppard L, Mills GH, Edbrooke DL. The cost of a hospital ward in Europe: is there a methodology available to accurately measure the costs? J Health Organ Manag. 2004;18(2–3):195–206.
31. Swanson J, Dorn R, Swartz M, Robbins P, Steadman H, Cguire T. The cost of assisted outpatient treatment: can it save states money? Am J Psychiatry. 2013;170(12):1423–32.
32. Amaddeo F, Beecham J, Bonizzato P, Fenyo A, Tansella M, Knapp M. The costs of community-based psychiatric care for first-ever patients. a case register study. Psychol Med. 1998;28(1):173–83.
33. Hastrup LH, Aagaard J. Costs and outcome of assertive community treatment (ACT) in a rural area in Denmark: 4-year register-based follow-up. Nord J Psychiatry. 2015;69(2):110–7.
34. Cousins SJ, Antonini VP, Rawson RA. Utilization, measurement, and funding of recovery supports and services. J Psychoactive Drugs. 2012;44(4):325–33.
35. Levin C, Chisholm D. Cost-effectiveness and affordability of interventions, policies, and platforms for the prevention and treatment of mental, neurological, and substance use disorders. In: Patel V, Chisholm D, Dua T, editors. Mental, neurological, and substance use disorders: disease control priorities. 3rd ed, volume 4. Washington, DC: The International Bank for Reconstruction and Development/The World Bank; 2016. [cited 14 Nov 2016]. p. 219–236. Available from: http://www.ncbi.nlm.nih.gov/pubmed/27227237.
36. Drummond M, Sculpher MJ. Common methodological flaws in economic evaluations. Med Care. 2005;43(suppl7):II5–14.
37. Husereau D, Culyer AJ, Neumann P, Jacobs P. How do economic evaluations inform health policy decisions for treatment and prevention in Canada and the United States? Appl Health Econ Health Policy. 2015;13(3):273–9.
38. Furber G, Brann P, Skene C, Allison S. Benchmarking the cost efficiency of community care in Australian child and adolescent mental health services: implications for future benchmarking. Australas Psychiatry. 2011;19(3):226–31.
39. Bower P. Primary care mental health workers: models of working and evidence of effectiveness. Br J Gen Pract. 2002;52(484):926–33.
40. Salvador-Carulla L, Haro JM, Cabases J, Madoz V, Sacristan JA, Vazquez-Barquero JL. Service utilization and costs of first-onset schizophrenia in two widely differing health service areas in North-East Spain. PSICOST Group. Acta Psychiatr Scand. 1999;100(5):335–43.
41. Mihalopoulos C, Chatterton ML. Economic evaluations of interventions designed to prevent mental disorders: a systematic review. Early Interv Psychiatry. 2015;9:85–92.
42. Hastrup LH, Kronborg C, Bertelsen M, Jeppesen P, Jorgensen P, Petersen L, et al. Cost-effectiveness of early intervention in first-episode psychosis: economic evaluation of a randomised controlled trial (the OPUS study). Br J Psychiatry. 2013;202(1):35–41.
43. Rosenheck R. Cost-effectiveness of services for mentally ill homeless people: the application of research to policy and practice. Am J Psychiatry. 2000;157(10):1563–70.
44. Mihalopoulos C, Vos T, Pirkis J, Carter R. The economic analysis of prevention in mental health programs. Annu Rev Clin Psychol. 2011;7:169–201.
45. Mansel J, Beadle-Brown J. Deinstitutionalisation and community living: position statement of the comparative policy and practice special interest research group

of the international association for the scientific study of intellectual disabilities. J Intellect Disabil Res. 2010;54(2):104–12.
46. McCrone P, Weich S. Mental health care costs: paucity of measurement. Soc Psychiatry Psychiatr Epidemiol. 1996;31(2):70–7.
47. Van Citters AD, Bartels SJ. A systematic review of the effectiveness of community-based mental health outreach services for older adults. Psychiatr Serv. 2004;55(11):1237–49.
48. Vos T, Haby MM, Magnus A, Mihalopoulos C, Andrews G, Carter R. Assessing cost-effectiveness in mental health: helping policy-makers prioritize and plan health services. Aust N Z J Psychiatry. 2005;39(8):701–12.
49. Leff J, Trieman N, Knapp M, Hallam A. The TAPS project. Psychiatr Bull. 2000;24:165–8.
50. Mogyorosy Z, Smith P. The main methodological issues in costing health care services. York: Centre for Health Economics, University of York; 2005.
51. Chisholm D, MKH K, Amaddeo F, Gaite L, Winjgaarden B. Client socio-demographic service receipt inventory European version: development of one instrument for international research. Br J Psychiatry. 2000;177(39):s28–33.
52. Sousa A, Cardoso A, Gregório G, Mari J, Razzouk D. Instrumento padronizado para medir custos e utiliação de serviços em saúde mental: versão brasileira, adaptação cultural e testagem do Client Socio-demografic and Service Receipt Inventory [Internet]. ISPOR: News across Latin America 1; 2013. https://www.ispor.org/consortiums/latinamerica/articles/Vol1Issue5_outcomesresearch_portuguese.asp
53. McFarkand B, Smith J, Bigelow D, Mofidi A. Unit of costs of community mental health services. Admin Pol Ment Health. 1995;23(1):27–42.
54. Oostenbrink JB, Oopmanschap MA, Rutten FF. Standardisation of costs: the Dutch manual for costing in economic evaluations. Pharmacoeconomics. 2002;20(7):443–54.
55. Amaddeo F, Grigoletti L, De GG, Picardi A, Santone G. Which factors affect the costs of psychiatric residential care? findings from the Italian PROGRES study. Acta Psychiatr Scand. 2007;115(2):132–41.
56. Beecham J, Knapp M, Mc Gilloway S, Kavanagh S, Fenyo A, Donnell M, et al. Leaving hospital II: the cost-effectiveness of community care for former long-stay psychiatric hospital patients. J Ment Health. 1996;5(4):379–94.

Estimating Costs of Residential Services

16

Denise Razzouk

Abstract

This chapter presents a definition of residential care according to the community mental health care model and describes types of services according to size, staff, and structure. A brief review of varying costs of residential services in the literature is presented to explore the main research questions related to this issue and which factors are involved with their costs. Costing method involves transparency about results and methods used, comprehensiveness of data collection, and characterization of services and resident profiles. Crucial steps for estimating resident services should be based on determining the main question related to the costs of services; defining the study perspective, the time horizon for collecting data, and data collection methods; identifying services components of costs; estimating unit costs; and, ultimately, proceeding with cost analysis. We present one example of costing residential services following these steps using data from a Brazilian study of costing residential services in the city of São Paulo.

Key Points Summary

- Definition of residential care
- Types of residential services
- Variation of residential care costs
- Costing method for residential services
- Step-by-step example for estimating residential costs

D. Razzouk (✉)
Centre of Economic Mental Health, Department of Psychiatry, Universidade Federal de Sao Paulo, Rua Borges Lagoa 570, 1° andar, São Paulo 04038-000, Brazil
e-mail: drazzouk@gmail.com

D. Razzouk (ed.), *Mental Health Economics*, DOI 10.1007/978-3-319-55266-8_16

16.1 Introduction

Residential services are part of community mental healthcare and are addressed to accommodate people with mental disorders without family or social support [1, 2]. These services have been provided mainly for people discharged from long-term hospitalization in psychiatric hospitals or for individuals with mental illness who have a low or no income and have special self-care needs, such as severe mental retardation and schizophrenia [3]. The definition of community living is linked with the idea of offering housing available to the ordinary public to people with mental illness and also to provide all needed support for living independently [4]. In practice, services vary extensively in term of definition, goals, and structure [1, 5, 6]. A variety of these services deliver interventions and care shaped by a model of care according to the health system infrastructure of each country [7]. For instance, Macpherson et al. [1] identified at least five modalities of residential care or supported accommodation in the United Kingdom: high- and medium-staffed hostels, low-staffed hostels, staffed care homes, group homes (GHs), and core and cluster high-dependency housing (see Box 16.1). Terms associated with accommodation and residential care vary widely for people with mental disorders: "group homes," "cluster housing," "dispersing houses," "supported living," "semi-independent living," "shelter homes," "staffed homes" [5]. Yet, these services vary in terms of structure and resources even though they target similar goals and populations.

Moreover, these services may vary according to distribution within the community: campus-style residential or village communities and community-based dispersing houses [8]. Campus-style residence is a generic term encompassing all types of 24-h sharable residential services offered to a group of patients with intellectual disabilities. Community-based dispersing houses are used for services with long-term residential supports in domestic-style housing for up to eight residents.

In this chapter we present a brief review of the literature about costs of residential services and then address each of these items, illustrating with research on residential costs analysis carried out in São Paulo City, Brazil.

Box 16.1 Types of Supported Accommodation in the Community (Residential Care) in the United Kingdom [1]

Medium- and high-staffed houses (nursing homes, residential care) comprise a 24-h service with 2 to 20 workers per unit caring for between 6 and 12 patients.

Low-staffed hostels comprise a day service with two or three lay-caregivers run by the private sector.

Staffed care homes comprise 24-h service with lay-caregivers caring for between 3 and 12 residents.

Group homes are homes without staff and support up to five residents, who receive regular visits by mental health professionals.

Core and cluster high-dependency housing comprises individual flats with regular visits by mental health professionals.

16.2 How Residential Costs Vary in the Literature

Therefore, the variability of terms and classifications of residential care hinders comparability among services. Costs of residential services vary accordingly with the level of service complexity, service size, type and quantity of interventions delivered, and geographic location [9–11]. Moreover, new services are usually more expensive because of initial capital costs and costs to train staff [12]. Knapp et al. [13, 14] emphasized that residential costs varied between 65% and 95% of the total costs of an individual care package.

We reviewed how costs of residential care vary in the literature using the MEDLINE, Embase, and LILACS databases through 2012. Our search resulted in 754 articles, of which 31 studies have at least one measure of costs. From these, eight studies focused specifically on the costs of residential care, and 15 compared residential costs with costs of psychiatric hospitals.

These eight studies evaluated the costs of residential services considering four aspects: (a) comparison of costs among different types of residential services; (b) comparison of accommodation and nonaccommodation costs according to the type of residential facility (RF); (c) cost-consequence analysis (CCA) among different types of residential services; and (d) identification of resident profiles that could contribute to residential costs.

16.2.1 Comparison of Costs Among Different Types of Residential Services

Four studies compared direct costs among residential services [15–20]. Dockrell et al. [15] compared direct costs among three accommodation services in the United Kingdom: hospital homes, campus homes, and community homes for people hospitalized in Mental Impairment Evaluation and Treatment (MIET) Services hospital (this institution prepares people with learning disabilities and challenging behavior to be discharged into the community over 18 months). They found that the transfer of such people to the community was more costly in community homes (which house up to four people in the community) and less costly in hospital homes (small and medium-sized units on the grounds of a hospital).

Dickey et al. [17] compared the costs of shared housing and independent-living apartments among homeless people with mental disorders, and they found that the annual housing costs per person were U$25,000 higher in shared housing than in independent-living apartments. Staff expenses in shared homes were the main component of the total cost.

Chisholm et al. [16] found that accommodation costs were greater among highly staffed homes than in low- and nonstaffed homes. Felce et al. [19] found that costs of fully staffed homes were threefold more expensive than semi-independents homes in the United Kingdom. In this case, costs were lower in terms of direct-staff costs, nonstaff costs, and agency overhead.

16.2.2 Comparison of Accommodation and Nonaccommodation Costs According to the Type of Residential Facility

While in psychiatric hospitals "accommodation" and "treatment" are delivered together, in the community, accommodation and treatment are delivered through multiple services. Costing the direct costs of patients living in the community requires verifying all services delivered for each individual. Yet, some RFs provide rehabilitation care while others do not. Therefore, costs should be measured in a comprehensive way, that is, considering all costs involved in the package of care and services used. Residential costs then encompass accommodation costs related exclusively to residential costs and nonaccommodation costs related to treatment and all services consumed. Regarding patients discharged from long stays in psychiatric hospitals, direct costs would fall in these two categories of costs, though the available intervention varies somewhat: accommodation and nonaccommodation costs.

Chisholm et al. [16] found that accommodation costs were greater among highly staffed homes than in low- and nonstaffed homes in the United Kingdom. On the other hand, nonaccommodation costs such as community services use were greater in nonstaffed homes than in other residential homes.

16.2.3 Cost-Consequence Analysis among Different Types of Residential Services

Despite many criticisms against CCA because it does not allow objective results for supporting decision-making, these studies explore advantages and disadvantages in terms of outcomes and costs among different service modalities. Because there is no gold standard or consensus to determine the most appropriate RF for people with mental disorders, these studies are useful to evaluate which benefits and harms are involved in care considering residents' profiles and needs. Three studies used CCA to compare residential services according to the staff present and the number of residents (a group or individuals).

Emerson et al. [18] used a CCA to compare GHs (small and large) and supported-living residences (SLRs) using a sample of 300 people with mental retardation in the United Kingdom. SLRs were more costly in terms of accommodation costs and less costly in terms of nonaccommodation costs when compared with GHs, but no significant differences in total costs were found among the three facilities. SLRs were associated with more choice, a larger number of community-based activities, and a higher risk of exploitation and victimization. The small GH was associated with larger social networks and less risk of abuse when compared with the larger GH.

Hallam et al. [20] used CCA to compare different models of residential services for 500 people with mental illness in the United Kingdom. Three modalities of 24-h support services were compared: campus-style residence, village communities, and community-based dispersing houses. The mean cost per week of accommodation and care per resident was higher in the residential campus (£931.00) and dispersing housing (£901.00) than in village communities (£637.00). Almost 40% of the total costs were explained by 14 high-cost predictor variables: low ability and severe challenging behavior, younger age, predominance of men, and fewer arrangements for training and supervising the staff. Regarding outcomes, compared with other residential services, people living in dispersed housing schemes experienced more choice, more social networks, an active physical life, few accidents in the home, and a larger number of leisure activities. On the other hand, people living in residential campuses experienced more exposure to crime and abuse, more domestic accidents, and smaller social networks.

Felce et al. [19] performed a CCA comparing outcomes (quality of life, money management, safety, healthcare, lifestyle measures, social networks) and direct costs between fully staffed homes and semi-independent living for people with intellectual disabilities and mental illness in the United Kingdom. Costs of fully staffed homes were threefold higher than costs for the semi-independent homes. However, both accommodations provided different benefits: residents in semi-independent homes were able to make more choices and choose from more community activities than residents in fully staffed homes. However, the latter had fewer problems with managing money and safety, and had better physical health indicators. The authors concluded that semi-independent living might be cost-effective compared with fully staffed homes, but the differences between these services might be associated to intrinsic characteristics of the sample.

16.2.4 The Influence of Residents' Profiles on Residential Costs

Amaddeo et al. [21] and Chisholm et al. [16] investigated which resident characteristics could be correlated with residential costs. Chisholm et al. found that residential costs were correlated with younger age, having a diagnosis of schizophrenia/paranoid state or affective disorder, being female, exhibiting aggressive behavior, and having fewer living skills. Amaddeo et al. evaluated the accommodation and service use costs for 2962 residents from 265 Italian RFs. RF costs were correlated with young men in residence, fewer living skills, and having a diagnosis of schizophrenia or an affective disorder, whereas costs of community services use were correlated with poor functioning, having a diagnosis of personality disorder, and younger age. They also found that RF costs varied according to geographic region and RF size. The costs of accommodation were lower in the smallest RF and were higher with community psychiatric care.

16.3 Cost-Savings and Cost-effectiveness of Residential Care

Since the beginnings of deinstitutionalization, multiple studies have emerged comparing costs between psychiatric hospitals and community mental health services, including residential care [7, 10, 12, 22–32]. However, the majority of studies pursued cost-savings, that is, reducing costs without taking into account the potential benefits and advantages of different models of care [33]. Moreover, the costing methodology of such services has been poorly described and lacks accuracy. Costs are not directly related to health service quality and efficiency. One service can be more expensive because of its characteristics, its good quality (see Chap. 12), and the cost-effectiveness of the intervention; on the other hand, a service can be costly because of poor management and resource waste [33]. Therefore, costs alone do not allow services to be compared in terms of quality and cost-effectiveness. Also, it is important to bear in mind that patients living in residential facilities outside hospitals may need other nonpsychiatric healthcare services, and this should be measured as well [25, 28, 30]. Therefore, good descriptions reporting which services were measured are crucial for estimating costs.

It is challenging to conduct cost-effectiveness studies comparing the costs and benefits of residential services because a set of relevant outcomes is involved, and the choice of a single outcome might be not enough to evaluate services. Longitudinal studies and CCA usually are used to measure potential outcomes associated with the type of service and costs [34]. Some reviews assess the potential cost-effectiveness of residential services over hospital care and compare different provisions of residential care, but these results are not based on cost-effectiveness ratios but on comparing a specific set of outcomes and costs among services [7, 19, 22, 25, 35]. Moreover, some studies assessed effectiveness based on admission rate, which is not an outcome representing mental health improvements. A systematic review of the cost-effectiveness of acute residential services compared with a hospital found that on average there was no significant difference in effectiveness between the services, but users' satisfaction was greater and costs were lower in the former in some studies [36]. This kind of evidence is not definitive because it is necessary to identify which user receive more benefit from the type of service.

16.4 Costing Residential Facilities

The variability in the structure and complexity of residential facilities are not the only challenge for costing such services. Several factors can exert influence on estimating these costs, such as period of time, resident profiles and needs, and region, among others [7]. Comparing costs among services is not useful if outcomes and resident needs are not taken into account [12]. Also, the poor description of methodology for costing services in studies published in the literature and the lack of standardized methodology and consensus in the field represent major constraints in estimating residential costs [23, 33].

Before estimating residential costs, it is necessary to follow some crucial steps: (a) define the main question related to the costs of services; (b) define the perspective of the study; (c) define the time horizon for collecting data; (d) identify services' cost components; (e) define the data collection method; (f) estimate unit costs; and (g) estimate and analyze costs.

16.5 Residential Costs Step by Step: The Case of Residential Services in São Paulo Services

16.5.1 Defining the Main Question

At least three main questions are related to residential costs. The first issue is related to the costs of one or more residential services and the comparison of them. The second issue is related to client characteristics and outcomes and the care package. For example, one might wish to explore whether residential costs for people with severe schizophrenia differ from those of people with moderate schizophrenia. It is possible to verify how residents' profiles affect total costs of residential services. The third issue might be verifying the cost-effectiveness of different residential service modalities to achieve one outcome in a specific sample.

Importantly, once the main question is delineated, each subsequent step is tailored accordingly. In our example, we describe the method used to estimate the total costs of 20 residential services and their components in the city of São Paulo.

16.5.2 Study Perspective

We adopted the perspective of a public health provider. This service is funded by resources from the Ministry of Health and from the Mayor of the City of São Paulo. All residents' needs (health, accommodation, and self-care) are enabled through public provisions. Also, the majority of residents receive welfare or social benefits to cover personal expenses.

16.5.3 Defining the Time Horizon for Data Collection

The ideal time horizon for evaluating services is more than 1 year. However, in this case a prospective study was not feasible for several reasons. Notwithstanding of this limitation, we decided to collect data for 1 month because of recall bias and the lack of medical records.

16.5.4 Identifying Service Components of Costs

The identification of component of costs cost components depends on knowing well the structure and function of a health service, because each varies in terms of complexity, the type of interventions available, and its components of costs. Also, the choice of components of costs would be different according to the research question. For instance, if the goal is to determine costs according to an individual's profile on the consumption of health services, all relevant costs related to individual variations should be computed. On the other hand, if the objective is to estimate fixed costs that are equally sharable among all individuals, then it is acceptable to consider the total cost of one component or package of care and then to estimate average costs per person. Once components of costs are listed, the next step is to select all relevant costs and to classify costs as fixed or variable, direct or indirect, and sharable and not sharable. Yet, it is important to verify how these common costs are sharable among individuals and among health service units, for instance, the consumption of electricity and food in a hospital or a residential service.

16.5.4.1 Describing the Structure and Function of Residential Services

In 2010, when this study was carried out, 20 type-2 residential services, with eight residents each, could be found in the city of São Paulo. These services were created between 2008 and 2009. A type-2 RF is a home that is fully staffed, 24 h a day, with a team of lay-caregivers and one coordinator. All these houses were rented in different regions of the city by the Secretary of Health of the Mayor of the City of São Paulo. The caregivers' role was to assist up to eight residents with mental disorders in their daily routine activities, such as self-care, cleaning, cooking, delivering medications, getting out for consultations, and other needs. All medical and psychosocial interventions were delivered by mental health professionals in the Centre of Psychosocial Care (CAPS), an outpatient health service that is usually close to residential services. Residents originally experienced long-term hospitalization in psychiatric hospitals before moving to the RF.

16.5.4.2 Components of Costs

We identified two major categories of costs: accommodation costs and package of care (non-accommodation) costs. To estimate the costs of residential services, we focused on accommodation cost components: house rent, equipment, transport, repair services, food and supplies, human resources, consumables, and caregivers and their training (Table 16.1). Nonaccommodation costs comprised the package of care with the following

Table 16.1 Description of accommodation costs

	Description	Cost classification
Capital costs: Equipment	All houses received the same items in the same year using a fixed budget (refrigerator, microwave, TV, sound system, washing machine, furniture, kitchen, and other supplies)	Fixed
Capital costs: Rent	Rent on a house in the community was paid monthly by the mayor and was unchanged for 1 year. Prices followed the local market	Fixed for 1 year
Transport (car)	One car was rented by agreement with a third party at a fixed price (independent of usage) for each residential house. Consumption varied on average from 3 to 10 h/week. Car rent was fixed but the price contracted varied from one residence to another, according to the management agency. According to the mayor, these cars were not sharable with other services. Also, when cars were not available full time, taxi costs were collected directly from coordinators of residencies	Variable
Repair service	An agreement existed between the mayor and a third-party company for repairs on an on-call basis (monthly expenses were paid independent of consumption). The same cost was used for each house, independent of usage. Only two residential services had a different fixed price for this service. It was not possible to obtain data on the usage of such services, but we included any extra costs in each service	Fixed
Food and supplies	Each coordinator received funding from the mayor to buy food and supplies as necessary (up to R$2200.00 per month)	Variable
Utilities (e.g., electricity, telephone, water)	Each coordinator used mayoral funding to pay for these services and taxes. Gas costs were not available for all services and were irrelevant compared with other costs, and therefore they were excluded from the cost analysis	Variable
Staff	Six to nine lay professionals worked as caregivers (worked 12-h periods, three to four4 times a week, with 36-h rest intervals). One coordinator (a psychologist or occupation therapist) worked 20–40 h/week).Salaries were paid by the mayor through management agencies	Fixed
Overhead	7–8% of residential total expenditures and were obtained from the management agency	Variable
Carer training	One workshop training on mental health concepts for each new caregiver starting in a job function, lasting 40 h during a 1-week period	Information not available

components: medication, psychosocial intervention, health center visits, hospitalizations, and emergency care. In this chapter we describe only accommodation costs.

16.5.4.2.1 Capital Costs: House Rent

All houses, located in the main neighborhoods of the city of São Paulo, had at least three bedrooms, a living room, a kitchen, two bathrooms, and a garden. Rent varied according to availability of houses with these characteristics in the region and within the local market. Renewable agreements between the mayor and the landlord, renewable after 1 year, were carried at fixed costs during this period. House rent was obtained directly from the coordinator of each residential service and checked with the management agency.

16.5.4.2.2 Capital Costs: Equipment

All houses received the same amount of funding from national and local governments to buy standard equipment when the services were created. There were two main categories: furniture and devices (TV, washing machine, wardrobes, beds, refrigerator, microwave, etc.). The management agency delivered a list of 106 items, with a total cost of R$39,043.89 per residential service in 2009, and this value was converted to the equivalent annual annuity, or R$9,018.15 per year. It was not feasible to check whether all houses received the same items and equipment at the same price; for this reason we used the same value for all of them.

16.5.4.2.3 Transport

One car was rented by the mayor for each house to cover residents' transportation to healthcare centers and exams. The consumption of this service varied, on average, between 3 and 10 h a week, though expenditures for the rented cars were similar at all residences. Because this service was not sharable with other services and coordinators did not know the precise periods of time the cars were used, we considered the same costs for all residential services, independent of usage. Occasional use of taxi services were computed individually for each service.

16.5.4.2.4 Repair Services

A third-party commercial agreement existed between the mayor and a private agency for house repairs. This agreement was paid at a fixed price on a monthly basis. Expenditures related to this agreement were similar (R$890) for all residential services except those in the south (R$972 and R$1392). Because it was not possible to estimate individually the usage of this service, we considered the cost for each residential service according to the agreement mentioned above. In addition, extra costs for small repairs occurred independent of this agreement, and we added that value to the total repair costs according to data provided by each residential service coordinator.

16.5.4.2.5 Food and Supplies

Each residential services coordinator received funding for food, market, cleaning, and other daily expenses in the house. We checked the total consumption for each service.

16.5.4.2.6 Human Resources

Two caregivers worked for 12-h periods on a duty schedule, and one coordinator (a psychologist or occupational therapist) worked for 20–40 h per week at each house. The number of caregivers by house varied from six to nine. All wages and taxes were paid directly by the management agency for each residential service.

16.5.4.2.7 Utilities and Other Services

Utilities such as gas, electricity, telephone, and gardening were paid for by the mayor, and we checked all individual costs per house. Gas costs were not available for the majority of houses, however, and we decided to exclude those from the analysis.

16.5.4.2.8 Overhead

Three management agencies operated residential budgets, and they received 7– 8% of the total residential costs for management and overhead. We obtained these data directly from the respective agencies.

16.5.4.2.9 Caregiver Training

Each caregiver received 40 h of training in mental health before working with residents. No information was available on the costs for this training.

16.5.5 Definition of Method for Data Collection

Two methods are used to collect data: the top-down and bottom-up approaches (see Chaps. 2 and 13). However, mixed methods are commonly used for practical reasons and to save time. We used the ISDUCS questionnaire (see Chap. 13) and the bottom-up approach to estimate housing costs for the following items: rent, consumables, food and supplies, medicines, overhead, and human resources. We obtained data on costs directly from the mayor's agency, and we used the top-down approach to estimate costs for transportation, house repairs, and equipment and furniture for each house.

16.5.6 Estimation of Unit Costs

The estimation of unit cost is complex, and each item deserves careful and transparent consideration and description. Table 16.2 presents the units of cost per a month for residential services for July 2011. In this case, capital costs involve rent, equipment, furniture, and other supplies needed to create residential services. The amount invested in all residential services at the date of

Table 16.2 Capital and running costs per residential service and per resident (Costs are expressed in Brazilian currency BRL$, for the year 2011)

	Total costs for all residential services (N = 20) per month (BRL$)	Unit costs per residential service per month (n = 20) BRL$	Unit costs per resident per month (n = 160) BRL$
	Capital costs		
Rent	60,932.67	3,046.63	380.82
Equipment	15,030.25	751.51	93.94
Total capital costs	75,962.92	3,798.14	474.76
Revenue costs			
Human resources	348,835.50	17,441.76	2,180.22
Transport	21,174.40	1,058.72	132.34
Repair services	19,244.51	962.23	120.29
Food and supplies	50,642.22	2,532.11	316.50
Utility services	24,396.10	1,219.80	152.47
Overhead	37,358.09	1,867.05	233.48
Total revenue costs	501,651.01	25,082.55	3,135.31
Full total costs (1 month)	567,595.32	28,380.11	3,610.87
Social benefits (for personal expenditures)[a]	51,200.00	2,560.00	320.00

[a]People discharged from a long-term stay in a psychiatric hospital were allowed to receive monthly social disability benefit (BRL$320.00) for personal living expenses. One-third of them did not receive any social benefits

their creation was available for 2009; this value was annuitized using equivalent annual costs at a discount rate of 5%, and considered a lifetime use of 5 years for all equipment [37]. We used a top-down approach to estimate units of costs for capital costs, transport, and house repairs for residential services. The top-down approach was used to estimate units of costs for all components of accommodation costs per resident, considering that each residential service comprised eight residents. The bottom-up approach was used to estimate the units of cost for the remaining items. Social benefits are described in Table 16.2, but these costs were not included in the full costs.

16.5.7 Estimation of Costs and Cost Analysis

It is important to distinguish between full costs and revenue costs. Full costs involve capital and revenue costs, and they might also include social benefits for individual expenditures, depending on the perspective of the study. Long-run marginal analysis of opportunity costs considers full costs because the goal is to verify the additional costs of including one more resident and the resources invested in terms of opportunity costs. Therefore, isolated revenue costs are not appropriate in terms of estimating the investment for a new service [38]. When estimating costs of services, two main aspects must be considered: costs of services from the provider perspective, and costs of the package of care. When costing a residential service alone, costs related to treatment and other services used are not taken into account. However, when estimating residents' costs, accommodation and nonaccommodation (package of care) costs should be estimated. The package of care should be estimated using the bottom-up approach to consider individual variations. In this chapter we present only accommodation costs.

After determining the unit of cost for all cost components, the next step is to estimate the cost of each component based on consumption. The bottom-up approach is the most accurate method to verify individual consumption of a service, by calculating the product of the quantity consumed and the unit costs. In Table 16.3, costs for variable consumption of services per residential service per month, and the full costs, are described

Table 16.3 Costs per residential service per month (in BRL$[a])

Residence region	Full costs (per month)	Capital costs		Human resources	Food and supplies	House repairs	Utility services	Transport	Overhead
		Equipment	Rent						
N1	26,159.05	751.51	1,654.05	16,395.44	2,452.90	1,033.35	1,165.00	1,054.00	1,652.80
N2	26,939.09	751.51	3,264.13	16,396.44	2,073.91	890.00	933.00	917.00	1,713.14
N3	29,246.50	751.51	3,200.00	18,277.26	2,298.57	890.00	1,018.00	947.00	1,864.16
N4	30,296.70	751.51	3,550.00	18,277.26	2,643.59	1,087.39	1,002.00	1,065.00	1,919.95
N5	30,693.62	751.51	3,000.00	18,277.26	2,632.53	1,066.00	1,963.00	1,056.00	1,947.32
CW1	26,567.48	751.51	1,719.58	16,395.44	2,696.41	1,020.07	1,262.08	1,042.00	1,680.39
CW2	26,965.18	751.51	3,344.97	16,395.44	2,307.59	890.00	643.76	917.00	1,714.91
CW3	28,131.40	751.51	3,308.00	16,395.44	2,273.70	906.80	1,583.84	1,122.00	1,790.11
CW4	29,933.27	751.51	4,631.41	16,395.44	2,591.22	900.00	1,214.42	980.00	1,869.17
CW5	29,392.31	751.51	5,000.00	16,395.44	2,237.70	959.90	1,054.27	1,122.00	1,871.48
SE1	28,865.99	751.51	2,170.33	18,277.26	2,393.30	895.80	1,538.44	1,004.00	1,835.35
SE2	29,153.17	751.51	2,384.57	18,277.26	2,568.36	890.00	1,347.82	1,075.60	1,858.05
SE3	28,379.06	751.51	3,308.15	18,277.26	2,208.78	890.00	1,023.93	1,046.60	1,872.83
SE4	29,997.95	751.51	3,600.00	18,277.26	2,445.19	897.20	1,122.13	989.20	1,915.46
SE5	30,946.79	751.51	3,905.48	18,277.26	2,177.95	890.00	1,927.10	1,042.00	1,975.49
S1	31,137.85	751.51	2,605.00	18,823.00	2,835.00	1,392.00	1,148.00	1,344.00	2,249.35
S2	33,971.91	751.51	3,787.00	19,839.00	3,624.00	1,076.00	1,060.00	1,344.00	2,490.400
E1	26,211.08	751.51	1,800.00	16,395.44	2,591.22	890.00	1,144.24	973.00	1,665.67
E2	26,577.67	751.51	1,900.00	16,395.44	2,930.30	890.00	1,030.28	967.00	1,713.14
E3	27,637.87	751.51	2,800.00	16,395.44	2,660.00	890.00	1,215.00	1,167.00	1,758.92

[a]US$1 = BRL$1.55 as of July 1st, 2011. The Brazilian per capita income in 2011 was BRL$22,157.00.
N North region in São Paulo city, *CW* Center West, *E* East, *SW* Southwest, *SE* Southeast

in Brazilian reals. Medication costs were not included in this cost analysis because medications were provided in outpatient care and were estimated as part of nonaccommodation costs (package of care per resident).

The full costs of residential services varied from BRL$26,159.05 to BRL$33,971.91 for a 1-month period in 2011. The main component of costs was human resources, corresponding almost to 61.4% of the total costs (Table 16.2). Capital costs accounted for 13.4%. Among revenue costs, food costs accounted for almost 9%, and transport and house repair together accounted for 6.4% of total costs, though this amount corresponded to expenditures rather than the real cost because individual consumption was not available. Therefore, monthly full accommodation costs per capita were, on average, BRL$3610.87, considering 160 people living in residential services.

16.6 Discussion

Our results showed than the full costs for residential services were, on average, BRL$28,380.00 per month. The main component of cost was staff, similar to the main cost components found in the literature in other countries [14, 16, 17, 21]. Of interest, these costs might be overestimated because accurate data on the consumption of transport and house repairs were not available, and costs were based on fixed agreements with third parties. These costs corresponded to 6% of total costs for residential services, and it is likely that consumption of such services is lower than monthly expenditures assume.

Therefore, accommodation costs per resident per month were, on average, BRL$3610.00. To put this into perspective, when extrapolating this amount for a whole year (without taking into account inflation and other variations in costs), annual costs per resident would roughly reach up to approximately BRL$42,570.00. This means that one resident living in a residential service would cost, in terms of accommodation, an average of 2.1 Brazilian income per capita in the year of 2011, without considering the package of care (other healthcare services, medications, exams, and so on). Although nonaccommodation costs are not described in this chapter, our data show that residential services correspond to 90% of the full package of care (accommodation plus nonaccommodation costs).

Limitations

Some methodological limitations exist regarding estimation of costs in this study. Because costing methods require accounting for all cost differences among services and all issues related to time, this study presents one limitation regarding the accuracy of measuring consumption of items such as transportation, house repairs, and equipment and furniture. Expenditures for car leases are likely greater than the real costs because the usage of such service was much smaller than car availability. Similarly, we considered fixed expenditures for house repairs and did not collect the real costs of repairs made because of a lack of information. Yet, furniture and equipment were standardized and bought by the same mayor's agency, during the same period of time; therefore we considered the same costs for all services. Moreover, the costs of training caregivers at the start-up of residential services were not available, and the lack of accurate information hindered any estimation of costs in this case. Another limitation was related to issue of time; that is, all data collected for cost estimation were based on 1 month, and we did not take into account whether these costs varied substantially over time. However, variable costs such as utilities, food, and supplies accounted for a tiny part of the total costs of residential services.

16.7 Conclusion

The majority of economic evaluation studies in the literature have not described costing methods in detail, especially in terms of costing methods applied to estimate full costs, revenue costs, and packages of care. Accommodation costs correspond to the largest portion of full costs in community mental healthcare. The lack of standardized methods, gold standards, and transparency in describing results jeopardize the accuracy of cost estimation and, as a result, the validity of results from economic evaluation studies. Cost estimations vary substantially regarding the inclusion of relevant components of costs, the discount factor applied (3–5%), capital cost estimations, lifetime use of equipment, currency, year when costs are estimated, unit cost estimation, and data collection period. Moreover, comparability among services is challenging because residential services vary enormously in terms of size, structure, and complexity of care delivery.

Key Messages

- Costs of residential services vary according to the level of complexity, local characteristics, and the health system framework.
- Six basic steps must be followed before estimating costs of residential services: delineation of the main question, identification of the perspective of the study, identification of components of costs, determination of data collection method and unit costs, and data collection.
- Human resources are the key element of the total costs for residential services, corresponding to more than 60% of the total accommodation costs.
- Costs of residential services might vary over the time and should be assessed regularly.

References

1. Macpherson R, Shepherd G, Edwards T. Supported accommodation for people with severe mental illness: a review. Adv Psychiatr Treat. 2004;10:180–8.
2. Lelliott P, Audini B, Knapp M, Chisholm D. The mental health residential care study: classification of facilities and description of residents. Br J Psychiatry. 1996;169(2):139–47.
3. Randolph FL, Lindenberg RE, Menn AZ. Residential facilities for the mentally ill: needs assessment and community planning. Community Ment Health J. 1986;22(2):77–93.
4. Mansell J, Beadle-Brown J. Deinstitutionalisation and community living: position statement of the comparative policy and practice special interest research group of the international association for the scientific study of intellectual disabilities. J Intellect Disabil Res. 2010;54(2):104–12.
5. The Community Living Research Project. Residential options for adults with developmental disabilities: quality and cost outcomes. Vancouver: The University of British Columbia; 2006.
6. Burns T, Knapp M, Catthy J, Healey A, Henderson J, Watt H, et al. Home treatment for mental health problems: a systematic review. Health Technol Assess. 2001;5(15):1–139.
7. Mansel J, Beadle-Brown J. Deinstitutionalisation and community living: position statement of the comparative policy and practice special interest research group of the international association for the scientific study of intellectual disabilities. J Intellect Disabil Res. 2010;54(2):104–12.
8. Hallam A, Knapp M, Jarbrink K, Netten A, Emerson E, Robertson J, et al. Costs of village community, residential campus and dispersed housing provision for people with intellectual disability. J Intellect Disabil Res. 2002;46(Pt 5):394–404.
9. De GG, Picardi A, Micciolo R, Falloon I, Fioritti A, Morosini P. Residential care in Italy. national survey of non-hospital facilities. Br J Psychiatry. 2002;181:220–5.
10. Beecham J, Knapp M, Mc Gilloway S, Kavanagh, Fenyo A, Donnell M, et al. Leaving hospital II: the cost-effectiveness of community care for former long-stay psychiatric hospital patients. J Ment Health. 1996;5(4):379–94.
11. Harkness J, Newman S, Salkever D. The cost-effectiveness of independent housing for the chronically mentally ill: do housing and neighborhood features matter? Health Serv Res. 2004;39(5):1341–60.
12. Knapp M, Beecham J, McDaid D, Matosevic T, Smith M. The economic consequences of deinstitutionalisation of mental health services: lessons from a systematic review of European experience. Health Soc Care Community. 2011;19(2):113–25.
13. Knapp M, Beecham J, Fenyo A, Hallam A. Community mental health care for former hospital in-patients. predicting costs from needs and diagnoses. Br J Psychiatry. 1995; Suppl(27):10–18.
14. Knapp M, Chisholm D, Astin J, Lelliott P, Audini B. The cost consequences of changing the hospital-community balance: the mental health residential care study. Psychol Med. 1997;27(3):681–92.
15. Dockrell JE, Gaskell GD, Normand C, Rehman H. An economic analysis of the resettlement of people with mild learning disabilities and challenging behaviour. Soc Sci Med. 1995;40(7):895–901.
16. Chisholm D, Knapp MR, Astin J, Lelliott P, Audini B. The mental health residential care study: predicting costs from resident characteristics. Br J Psychiatry. 1997;170:37–42.

17. Dickey B, Fisher W, Siegel C, Altaffer F, Azeni H. The cost and outcomes of community-based care for the seriously mentally ill. Health Serv Res. 1997;32(5):599–614.
18. Emerson E, Robertson J, Gregory N, Hatton C, Kessissoglou S, Hallam A, et al. Quality and costs of community-based residential supports, village communities, and residential campuses in the United Kingdom. Am J Ment Retard. 2000;105(2):81–102.
19. Felce D, Perry J, Romeo R, Robertson J, Meek A, Emerson E, et al. Outcomes and costs of community living: semi-independent living and fully staffed group homes. Am J Ment Retard. 2008;113(2):87–101.
20. Hallam A, Knapp M, Jarbrink K, Netten A, Emerson E, Robertson J, et al. Costs of village community, residential campus and dispersed housing provision for people with intellectual disability. J Intellect Disabil Res. 2002;46(Pt 5):394–404.
21. Amaddeo F, Grigoletti L, de GG, Picardi A, Santone G. Which factors affect the costs of psychiatric residential care? findings from the Italian PROGRES study. Acta Psychiatr Scand. 2007;115(2):132–41.
22. Rothbard AB, Schinnar AP, Hadley TP, Foley KA, Kuno E. Cost comparison of state hospital and community-based care for seriously mentally ill adults. Am J Psychiatry. 1998;155(4):523–9.
23. Walsh KK, Kastner TA, Green RG. Cost comparisons of community and institutional residential settings: historical review of selected research. Ment Retard. 2003;41(2):103–22.
24. Pijl YJ, Sytema S, Barels R, Wiersma D. Costs of deinstitutionalization in a rural catchment area in the Netherlands. Psychol Med. 2002;32(8):1435–43.
25. Mansell J, Knapp M, Beadle-Brown J, Beecham J. Deinstitutionalization and community living outcomes and costs: reports of European study. Volume 2: main report. Report No. 2. Canterbury: Tizard Centre, University of Kent; 2007.
26. McCartney PL. Does deinstitutionalization cost state mental health authorities more? Admin Pol Ment Health. 1994;21(6):479–86.
27. Knapp M, Beecham J, Koutsogeorgopoulou V, Hallam A, Fenyo A, Marks IM, et al. Service use and costs of home-based versus hospital-based care for people with serious mental illness. Br J Psychiatry. 1994;165(2):195–203.
28. Rothbard AB, Kuno E, Schinnar AP, Hadley TR, Turk R. Service utilization and cost of community care for discharged state hospital patients: a 3-year follow-up study. Am J Psychiatry. 1999;156(6):920–7.
29. Knapp M, Chisholm D, Astin J, Lelliott P, Audini B. The cost consequences of changing the hospital-community balance: the mental health residential care study. Psychol Med. 1997;27(3):681–92.
30. Salize HJ, Rossler W. The cost of comprehensive care of people with schizophrenia living in the community. a cost evaluation from a German catchment area. Br J Psychiatry. 1996;169(1):42–8.
31. Amaddeo F, Beecham J, Bonizzato P, Fenyo A, Tansella M, Knapp M. The costs of community-based psychiatric care for first-ever patients. a case register study. Psychol Med. 1998;28(1):173–83.
32. Glennerster H. The costs of hospital closure: reproviding services for the residents of Darenth Park hospital. Psychiatr Bull. 2011;14:140–3.
33. Rubin J. Cost measurement and cost data in mental health settings. Hosp Community Psychiatry. 1982;33(9):750–4.
34. Robertson J, Emerson E, Pinkney L, Caesar E, Felce D, Meek A, et al. Quality and costs of community-based residential supports for people with mental retardation and challenging behavior. Am J Ment Retard. 2004;109(4):332–44.
35. Reinharz D, Lesage AD, Contandriopoulos AP. Cost-effectiveness analysis of psychiatric deinstitutionalization. Can J Psychiatr. 2000;45(6):533–8.
36. Thomas KA, Rickwood D. Clinical and cost-effectiveness of acute and subacute residential mental health services: a systematic review. Psychiatr Serv. 2013;64(11):1140–9.
37. Drummond MF, Sculpher MJ, Torrance GW, BJ O'B, Stoddart GL. Methods for the economic evaluation of health care programmes. 3rd ed. Oxford: Oxford University Press; 2007.
38. Knapp M. The economic evaluation of mental health care. 1st ed. Brookfield: Ashgate Publishing Limited; 1995.

Quantifying Informal Care for Economic Evaluation in Mental Health

17

Helen Weatherly, Rita Faria, and Bernard van den Berg

Abstract

Informal caregivers make a substantial contribution to the care of people with mental health disorders, enabling them to continue living in the community. To provide care, individuals may reduce their paid working hours or leave their jobs, take less leisure time, incur out-of-pocket costs, and experience changes in their health and well-being. The value of this care is widely acknowledged but rarely quantified.

Based on an economic evaluation framework, it is possible to quantify the contribution of informal caregivers' time by measuring and valuing the care they offer. In practice, few economic evaluations include informal care, and this may reflect that most studies are undertaken from the perspective of a decision maker allocating funding within the public sector. Cost-effectiveness results would differ if caregivers were included, with implications for decision making. This chapter reviews methods to measure informal care time, as well as monetary and nonmonetary approaches to quantifying informal care. Little guidance is available about whether or how to include informal care contributions within economic evaluations. This chapter suggests that it might be important to reflect informal care contributions when the intervention being evaluated is for the caregiver, when the intervention is for the care recipient but with effects on the caregiver, and in order to test the cost-effectiveness of targeting services, with different levels of access to more formal paid care. Formal guidance on when and how to include informal care in economic evaluations would aid greater consistency in the methods applied across evaluations and therefore enhance comparability across evaluations.

H. Weatherly (✉) • R. Faria
Centre for Health Economics, Heslington Road, University of York, York, UK
e-mail: helen.weatherly@york.ac.uk; rita.nevesdefaria@york.ac.uk

B. van den Berg (✉)
Faculty of Economics and Business, University of Groningen, Nettelbosje 2, Groningen, 9747 AE Netherlands
e-mail: bernard.van.den.berg@rug.nl

D. Razzouk (ed.), *Mental Health Economics*, DOI 10.1007/978-3-319-55266-8_17

Key Points Summary

- Informal caregivers provide substantial input into the care of people with mental health disorders, enabling them to continue living in the community.
- Few economic evaluations quantify informal care, which means that the contribution and impact on caregivers is not considered. Cost-effectiveness results would differ if they were included, with implications for decision making.
- Valuation of informal care contributions is essential when the intervention being evaluated is directly for the informal caregiver, for example, respite care for caregivers, but it can also be informative when the intervention is for the care recipient when there is an impact on the caregiver, or when access to care is being considered.
- A number of monetary and nonmonetary approaches are available to quantify informal care.
- Little guidance is available about whether and how to include informal care contributions within economic evaluations.

17.1 Introduction

Financial and human resources for mental health tend to focus on formal care provided by health and social care professionals [1], but informal care is widely acknowledged. In the United States, the 2015 National Family Caregiving Survey found that an estimated 17% of the adult population (39.8 million adults) provided informal care for another adult [2]. In the United Kingdom, the Office of National Statistics found that informal care time increased from 5.2 billion hours in 1995 to 7.6 billion hours in 2010, although the number of adults receiving informal care remained stable at approximately 2 million people [3].

In mental health in particular, the contribution of informal care can be substantial, and when undertaking caregiving, other activities and choices are given up. Caregivers may reduce their paid working hours or leave their jobs, take less leisure time, incur out-of-pocket costs, and experience changes in their health and well-being in order to provide care [4–9]. In schizophrenia, for example, a study in Spain found that informal caregivers were likely to care for over 70 hours a week [6]. In the United States, more informal care time was typically used by older people with depression compared with those with no depressive symptoms, averaging 4.3–6.0 and 2.9 h/week, respectively, varying by severity of symptoms [7]. Wimo et al. [9] estimated the hours per day that informal caregivers assisted people with dementia worldwide. On average, 3.6 h/day were spent on activities of daily living, including personal care, shopping, food preparation, and transport, and 2.6 h/day on supervision.

Informal care provision can affect caregiver health, including physical health and injury, as well as mental health and well-being. For example, Schultz and Beach [10] reported that caring increased mortality risk, although this was only significant for caregivers with mental or emotional strain. Pinquart and Sörensen [11] conducted a meta-analysis of studies of the differences between caregivers and noncaregivers in perceived stress, depression, general subjective well-being, physical health, and self-efficacy. They found that caregivers were more likely to report depression and poorer self-efficacy and general subjective well-being, particularly those providing care of people with dementia. In another meta-analysis, Vitaliano et al. [12] found that caregivers were at greater risk of having health problems. Hughes et al. [13] found that caring may have a direct effect on caregivers' health-related quality of life (HRQoL). Furthermore, there is evidence that the burden of informal care increases the risk of having health problems [12, 14]. Typically, the impact of providing informal care on caregivers' health and well-being is intensified in older, poorer, and more isolated caregivers [15].

Most economic evaluations that include informal care quantify their contribution as a cost within the analysis [16]. As noted above, however, the provision of informal care also has consequences for caregiver health and well-being, and this could be quantified as an outcome or (dis) benefit within the analysis. Although informal caregivers' contributions are widely recognized, many economic evaluation studies, including those in mental health, do not reflect this contribution in the analysis. This might be because of the lack of prescriptive guidance on how to include informal care in an economic evaluation. Also, most studies are undertaken from the perspective of a decision maker allocating funding within the public sector. Two recent reviews examined whether and how applied economic evaluations have included informal care [17, 18]. Both concluded that informal care is rarely and inconsistently included in economic evaluation studies, and the impact of its inclusion may differ by context, intervention, and disease [17]. The inclusion of informal care costs can change results.

Many jurisdictions are moving toward supporting care in the community whereby informal caregivers make a greater contribution to the overall level of care. This might result in a shift in the use of resources from a reduction in use of public services and greater consequences for informal caregivers. In general, it might be important to reflect informal caregivers' contributions when the intervention being evaluated is for the caregiver (e.g., caregiver support), when the intervention is for the care recipient but with impacts on the caregiver, and in order to test the cost-effectiveness of targeting services with different levels of access to more formal input.

This chapter provides an overview of the methods available to analysts to quantify informal care for use in economic evaluation. It starts by discussing the concept of informal care and identifying what counts as care (Sect. 17.2). It then describes the methods for measuring informal care as a time input (Sect. 17.3), and for valuing informal care time in monetary terms (Sect. 17.4). It discusses the measurement and valuation of informal care in terms of (dis)benefits (Sect. 17.5). The chapter concludes by discussing the implications of quantifying informal care in economic evaluations.

17.2 Conceptualization of Informal Care

Informal caregivers are a major nonmarket contributor to healthcare programs, providing care to individuals who might not be able to manage in the community without them. Table 17.1 reports a few definitions. Informal care may be provided by children and adults, and it may be provided by one or more people who may or may not live with the care recipient. Informal care can be very heterogeneous. Examples of tasks that informal caregivers might undertake include personal care such as washing and dressing, domestic tasks such as cooking and cleaning, administrative tasks such as organizing finances and coordinating care, and assisting the care recipient to be involved in the community and leisure activities.

Table 17.1 Definitions of informal care

Definition	Source
A nonmarket or quasi-market commodity consisting of heterogeneous tasks produced unpaid or paid (receiving some nominal payment or state benefits) and provided by one or more of the social network of the care recipient (relatives, friends, or volunteers)	Van den Berg et al. [20]
Unpaid care to a relative or friend 18 years or older to help them take care of themselves. This may include helping with personal needs or household chores. It might be managing a person's finances, arranging for outside services, or visiting regularly to see how they are doing. This adult need not live with you	U.S. National Family Caregiving Survey [2]
Any help received either from members of one's own household or from members of other households	U.K. Office for National Statistics [3]
An adult who provides or intends to provide care for another adult [unless] it is under or by virtue of a contract or as voluntary work	U.K. government [21]
A person, such as a family member, friend or neighbor, who provides regular and sustained care and assistance to the person requiring support	Australian government [22]

In middle- and low-income countries, informal care might also include more medically related tasks, as identified by Riewpaiboon et al. [19]. Care typically is unpaid; however, some caregivers may receive a nominal payment, and therefore, ideally, definitions should avoid restricting informal care to unpaid care [21].

Some tasks may involve "joint production" [20] whereby informal caregivers undertake other beneficial, nonmarketed tasks concurrently. For example, they may be responsible for cooking but may also benefit from it if the meal is shared. The caregiver may accompany the care recipient in leisure activities, and in doing so also enjoy the activities. The caregiver may be sleeping but still aware of their supervisory role, which may be called for by the care recipient. This has implications for quantifying the time a caregiver spends on these tasks, and the estimates obtained can differ considerably depending on how such questions are asked.

Another consideration is that a care recipient may receive care from numerous people such as family members, friends, and volunteers, especially over the long term. Within a research study, however, it may not be practical to collect data on all informal care provided. Furthermore, the degree to which a caring task might affect the caregiver might be influenced by the duration of time over which the care is provided, the frequency of care, and the type of task undertaken.

To date, no formal guidance about what counts as care is available; therefore analysts should frame their analyses by specifying what they are counting as informal care and justifying the appropriateness of its inclusion. The transparency of the analysis is enhanced if details are provided regarding the specific organizational and cultural contexts in which the care takes place, such as the way the health and long-term care systems are organized. By making these considerations explicit, the methods used to quantify informal care are clearer and more amenable to scrutiny. In turn, clarity in methods should enhance transparency in decision making, based on an economic evaluation framework, and to enhance the comparability of findings across studies.

17.3 Measuring Informal Care Time

Once the informal care tasks are identified, the time spent on these tasks can be measured. Four approaches for doing so are summarized next.

17.3.1 Time Diary Method

This method requires the caregiver to indicate, often at multiple time points, all the caring activities they undertake, as well as the time required, for a specified period of time. Examples of this method are described by Van den Berg and Spauwen [23] and Goossens et al. [24].

The time diary method is considered the gold standard because it supports systematic data collection. By asking respondents to complete the diary close to the time activities take place, it might also reduce issues associated with recall bias. If a caregiver undertakes more than one activity at a time, this can be specified to take account of joint production. There is no consensus, however, about how to account for joint production when measuring time. The diary method can be time-consuming to report and can affect time spent caring, which could affect compliance.

17.3.2 Recall/Stylized Questionnaire Method

This method is the most commonly used approach to time measurement. Caregivers may be asked to recall the amount of time that was spent on a particular caring activity and the frequency of the activity given a specified time frame, such as last week or the previous day. Van den Berg and Spauwen [21] compared this method with the time diary method and found that this approach is less time-consuming, which might enhance compliance; however, there may be more recall bias as caregivers try to remember past activities [23]. An example of a recall questionnaire that measures caregiver time is the Caregiver Activity Survey [25, 26]. It measures time spent caring for people with Alzheimer disease in the previous

24 h based on six activities: communication, transportation, eating, dressing, appearance, and supervision. Hassink and Van den Berg [27] showed that informal care tasks can be shifted within and across days; if so, the data collection time should be sufficiently long enough to get an accurate picture of informal care provision.

17.3.3 Experience Sampling/Beeper/Buzzer Method

Experience sampling can be used to alert caregivers to record their caring activities and time spent on them as soon as they receive a signal from an electronic device. The intervals at which signals are sent might be set at random, over a defined period of time. The method is less prone to recall bias than the previous two methods given that caregivers record the current caring task(s); however, it can intrude in a caregiver's daily life, which might reduce compliance and be more costly to perform, including the cost of the electronic devices. To our knowledge, this method had not yet been applied to measure informal care or tasks [3].

17.3.4 Direct Observation/Continuous Observation/Outsider Method

This method involves an independent observer recording activities undertaken by the caregiver. While it is potentially very accurate, considerable amounts of observer time might be required, with resource and cost implications. In addition, caregivers may find direct observation intrusive. We are not aware of studies using this approach to measure informal care tasks or time.

17.4 Valuing Informal Care in Monetary Terms

Once informal care time is measured, this time can be valued in monetary terms. Time spent on informal care is multiplied by the value of that time, for example, the value per hour of informal care. This multiplication is called valuing informal care in monetary terms. The monetary value of informal care can be included in the cost side of an economic evaluation. It is important to note, though, that the majority of the methods presented next value not just the costs of informal care but also the consequences of informal care, in monetary terms, from the perspective of the caregiver.

17.4.1 Discrete Choice Experiment/Conjoint Measurement/Conjoint Analysis

Discrete choice experiment (DCE) is used to elicit the relative value caregivers place on different scenarios presented to them. A few studies in the published literature value informal care using this approach [28, 29]. For example, Mentzakis et al. [29] used DCE to value informal care tasks by including an attribute for the money required as compensation per hour for the care the caregivers provided. Attributes comprised different levels of personal care, supervision, household tasks, formal care, and monetary compensation [29]. Respondents were faced with a number of choice sets, each containing two caring scenarios, from which they were asked to choose their preferred option from a third-person perspective. This method can be cognitively burdensome and compliance can be an issue.

17.4.2 Contingent Valuation

Two main approaches to contingent valuation (CV) are relevant, that is, (a) the minimum monetary amount the caregiver is willing to accept to compensate for supplying more care, or (b) the maximum they are willing to pay for a reduction in caring activities. Adapted from Van den Berg et al. [30], a willingness to accept question could be, "Suppose your care recipient needs 1 hour of extra care per week and the government compensates you for this. What is the minimum amount of money you would want to receive from the government net of taxes to provide this additional hour of care?" An example of a willingness to pay question might be, "Suppose there is a possibility for you to provide 1 hour less informal care per week. Someone else will replace you, so the total amount of care for the care recipient remains the same. What is the maximum amount of money you would want to pay in order that someone else takes over this hour of care?"

A number of studies in the published literature have used CV to value informal care [30–34]. When applying CV questions to monetarily value informal care, it can be beneficial to avoid asking caregivers to imagine they get paid by their care recipient, particularly as caregivers are unlikely to consider their caring role in terms of a monetary value because money may have low importance for caregivers, and these issues may result in noncompliance [35]. To overcome this issue, CV questions could be framed by asking caregivers to imagine that the government would compensate them using a willingness-to-accept approach [36] (see Chap. 4). In a subsequent article, Van den Berg et al. [30] applied the willingness-to-pay and willingness-to-accept approaches to the same issue, and the results from both analyses were similar. This finding is not consistent with much of the literature using the CV method in health economics and environmental economics, suggesting that willingness-to-accept results tend to be higher than willingness-to-pay estimates, which is considered to be inconsistent with standard economic theory and therefore questions the validity of the CV method. Van den Berg et al. suggested that while there might be disparity in these estimates in something as abstract as, for example, the environment, in informal care, time spent on care is likely to be a familiar concept to caregivers, who are therefore in a strong position to value it.

17.4.3 Proxy Good Method/ Replacement Cost Method

The proxy good method values informal care time at the price of a close substitute activity. Examples of this are given in Table 17.2. The wage of a cleaner or housekeeper might be used for time spent on domestic duties, whereas the wage of a formal/paid caregiver may be appropriate for personal care activities. This approach requires information on the activity undertaken, the duration of the activity, and proxy values for each substitute activity. It assumes that the work the replacement employee undertakes and the wage they obtain is a perfect substitute for the activity the caregiver performs. It also assumes that the price/wage in the marketplace for the replacement employee appropriately reflects value.

Table 17.2 Examples of applied economic evaluations in mental health using the proxy good method to monetarily value informal care time

Disease area	Country	Proxy good	Monetary values as reported (financial year)	Study
Depression	India	Unskilled, manual labor or housework	100 rupees/day; financial year not given Data collection was completed in 1999	Patel et al. [37]
Dementia	United States	Home care aide	$8.12/h; financial year not given Data collection was completed in 2004	Nichols et al. [38]
Dementia	The Netherlands	Cleaner	$12/h; financial year not given Data collection was completed in 2005	Graff et al. [39]

Table 17.3 Examples of the opportunity cost method of valuing informal care time used in economic evaluations in mental health

Disease area	Country	Source	Unit cost reported (financial year)	Study
Substance misuse	United States	Average wage of people of the same sex and similar age as the caregiver	Not reported	Clark et al. [40]
Dementia	United Kingdom	Minimum wage	£5.30/h (2007)	Getsios et al. [41]
Depression	Germany	Average wage	€18/h (2008)	Egger et al. [42]

17.4.4 Opportunity Cost Method

This approach values informal care as the income that the caregiver would have received had they not spent time caring. Forgone income would be the current wage of the caregiver if employed, their past wage if they used to work but are not currently employed, or the wage of people with similar sociodemographic characteristics if they have never worked. The value of children and young people's care provision is less clear, and the opportunity cost of time spent on caring now could reduce time spent on gaining an education, with possible future implications for career options.

The opportunity cost method results in different values for caregiver time among caregivers with different wages and earning capacity. Because time is spent on other activities, such as leisure, it is not clear that the time spent on caring, which replaces leisure, has the same marginal value. The wage rate used should reflect the perspective of the analysis, so from a societal perspective, the gross wage rate would be appropriate to reflect the opportunity cost to society, whereas from a caregiver perspective, the net wage rate would be appropriate. Table 17.3 reports examples of the opportunity cost method of valuing informal care time used in economic evaluations in mental health.

17.4.5 Well-being Valuation Method

The well-being valuation method uses regression analysis to calculate the monetary value of informal care. It estimates the caregiver's subjective well-being as a function of time spent providing informal care and of income, among other things. An example involves asking about the caregiver's level of satisfaction with their life in general, on a scale of 1 to 10, with 1 meaning that they are completely dissatisfied and 10 meaning they are completely satisfied. It is also necessary to collect information on informal care time and on income. Other information may be collected, such as the relationship to the care recipient and the presence of other caregivers. A monetary value for caregiver input is calculated as the regression coefficient of informal care time divided by the regression coefficient of income, which derives the marginal rate of substitution between the two. This approach was taken by Van den Berg and Ferrer-i-Carbonell [43] and Van den Berg et al. [44] to establish how much monetary compensation a caregiver would require to have the same level of life satisfaction (subjective well-being) as without caregiving.

17.5 Nonmonetary Valuation of Informal Care

Informal care can also be included as an outcome component of the cost-effectiveness of an intervention, either as an effectiveness measure or as a preference-based measure. Effectiveness measures in informal care include both objective and subjective measures of burden, and measures of feelings about caring, coping, and distress. In practice, burden does not include valuation, so it is not reviewed in the section below; however, it has been used as an outcome instrument in many studies and is therefore worth noting. It focuses on quantifying physical, psychological, social, and financial aspects of caring and traditionally focuses on negative aspects of caring, but there have been attempts to incorporate more positive benefits, for example, the Caregiver Reaction Assessment [45] and process utility [46]. Harvey et al. [47] reviewed instruments developed to measure outcomes for caregivers of people with mental health problems. Hastrup et al. [48], using the Caregiver Strain Index, showed that providing informal care to people with mental illness – and especially the combination of caring for people with mental and somatic illnesses – resulted in more burden compared with providing informal care to people with only somatic illness.

In economic evaluation, the outcome measure should ideally reflect the preference of individuals for one situation over another, and how they are willing to trade-off some characteristics over others. For this reason, this section focuses on preference-based measures that are specific to informal caregivers. Nonetheless, it is important to emphasize that generic preference-based measures, namely, HRQoL measures such as the EuroQol five-dimension questionnaire (EQ-5D), alone or in combination with length of life in quality-adjusted life years (QALYs), are relevant and can be appropriate to capture the impact of informal care on caregivers. Some relatively new caregiver-specific measures have been designed, such as the Adult Social Care Outcomes Toolkit (ASCOT). Caregiver-specific measures are not reviewed further here because, to date, preference weights/valuations are not currently available, but these may be used to generate social care–related quality of life estimates in the future. In addition, caregiver burden, stress, and coping type are not reviewed because they are not based on preferences; however, they can be used in cost-effectiveness analyses to determine the optimal allocation of a budget aiming to reduce caregiver burden. Finally, process (dis)utility or the distinction between the positive and negative aspects of caring is not reviewed because it is often considered to be an interim outcome, such as a proxy value.

17.5.1 Informal Caregivers' Health-Related Quality of Life

The nonmonetary valuation of informal care could be based on HRQoL assessment. The HRQoL of caregivers can be assessed using QALYs based on generic HRQoL instruments, including the EQ-5D and the SF-6D health state descriptors, and converted to HRQoL weights (see Chap. 6). Different instruments have different valuation sets based on the visual analog scale (VAS), the time-trade off (TTO), and the standard gamble (SG) approaches (see Chap. 3). VAS and TTO are less complex cognitively; however, because the SG considers uncertainty, it is considered to be the gold standard approach to valuation (see Chap. 3). Most use the valuations of a representative sample of the general population to value health states.

Table 17.4 reports examples of applied economic evaluation studies that have used generic preference-based measures of HRQoL to capture the impact of informal care on caregivers. The advantage of using generic measures is that they ensure comparability across disease areas.

17.5.2 Caregiver-Related Quality of Life

Mohide et al. [52] were the first researchers to develop the concept of caregiver-related quality of life (CRQoL) based on the belief that at that time no instrument was available to value the full contributions of caregivers to the elderly. The dimensions selected for CRQoL were based on the literature and expert advice, and comprised asking whether in caring situations the caregiver feels physically well and energetic, feels happy and free from worry or frustration, has sufficient time to socialize with family and friends, gets an adequate amount of undisturbed sleep, and gets along well with the person being cared for. The weights or utilities were calculated using time equivalence scales and a TTO approach to valuation using a sample of family caregivers and relatives of well older people. In the TTO exercise, caregivers were asked to indicate the number of years of future life in the burdened state that they would be willing to exchange for a year in the ideal state [52].

17.5.2.1 Carer Experience Scale

The Carer Experience Scale (CES) measures CRQoL in a profile comprising six dimensions including activities outside caring, support from

Table 17.4 Examples of studies using generic preference-based HRQoL measures to capture the impact of informal care

Disease area	Country	Measure	Study
Dementia	United Kingdom	EQ-5D	Livingston et al. [49]
Dementia	United Kingdom	EQ-5D	Woods et al. [50]
Dementia	The Netherlands	EQ-5D	Meeuwsen et al [51]

family and friends, assistance from organizations and the government, fulfillment from caring, control over caring, and getting along with the care recipient. These were selected in a metaethnography, used to synthesize qualitative studies, each with three levels (few/a little, some, a lot/most) [53, 54]. A preference-based tariff is available for the CES using profile best-worst scaling. In profile best-worst scaling, respondents are asked to choose the most desirable (best) attribute and the least desirable (worst) attribute from the attributes in a profile. These are the pair of attributes with the maximum difference in well-being between them. The dimensions provide a profile of the caregiver that can be scored on a scale of 0 to 100 and represents the CRQoL. To calculate the score for an individual, the analyst starts from a score of zero and adds up the tariff per category for all CES dimensions.

17.5.2.2 CarerQol

The CarerQol instrument consists of seven dimensions to measure informal caregiver quality of life (CarerQol 7D). The instrument also includes a VAS to quantify the caregiver's happiness (the CarerQol VAS). The dimensions comprise fulfillment with care tasks, relational problems with care recipient, the caregiver's own mental health problems, problems combining care tasks with daily activities, financial problems due to care tasks, support when required, and the caregiver's own physical health problems. An interaction term was included to adjust for no mental health problems and no physical health problems. The dimensions were selected from a literature review and tested in a pilot study, then scored over three levels (none, some, a lot) [55]. The CarerQol 7D can be converted into a preference-based score using a recently developed tariff [56]. To calculate the score for an individual, the analyst must start from a score of zero and add up the tariff per category across all of the CarerQoL 7D dimensions. A tariff was calculated from a DCE, where respondents were asked to choose their preferred situation among a set of two informal care situations, which were described using the CarerQol 7D.

17.6 Discussion

Informal caregivers are an essential component in the care of people with mental health disorders. Using an economic evaluation framework, informal care provision in mental health can be incorporated in the analysis of monetary and nonmonetary values. Monetary approaches to include informal care are the opportunity cost method, the proxy good method, the CV method, DCEs, and the well-being valuation method. Nonmonetary approaches are HRQoL and CRQoL.

The opportunity cost and the proxy good methods involve identifying informal care tasks, measuring the time spent on them, and valuing this time using the relevant monetary valuation method. Methods to measure time include diary, recall, experience sampling, and direct observation.

Informal care can be incorporated as a consequence component using an effectiveness measure such as measures of caregiver burden, or valuation methods like HRQoL or CRQoL. An example of the HRQoL is the EQ-5D, and examples of CRQoL instruments include the CES and the CarerQol.

It also is possible to apply the opportunity cost or the proxy good approaches, focusing as they do on foregone wages and market substitutes, and complement them by measuring health- and care-related quality of life using nonmonetary valuation methods such as HRQoL or CRQoL; however, this could result in double counting. For example, combining the opportunity cost method and the EQ-5D could generate an overestimate, as the wages of the informal caregiver might also be captured in the QALYs of the EQ-5D, given there may be an effect on the usual activities domain.

The CV method, DCEs, and the well-being method evaluate how individuals trade off income with the provision of informal care. These methods assume that people take other factors – like their leisure time, health, and the health of the care recipient – into consideration when evaluating the trade-off between informal care and income. Therefore they capture the full impact of providing informal care on the caregiver. These methods should not be complemented by nonmonetary valuation methods to avoid double counting. The main advantage of these methods is that they capture the full impact of providing informal care in monetary terms, which allows the analyst to include them on the cost side of the economic evaluation.

Caution is required when comparing estimates obtained using different preference-based quality of life instruments. For instance, the CarerQol 7D uses an approach to valuation that is not anchored at zero death, unlike the EQ-5D, which means that the findings are valued differently to HRQoL weights. The implication of this is that the estimates cannot be compared or aggregated with health-based QALYs. Weatherly et al. [57] compared the domains of caregiver quality of life instruments. Although there is some overlap in the domains that are covered using different instruments, it would not be appropriate to aggregate preference-based measures calculated based on each of the instruments, as the domains that are covered differ across instruments. Aggregating outcomes can be a real issue in this area, and analysts need to avoid double counting them within their analyses. If the CRQoL instrument were to be used in a cost utility–type analysis (see Chap.r 6), it might be appropriate for use only as a replacement for a QALY when the interventions being compared focus on the caregiver, and when this was related to a budget that was earmarked and fixed for supporting caregivers.

There is increasing interest in the economic evaluation of social care interventions as an aid to decision-making. In 2013, for example, the National Institute for Health and Care Excellence was conferred the responsibility to offer quality assurance and guidance on interventions with a social care focus. In contrast to healthcare interventions, where the perspective on costs comprises healthcare and personal social services, social care interventions support a wider perspective [58]. This includes consideration of the costs falling on the public sector, including the National Health Service, personal social services, local authorities, and other public-sector agencies as appropriate; and non-public-sector funding, including family funding and the costs of informal care, which fall in the private sphere, if these contribute to outcomes [58]. In terms of outcomes, the guideline recommends that for social care interventions, effects on people to whom services are delivered (users, caregivers) might be included when relevant. In summary, the guideline acknowledges the potential contribution of informal caregivers without prescribing methods for measuring and valuing informal care.

HRQoL health-related quality of life, *QALY* quality-adjusted life year, *TTO* time trade-off

A few economic evaluations have been undertaken that quantify the impact of informal care. Some examples are reported in Table 17.5. The incorporation of informal care in economic evaluation remains an area of active research. There is no consensus on whether and how to incorporate informal care in economic evaluation. In principle, informal care should be included in any economic evaluation adopting a broad perspective, such as a societal perspective, which includes costs falling on patients' and their caregivers' budgets, among other relevant statutory and nonstatutory costs. It is worth noting that in practice there is no 'societal' decision maker in social care or more generally, so there is a separate question about the relevance of this perspective. If informal care is seen as a care input, however, arguably it could be included under a healthcare perspective because the formal care

Table 17.5 Examples of economic evaluations quantifying the impact of informal care

Author	Intervention focus	Instrument/s
Drummond et al. [59]	Support program for *caregivers* of elderly patients with dementia	HRQoL Caregiver Quality of Life Instrument (CQLI) estimates, valued using TTO to calculate QALYs Center for Epidemiological Studies Depression Scale (CES-D) State-trait Anxiety Inventory (STAI)
Gaugler et al. [60]	Evaluating community-based programs for *caregivers* to patients with dementia	Proxy good method Hourly rate per type of activity
Gustavsson et al.[32]	Estimating the value of *informal caregivers* in Alzheimer disease	Contingent valuation Caregivers' monthly willingness to pay for 1 h/day of a reduction in informal care
Meeuswen et al. [51]	Dementia follow-up care and impact on *caregivers and care recipients*	Proxy good and HRQoL Hourly wage of a cleaner EQ-5D-based QALYs combining care recipient and caregiver HRQoL weights
Wilson et al.) [61]	Befriending *caregivers* of people with dementia	Opportunity cost method Average gross hourly wage rate
Wu et al [62]	Cholinesterase inhibitors in mild to moderate dementia; *care recipient*	Contingent valuation: willingness to pay

HRQoL health-related quality of life, *QALY* quality-adjusted life year, *TTO* time trade-off

sector would need to substitute this care for individuals who do not have access to informal care. Furthermore, excluding the health effects and costs of providing informal care involves the issue that economic evaluations recommend funding interventions that shift costs to the social networks of care recipients [20].

The valuation of informal care in economic evaluation might also have consequences for the cost-effectiveness threshold. In an economic evaluation undertaken from a healthcare perspective, the threshold represents the health opportunity cost of healthcare expenditure – that is, the health foregone by investing in the new intervention, rather than by investing in the next best alternative intervention, and given a fixed health care budget. The downstream consequences of including informal care contributions require further investigation.

The approaches reviewed here focus on direct estimation of a caregiver's contribution. It is worth noting that Rowen et al. [63] recently estimated informal care usage associated with the health of the care recipient based on linking informal caregiver time, EQ-5D, and *International Classification of Disease* chapter. Regression analysis was used to predict informal care time; hence the impact of health technologies on informal caregiver time may be predicted via their impact on the care recipient's health. Informal care time can then be given a monetary value using the monetary valuation methods reviewed above.

Guidance on methods for quantifying the contribution of informal care tends to be less prescriptive than for other methods. The method most commonly used to measure and value informal care is the proxy good (also known as replacement cost) method; however, other methods are available, some of which are more technically advanced and may offer some advantages. This chapter provides an overview of available methods that could be used by analysts in the area of mental health to measure and value informal care for use in economic evaluation.

Key Messages

- Informal caregivers make a significant contribution to the care of people with mental health issues. Using an economic evaluation framework, many methods are available to value this contribution.
- Most economic evaluations that include informal care contributions tend to cost their time based on the proxy good (replacement) method; however, more advanced methods are available that might offer additional advantages.
- More prescriptive methods and guidance on how to value informal care contributions would aid greater consistency in methods applied across evaluations and therefore enhance comparability across evaluations.

References

1. WHO. Mental health atlas. Geneva: World Health Organisation; 2015.
2. Associates Ga. Caregiving in the US. Executive summary: national alliance for caregiving and the AARP Public Policy Institute; 2015 (Updated 9 Nov 16 http://www.caregiving.org/wp-content/uploads/2015/05/2015_CaregivingintheUS_Executive-Summary-June-4_WEB.pdf)
3. Foster R., Fender V. Valuing informal adultcare in the UK London: Office of National Statistics; 2013. Available from: http://webarchive.nationalarchives.gov.uk/20160105160709/http://www.ons.gov.uk/ons/dcp171766_315820.pdf.
4. Allegri RF, Butman J, Arizaga R, Machnicki G, Serrano C, Taragano F, et al. Economic impact of dementia in developing countries: an evaluation of costs of Alzheimer-type dementia in Argentina. Int Psychogeriatr. 2007;19(4):705–18.
5. Parabiaghi A, Lasalvia A, Bonetto C, Cristofalo D, Marrella G, Tan-sella M, et al. Predictors of changes in caregiving burden in people with schizophrenia: a 3-year follow-up study in a community mental health service. Acta Psychiatr Scand. 2007;116(Suppl. 437):66–76.
6. Aranda-Reneo I, Oliva-Moreno J, Vilaplana-Prieto C, Hidalgo-Vega Á, González-Domínguez A. Informal care of patients with schizophrenia. J Ment Health Policy Econ. 2013;16(3):99–108.
7. Langa KM, Valenstein MA, Fendrick AM, Kabeto MU, Vijan S. Extent and cost of informal caregiving for older Americans with symptoms of depression. Am J Psychiatr. 2004;161(5):857–63.
8. Van Asselt A, Dirksen CD, Arntz A, Severens JL. The cost of borderline personality disorder: societal cost of illness in BPD-patients. Eur Psychiatry. 2007;22(6):354–61.
9. Wimo A, Jönsson L, Bond J, Prince M, Winblad B, International AD. The worldwide economic impact of dementia 2010. Alzheimer's Demen. 2013;9(1):1–11. e3
10. Schulz R, Beach SR. Caregiving as a risk factor for mortality: the Caregiver Health Effects Study. JAMA. 1999;282(23):2215–9.
11. Pinquart M, Sörensen S. Differences between caregivers and noncaregivers in psychological health and physical health: a meta-analysis. Psychol Aging. 2003;18(2):250.
12. Vitaliano PP, Zhang J, Scanlan JM. Is caregiving hazardous to one's physical health? A meta-analysis. Psychol Bull. 2003;129(6):946.
13. Hughes SL, Giobbie-Hurder A, Weaver FM, Kubal JD, Henderson W. Relationship between caregiver burden and health-related quality of life. The Gerontologist. 1999;39(5):534–45.
14. Burton LC, Zdaniuk B, Schulz R, Jackson S, Hirsch C. Transitions in spousal caregiving. The Gerontologist. 2003;43(2):230–41.
15. Schulz R, Sherwood PR. Physical and mental health effects of family caregiving. Am J Nurs. 2008;108(9 Suppl):23.
16. Drummond MF, Sculpher MJ, Claxton K, Stoddart GL, Torrance GW. Methods for the economic evaluation of health care programmes. Oxford: Oxford University Press; 2015.
17. Krol M, Papenburg J, van Exel J. Does including informal care in economic evaluations matter? A systematic review of inclusion and impact of informal care in cost-effectiveness studies. PharmacoEconomics. 2015;33(2):123–35.
18. Goodrich K, Kaambwa B, Al-Janabi H. The inclusion of informal care in applied economic evaluation: a review. Value Health. 2012;15(6):975–81.
19. Riewpaiboon A, Riewpaiboon W, Ponsoongnern K, Van den Berg B. Economic valuation of informal care in Asia: a case study of care for disabled stroke survivors in Thailand. Soc Sci Med. 2009;69:648–53.
20. Van den Berg B, Brouwer WB, Koopmanschap MA. Economic valuation of informal care. Eur J Health Econ, formerly: HEPAC. 2004;5(1):36–45.
21. Care Act 2014, Part 1 Assessing needs – Section 10 (2014).
22. Australian Institute of Health and Welfare. Informal care 2016. Available from: http://www.aihw.gov.au/informal-care-ageing/.
23. Van den Berg B, Spauwen P. Measurement of informal care: an empirical study into the valid measurement of time spent on informal caregiving. Health Econ. 2006;15(5):447–60.

24. Goossens ME, Rutten-van Mölken MP, Vlaeyen JW, van der Linden SM. The cost diary: a method to measure direct and indirect costs in cost-effectiveness research. J Clin Epidemiol. 2000;53(7):688–95.
25. Davis KL, Marin DB, Kane R, Patrick D, Peskind ER, Raskind MA, et al. The Caregiver Activity Survey (CAS): development and validation of a new measure for caregivers of persons with Alzheimer's disease. Int J Geriatr Psychiatry. 1997;12(10):978–88.
26. Marin DB, Dugue M, Schmeidler J, Santoro J, Neugroschl J, Zaklad G, et al. The Caregiver Activity Survey (CAS): longitudinal validation of an instrument that measures time spent caregiving for individuals with Alzheimer's disease. Int J Geriatr Psychiatry. 2000;15(8):680–6.
27. Hassink WH, Van den Berg B. Time-bound opportunity costs of informal care: consequences for access to professional care, caregiver support, and labour supply estimates. Soc Sci Med. 2011;73(10):1508–16.
28. Van Den Berg B, Al M, Van Exel J, Koopmanschap M, Brouwer W. Economic valuation of informal care: conjoint analysis applied in a heterogeneous population of informal caregivers. Value Health. 2008;11(7):1041–50.
29. Mentzakis E, Ryan M, McNamee P. Using discrete choice experiments to value informal care tasks: exploring preference heterogeneity. Health Econ. 2011;20(8):930–44.
30. Van den Berg B, Bleichrodt H, Eeckhoudt L. The economic value of informal care: a study of informal caregivers' and patients' willingness to pay and willingness to accept for informal care. Health Econ. 2005;14(4):363–76.
31. Chiwaula LS, Revill P, Ford D, Nkhata TM, Hakim J, Kityo C, et al. Measuring and valuing informal care for economic evaluation of HIV/AIDS interventions: methods and application in Malawi. Value Health Reg Issues. 2016. http://dx.doi.org/10.1016/j.vhri.2016.08.002http://www.sciencedirect.com/science/article/pii/S2212109916300164. Accessed July 2016.
32. Gustavsson A, Jönsson L, McShane R, Boada M, Wimo A, Zbrozek AS. Willingness-to-pay for reductions in care need: estimating the value of informal care in Alzheimer's disease. Int J Geriatr Psychiatry. 2010;25(6):622–32.
33. Garrido-García S, Sánchez-Martínez F-I, Abellán-Perpiñán J-M, van Exel J. Monetary valuation of informal care based on carers' and noncarers' preferences. Value Health. 2015;18(6):832–40.
34. Gervès-Pinquié C, Bellanger MM, Ankri J. Willingness to pay for informal care in France: the value of funding support interventions for caregivers. Heal Econ Rev. 2014;4(1):1.
35. Smith K, Wright K. Informal care and economic appraisal: a discussion of possible methodological approaches. Health Econ. 1994;3(3):137–48.
36. Van den Berg B, Brouwer W, Van Exel J, Koopmanschap M. Economic valuation of informal care: the contingent valuation method applied in informal caregiving. Health Econ. 2005;14:169–83.
37. Patel V, Chisholm D, Rabe-Hesketh S, Dias-Saxena F, Andrew G, Mann A. Efficacy and cost-effectiveness of drug and psychological treatments for common mental disorders in general health care in Goa, India: a randomised, controlled trial. Lancet. 2003;361(9351):33–9.
38. Nichols LO, Chang C, Lummus A, Burns R, Martindale-Adams J, Graney MJ, et al. The cost-effectiveness of a behavior intervention with caregivers of patients with Alzheimer's disease. J Am Geriatr Soc. 2008;56(3):413–20.
39. Graff MJL, Adang EMM, Vernooij-Dassen MJ M, Dekker J, Jonsson L, Thijssen M, et al. Community occupational therapy for older patients with dementia and their care givers: cost effectiveness study. BMJ. 2008;336(7636):134–8.
40. Clark RE, Teague GB, Ricketts SK, Bush PW, Xie H, McGuire TG, et al. Cost-effectiveness of assertive community treatment versus standard case management for persons with co-occurring severe mental illness and substance use disorders. Health Serv Res. 1998;33(5 Pt 1):1285.
41. Getsios MD, Blume S, Ishak KJ, Maclaine GD. Cost effectiveness of donepezil in the treatment of mild to moderate Alzheimer's disease. PharmacoEconomics. 2010;28(5):411–27.
42. Egger N, Konnopka A, Beutel ME, Herpertz S, Hiller W, Hoyer J, et al. Short-term cost-effectiveness of psychodynamic therapy and cognitive-behavioral therapy in social anxiety disorder: results from the SOPHO-NET trial. J Affect Disord. 2015;180:21–8.
43. Van den Berg B, Ferrer-i-Carbonell A. Monetary valuation of informal care: the well-being valuation method. Health Econ. 2007;16(11):1227–44.
44. Van den Berg B, Fiebig DG, Hall J. Well-being losses due to care-giving. J Health Econ. 2014;35:123–31.
45. Deerken JTL, Mangan P, Yabroff R, Ingham J. Care for the caregivers: a review of self-report instruments developed to measure the burden, needs, and quality of life of informal caregivers. J Pain Symptom Manag. 2003;26:922–53.
46. Brouwer WB, van Exel NJA, van den Berg B, van den Bos GA, Koopmanschap MA. Process utility from providing informal care: the benefit of caring. Health Policy. 2005;74(1):85–99.
47. Harvey K, Catty J, Langman A, Winfield H, Clement S, Burns E, et al. A review of instruments developed to measure outcomes for carers of people with mental health problems. Acta Psychiatr Scand. 2008;117(3):164–76.
48. Hastrup LH, Van Den Berg B, Gyrd-Hansen D. Do informal caregivers in mental illness feel more burdened? A comparative study of mental versus somatic illnesses. Scand J Public Health. 2011;39(6):598–607.
49. Livingston G, Barber J, Rapaport P, Knapp M, Griffin M, King D, et al. Long-term clinical and cost-effectiveness of psychological intervention for family carers of people with dementia: a single-blind, randomised, controlled trial. Lancet Psychiatry. 2014;1(7):539–48.

50. Woods RT, Orrell M, Bruce E, Edwards RT, Hoare Z, Hounsome B, et al. REMCARE: pragmatic multi-centre randomised trial of reminiscence groups for people with dementia and their family carers: effectiveness and economic analysis. PLoS One. 2016;11(4):e0152843.
51. Meeuwsen E, Melis R, van der Aa G, Golüke-Willemse G, de Leest B, van Raak F, et al. Cost-effectiveness of one year dementia follow-up care by memory clinics or general practitioners: economic evaluation of a randomised controlled trial. PLoS One. 2013;8(11):e79797.
52. Mohide E, Torrance G, Streiner D, Pringle D, Gilbert R. Measuring the wellbeing of family caregivers using the time trade-off technique. J Clin Epidemiol. 1988;41:475–82.
53. Al-Janabi H, Coast J, Flynn TN. What do people value when they provide unpaid care for an older person? A meta-ethnography with interview follow-up. Soc Sci Med. 2008;67(1):111–21.
54. Al-Janabi H, Flynn TN, Coast J. Estimation of a preference-based carer experience scale. Med Decis Mak. 2011;31(3):458–68.
55. Brouwer W, Van Exel N, Van Gorp B, Redekop W. The CarerQol instrument: a new instrument to measure care-related quality of life of informal caregivers for use in economic evaluations. Qual Life Res. 2006;15(6):1005–21.
56. Hoefman RJ, van Exel J, Rose JM, Van De Wetering E, Brouwer WB. A discrete choice experiment to obtain a tariff for valuing informal care situations measured with the CarerQol instrument. Med Decis Mak. 2014;34(1):84–96.
57. Weatherly H, Faria R, Van Den Berg B. Valuing informal care for economic evaluation. In: Encyclopedia of health economics [Internet]. Vol. 1. San Diego: Elsevier. 2014. p. 459–67.
58. NICE. The social care guidance manual. http:\\www.nice.org.uk/process/pmg10: National Institute for Health and Care Excellence, 2016.
59. Drummond MFME, Tew M, Streiner DL, Pringle DM, Gilbert JR. Economic evaluation of a support program for caregivers of demented elderly. Int J Technol Assess Health Care. 1991;7(2):209–19.
60. Gaugler JZS, Townsend A, Parris Stephens MA, Greene R. Evaluating community based programs for dementia caregivers: the cost implications of adult day services. J Appl Gerentol. 2003;22(1):118–33.
61. Wilson E, Thalanany M, Shepstone L, Charlesworth G, Poland F, Harvey I, et al. Befriending carers of people with dementia: a cost utility analysis. Int J Geriatr Psychiatry. 2009;24(6):610–23.
62. Wu GLK, Herrmann N, Moosa S, Oh PI. The cost-benefit of cholinesterase inhibitors in mild to moderate dementia: a willingness-to-pay approach. CNS Drugs. 2003;17(14):1045–57.
63. Rowen D, Dixon S, Hernandez-Alava M, Mukuria C. Estimating informal care inputs associated with EQ-5D for use in economic evaluation. Eur J Health Econ. 2016;17:733–44.

Part III

Economic Evaluation of Treatment of Mental Disorders

Cost-Effectiveness of Interventions for Anxiety and Depressive Disorders

18

Cathrine Mihalopoulos and Mary Lou Chatterton

Abstract

Depression and anxiety disorders are highly prevalent diagnoses associated with significant morbidity and economic burden to healthcare systems and society. It is important to consider the costs and outcomes of the various pharmacologic and psychologic therapies available for the treatment and prevention of these diagnoses in order to provide services in the most efficient way. This chapter reviews the numerous economic evaluations previously undertaken to evaluate medications and the psychological (both in-person and Internet-based) and combination therapies used as treatments for diagnosed depression and anxiety. It also reviews the growing literature on interventions for the prevention of these conditions. A discussion of methodologic concerns is included to provide guidance for interpreting the existing evidence and as a basis for the design of future evaluations.

Key Points Summary

- What are depression and anxiety, and what disease burden is associated with both disorders?
- What are the cornerstones of treatment?
- What evidence of cost-effectiveness exists for the main treatments recommended for depression and anxiety?
- Some methodological considerations

C. Mihalopoulos (✉) • M.L. Chatterton
Deakin Health Economics, Centre for Population Health Research, School of Health and Social Development, Deakin University,
221 Burwood Hwy, Melbourne, VIC, Australia
e-mail: cathy.mihalopoulos@deakin.edu.au; m.chatterton@deakin.edu.au

D. Razzouk (ed.), *Mental Health Economics*, DOI 10.1007/978-3-319-55266-8_18

18.1 Introduction

18.1.1 What Are Depressive and Anxiety Disorders?

There is little doubt that depressive and anxiety disorders are highly prevalent among almost all countries worldwide, and that they result in a large disease burden and are associated with substantial economic costs. While most of us are familiar with the more minor symptoms of depression (e.g., sadness) and anxiety (e.g., feeling nervous), the focus of this chapter is on the more severe clinical manifestations of both anxiety and depression.

The most commonly used reference for the clinical diagnosis of mental disorders is the *Diagnostic and Statistical Manual of Mental Disorders* (DSM). The most recent edition of this manual, published in 2013 [1], states that major depressive disorder (MDD; sometimes also referred to as clinical depression) is characterized by episodes (lasting longer than 2 weeks) of five or more symptoms of depressed mood or loss of interest or pleasure (at least one of these must be present), along with at least four of the following: significant weight loss not associated with dieting (or marked reduction in appetite), insomnia (or hypersomnia), psychomotor retardation/agitation, fatigue, feelings of worthlessness (or excessive inappropriate guilt), diminished ability to think, and recurrent thoughts of death. Weight change and suicidal ideation do not need to be present every day. Furthermore, the symptoms must cause significant impairment in functioning and not be caused by the physiological effects of another disorder.

Anxiety disorders include disorders that share the main features of fear and anxiety. Fear is characterized by the emotional response to a threat, whether real or perceived, and anxiety is associated with the anticipation of a future threat. A number of anxiety disorders can be diagnosed, and common ones include separation anxiety disorder (quite common in children), phobias, social anxiety disorder, generalized anxiety disorder, panic disorder, and agoraphobia. The symptoms for each disorder usually should be present for around 6 months, although the symptoms for panic disorder must be present for 1 month. Like depression, to qualify for a diagnosis the symptoms must cause significant impairment in functioning.

Even though there has been a shift to the newer DSM-V for disorder classification, it is important to note that only minor changes have been made in the main diagnostic criteria for depressive and anxiety disorders [2]; therefore, prior scientific studies that used previous versions of the DSM (e.g., DSM-IV) to classify people with or without disorders are still relevant. While such disorders can occur on their own, considerable comorbid conditions occur (when people meet the criteria for both depression and anxiety) [3]. Such disorders are often also comorbid with substance use disorders [3].

18.1.2 What Are the Prevalence and Disease Burden of Depression and Anxiety Disorders?

Recent burden of disease studies have continued to show that mental disorders are highly prevalent and associated with considerable disease burden. The global point prevalence of MDD is reported to be 4.7% (95% confidence interval: 4.4–5.0%), the 12-month prevalence is 3.7% (2.7–5.0%), and the pooled annual incidence is 3.0% (2.4–3.8%) [4]. Of course, country-specific variations exist around these estimates; for example, in Africa, the point prevalence estimate is 6.6% (5.3–8.3) [4]. Anxiety disorders are associated with higher prevalence rates and are considered to be the most common mental disorder [5]. The global point prevalence of anxiety disorders is 7.3% (4.3–10.9%), ranging from 5.3% in African cultures to 10.4% in European/Anglo cultures [5]. Alarmingly, both depression and anxiety are associated with an increased risk of suicide [6].

More concerning is the considerable disease burden associated with both depression and anxiety. As discussed elsewhere in this book (see Chap. 25), mental and behavioral disorders are the leading cause of years lost to disability globally [7]. Within the mental disorders category, the leading cause of disease burden is depression (accounting for 40.5% of the disease burden), followed by anxiety disorders (accounting for 14.6% of the disease burden) [7]. The highest proportion of total disability-adjusted life years attributable to mental disorders accrued in young people aged 10–29 years of age, highlighting the fact that for many people the onset of such disorders occurs at a younger age [7]. Figure 18.1 highlights the age distributions of the main mental disorders included in the burden of disease studies.

While the "formal" measured disease burden of mental disorders strikingly highlights the substantial burden associated with such disorders, it is also important to note that many other individual and society-level implications are associated with the advent of depression and anxiety. For example, such disorders can have a negative impact on educational attainment, employment, and caregivers and span the entire life course; these have been well demonstrated in a number of epidemiological studies.

The economic costs associated with depression and anxiety are also formidable. For example, in a review of existing cost-of-illness studies for depression, Luppa et al. [8] found that the average annual direct treatment costs per person associated with depression ranged from $US1000–2500 (reference year 2003), whereas the indirect costs (largely associated with morbidity-related consequences such as reduced productivity) are higher at $2000–$3700. A recent study conducted in Australia used data from the most recent National Survey of Mental Health and Wellbeing found that highly prevalent disorders (including depression, anxiety, and substance use disorders) were associated with a total annual health sector cost of AU$1 billion(reference year 2013) and AU$12 billion in lost productivity (absenteeism and reduced workforce participation) [9]. While these numbers include respondents who abuse substances, it is important to note that substance abuse was a substantial comorbidity with anxiety and depression, and 81% of the total healthcare costs can be attributed to people with either MDD, anxiety disorder, or comorbid depression and anxiety (with no substance use disorder).

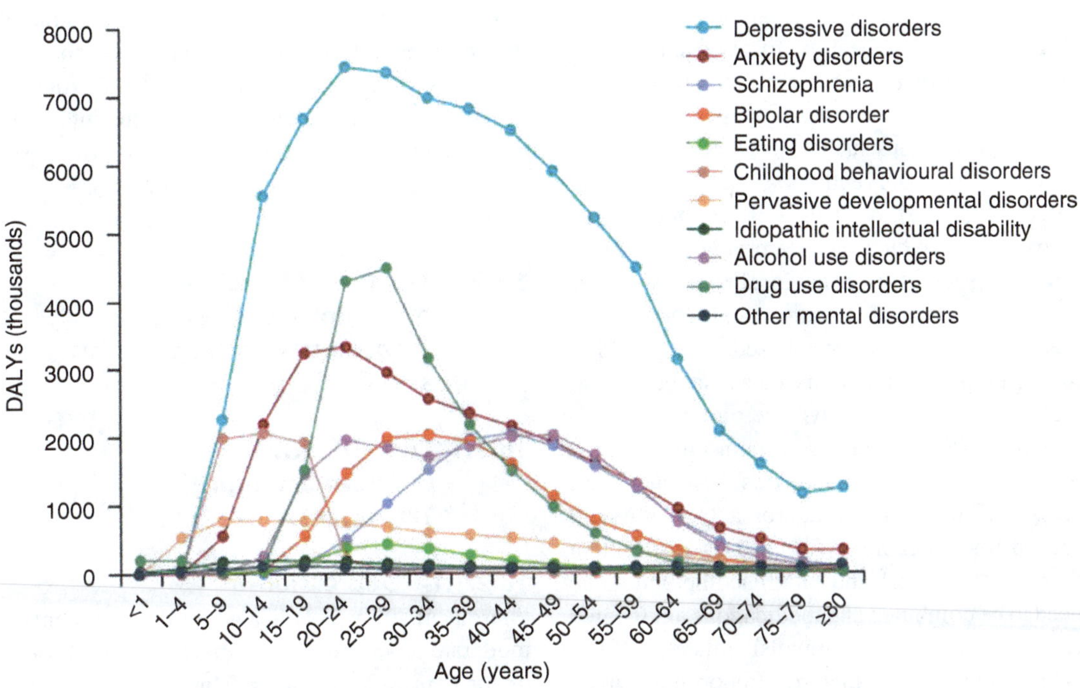

Fig. 18.1 Disability-adjusted life years (DALYs) for mental and substance use disorders in 2010, by age (Reproduced with permission from [7], p. 1580)

18.1.3 Treatments for Anxiety and Depressive Disorders

A number of effective, evidence-based psychosocial and pharmacological interventions exists for both depressive and anxiety disorders. It is beyond the scope of this chapter to review all these guidelines, but interested readers are referred to well-known organizations including, but certainly not limited to, the National Institute of Health and Care Excellence (NICE) in the United Kingdom (https://www.nice.org.uk/); the Royal Australian and New Zealand College of Psychiatrists in Australia (https://www.ranzcp.org/Home.aspx), and the Agency for Healthcare Research and Quality in the in the United States (http://www.ahrq.gov/).

Most of these guidelines cite a number of evidence-based psychosocial and pharmacological interventions for the treatment of both depression and anxiety disorders. An excellent recent publication regarding the treatment of MDD advocated a three-step approach to treatment [10]. The first step (called step 0) includes ensuring that any substances that can lower mood are tapered and ceased, that good sleep hygiene is initiated, and that healthy lifestyle choices are implemented (e.g., exercise). If step 0 is not sufficient, then step 1 includes more generic psychosocial interventions such as psychoeducation and low-intensity interventions (such as Internet-based education), as well as formulation-based interventions, which include psychological therapy (e.g., cognitive behavioral therapy), interpersonal therapy, acceptance and commitment therapy, and mindfulness-based therapy. Pharmacotherapy interventions can also be considered, including selective serotonin reuptake inhibitors (SSRIs) and serotonin-noradrenaline reuptake inhibitors (SNRIs) as first-line therapies, and tricyclic antidepressants (TCAs) as second-line therapies. If step 1 is insufficient, then psychological and pharmacotherapies may need to be combined and medications augmented. If all else fails, electroconvulsive therapy (ECT) is the final step of therapy. Importantly, many guidelines also differentiate between severities of illness, stipulating that pharmacotherapies and intensive psychological treatments should be reserved for more severe cases of depression. A recent review of the published controlled trials of stepped care approaches found that there have been 14 studies of stepped care interventions in depression published, and an overall pooled effect size of 0.34 (Cohen *d*; 95% CI 0.2–0.8) was observed across all the trials, suggesting a moderate impact [11]. Unfortunately, however, the study concluded that the evidence base was not strong because of substantial variability in how stepped care was operationalized across the different studies and because of the large variations in treatments offered in terms of steps, the professionals delivering the treatment, and step-up criteria.

The treatment guidelines for common anxiety disorders do not differ substantially from those for MDD in that a mix of psychological and pharmacological interventions are advocated [12].

Importantly, while such published guidelines usually include a comprehensive selection of evidence-based treatments, they do not usually refer to the value-for-the-money credentials of such treatments. In healthcare systems, which often face constrained resources, the question of which interventions offer good value for the money is an important consideration. Certainly, as will be discussed below, some of the interventions cited have strong credentials of cost-effectiveness, whereas others do not.

18.2 The Cost-Effectiveness of Commonly Used Treatments for Depression and Anxiety

18.2.1 Cost-Effectiveness of Pharmacological Treatments

18.2.1.1 Depression

Pharmacotherapy is indicated for the treatment of moderate to severe depression as well as chronic major depressive disorder. Many of the second-generation antidepressants, including the SSRIs (citalopram, fluoxetine, etc.), reboxetine, agomelatine, and bupropion, are recommended as first-line therapy. Older antidepressants including the TCAs (amitriptyline, imipramine, etc.) and monoamine oxidase inhibitors (phenelzine, tranylcypromine, moclobemide) are also available but less commonly prescribed because of their side effects, drug interactions, and frequent dosing regimens [10].

Two reviews focused on model-based economic evaluations of therapies for MDD were published in 2012 [13, 14]. Zimovetz et al. [14] identified 37 modeled economic evaluations of MDD interventions, whereas Afzali et al. [13] focused on 14 modeled cost-utility analyses (CUA). The majority of the evaluations included second-generation antidepressants. Several factors were identified that affected the outcome of modeled economic evaluations: the choice of effectiveness data, model structure, perspective, time horizon, and measurement of response and remission. Approximately two-thirds of the models used meta-analyses or pooled study results, which provide more robust estimates of effectiveness than models based on the results of a single study. Many models used decision trees rather than a Markov structure, which is better suited to chronic conditions. This seemed to be because of the clinical trial data used in the models, which typically covered the acute treatment and continuation phases over 6–12 weeks. Less than half of the modeled evaluations (see Chap. 7) used a societal perspective, which was found to have a substantial effect on the outcome of the analysis. The societal perspective includes the cost of the intervention as well as the cost of lost productivity (see Chap. 29), which can be affected by MDD and its treatment. Response was defined in many evaluations as 50% or greater improvement in the Montgomery Asberg Depression Rating Scale or Hamilton Rating Scale for Depression, but some varied this definition, which effects the results of different evaluations. Similarly, remission was defined by achieving a Montgomery Asberg Depression Rating Scale or Hamilton Rating Scale for Depression cutoff; however, the cutoff score between evaluations showed variability. The possibility of relapse was not included in all models and would favor medications with higher remission rates. Not all models included treatment options after initial treatment failure, which would affect the cost-effectiveness results, and only three models included the effects of specific adverse events on costs and utilities.

A third systematic review undertaken by Pan et al. [15] focused on cost and cost-effectiveness evaluations for antidepressants from databases and randomized and naturalistic trials. A relatively large number of the 40 peer-reviewed publications were industry-sponsored evaluations, with many of the database analyses conducted in the United States and Canada. Similar to the modeled evaluations, people prescribed escitalopram had lower healthcare costs and better outcomes than those prescribed many other SSRIs. Some studies also showed that people receiving escitalopram had lower healthcare costs compared with those receiving venlafaxine. The results from the evaluations of SSRIs versus TCAs varied. In database analyses, people using TCAs had healthcare costs comparable to those using SSRIs; in some studies, however, higher non-depression-related costs were found among TCA users. Other database studies reported that SSRI users had greater treatment persistence and lower total healthcare costs than TCA users. Pragmatic trials conducted across several countries (Spain, United Kingdom, Czech Republic, United States), showed that from a healthcare payer perspective, patients prescribed TCAs had costs and outcomes comparable with those of SSRI users, but from a societal perspective, TCA users had similar or even better outcomes, but lower total costs, than SSRI users. The inconsistency between the study results was likely the result of variation in study populations, which have differing illness severity, comorbidities, prior treatments, and treatment response. Differences in healthcare provision and attitudes regarding mental illness affecting treatment-seeking behavior across different countries may also be a factor in the different results.

A meta-analysis comparing multiple treatments was undertaken to determine the relative efficacy of remission for 10 antidepressants (citalopram, duloxetine, escitalopram, fluoxetine, fluvoxamine, mirtazapine, paroxetine, reboxetine, sertraline, and venlafaxine) [16]. The remission rates were then applied in a decision-analytic model to estimate costs and quality of life related to these treatments as fist-line pharmacologic therapy for people with moderate to severe depression treated in a primary care setting over 1 year. Consistent with the previous evaluations, escitalopram had the lowest cost from a societal perspective (€15,000) and the second lowest cost from a healthcare perspective (€5,000). It also delivered the highest quality-adjusted life year (QALY) value (0.6978) of the antidepressants evaluated (utilities were derived from the EQ-5D). This resulted in escitalopram being dominant over all the other comparators from a societal perspective. From a healthcare perspective, escitalopram had an incremental cost-effectiveness ratio (ICER) of €3700/QALY compared with venlafaxine, with both agents dominating the remaining antidepressants.

18.2.1.2 Anxiety

The medications used to treat anxiety vary with regard to their pharmacologic properties and include antidepressants, benzodiazepines, buspirone, anticonvulsants, antipsychotics, and other miscellaneous agents (antihistamines, β-blockers, and prazosin). Some have the potential for abuse and dependence, such as the benzodiazepines, whereas others seem to be non-habit-forming (e.g., antidepressants, buspirone). Benzodiazepines are effective upon the first dose of medication, whereas antidepressant therapy may take several weeks to achieve a therapeutic effect.

Ten studies have evaluated the cost-effectiveness of medications for the treatment of anxiety disorders, and an additional 11 studies compared medications with psychosocial therapies (up to December 2015). The studies are discussed below, focusing first on the evaluation of medications. The studies have been divided into two groups depending on the type of evaluation (CUA or cost-effectiveness analysis [CEA]). The studies evaluating a mix of psychosocial and pharmacologic therapies are then discussed separately using a similar grouping based on outcome. Studies that included costs only or those without a comparator are not considered full economic evaluations and have not been included.

18.2.1.2.1 Cost-Utility Studies of Anxiety Medications

Six publications undertook evaluations of pharmacologic therapies for anxiety disorders using a CUA approach. Two of these studies used a case-control design using subjects from an observational study in Spain to evaluate the use of pregabalin (an anticonvulsant) in refractory outpatients with generalized anxiety disorder (GAD) compared with usual care [17]and compared specificallywith SSRIs/SNRIs [17]. Two additional publications evaluated the use of pregabalin compared with venlafaxine extended release (an SNRI) for the treatment of GAD using simulation models [19, 20]. All four evaluations found that pregabalin delivered additional QALYs but at a high cost. The incremental cost-utility ratios ranged from €33,000/QALY when compared with venlafaxine extended release in Spain [20], to €27,000/QALY compared with venlafaxine in Portugal [19]. The ICER was €16,000/QALY when compared with usual care and €25,000/QALY when compared with SSRIs/SNRIs.

Another publication reported the results of a modeled analysis comparing the use of imipramine (a TCA) plus different maintenance strategies for the treatment of panic disorder from the perspective of the US mental healthcare system. They found that two maintenance regimens (full- and half-dose imipramine) were dominant compared with acute imipramine therapy with no maintenance regimen [21]. They found that two maintenance regimens (full-dose imipramine [2.25 mg/kg/day] and half-dose imipramine) were dominant compared with acute imipramine therapy with no maintenance regimen [21].

Mavranezouli et al. [22] used a decision-analytic model to evaluate six drugs used as monotherapy (duloxetine, escitalopram, paroxetine, pregabalin, sertraline, and venlafaxine extended release) compared with no pharmacologic treatment in people with GAD. Sertraline was the dominant strategy, producing the lowest costs and highest QALYs, and had a 75% probability of being the most cost-effective option when the willingness to pay was £20,000/QALY.

All these modeled evaluations took a limited healthcare perspective. The four evaluations of pregabalin used short time horizons (6 months to

1 year), whereas Mavissakalian et al. [21] evaluated an 18-month time horizon and Mavranezouli et al. [22] took a slightly longer window of 3.5 years. In the four studies evaluating pregabalin [17–20], QALYs were measured using the EQ-5D, whereas Mavranezouli et al. [21] usedShort Form 36-item (SF-36) data from a trial of escitalopram, and the remaining study [21] used clinical judgements to derive the QALY weights associated with the health states captured in the model (see Chap. 6). These different methods for valuation of utility values can result in quite different outcomes and should be considered when comparing these evaluations for healthcare decision making (more on this issue below in Sect. 18.3, "Methodological Considerations").

18.2.1.2.2 Cost-Effectiveness Studies of Anxiety Medications

Mihalopoulos et al. [23] reviewed the economic evaluation evidence base for interventions targeting anxiety disorders and found four studies that evaluated pharmacological interventions for anxiety disorders using a CEA framework. Two compared the SSRIs escitalopram and paroxetine [24, 25], one evaluated the SNRI venlafaxine compared with diazepam (a benzodiazepine) [26], and the final study evaluated controlled-release versus immediate-release paroxetine [27]. Three of the evaluations were model based, whereas one was based on data from a retrospective database analysis. The studies covered short time horizons (3–9 months). Two studies took a narrow health sector perspective and the remaining studies took a societal perspective that included productivity costs. The outcomes used included symptom-free days [24], discontinuation rates [27], and remission [25, 26].

The results of the studies suggest that escitalopram may cost less and be more effective than paroxetine, particularly when effects on productivity are included in the analysis [24, 25]. Venlafaxine costs more but is more effective than diazepam [26]. The results also suggest that controlled-release paroxetine is less costly and has a lower discontinuation rate that the immediate release formulation [27]. It is important to note that for several economic evaluations of pharmacologic interventions, many authors were employees of pharmaceutical companies or consultants paid by these companies, raising doubt about the independence of such studies.

18.2.2 Cost-Effectiveness of Psychological/Psychosocial Treatments

18.2.2.1 Depression

18.2.2.1.1 Cognitive Behavioral Therapy

Cognitive behavioral therapy (CBT), along with the pharmacological therapies detailed above, is perhaps one of the major cornerstones of treatment for depression. CBT aims to assist people in first identifying thoughts and behaviors that are unhelpful and learn better ways of managing both thoughts and behavior. CBT is a recommended treatment approach in almost all major clinical guidelines internationally. Individualized, group and even Internet-based CBT all have strong evidence of effect, particularly among people (including children and adults) with mild to moderate depression [28–30].

A recent review of the CUA studies of CBT for the treatment of depression found 22 available studies (until July 2013) [31]. The review found that studies were generally of a reasonably high standard using published quality criteria for economic evaluations (86% of the criteria were met overall). Health sector costs were widely included in almost all the studies, with patient time and travel costs included in about half of studies and a smaller proportion including effects on productivity. The conclusions of the review found that individualized CBT for adults as a stand-alone treatment (either individual therapy or group therapy) or in combination with pharmacological treatments (usually SSRIs)[1] seemed to be generally cost-effective. The results for children were far less uniform. For studies of children, the results ranged from dominant (that is, the intervention cost less and had greater ben-

[1] Economic evaluations of combination therapies (psychological plus pharmacological) are discussed further below.

efits) to not cost-effective (ICERs fell above the normally accepted value-for-money thresholds such as £30,000/QALY in the United Kingdom or $50,000/QALY in Australia) to dominated (that is, the intervention cost more and had less benefits than the comparator). The conclusions of this recent review are similar to those of older reviews of the cost-effectiveness of CBT for depression and other mental disorders.

However, a number of methodological issues were raised by the reviews considered above. For example, the short time horizon of many of the studies was discussed (no study tracked costs or benefits beyond 5 years), very few studies included broader societal costs (such as productivity), and the way which missing data were handled in some of the studies. Another important issue that needs to be highlighted is that the comparator condition in many of these studies must be considered. For example, while treatment as usual (TAU) is a common comparator, it can vary considerably both within and across different countries and contexts. This is important, as TAU can incur quite different costs and of course benefits, thus influencing the ICER. Furthermore, each jurisdiction responsible for decision-making needs to know whether the comparator conditions in studies are broadly representative of their own jurisdiction.

18.2.2.1.2 Other Treatment Approaches

As mentioned previously, stepped care approaches for the treatment of depression are currently receiving much attention and feature relatively prominently in many of the treatment guidelines discussed above. Unfortunately, there is almost no evidence of the cost-effectiveness of such stepped care approaches versus other treatment approaches.

The cost-effectiveness of collaborative care approaches, which are much less defined than stepped care approaches and tend to be recommended for people in whom prior (simpler) treatments have not worked, have recently been reviewed [32]. *Collaborative care* is loosely defined as a multidisciplinary approach, usually set in primary care, targeting the patient, doctor, and healthcare system. Basically, a care coordinator coordinates the care of the patient and guides treatment decision-making in an organized and informed way between all treating professionals (e.g., the general practitioner, psychologists, and psychiatrists). This review included 19 published studies in which usual care was the most common comparator. The overriding conclusion of the review was that the existing evidence base of economic evaluations of collaborative care is highly variable in terms of final results, with results ranging from dominance to a cost per QALY of nearly US$900,000. The review concluded that there is still substantial uncertainty regarding the cost-effectiveness of collaborative care, and further research needs to measure QALYs directly and to adopt longer time horizons (beyond 1 year). An earlier related review of the management of depression in a primary care setting concluded that such collaborative care can return a positive cost-to-benefit ratio when the outcomes are expressed in monetary units (largely by monetizing the value of the QALY in CUA studies) [33].

The cost-effectiveness of other, lesser known/discussed therapies have also been recently investigated. For example, the cost-effectiveness of art therapy was recently investigated using modeling and found to be cost-effective compared with a waitlist comparator, but it may be dominated (i.e., more expensive and less effective) when compared with verbal psychological therapy [34].

A recent modeled economic evaluation study set within the Spanish context evaluated the cost-effectiveness of ECT compared with repetitive transcranial magnetic stimulation for the treatment of treatment-resistant severe depression. The study found that ECT was likely to be the most cost-effective option at a willingness-to-pay threshold of €30,000/QALY [35]. Importantly, this study also had a short time horizon of 1 year under a limited National Health Service perspective. However, previous research using economic modeling conducted in the United Kingdom concluded that ECT is likely to be as cost-effective as pharmacological treatment, although the model upon which this conclusion is based has been seriously critiqued [36].

Longer-term and more intensive psychotherapeutic approaches (such as psychodynamic therapy, as opposed to more discrete approaches such as CBT) have been found to be more effective for subsets of people with depressive disorders (such as those with comorbid personality disorders or perfectionistic tendencies); however, the evidence base regarding the cost-effectiveness of such approaches is not strong, since very few cost-effectiveness studies have been undertaken [37].

18.2.2.2 Anxiety

There are substantially more reviews of economic evaluations of interventions targeting depression compared with anxiety. In a recent publication, Mihalopoulos et al. [23] reviewed the economic evaluation evidence base for interventions targeting anxiety disorders and found 18 studies of non-pharmacological interventions. That chapter presented an update of studies previously published in a review by Konnopka et al. [38], which identified only 11 cost-effectiveness studies. Twelve of the studies identified by Mihalopoulos et al. were CEA studies and the remainder were CUA studies. The CUA studies evaluated a range of interventions, largely based on CBT principles (e.g., family-based CBT, Internet-based CB,T and stepped care treatment, also including lower-dose and more intensive types of CBT). As for depression, most of the studies were in adults and evaluated either generic anxiety disorders or panic disorders. The study perspectives were largely those of the health sector, with the occasional addition of effects on productivity, and the types of analyses were largely trial-based economic evaluations. The vast majority of studies used the EQ-5D to measure QALYs (see Chap. 6), which does help to aid comparability between studies, at least on the outcome side. Again, similar to depression, the studies overwhelming suggested that the interventions evaluated were very cost-effective compared with TAU at commonly accepted value-for-money thresholds.

Of the cost-effectiveness studies, half of the studies targeted people with just anxiety disorders and the other half included people with affective disorders as well as other mental disorders. The range of interventions evaluated in these studies were broader than in the CUA studies and included, for example, a shyness program for social phobia, collaborative care in primary care, and psychodynamic therapy. A variety of outcome measures were used, including symptom severity scales and anxiety-free days. While the value-for-money credentials of interventions using a CEA framework are difficult to determine, this review noted that studies of stepped care approaches and self-directed CBT in fact save costs compared with more traditional forms of therapy.

The limitations of this evidence base were largely the same as the limitations identified for interventions targeting depression: short time horizons, limited perspectives, and an unclear definition of TAU comparators.

18.2.3 Cost-Effectiveness Studies Comparing Psychosocial Therapies and Medications

Other recent evidence has assessed the cost-effectiveness of pharmacotherapy compared with CBT and combination therapy for the treatment of moderate to severe depression in the United Kingdom [39]. This study was undertaken in part to fulfill the lack of cost-effectiveness evidence underpinning many of the treatment guidelines that recommend combination therapy for the treatment of severe to moderate depression. This study used a decision-tree framework (see Chap. 7) over a 27-month time horizon constructed from the National Health Service perspective in the United Kingdom. The study concluded that CBT monotherapy was likely to be the most cost-effective option that dominated combination therapy and had an ICER of around £20,000/QALY compared with pharmacotherapy. Similarly, a recent study also found that adding CBT to pharmacological regimes for those who are resistant to treatment is also likely to be a cost-effective option at commonly accepted WTP thresholds (e.g., £20,000–30,000/QALY in the United Kingdom) [40].

For anxiety disorders, the review by Mihalopoulos et al. [41] identified two studies that assessed both pharmacological and nonpharmacological studies in the same study context

[42, 43]. The first evaluation compared CBT and pharmacotherapy for the treatment of people with panic disorder in a speciality anxiety treatment center in the United States [43]. The CBT was manualized, but the choice of medication was left to the treating clinician. The next evaluation compared CBT with imipramine and paroxetine as monotherapy, as well as two combination therapies – CBT plus imipramine and CBT plus paroxetine – again in people with a diagnosis of panic disorder [42]. The studies seemed to take a health sector perspective and included only direct medical costs and limited time frames of 6 months to 1 year. Otto et al. [43] used the Clinician Global Impression of Severity scale, whereas McHugh et al. [42] used the panic disorder severity scale for effectiveness measures. Both studies found that CBT had the most favorable cost-effectiveness ratios [42, 43]. The main obvious problems for decision makers attempting to use these evaluations is whether the various outcome measures are comparable and what is a reasonable cost to pay for a point change in a symptom scale.

18.2.4 Cost-Effectiveness of Preventive Interventions for Depression and Anxiety

Mihalopoulos and Chatterton [44] recently systematically reviewed the economic evidence base of preventive interventions for mental disorders. This review included nine studies that were largely found to be of fairly good quality. Six of these studies were designed to prevent depression and two to prevent childhood anxiety disorders. The review concluded that the most effective and cost-effective preventive interventions for depression in both children and adults were indicated[2] types of CBT-based interventions. Such interventions largely consist of screening people for signs of depression and then providing to those who have elevated symptoms but do not yet meet all the criteria for MDD a therapeutic intervention such as group-based CBT. Half of the studies were CUAs, and the results of those studies all showed that these interventions fell well below the normally accepted criteria of cost-effectiveness. However, the CUAs were all modeled economic evaluations. Mihalopoulos et al. [46] recently evaluated the cost-effectiveness of a preventive parenting intervention for shy, preschool-age children and showed that this intervention is also likely to be very good value for the money. The review concluded that future research needs to integrate economic evaluations within trials so that broader assessments of economic effects can be attained, at least in the short term. Furthermore, longer-terms assessments of study participants, particularly in interventions targeting children and adolescents, should be undertaken to demonstrate to what extents effects can be maintained into adulthood.

Another area that is recently receiving considerable attention is the poor physical health of people with mental disorders, which is highlighted by the sobering statistics showing the much-reduced life expectancy of people with serious mental disorders that is not related to increased risk of suicide [47]. Because such interventions that specifically target the physical health of those with mental disorders are now receiving more attention, the cost-effectiveness of such interventions is also being evaluated. In a review of this evidence base, Park et al. [48] identified studies that targeted the physical health of people with depressive disorders and concluded that, in general, such interventions provide good value for the money at commonly accepted value-for-money thresholds. However, many studies were very context specific, and the issues of treatment fidelity, uptake, and adherence in particular need to be better accounted for.

18.2.5 Cost-Effectiveness of Internet-Based Therapies

Donker et al. [49] evaluated the existing economic evaluations of Internet interventions for mental disorders, which have been conducted

[2]"Indicated prevention" refers to preventive interventions targeting people with some symptoms of a mental disorder but who do not yet meet all criteria. This definition is contrasted with universal preventive interventions, which target entire populations, and selective interventions, which target "at-risk" populations [45].

alongside trials of such interventions. Sixteen studies met the review's inclusion criteria, and most were of a reasonable standard. Of those 16 studies, 4 targeted depression, 3 social phobia, 1 panic disorder, 1 health anxiety, and 1 generic anxiety. The majority of studies used CBT as the therapeutic intervention and were supported or guided by therapists. The evaluations that were targeted to depression showed a reasonable probability of being cost-effective when compared with waitlist controls, although compared with other comparators, the results were more mixed. For anxiety disorders, some of the studies demonstrated that guided integrated CBT might be dominant (cost less and have greater benefits) compared with other active interventions or attention controls. Importantly, however, this review excluded modeled economic evaluations on the basis that the methods included in these studies are different from those of economic evaluations undertaken alongside randomized trials. At the time of this review, 10 modeled economic evaluations ofInternet-based CBT were identified and excluded.

Another published review of Internet-based psychological therapies in children/adolescents in particular cautioned that the evidence base of such therapies (in terms of cost-effectiveness) is not strong and is an area that future research must urgently address [50].

18.3 Methodological Considerations

In this section, some of these more important methodological considerations in economic evaluation studies of interventions targeting depression and anxiety are discussed, along with their implications for the results of cost-effectiveness studies. Many of the reviews discussed earlier in this chapter highlight that costs are often measured from limited economic perspectives (largely that of the health sector), and broader (i.e., societal) perspectives usually only include health sector costs and effects on productivity. Traditionally, it has been argued that the starting perspective of economic evaluations should be societal, with all costs and consequences – no matter to whom they accrue – included in the evaluation [51]. The main reason for this is that important and potentially unknown costs (and consequences) are accounted for, and there is less chance of biased results. There is, however, always a balance between the pragmatic requirements of studies and theoretical methodological rigor. The Second Panel on Cost-Effectiveness in Health and Medicine recently highlighted the fact that many international decision-making agencies in Europe, Australia, and elsewhere have stipulated that a health sector perspective be adopted in the base case results of cost-effectiveness studies and wider societal impacts be included as supplementary analyses (if there is adequate evidence) [52]. Further, the panel highlighted the continued theoretical challenges that beset aggregation of the costs and consequences that accrue in different contexts. As such, the panel's recommendation is that all cost-effectiveness studies adopt a health sector perspective as the reference case, with another reference case adopting a societal perspective. Within the health care perspective, the panel recommends including all formal health sector costs (e.g., hospitalizations, medicines, community health care), regardless of whether they are reimbursed by a third-party payer or the individual. Interestingly, the panel also recommends all future related and unrelated healthcare costs be included in the evaluation. Societal costs include both time costs of patients seeking/receiving care, caregiver time, travel costs, effects on productivity, and any other non-–health sector costs and impacts (e.g., criminal justice). It has also been demonstrated that the inclusion in economic evaluations of the effects of interventions targeting depression on productivity can substantially alter the results of the study, with up to 60% of costs attributable to effects on productivity [53] (see Chaps. 28 and 29). Interestingly, while it is almost assumed that productivity costs should decrease with effective interventions, instances exist where they can increase (e.g., in a multimodal study, described in this review, that evaluated psychotherapy combined with pharmacotherapy, productivity costs increased because of the extra time associated with a more intensive intervention). However, future research needs to ensure that costs are indeed comprehensively measured in order to ensure that no unintended cost consequences or implications associated with various interventions are missed. Certainly, this has been highlighted as a limitation in many of the reviews discussed above.

In many respects, however, the measurement of benefit is just as important and needs to be carefully considered in each study. Many international decision-making authorities have stipulated that QALYs should be the main outcome included in the base case analyses of cost-effectiveness studies. The Second Panel on Cost-Effectiveness in Health and Medicine also recommended that the reference case analysis of cost-effectiveness studies should measure outcomes in QALYs [52]. As described in greater detail elsewhere in this book, QALYs are a generic outcome measure that combine mortality and morbidity into a single numeric unit, whereby the amount of time spent in a health state is multiplied by a weight (bounded by 0 and 1), which denotes the strength of preference for that health state. Various techniques are available to determine the utility weights for different health states; however, the most commonly used technique is preference-based health-related quality of life measures (also called multiattribute utility measures) (see Chaps. 3 and 6). These measures are simply health-related quality-of-life questionnaires with an added utility scoring algorithm, which gives preference weights to the various dimensions in the questionnaires. In a systematic review of utility weights used in economic evaluations of mental disorders, Sonntag et al. [54] found that of the 227 existing studies included in the review (127 model-based evaluations and 100 empirical evaluations), the majority of the empirical studies used such preference-based measures to estimate health state utilities. Of those, the most commonly used instruments were the EQ-5D and the SF-6D. The choice of instrument used in cost-utility studies is not trivial; previous research has unequivocally demonstrated that the choice of preference-based health-related quality-of-life instrument used to assess QALYs can have a major impact on results. A recent study compared the main preference-based utility measures used to assess QALYs with two commonly used outcome measures in studies of depression (the Kessler Psychological Distress Scale [K10] [55] and the 21-item Depression and Anxiety Stress Scale) [56, 57]; it found that while all the instruments discriminated between severity levels measured by the two clinical measures, they were certainly not uniform. For example, the difference in utility going from mild to severe health states as measured by the K10 was 0.3 for the HUI3, 0.2 for the eight-dimension Assessment of Quality of Life instrument and the EQ-5D, and 0.1 for the SF-6D and the 15D. This means that there could be a threefold difference in results if an intervention moved people from mild to severe psychological distress (as measured by the K10) simply based on the choice of outcome measure. This study found that while all instruments had acceptable construct validity that seemed to reflect depression severity levels, the eight-dimension Assessment of Quality of Life instrument seemed to have the best statistical fit with the clinical measures when compared with the other preference-based measures. It is imperative that such comparative studies be undertaken for all utility measures in order to ensure that they are indeed discriminatory compared with routinely used clinical measures. This is particularly urgent for measures used to assess QALYs in children with mental disorders, among whom very few quality construct validity studies have been conducted.

A review of the methodological considerations of modeled cost-effectiveness studies for depression concluded that many of the models published up to 2010 were largely cohort, Markov-type models, had a short time duration (usually 1 year), used limited costing perspectives, and differentially determined benefit both in terms of the health states used in the models and the source of the health state utilities [14]. Recent studies, however, have started to use more sophisticated forms of modeling that attempt to account for patient heterogeneity and can track costs and benefits over a longer time horizon [58]. While the development of such models is a welcome addition to the literature, caution must be exercised because models are only as good as the input parameters, and assumptions are made in estimating both the costs and benefits of the interventions as well as the progression of the disease. However, given that patient heterogeneity has been identified as an important variable to be considered in cost-effectiveness models [59], more complicated models such as the discrete event simulation (DES) model (a type of microsimulation model) are now starting to be developed within the mental health context (see Chap. 7). This type of modeling differs from more traditional deterministic cohort models or even Markov processes in that DES models simulate individual patient trajectories rather than "averages" among cohorts, thus allowing more complex characteristics of systems to be captured [60]. Within a DES model, an individual basically moves through the model, experiencing events at any discrete period after the previous event (using mathematical formulas). The timing of events is important, and different events can occur at different times for different people. This model is much more flexible and allows individual patient heterogeneity to be incorporated within the analysis. More complex agent-based models can even incorporate interactions between people (that is, agents).

The above discussion includes evidence of cost-effectiveness mostly from evaluations that evaluate one intervention compared with another. However, one of the largest limitations in many such studies is the issue of direct comparability. Even when individual studies are of high quality, differences in methods – such as perspective, collection of resource use data, utility measurement, time horizon, and so on – can mean that the ICER results of studies are not directly comparable. For this reason, broader priority-setting approaches have been developed (see Carter et al. [61] for a general discussion and Mihalopoulos et al. [62] for a review of such approaches within the mental health context). In these broader studies, the cost-effectiveness of interventions is reevaluated using modeling techniques that have comparableassumptions. For example, a consistent set of disease weights may be used, or resource use and unit costs from a particular context (e.g., Australia) are used. Examples of such approaches are the Assessing Cost Effectiveness Approach and the Avertable Burden studies, both from Australia, and the generalized cost-effectiveness approach from the World Health Organization. All of these priority-setting approaches are described by Mihalopoulos et al. [41]. What is notable from these studies is that the vast majority of interventions for depression and anxiety evaluated (many of which are also discussed above) where found to have extremely favorable cost-effectiveness ratios at commonly accepted value-for-money thresholds. Furthermore, many of these studies found that if cost-effective treatments are offered to those who are already accessing treatment and are not receiving evidence-based, cost-effective care, a substantial amount of disease burden can be averted at no extra cost [63, 64].

18.4 Conclusions

Lastly, much of what has been briefly discussed and reviewed in this chapter relates to interventions that tend to cost more than the comparator conditions but usually bestow some benefit. What is less often discussed, however, is that instances may occur when it is best to disinvest from some healthcare interventions, if the opportunity costs of doing so are not too onerous. In this instance, disinvestment may lead to substantial cost savings, with only minor health losses. These cost savings could theoretically be invested in other healthcare technologies (if the opportunity cost of doing so is acceptable). Nelson et al. [65] found that disinvestment from transcranial magnetic stimulation for people with treatment-resistant depression can lead to considerable cost savings, with minor QALY losses. However, very few interventions evaluated in existing reviews of economic evaluations of interventions targeting depression and anxiety fit into this category.

Finally, it is now fair to conclude that there exists sufficient evidence demonstrating the effectiveness and cost-effectiveness of both pharmacological and psychosocial treatments for both depression and anxiety. However, a major problem is that people who might benefit from these therapies are still not receiving them, even in well-resourced countries such as Australia. Compelling evidence shows that even when people access care, many, if not the majority, still do not receive even minimally adequate care, let alone evidence-based care. For example, Harris et al. [66] found that, in Australia, among people meeting criteria for affective and/or anxiety disorders, fewer than half sought treatment (39%); of those who sought treatment, only 16% received minimally adequate treatment. An urgent issue for future research needs to be how interventions that are known to work and are cost-effective can be properly provided to everyone who needs them.

Key Messages

- Many studies evaluate the cost-effectiveness of both psychological and pharmacological treatments for depression and anxiety.
- Outcome measurement in economic evaluations of mental health conditions can vary, requiring careful interpretation of results across studies and the contexts in which they have been evaluated.
- Future research needs to determine how to best ensure that people with depression and anxiety receive effective and cost-effective care when accessing treatment.

References

1. American Psychiatric Association. Diagnostic and statistical manual of mental disorders (DSM-5). 5th ed. Arlington: American Psychiatric Association; 2013.
2. Grohol J. DSM-5 changes: depression & depressive disorders. Psych Central [Internet]. 8 June 2013. 2016. Available from: http://pro.psychcentral.com/dsm-5-changes-depression-depressive-disorders/004259.html
3. Tiller JWG. Depression and anxiety. Med J Aus. 2012;1:28–31.
4. Ferrari AJ, Somerville AJ, Baxter AJ, Norman R, Patten SB, Vos T, et al. Global variation in the prevalence and incidence of major depressive disorder: a systematic review of the epidemiological literature. Psychol Med. 2013;43(3):471–81.
5. Baxter AJ, Scott KM, Vos T, Whiteford HA. Global prevalence of anxiety disorders: a systematic review and meta-regression. Psychol Med. 2013;43(5):897–910.
6. Charlson FJ, Baxter AJ, Dua T, Degenhardt L, Whiteford HA, Vos T. Excess mortality from mental, neurological, and substance use disorders in the Global Burden of Disease Study 2010. In:Mental, neurological, and substance use disorders: disease control priorities, vol. 4. 3rd ed; 2016.
7. Luppa M, Heinrich S, Angermeyer MC, Konig HH, Riedel-Heller SG. Cost-of-illness studies of depression - A systematic review. Journal of Affective Disorders 2007; 98(1-2):29-43. Whiteford HA, Degenhardt L, Rehm J, Baxter AJ, Ferrari AJ, Erskine HE, et al. Global burden of disease attributable to mental and substance use disorders: findings from the global burden of disease study 2010. Lancet (Lond. Eng). 2013;382(9904):1575–86.
8. Leichsenring F, Rabung S. Effectiveness of long-term psychodynamic psychotherapy: a meta-analysis. JAMA. 2008;300(13):1551–65.
9. Malhi GS, Bassett D, Boyce P, Bryant R, Fitzgerald PB, Fritz K, et al. Royal Australian and New Zealand College of Psychiatrists clinical practice guidelines for mood disorders. Aust N Z J Psychiatry. 2015;49(12):1087–206.
10. van Straten A, Hill J, Richards DA, Cuijpers P. Stepped care treatment delivery for depression: a systematic review and meta-analysis. Psychol Med. 2015;45(2):231–46.
11. Royal Australian New Zealand College of Psychiatrists Clinical Practice Guidelines Team for Panic Disorder Agoraphobia. Australian and New Zealand clinical practice guidelines for the treatment of panic disorder and agoraphobia. Aust N Z J Psychiatry. 2003;37(6):641–56.
12. Afzali HHA, Karnon J, Gray J. A critical review of model-based economic studies of depression: modelling techniques, model structure and data sources. PharmacoEconomics. 2012;30(6):461–82.
13. Zimovetz EA, Wolowacz SE, Classi PM, Birt J. Methodologies used in cost-effectiveness models for evaluating treatments in major depressive disorder: a systematic review. Cost Eff Resour Alloc. 2012;10(1):1.
14. Pan Y-J, Knapp M, McCrone P. Cost-effectiveness comparisons between antidepressant treatments in depression: evidence from database analyses and prospective studies. J Affect Disord. 2012;139(2):113–25.
15. Ramsberg J, Asseburg C, Henriksson M. Effectiveness and cost-effectiveness of antidepressants in primary care: a multiple treatment comparison meta-analysis and cost-effectiveness model. PLoS One. 2012;7(8):e42003.
16. De Salas-Cansado M, Alvarez E, Olivares JM, Carrasco JL, Ferro MB, Rejas J. Modelling the cost-effectiveness of pregabalin versus usual care in daily practice in the treatment of refractory generalised anxiety disorder in Spain. Social psychiatry and psychiatric epidemiology 2013; 48(6): 985-96.Kyu

HH, Pinho C, Wagner JA, Brown JC, Bertozzi-Villa A, Charlson FJ, et al. Global and national burden of diseases and injuries among children and adolescents between 1990 and 2013: findings from the global burden of disease 2013 study. JAMA Pediatr. 2016;170(3):267–87.

17. De Salas-Cansado M, Olivares JM, Alvarez E, Carrasco JL, Barrueta A, Rejas J. Pregabalin versus SSRIs and SNRIs in benzodiazepine-refractory outpatients with generalized anxiety disorder: a post hoc cost-effectiveness analysis in usual medical practice in Spain. ClinicoEconomics and outcomes research : CEOR 2012; 4: 157-68.Silva Miguel L, Silva Miguel N, Ines M. A cost-utility analysis of pregabalin versus venlafaxine XR in the treatment of generalized anxiety disorder in Portugal. Cost Eff Resour Alloc. 2013;11(1):8.
18. Vera-Llonch M, Dukes E, Rejas J, Sofrygin O, Mychaskiw M, Oster G. Cost-effectiveness of pregabalin versus venlafaxine in the treatment of generalized anxiety disorder: findings from a Spanish perspective. The European journal of health economics : HEPAC : health economics in prevention and care 2010; 11(1): 35-44.Baxter AJ, Vos T, Scott KM, Norman RE, Flaxman AD, Blore J, et al. The regional distribution of anxiety disorders: implications for the global burden of disease study, 2010. Int J Methods Psychiatric Res. 2014;23(4):422–38.
19. Silva Miguel L, Silva Miguel N, Ines M. A cost-utility analysis of pregabalin versus venlafaxine XR in the treatment of generalized anxiety disorder in Portugal. Cost Eff Resour Alloc. 2013;11(1):8. Murray CJL, Vos T, Lozano R, Naghavi M, Flaxman AD, Michaud C, et al. Disability-adjusted life years (DALYs) for 291 diseases and injuries in 21 regions, 1990–2010: a systematic analysis for the global burden of disease study 2010. Lancet. 2012;380(9859):2197–223.
20. Mavissakalian MR, Schmier JK, Flynn JA, Revicki DA. Cost effectiveness of acute imipramine therapy versus two imipramine maintenance treatment regimens for panic disorder. Pharmacoeconomics 2000; 18(4): 383-91.21.Mavranezouli I, Meader N, Cape J, Kendall T. The cost effectiveness of pharmacological treatments for generalized anxiety disorder. PharmacoEconomics. 2013;31(4):317–33.
21. Mihalopoulos C, Baxter AJ, Whiteford H, Vos T. The cost-effectiveness of treatments for anxiety disorders. In: Emmelkamp P, Ehring T, editors. The Wiley handbook of anxiety disorders. 1st ed. West Sussex: Wiley & Sons Ltd; 2014.
22. Drummond M, Sculpher M, Torrance G, O'rien B, Stoddart G. Methods for the economic evaluation of health care programmes. 4th ed. Oxford: Oxford University Press; 2015.
23. Carter R, Vos T, Moodie M, Haby M, Magnus A, Mihalopoulos C. Priority setting in health: origins, description and application of the Australian assessing cost effectiveness (ACE) initiative. Expert Rev Pharmacoecon Outcomes. 2008;8(6):593–617.
24. Mihalopoulos C, Carter R, Pirkis J, Vos T. Priority-setting for mental health services. J Mental Health. 2013;22(2):122–34.
25. Sheehan DV, Eaddy M, Sarnes M, Vishalpura T, Regan T. Evaluating the economic consequences of early antidepressant treatment discontinuation: a comparison between controlled-release and immediate-release paroxetine. J Clin Psychopharmacol. 2004;24(5):544–8.
26. NICE. CG28: depression in children andyoung people: NICE guideline. National Institute for Health and Clinical Excellence; 2010.
27. Butler AC, Chapman JE, Forman EM, Beck AT. The empirical status of cognitive-behavioral therapy: a review of meta-analyses. Clin Psychol Rev. 2006;26(1):17–31.
28. Foroushani PS, Schneider J, Assareh N. Meta-review of the effectiveness of computerised CBT in treating depression. BMC Psychiatry. 2011;11:131.
29. Brettschneider C, Djadran H, Härter M, Löwe B, Riedel-Heller S, König H-H. Cost-utility analyses of cognitive-behavioural therapy of depression: a systematic review. Psychother Psychosomat. 2015;84(1):6 21.
30. Grochtdreis T, Brettschneider C, Wegener A, Watzke B, Riedel-Heller S, Harter M, et al. Cost-effectiveness of collaborative care for the treatment of depressive disorders in primary care: a systematic review. PLoS One. 2015;10(5):e0123078.
31. Glied S, Herzog K, Frank R. The net benefits of depression management in primary care. Med Care Res Rev. 2010;67(3):251–74.
32. Uttley L, Scope A, Stevenson M, Rawdin A, Buck ET, Sutton A, et al. Systematic review and economic modelling of the clinical effectiveness and cost-effectiveness of art therapy among people with non-psychotic mental health disorders. Health Technol Asses. 2015;19(18):1.
33. Vallejo-Torres L, Castilla I, González N, Hunter R, Serrano-Pérez P, Perestelo-Pérez L. Cost-effectiveness of electroconvulsive therapy compared to repetitive transcranial magnetic stimulation for treatment-resistant severe depression: a decision model. Psychol Med. 2015;45(7):1459–70.
34. McDonald WM. Is ECT cost-effective? A critique of the National Institute of health and clinical Excellence's report on the economic analysis of ECT. J ECT. 2006;22(1):25–9.
35. Lazar SG. The cost-effectiveness of psychotherapy for the major psychiatric diagnoses. Psychodynam Psychiatry. 2014;42(3):423–57.
36. Konnopka A, Leichsenring F, Leibing E, König H-H. Cost-of-illness studies and cost-effectiveness analyses in anxiety disorders: a systematic review. J Affect Disord. 2009;114(1–3):14–31.
37. Koeser L, Donisi V, Goldberg DP, McCrone P. Modelling the cost-effectiveness of pharmacotherapy compared with cognitive-behavioural therapy and combination therapy for the treatment of moderate to severe depression in the UK. Psychol Med. 2015;45(14):3019–31.

38. Hollinghurst S, Carroll FE, Abel A, Campbell J, Garland A, Jerrom B, et al. Cost-effectiveness of cognitive-behavioural therapy as an adjunct to pharmacotherapy for treatment-resistant depression in primary care: economic evaluation of the CoBalT trial. Br J Psychiatry J Mental Sci. 2014;204(1):69–76.
39. McHugh RK, Otto MW, Barlow DH, Gorman JM, Shear MK, Woods SW. Cost-efficacy of individual and combined treatments for panic disorder. J Clin Psychiatry. 2007;68(7):1038–44.
40. Otto MW, Pollack MH, Maki KM. Empirically supported treatments for panic disorder: costs, benefits, and stepped care. J Consul Clin Psychol. 2000;68(4):556–63.
41. Mihalopoulos C, Chatterton ML. Economic evaluations of interventions designed to prevent mental disorders: a systematic review. Early Interven Psychiatry. 2015;9(2):85–92.
42. Mrazek PJ, Haggerty RJ. In: Committee on Prevention of mental Disorders DoBSaMD, Institute of Medicine, editor. Reducing risks for mental disorders: frontiers for preventative intervention research. Washington, DC: National Academy Press; 1994.
43. Mihalopoulos C, Vos T, Rapee RM, Pirkis J, Chatterton ML, Lee YC, et al. The population cost-effectiveness of a parenting intervention designed to prevent anxiety disorders in children. J Child Psychol Psychiatry. 2015;56(9):1026–33.
44. Chesney E, Goodwin GM, Fazel S. Risks of all-cause and suicide mortality in mental disorders: a meta-review. World Psychiatry. 2014;13(2):153–60.
45. Park AL, McDaid D, Weiser P, Von Gottberg C, Becker T, Kilian R. Examining the cost effectiveness of interventions to promote the physical health of people with mental health problems: a systematic review. BMC Public Health. 2013;13:787.
46. Arnberg FK, Linton SJ, Hultcrantz M, Heintz E, Jonsson U. Internet-delivered psychological treatments for mood and anxiety disorders: a systematic review of their efficacy, safety, and cost-effectiveness. PLoS One. 2014;9(5):e98118.
47. Sanders GD, Neumann PJ, Basu A, Brock DW, Feeny D, Krahn M, et al. Recommendations for conduct, methodological practices, and reporting of cost-effectiveness analyses: second panel on cost-effectiveness in health and medicine. JAMA. 2016;316(10):1093–103.
48. Krol M, Papenburg J, Koopmanschap M, Brouwer W. Do productivity costs matter? The impact of including productivity costs on the incremental costs of interventions targeted at depressive disorders. PharmacoEconomics. 2011;29(7):601–19.
49. Sonntag M, König H-H, Konnopka A. The estimation of utility weights in cost-utility analysis for mental disorders: a systematic review. PharmacoEconomics. 2013;31(12):1131–54.
50. Kessler RC, Barker PR, Colpe LJ, Epstein JF, Gfroerer JC, Hiripi E, et al. Screening for serious mental illness in the general population. Arch Gen Psychiatry. 2003;60(2):184–9.
51. Lovibond SH, Lovibond PF. Manual for the depression anxiety stress scales. 2nd ed. Psychology Foundation: Sydney; 1995.
52. Mihalopoulos C, Chen G, Iezzi A, Khan MA, Richardson J. Assessing outcomes for cost-utility analysis in depression: comparison of five multi-attribute utility instruments with two depression-specific outcome measures. Br J Psychiatry J Mental Sci. 2014;205(5):390–7.
53. Vataire A-L, Aballéa S, Antonanzas F, Roijen LH-V, Lam RW, McCrone P, et al. Core discrete event simulation model for the evaluation of health care technologies in major depressive disorder. Value Health. 2014;17(2):183–95.
54. Rodgers M, Asaria M, Walker S, McMillan D, Lucock M, Harden M, et al. The clinical effectiveness and cost-effectiveness of low-intensity psychological interventions for the secondary prevention of relapse after depression: a systematic review. Health Technol Asses. 2012;16(28):1–130.
55. Karnon J. Alternative decision modelling techniques for the evaluation of health care technologies: Markov processes versus discrete event simulation. Health Econ. 2003;12(10):837–48.
56. Andrews G, Issakidis C, Sanderson K, Corry J, Lapsley H. Utilising survey data to inform public policy: comparison of the cost-effectiveness of treatment of ten mental disorders. Br J Psychiatry. 2004;184:526–33.
57. Vos T, Haby MM, Magnus A, Mihalopoulos C, Andrews G, Carter R. Assessing cost-effectiveness in mental health: helping policy-makers prioritize and plan health services. Aus N Z J Psychiatry. 2005;39(8):701–12.
58. Nelson AL, Cohen JT, Greenberg D, Kent DM. Much cheaper, almost as good: decrementally cost-effective medical innovation. Ann Intern Med. 2009;151(9):662–7.

Cost-Effectiveness of Treatment for Bipolar Disorders

19

Ana Flávia Barros da Silva Lima, Luciane Cruz, Mírian Cohen, Jacques José Zimmermann, and Sandro René Pinto de Sousa Miguel

Abstract

This chapter focuses on a review the cost-effectiveness studies of bipolar disorder (BD) published in the past 10 years in order to present the main methodological issues related to economic evaluations of this topic. A systematic search of the was performed to include articles on the cost-effectiveness of any management strategy for BD, published in English, and spanning the period of January 2005 to June 2016. Five electronic databases were assessed, namely, the National Health Services–Health Economic Evaluation Database, the Health Technology Assessment Database, MEDLINE, and the Cumulative Index to Nursing and Allied Health Literature. A total of 141 citations were found. After screening, 24 studies were selected, of which 18 were original articles and 6 were systematic reviews. Of the eligible studies, the majority were from the United Kingdom and United States. Few studies were not funded by the pharmaceutical industry. Considering methodology, four studies were trial-based economic evaluations and the others were model-based economic evaluations. The number of subjects enrolled in the reported trials varied from 103 to 431. Most studies focused on the maintenance phase of BD treatment. New atypical antipsychotics were the most commonly evaluated interventions, with placebo and traditional treatments as comparators. Few articles evaluated classical mood stabilizers (lithium, valproate,

A.F.B. da Silva Lima (✉) • J.J. Zimmermann
Institute for Health Technology Assessment (IATS/CNPq), Rua Ramiro Barcelos 2359 Prédio 21 sala 507, 90035-903 Porto Alegre, Brazil
e-mail: afbslima@gmail.com; zimmermann@ig.com.br

L. Cruz • S.R.P. de Sousa Miguel
Hospital Moinhos de Vento, Porto Alegre, Brazil

Institute for Health Technology Assessment (IATS/CNPq), Rua Ramiro Barcelos 2359 Prédio 21 sala 507, 90035-903 Porto Alegre, Brazil
e-mail: lucianecrz@gmail.com; sandropsm@gmail.com

M. Cohen
Institute for Health Technology Assessment (IATS/CNPq), Rua Ramiro Barcelos 2359 Prédio 21 sala 507, 90035-903 Porto Alegre, Brazil

Health Department of Rio Grande do Sul State, Hospital Psiquiátrico São Pedro, Porto Alegre, Brazil
e-mail: mirian.cohen@22c.com.br

D. Razzouk (ed.), *Mental Health Economics*, DOI 10.1007/978-3-319-55266-8_19

carbamazepine) in an economic assessment. Atypical antipsychotics were the most cost-effective intervention studied. When one considers the economic evaluations, quetiapine, olanzapine, and aripiprazole are considered to be good strategies in the maintenance treatment of BD.

Key Points Summary

- Introduction to bipolar disorder (BD) clinical characteristics and epidemiology
- A brief contextualization of impacts and economic issues of BD treatments
- Review of up-to-date treatments and cost-effectiveness evidence in BD
- A critical discussion of the many challenges, limitations, and research aspects presented in current cost-effectiveness studies for BD
- Considerations for future studies and decision-making policies

19.1 Introduction

Bipolar disorder (BD) is a chronic mood disorder characterized by fluctuations in mood, from depressive to irritable or elated temper. Affected subjects can present depressive or hypomanic/manic episodes throughout their lifetime. In depressive episodes, symptoms such as low energy, low mood, anhedonia, loss of interest or pleasure, sleep disturbances, and difficulties concentrating could affect the individuals. Hypomanic and manic episodes are associated with expansive or irritable mood, increased energy and activity, distractibility, decreased need for sleep, inflated self-esteem, and grandiosity, all of which differ in terms of severity and duration. Manic episodes need to last at least 1 week and lead to marked impairment in social or occupational functioning, hospitalization, or psychosis. Hypomanic episodes have a minimal duration of 4 days and do not present the severity described for manic episodes. Bipolar I disorder (BD I) and bipolar II disorder (BD II) are the most defined and studied subtypes. Patients with BD I must present at least one manic episode during their lifetime, with or without major depressive episodes, and those with BD II need to present at least one hypomanic episode and one major depressive episode [1].

The lifetime prevalence of BD types I and II within the general population is more than 1%, irrespective of socioeconomic level, culture, and nationality. BD I affects men and women equally; however, BD II is more frequent in women [2]. Psychiatric and medical comorbidities are highly prevalent, more frequently co-occurring with anxiety disorders, substance abuse disorders, metabolic syndrome, and cardiovascular disorders [2, 3]. The chronic course of illness associated with partial remission of symptoms, high rates of comorbidities, and a complex clinic presentation implicates the significant utilization of inpatient and outpatient services, as well as medications and psychosocial interventions [4].

There is an average delay of 5–10 years from symptom onset to the beginning of treatment in this population [2, 3]. This delay, associated with high rates of comorbidities and poor treatment compliance, is extremely important in the resulting impairments, such as limited functional outcome, cognitive dysfunction, decrease in physical health, and high mortality caused by both medical conditions and suicide rates [3]. The incidence of death by suicide is high– it can be more than 20 times higher than in the general population – and 30–50% of patients with BD attempt suicide at least once in their lifetime. About 20% succeed [2, 5].

BD is one of the major causes of disability worldwide, according to the Global Burden of Disease Study [6]. It is considered a severe psychiatric disorder that often causes not only a major impact on patient well-being but also an emotional overload on the patients' family and an economic burden for society [3, 4]. Treatment involves pharmacotherapy with mood stabilizers frequently associated with other strategies: antipsychotics and/or antidepressants, electroconvulsive therapy, and psychotherapies. The treatment of BD remains a challenge, with studies showing that fewer than half of patients present a good response to treatment, and most achieve only partial remission [4].

At a societal level, people with this illness induce enormous direct and indirect costs [3]. Studies demonstrate that they use almost four times more healthcare resources than and cost more than four times more than people without BD [5]. Indirect costs due to morbidity, premature mortality, and loss of productivity make it an important public health issue. It is important to highlight that intangible costs exist, such as family burden and impaired health-related quality of life [4].

With a wide range of interventions to treat BD, from pharmacological to psychosocial approaches, and limited healthcare budgets, it is important for stakeholders to allocate scarce resources to understanding the additional value of new interventions. Economic evaluation methods are used to compare costs and benefits between different interventions and to support the decision of whether alternative interventions represent an efficient use of resources. Cost-effectiveness analysis is a type of economic evaluation that provides information on the costs and benefits of competing interventions, measured by resource use and impact on mortality and morbidity in a certain population. Many outcome measures can be used, but regulatory agencies have recently recommended the use of quality-adjusted life years (QALYs) [5, 7]. Considering the perspective of a broad spectrum of effective interventions, economic evaluations are increasing in the literature because of their relevance in assisting decision makers in creating health policies.

19.2 Bipolar Disorder Treatment: Cost-Effectiveness Evidence

For this chapter, a systematic search of the literature was undertaken to identify English-language articles published between January 2005 and June 2016 that provided data on the cost-effectiveness of any management strategy for BD. This date restriction was enforced in order to obtain data likely to be relevant to current healthcare settings and costs. In total, five electronic databases were searched: the National Health Services–Health Economic Evaluation Database, the Health Technology Assessment Database, MEDLINE, and the Cumulative Index to Nursing and Allied Health Literature. In addition, reference lists of key articles were searched and recent reviews were checked for further relevant publications. The search strategies included both key words in text and corresponding medical subject headings.

A search of the five electronic databases yielded a total of 141 citations. After managing duplicate records and screening titles and abstracts, 24 studies were selected, 18 of which were original articles and 6 were systematic reviews. Of the final reading, two originals were excluded for not presenting comparable interventions, and four reviews were not cost-effectiveness reviews. Of the eligible studies, the majority were from the United Kingdom and United States. Few studies (four trials) were not funded by the pharmaceutical industry. Most studies focused on the maintenance phase of BD treatment. Considering the methodology, four studies were trial-based economic evaluations, whereas the other studies were model-based economics evaluations. The number of individuals included in the studies trials varied from 103 to 431 participants. New atypical antipsychotics were the interventions of choice, with placebo and traditional treatments as comparators. Only two studies compared nonpharmacological and pharmacological interventions. The common characteristics between the studies are listed below. The main findings of the studies are summarized in Table 19.1.

Table 19.1 Summary of economic evaluation studies for bipolar disorder treatment

Study	Sample/design	Interventions	Costs	Outcomes	Results	Sensitivity analysis	Conclusions
Revicki et al. [8] Funding: Abbott Laboratories, USA	Open-label pragmatic RCT Inpatients aged ≥18 years with BD I (acute mania or mixed episode) Follow-up: NR Study type: CEA Perspective: NR Time Horizon: NR	Li 1800 mg/day (acute phase) or Li 900–1200 mg/day (remission) (97 patients) Comparator:DVP 15–20 mg/kg/day (104 patients)	$US Cost year: 1997 Direct costs	(a) No. of bipolar-free months (b) MCS scores of SF-36	No statistically significant differences between groups for primary outcomes and costs	NR	DVP is comparable to Li in terms of costs and effectiveness outcomes
Lam et al. [9] Funding: Centre for the Economics of Mental Health, Health Services Research Department, UK	Open-label pragmatic RCT Outpatients with BD I (maintenance phase) Follow-up: 12 and 30 months Study type: CEA Perspective: UK NHS Time Horizon: 30 months	CBT + CAU (51 patients) Comparator: CAU (52 patients)	GBP Cost year: NR Direct costs	No. of bipolar- free days	CBT group spent 62.3 fewer days with BD episodes in 12 months. In 30 months the CBT group spent 110 fewer days with bipolar episodes than CAU group. The cost-effectiveness acceptability curves showed an 85% chance for the 12-month and 80% chance for the 30-month follow-up that CBT is more cost-effective than standard care	Univariate and Probability Sensitivity analysis	The addition of CBT is cost-effective compared with usual care. CBT is useful for relapse prevention in BD
Calvert et al. [10] Funding: GlaxoSmithKline, USA	Simulated cohort Patients with BD I aged ≥18 years who start in a euthymic state Study type: CEA/CUA Design: Markov model Perspective: Society Time horizon: 18 months Transition period: biweekly cycles	LAM 200 mg/day (1000 patients) Comparator: No treatment (1000 patients)	US$ Cost year: 2004 Direct costs	(a) No. of episodes (b) No. of euthymic days (c) QALYs	LAM dominated placebo and OLZ for all the three outcomes. The ICER of LAM versus Li was $2400 per episode avoided, $30 per euthymic day gained, and $26,000 per QALY	Univariate and bivariate Sensitivity analyses	Using conventional WTP thresholds, LAM is the cost-effective strategy
NICE Economic Model [11] Funding: NICE, UK	Simulated cohort Patients with BD I aged ≥18 years who start in a euthymic state Study type: CEA/CUA Design: Markov model Perspective: UK NHS Time horizon: 5 years Transition period: monthly cycles	Li 1000 mg/day orDVP 1250 mg/day or OLZ 10 mg/day (1000 patients) Comparator: Placebo (1000 patients)	GBP Cost year: 2004–2005 Direct costs	(a) No. of acute episodes averted (b) No. of days free from acute episodes (c) QALYs	Li is a cost-effective long-term treatment option when WTP for an additional episode averted or an additional day free from episode is below £17,500 and £150, respectively. 90% probability that OLZ is the most cost-effective option among all treatments for all patients at a WTP threshold of £20,000/QALY	Univariate and probability sensitivity analyses	Using conventional WTP thresholds, OLZ is the most cost-effective strategy

Klok et al. [12] Funding: AstraZeneca, the Netherlands	Simulated cohort Inpatients with BD I (acute mania) Study type: CEA Design: DES Perspective: Healthcare provider Time horizon: 100 days	QTP 600 mg/day or Li 800 mg/day or DVP 1000 mg/day or QTP 600 mg/day + Li 800 mg/day or OLZ 15 mg/day + Li 800 mg/day or RIS 6 mg/day + Li 800 mg/day (10,000 patients) Comparator: Placebo or Li 300–1800 mg/day (10,000 patients)	Euros Cost year: 2003 Direct costs	(a) Time to remission (b) Time to response (c) Length of stay (d) Proportion with ≥50% improvement from baseline YMRS score (e) No. of serious side effects	Combination therapy options were cheaper and more efficacious than placebo and monotherapies. QTP + Li was associated with the highest proportion of responders (54.7%; $P < 0.05$). Time to response was 21.2, 21.6, and 21.4 days for QTP + Li, OLZ + Li, and RIS + Li combinations, respectively. QTP + Li ICER of €1203/serious adverse event prevented against RIS + Li, and ICER of €3481/serious adverse event prevented in comparison with OLZ + Li combination	Univariate and probability sensitivity analyses	QTP + Li is more cost-effective than the combination of Li with OLZ or RIS
Soares-Weiser et al. [13] Funding: NIHR HTA Program, UK	Simulated cohort Stabilized patients with BD Ifollowing an acute episode Study type: CUA Design: Markov model Perspective: UK NHS Time horizon: 60 years Transition period: annual	Li 800 mg/day or DVP 1250 mg/day or OLZ 10 mg/day or CBZ 600 mg/day or LAM 200 mg/day or IMI 150 mg/day or Li + IMI Comparator: Placebo + Li or DVP combination	GBP Cost year: 2004–2005 Direct costs	(a) No. of acute episodes averted (b) No. of days free from acute episodes (c) QALYs	For patients with a recent depressive episode, DVP was the cheapest nondominated option. Against DVP, Li generated an ICER of £10,409/QALY. Against Li, Li + IMI generated an ICER of £21,370/QALY. PSA indicated a 41% probability for Li and 53% for Li + IMI being cost-effective at a threshold of £30,000	Univariate and probability sensitivity analyses	Using conventional WTP thresholds, Li + IMI is the most cost-effective strategy for patients with a recent depressive episode. For patients with a history of manic episode, Li is the most cost-effective strategy
McKendrick et al. [14] Funding: Eli Lilly, UK	Double-blind RCT Maintenance treatment for patients with BD I Study type: CEA Design: Markov model Perspective: UK NHS Time Horizon: 12 months Transition period: NR	431 patients OLZ 5–20 mg/day Comparator: Li 300–800 mg/day	GBP Cost year: NR Direct Costs	(a) No. of mood episodes avoided (b) No. of days in a hospital	Compared with Li, OLZ significantly reduces the number of acute mood episodes per patient from 0.81 to 0.58 (difference: 0.23; 95% CI: 0.34, 0.12). OLZ decreased the average annual costs per patient for the maintenance treatment of BD I by £799 compared with Li (95% CI: £1824–£59)	Univariate and probability sensitivity analyses	OLZ is more cost-effective compared with Li in preventing the number of acute mood episodes
Fajutrao et al. [15] Funding: AstraZeneca, UK	Double-blind RCT Patients with BD I who start in a euthymic state (maintenance phase) Study type: CEA/CUA Design: Markov model Perspective: UK NHS Time horizon: 2 years Transition period: NR	1326 patients QTP 400–800 mg/day + Li/DVP Comparator: Placebo + Li/DVP	GBP Cost year: NR Direct Costs	(a) No. of acute mood episodes (b) No. of acute mood event-related hospitalizations (c) QALYs	QTP + Li/DVP dominated placebo + Li/DVP, presenting lower costs and higher QALYs, and lower numbers of acute mood episodes and hospitalizations. ICER£506 for an additional acute mood event prevented, ICER –£4261 for an additional hospitalization prevented, ICER –£7453 for an additional QALY gained	Univariate and probability sensitivity analyses	Adjunctive QTP and mood-stabilizer therapy with Li/DVP is more cost-effective compared with mood-stabilizer therapy alone in the maintenance treatment of patients with BD I

(continued)

Table 19.1 (continued)

Study	Sample/design	Interventions	Costs	Outcomes	Results	Sensitivity analysis	Conclusions
Woodward et al. [16] Funding: AstraZeneca, USA	Simulated cohort Stabilized patients with BD I who start in a euthymic state Study type: CEA/CUA Design: Markov model Perspective: TPP and societal Time horizon: 24 months Transition period: biweekly cycles	QTP (400–800 mg/day) + Li (0.5–1.2 mEq/L) or DVP (50–125 g/mL) (1000 patients) Comparator: placebo + Li/DVP combination, or no maintenance treatment, or Li or LAM 200 mg/day, or OLZ 12.5 mg/day, or ARP 30 mg/day (1000 patients)	US\$ Cost year: 2007 Direct costs	Costs per QALY	QTP + Li or DVP combination dominates (i.e., is cost saving and produces more QALYs) than placebo + Li/DVP. While the QTP + Li or DVP combination generates 1.49 QALYs at a cost of US\$12,930, placebo + Li/DVP generated 1.44 QALYs at a cost of US\$12,937 over a 2-year period	Univariate and probability sensitivity analyses	QTP + Li/DVP combination is more cost-effective than Li or DVP alone
Woodward et al. [17] Funding: AstraZeneca, USA	Simulated cohort Stabilized patients with BD I (maintenance phase) Study type: CUA Design: Markov model Perspective: TPP and societal Time horizon: NR Transition period: NR	QTP XR + Li/DVP (1000 patients) Comparator: placebo + Li/DVP or LAM or OLZ or ARP (1000 patients)	US\$ Cost year: 2009 Direct and indirect costs	(a) No. of acute mood episodes (b) No. of hospitalizations due to an acute mood event (c) costs per QALY	QTP XR + Li/DVP ICER US\$22 959/QALY compared with placebo + Li/DVP. QTP XR + Li/DVP dominated all other comparators	Univariate and probability sensitivity analyses	QTP XR+ Li/DVP may be a cost-effective maintenance treatment option for patients with BD I
Kasteng et al. [18] Funding: Bristol-Myers Squibb, Sweden	Simulated cohort Patients with BD I who start either in a "no metabolic syndrome" or "metabolic syndrome" state Study type: CUA Design: Markov model Perspective: societal Time horizon: lifetime Transition period: annual	OLZ 10 mg/day or ARP Comparator: No maintenance treatment	krSEK Cost year: 2009 Direct and indirect costs	QALYs	ARP combination dominates OLZ. When compared with OLZ, ARP generates an incremental cost savings of 28,447 SEK while producing 0.04 additional life years and 0.09 additional QALYs	Univariate and probability sensitivity analyses	ARP is more cost-effective than OLZ in terms of metabolic side effects
Ekman et al. [19] Funding: AstraZeneca, UK	Simulated cohort Patients with BD I and BD II (maintenance phase) Study type: CEA/CUA Design: DES Perspective: UK NHS Time horizon: 5 years Transition period: NR	QTP 300–600 mg/day (10,000 patients) Comparator: OLZ 15 mg/day or OLZ 15 mg/day + Li 1000 mg/day or ARP 15 mg/day or RIS 2 mg/day or DVP 1250 mg/day or LAM 200 mg/day or VEN 187.5 mg/day + Li or PAR 30 mg/day + Li (10,000 patients)	GBP Cost year: NR Direct costs and indirect costs	(a) QALYs (b) No. of mood episodes	*Depressive episode* QTP was cost-effective compared with OLZ (all phases) (ICER: £8600/QALY). *Remission* QTP was cost-effective compared with OLZ(ICER: £27,400/QALY)	Univariate and probability sensitivity analyses	Compared with OLZ, the results suggest that QTP is more cost-effective for BD treatment

Chisholm et al. [20] Funding: WHO Two WHO sub regions (sub-Saharan Africa & Southeast Asia) primary/secondary care	Simulated cohort Patients with BD I Study type: CUA Design: Markov model Perspective: healthcare provider Time horizon: lifetime Transition period: NR	1 million patients Li 1200 mg/day or Li + psychosocial care or DVP or DVP + psychosocial care Comparator: placebo	International $ (adjusted for PPP) Cost year: 2000 Direct costs	DALYs	Li and Li + psychological care dominated the rest of the strategies	Univariate and probability sensitivity analyses	At a national GDP per capita threshold of $ 2000, use of Li in a community settings was cost-effective
Sawyer et al. [21] Funding: Lundbeck, France/UK	Simulated cohort Patients with BD I mixed episodes (all phases) Study type: CUA Design: Markov model Perspective: UK NHS Time horizon: 5 years Transition period: NR	ASE Comparator: OLZ or OLZ + DVP or OLZ + Li	GBP Cost year: NR Direct and indirect costs	QALYs	ASE was more cost-effective compared with OLZ (ICER £1302/QALY) (costs for ASE are higher for both the acute and maintenance phases). Savings by avoiding prolonged hospitalization (£2000 over 5 years) are sufficient to offset all of the extra drug costs among patients with mixed episodes	Univariate and probability sensitivity analyses	ASE is a cost-effective alternative to OLZ in the treatment of patients with mixed-episode BD I
Caresano et al. [22] Funding: Lundbeck, Italy	Simulated cohort Patients with mixed episodes of BD I Study type: CUA Design: Markov model Perspective: Italian NHS Time horizon: 5 years Transition period: 4 weeks	ASE or ASE + DVP or ASE + Li Comparator: OLZ or OLZ + DVP or OLZ + Li	Euros Cost year: NR Direct costs	QALYs	ASE dominated OLZ. ASE (ICER €1134.5) saves costs by avoiding hospitalization. ASE generates greater benefits than OLZ (0.0045 more QALY and 0.0041 more QALY when the impact of adverse events is excluded) at lower costs (€1065.4 less)	Univariate and probability sensitivity analyses	Patients with mixed episodes of BD I using ASE as an alternative to OLZ can lead to cost savings for the Italian NHS and improve patients quality of life
Lachaine et al. [23] Funding: Lundbeck S.A.S. Canada	Simulated cohort Patients with BD I Study type: CEA/CUA Design: Markov model Perspective: Canadian NHS and societal Time horizon: 1–5 years Transition period: NR	10,000 patients ASE or ARP Comparator: OLZ	CAD Cost year: NR Direct and indirect costs	(a) QALYs (b) Mortality rates (suicide)	Costs with ASE are lower than with OLZ. Decrease in cost of CAD3,847,300 from an NHS perspective, decrease of CAD3,878,343 from a societal perspective. The number of QALYs with ASE is higher than with OLZ (84.84 QALYs gained)	Univariate and probability sensitivity analyses	This economic evaluation showed that ASE is a dominant alternative over OLZ in the treatment of BD, from both NHS and societal perspectives

ARP aripiprazole, *ASE* asenapine, *BD* bipolar disorder, *BD I* bipolar disorder type I, *CAU* care as usual, *CBT* cognitive-based therapy, *CBZ* carbamazepine, *CEA* cost-effectiveness analysis, *CI* confidence interval, *CUA* cost-utility analysis, *DALY* disability-adjusted life year, *DES* discrete event simulation, *DVP* divalproate, *GBP* Great Britain pound, *GDP* gross domestic product, *HTA*Health Technology Assessment, *ICER* incremental cost-effectiveness ratio, *IMI* imipramine, *KrSEK* Swedish Krona, *LAM* lamotrigine, *Li* lithium, *MCS* Mental Component Scale, *NIHR* National Institute for Health Research, *NHS* National Health System, *NICE* National Institute for Health and Care Excellence, *NR* not reported, *OLZ* olanzapine, *PAR* paroxetine, *PPP* purchasing power parity, *QALY* quality-adjusted life year, *QTP* quetiapine, *QTP XR* Quetiapine Extended Release, *PSA* Probabilistic Sensitivity Analysis, *RCT* randomized clinical trial, *RIS* risperidone, *SF-36* 36-item Short Form Health Survey, *TPP* taxpayer perspective, *VEN* venlafaxine, *WHO* World Health Organization, *WTP* willingness to pay, *YMRS* Young Mania Rating Scale

Study Characteristics

- Similar costs between interventions
- Direct and indirect costs included
- Few cost analyses associated with drugs' adverse effects
- Healthcare payer perspective
- Main outcomes: QALYs, number of days with mood events, number of days free of a bipolar episode, and number of days in inpatient treatment
- Follow-up time: ~12 weeks for acute phase and ~5 years for maintenance phase (model)
- Few willingness-to-pay evaluations performed
- Data origin from meta-analysis, randomized controlled trials, or national guidelines
- Statistical analyses included bootstrapping, regression modeling, Markov models, and discrete event simulation
- All undertook sensitivity analyses.

19.2.1 Cost-Effectiveness of Classical Mood Stabilizers

Classical mood stabilizers (lithium, valproate, carbamazepine) were less studied as BD treatments in the time frame used for this review. Only one systematic review was thoroughly concerned with assessing the economics of older stabilizers. The results from a 2007 economic analysis of patients with a BD depressive episode from the National Institute for Health and Care Excellence suggested that valproate, lithium, and the combination of lithium and imipramine were potentially cost-effective, depending on the willingness to pay (WTP) for additional health gained. Using the U.K. National Health Service threshold (£20,000–40,000 per QALY), no treatment was ruled out on dominance grounds. The incremental cost-effectiveness ratio (ICER) of lithium monotherapy compared with valproate was £10,409 per additional QALY, and the ICER of the combination of lithium and imipramine compared with lithium monotherapy was £21,370 per additional QALY. Thus if the U.K. National Health Service was prepared to pay less than their WTP threshold, then lithium seemed cost-effective, but if more than the WTP was considered, then lithium plus imipramine would be cost-effective. For patients with manic episode, the authors of the 2007 National Institute for Health and Care Excellence study found that lithium monotherapy was more costly and more effective than olanzapine (ICER £11,359 per additional QALY). Hence, using the U.K. threshold as a reference point, the results suggest that lithium was the optimal cost-effective therapy. The study model sensitivity analysis results suggest a number of assumptions: they were markedly altered when lithium was assumed to have a effect on mortality similar to that of the other pharmacological treatments. Specifically, if in the analyses the lithium strategies were not associated with additional mortality effects (e.g., decrease in suicide mortality rates), then valproate would be the dominant strategy for a depressive episode, and all strategies would be dominated by olanzapine for a manic episode. This suggests that the mortality benefit associated with lithium was also central to its cost-effectiveness [13].

19.2.2 Cost-Effectiveness of Atypical Antipsychotics

Current cost-effectiveness studies (2005–2016) of treatments for BD mostly assess recent atypical antipsychotics such as quetiapine, asenapine, and olanzapine. Regarding treatment with quetiapine, five cost-effectiveness analyses and one systematic review were found. Quetiapine monotherapy dominated olanzapine, lithium, and divalproate comparators for all phases of maintenance treatment [16, 19]. As adjunctive therapy, quetiapine in combination with mood stabilizers (lithium/divalproate) was more cost-effective than monotherapy with a mood stabilizer [15, 17, 24]. Plosker [24] showed that quetiapine as monotherapy for a BD episode had more favorable results in comparison with more traditional interventions (venlafaxine + lithium, paroxetine + lithium) [24], but less favorable ones in comparison with aripiprazole [17]. For manic episodes, risperidone and aripiprazole were dominated by quetiapine [24].

Three studies evaluated the cost-effectiveness of asenapine in comparison with that of olanzapine for BD treatment. In the economic model used by Caresano et al. [22], asenapine was the dominant strategy (lower costs and higher effectiveness) in BD mixed episodes. This intervention decreased the duration of hospitalizations, saving €1588.8 over 5 years [22]. Sawyer et al. [21] demonstrated that asenapine was also a cost-effective alternative to olanzapine in the maintenance treatment of mixed episodes and saved costs, avoiding prolonged hospitalization (decreased time hospitalized, saving £2000 over 5 years). The economic evaluation by Lachaine et al. [23] showed that asenapine is a dominant alternative over olanzapine, presenting higher QALYs. The authors included extrapyramidal symptoms, weight gain, and long-term metabolic complications in the model [23].

Pari et al. [25] reviewed five studies of olanzapine's cost-effectiveness in BD treatment. For treatment of manic episodes, the results suggested that olanzapine was less cost-effective than haloperidol and quetiapine + lithium, and equally effective as valproate per additional QALY. However, for maintenance therapy, olanzapine was more cost-effective than lithium in preventing mood episodes [14, 25]. Metabolic side effects were evaluated as outcomes by Kasteng et al. [18], demonstrating that aripiprazole was more cost-effective than olanzapine, with more QALYs gained.

19.2.3 Other Treatments

The cost-effectiveness of electroconvulsive therapy in BD treatment was evaluated by Greenhalgh et al. [26]. They found no conclusive results regarding the cost-effectiveness of electroconvulsive therapy in manic episodes. The authors suggested that this was because of the lack of primary data (from randomized controlled trials) to create adequate uncertainty parameters for the economic model. Only one study assessing psychotherapy was obtained. In the study by Lam et al [9], cognitive behavioral therapy was useful for preventing relapse in BD and was more cost-effective compared with usual care [9].

19.3 Challenges, Gaps, and Limitations of Cost-Effectiveness Studies in Bipolar Disorder

As seen in the previous sections, cost-effectiveness analyses are increasingly common in the literature as decision support tools. These analyses are broadly applicable and can be used in a variety of contexts. However, many gaps, challenges, and limitations can be identified in the published studies reporting economic analysis in BD. Most studies focus on pharmacotherapy. Little is invested in the economic assessment of psychosocial interventions and cost-effectiveness and cost-benefit analyses [27]. In the past decade, the number of complete economic analysis in BD has been growing, and recent systematic and critical reviews of these analyses have demonstrated some important issues with that evidence; these are related not only to methodological challenges but also to the complexity of this severe mental disorder. Some relevant topics calling into question different steps in a cost-effectiveness study in BD are described in the subsequent sections.

19.3.1 Issues Related to the Choice of Comparative Alternatives

Many cost-effectiveness studies in BD compare a range of different classes of drugs through mixed treatment comparisons (MTC) and head-to-head trials, but a smaller number of studies evaluates combinations of medicines (e.g. a mood stabilizer plus an antipsychotic), the use of which is very common in clinical practice. An economic analysis needs to reflect the reality of healthcare interventions in order to be a useful tool for decision makers when planning health policy. In addition, many studies did not justify the choice of alternative interventions in their analysis [5].

19.3.2 Issues Related to Outcomes

Considering that BD figures among mental diseases with high mortality rates (suicide, all causes), mortality would represent an important outcome to consider as an input parameter in cost-effectiveness studies. However, Mohiuddin [5], in a critical review of cost-effectiveness studies of pharmacological treatments in BD, found that half of the revised studies did not include the risk of mortality in their analysis. This gap probably leads to an underestimation of the impact of the disease, as well as biased estimates of the effectiveness of interventions.

The same author reported that none of the studies included in the systematic review considered the possibility of patients having a mixed episode, which can occur in 30–40% of BD populations, making it difficult to judge the consistency of the conclusions of cost-effectiveness studies in this area [5]. We found just two studies that reported results from patients with mixed episodes.

Many cost-effectiveness studies use efficacy measures based on patients' symptom improvement (as response rates or disease-free days). This specific outcome limits comparisons with other healthcare interventions that report using a similar measure. Regulatory agencies and guidelines for cost-effectiveness studies have recommended QALY as the generic outcome measure in cost-effectiveness studies in order to facilitate a wide range of comparisons across different conditions [5]. This is a challenge in BD, since the most popular generic quality-of-life instruments, such as the SF-6D (derived from the SF-36) and EQ-5D, have demonstrated some limitations in some groups with BD. Brazier et al. [28], in a recent systematic review of the validity and responsiveness of generic preference-based measures, reported some concerns in the population with BD: it is unclear whether this instrument is valid in manic or hypomanic individuals; generic measures reflected known differences in clinical measures of depression, but not mania; and the generic measures fail to capture many of the problems that arose in the interviews with patients with BD; this is reflected in the psychometric evidence on validity and responsiveness results. Furthermore, some concern exists around how to obtain reliable information from manic or hypomanic patients when using a self-report questionnaire [28] (see Chap. 6).

19.3.3 Issues Related to the Modelling Technique

BD is a progressive and long-term disease, and in order to accurately represent its progression over time and its economic implications, a modeling framework must be supported by appropriate modeling techniques, model structure, and input parameters.

The choice of modeling techniques in BP is challenging because the natural history of the disease is unpredictable, even in one particular individual; therefore, comparing the follow-up of two different patients can be challenging since they can have completely different patterns of the disorder. The use of a decision tree or Markov model may not adequately represent the heterogeneity between patients because of the restricted ability to capture the reality of BD. Discrete event simulation could be an alternative; it can be used to replicate the time-dependent stochastic behavior of patients at an individual level. However, this method requires expert knowledge to construct a model in an explicit and effective way [5]. So, it is advisable that researchers spend time planning their modeling techniques, considering the pros and cons of each model to judge which one best fits their data. When authors write their articles, it is important to justify the choice of modeling technique used.

19.3.4 Issues Related to the Time Horizon

BD is a lifelong chronic illness, demanding a longer time horizon in economic analysis in order to represent a realistic scenario of the disorder. The use of a short time frame may introduce potential bias, as occurs in some cost-effectiveness studies in this area [5].

In addition to these methodological issues in the cost-effectiveness literature about BD disorder, development of recommendations to support the prioritization of investments in the prevention or treatment of mental illness is challenging not only because of the dearth of studies, but also because of the distinctive characteristics inherent to each population [27]. Economic evaluations are commonly expensive, time-consuming, and demanding in terms of trained human resources with skills in the area. As a consequence, it would be impossible to conduct an economic analysis for every health care intervention. Frequently, decision makers need to assess health technology assessment information from international studies [29].

Geographical transferability of economic data can represent a way of making more efficient use of existing studies and may be the only alternative for some countries where information is scarce. However, the potential applicability of the results from one country to another must be considered carefully. Clinical trials are frequently carried out in populations with genetic, demographic, and cultural characteristics that can present huge differences between countries. Such differences can significantly change parameters such as efficacy, effectiveness, and preferences [29].

Political differences can also be a barrier for the transferability of economic data. While countries such as Canada, the United Kingdom, and Australia have guidelines and economic evaluation studies for the treatment of psychiatric disorders, Brazil, for example, still does not have a policy for the majority of mental diseases.

There seems to be a consensus on the best practices to be adopted for technology transfer. The adoption of clear best practices for internationally recognized economic modeling, the use of the highest-quality evidence, the use of deterministic sensitivity analyses in order to explore potential biases, and the use of probabilistic sensitivity analyses for a broad evaluation of the model are examples of best practices. In line with this, the International Society for Pharmacoeconomics and Outcomes Research Task Force determined that an economic evaluation would be "generalizable" if it were applied to other contexts without adjustments. The group highlighted that many of the studies classified as economic analyses have questionable quality and usefulness for decision making and, as a result, would have very limited applicability. They also found that the perspective of the analysis, discount rates, and approach for assessing the incidence costs and prevalence of diseases are not suitable for all contexts [29].

In this context, several organizations have endeavored to bridge this gap by conducting economic evaluation research. At the international level, these organizations include the World Health Organization (WHO) and its Choosing Interventions that are Cost Effective program, the U.K. National Institute for Health Research Health Technology Assessment program, and the Canadian Agency for Drugs and Technologies in Health. Based on the assumption that the results of cost-effectiveness studies are not equally applicable to all countries and that pooling these results at a single clearinghouse would be useful to researchers and health administrators alike, in 1998, the WHO Choosing Interventions that are Cost Effective program created a database of cost-effectiveness results divided into 14 WHO subregions that have similar epidemiological, infrastructure, and economic characteristics. The program has published results for several mental health topics in the "AMR B" subregion, which includes Brazil. These topics have included measures for reducing hazardous alcohol use, determining the cost-effectiveness of schizophrenia treatment, and developing clinical interventions for reducing the consequences of BD and depression [5].

19.4 Limitations in the Review Studies Cited in This Chapter

Many studies evaluated here were limited regarding design choices, comparator evaluation, outcome measures, and data management. One of the most frequent limitations found was that studies did not describe drug dosages and titration for interventions and comparators. As is known by clinical psychiatrists and presented by randomized controlled trial data, several psychotropic medications need to be used at particular dosages to be capable of decreasing or resolving symptoms. By choosing to not show dose values, studies introduce some degree of uncertainty to the effectiveness of the data they present, since lower than recommended doses may falsely represent less drug efficacy and higher than recommended doses may increase side effects.

Few reviewed studies compared classical mood stabilizers with atypical antipsychotics. Even today, most assistant psychiatrists use lithium, valproate, and carbamazepine to treat BD. Although efficacy and effectiveness of atypical antipsychotics have been established for BD treatment, current guidelines still recommend classical mood stabilizers as treatment first choice [30, 31]. The lack of comparisons with them may poorly represent clinical practice and incorrectly identify a lack of cost-effectiveness for this type of drug. In addition, most proposed interventions were not in concordance with well-established guidelines, which can cause a possible misinterpretation of the effectiveness results.

From an external validation perspective, the fact that the majority of results were extracted from secondary and indirect sources produces a less robust and consistent interpretation of the results. This is an inherited limitation of simulation studies and is an important observation that points to the lack of primary data found in psychiatry, particularly on treatment for BD.

19.5 Conclusions

A central challenge for decision-making is heterogeneity among published studies, with a paucity of analyses comparing a wide range of therapeutic alternatives for BD treatment. All drug alternatives reviewed were cost-effective; nonetheless, it is important to note that mainly atypical antipsychotics were the selected strategy. Interests of industries and authors guided drug and protocol choices – decisions that could be based on biased assumptions and decision-making processes.

Conclusions regarding which treatments for BD are "best" in terms of effectiveness ratio is difficult because it depends on the WTP for mental health treatments in each healthcare system. When planning cost-effectiveness studies in BD, researchers need to be aware of the knowledge required to develop advanced models (e.g., discrete event simulation) that are able to represent the reality of this long-term disease, with a wide variability of outcomes during follow-up (see Chap. 7).

Key Messages

- BD is a complex condition presenting many challenges for economic evaluation and modeling.
- Atypical antipsychotics seem to be the optimal cost-effective interventions when compared with traditional mood stabilizers, per the reviewed studies presented here.
- Minimal or null cost-effective evidence for nonpharmacological strategies is available.

References

1. American Psychiatric Association. Diagnostic and statistical manual of mental disorders, fifth edition (DSM-V). Washington: American Psychiatric Publishing; 2013.
2. Grande I, Berk M, Birmaher B, Vieta E. Bipolar disorder. Lancet. 2016;387(10027):1561–72.
3. Conus P, Macneil C, McGorry PD. Public health significance of bipolar disorder: implications for early intervention and prevention. Bipolar Disord. 2014;16(5):548–56.
4. Kleinman L, Lowin A, Flood E, Gandhi G, Edgell E, Revicki D. Costs of bipolar disorder. PharmacoEconomics. 2003;21(9):601–22.
5. Mohiuddin S. A systematic and critical review of model-based economic evaluations of pharmacotherapeutics in patients with bipolar disorder. Appl Health Econ Health Policy. 2014;12(4):359–72.
6. World Health Organization. The global burden of disease: 2004 update. Geneva: WHO Press; 2008.
7. Weinstein MC, Siegel JE, Gold MR, Kamlet MS, Russell LB. Recommendations of the panel on cost-effectiveness in health and medicine. JAMA. 1996;276(15):1253–8.
8. Revicki DA, Hirschfeld RM, Ahearn EP, Weisler RH, Palmer C, Keck Jr PE. Effectiveness and medical

costs of divalproex versus lithium in the treatment of bipolar disorder: results of a naturalistic clinical trial. J Affect Disord. 2005;86(2–3):183–93.

9. Lam DH, McCrone P, Wright K, Kerr N. Cost-effectiveness of relapse-prevention cognitive therapy for bipolar disorder: 30-month study. BrJ Psychiatry. 2005;186:500–6.
10. Calvert NW, Burch SP, Fu AZ, Reeves P, Thompson TR. The cost-effectiveness of lamotrigine in the maintenance treatment of adults with bipolar I disorder. J Manag Care Pharm: JMCP. 2006;12(4):322–30.
11. National Institute for Health and Clinical Excellence. Bipolar disorder: the Management of Bipolar Disorder in adults, children and adolescents, in primary and secondary care. Leicester: National Institute for Health and Clinical Excellence; 2006.
12. Klok RM, Al Hadithy AF, van Schayk NP, Antonisse AJ, Caro JJ, Brouwers JR, et al. Pharmacoeconomics of quetiapine for the management of acute mania in bipolar I disorder. Expert Rev Pharmacoecon Outcomes Res. 2007;7(5):459–67.
13. Soares-Weiser K, Bravo Vergel Y, Beynon S, Dunn G, Barbieri M, Duffy S, et al. A systematic review and economic model of the clinical effectiveness and cost-effectiveness of interventions for preventing relapse in people with bipolar disorder. Health Technol Assess. 2007;11(39):iii–iv, ix–206.
14. McKendrick J, Cerri KH, Lloyd A, D'Ausilio A, Dando S, Chinn C. Cost effectiveness of olanzapine in prevention of affective episodes in bipolar disorder in the United Kingdom. J Psychopharmacol. 2007;21(6):588–96.
15. Fajutrao L, Paulsson B, Liu S, Locklear J. Cost-effectiveness of quetiapine plus mood stabilizers compared with mood stabilizers alone in the maintenance therapy of bipolar I disorder: results of a Markov model analysis. Clin Ther. 2009;31(Pt 1):1456–68.
16. Woodward TC, Tafesse E, Quon P, Kim J, Lazarus A. Cost-effectiveness of quetiapine with lithium or divalproex for maintenance treatment of bipolar I disorder. J Med Econ. 2009;12(4):259–68.
17. Woodward TC, Tafesse E, Quon P, Lazarus A. Cost effectiveness of adjunctive quetiapine fumarate extended-release tablets with mood stabilizers in the maintenance treatment of bipolar I disorder. PharmacoEconomics. 2010;28(9):751–64.
18. Kasteng F, Eriksson J, Sennfalt K, Lindgren P. Metabolic effects and cost-effectiveness of aripiprazole versus olanzapine in schizophrenia and bipolar disorder. Acta Psychiatrica Scandinavica. 2011;124:214–225.
19. Ekman M, Lindgren P, Miltenburger C, Meier G, Locklear JC, Chatterton ML. Cost effectiveness of quetiapine in patients with acute bipolar depression and in maintenance treatment after an acute depressive episode. PharmacoEconomics. 2012;30(6):513–30.
20. Chisholm D, van Ommeren M, Ayuso-Mateos JL, Saxena S. Cost-effectiveness of clinical interventions for reducing the global burden of bipolar disorder. Br J Psychiatry. 2005;187:559–67.
21. Sawyer L, Azorin JM, Chang S, Rinciog C, Guiraud-Diawara A, Marre C, et al. Cost-effectiveness of asenapine in the treatment of bipolar I disorder patients with mixed episodes. J Med Econ. 2014;17(7):508–19.
22. Caresano C, Di Sciascio G, Fagiolini A, Maina G, Perugi G, Ripellino C, et al. Cost-effectiveness of asenapine in the treatment of patients with bipolar I disorder with mixed episodes in an Italian context. Adv Ther. 2014;31(8):873–90.
23. Lachaine J, Beauchemin C, Mathurin K, Gilbert D, Beillat M. Cost-effectiveness of asenapine in the treatment of bipolar disorder in Canada. BMC Psychiatry. 2014;14:16.
24. Plosker GL. Quetiapine: a pharmacoeconomic review of its use in bipolar disorder. PharmacoEconomics. 2012;30(7):611–31.
25. Pari AA, Simon J, Wolstenholme J, Geddes JR, Goodwin GM. Economic evaluations in bipolar disorder: a systematic review and critical appraisal. Bipolar Disord. 2014;16(6):557–82.
26. Greenhalgh J, Knight C, Hind D, Beverley C, Walters S. Clinical and cost-effectiveness of electroconvulsive therapy for depressive illness, schizophrenia, catatonia and mania: systematic reviews and economic modelling studies. Health Technol Assess. 2005;9(9):1–156, iii–iv.
27. Lima AF, Cruz LN, Polanczyk CA, Maia CR. Economic evaluation in the field of mental health: conceptual basis. Rev Bras Psiquiatr. 2013;35(2):186–92.
28. Brazier J, Connell J, Papaioannou D, Mukuria C, Mulhern B, Peasgood T, et al. A systematic review, psychometric analysis and qualitative assessment of generic preference-based measures of health in mental health populations and the estimation of mapping functions from widely used specific measures. Health Technol Assess. 2014;18(34):vii–viii, xiii–xxv, 1–188.
29. Cruz L, Lima AF, Graeff-Martins A, Maia CR, Ziegelmann P, Miguel S, et al. Mental health economics: insights from Brazil. J Ment Health. 2013;22(2):111–21.
30. Yatham LN, Kennedy SH, Schaffer A, Parikh SV, Beaulieu S, O'Donovan C, Young LT. Canadian Network for Mood and Anxiety Treatments (CANMAT) and International Society for Bipolar Disorders (ISBD) collaborative update of CANMAT guidelines for the management of patients with bipolar disorder: update 2009. Bipolar Disord. 2009;11(3):225–55.
31. National Collaborating Centre for Mental Health – UK. Bipolar disorder: The management of bipolar disorder in adults, children and adolescents, in primary and secondary care. British Psychological Society. 2006. https://www.ncbi.nlm.nih.gov/books/n/nicecollect/

20 Cost-Effectiveness of Antipsychotics in the Treatment of Schizophrenia Disorders

Mônica Kayo and Denise Razzouk

Abstract

The aim of this chapter is to provide a critical overview of cost-effectiveness studies of antipsychotics in the treatment of psychotic disorders. Relevant studies were briefly reviewed and analyzed according to perspective, funding sources, outcomes, comparators, and time horizon. Differences in the cost-effectiveness of older, first-generation antipsychotics and the newer second-generation drugs are still a matter of debate. Several methodological issues limit the generalization of cost-effectiveness studies across countries.

Key Points Summary

- Characteristics of economic evaluations of antipsychotics
- The burden of schizophrenia
- Guidelines and treatment algorithms
- Outcomes
- Funding
- Perspective
- Time horizon
- Comparators
- What is a cost-effective antipsychotic?

20.1 Introduction

The use of antipsychotics in psychiatric practice began in the 1950s [1] with the introduction of chlorpromazine in the market. Since then, newer antipsychotics have been developed and adopted for the treatment of psychotic disorders. Until the early 1990s, drug choice was based mainly on efficacy and tolerability criteria; clozapine was the only atypical antipsychotic available at that time, and its use was restricted to treatment-resistant schizophrenia. Although clozapine has been proven to have superior efficacy for treatment of severe psychosis, life-threatening risks due to adverse events – namely, agranulocytosis – became the main restriction to its widespread use [2]. Therefore, pharmaceutical companies began racing to find the ideal antipsychotic, which should combine the efficacy of clozapine and no hematological side effect. As a result, several newer antipsychotic drugs were

M. Kayo (✉) • D. Razzouk
Centre of Economic Mental Health, Department of Psychiatry, Universidade Federal de Sao Paulo, Rua Borges Lagoa 570, 1° andar, São Paulo, Brazil
e-mail: monica.kayo@gmail.com; drazzouk@gmail.com

D. Razzouk (ed.), *Mental Health Economics*, DOI 10.1007/978-3-319-55266-8_20

Table 20.1 First-generation antipsychotics (FGAs) and second-generation antipsychotics (SGAs)

	First-generation antipsychotics (typicals)	Second-generation antipsychotics (atypicals)
Oral	Chlorpromazine Levomepromazine Thioridazine Trifluoperazine Pimozide Sulpiride Zuclopenthixol	Amisulpride Aripiprazole Asenapine Clozapine Lurasidone Olanzapine Paliperidone Quetiapine Quetiapine XR (extended release) Risperidone Sertindole Ziprasidone
Injectable	Fluphenazine long-acting injectable Haloperidol decanoate Pipothiazine depot Zuclopentixol decanoate	Aripiprazole long-acting injectable Olanzapine long-acting injectable Paliperdione long-acting injectable Risperidone long-acting injectable

launched after the 1990s, starting with risperidone, followed by olanzapine, ziprasidone, and quetiapine, among others. The newer drugs were classified as atypicals, or second-generation antipsychotics (SGAs), and, as a rule, and independent of their similar comparative efficacy and tolerability, they had higher prices than older, first-generation antipsychotics (FGAs) such as haloperidol and chlorpromazine [3]. In Table 20.1 the most common FGAs and SGAs available worldwide are listed.

The emergence of new and expensive antipsychotics challenged stakeholders involved in the treatment of schizophrenia and other psychoses, who questioned whether it would be worthwhile to pay more for the newer drugs [4–6]. One of the main concerns for public policies regarding rational resource allocation is the remarkable differences in prices among antipsychotics: costs for atypicals can be 167 times greater than cost for typicals; even among atypicals, one study found unit costs for olanzapine to be 400 times higher than unit costs for risperidone [6]. However, focusing exclusively on costs does not allow for the best choices because schizophrenia imposes diverse costs in multiple sectors. Expensive treatment would be acceptable if it provided better outcomes in comparison with cheaper available treatments, that is, cost-effectiveness [5] (see Chap. 5). Yet, health economics questions have arisen regarding which outcome could be measured (and how) to verify the best value for the money that is, the best treatment for a fair price? By "stakeholders" we mean payers, patients and caregivers, healthcare professionals, policymakers, and healthcare providers. The answers to these queries should come from economic analyses.

20.2 Characteristics of Economic Evaluations of Antipsychotics

Economic evaluations measure costs and outcomes, allowing two or more competing alternatives to be compared, and they are a powerful tool for decision-making in healthcare [7]. The two main economic evaluations used to support the decision-making process in health field are cost-effectiveness analysis (CEA) and cost-utility analysis (CUA) (see Chaps. 5 and 6). The World Bank and the World Health Organization recommend the use of cost-effectiveness studies for decision-making and budget allocation, especially for countries with scarce resources [8]. However, there is a paucity of economic evaluation in the majority of countries, especially among low- and middle-income countries. Similarly, the majority of clinical trials published in the literature has not added an economic component, though there is a growing trend to incorporate one [9].

Likewise, economic evaluations are scarce in the field of Psychiatry, and the majority of data published on this topic come from modeling studies (Chap. 7). The main limitation in this regard is the use of data extracted from multiple sources, including clinical trials (when available), which may not necessarily reflect the real world (see Chap. 7). Because economic modeling carries all the limitations from the extrapolation of data from clinical trials, the ideal economic evaluation regarding comparison among antipsychotics is empirical, head-to-head trials designed for such a purpose, .

According to the Consolidated Health Economics Evaluation Reporting Standards checklist, some items are crucial for reporting and analyzing CEA studies: outcomes, comparators, perspective, time horizon, and funding [10]. In the case of schizophrenia disorders and antipsychotics, CEA studies should consider factors such as stage of the disease, because response to treatment is different as disease progresses. Moreover, the burden of schizophrenia [5, 11] is reflected on other sectors of society, and non–health-related costs and outcomes should be taken into account, as well as the need for broader perspectives should be considered.

20.3 The Burden of Schizophrenia

The early onset and chronic course of schizophrenia are responsible for its enormous burden, in spite of its relatively low prevalence. The burden of schizophrenia affects patients, caregivers, healthcare systems, and society.

The economic burden of schizophrenia comes from direct costs, indirect costs, and intangible costs [4, 5].Among direct health costs, hospital care is the main driver and can range from 19% (in the United States) to 92% (in Belgium), demonstrating a great variability in treatment patterns [12]. In the 1990s, the World Health Organization estimated that direct costs of schizophrenia in Western countries ranged from 1.6% to 2.6% of total healthcare expenditures [13].

Indirect costs of schizophrenia are those related to loss of productivity, unemployment, loss of caregiver productivity and time, increased morbidity, and premature mortality [4, 14] (see Chap. 25). From a societal perspective, the main contributor to schizophrenia costs are indirect costs, accounting for 50–85% of total costs [14]. Intangible costs are those related to the deterioration in quality of life of patients, families, and friends as a result of other factors such as pain and suffering.

The total costs of schizophrenia in the United States in 2002 were estimated to be US$62.7 billion [15]. Interestingly, from 1991 to 2002, inpatient costs decreased while outpatient and medication costs increased in the United States. This decrease in inpatient costs can be explained by changes in Medicaid payment practices and the expansion of managed care programs that incentivize clinical staff to return patients to outpatient status as soon as possible. The use of clozapine has also been mentioned as a factor of decreased inpatient costs, as this drug is associated with lower hospitalization rates among patients who otherwise would have been chronically hospitalized [15].

20.4 Guidelines and Treatment Algorithms

Several guidelines exist for the treatment of schizophrenia [16–19]. They all share the following recommendations: antipsychotic monotherapy is preferred over polytherapy, and clozapine should be given to patients with treatment-resistant schizophrenia. The Schizophrenia Patient Outcomes Research Team [17] recommendations include avoiding olanzapine as a first choice for young patients because of the risk of metabolic adverse events [20]. The use of antipsychotic polytherapy is not recommended as first- or second-line treatment by any guideline because there is no proven benefit to combining antipsychotics; rather, the association increases adverse events and costs [6]. The exception is in the super-refractory population, that is, those refractory to clozapine. In such cases, adding another antipsychotic to clozapine could be attempted to augment clozapine's efficacy, but even this strategy is not fully supported by clinical evidence [21].

All the guidelines recommend, based on efficacy, either FGAs (typicals) or SGAs (atypicals). The guidelines do not take into account cost-effectiveness of the available pharmacological treatments. Since the differences among the antipsychotics are mainly based on effectiveness, which includes not only efficacy but also tolerability and adherence aspects, which outcomes should be pursued when analyzing cost-effectiveness? Which outcomes could really influence resource allocation? Which analyses could better support decision-making in low- and middle-income countries? What are the risks in using data from high-income countries?

20.5 Outcomes

The purpose of economic evaluation is to support decisions to achieve the best possible intervention for a patient using available resources. Because both typical and atypical antipsychotics are efficacious in reducing psychotic symptoms but have different side effect profiles, the outcome should reflect the information required for decision-making.

The choice of outcome in mental health is not straightforward (see Chap. 3), and in the case of schizophrenia it is even more complex. Economic evaluation can provide different levels of information in this regard. CEAs are useful for comparing two or more treatments oriented mostly toward clinical outcomes (e.g., psychotic symptoms, negative symptoms). These outcomes are measured by specific scales for psychosis, such as the Positive and Negative Syndrome Scale. However, CEAs are too narrow in terms of capturing all the benefits of treatments; CEAs require only one outcome. Then, depending on the choice of outcome and which drugs are compared, one drug can or cannot be cost-effective. However, it is important to note that in this case a drug would be cost-effective for one outcome, and potential benefits from changing other outcomes are not included. The majority of CEA studies use a healthcare provider perspective and do not include indirect costs; therefore, in terms of resource allocation, it might be said that good treatments in terms of generating benefits are not necessarily cost-effective [5]. In schizophrenia disorder, multidimensional evaluations are essential, rather than focusing only on improving psychotic symptoms.

One alternative to CEA is CUA using generic indicators, usually encompassing multiple dimensions. The most known are quality-adjusted life years (QALYs) and disability-adjusted life years. Regarding QALYs, the use of CUA for capturing changes in outcomes and QALYs in schizophrenia have many methodological restrictions (see Chaps. 3 and 5). While CUA information is useful to determine resource allocation between different programs and diseases, it is not "fair" in the case of schizophrenia because the potential benefits of treatment are not appropriately captured using QALY measurements. In this regard, disability-adjusted life years better address reduction of the disability caused by schizophrenia, though some methodological issues have been raised for this process, too.

The only economic evaluation able to capture all the benefits of schizophrenia treatments is cost-benefit analysis (CBA). CBA adopts a societal perspective and computes indirect costs, direct costs, informal care costs, spillover effects, and gains to individuals and to society; for this reason CBA is the best economic evaluation for providing accurate information for resource allocation. However, applying CBA methods in health, especially in mental health, has methodological constraints. Because of the cognitive impairments in and some peculiarities of people with schizophrenia, the use of willingness-to-pay techniques were difficult to apply, though this kind of obstacle has also occurred with time trade-off and standard gamble (see Chaps. 3, 4 and 6). Discrete choice experiments have recently been tested in the Mental Health field, and with schizophrenia disorder in especial, showing some promising results (see Chap. 4).

New approaches have more recently been proposed as alternatives to economic evaluation; one example is the capability approach (see Chap. 9), in which several dimensions are considered in terms of having minimal capability for living at decent standards. However, it is still premature to affirm that this approach is the best alternative, and studies of this are still in progress.

Another important issue is the choice of intermediate outcomes for CEA studies, such as hospitalization rates or length of hospitalization. These are not actually "intermediate" outcomes because they are not necessarily related to the improvement of users' mental health. In fact, economic evaluation requires primary outcomes. If one treatment claims superiority over another because it decreases the number of days of hospitalization, several aspects should be taken into account before making this conclusion: the healthcare system, the treatment setting, access to hospitals, and the costs of hospitalization. Moreover, such studies define hospitalization rates the same way they define relapse rates, which is not necessarily true. A patient's symptoms may worsen without them being hospitalized; conversely, hospitalization may occur for reasons other than a relapse. Economic modeling usually extracts data from randomized clinical trials to make an assumption about hospitalization rates, which is another reason to interpret the results with caution. Decision models using rehospitalizations as outcomes found that SGAs are dominant in comparison with haloperidol (i.e., SGAs were less costly and more effective) [22, 23], but such results were not confirmed by clinical trials that used broader outcomes such as QALYs, quality of life, and quality of well-being [24–26].

In summary, it is important to verify the real meaning of the outcome presented in an study and explain how assumptions were made.

20.6 Funding

The funding of a study is an important source of bias. Results of industry-funded studies significantly favor expensive atypical antipsychotics over typical antipsychotics when compared with non–industry-funded studies [27]. In 90.0% of studies, the reported overall outcome is in favor of the sponsor's drug [28].

The majority of published cost-effectiveness studies are conducted by pharmaceutical companies, mainly in high-income countries. The concentration of studies in high-income countries might occur because of the demands of regulatory agencies such as the U.S. Food and Drug Administration, the European Medicines Agency, and the National Institute for Health and Clinical Excellence, which provides guidance on health technology and clinical practice to the National Health Service in England and Wales. This scenario raises the need for conducting more independent analyses and more cost-effectiveness studies in low- and middle-income countries, where healthcare systems have particular characteristics; this should prevent decision-makers from importing data from high-income countries. The paucity of economic evidence in the published literature using data from developing countries has been observed in other healthcare areas, as critically stated by Mulligan et al. [29], who were alert to the need for economic evaluation with a broader view and transparency that takes into account local constraints.

Many industry-sponsored clinical trials indicate that atypicals are superior to typicals in terms of efficacy and tolerability. However, in addition to the sponsorship bias, such trials are often too short or include a highly selected population that does not reflect reality. SGAs replaced the FGAs without superior cost-effectiveness proven by large-scale studies [5].

Two pragmatic clinical trials not sponsored by pharmaceutical companies were carried out to look for data that could help in decision-making, especially in the public health setting: the Clinical Antipsychotic Trials of Intervention Effectiveness (CATIE) study [25] and the Cost Utility of the Latest Antipsychotic drugs in Schizophrenia Study (CUtLASS) [26, 30]. The characteristics of both studies are summarized in Table 20.2.

Analysis of the cost-effectiveness of SGAs and perphenazine using data from the CATIE trial, with QALY as the outcome, concluded that the average total monthly healthcare costs were US$300–600 (20–30%) lower for perphenazine

Table 20.2 CATIE and CUtLASS characteristics [25, 26, 30]

Study	CATIE	CUtLASS
Subjects (N)	1493	227
Design	Double-blind, randomized, multicenter	Randomized, rater-blinded, multicenter
Setting	57 clinical sites in the United States, including university clinics, Veterans Affairs centers, and private clinics	Five medical schools in England
First-generation (typical) antipsychotic	Perphenazine	Several (mostly sulpiride)
Second-generation (atypical) antipsychotics	Olanzapine, quetiapine, risperidone, ziprasidone	Amisulpride, olanzapine, quetiapine, risperidone
Duration of the study	18 months	12 months
Population	Schizophrenia (excluding subjects with schizoaffective disorders) (DSM-IV)	Schizophrenia, schizoaffective disorders, and delusional disorder (DSM-IV)
Age	18–65 years	18–65 years
Primary outcome	Discontinuation of treatment for any cause	QLS
Primary outcome (cost-effectiveness)	QALY	QLS
Secondary outcomes	PANSS CGI	PANSS Calgary Depression Scale Adherence Extrapyramidal symptoms Participant satisfaction
Funding	National Institute of Mental Health	UK National Health Services

CGI clinical global impression, *DSM-IV Diagnostic and Statistical Manual of Mental Disorders*, 4th ed., *PANSS* Positive and Negative Syndrome Scale, *QALY* quality-adjusted life year, *QLS* quality of life scale

than for SGAs because of lower drug costs, and found no significant differences between perphenazine and any of the SGAs, either in QALY ratings or PANSS ratings [25].

CUtLASS came to somewhat similar conclusions. The study found no disadvantage in terms of quality of life, symptoms, or associated costs of care over 1 year when starting treatment with FGAs rather than SGAs in people with schizophrenia [26].

CATIE and CUtLASS are mentioned in this section to challenge the importance of study funding. It is interesting that these two non–industry-funded trials favored older, cheaper antipsychotics rather than newer SGAs. However, both studies have limitations: they were not long enough to detect differences in longer-term side effects such as tardive dyskinesia or metabolic syndrome.

SGAs are an important advance in the treatment of schizophrenia and other psychoses, but the differences between SGAs and FGAs in terms of clinical effectiveness and relapse prevention may not be as great as previously believed. From an individual patient perspective, the multiple choices are an advantage, but from a societal perspective, the heterogeneity of the antipsychotics, even within the same class (typicals or atypicals), adds complexity to analyses.

20.7 Perspective

When analyzing a cost-effectiveness study, it is fundamental to determine the study's perspective. However, in a review of the global burden of schizophrenia, the authors found that fewer than half (23/56; 41%) of the studies included in the review explicitly stated the perspective taken [14]. Keep in mind that the answer to the question, "How much is a symptom-free day worth?" varies depending on the perspective [15]. For the calculation of burden and cost of illness, the societal and payer perspectives are the most used [14]; when speaking of cost-effectiveness studies, however, the majority are conducted from the payer (either public or private) perspective. The reason for the predominance of the payer perspective is probably because such studies (usually based on modeling) are motivated by the possibility of obtaining reimbursement from healthcare providers and to convince policymakers.

Studies using a patient perspective are rare. Specifically, costs from a patient perspective are typically expenses that patients pay for medical products or healthcare services not covered by their health insurance [31]. Understanding and comparing the costs across different perspectives may help to identify areas where costs shift and may result in better health policies.

20.8 Time Horizon

Schizophrenia is a chronic illness, with onset commonly in early adulthood. Each stage of schizophrenia has particular features: the age of the patient, the caregiver situation, the most appropriate treatment (psychosocial and pharmacological), and the disease severity. The disease is characterized by acute episodes of psychosis and periods of relative stability. In summary, the disease changes over time, and each period has distinct needs and requires specific solutions.

A cost-effectiveness study is limited by its time horizon. Studies should be carried out over a time frame long enough to capture the longer-term consequences of an outcome. We cannot make conclusions about schizophrenia by considering its full course. For instance, an SGA may be more cost-effective than an FGA in a 6-month study. However, the metabolic side effects related to some SGAs may not be observed in the short term, which could affect morbidity and adherence. We can also consider the CATIE trial and CUtLASS, which did not find differences in effectiveness between SGAs and FGAs, but the time horizon did not allow the impact of tardive dyskinesia to be observed, which could favor the SGAs [25, 26].

20.9 Comparators

A cost-effectiveness study should ideally compare a new intervention with the best available alternative, or at least with the choices available to physicians. However, few trials include a comparator that represents the standard therapy [32]. The choice of comparator is influenced by many factors, from the purpose and perspective of the study to the organization of the healthcare system.

Cost-effectiveness studies comparing a new intervention with another relatively new and expensive intervention are common, for instance, studies comparing the paliperidone long-acting injectable with the olanzapine long-acting injectable or the risperidone long-acting injectable [33–36] (usually in modeling studies). It is noteworthy that in the absence of data from clinical trials, models are based on expert opinion about the likely effect(s) of the studied drug.

Taking into account the limitation of the models, the Veteran Affairs Administration decided to conduct a naturalistic randomized clinical trial to assess the cost-effectiveness of long-acting risperidone, comparing this drug to oral antipsychotics (mostly SGAs but also FGAs) [24]. The study enrolled patients with poor medication adherence, higher hospitalization rates, and significant comorbidities. Different from studies based on modeling, this trial did not find any additional benefit in effectiveness among patients taking long-acting risperidone. The authors concluded that the risperidone long-acting injectable did not improve clinical outcomes or decrease hospitalization costs; in fact, it added US$4060 to annual pharmacy costs, and excluding it from formularies would save costs without affecting patient welfare [24]. This study compared the new intervention with available antipsychotics and challenged statements from previous studies that long-acting injectable SGAs decreased costs through lower hospitalization rates resulting from higher adherence to treatment. The conclusions of the Veteran Affairs study cannot be generalized, as they reflect a specific system within the United States. Patients covered by the Veterans Health Administration are usually older and have a higher income than patients with other types of insurance.

Cost-effectiveness studies of lurasidone (an SGA) have proven its favorable cost-effectiveness in comparison with quetiapine extended release [37] and aripiprazole [38], two other expensive SGAs. It is not a surprise that the results favored the sponsor's drug, since as we previously discussed a study's source of funding is an important source of bias [27, 28].

We are not saying here that industry-sponsored studies do not have a role. Instead, our recommendation is to always pay attention to the final purpose of the study and its characteristics, such as the chosen comparator, perspective, outcome, type of study (clinical trial or modeling), and time horizon, in addition to the funding source. A critical analysis is fundamental to good decision-making.

20.10 What Is a Cost-Effective Antipsychotic?

The cost-effectiveness of an antipsychotic or any other drug depends on several factors: the comparator, outcomes, perspective, and time horizon. Clinical trials are better than modeling studies in terms of accuracy, but they are more expensive and findings are not generalizable. The particularities of each country require specific analyses and are seldom answered by imported studies and models. Low- and middle-income countries have different needs in comparison with high-income countries. Various methodological issues in cost-effectiveness studies limit the conclusions that can be drawn.

Until now, no conclusive evidence on the cost-effectiveness of SGAs has been found, and the comparisons between FGAs and SGAs are still a matter of debate [5, 32]. Clozapine seems to be an exception, with proven cost-effectiveness for treatment-resistant patients, particularly those with high use of inpatient services [5, 32, 39].

In summary, it is not possible – nor was it our intention – to state which antipsychotics are most cost-effective. Instead, it is important to always make critical use of available studies, especially when data are not generated locally.

Key Messages

- The main component of schizophrenia burden is indirect costs.
- Head-to-head comparison in clinical trials is a more accurate method to assess cost-effectiveness, though results are not generalizable.
- The funding of a study is an important source of bias.
- The majority of cost-effectiveness studies have been done in high-income countries.
- Treatment guidelines usually do not account for cost-effectiveness.
- Cost-effectiveness depends on the context, the healthcare system, and the stage of the disease.
- Until now, there has been no convincing evidence that SGAs are more cost-effective than FGAs.
- Results from cost-effectiveness studies cannot be generalized.

References

1. Ban TA. Fifty years chlorpromazine: a historical perspective. Neuropsychiatr Dis Treat. 2007;3(4):495–500.
2. Warnez S, Alessi-Severini S. Clozapine: a review of clinical practice guidelines and prescribing trends. BMC Psychiatry. 2014;14:102.
3. Kendall T. The rise and fall of the atypical antipsychotics. Br J Psychiatry. 2011;199(4):266–8.
4. Knapp M, Razzouk D. Costs of schizophrenia. Psychiatry. 2008;7(11):491–4.
5. Knapp M, Razzouk D. Economic evaluation and schizophrenia. In: Kasper S, Papadimitriou GN, editors. Schizophrenia: biopsychosocial approaches and current challenges. 2nd ed. London: Informa Healthcare; 2009. p. 347–61.
6. Razzouk D, Kayo M, Sousa A, Gregorio G, Cogo-Moreira H, Cardoso AA, et al. The impact of antipsychotic polytherapy costs in the public health care in Sao Paulo, Brazil. PLoS One. 2015;10(4):e0124791.
7. Drummond MF, Sculpher MJ, Torrance GW, BJ O'B, Stoddart GL. Methods for the economic evaluation of health care programmes. 3rd ed. Oxford: Oxford University Press; 2007.

8. World Health Organization. Making choices in health: the WHO guide to cost-effectiveness analysis. WHO Publications, 2003. World Health Organization; 2003.
9. Knapp M. Economic evaluation and mental health: sparse past. Fertile future? J Ment Health Policy Econ. 1999;2(4):163–7. www.ipap.org/schiz/index.php
10. Husereau D, Culyer AJ, Neumann P, Jacobs P. How do economic evaluations inform health policy decisions for treatment and prevention in Canada and the United States? Appl Health Econ Health Policy. 2015;13(3):273–9.
11. Knapp M. Economic outcomes and levers: impacts for individuals and society. Int Psychogeriatr. 2007;19(3):483–95.
12. Charrier N, Chevreul K, Durand-Zaleski I. The cost of schizophrenia: a literature review. Encephale. 2013;39(Suppl 1):S49–56.
13. Barbato A. WHO. Nations for mental health: schizophrenia and public health. Geneva: World Health Organization; 1998.
14. Chong HY, Teoh SL, Wu DB, Kotirum S, Chiou CF, Chaiyakunapruk N. Global economic burden of schizophrenia: a systematic review. Neuropsychiatr Dis Treat. 2016;12:357–73.
15. McEvoy J. The costs of schizophrenia. J Clin Psychiatry. 2007;68(suppl 1):4–7.
16. IPAP. The international psychiopharmacology algorithm project (IPAP): schizophrenia algorithm; 2006. www.ipap.org/schiz/index.php
17. Buchanan RW, Kreyenbuhl J, Kelly D, Noel J, Boggs D, Fischer B, et al. The 2009 schizophrenia PORT psychopharmacological treatment recommendations and summary statements. Schizophrenia bulletin. Schizophr Bull. 2010;36(1):71–93.
18. Moore TA, Buchanan RW, Buckley PF, Chiles JA, Conley RR, Crismon ML, et al. The Texas medication algorithm project antipsychotic algorithm for schizophrenia: 2006 update. J Clin Psychiatry. 2007;68(11):1751–62.
19. Hasan A, Falkai P, Wobrock T, Lieberman J, Glenthoj B, Gattaz W, et al. World Federation of Societies of Biological Psychiatry (WFSBP) guidelines for biological treatment of schizophrenia, part 2: update 2012 on the long-term treatment of schizophrenia and management of antipsychotic-induced side effects. World J Biol Psychiatry. 2013;14(1):2–44.
20. Correll CU, Frederickson AM, Kane JM, Manu P. Does antipsychotic polypharmacy increase the risk for metabolic syndrome? Schizophr Res. 2007;89(1–3):91–100.
21. Barbui C, Signoretti A, Mulè S, Boso M, Cipriani A. Does the addition of a second antipsychotic drug improve clozapine treatment? Schizophr Bull. 2009;35(2):458–68.
22. Bounthavong M, Okamoto MP. Decision analysis model evaluating the cost-effectiveness of risperidone, olanzapine and haloperidol in the treatment of schizophrenia. J Eval Clin Pract. 2007;13(3):453–60.
23. Garcia-Ruiz AJ, Perez-Costillas L, Montesinos AC, Alcalde J, Oyaguez I, Casado MA. Cost-effectiveness analysis of antipsychotics in reducing schizophrenia relapses. Health Econ Rev. 2012;2(1):8.
24. Barnett PG, Scott JY, Krystal JH, Rosenheck RA. Cost and cost-effectiveness in a randomized trial of long-acting risperidone for schizophrenia. J Clin Psychiatry. 2012;73(5):696–702.
25. Rosenheck R, Swartz M, McEvoy J, Stroup TS, Davis S, Keefe RS, et al. Second-generation antipsychotics: reviewing the cost-effectiveness component of the CATIE trial. Expert Rev Pharmacoecon Outcomes Res. 2007;7(2):103–11.
26. Jones PB, Barnes TR, Davies L, Dunn G, Lloyd H, Hayhurst KP, et al. Randomized controlled trial of the effect on quality of life of second- vs first-generation antipsychotic drugs in schizophrenia: cost utility of the latest antipsychotic drugs in schizophrenia study (CUtLASS 1). Arch Gen Psychiatry. 2006;63(10):1079–87.
27. Montgomery JH, Byerly M, Carmody T, Li B, Miller DR, Varghese F, et al. An analysis of the effect of funding source in randomized clinical trials of second generation antipsychotics for the treatment of schizophrenia. Control Clin Trials. 2004;25(6):598–612.
28. Heres S, Davis J, Maino K, Jetzinger E, Kissling W, Leucht S. Why olanzapine beats risperidone, risperidone beats quetiapine, and quetiapine beats olanzapine: an exploratory analysis of head-to-head comparison studies of second-generation antipsychotics. Am J Psychiatry. 2006;163(2):185–94.
29. Mulligan J-A, Walker D, Fox-Rushby J. Economic evaluations of non-communicable disease interventions in developing countries: a critical review of the evidence base. Cost Eff Resour Alloc. 2006;4(7):1–10. https://www.ncbi.nlm.nih.gov/pmc/articles/PMC1479369/pdf/1478-7547-4-7.pdf
30. Lieberman JA. Effectiveness of antipsychotic drugs in patients with chronic schizophrenia: efficacy, safety and cost outcomes of CATIE and other trials. J Clin Psychiatry. 2007;68(2):e04.
31. Bilvick Tai BW, Bae YH, Le QA. A systematic review of health economic evaluation studies using the Patient's perspective. Value Health. 2016;19(6):903–8.
32. Ohlsen R, Taylor D, Tandon K, Aitchison K. Returning to the issue of the cost-effectiveness of antipsychotics in the treatment of schizophrenia. Clin Neuropsychiatry. 2008;5(4):184–94.
33. Einarson TR, Zilbershtein R, Skoupa J, Vesela S, Garg M, Hemels ME. Economic and clinical comparison of atypical depot antipsychotic drugs for treatment of chronic schizophrenia in the Czech Republic. J Med Econ. 2013;16(9):1089–95.
34. Mehnert A, Nicholl D, Pudas H, Martin M, McGuire A. Cost effectiveness of paliperidone palmitate versus risperidone long-acting injectable and olanzapine pamoate for the treatment of patients with schizophrenia in Sweden. J Med Econ. 2012;15(5):844–61.
35. Zeidler J, Mahlich J, Greiner W, Heres S. Cost effectiveness of paliperidone palmitate for the treatment of schizophrenia in Germany. Appl Health Econ Health Policy. 2013;11(5):509–21.

36. Einarson TR, Pudas H, Zilbershtein R, Jensen R, Vicente C, Piwko C, et al. Cost-effectiveness analysis of atypical long-acting antipsychotics for treating chronic schizophrenia in Finland. J Med Econ. 2013;16(9):1096–105.
37. Rajagopalan K, Hassan M, O'Day K, Meyer K, Grossman F. Cost-effectiveness of lurasidone vs aripiprazole among patients with schizophrenia who have previously failed on an atypical antipsychotic: an indirect comparison of outcomes from clinical trial data. J Med Econ. 2013;16(7):951–61.
38. Rajagopalan K, O'Day K, Meyer K, Pikalov A, Loebel A. Annual cost of relapses and relapse-related hospitalizations in adults with schizophrenia: results from a 12-month, double-blind, comparative study of lurasidone vs quetiapine extended-release. J Med Econ. 2013;16(8):987–96.
39. Essock SM, Frisman LK, Covell NH, Hargreaves WA. Cost-effectiveness of clozapine compared with conventional antipsychotic medication for patients in state hospitals. Arch Gen Psychiatry. 2000;57(10):987–94.

21 Cost-Effectiveness of Interventions for the Treatment of Alcohol and Other Substance Use Disorders

Paula Becker and Monica Kayo

Abstract

In this chapter we discuss methodological issues regarding cost-effectiveness research on treatment strategies for alcohol and other substance use disorders. Alcohol and substance use disorders have been included in public health policy agendas because of their high prevalence and economic burden to society. However, important issues must still be considered in economic evaluations of this topic, such as adopting an appropriate perspective that takes into account all social burdens due to these disorders, that is, including indirect costs of and social gains achieved by the treatments available. User profiles and high dropout are the main hindrances in conducting cost-effectiveness studies aside clinical trials. The cost-effectiveness of the main pharmacological and nonpharmacological approaches is described in this chapter, as is the research challenges when considering targeting a population profile.

Key Points Summary

- Definition of substance-related disorders
- Health and nonhealth outcomes of alcohol and substance use disorders
- The challenge of conducting cost-effectiveness analysis in samples of alcohol and drug users using Health Economics methods
- Cost-effectiveness of pharmacological, nonpharmacological, and mixed strategies for the treatment of alcohol and substance use disorders
- Research challenges

P. Becker (✉) • M. Kayo
Centre of Economic Mental Health, Department of Psychiatry, Universidade Federal de São Paulo, Rua Borges Lagoa 570, 1° andar Vila Clementino, 04038-000 São Paulo-SP, Brazil
e-mail: pbecker259@gmail.com; monica.kayo@gmail.com

D. Razzouk (ed.), *Mental Health Economics*, DOI 10.1007/978-3-319-55266-8_21

21.1 Introduction

The interest in interventions in alcohol and other drug use disorders has been increasing among researchers. The discussion is still open regarding the efficacy and cost-effectiveness of available treatments. Cost-effectiveness provides arguments for an evidence-based decision-making, ensuring the accuracy of resource allocation by policymakers, purchasers, and providers.

Thus, this chapter aims to present an updated overview of the cost-effectiveness of nonpharmacological, pharmacological, and mixed treatments for substance-related disorders through a review of the literature in the PubMed database in the past 10 years. This review is focused on studies related to the use of alcohol, cannabis, cocaine, crack, amphetamines, and opioids.

21.2 Definition of Substance-Related Disorders

The World Health Organization estimates that 15.3 million people suffer from drug addiction [1]. In 2010, mental and substance use disorders were the fifth leading disorder category of global disability-adjusted life years (DALYs) and were the leading global cause of all nonfatal burden of disease (years lived with disability). The burden of drug use disorders was greatest among young adults (ages 15–29 years), and for alcohol use disorders the largest burden occurred at ages 25–55 years, followed by a gradual decline [2] (see Chap. 26).

No other drug surpasses the prevalence of alcohol consumption: 37.3% of world population consumed alcohol at least one time in the past 12 months; alcohol abuse and dependence caused about 3.3 million deaths, accounting for 5.9% of all global deaths. Cannabis is also commonly used (129–190 million people), followed by amphetamines, cocaine, and opioids. A discussion of tobacco use is not included in this chapter.

The diagnostic criteria adopted for substance-related disorders are the *Diagnostic and Statistical Manual of Mental Disorders* (DSM) and the *International Classification of Diseases and Related Health Problems* (ICD). Up to the 4th edition of the DSM, drug dependence and drug abuse were distinct diagnoses. In this context, drug dependence was defined as a maladaptive pattern of substance use leading to clinically significant impairment or distress, as manifested by three (or more) symptoms such as cravings, a persistent desire to cut down or regulate substance use, multiple reported unsuccessful efforts to decrease or discontinue use, tolerance, withdrawal, among others, occurring at any time in the same 12-month period.

However, the latest version, the DSM-V [3], merged categories of abuse and dependence into a single disorder, toward a continuum measurement from mild to severe disorder. Therefore, in this most recent version, drug abuse was considered as mild substance use disorder. The 10th revision of the ICD defines dependence syndrome as "a cluster of physiological, behavioural, and cognitive phenomena in which the use of a substance or a class of substances takes on a much higher priority for a given individual than other behaviours that once had great value."

The problematic of substance-related disorders has been widely investigated by health professionals interested in explaining how these drugs affect the health of the users, and many efforts have been directed toward understanding the physiological processes of drug dependence and pharmacological therapeutic modalities. However, the conclusion was that social issues could act as one of the main causes of the disease and could be influenced by health treatments proposed so far.

21.3 Health and Nonhealth Outcomes of Alcohol and Drugs Disorders

Notably, psychoactive substance abuse and dependence affect society in different ways, burdening all countries across the globe and challenging stakeholders and managers to determine the best coping strategy. Beyond users' health, substance-related disorders also affect society as a whole in areas such as education, social care, criminal justice, the workplace, and early retirement. Therefore, the choice of outcome in studies interested in analyzing or determining casuistic conditions of this disease or effects of new treatments should consider the magnitude of the target problem. A study aiming to verify whether an intervention promotes users' motivation to abandon or reduce the use of their preferred drug would usually choose the number of days per month of alcohol/drug use as the outcome. However, other nonclinical outcomes that could be influenced by the intervention would be not assessed, though they could be relevant proxies of burden measurement, such as enhanced social participation, reduced work absenteeism, productivity and income gains, fewer illegal activities, and overall family well-being. Moreover, cost-effectiveness studies allow only one outcome to be assessed at a time, and in this case, multidimensional aspects drug and alcohol use are not verified. Therefore, the cost-effectiveness of interventions might be underestimated.

Therefore, nonhealth outcomes may be a good outcome option to be assessed in cost-effectiveness studies, especially if a multidimensional scale or measurement is chosen [4]. For instance, the most prevalent mental disorder in the workplace is alcohol misuse [2], and the cumulative overall effect of this kind of mental disorder in terms of lost economic output could reach $16 trillion over the next 20 years, equivalent to 25% of the global gross domestic product in 2010 [5]. In other words, treatments that improve patterns of alcohol use may affect non-health-related outcome measures such as job loss, presenteeism, and absenteeism (see Chap. 28).

By contrast, a generic health-related outcome largely used in cost-utility studies is quality-adjusted life years (QALYs), which have been the focus of extensive debate in terms of their conceptualization, the appropriateness of their application according to context, and, most important, regarding their use to guide health resource allocation [6] (see Chaps. 9 and 10). Briefly, the discussion points out that, although health systems aim to maximize the health of the population and of individuals, equity and social justice are prominent considerations in the allocation of healthcare resources, and the QALY, in its current conception, may not represent them (see Chap. 9).

21.4 The Challenge of Conducting Cost-Effectiveness Studies in Alcohol- and Drug-Related Disorders Using Health Economics Methods

Designing and conducting cost-effectiveness studies among people with substance-related disorders entail many challenges because of some characteristics of this population. The dropout rate usually decreases the statistical power of the studies, and the main cause of this is the significant disruption of routine and the users' psychological characteristics, which leads them to low rates of adherence to treatment programs. Hence, the use of refined methodologies such as randomized controlled trials or cohort studies are often compromised. Previous data indicate dropout rates ranging between 12 and 67% in clinical trials of people with substance use disorders. Some dropout predictors are younger age, female sex, and maladaptive personality functioning [7, 8].

Another significant challenge is the meaningful and comprehensive indirect costs of this disease. For instance, while conducting cost-effectiveness analysis (CEA) of a psychosocial treatment among people with substance-related disorders, the societal perspective is the most recommended because of its broad impact on the sectors of society: criminal justice use [9–11], presenteeism and absenteeism [12, 13], car accidents [3], job losses, and infectious diseases such as AIDS and hepatitis C [15–17], among others. As another example, crack users are more likely to be involved in sex-related work, participate in risky behaviors, and engage in criminal activity, whereas they are less likely to access social and health services [18]. In the United States and Europe, among injection drug users, an estimated 50–90% of those who are HIV-positive also have hepatitis C; and sharing needles is the leading route of HIV transmission in men and women [10, 17]. In other words, when choosing the societal perspective, with the objective of conducting a pragmatic analysis of the reality of this population and the effects of the available treatment, investigators are challenged to find feasible methods of measuring direct and

Table 21.1 Characteristics of cost-effectiveness studies in samples of alcohol and drug users

Authors	Follow-up	Intervention	Comparator	Primary outcome	Drug (s) analyzed	Perspective	CE results
Grahan et al. [21]	3 months	Brief integrated motivational intervention in an adult mental health inpatient unit	TAU	Substance abuse treatment scale	Alcohol and other drugs	Not specified	Pilot study phase, results not computed
Neighbors et al. [23]	6 months	Motivational interviewing among youths in an emergency department	TAU	Young adult drinking and driving questionnaire, vehicular citations from public database, adolescent injury checklist, health behavior questionnaire	Alcohol	Not specified for CEA	CE across all outcomes
Angus et al. [28]	30 years	Screening and brief intervention in primary healthcare	"Do nothing" scenario	42 Alcohol-attributable health conditions from WHO's work on global burden of disease due to alcohol	Alcohol	Healthcare system	CE
Walters et al. [37]	12 weeks	CBT combined with naltrexone	CBT alone	"Success Treatment outcome": alcohol timeline follow-back and recorded attendance across all eight sessions provided	Alcohol	Not specified for CEA	CE
Palmer et al. [45]	48 weeks	Standard counseling therapy plus acamprosate	Standard counseling therapy	Life years gained	Alcohol	German health insurance	CE
Sindelar et al. [40]	7 months	Standard outpatient counseling plus a case manager and access to prepaid social services	Standard outpatient counseling	Addiction Severity Index (multiple) domains	Alcohol and other drugs	Healthcare system	CE for indicator related to alcohol and drug dependence; not CE for other outcomes
Purshouse et al. [13]	30 years	Screening and brief intervention in primary healthcare	TAU	Health-related quality of life	Alcohol	Healthcare system	CE

CBT cognitive behavioral therapy, *CE* cost-effective; *CEA* cost-effectiveness analysis, *TAU* treatment as usual, *WHO* World Health Organization indirect costs and all possible effects involved (for more information, see Chap. 29).

Table 21.1 lists some studies that illustrate our findings in the literature regarding CEA in samples of alcohol and other drugs users. It can be observed that some studies do not clearly specify which perspective they adopted for their economic analysis, whereas others choose more than one primary outcome (which is contradictory in CEAs); modeling studies are widely used for CEA.

21.5 The Cost-Effectiveness of Distinct Treatments for Alcohol and Substance Use Disorders

Engagement with treatment is essential to the well-being and social performance of those who experience substance-related disorders, and is associated with reduced criminality, improved health, and increased employment rates [19].

The most-studied nonpharmacological interventions are motivational interviewing, screening and brief interventions, harm reduction, cognitive behavioral therapy (CBT), and pharmacological treatments.

21.5.1 Nonpharmacological Treatments for Alcohol and Substance Use Disorders

21.5.1.1 Motivational Interviewing

In 1983, Miller proposed a therapeutic intervention called motivational interviewing (MI) for use with people with alcohol-related disorders; this intervention aimed to a change behavior [20]. Later, the principles and clinical procedures of this theory were enhanced by Miller and Rollnick [61]. Miller wrote down a conceptual model and described some clinical guidelines for MI, which is very peculiar when compared with existing theories.

MI is a particular kind of conversation about change, responding differentially to the client's speech within a generally empathic, person-centered style. It is collaborative, putting the client at the center of his or her own therapeutic program and giving them autonomy to decide about their own lives; it is also evocative, seeking to call forth the person's own motivation and commitment [20].

MI can also be applied in brief forms of interventions, as Graham et al. [21] did in their study. They called it the Brief Motivational Intervention, characterized by four to six sessions, 15–30 min each, over 2 weeks. These sessions occurred in parallel with usual treatment at an inpatient service for alcohol and drug users. At the end, the Brief Motivational Intervention demonstrated good results across a range of substances and was often equivalent to long-term interventions [21].

MI has over time become a model for intervention in drug-dependent individuals and is widely applied in therapeutic settings. Bachiller et al. [22] described a successful experience with the application of an MI group at an inpatient service for detoxification. The MI group took place three times a week during an average 12.2-day hospitalization, and it was related to a greater likelihood of maintaining abstinence and subsequent treatment adherence 2 months after discharge. The positive predictive factors were being male, being satisfied with group therapy and the therapist during hospitalization, and being at a maintenance stage at discharge. However, this study did not include a control group for further comparisons.

The efficacy of MI is widely discussed in the literature, but few cost-effectiveness studies can be found. Neighbors et al. [23] analyzed data from a CEA of a previous clinical trial conducted at an emergency department trauma center for drinking-related injuries. The study aimed to examine the cost-effectiveness of conducting brief alcohol intervention by adopting strategies from MI for use with high-risk teens, from the provider perspective, and a cost-utility analysis. The control group received usual advice to reduce alcohol-related risk while waiting for medical evaluation or treatment; the intervention group received counseling from trained staff who provided the brief MI assessment and intervention, in addition to handouts on the effects of alcohol and local alcohol treatment facilities, in the same period at that service at baseline, among youths aged 18–19 years. Three- and 6-month follow-ups were conduct by phone and in person, respectively. For the CEA, four outcomes were considered: incidence of drinking and driving, alcohol-related injuries, vehicle citations, and alcohol-related problems. The time spent by staff in the control group was estimated at 5 min with the nurse providing usual service, representing personnel costs of $3.81, whereas the costs of the MI were calculated based on the time spent by the trained staff (administrative paperwork, preparatory procedures, and waiting for client availability, plus 30 min of direct contact with the clients and 15 min of supervisory time per client) added to the cost of the handouts. The total cost per client for the MI intervention was $170.00 and for usual care was $81.00. The authors concluded that the cost-effectiveness ratios for MI were more favorable than those for standard care across all study outcomes. Although this study brings to light important methodological aspects of the application and evaluation of MI programs, it has some limitations, such as the short time horizon (6 months), small sample size, and that the approach to estimating QALYs gained derived from population-based studies rather than directly from study data.

Several cost-effectiveness studies considering MI and brief interventions are being conducted [24–26], including with young heavy or harmful drinkers, which are a group being focused on by governments and public health policy, considering that alcohol consumption and related harms are a major preventable cause of injury, disability, and death in young people [25, 26]. However, those studies are still in the protocol phase, and their cost-effectiveness has not yet been clarified.

21.5.1.2 Screening and Brief Interventions

Brief interventions can be classified into two main types: (a) structured brief advice, which involves a short conversation between a practitioner and a client, providing practical advice on how to reduce consumption and giving the client a self-help leaflet or workbook; and (b) extended brief intervention, which typically involves one to five counseling sessions based on MI principles [13]. Screening is typically conducted by the application of a structured instrument, such as the Alcohol, Smoking and Substance Involvement Screening Test for alcohol and drug abusers. Therefore, screening and brief intervention (SBI) is the sum of both approaches into a single intervention.

Solberg et al. [27], in a systematic review of the literature used to investigate primary care intervention to reduce clinically preventable burden of alcohol misuse, pointed out that screening with brief instruments followed by brief counseling saved costs from a societal perspective and had a cost-effectiveness ratio of $1755/QALY saved from a health system perspective. The authors also make an important caveat, emphasizing that the time horizon is an important factor to be considered regarding analysis of SBI intervention effects.

The first step for a cost-effectiveness evaluation is a cost analysis, and regarding SBI, these data vary widely and are generally not comparable among studies because of differences between settings, staffing, screening tools, delivery, or target populations [28]. In addition to these possible variations in cost analysis, the study outcome also should be carefully observed. The most used is drinks per week or days of use of any other drug, but SBI may generate other worthwhile outcomes, and the literature has yet to agree on a standard and aggregated outcome that could represent the clinical and social effects of the intervention.

Despite the vast literature about SBI with those who abuse and are dependent on alcohol, there is no robust cost-effectiveness evidence of SBI for the abuse and dependence of substances such as cocaine, crack, heroin, methamphetamines, or marijuana.

21.5.2 Mixed Treatments for Alcohol and Drugs Disorders

In this section the name *mixed treatment* is given to interventions that combine more than one approach into a single form of treatment, for instance, when evaluating psychotherapy and pharmacological intervention as an intervention package offered to patients, or a psychosocial rehabilitation package of care. Next, we present data on mixed treatments most discussed in the literature.

21.5.2.1 Harm Reduction

When eliminating the abuse or dependence of alcohol or other drugs seems to be improbable, an alternative approach is harm reduction, which addresses methods to improve clinical health and reduce social and economic harms that individuals experience as a result of engaging in risky activities related to substance use disorders [29].

Its first introduction occurred as a response to the AIDS endemic in the mid-1980s in the Netherlands, the United Kingdom, and Australia. The concern about reducing the transmission rates of infectious diseases, such as hepatitis C, remains one of the main focuses of this modality of care.

Harm reduction strategies usually are associated with the crucial issue of HIV transmission by injection drug users. Injection drug use is estimated to be responsible for around 10% of all HIV contamination worldwide [30], and HIV prevalence worldwide among people who inject drugs is around 19% [29]. In this context, harm reduction often includes needle/syringe programs (NSPs) and opioid substitution therapy.

A study conducted in the Ukraine by Alistar et al. [31] confirmed that methadone substitution therapy is a very cost-effective option for the growing mixed HIV epidemic in the country, and a strategy that expands both methadone substitution therapy and antiretroviral therapy to high levels is the most effective intervention, evaluated by the World Health Organization as a cost-effective approach according to their criteria.

Opioid substitution therapy is effective but seems to be costly when only HIV transmission rates are considered as an outcome; however, when other societal outcomes are considered, its cost-effectiveness ratio improves.

NSPs have been shown to be an effective and safe strategy in reducing HIV transmission among injection drug users [29]. Many studies have shown NSPs, when implemented, do not result in a decreased number of people dependent on injectable drugs, but rather in a reduction of HIV transmission among users. A review of ecological data from 81 cities across Europe, Asia, and North America found that HIV prevalence increased by an average of 5.9% per year in 52 cities without an NSP, whereas the prevalence of HIV decreased by 5.8% per year in the 29 cities with an NSP [29, 32]. Studies also showed that implementing an NSP is an inexpensive alternative, having an average cost of US$23–71 per person per year, though this varies according to world region and delivery system [29, 30]. Therefore, NSPs are recognized as one of the most cost-effective public health interventions in the field of substance abuse [33].

A study conducted in Bangladesh [16] aimed to provide information on costs of HIV prevention programs for injection drug users in South Asia and the potential gains to be made by intervening early and maintaining these programs from a provider perspective. The cost-effectiveness ratio was calculated for three scenarios: (1) over the first 3 years of the program operation; (2) continuing the intervention to year 4 compared with stopping at the end of year 3; (3) and whether the CE would have been affected if the program was implemented when HIV had taken hold in the injection drug user population. The capital costs considered were buildings, furniture, equipment, and vehicles, using a standard discount rate of 3%. Other costs considered were staff training, condoms, needles and syringes (current market prices) delivered, sessions provided by the sexually transmitted infections services (sessions per year × the rate per session), and abscess management (cost of management × the number of abscesses treated). The cost-effectiveness ratio was calculated as the total costs divided by the total HIV infections averted. The cost per DALY was calculated for comparison with other health services, although the study does not specify them. The study demonstrated that a harm reduction program based on an NSP is cost-effective as an early intervention for reducing DALYs and the incidence of infections when compared with other HIV prevention activities in South Asia. The study confirmed that even if HIV prevalence had reached 40% among injection drug users before the intervention was started, the cost per HIV infection averted for the harm reduction program was as low as U$228.00, and therefore was cost-effective in comparison with other projects reported within the same population.

Another alternative harm reduction action plan is, for instance, a supervised smoking facility (SSF) for cocaine, methamphetamine, and heroin users; the goal is to avoid sharing needles or pipes, thus preventing HIV and hepatitis C transmission by providing a safe place that could avoid deaths by overdoses. An experience in Vancouver, Canada, conducted by Jozaghi [18], investigated whether an already existing SSF would have had a net positive fiscal impact on Canadian society and whether this policy initiative would save public healthcare resources by averting new HIV and hepatitis C infections. The results showed that the SSF not only saved money for taxpayers but also deserved to be expanded, since the marginal cost-effectiveness ratio ranged from \$1.705 to \$97.203, and the SSF saved CAD1.8 million for taxpayers annually.

Another important strategy to reduce harms associated with alcohol abuse [1] is making it more expensive and less available, and banning alcohol-related advertising. A study conducted by Anderson, Chishom and Fuhr [14] confirms that banning alcohol advertising, implementing drunk-driving countermeasures, and providing individually directed interventions to drinkers already at risk are also cost-effective approaches for reducing harm.

21.5.2.2 Cognitive Behavioral Therapy

Plenty of studies have been published on the cost-effectiveness of CBT in the treatment of depression and anxiety disorders (see Chap. 18), but this scenario does not reflect the cost-effectiveness evaluation of CBT in the field of substance-related disorders. Some studies have been developed comparing CBT alone and CBT plus pharmacological therapy in people with substance abuse disorders, especially alcohol users. As we will see, CBT has been proven to be effective when aggregated with pharmacological treatment, and CEA studies usually consider these two approaches as a single package of care.

CBT is effective in helping individuals to reduce substance consumption by anticipating problems and developing an effective coping strategy, examining the positive and the negative consequences of drug abuse and dependence, and identifying situations that may trigger substance use. CBT has become the leading treatment approach in a variety of psychological disorders [34, 35]. As the Center for Substance Abuse Treatment [36] states, “cognitive factors mediate all interactions between the individual, situational demands, and the person’s attempts to cope effectively”, and individuals who want to change behavior need to modify their beliefs, thoughts, self-perceptions, external environment. The therapist helps clients to learn to recognize triggering events, automatic thoughts regarding such events, emotional and behavioral responses, and, in certain situations, their underlying core beliefs. The main objective is to empower the client to identify this process, after which they can work toward changing their emotions and behaviors by altering their automatic cognitions [34].

Walters et al. [37] evaluated the cost-effectiveness of treating alcohol dependence using CBT alone compared with CBT combined with naltrexone. The “success treatment outcome” was considered as attending all eight sessions and remaining abstinent over the 12-week program (estimated by a combination of patient self-report, clinic visit, breathalyzation, monthly serum transaminase, and monthly serum carbohydrate deficient transferrin estimation). The costs analyzed were those for personnel, supplies and materials, major equipment, contracted services, buildings and facilities, miscellaneous resources, and other costs according to the Drug Abuse Treatment Costs Analysis Program in Australia. The study perspective was not mentioned. The authors pointed out that CBT plus naltrexone introduced additional treatment cost and was 54% more costly than CBT alone, but it was also more cost-effective than CBT alone. According to that study, in order to achieve 100 abstainers over a 12-week program, 280 patients treated with CBT would be needed, in comparison with 160 treated with CBT plus naltrexone.

A relevant cost-effectiveness study was conducted by the London School of Hygiene and Tropical Medicine Research Group [35]: a pragmatic, randomized, multicenter, parallel group design comparing CBT plus methadone maintenance treatment (MMT) with MMT alone; the primary outcome was heroin use (percentage of days abstinent and the amount spent on heroin in the past 180 days), and the secondary outcomes were the addiction severity, severity of drug dependence, quality of life, psychological symptoms, and compliance with methadone treatment. The CBT intervention consisted of weekly sessions (each 50 min) up to 24 sessions over 6 months. The authors affirm that CBT has a mean cost-saving advantage of €7000 per patient compared with MMT alone (not statistically significant) and a simulated incremental cost effectiveness ratio (ICER) confirmed that, at a threshold value of €30,000 per QALY, CBT would be preferred to MMT 74% of the time by policymakers.

21.5.2.3 Community-Based Mental Health Network

Mental health interventions embrace much more than treatment approaches, and have been further studied over the years; it also encompasses a wide range of strategies such as legislative and regulatory frameworks, prevention, promotion, rehabilitation [38], and social inclusion.

With the advance of psychiatric reform worldwide, with mental hospital–based services being closed and replaced by community-based services, different modalities of care have been offered. Interest is increasing in the way in which mental health systems are organized and financed, and in the use of CEA for resource allocation, which is frequently scarce. Roberts et al. [39], in a literature review, found that community-based mental health services have been shown to be more cost-effective than inpatient treatment, but the studies did not totally clarify in which level of care is most effective. For the same authors, substantial methodological problems are frequently found in economic evaluation studies in the field of community based treatment: costs are often not completely specified (especially indirect costs from a societal perspective), and the lack of a natural outcome measure in mental health makes the comparability of CEA studies with other health conditions a challenge [39].

Sindelar et al. [40] discussed the issue of choosing a natural outcome for cost-effectiveness studies of treatment for substance-related disorders, showing concern about how to consider the multiple and important outcomes in economic evaluations, especially in cost-effectiveness studies, which could be affected by treatments for substance-related disorders. To illustrate this matter, the authors conducted a CEA of two modalities of substance-related disorder treatment in a community, comparing standard outpatient counseling versus the same treatment enhanced using a case manager and access to prepaid social services at nine abstinence-based outpatient treatment programs in North and West Philadelphia, six of which received enhancements. The Drug Abuse Treatment Cost Analysis Program was applied to measure costs; this tool is an on-site data collection instrument that comprises categories such as personnel, supplies and materials, contracted services, buildings and facilities, equipment, and miscellaneous items. The primary outcome was selected variables from the seven domains of the Addiction Severity Index (see Chap. 5), and effectiveness for each outcome was the change from baseline to 6 months' follow-up. The main question of this study was to verify whether a reduction in drug use was a significant predictor of change in other outcomes measures from the Addiction Severity Index. However, the results showed that drug use may not be a sufficient predictor of changes in other outcomes such as employment, family, social, and psychiatric problems. So, using the reduction of drug use as a single outcome in CEA of treatments for substance-related disorders might be a problem. For all indicators related to drug and alcohol dependence, enhanced care is more cost-effective for showing a lower cost for a unit of effect achieved. On the other hand, for outcomes such as family relationships, physical health problems, employment, and days of illegal activity, the standard care was cost-effective for being cheaper and more effective than or equally as effective as enhanced care.

21.5.3 Cost-Effectiveness of Pharmacological Treatments

The pharmacotherapy of alcohol and substance disorders may target distinct outcomes, including the reduction of use, relief of withdrawal symptoms, reduction of the risk of infection from stopping injections, short- and long-term substitution, and the maintenance of abstinence. The outcome may be also concerned with societal gains, such as the reduction of criminality; however, studies using nonhealth outcomes are scarce. Here we focus only on commercially approved pharmacological therapies for treatment of alcohol and substance dependence. Although it is recognized that pharmaceutical approaches may be useful in cases of harmful use, the lack of clinical trials does not allow the cost-effectiveness of pharmacotherapy to be analyzed in those cases. It is not the aim of this chapter to analyze the cost-effectiveness of interventions for tobacco dependence, nor to point out which pharmacotherapy is the most cost-effective for alcohol and substance use disorders.

Four agents are approved used to treat alcohol dependence: acamprosate, disulfiram, oral naltrexone, and extended-release naltrexone (naltrexone XR, a once-monthly intramuscular injection) [41]. To treat opioid dependence, the pharmacological alternatives are methadone, buprenorphine, oral naltrexone, and naltrexone XR [41]. To date, no pharmacological intervention is formally approved for the treatment of cannabis dependence, although some empirical data exist for some pharmacotherapies.

It is explicitly recommended that all pharmacological approaches for the treatment of alcohol dependence must be combined with psychosocial treatments [42], although it is not specified which psychosocial therapy is the most effective for each type of drug dependence. Although the efficacy and safety of pharmaceutical interventions has been studied and its use should be offered to all patients who are undergoing treatment drug dependence, pharmacotherapy is still underused [41]. The U.K. National Institute for Health and Care Excellence guidelines recommend that oral naltrexone or acamprosate should be used after successful withdrawal for people with moderate and severe alcohol dependence [42].

Acamprosate reduces the hyperglutamatergic state during alcohol withdrawal. As a result, acamprosate is effective in supporting continuous abstinence after detoxification in alcohol-dependent patients [43].

In terms of budget impact, the use of acamprosate in the treatment of alcohol dependence seems to save costs according to economic models that considered the perspectives of the Italian National Health Service. However, no CEA was conducted in this case [44]. Acamprosate was considered cost-effective from the perspective of German health insurance [45]. A computer model with decision analysis showed a higher abstinence rate when acamprosate was added to standard counseling therapy. The lower incidence of clinical complications included in the model, such as fatty liver, cirrhosis, pancreatitis, and alcoholic cardiomyopathy led to an increase in life expectancy (life years gained), and the acquisition costs of acamprosate were lower than the costs of clinical complications [45].

Disulfiram is a drug used to support the maintenance of abstinence from alcohol. It blocks aldehyde dehydrogenase, causing accumulation of acetaldehyde if alcohol is consumed, resulting in nausea, flushing, and palpitations. Because of such unpleasant effects, the patient avoids drinking alcohol. To our knowledge, there is no cost-effectiveness analysis of disulfiram to date in the treatment of alcohol dependence.

Oral naltrexone, a μ-opioid receptor antagonist, is another effective pharmacotherapy to improve abstinence rates and reduce the risk of relapse in people with alcohol dependence. By blocking opioid receptors, naltrexone reduces the rewarding effects of alcohol as well as motivation to drink or "cravings." Its effectiveness seems to be similar to that of acamprosate [46]. The largest amount of data on cost-effectiveness comes from a randomized study conducted in the United States, the COMBINE study [47]. This study included 1383 subjects and had nine treatment arms: four arms received medical management (MM) with 16 weeks of naltrexone (100 mg/day) or acamprosate (3 g/day), both, and/or placebo; four arms received the same options as above but delivered with combined behavioral intervention; and one arm received combined behavioral intervention only [47]. The data from COMBINE showed that in terms of cost-effectiveness, oral naltrexone was cost-effective when combined with MM. From a patient perspective, MM with oral naltrexone was more cost-effective than MM + placebo or MM + naltrexone and acamprosate, when considering a willingness to pay between US$1000.00 and US$1500.00 per 16 weeks of treatment. The outcomes used in this study were the proportion of subjects avoiding heavy drinking, the percentage point increase in percentage of days abstinent, and patients achieving a good clinical outcome. The patients' out-of-pocket expenses were medication costs (expected prescription copayments) and costs for session visits (expected office visit copayments). An ICER was computed for each of those outcomes. The ICER moving from MM + placebo to MM + naltrexone was $575 per patient achieving a good clinical outcome, $1023 per patient avoiding a return to heavy drinking, and $15 per patient for a percentage point increase in percentage of days abstinent. The ICER moving from MM + naltrexone and acamprosate was $1243 per patient achieving a good clinical outcome, $1243 per patient avoiding a return to heavy drinking, and $99 per patient for a percentage point increase in percentage of days abstinent [48]. From a provider perspective, and following the same outcomes, MM combined with naltrexone was considered the most cost-effective treatment. However, based on the joint distribution of cost and effectiveness, MM + naltrexone + acamprosate may be a cost-effective choice, depending on whether the cost of the incremental increase in mean effectiveness is worth it to the decision maker. Adding acamprosate to MM plus naltrexone has only a slightly larger mean effectiveness than MM + naltrexone in the percentage of days abstinent, but has an approximately 50% higher mean cost per patient. In this study, from the provider perspective, the MM + naltrexone cost $671 per patient), whereas MM + naltrexone + acamprosate cost $1003 per patient. The estimated costs were the sum of medication, labor, space, and laboratory costs for each treatment condition [49].

Naltrexone XR is a once-monthly intramuscular injection that is also used to improve abstinence rates in alcohol dependence. An analysis of a commercial insurance database (n = 2977) reviewed the costs of patients with alcohol dependence treated with naltrexone XR, oral naltrexone, acamprosate, and disulfiram [50]. The costs for inpatient detoxification days and alcoholism-related admissions were measured by multiplying charges per day by the number of inpatient detoxification days or alcoholism-related inpatient days. Charges for inpatient treatment were determined using the Healthcare Cost and Utilization Project National Inpatient Sample data set, the largest all-payer inpatient care database in the United States. The patients were not prospectively randomized, but rather chose or were prescribed their respective treatments naturalistically. Patients who received alcoholism medications had fewer inpatient detoxification days (706 vs. 1163 days/1000 patients; $P < 0.001$), alcoholism-related inpatient days (650 vs. 1086 days; $P < 0.001$), and alcoholism-related emergency department visits (127 vs. 171; $P = 0.005$). The inpatient detoxification days cost $1,890,822 per 1000 patients treated with any alcoholism medication and $3,113,389 per 1000 patients treated with no alcoholism medication. The group that received naltrexone XR had fewer alcoholism-related inpatient days than the groups receiving disulfiram or acamprosate. The authors' conclusion was that patients who received an alcoholism medication had lower healthcare utilization than patients who did not. Naltrexone XR showed an advantage over oral medications in healthcare utilization and costs [50].

Acamprosate and oral naltrexone seem to have the best evidence for improving abstinence rates and prolonging abstinence periods [51]. However, current CEAs are scarce and limited to outcomes that do not reflect the societal costs of alcohol dependence, and the differences among healthcare systems do not allow extrapolation of the conclusions. In addition, we still do not have an answer to the question, "Who is likely to benefit from which pharmacotherapy?" [42].

If the cost-effectiveness studies of pharmacotherapies for alcohol dependence are scarce, the situation with other substance use disorders is even more limited. The difficulties of conducting trials in those populations are huge, and the outcomes are complex.

The most studied intervention for opioid dependence is MMT. Methadone is a μ-opioid receptor agonist with a much longer half-life than heroin; it is used to replace heroin and other opioids. MMT should be administered under supervision, and the main outcomes in related clinical studies are patient retention in treatment and the reduction in the use of illicit opioid drugs [41]. Methadone is available in oral (liquid and tablet) formulations and as an injectable preparation. Injection drug use is an important route of HIV transmission. Replacing injection with oral methadone reduces drug-related behaviors with a high risk of HIV transmission [52]; therefore MMT has been extensively studied in populations with HIV. The cost-effectiveness of MMT was assessed in Canada [53], the United States [54], and the United Kingdom [55]; however, it is almost impossible to compare the results, given the important differences among healthcare in those countries. The majority of studies point out that MMT is more cost-effective than no drug therapy among subjects with opioid dependence. An important factor that has a positive impact on the cost-effectiveness is that MMT programs are more effective when the targets are individuals located in high-risk networks, rather than when they reach individuals at the periphery of such networks [54].

A study conducted in Vietnam assessed the impact of MMT on health utility, healthcare service utilization, and out-of-pocket health expenditures among drug users with HIV/AIDS, and concluded that MMT was associated with a clinically important difference in health utility and large reductions in healthcare service utilization and out-of-pocket health expenditures in HIV-positive drug users [56]. In that study, utility was measured using the five-dimension, five-level EuroQOL and a visual analog scale. A 66.7% reduction in out-of-pocket health expenditures related to MMT was observed.

Buprenorphine is a semisynthetic derivative of the opiate alkaloid thebaine, which is isolated from the poppy *Papaver somniferum*. It is a potent but partial agonist of the μ-opioid receptor, with a high affinity but low intrinsic activity. High potency and slow off-rate (the half-life of association/dissociation is 2–5 h) help buprenorphine displace other μ-agonists such as morphine and methadone from their receptors [57]. Buprenorphine is used in the same way as methadone – as a replacement therapy. No consistent evidence shows that buprenorphine maintenance therapy (BMT) is superior to MMT in terms of retention in treatment or the use of drugs. Both flexible-dose MMT and BMT are more clinically effective and more cost-effective than no drug therapy in people with opioid dependence [55]. However, studies did not include safety outcomes, which may be a concern associated with these two drugs (e.g., constipation, drug interactions, and a possible higher mortality risk). Direct comparison of the results between studies of MMT and BMT is not possible because of their different approaches to modeling and different time horizons, comparators, perspectives, countries of origin, and sources of preference weights and effectiveness data used [55].

Oral naltrexone, which is mainly used to treat alcohol dependence, is also used to support the maintenance of abstinence from opioid drugs after detoxification in formerly dependent patients. However, evidence of the efficacy of naltrexone in the treatment of opioid dependence is weaker than in the alcohol-dependent population. Oral naltrexone treatment can be considered for formerly opioid-dependent people who are highly motivated to remain abstinent (level of recommendation D) [42]. Studies of the cost-effectiveness of the use of naltrexone in the treatment of opioid dependence are scarce [58]. One study showed that naltrexone is not cost-effective in comparison with either buprenorphine or placebo in heroin-dependent patients from Malaysia [59]. The primary outcome measures were days in treatment, maximum consecutive days of heroin abstinence, days to first heroin use, and days to heroin relapse. Secondary outcome measures included treatment retention, injection drug use, illicit opiate use, AIDS Risk Inventory total score, and drug risk and sex risk subscores. In spite of the higher cost of buprenorphine, it was dominant over naltrexone because of its superior effectiveness in all the primary and almost all secondary outcomes [59].

The cost-effectiveness of injectable naltrexone XR was analyzed with the use of a Markov model (see Chap. 7) and compared with MMT and BMT. The model analyzed the incremental cost per opioid-free day over a 6-month period among a simulated cohort of adult men aged 18–65 years, from a state health program perspective. In this case, naltrexone XR was a cost-effective medication for treating opioid dependence if state addiction treatment payers are willing to pay at least $72 per opioid-free day. The costs included costs of the drug, counseling (usually delivered in a group setting), medication management, and oversight [60]. It is important to note that MMT has been used for over 50 years and BMT for more than 10 years, and this model was based on a single clinical trial.

No convincing evidence exists to support the use of pharmacological treatment for amphetamine and cocaine abuse and dependence, nor for cannabis dependence [42]. Currently, no pharmacological treatment is approved for those indications, and psychosocial interventions remain the mainstay of treatment. Therefore, no economic evaluations of those pharmacological therapies are approached in this chapter.

In summary, in spite of the few cost-effectiveness studies of pharmacotherapies for the treatment of alcohol and substance use disorders, naltrexone and acamprosate were the pharmacotherapies with more evidence of cost-effectiveness for alcohol dependence in some countries, in comparison with placebo, and in a population with HIV and opioid dependence, MMT seems to be a cost-effective therapy in reducing the risk of infecting other people. It is important to keep in mind that the majority of studies were conducted in high-income countries, and cost-effectiveness studies always depend on the healthcare system of the particular country, so the results cannot be generalized.

21.6 Research Challenges

Several challenges exist in cost-effectiveness research with samples of alcohol and other drug users. These include the profile of the population, considering the high dropout rates that negatively affect the power of clinical trials, the perspective chosen, the indirect costs of disease, and the choice of the best primary outcome.

The choice of outcome should take into account the real dimension of the problem. For instance, an NSP can be cost-effective when the outcome is the reduction of HIV incidence; however, it may not be cost-effective when the outcome analyzed is the reduction of drug use.

The societal perspective is the most recommended for cost-effectiveness studies of alcohol and substance use because of the spillover effects of such disorders in criminality, productivity, social security, and other sectors. The time horizon should reflect the long-term impact of alcohol and substance use disorders.

Finally, cost-effectiveness studies of alcohol and substance use disorders are scarce and predominantly done in high-income countries. Because CEA depends on the structure of the country's healthcare system, it is fundamental to perform CEA in low- and middle-income countries, which are the most affected areas.

Key Messages

- Substance-related disorders are more costly to society when they are not treated.
- Substance-related disorders affect not only users' clinical and well-being outcomes, but also those of their families and society. In that case, the societal perspective is the most recommended for adoption in cost-effectiveness studies of this topic.

(continued)

(continued)

- The high dropout rate and users' characteristics are the main challenges for conducting cost-effectiveness studies. The choice of outcome is also critical.
- MI, harm reduction, and CBT have their cost-effectiveness analyzed, although it may vary according to the healthcare context in which they are applied.
- Naltrexone and acamprosate show some evidence of cost-effectiveness in supporting abstinence rates, but results cannot be generalized.
- MMT is the most studied pharmacological treatment for opioid dependence, and it is particularly cost-effective when outcomes include HIV costs.

References

1. World Health Organization. Facts and figures – The Bare Facts. Genebra: WHO. World Health Organization; 2014. Available from:http://www.who.int/substance_abuse/facts/en/
2. Whiteford HA, Degenhardt L, Rehm J, Baxter AJ, Ferrari AJ, Erskine HE, et al. Global burden of disease attributable to mental and substance use disorders: findings from the global burden of disease study 2010. Lancet. 2013;382(9904):1575–86.
3. American Psychiatric Association. Diagnostic and statistical manual of mental disorders. 5th ed. [Internet]. Arlington: American Psychiatric Association; 2013 [cited 31 Mar 2016]. p. 970. Available from: http://psy-gradaran.narod.ru/lib/clinical/DSM5.pdf
4. Inocencio TJ, Carroll NV, Read EJ, Holdford DA, Health A. The economic burden of opioid-related poisoning in the United States. Pain Med. 2013;14:1534–47.
5. Bloom DE, Cafiero E, Jané-Llopis E, Abrahams-Gessel S, Reddy Bloom L, Fathima S, et al. The global economic burden of noncommunicable diseases. World Econ Forum [Internet]. 2011;September:1–46. Available from: http://ideas.repec.org/p/gdm/wpaper/8712.html
6. Drummond M, Brixner D, Gold M, Kind P, McGuire A, Nord E. Toward a consensus on the QALY. Value Health [Internet]. 2009;12(1):S31–5. Available from: http://eprints.whiterose.ac.uk/51591/
7. Chen Y-C, Chen C-K, Wang L-J. Predictors of relapse and dropout during a 12-week relapse prevention program for methamphetamine users. J Psychoactive Drugs [Internet]. 2015;47(4):317–24. Available from: http://www.ncbi.nlm.nih.gov/pubmed/26267045
8. McKellar J, Kelly J, Harris A, Moos R. Pretreatment and during treatment risk factors for dropout among patients with substance use disorders. Addict Behav. 2006;31(3):450–60.
9. Schwartz RP, Alexandre PK, Kelly SM, O'Grady KE, Gryczynski J, Jaffe JH. Interim versus standard methadone treatment: a benefit–cost analysis. J Subst Abuse Treat [Internet]. 2014 [cited 2 Oct 2015];46(3):306–314. Available from: http://www.pubmedcentral.nih.gov/articlerender.fcgi?artid=3947051&tool=pmcentrez&rendertype=abstract
10. Center for Behavioral Health Statistics and Quality. Behavioral health trends in the United States: results from the 2014 national survey on drug use and health [Internet]. 2015. Available from: http://www.samhsa.gov/data/sites/default/files/NSDUH-FRR1-2014/NSDUH-FRR1-2014.pdf\nhttp://www.samhsa.gov/data/
11. Durbeej N, Palmstierna T, Rosendahl I, Berman AH, Kristiansson M, Gumpert CH. Mental health services and public safety: substance abuse outpatient visits were associated with reduced crime rates in a Swedish cohort. PLoS One. 2015;10(9):1–17.
12. van Amsterdam J, van den Brink W. The high harm score of alcohol. time for drug policy to be revisited? J Psychopharmacol [Internet]. 2013 [cited 18 Jan 2016];27(3):248–255. Available from: http://www.ncbi.nlm.nih.gov/pubmed/23325370
13. Purshouse RC, Brennan A, Rafia R, Latimer NR, Archer RJ, Angus CR, et al. Modelling the cost-effectiveness of alcohol screening and brief interventions in primary care in England. Alcohol Alcohol [Internet]. [cited 15 Jan 2016];48(2):180–188. Available from: http://www.ncbi.nlm.nih.gov/pubmed/23015608
14. Anderson P, Chisholm D, Fuhr DC. Effectiveness and cost-effectiveness of policies and programmes to reduce the harm caused by alcohol. Lancet [Internet]. 2009 [cited 13 Jun 2015];373(9682):2234–2246. Available from: http://www.ncbi.nlm.nih.gov/pubmed/19560605
15. Li J, Gilmour S, Zhang H, Koyanagi A, Shibuya K. The epidemiological impact and cost-effectiveness of HIV testing, antiretroviral treatment and harm reduction programs. AIDS [Internet]. 2012 [cited 18 Jan 2016];26(16):2069–2078. Available from: http://www.ncbi.nlm.nih.gov/pubmed/22781221
16. Guinness L, Vickerman P, Quayyum Z, Foss A, Watts C, Rodericks A, et al. The cost-effectiveness of consistent and early intervention of harm reduction for injecting drug users in Bangladesh. Addiction [Internet]. 2010 [cited 18 Jan 2016];105(2):319–328. Available from: http://www.ncbi.nlm.nih.gov/pubmed/19922513
17. Ruger JP, Abdallah A Ben, Ng NY, Luekens C, Cottler L. Cost-effectiveness of interventions to prevent HIV and STDs among women: a randomized controlled trial. AIDS Behav [Internet]. 2014 [cited 2

Dec 2015];18(10):1913–1923. Available from: http://www.ncbi.nlm.nih.gov/pubmed/24699712

18. Jozaghi E. A cost-benefit/cost-effectiveness analysis of an unsanctioned supervised smoking facility in the downtown eastside of Vancouver, Canada. Harm Reduct J [Internet]. 2014 [cited 18 Jan 2016];11(1):30. Available from: http://www.pubmedcentral.nih.gov/articlerender.fcgi?artid=4251950&tool=pmcentrez&rendertype=abstract
19. Basu A, Paltiel AD, Pollack HA. Social costs of robbery and the cost-effectiveness of substance abuse treatment. Health Econ [Internet]. 2008 [cited 18 Jan 2016];17(8):927–946. Available from: http://www.pubmedcentral.nih.gov/articlerender.fcgi?artid=3512566&tool=pmcentrez&rendertype=abstract
20. Miller W, Rose G. Toward a theory of motivational interviewing MI was not founded on theory. Am Psycho. 2009;64(6):527–37.
21. Graham HL, Birchwood M, Griffith E, Freemantle N, McCrone P, Stefanidou CA, et al. A pilot study to assess the feasibility and impact of a brief motivational intervention on problem drug and alcohol use in adult mental health inpatient units: study protocol for a randomized controlled trial. Trials [Internet]. 2014 [cited 2 Dec 2015];15:308. Available from: http://www.pubmedcentral.nih.gov/articlerender.fcgi?artid=4124140&tool=pmcentrez&rendertype=abstract
22. Bachiller D, Grau-López L, Barral C, Daigre C, Alberich C, Rodríguez-Cintas L, et al. Motivational interviewing group at inpatient detoxification, its influence in maintaining abstinence and treatment retention after discharge. Adicciones [Internet]. 2015;27(2):109–18. Available from: http://www.ncbi.nlm.nih.gov/pubmed/26132300
23. Neighbors CJ, Barnett NP, Rohsenow DJ, Colby SM, Monti PM. Cost-effectiveness of a motivational intervention for alcohol-involved youth in a hospital emergency department. J Stud Alcohol Drugs [Internet]. 2010 [cited 18 Jan 2016];71(3):384–394. Available from: http://www.pubmedcentral.nih.gov/articlerender.fcgi?artid=2859787&tool=pmcentrez&rendertype=abstract
24. Ruger JP, Weinstein MC, Hammond SK, Kearney MH, Emmons KM. Cost-effectiveness of motivational interviewing for smoking cessation and relapse prevention among low-income pregnant women: a randomized controlled trial. Value Health [Internet]. [cited 18 Jan 2016];11(2):191–198. Available from: http://www.pubmedcentral.nih.gov/articlerender.fcgi?artid=2775431&tool=pmcentrez&rendertype=abstract
25. Deluca P, Coulton S, Alam MF, Cohen D, Donoghue K, Gilvarry E, et al. Linked randomised controlled trials of face-to-face and electronic brief intervention methods to prevent alcohol related harm in young people aged 14-17 years presenting to emergency departments (SIPS junior). BMC Public Health [Internet]. 2015 [cited 15 Oct 2015];15:345. Available from: http://www.pubmedcentral.nih.gov/articlerender.fcgi?artid=4394590&tool=pmcentrez&rendertype=abstract
26. Hides L, Kavanagh DJ, Daglish M, Cotton S, Connor JP, Barendregt JJ, et al. The quik fix study: a randomised controlled trial of brief interventions for young people with alcohol-related injuries and illnesses accessing emergency department and crisis support care. BMC Emerg Med [Internet]. 2014 [cited 18 Jan 2016];14:19. Available from: http://www.pubmedcentral.nih.gov/articlerender.fcgi?artid=4136406&tool=pmcentrez&rendertype=abstract
27. Solberg LI, Maciosek M V, Edwards NM. Primary care intervention to reduce alcohol misuse ranking its health impact and cost effectiveness. Am J Prev Med [Internet]. 2008 [cited 18 Jan 2016];34(2):143–152. Available from: http://www.ncbi.nlm.nih.gov/pubmed/18201645
28. Angus C, Scafato E, Ghirini S, Torbica A, Ferre F, Struzzo P, et al. Cost-effectiveness of a programme of screening and brief interventions for alcohol in primary care in Italy. BMC Fam Pract [Internet]. 2014 [cited 14 Dec 2015];15:26. Available from: http://www.pubmedcentral.nih.gov/articlerender.fcgi?artid=3936801&tool=pmcentrez&rendertype=abstract
29. Wilson DP, Donald B, Shattock AJ, Wilson D, Fraser-Hurt N. The cost-effectiveness of harm reduction. Int J Drug Policy [Internet]. 2015 [cited 18 Jan 2016];26 Suppl 1:S5–11. Available from: http://www.ncbi.nlm.nih.gov/pubmed/25727260
30. UNAIDS. UNAIDS reporte on the global AIDS epidemic [Internet]. 2012. Available from: https://papers2://publication/uuid/4467B415-2E9B-472A-89EF-B30E692EFE5C
31. Alistar SS, Owens DK, Brandeau ML. Effectiveness and cost effectiveness of expanding harm reduction and antiretroviral therapy in a mixed HIV epidemic: a modeling analysis for Ukraine. PLoS Med [Internet]. 2011 [cited 18 Jan 2016];8(3):e1000423. Available from: http://www.pubmedcentral.nih.gov/articlerender.fcgi?artid=3046988&tool=pmcentrez&rendertype=abstract
32. Hurley SF, Jolley DJ, Kaldor JM. Effectiveness of needle-exchange programmes for prevention of HIV infection. Lancet (London, England) [Internet] Elsevier. 1997 [cited 5 May 2016];349(9068):1797–800. Available from: http://www.thelancet.com/article/S0140673696113805/fulltext
33. Stoicescu C. The global state of harm reduction. Harm Reduction International: London; 2012.
34. Windsor LC, Jemal A, Alessi E. Cognitive behavioral therapy: a meta-analysis of race and substance use outcomes. Cult Divers Ethn Minor Psychol. 2015;21(2):356–72.
35. Drummond C, Kouimtsidis C, Reynolds M, Russell I, Godfrey C, Mccusker M et al. The effectiveness and cost effectiveness of Cognitive Behaviour Therapy for opiate misusers in methadone maintenance treatment: A multicentre, randomised, controlled trial. UKCBTMM Study: United Kingdom Cognitive Behaviour Therapy Study in Methadone Maintenance Treatment. Drugs: education, prevention and policy. 2005;12:69–76.

36. Center for Substance Abuse Treatment. Brief cognitive-behavioral therapy. brief interventions and brief therapies for substance abuse. Rockville: Substance Abuse and Mental Health Services Administration (US); 1999.
37. Walters D, Connor JP, Feeney GFX, Young RM. The cost effectiveness of naltrexone added to cognitive-behavioral therapy in the treatment of alcohol dependence. J Addict Dis [Internet]. 2009 [cited 18 Jan 2016];28(2):137–144. Available from: http://www.ncbi.nlm.nih.gov/pubmed/19340676
38. Chisholm D, Saxena S, Ommeren M van. Economic aspects of the mental health system: Key messages to health partners and policy-makers [Internet]. Geneva; 2006. Available from: http://www.who.int/mental_health/economic_aspects_of_mental_health.pdf
39. Roberts E, Cumming J, Nelson K. A review of economic evaluations of community mental health care. Med Care Res Rev [Internet]. 2005;62(5):503–43. Available from: http://mcr.sagepub.com/cgi/doi/10.1177/1077558705279307
40. Sindelar JL, Jofre-Bonet M, French MT, McLellan AT. Cost-effectiveness analysis of addiction treatment: paradoxes of multiple outcomes. Drug Alcohol Depend [Internet] Elsevier. 2004 [cited 30 Nov 2016];73(1):41–50. Available from: http://www.drugandalcoholdependence.com/article/S037687160300259X/fulltext
41. Gastfriend DR. A pharmaceutical industry perspective on the economics of treatments for alcohol and opioid use disorders. Ann N Y Acad Sci. 2014;1327:112–30.
42. Lingford-Hughes AR, Welch S, Peters L, Nutt DJ. BAP updated guidelines: evidence-based guidelines for the pharmacological management of substance abuse, harmful use, addiction and comorbidity: recommendations from BAP. J Psychopharmacol. 2012;26(7):899–952.
43. Rosner S, Hackl-Herrwerth A, Leucht S, Lehert P, Vecchi S, Soyka M. Acamprosate for alcohol dependence. Cochrane Database Syst Rev England. 2010;(9):CD004332.
44. Colombo GL, Di Matteo S, Bruno G. Acamprosate in the treatment of alcoholism: a budget impact analysis for the national health service in Italy. Subst Abuse Rehabil. New Zealand. 2012;3:73–9.
45. Palmer AJ, Neeser K, Weiss C, Brandt A, Comte S, Fox M. The long-term cost-effectiveness of improving alcohol abstinence with adjuvant acamprosate. Alcohol Alcohol. England. 2000;35(5):478–92.
46. Feeney GFX, Connor JP. Acamprosate reduces risk of return to drinking after detoxification, but is similarly effective to naltrexone. Evid Based Ment Health England. 2011;14(1):22.
47. Gueorguieva R, Wu R, Donovan D, Rounsaville BJ, Couper D, Krystal JH, et al. Baseline trajectories of heavy drinking and their effects on postrandomization drinking in the COMBINE study: empirically derived predictors of drinking outcomes during treatment. Alcohol. 2012;46(2):121–31.
48. Dunlap LJ, Zarkin GA, Bray JW, Mills M, Kivlahan DR, McKay JR, et al. Revisiting the cost-effectiveness of the COMBINE study for alcohol dependent patients: the patient perspective. Med Care. 2010;48(4):306–13.
49. Zarkin GA, Bray JW, Aldridge A, Mitra D, Mills MJ, Couper DJ, et al. Cost and cost-effectiveness of the COMBINE study in alcohol-dependent patients. Arch Gen Psychiatry. 2008;65(10):1214–21.
50. Mark TL, Montejano LB, Kranzler HR, Chalk M, Gastfriend DR. Comparison of healthcare utilization among patients treated with alcoholism medications. Am J Manag Care. 2010;16(12):879–88.
51. Jonas D, Amick H, Feltner C, Bobashev G, Thomas K, Wines R, et al. Pharmacotherapy for Adults With Alcohol-Use Disorders in Outpatient Settings: a systematic review and meta-analysis. JAMA. 2014;311(18):1889–900.
52. Gowing L, Farrell MF, Bornemann R, Sullivan LE, Ali R. Oral substitution treatment of injecting opioid users for prevention of HIV infection. Cochrane Database Syst Rev. 2011;(8):CD004145.
53. Zaric GS, Brennan AW, Varenbut M, Daiter JM. The cost of providing methadone maintenance treatment in Ontario, Canada. Am J Drug Alcohol Abuse. 2012;38(6):559–66.
54. Zaric GS, Barnett PG, Brandeau ML. HIV transmission and the cost-effectiveness of methadone maintenance. Am J Public Health. 2000;90(7):1100–11.
55. Connock M, Juarez-Garcia A, Jowett S, Frew E, Liu Z, Taylor RJ, et al. Methadone and buprenorphine for the management of opioid dependence: a systematic review and economic evaluation. Health Technol Assess. 2007;11(9):1–171, iii–iv.
56. Tran BX, Nguyen LT. Impact of methadone maintenance on health utility, health care utilization and expenditure in drug users with HIV/AIDS. Int J Drug Policy Netherlands. 2013;24(6):e105–10.
57. Virk MS, Arttamangkul S, Birdsong WT, Williams JT. Buprenorphine is a weak partial agonist that inhibits opioid receptor desensitization. J Neurosci. 2009;29(22):7341–8.
58. Adi Y, Juarez-Garcia A, Wang D, Jowett S, Frew E, Day E, et al. Oral naltrexone as a treatment for relapse prevention in formerly opioid-dependent drug users: a systematic review and economic evaluation. Health Technol Assess. 2007;11(6):iii–iv, 1–85.
59. Ruger JP, Chawarski M, Mazlan M, Ng N, Schottenfeld R. Cost-effectiveness of buprenorphine and naltrexone treatments for heroin dependence in Malaysia. PLoS One. 2012;7(12):e50673.
60. Jackson H, Mandell K, Johnson K, Chatterjee D, Vanness DJ. Cost-effectiveness of injectable extended-release naltrexone compared with methadone maintenance and buprenorphine maintenance treatment for opioid dependence. Subst Abus. 2015;36(2):226–31.
61. William R, Miller SR. Motivational Interviewing: helping people change. 3rd ed. The Guilford Press; 2012. 482 p.

Cost-Effectiveness of Interventions for the Treatment of Dementia Disorders

22

Dominic Trépel

Abstract

By 2050, dementia is anticipated to cost $2 trillion per year globally. Strategic investment is required to mitigate the health and economic consequences of dementia. Projections suggest that, by the middle of the century, 68% of all cases of dementia worldwide will occur in low- and middle-income countries. Cost-effectiveness analysis of dementia requires more research to inform policy. To date, cost-effectiveness analysis has focused on pharmacological and nonpharmacological management. Whether pharmacological agents for dementias (e.g., acetylcholinesterase inhibitors and N-methyl-D-aspartate receptor antagonists) are cost-effective is an area of ongoing contentious debate, but increasing evidence supports that they represent value for the money. An increasing number of on-pharmacological treatments are also considered cost-effective in certain circumstances (e.g., cognitive stimulation therapy, tailored activity programs, gingko biloba in occupational therapy, reminiscence therapies, and interventions for agitation). The potential gains from treating dementia diminish as dementia progresses, and measuring individuals' outcomes becomes increasing difficult as symptoms worsen. Current evidence suggests that a focus on the relative value of *prevention* strategies is required, as averting dementias would avoid significant suffering and may offset substantial costs, thus justifying larger investments. As dementia progresses over a number of years and through a number of stages, cost-effectiveness analysis based on primary data sources presents methodological issues; however, increased scientific attention is required to improve the methods and the evidence base to inform better decision-making on dementia.

D. Trépel, Ph.D (✉)
Global Brain Health Institute (GBHI), Trinity College Dublin, Dublin, Ireland

The Irish Longitudinal Study on Ageing (TILDA), Trinity College Dublin, Dublin, Ireland
e-mail: dominic.trepel@gbhi.org

D. Razzouk (ed.), *Mental Health Economics*, DOI 10.1007/978-3-319-55266-8_22

Key Points Summary

- What is dementia and what is the associated economic consequences?
- How are dementia disorders treated and what are successful outcomes?
- What evidence of cost-effectiveness is there for dementia interventions?
- Methodological considerations

22.1 Introduction

22.1.1 What Is Dementia?

Worldwide, life expectancy is increasing, the elderly population is growing [1], and dementia is becoming a major health and economic issue. In 2015 there were estimates of 46.8 million people worldwide with dementia, and this number will double over the next 20 years [2]. By 2018, the total costs associated with dementia worldwide are predicted to reach US$1 trillion, and based on projected changes, by 2030, costs will double yet again.

But what is dementia, why does it have such substantial cost implications, and what economic research does society need for this economic phenomenon?

Dementia disorders are a broad set of neurological diseases that often cause a gradual and progressive decline in cognitive ability and daily functioning. The American Psychiatric Association's *Diagnostic and Statistical Manual of Mental Disorders*, 5th edition, or DSM-5, now classifies dementia as a major neurocognitive disorder [3]. This is a recent reclassification, however, and it is anticipated that the forthcoming *International Classification of Diseases, 11th Revision*, is likely to categorize dementia as a neurocognitive disorder [4].

Many economic consequences are the direct result of the etiology and symptoms of dementia, which are onerous to formal healthcare [5] and place many demands on families [6]. The gradual damage to the brain caused by dementia (most often by degeneration of brain cells) leads to reduced cognitive ability and, in certain cases, physical function, and ultimately disrupts individuals' daily lives.

Dementia is an umbrella term encompassing a number of disease states; the common forms are Alzheimer disease and vascular dementia (comprising around 90% of cases), followed by Lewy body and frontotemporal dementias. Furthermore, boundaries between the varying forms of dementia are not necessarily distinct. While the symptoms of each type of dementia vary, they generally include loss of memory, impaired judgment, loss of daily functioning, and inappropriate behavior.

As conditions progress and symptoms worsen, people with dementia become increasingly reliant on other people's help because of the loss of their physical and mental abilities [7]. This creates demands for care and supervision from formal services, families, and the wider community.

While there is no known cure, risks of dementia attributable to the population (e.g., diabetes, midlife hypertension, midlife obesity, physical inactivity, depression, smoking, and low educational attainment) are considered potentially reversible, and estimates suggest that 28.2% (95% confidence interval, 14,2–41.5) of projected cases worldwide in the next two decades may be prevented by public health interventions [8].

Upon diagnosis, a variety of treatments are proven to be clinically effective and cost-effective in slowing disease progression and managing symptoms [9]. Furthermore, people living with dementia require organized care, and society must optimize arrangements for formal care and also monitor adverse health risks experienced by informal caregivers [10].

An identified paucity of evidence exists to inform policies on dementia [11], and dementia research remains underfunded [12]. National and international agencies are increasingly agreeing on the need for better, evidence-based dementia strategies; given the economic consequences, evidence on the cost-effectiveness of dementia interventions is becoming increasingly important.

22.1.2 What Are the Current and Projected Prevalences of Dementia?

Before considering strategies that might represent value for money or indeed economic consequences of dementia that may be averted, it is important to contextualize the challenges that dementia is placing on current and future society.

With 46.8 million people with dementia worldwide, variation in the prevalence of dementia is driven by country-level demographics of the aging population [2]. The likelihood of dementia doubles with every 5-year increase over 65 years of age [13], and forecasted global changes form an important indicator for strategic initiatives and research. HelpAge International's Global AgeWatch Index (2015; available from http://www.globalagewatch.org) illustrates the proportion of the worldwide population aged 60 years or older in 2014 compared with expected proportions in 2050 (see Fig. 22.1).

Today, worldwide aging may primarily concern more developed economies, but over the next three decades, it will increasingly affect less developed economies. It is estimated that by 2050, 68% of all dementia cases will be found in low- and middle-income countries [2].

The World Health Organization "Strategy and Plan of Action on Dementias in Older Persons (2015–2019)" recognizes threats imposed by projected changes in age profiles and proposes a strategic "plan of action on dementia," with objectives seeking "'multisectoral care and training programs for informal and formal caregivers." High-level calls to action seek to address consequences of dementia (https://worlddementiacouncil.org/), and any international or national recommendations necessitate sustainability and efficiency in their design.

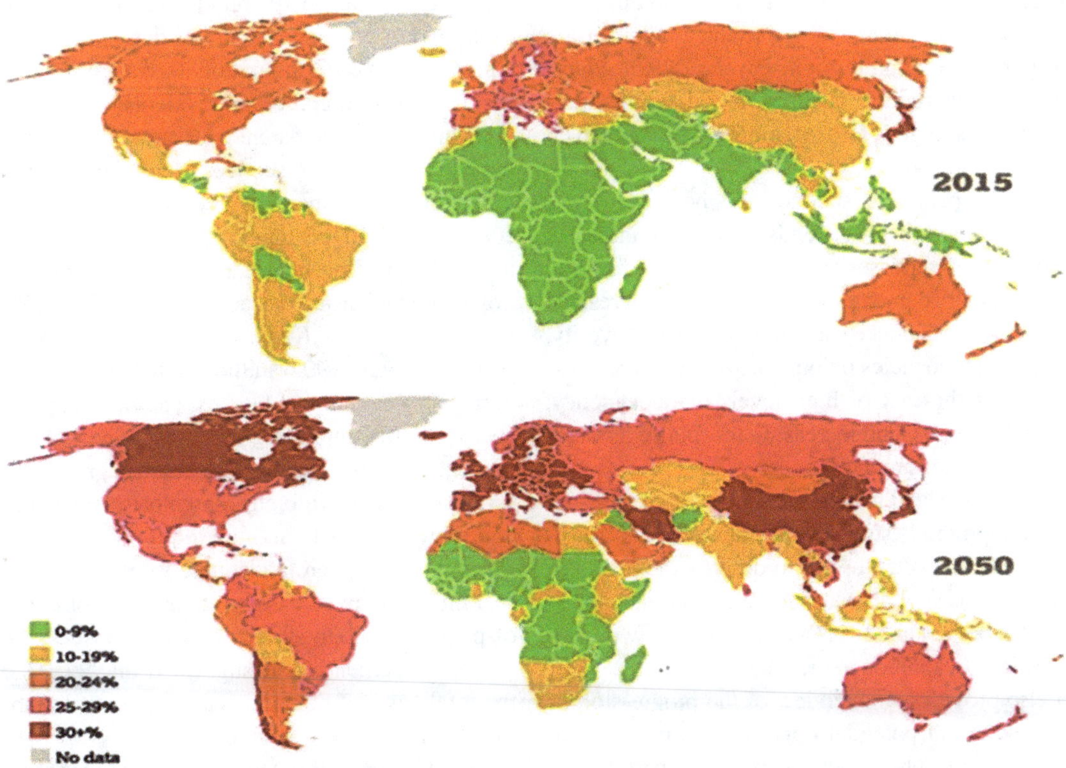

Fig. 22.1 Proportions of the population aged older than 60, by country (Source: *International Global AgeWatch Index 2015*, Age International, London)

To position strategies for dementia and what may constitute successful outcomes, the following section presents the known consequences associated with dementia to economies and society.

22.1.3 What Are the Associated Economic Consequences of Dementia?

Dementia has consequences to the person, their family and friends, and the wider community. Symptoms of dementia may be categorized into four broad areas: cognitive, functional, behavioral, and psychological effects. *Cognitive effects* relate to the loss of processes required to recognize people and places, to remember things, and to concentrate. *Functional effects* create difficulties completing everyday tasks and activities (e.g., cooking, cleaning, and managing personal finances). *Behavioral problems* are associated with a loss of social skills and may manifest as repetition of patterns of behavior, inappropriate responses, and aggression. *Psychological effects* include frustration, irritation, mood swings, personality changes, loss of motivation, and even depression.

Every person is unique, and how quickly a dementia progresses depends on the individual. As the illness progresses and symptoms manifest, the person with dementia experiences a progressive loss of independence and, with increasing severity, forms dependencies on others. As dementia worsens, it is the mix of high levels of dependency, complex needs, and increasing morbidity that creates a unique demand for care.

To understand this progression of dementia and have appropriate strategies to manage these consequences, it is often useful to describe dementia in stages. The Global Deterioration Scale developed by Reisberg et al. [14] is a useful overview of progression. In addition to the clinical use of the scale, it also provides an overview of the progression of dementia and potential opportunities to invest in and to delay subsequent stages; this is particularly useful where economic models may seek to extrapolate cost and outcomes in the long term.

To explore care provision, Fig. 22.2 presents costs of dementia care by country income and by the three of the most common sources of care: medical, social, and informal care.

The most common response to the loss of independence from dementia is *informal care*, defined as care provided by a family member or another person who is close to the care receiver (Act on Support for Informal Care [937/2005], Finland, 2006 (see Chap. 17), and is consistently a more utilized resource across all countries. However, proportions decline as the country income increases (suggesting substitution by increased spending on social care services). Interestingly, the proportion of dementia costs put toward medical care is approximately 20% across all country income levels, but this depends how much governments spend to provide support for people with dementia and their families. This raises significant concerns regarding financial protection against catastrophic expenditure in lower-income areas; for example Mould-Quevedo et al. [15] found that the average monthly out-of-pocket costs for dementia care in China may exceed the national average monthly incomes of rural and urban residents.

While it is not apparent from these figures, voluntary and charitable services often play a significant role in dementia, providing services to communities, advocating for the needs of individuals, and providing respite to informal caregivers. For example, in annual accounts for 2014/2015, trustees for the U.K. charity Alzheimer Society report receiving £90.6 million in income and suggest that, for every "£1 of expenditure, 89p was spent towards improving the lives of people with dementia" (https://www.alzheimers.org.uk/site/scripts/download_info.php?downloadID=1976).

Finally, access to and the required quantity of formal care is often inadequate to meet demand, so families may often also incur additional out-of-pocket costs to obtain private services. For example, Dementia UK suggested that 22.1% of the total costs of dementia care were attributable to privately funded "social" care.

In addition to the economic consequences of dementia care, dementia may also have wider economic consequences. One consideration is

Fig. 22.2 Percentages of the total cost of dementia care divided by country income (based on current World Bank country classification) and by cost subcategories (medical, social, and informal) (Source: World Alzheimer Report 2015 [2])

A summary of stages related to disease progression

Stage 1: No cognitive decline
- No problems experienced in daily living.
- ⇨ Associated diagnosis: No dementia.

Stage 2: Very mild cognitive decline
- Forgets names and locations of objects.
- Trouble finding words.
- ⇨ Associated diagnosis: No dementia.

Stage 3: Mild cognitive decline
- Difficulty travelling to new locations.
- Difficulty handling problems at work.
- ⇨ Associated diagnosis: No dementia.
- ⇨ Estimated mean duration: 7 years before onset of dementia

Stage 4: Moderate cognitive decline
- Difficulty with complex tasks (finances, shopping, planning).
- ⇨ Associated diagnosis: Early-Stage dementia.
- ⇨ Estimated mean duration: 2 years

Stage 5: Moderately severe cognitive decline
- Help required to choose clothing.
- Requires reminders for bathing.
- ⇨ Associated diagnosis: Mid-Stage dementia.
- ⇨ Estimated mean duration: 1.5 years

Stage 6: Severe cognitive decline
- Loss of awareness of recent events and experiences.
- Assistance is required to bathe.
- Decreased ability to use the toilet or may become incontinent.
- ⇨ Associated diagnosis: Mid-Stage dementia.
- ⇨ Estimated mean duration: 2.5 years

Stage 7: Very severe cognitive decline
- Limitations in vocabulary with eventual loss of speech.
- Loss of psychomotor skills (i.e. ability to walk and sit).
- Requires help with eating.
- ⇨ Associated diagnosis: Late-Stage dementia.
- ⇨ Estimated mean duration: 2.5 years

that dementia reduces individuals' and their caregivers' opportunities to be productive. One important potential productivity loss is the level of labor force participation, which produces income for households, taxes to fund public goods, and the production of market goods and services (required to drive the economic performance of any given country). Suffering from dementia often means that individuals can no longer undertake paid employment; furthermore, with increasing demand for informal care, family members may also be absent from work (absenteeism), their productivity while at work may diminishes as a direct result of high demand being placed on the informal caregiver (presenteeism), or they may reduce their hours or be forced to take early retirement to care for their loved ones.

In summary, the economic consequences of dementia are substantial and present a significant consideration for policymakers worldwide. This raises questions for policy on how society should intervene in dementia and what represents successful outcomes for any given intervention.

22.1.4 Interventions and Outcomes for Dementia Disorders

Most types of dementia are currently incurable. However, strategies exist that may prevent symptoms worsening or avert degeneration of brain tissue or nerves. At an individual level, the approach taken to intervene is highly contingent on the stage of dementia (see Fig. 22.2) and the degree to which risk factors may be modified (particularly in the earlier stages).

Current evidence-based guidelines are increasingly recognizing the complexity of dementias, and care pathways extensively describe how dementia should be approached within an integrated care system. For example, the National Institute for Health and Care Excellence (NICE) produced guidelines that account for prevention (in relation to midlife risk factors), early detection, diagnosis and assessment, patient choice, and ultimately approaches to intervention. Their current recommendations for interventions also seek to compartmentalize treatment into three groups: (1) cognitive symptoms with functional maintenance, (2) noncognitive symptoms with behavioral challenges, and (3) comorbid emotional disorders. Across the board, pharmacological interventions have various roles and nonpharmacological interventions are increasingly being recommended (e.g., structured group cognitive stimulation programs). Furthermore, guidelines are now advising on the appropriate means to support caregivers, appropriate end-of-life care, and pain relief.

Allocating resources to dementia care necessitates forgoing some alternative investment decisions. Ideally, healthcare provided for dementia should tangibly produce sufficient health to justify investment compared with a competing health state (e.g., cancer). Here we overview some potential outcomes that may be relevant to contrast healthcare decisions in dementia.

A common currency used in cost-utility analysis is the quality-adjusted life year (QALY), which provides a preference-weighted unit of generic health that can be compared across various healthcare decisions (see Chap. 6). In the case of dementia, however, the QALY framework presents several methodological challenges. For example, many patients may find it difficult to complete questionnaires required to estimate QALYs, and a proxy may be required to provide the required information.

If it is important to decision makers that generic health be expressed in QALYs (e.g., NICE), condition-specific instruments are considered more suitable than generic tools (e.g., the EuroQol five-dimension questionnaire). The Health Economic Research Centre database of mapping studies indicates methods to map health state utilities from condition-specific measures [16].

DEMQOL is a condition-specific measure of health-related quality of life that aims to provide an alternative method to estimate QALYs in dementia [17]. The DEMQOL proxy aims to assess QALYs during later stages of dementia, when verbal ability diminishes and can only be elicited from a proxy (e.g., a caregiver). Psychometric analysis analyzed the dimensional structure and performance and resulted in final health state classification systems for five dimensions for the DEMQOL-U (i.e., positive emotion, cognition, relationship, negative emotion, and loneliness) and four for the DEMQOL-Proxy-U (i.e., positive emotion, cognition, appearance, and negative emotion) [17]. The health state classification provides a means to use DEMQOL and DEMQOL-Proxy data and examine the cost-effectiveness of various interventions in dementia.

Alternatively, because the economic consequences of dementia are particularly important to policymakers, the relative benefits of intervention for dementia may more readily be expressed directly in monetary terms. Such approaches may be particularly useful in cost-benefit analysis or cost consequence analysis (CCA) (see Chaps. 1, 4, and 5). For example, the ENABLE trial evaluated assisted technologies using cost-benefit methods to analyze whether the benefits of technologies exceed their costs and resulted in positive net social gains [18]; such analysis is cited as identifying areas for improvements and possible cost savings in care delivery [19]. Similarly, CCA examines economic argument based solely on cost (e.g., where no summary measures of health benefit are used in the economic evaluation). One example of CCA applied in dementia is the evaluation of a psychogeriatric day center versus community care; these varying arrangements of care, while not directly altering the health state, considered that caregivers' lost productivity might influence the total cost of care [20].

The next section reviews cost-effectiveness evidence for commonly used interventions for dementia disorders, highlighting current sources of supporting evidence and discussing the quality of evidence.

22.2 The Cost-Effectiveness of Commonly Used Treatments for Dementia Disorders

Cost-effectiveness analysis is relatively less common in dementia compared with other health conditions. Systematic searches are applied to identify, quantify, and appraise the evidence [21], and despite numerous reviews over the past decade [22–26], there remains a paucity of economic evaluations in dementia.

Most recent is the study by Knapp et al. [24], who reviewed dementia studies containing both costs and outcomes [24]. They searched six electronic databases (PubMed, Embase, PsycINFO, EconLit, The Cochrane Library, Centre for Reviews and Dissemination [including DARE, NHSEED, HTA]) and a limited number of salient websites (e.g., NICE, Alzheimer's Society, and the Bradford Dementia Group at Bradford University). Searches were restricted to studies published between January 1, 2005, and December 31, 2011. These searches yielded 2731 potentially relevant studies, and after screening titles and abstracts, they identified 329 articles considered relevant for full-article screening. Upon appraisal of these full articles, 56 were included in the final literature review (258 studies were rejected after full-text appraisal and 71 studies were rejected because full-text articles could not be found).

In addition to previous reviews, this section presents the literature published since January 1, 2012. No formal quality assessment of cost-effectiveness studies is presented (our quality assessment of the literature will be presented elsewhere); however, previous reviews concur on the paucity of available studies and that included studies commonly have issues with the methodological quality.

The remainder of this section reviews cost-effectiveness studies of (a) pharmacological and (b) nonpharmacological interventions for dementia disorders.

22.2.1 Pharmacological Interventions

While there is presently no cure for dementia, two main pharmacological options that are currently believed to alter the course of the disease's progress:

- *Acetylcholinesterase inhibitors (AChEIs)* address deficits in cerebral acetylcholine by inhibiting the breakdown of and increasing the concentration of acetylcholine in brain synapses. Three licensed AChEIs are current available on the market (donepezil, galantamine and rivastigmine), and evidence suggests these are most effective in earlier stages, such as mild to moderate Alzheimer disease.
- *N-methyl-D-aspartate (NMDA) receptor antagonists* selectively inhibit the production of glutamate, which is released in excess in Alzheimer disease and is believed to be associated with brain damage during the course of the disease. Memantine is currently the only NMDA receptor antagonist licensed for use as treatment, with indications in moderate to severe Alzheimer disease.

In the United Kingdom, this range of pharmaceutical interventions was the basis of potentially the most heated debate on the grounds of unfavorable cost-effectiveness evidence. In 2004, NICE appraised the market for AChEIs and NMDA receptor inhibitors and, following a judicial review, restricted the use of memantine on the basis of uncertainty surrounding its clinical and cost-effectiveness [27]. As a result, memantine was licensed for used *only in research* such as clinical trials [28]. As part of planned updates and under increasing political pressure, NICE guidance was updated in 2010, broadening the indication for AChEIs and allowing use of NMDA receptor antagonists in routine practice.

The majority of economic evidence for dementia care relates to pharmacotherapy, and by far the majority relates to AChEIs, predominantly for the treatment of Alzheimer disease.

In 2008, a systematic review of economic evaluations of Alzheimer disease medications found very few randomized controlled trials (RCTs) that collected resource use data and recommended, in addition to clinical trials, that future RCTs include a mechanism to record patient resource use [26]. Our review of the literature finds little evidence of within-trial economic evaluations. The majority of publications have been economic modeling studies bringing together evidence on effectiveness with costs funded by manufacturers, raising questions regarding potential conflicts of interest. As a result, NICE developed the "Assessment of Health Economics in Alzheimer's Disease" model; however, the model received criticism given its attempt to replicate the findings and drew into question the model's conclusions [29]. Ultimately, earlier models have attracted controversy given the limited amount of available data, and more recent discussions have questioned how the underlying evidence has changed to support guidance issued in 2010 [30]. By 2010, the change in the economic argument supporting AChEIs as given larger cost offsets when compared with comparators (defined as "best supportive care" in the systematic review). Table 22.1 summarizes the effectiveness and cost-effectiveness of drugs to treat Alzheimer disease in 2004 and 2010.

NICE has an explicit reimbursement threshold (£20,000–£30,000 per QALY) and, as Hyde et al. [31] show, estimates in 2004 were all above the NICE threshold. However, updated estimates of cost effectiveness in 2010 suggest that all AChEIs (i.e., donepezil, galantamine, and rivastigmine) dominated the comparator (i.e., had improved clinical outcomes and cost less), and memantine was borderline cost-effective. Analysis of the underlying drivers for changes in clinical and cost-effectiveness suggest that emerging evidence altered the confidence intervals in the clinical effect size (in particular with regard to function and global impact), and changes in cost effectiveness of AChEIs were largely the result of reduction in the "modelled costs of introducing the drugs, particularly drug acquisition and the costs of full time institutionalised care." Limitations of these cost-effectiveness estimates are cited as results of (a) "time to institutionalization" being almost wholly driven from model-based predictions (which no emerging clinical evidence had observed), and (b) disputed evidence on drug-related cost-offsets for full-time care, and (c) that changes in the incremental cost-effectiveness ratio were largely the result of small changes in mean costs and benefits.

Given the complexity of reviewing various economic models, this chapter does not provide full treatment of this evidence base; for comprehensive discussions of cost-effectiveness models (and industry submissions), we recommend reading the Health Technology Assessment entitled "'The effectiveness and cost-effectiveness of

Table 22.1 Comparison of the effectiveness and cost effectiveness of drugs to treat Alzheimer disease in 2004 and 2010

Drug compared with best supportive care	2004			2010		
	Cost	QALY	ICER (per QALY)	Cost	QALY	ICER (per QALY)
Donepezil	£2895	0.036	£80,941	−£588	0.036	Dominates
Galantamine	£2648	0.039	£68,042	−£620	0.033	Dominates
Rivastigmine	£2121	0.037	£57,985	−£534	0.029	Dominates
Memantine	a	NR	£37–53,000	£405	0.013	£32,100

ICER incremental cost-effectiveness ratio, *NR* not reported, *QALY* quality-adjusted life year
Source: Hyde et al. [31]

donepezil, galantamine, rivastigmine and memantine for the treatment of Alzheimer's disease (review of Technology Appraisal No. 111): a systematic review and economic model" [32].

22.2.2 Nonpharmacological Interventions

Limited published economic research describes nonpharmacological interventions for people with dementia. A review by Knapp et al. [24] found that cognitive stimulation therapy, tailored activity programs, and occupational therapy were more cost-effective than usual care. Since 2012, we also identified three further studies evaluating the cost-effectiveness of gingko biloba, reminiscence therapies, and interventions for agitation. It is worth noting that studies of cost-effectiveness commonly compare the particular intervention to "usual care" and are therefore inherently context specific; thus the following review of the evidence is primarily relevant to the setting of the study.

Cognitive stimulation therapy involves group activities and exercises designed to help people with memory and communication. One RCT conducted in England studied 91 community-dwelling people with dementia receiving twice-weekly group sessions for 8 weeks; these people were compared with 70 people with dementia who received treatment as usual [33]. The aim of the intervention focused on stimulating the "senses, remembering the past, people and objects and everyday practical issues." The findings suggest that providing group sessions did not significantly change overall costs but had benefits to cognition and quality of life in dementia and therefore represent value for the money to the English National Health Service.

Occupational therapy in dementia aims to improve "daily functioning, social participation, and wellbeing in people with dementia living in the community." It can also improve the "'sense of competence and wellbeing of their primary care givers." In an RCT conducted in Holland, people with dementia were allocated ten 1-h sessions of occupational therapy delivered in their homes [34]. Intervention included an evaluation of the degree of disability and daily function, and implemented changes in the home to "train patients in the use of aids to compensate for cognitive decline and care givers in coping behaviours and supervision." At 3 months, through assessing improvement in patients' daily functioning and caregivers' sense of competence, the study concluded that "there was a significant difference in proportions of successful treatments of 36%." (In this case, *successful treatment* was defined as "a combined patient and caregiver outcome measure of clinically relevant improvement on process, performance, and competence scales.") Cost consequence analysis also reveal average savings of €1748 (£1279, $2621) per couple successfully treated with occupational therapy through reductions in nursing home care, domestic home care, social worker and physiotherapist time, day care, and Meals on Wheels.

Tailored activity programs are a home-based occupational therapy intervention that identifies and develops tailored activities based on the interest of the person with dementia and trains families to use the activities in their daily lives. One RCT in the United States included people with dementia and their caregivers, and evaluated the cost-effectiveness of home-based occupational therapy delivered in eight sessions (six home/two telephone contacts) over 4 months; these sessions were delivered by occupational therapists [35]. The aim of the intervention was to preserve "capabilities, roles, habits and interests, as well as train families to do them." Taking two items from the Caregiver Vigilance Scale [36], the study found that, compared with the control group, caregivers had reduced their average time "doing things" (intervention: 5.4 h vs. control: 8.6 h) and also had a significant reduction in time "on duty" (intervention: 13.4 h vs. control: 17.6 h). The cost of providing the program was US$942 and every hour per day saved "doing things" cost $2.37 per day, and every hour per day "being on duty" cost of $1.10 per day. Analysis of uncertainty suggested that the probability that the program is cost effective was 79.2%.

Gingko biloba has an (arguably) nonpharmacological extract, EGb 761, that is considered a herbal remedy for dementia and cognitive impairment.

The extract was investigated in three clinical trials in Austria, and findings were used to investigate the pharmacoeconomic implications [37]. The study found that deterioration in activities of daily living were delayed by an average of 22.3 months in comparison with placebo, resulting in overall net savings ranging between €3,692 and €29,577. The economic evaluation assessed costs of drug reimbursement, physician fees, and federal subsidies. The evaluation determined that, when compared with placebo, the extract was associated with cost savings ranging from €3,692 to €29,577 (largely as a result of reductions in subsidies).

Reminiscence therapies for people with dementia aim to stimulate memories and events from the past. REMCARE was a pragmatic, multicenter randomized trial evaluating the clinical and cost-effectiveness of reminiscence groups for people with dementia and their family caregivers. As the primary clinical outcome in patients with dementia, quality of life was measured using the QoL-AD [38], and to measure the general health of caregivers the 28-item General Health Questionnaire was used [39]. The economic evaluation ascertained health-state utilities separately in patients and caregivers using the EQ-5D [40] to estimate QALYs, and cost analysis measured the types and quantities of resource inputs using an adapted CSRI as part of microcosting [41] (see Chap. 13). Despite the quality of the methodological design, the reminiscence intervention did not demonstrate effectiveness with the clinical outcomes, nor did the economic evaluation demonstrate cost-effectiveness using costs and QALYs.

Agitation is common in people with dementia and may result in restlessness, repetitiveness, and acts of aggression. In 2014 a review evaluated the evidence for nonpharmacological interventions for reducing agitation. The review included 160 of 1916 article screened and calculated standard effect sizes to compare heterogeneous interventions [42]. The study identified two health economic studies and, given the paucity of previous studies, developed an economic model based on the relationship between agitation and health and social care costs, and health-related quality of life (see the full study for details of the modeling strategy).

22.2.3 Summary of Economic Evidence

The disabilities associated with dementia create strong economic arguments to support interventions. Pharmacological therapies have historically dominated the literature and have largely been modeling studies to support industry submissions for reimbursement. More recently, research-funding bodies have increasingly supported cost-effectiveness studies examining nonpharmacological approaches in dementia, most often using within-trial cost-effectiveness analysis [43]. In the absence of cures, the literature has focused on alleviating cognitive, functional, behavioral, or psychological effects of dementia, often also considering how to reduce demands placed on informal caregivers (e.g., family, friends).

The diversity of clinical manifestations and the temporal factors of progression combined with complex economic issues raise various methodological considerations. Furthermore, it is envisaged that prevention will play an increasing role in dementia. The next section concludes this chapter with methodological considerations for future research.

22.3 Methodological Considerations

As with many chronic conditions [44], the objective should be to prevent the condition or, failing that, to prolong the quality and quantity of life by improving long-term care [45]. In 2007, the National Audit Office is cited as saying [46], "Parallels can be drawn between dementia now and cancer in the 1950s, when there were few treatments and patients were commonly not told the diagnosis for fear of distress."

To consider potential disparities in decisions about research investments, an analysis of research spending in the United Kingdom, published in 2014, examined government and charitable investments combined and determined that expenditures for cancer comprise 64%; those for chronic heart disease, 19%; dementia, 10%; and stroke, 7% (https://www.stroke.org.uk/sites/default/files/sa-research_spend_in_the_uk_apr2015_web.pdf). The report determines that, "for every £10 of health and social care costs attributable to the disease, cancer received £1.08 in research funding, CHD received £0.65, stroke received £0.19 (or £0.11 depending on care costs of stroke used) and finally *dementia received £0.08*."

The U.S. National Institutes of Health's "state-of-the-science conference" released a statement calling for increased research into the prevention of Alzheimer disease and cognitive decline. The panel determined the need for more large-scale, population-based studies and RCTs to investigate strategies to "maintain cognitive function in individuals at risk for decline, to identify factors that may delay the onset of Alzheimer's disease among persons at risk, and to identify factors that may slow the progression of Alzheimer's disease among persons in whom the condition is already diagnosed" [47]. Recent EU funded research suggests that the most likely risk factors for dementia prevention are depression, hypertension, physical inactivity, diabetes, obesity, hyperlipidemia, and smoking, and probable factors requiring further research including coronary heart disease, renal dysfunction, diet, and cognitive activity [48].

Furthermore, the Alzheimer's Drug Discovery Foundation convened an advisory panel to discuss the existing evidence and calls for increased comparative effectiveness research to learn whether routine clinical care decisions can protect against dementia and cognitive decline [49]. However, there exists an identified need for a greater consensus on the definition of quality of life [50], cost-effectiveness of interventions [51], and whether deploying resources to address modifiable risk factors will represent value for the money in preventing future dementia cases [8].

Investment in dementia is necessitated by the potential implications for society. Investment strategies for dementia require a unified framework, and the Global Deterioration Scale developed by Reisberg et al. [14] may prove useful in covering seven stages, although the value of intervention may differ substantially in each [14, 52]. As the timelines associated with this scale illustrate, the progression of dementia from early risk factors to death occurs over several decades; therefore is it any wonder that the number of good-quality RCTs is so limited? Methodological considerations need to reformat our conceptual framework, our views on required data, and our opinions on what constitutes an intervention.

22.4 Conclusion

Dementia prevalence is predicted to triple by 2050; as a result, global costs will reach an estimated $2 trillion. While various pharmacological and nonpharmacological strategies represent value for the money, the key to the agenda for future cost-effectiveness research in dementia may lie in prevention strategies. As we have learned, 30% of dementia cases worldwide are currently believed to be preventable by addressing midlife modifiable risk factors [8]. But what resources are required to realize this? Are investments in prevention economically viable? What is the appropriate research design to assess this?

As the Global Deterioration Scale highlights (see Fig. 22.3), temporal factors of dementia progression are key to the decision problems for policymakers, and appropriately targeting interventions across the various stages is required to ensure society achieves a maximum return on investment. A unified evaluation framework that considers the life course from health, through dementia, to death is required, particularly with regard to comparing the value of prevention and treatment strategies.

National dementia plans remain the single most powerful tool to transform national dementia care [54]; however, there is currently limited evidence that cost-effectiveness analysis is applied to inform policy development or indeed to evaluate the implementation of dementia strategies themselves. As national dementia strategies are being implemented worldwide, researchers need to develop *innovative* approaches to monitor whether investments are cost-effective uses of limited available resources. Methodological development of such evaluation frameworks also needs to consider translation to low- and middle-income countries, where estimates suggest 68% of all dementia will occur by 2050.

Cost-utility analysis is an important means of comparing disparate health decisions by estimating QALYs and costs. Dementia is problematic in

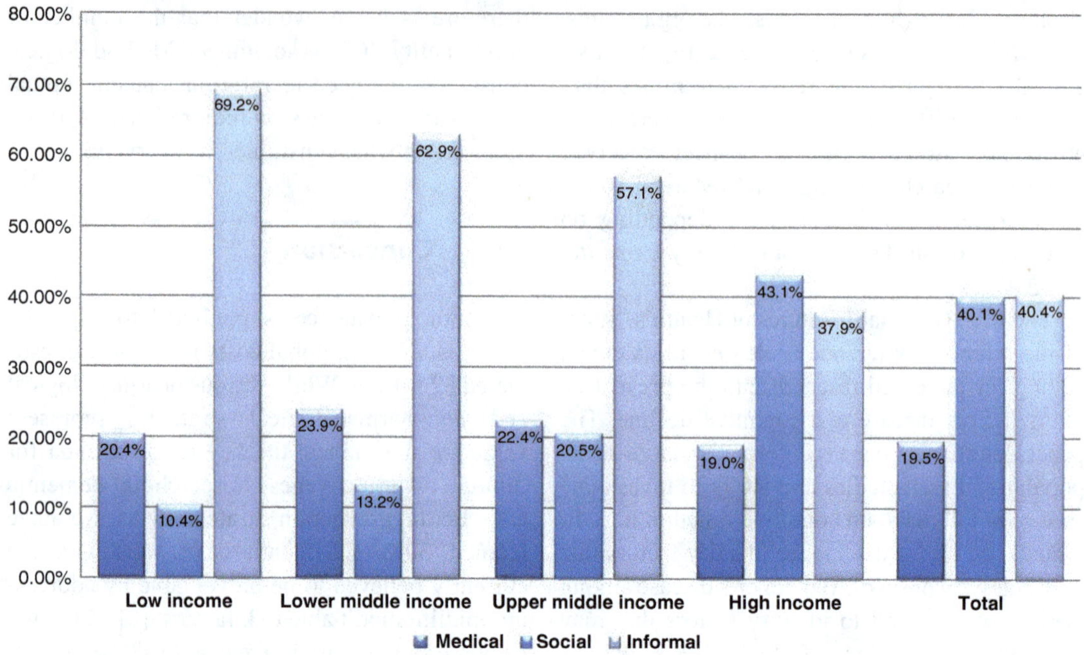

Fig. 22.3 A summary of the stages of dementia (Source: Global Deterioration Scale [14] and Clinical Stages of Alzheimer's Disease [52, 53]

outcome research, but condition-specific outcome measures are providing dementia health state classifications (e.g., DEM-QOL [17]). To fully implement economic evaluations in order to compare all investment decisions, countries need to establish preference weights for such emerging outcome measures.

The economic implications of dementia are mismatched to the level of dementia research. For example, in the United Kingdom, dementia receives only 10% of the proportion of research spent on cancer, chronic heart disease, dementia, and stroke combined, but consumes up to 50% of the total health and social care costs of these four conditions combined. Future economic evaluations need to present arguments intended to realign this disparity in society's scientific focus and demonstrate the value of information to inform dementia policy [55]. While the field of dementia research may prove eminently more challenging than research into other illnesses, sound economic reasoning can ensure the value of future research. The expected payoff from proposed research should set research priorities and should establish technically efficient designs to ensure the societal value of proposed research.

Key Messages

- Dementia is a major economic issue predicted to cost trillions every year over the next half century.
- When comparing the economic consequences of dementia with those of other disease states (e.g., cancer, chronic heart disease), dementia research is relatively underfunded.
- Cost-effectiveness analysis of dementia is an area requiring a larger amount of output to inform policy.

(continued)

(continued)

- Previous cost-effectiveness analysis has focused on pharmacological and non-pharmacological management, and there is a need for research on whether prevention strategies and national dementia plans represent value for the money.
- Economic research in dementia (e.g., cost-effectiveness analysis) presents methodological issues; however, increased scientific attention is required to address methodological issues and aid healthcare decision makers tackle this social and economic challenge.

References

1. United Nations, Department of Economic and Social Affairs, Population Division. World population prospects: the 2015 revision, key findings and advance tables. Working paper no. ESA/P/WP.241; 2015.
2. Martin Prince A, et al. World Alzheimer report 2015: the global impact of dementia: an Analysis of prevalence, incidence, cost and trends. London: Alzheimer's Disease International; 2015.
3. American Psychiatric Association. *Diagnostic and statistical manual of mental disorders*. Arlington: American Psychiatric Association; 2013.
4. WHO. The international classification of diseases 11th revision, WHO; 2016.
5. Burns A, Iliffe S. Dementia. *BMJ*. 2009;338:405–9.
6. Trépel D. Economic analyses of dementia care in Ireland and Europe: perception of services and care, the market value of informal care and changes in service utilisation; 2012. Retrieved from https://ulir.ul.ie/handle/10344/2462.
7. Trépel D. Informal cost of dementia care – a proxy-good valuation in Ireland. Econ Soc Rev (Irel). 2011;42(8):479–50357.
8. Norton S, Matthews FE, Barnes DE, Yaffe K, Brayne C. Potential for primary prevention of Alzheimer's disease: an analysis of population-based data. Lancet Neurol. 2014;13(8):788–94.
9. NICE. Dementia quality standard|Guidance and guidelines| NICE. NICE; 2010. Retrieved from https://www.nice.org.uk/guidance/qs1.
10. Trepel D, Crean M, Bedley E. An economic analysis of home care services for people with dementia [executive summary]. Dublin: Alzheimer Society of Ireland; 2015.
11. Rubinstein E, Duggan C, Van Landingham B, Thompson D, Warburton W. A call to action: the global response to dementia through policy innovation; 2015.
12. Luengo-Fernandez R, Leal J, Gray A. UK research spend in 2008 and 2012: comparing stroke, cancer, coronary heart disease and dementia. *BMJ Open*. 2015;5(4):e006648.
13. Gao S, Hendrie HC, Hall KS, Hui S. The relationships between age, sex, and the incidence of dementia and Alzheimer disease: a meta-analysis. Arch Gen Psychiatry. 1998;55(9):809–15.
14. Reisberg B, Ferris SH, de Leon MJ, Crook T. The global deterioration scale for assessment of primary degenerative dementia. Am J Psychiatry. 1982;139(9): 1136–9.
15. Mould-Quevedo JF, et al. The burden of caring for dementia patients: caregiver reports from a cross-sectional hospital-based study in China. Expert Rev Pharmacoecon Outcomes Res. 2013;13(5):663–73.
16. Dakin H, et al. Review of studies mapping from quality of life or clinical measures to EQ-5D: an online database. *Health Qual Life Outcomes*. 2013;11(1):151.
17. Mulhern B, et al. Development of DEMQOL-U and DEMQOL-PROXY-U: generation of preference-based indices from DEMQOL and DEMQOL-PROXY for use in economic evaluation. Health Technol Assess (Rockv). 2013;17(5):1–160.
18. Duff P, Dolphin C. Cost-benefit analysis of assistive technology to support independence for people with dementia – part 2: results from employing the ENABLE cost-benefit model in practice. *Technol Disabil*. 2007;19(2, 3):79–90.
19. Gibson G, Dickinson C, Brittain K, Robinson L. The everyday use of assistive technology by people with dementia and their family carers: a qualitative study. BMC Geriatr. 2015;15:89.
20. Artaso Irigoyen B, Martín Carrasco M, Cabasés Hita JM. Análisis coste-consecuencia de un centro de día psicogeriátrico. Rev Esp Geriatr Gerontol. 2002;37(6): 291–7.
21. Shemilt I, et al. Chapter 15: incorporating economics evidence. In: Higgins JPT, Green S, editors. Cochrane handbook for systematic reviews of interventions, vol. 4. Chichester: John Wiley & Sons; 2011. p. 449–80.
22. Laver K, Dyer S, Whitehead C, Clemson L, Crotty M. Interventions to delay functional decline in people with dementia: a systematic review of systematic reviews. *BMJ Open*. 2016;6(4):e010767.
23. Oremus M. Systematic review of economic evaluations of Alzheimer's disease medications. Expert Rev Pharmacoecon Outcomes Res. 2008;8(3):273–89.
24. Knapp M, Iemmi V, Romeo R. Dementia care costs and outcomes: a systematic review. Int J Geriatr Psychiatry. 2013;28(6):551–61.
25. NICE. Donepezil, galantamine, rivastigmine and memantine for the treatment of Alzheimer's disease| Guidance and guidelines|NICE; 2009. Retrieved from https://www.nice.org.uk/Guidance/ta217.
26. Walker S, Sculpher M, Claxton K, Palmer S. Coverage with evidence development, only in research, risk

sharing, or patient access scheme? A framework for coverage decisions. Value Health. 2012;15(3):570–9.
27. Getsios D, Migliaccio-Walle K, Caro JJ. NICE cost-effectiveness appraisal of cholinesterase inhibitors: was the right question posed? Were the best tools used? PharmacoEconomics. 2007;25(12):997–1006.
28. Loveman E, et al. The clinical and cost-effectiveness of donepezil, rivastigmine, galantamine and memantine for Alzheimer's disease. *Health Technol Assess.* 2006;10(1):iii–iv, ix–xi, 1–160.
29. Hyde C, et al. Evolution of the evidence on the effectiveness and cost-effectiveness of acetylcholinesterase inhibitors and memantine for Alzheimer's disease: systematic review and economic model. Age Ageing. 2013;42(1):14–20.
30. Bond M, et al. The effectiveness and cost-effectiveness of donepezil, galantamine, rivastigmine and memantine for the treatment of Alzheimer's disease (review of technology appraisal no. 111): a systematic review and economic model. Health Technol Assess. 2012;16(21):1–470.
31. Knapp M, et al. Cognitive stimulation therapy for people with dementia: cost-effectiveness analysis. Br J Psychiatry. 2006;188:574–80.
32. Graff MJL, et al. Community occupational therapy for older patients with dementia and their care givers: cost effectiveness study. BMJ. 2008;336(7636):134–8.
33. Gitlin LN, Hodgson N, Jutkowitz E, Pizzi L. The cost-effectiveness of a nonpharmacologic intervention for individuals with dementia and family caregivers: the tailored activity program. Am J Geriatr Psychiatry. 2010;18(6):510–9.
34. Mahoney DF, Jones RN, Coon DW, Mendelsohn AB, Gitlin LN, Ory M. The Caregiver Vigilance Scale: application and validation in the Resources for Enhancing Alzheimer's Caregiver Health (REACH) project. Am J Alzheimers Dis Other Demen. 18(1):39–48.
35. Rainer M, Mucke H, Schlaefke S. *Ginkgo biloba* extract EGb 761 in the treatment of dementia: a pharmacoeconomic analysis of the Austrian setting. Wien Klin Wochenschr. 2013;125(1–2):8–15.
36. Hoe J, Katona C, Roch B, Livingston G. Use of the QOL-AD for measuring quality of life in people with severe dementia--the LASER-AD study. Age Ageing. 2005;34(2):130–5.
37. Sterling M, et al. General health questionnaire – 28 (GHQ-28). *J Physiother*. 2011;57(4):259.
38. van Reenen M, Oppe M. EQ-5D-5L user guide: basic information on how to use the EQ-5D-5L instrument. Rotterdam: EuroQol Research Foundation; 2015.
39. Ridyard CH, Hughes DA, DIRUM Team. Taxonomy for methods of resource use measurement. Health Econ. 2015;24(3):372–8.
40. Livingston G, et al. A systematic review of the clinical effectiveness and cost-effectiveness of sensory, psychological and behavioural interventions for managing agitation in older adults with dementia. *Health Technol Assess (Rockv)*. 2014;18(39):1–226.
41. Glick H, Doshi J, Sonnad S, Polsky D. Economic evaluation in clinical trials. OUP Oxford, 2014.
42. Manton KG, Patrick CH, Stallard E. Mortality model based on delays in progression of chronic diseases: alternative to cause elimination model. Public Health Reports 95.6 (1980):580.
43. WHO. Preventing chronic diseases: a vital investment. Geneva: WHO; 2015.
44. Great Britain. National Audit Office. Improving services and support for people with dementia: report, The Stationery Office; 2007.
45. Daviglus ML, et al. NIH state-of-the-science conference statement: preventing Alzheimer's disease and cognitive decline. NIH Consens State Sci Statements. 2010;27(4):1–30.
46. Dacks PA, et al. A call for comparative effectiveness research to learn whether routine clinical care decisions can protect from dementia and cognitive decline. Alzheimers Res Ther. 2016;8:33.
47. Cooper C, et al. Systematic review of the effectiveness of non-pharmacological interventions to improve quality of life of people with dementia. Int Psychogeriatr. 2012;24(6):856–70.
48. Deckers K, Boxtel MP, Schiepers OJ, Vugt M, Muñoz Sánchez JL, Anstey KJ, et al. Target risk factors for dementia prevention: a systematic review and Delphi consensus study on the evidence from observational studies. Int J Geriatr Psychiatry. 2015;30(3):234–46.
49. Krzymińska E, Rossa G, Krzymiński S. The global deterioration scale (GDS) and functional assessment staging (FAST) in the diagnosis of Alzheimer type dementia. Psychiatr Pol. 1992;27(2):129–38.
50. Ettema TP, et al. The concept of quality of life in dementia in the different stages of the disease. Int Psychogeriatr. 2005;17(03):353–70.
51. De Leon MJ, Braak H. An atlas of Alzheimer's disease. New York: Parthenon Pub. Group; 1999.
52. Pot AM, Petrea I, Meerveld J. Improving dementia care worldwide: ideas and advice on developing and implementing a National Dementia Plan. London: Bupa/ADI; 2013.
53. Schaller S, Mauskopf J, Kriza C, Wahlster P, Kolominsky-Rabas PL. The main cost drivers in dementia: a systematic review. Int J Geriatr Psychiatry. 2015;30(2):111–29.
54. Claxton K, Neumann PJ, Araki S, Weinstein MC. Bayesian value-of-information analysis: an application to a policy model of Alzheimer's disease. Int J Technol Assess Health Care. 2001;17(1):38–55.
55. Tilford JM, et al. Preference-based health-related quality-of-life outcomes in children with autism spectrum disorders: a comparison of generic instruments. PharmacoEconomics. 2012;30(8):661–79.

23 Cost-Effectiveness of Interventions for Children and Adolescents with Psychiatric Disorders

Monica Kayo

Abstract

The objective of this chapter is to provide an overview of the cost-effectiveness of interventions for the major burdensome mental health disorders occurring during childhood and adolescence: autism spectrum disorders, attention-deficit/hyperactivity disorder, and conduct disorders. Interventions in childhood have a great impact on society as a whole, not just the children and their families. The costs of psychiatric disorders in children and adolescents are reflected in education, justice, and productivity over their lifetime. However, cost-effectiveness evaluations of mental health interventions in children are more rare than in adults.

Key Points Summary

- Burden of childhood and adolescent psychiatric disorders
- Cost-effectiveness of interventions for autism spectrum disorders
- Cost-effectiveness of interventions for attention-deficit/hyperactivity disorders
- Cost-effectiveness of interventions for conduct disorders

23.1 Introduction

Childhood psychiatric disorders have a significant impact not only in health services but also in education, justice, lost productivity, shorter life expectancy, and intangible costs (stigma, social exclusion, lower quality of life). Mental health problems in early childhood and adolescence may result in lower educational achievements, risky behavior, substance abuse, criminality, and other psychosocial complications. In addition to direct health costs, significant expenditures come from indirect costs and non–health-related direct costs. Therefore, the consequences of childhood psychiatric disorders could be better assessed in studies with a broader societal perspective. As in other areas of mental health, however, cost-effectiveness evaluations are scarce, with fewer studies of children than those of adults [1]. To determine the full

M. Kayo (✉)
Centre of Economic Mental Health, Department of Psychiatry, Universidade Federal de Sao Paulo, Rua Borges Lagoa 570, 1° andar, São Paulo 04038-000, Brazil
e-mail: monica.kayo@gmail.com

D. Razzouk (ed.), *Mental Health Economics*, DOI 10.1007/978-3-319-55266-8_23

costs and cost-effectiveness of interventions, a long evaluation period is needed, and because the potential future benefits take considerable time to come to fruition (such as savings from not using justice system services when conduct disorder is effectively prevented), this type of research is rare. Moreover, the majority of existing studies of costs and the burden of psychiatric disorders in children and adolescents were conducted in Europe and the United States [2]. In fact, less than 1% of research publications on mental health in low- and middle-income countries are dedicated to economic evaluations. A review of cost-of-illness studies of mental health found that only 1 of 39 studies performed in developed countries focused on children, whereas none of the 5 studies conducted in developing countries included any evidence of psychiatric disorders in children [3].

23.2 The Burden of Childhood and Adolescent Psychiatric Disorders

The median prevalence of childhood psychiatric disorders has been reported as 12% for prepubescent school-age children and 15% among adolescents [4]. Most studies focused the population between 4 and 17 years old, but it does not mean that the problems start at this age; one review considering epidemiological aspects of mental health problems and psychopathology in children aged 0–3 years found that a 2% incidence of mental health disorders, including mental retardation, diagnosed at a hospital in the first 3 years of life [5].

Few studies provide a broad picture of the costs of all child and adolescent psychiatric disorders [1]. The most studied conditions are attention-deficit/hyperactivity disorder (ADHD), autism spectrum disorder (ASD), and conduct disorder (CD), and the studies are usually conducted in children older than 3 years. Although a reasonable number of studies of depression and anxiety in adults exist, such conditions in children are less studied from an economic perspective.

A pan-European study assessed the costs of ADHD, ASD, and CD in childhood and estimated the total costs to be €21.3 billion per year in 2010 for an estimated 5,932,112 children with ADHD (age 6–17 years), CD (5–17 years), or ASD (2–17 years). The direct medical costs accounted for 12% and the nonmedical costs, including informal care, accounted for 88%. Indirect costs were not measured [6]. The average annual cost per child was €3595; this was lowest for ADHD (€781) and highest for ASD (€27,261). The costs per child with CD were €1735 [6].

When talking about total costs, the mean annual costs per child range from €7,376 to €64,703, depending on the ages included and the conditions examined [2]. Such estimates came from seven studies in a review that included different methods of cost estimates [7–13]. Five studies used the Client Service Receipt Inventory [14] (see Chap. 13, to collect cost data). The Client Service Receipt Inventory was adapted to suit the specific mental condition and age of the patients examined.

23.3 Cost-Effectiveness of Treatments for ASDs

23.3.1 Definition of Autism Spectrum Disorder

ASD is a group of developmental disabilities characterized by deficits in social communication skills and repetitive and stereotyped behaviors [15]. The fourth edition of the *Diagnostic and Statistical Manual of Mental Disorders* [16] used *pervasive developmental disorder* as the term for a group of five diagnoses: autistic disorder, Asperger disorder, Rett disorder, childhood disintegrative disorder, and pervasive developmental disorder – not otherwise specified. Such diagnoses had in common deficits in social communication skills and a limited range of repetitive or stereotyped activities and interests. The fifth edition of the *Diagnostic and Statistical Manual of Mental Disorders* [15] uses the term *autism spectrum disorders* to group those five conditions. The common core symptoms of this group are deficits in social communication skills and strict repetitive behavior. Most interventions address these core symptoms.

According to the U.S. Centers for Disease Control and Prevention, the estimated prevalence of ASD is 1 in 68 children (1.5%), based on tracking in 11 communities across the United States in 2012 [17]. In that study, conducted by the Centers for Disease Control and Prevention, concerns about the development of the children identified with ASD began by the age of 3 years [17], but a diagnosis is usually made when the child entrs school (64.9 months) [18].

23.3.2 Outcomes

Measuring health outcomes in children with ASD is a complex task because of the communication deficits and cognitive disabilities often present in this population. Although adolescents with ASD can report their own quality of life, proxy reporting by parents is needed for younger preschool children and toddlers.

Several generic tools are available for preference-weighting health outcomes to estimate quality-adjusted life years; however, the majority of them were not developed to be used in children, with the exception of the Health Utilities Index Marks 2 and 3 [19]. Therefore, two preference-based health-related quality of life instruments were developed to be used in children and adolescents: the EuroQol five-dimension questionnaire (EQ5D), youth version (EQ5D-Y) [20], and the nine-dimension Child Health Utility (CHU9D) questionnaire [21]. The EQ5D-Y is a modified version of the EQ5D, adapted to be used with children 8 years or older. Like the adult version, the EQ5D-Y includes five questions on current health status regarding mobility, self-care, usual activities, pain/discomfort, and anxiety/depression. The nine dimensions of the CHU9D are worried, sad, pain, tired, annoyed school/work, sleep, daily routine, and activities. Preference weights for the CHU9D were obtained from a sample of the U.K. general population using the recognized valuation technique of standard gamble [21]. Although the CHU9D has not been used in children with ASD, its domains are relevant to ASD symptoms. The CHU9D can be applied in children aged 7 years and older. The National Institute for Health and Care Excellence recommends the use of the HUI 2 [19], which was designed to be used in children [22].

An important aspect of cost-effectiveness evaluations in ASD is that any intervention that improves outcomes for children with ASD will have a "spillover effect" on the family, educational system, and social security. Therefore, if a study does not include such costs, the potential benefits of the intervention may be understated [23].

23.3.3 Cost-Effectiveness of Psychosocial Interventions

Psychosocial interventions in ASD comprise many approaches addressing several aspects of the condition: the core symptoms, challenging behaviors, coexisting conditions (e.g., speech and language problems, motor and sensory impairments), and improving the impact on the family [22]. In spite of the difficulties in comparing results from heterogeneous clinical trials [24], early intervention is recommended and possibly saves costs [1, 25].

Early diagnosis and intervention lead to a better prognosis in children with ASD [26]. Early intensive behavioral interventions (EIBIs) are approaches with more robust evidence of efficacy [27]. The Early Start Denver Model (ESDM) is a comprehensive EIBI for infants to preschool-aged children with ASD that integrates applied behavior analysis with developmental and relationship-based approaches. The ESDM can be used in children from 12 months of age. In one study, the intervention was initiated when children were younger than 2½ years old, and resulted in significant improvements in IQ, language, and adaptive behavior [27]. EIBIs are expensive interventions that require a minimum of 20 h/week of behavioral interventions from clinicians initiated at an early age (toddlers and preschool-aged children), and also involves parent training for at least 5 h/week. The costs of EIBIs range from US$20,000 to US$60,000 per child [28]. EIBIs last a minimum of 6 months, but can easily extend to 2 years.

Although several studies have measured the costs of ASD (mostly in the United Kingdom) [1, 2], only a few studies have addressed the cost-effectiveness of the interventions. Two Canadian studies analyzed the cost-effectiveness of EIBIs and are described below in sequence.

In 2006, Motiwala et al. [29] published a cost-effectiveness study based on a simulation model, comparing the expansion of EIBIs to all Ontario children with ASD to "no intervention" and to "status quo" (SQ). The modeling was to determine the incremental cost savings and gains in dependence-free life years (DFLYs). The authors concluded that the expansion of EIBIs to all children with ASD would save costs because of the gains in DFLYs, which in turn reduced costs during schooling (until age 18 years) and adulthood (ages 18–65 years). The primary reason for cost savings from the expansion of EIBIs (from no intervention to SQ and from SQ to expansion) was the change in the distribution of functional dependence. Increased provision of EIBIs resulted in a shift of individuals from the very dependent to the semidependent category and, to a lesser extent, from the semidependent to the normal-functioning group [29].

Penner et al. [30] compared the prediagnosis intensive ESDM, the prediagnosis parent-delivered ESDM, and the Ontario SQ, which meant limited access to EIBIs after diagnosis (in Ontario, the public health system provides EIBIs to individuals with severe ASD). The outcome was measured as DFLYs and the chosen perspectives were the government and society, to age 65. The time horizon included costs and benefits until the age of 65 because it is the traditional age of retirement. The probabilities of independent, semidependent, or dependent living based on projected IQ were estimated. The authors found that from a government perspective, the parent-delivered ESDM produced an additional 0.17 DFLYs for CAD$8600 less than SQ. From a societal perspective, the intensive ESDM produced an additional 0.53 DFLYs for CAD$45,000 less than SQ [30].

23.3.4 Cost-Effectiveness of Pharmacological Interventions in ASD

To date, there is no medication approved to treat the core symptoms of ASD. Risperidone and aripiprazole are approved by the U.S. Food and Drug Administration to treat irritability in ASD. Other drugs used in the treatment of challenging behaviors in ASD include other atypical antipsychotics, α2-agonists, mood stabilizers, stimulants, atomoxetine, and naltrexone [31]. Repetitive behaviors are often treated with selective serotonin reuptake inhibitors such as fluoxetine and fluvoxamine [31]. Oxytocin and glutamate-modulating agents have some potential efficacy for the treatment of social withdrawal and core deficits in ASD [32] and repetitive behaviors [31], but more randomized controlled trials are needed. No cost-effectiveness studies address the use of drug therapy in the treatment of core symptoms or challenging behaviors in ASD [22].

23.4 Cost-Effectiveness of Interventions for ADHD

23.4.1 Overview of ADHD

ADHD is a disorder marked by an ongoing pattern of inattention and/or hyperactivity/impulsivity that interferes with functioning or development. Some people with ADHD only have problems with one behavior, whereas others have both inattention and hyperactivity/impulsivity [15]. Most children have the combined type of ADHD.

The prevalences of ADHD reported in different countries differ, and two systematic reviews found different pooled prevalences of ADHD: Polanczyk et al. [33] estimated a pooled worldwide prevalence of 5.29%, and Thomas et al. [34] found a pooled estimate of 7.29%. It continues into adulthood in up to half of diagnosed cases.

The number of publications on ADHD has increased in the past 25 years, driven by the United States and pharmacological interventions [1].

Direct health costs vary from US$660 to US$3140 [1], but it is important to notice that such costs were measured in high-income countries.

Global spending on medication for ADHD increased ninefold between 1993 and 2003; the United States spends the most on medication [1]. Medication costs constitute approximately 20% of total health care costs.

Children with ADHD have a higher risk of having less skilled and lower-paying jobs in adulthood than their peers without ADHD, with a substantial economic impact as a result of absenteeism and lost productivity [35]. The disorder is also associated with increased mortality rates due to deaths from unnatural causes such as accidents [36]. In the United States, the annual societal costs of ADHD were estimated at US$42.5 billion in 2005.

23.4.2 Cost-Effectiveness of Interventions for ADHD

Cost-effectiveness evaluations of the treatment of ADHD (it is a treatable condition) are important to better allocate resources. However, such evaluations are rare [1] and are mostly related to drug treatments only.

Pharmacotherapy for ADHD is based on stimulants such as methylphenidate and lisdexamphetamine or nonstimulants such as atomoxetine, a selective noradrenaline reuptake inhibitor. A systematic review found consistent evidence that pharmacotherapies are cost-effective compared with no treatment, behavioral therapy, or community care among children and adolescents with ADHD [37]. Another systematic review also concluded that pharmacological treatment with methylphenidate or atomoxetine is probably cost-effective in the short term when compared with placebo or no treatment [38]. Both reviews concluded that adequate data are lacking to draw conclusions regarding the relative cost-effectiveness of different pharmacological agents, including new formulations and new drugs. Guanfacine extended release is the only medication approved as an adjunct to stimulants. When added to existing stimulant monotherapy, guanfacine was demonstrated to be cost-effective in a 1-year Markov model from a third-party payer perspective and using quality-adjusted life years as the outcome. The comparator was monotherapy alone [39].

Although a systematic review by Wu et al. [37] concluded that pharmacotherapy was cost-effective in comparison with behavioral therapy, Foster et al. [40] assessed the cost-effectiveness of different treatments in a clinical trial that randomized participants to one of four arms: routine community care, intensive medication management, multicomponent behavioral treatment, and a combination of behavioral treatment and medication. They adopted a payer perspective to analyze the data. The conclusion was that the preferred cost-effective treatment varies as a function of the child's comorbidity and of the policymaker's willingness to pay. In cases of ADHD without comorbidities, high-quality medication management seemed to be more cost-effective at all levels of willingness to pay. On the other hand, a policymaker willing to pay more now in expectation of future costs savings (involving, for example, juvenile justice) will recognize that the most cost-effective choice for comorbid conditions likely involves behavioral therapy, with or without medication [40].

It is not the aim of this chapter to determine which treatment for ADHD is most cost-effective. As with any other condition, the results cannot be generalized. Particularly in ADHD, it is common to find studies based on simulation models and review articles stating the superiority of pharmacological treatment over other modalities or no intervention [37, 38, 41]. However, it is important to keep in mind that the majority of studies were conducted in high-income countries, each with a particular healthcare system; the time horizons were short; and the studies usually excluded comorbid conditions.

23.5 Conduct Disorders

23.5.1 Overview of Conduct Disorders

CDs are characterized by a repetitive and persistent pattern of behavior that violates either the rights of others or major age-appropriate societal norms or rules. People with CD often are aggressive toward people and animals, destroy property, are deceitful, steal, and/or seriously violate rules. Lying, bullying, threats, and intimidation are common behaviors in children with CD. To be diagnosed with CD, the symptoms must significantly impair social, academic, or occupational functioning. The disorder is typically diagnosed before adulthood [15]. CD is one of the most common disorders of childhood, with a prevalence of 5%, and it is the most common reason for referral of children for psychiatric and psychological treatment [42]. CDs are more common in males than females, and the prognosis is usually poor, with delinquency and criminal behavior in adulthood.

The public costs of CD are huge. An analysis of the expenditures related to CD in multiple public sectors found that in a 7-year period the costs of CD are over US$70,000 in the United States [43]. The costs analyzed were distributed among mental health, general health, school, and juvenile justice, with the latter representing 20% of public expenditures. For comparison, the percentage of costs for juvenile justice in children and adolescents with oppositional defiant disorder was 11% [43].

It is interesting to notice the differences in the costs of CD in different countries. In the United Kingdom, the support costs for children with CD are lower than the costs of ADHD, whereas in the United States the support costs of CD are higher than the costs of ADHD [1]. Societal costs of CD are consequences of crimes, drug abuse, and school dropout [44]. Early treatment and prevention seem to be the key to reducing costs.

23.5.2 Cost-Effectiveness of Interventions for CDs

A Cochrane review conducted by Furlong et al. [45] assessed the effectiveness and cost-effectiveness of behavioral and cognitive-behavioral, group-based parenting programs for improving child conduct problems, parental mental health, and parenting skills. The treatments were directed to children aged 3–12 years. The review included 13 trials, but only 2 economic evaluations based on 2 of the trials were included, which evaluated parenting programs in comparison with a waiting list [46, 47]. Effectiveness was measured by reductions in the intensity and problem scores of the Eyberg Child Behavior Inventory, a commonly used outcome measure in clinical trials of child behavior interventions. The results of the economic evaluations were not pooled because the outcomes were country-specific and not comparable. One study showed that the parenting program improved children's behavior at a cost of £1344 (€2006) per child. The comparator was a waiting list (no intervention) [46]. The other study included in the review found that it would cost €7848 to bring the child with the highest intensity score to within the nonclinical limits of the intensity score, and €2232 to return the average child in the intervention group to the nonclinical range. Such costs seem to be modest when compared with the long-term social, educational, and legal costs of CD [45].

Foster and Jones [44] evaluated the cost-effectiveness of the Fast Track Program, an intensive, multicomponent intervention targeted at preventing aggression in young children in the United States; the Fast Track Program targets parenting, peer relations, and social-cognitive and cognitive skills. The study evaluated the cost-effectiveness according to three outcomes, calculating the incremental cost-effectiveness ratios (ICERs) for each. A public payer perspective was adopted over a 10-year time horizon. The three long-term outcomes were

diagnosis of CD, defined as "a repetitive and persistent pattern of behaviour in which the basic rights of others or major age-appropriate societal norms or rules are violated"; Index Criminal Offenses, a 13-item scale that includes items such as "stolen an item greater than a hundred dollars in value" and "sold heroin or LSD"; and Interpersonal Violence, a 6-item scale that includes items such as "attacked someone with intent to hurt" and "had sex with someone against their will."

Children were grouped according to their initial risk for developing CD. The lower-risk group had negative ICERs for all three outcomes. By contrast, the higher-risk children had positive ICERs for all three outcomes. For the CD and index crime outcomes among the higher-risk group, the ICERs was cost-effective (less than the $1 million and $160,000 thresholds, respectively) [44].

When speaking of cost-effectiveness of treatments for CD, prevention of consequences in adulthood is key, particularly outcomes related to criminal justice.

Key Messages

- Psychiatric disorders are common among children and adolescents.
- The costs of psychiatric disorders among children and adolescents are huge, and estimating them is a complex task because they are reflected in adulthood and spill over to justice and education.
- Cost-effectiveness studies of mental health interventions for children and adolescents are rare.
- The vast majority of cost-effectiveness studies were done in high-income countries.
- The interventions for children and adolescents are costly, but so are the consequences of no intervention, which makes cost-effectiveness studies fundamental for decision-making.

References

1. Beecham J. Annual research review: child and adolescent mental health interventions: a review of progress in economic studies across different disorders. J Child Psychol Psychiatry. [Internet]. 2014 [cited 20 Nov 2016];55:714–32. Available from: http://www.pubmedcentral.nih.gov/articlerender.fcgi?artid=4657502&tool=pmcentrez&rendertype=abstract
2. Suhrcke M, Pillas D, Selai C. Economic aspects of mental health in children and adolescents [Internet]. Who.backgr. Pap. 2007. p. 43–64. Available from: http://www.euro.who.int/__data/assets/pdf_file/0003/76485/Hbsc_Forum_2007_economic_aspects.pdf
3. Shah A, Jenkins R. Mental health economic studies from developing countries reviewed in the context of those from developed countries. Acta Psychiatr Scand [Internet]. 2000 [cited 11 Dec 2016];101:87–103. Available from: http://www.ncbi.nlm.nih.gov/pubmed/10706008
4. Roberts RE, Attkisson CC, Rosenblatt A. Prevalence of psychopathology among children and adolescents. Am J Psychiatry [Internet]. 1998 [cited 20 Nov 2016];155:715–25. Available from: http://www.ncbi.nlm.nih.gov/pubmed/9619142
5. Skovgaard AM. Mental health problems and psychopathology in infancy and early childhood. An epidemiological study. Dan Med Bull [Internet]. 2010 [cited 11 Dec 2016];57:B4193. Available from: http://www.ncbi.nlm.nih.gov/pubmed/21040689
6. Gustavsson A, Svensson M, Jacobi F, Allgulander C, Alonso J, Beghi E, et al. Cost of disorders of the brain in Europe 2010. Eur Neuropsychopharmacol [Internet]. 2011 [cited 11 Dec 2016];21:718–79. Available from: http://www.ncbi.nlm.nih.gov/pubmed/21924589
7. Barrett B, Byford S, Chitsabesan P, Kenning C. Mental health provision for young offenders: service use and cost. Br J Psychiatry [Internet]. 2006 [cited 11 Dec 2016];188:541–6. Available from: http://www.ncbi.nlm.nih.gov/pubmed/16738344
8. Minnis H, Everett K, Pelosi AJ, Dunn J, Knapp M. Children in foster care: mental health, service use and costs. Eur Child Adolesc Psychiatry [Internet]. 2006 [cited 11 Dec 2016];15:63–70. Available from: http://www.ncbi.nlm.nih.gov/pubmed/16523249
9. Romeo R, Knapp M, Scott S. Economic cost of severe antisocial behaviour in children – and who pays it. Br J Psychiatry [Internet]. 2006 [cited 10 Oct 2016];188:547–53. Available from: http://www.ncbi.nlm.nih.gov/pubmed/16738345
10. Clark AF, O'Malley A, Woodham A, Barrett B, Byford S. Children with complex mental health problems: needs, costs and predictors over one year. Child Adolesc Ment Health [Internet]. 2005 [cited 11 Dec 2016];10:170–8. Available from: http://doi.wiley.com/10.1111/j.1475-3588.2005.00349.x
11. Muntz R, Hutchings J, Edwards R-T, Hounsome B, O'Céilleachair A. Economic evaluation of treatments for children with severe behavioural problems. J Ment Health Policy Econ [Internet]. 2004 [cited 11 Dec 2016];7:177–89. Available from: http://www.ncbi.nlm.nih.gov/pubmed/15701933
12. Järbrink K, Fombonne E, Knapp M. Measuring the parental, service and cost impacts of children with autistic spectrum disorder: a pilot study. J Autism Dev Disord [Internet]. 2003 [cited 11 Dec 2016];33:395–402. Available from: http://www.ncbi.nlm.nih.gov/pubmed/12959418
13. Beecham J, Chadwick O, Fidan D, Bernard S. Children with severe learning disabilities: needs, services and costs. Child. Soc. [Internet]. 2002 [cited 11 Dec 2016];16:168–81. Available from: http://doi.wiley.com/10.1002/chi.690
14. Chisholm D, Knapp MR, Knudsen HC, Amaddeo F, Gaite L, van Wijngaarden B. Client socio-demographic and service receipt inventory – European version: development of an instrument for international research. EPSILON Study 5. European psychiatric services: inputs linked to outcome domains and

needs. Br. J. Psychiatry. Suppl. [Internet]. 2000 [cited 22 Nov 2014];s28–33. Available from: http://www.ncbi.nlm.nih.gov/pubmed/10945075

15. American Psychiatric Association. Diagnostic and statistical manual of mental disorders. 5th ed. Washington, DC: American Psychiatric Press; 2013.
16. American Psychiatric Association. Diagnostic and statistical manual of mental disorders. 4th-Revise ed. Washington, DC: APA; 2000.
17. Center for Disease Control and Prevention. Autism spectrum disorder (ASD) [Internet]. 2016. Available from: http://www.cdc.gov/ncbddd/autism/index.html
18. Mandell DS, Morales KH, Xie M, Lawer LJ, Stahmer AC, Marcus SC. Age of diagnosis among medicaid-enrolled children with autism, 2001–2004. Psychiatr. Serv. [Internet]. 2010 [cited 17 Dec 2016];61:822–9. Available from: http://www.pubmedcentral.nih.gov/articlerender.fcgi?artid=2966012&tool=pmcentrez&rendertype=abstract
19. Horsman J, Furlong W, Feeny D, Torrance G. The Health Utilities Index (HUI): concepts, measurement properties and applications. Health Qual. Life Outcomes [Internet]. 2003 [cited 18 Dec 2016];1:54. Available from: http://www.pubmedcentral.nih.gov/articlerender.fcgi?artid=293474&tool=pmcentrez&rendertype=abstract
20. Wille N, Badia X, Bonsel G, Burström K, Cavrini G, Devlin N, et al. Development of the EQ-5D-Y: a child-friendly version of the EQ-5D. Qual. Life Res. [Internet]. 2010 [cited 18 Dec 2016];19:875–86. Available from: http://www.pubmedcentral.nih.gov/articlerender.fcgi?artid=2892611&tool=pmcentrez&rendertype=abstract
21. Stevens K. The child health utility 9D (CHU9D). A new, paediatric, preference-based measure of health related quality of life. Patient Rep. Outcomes [Internet]. Lyon; 2010;43:11–2. Available from: http://www.pro-newsletter.com/images/PDF/pron43-final.pdf
22. National Collaborating Centre for Mental Health. Autism: the management and support of children and young people on the autism spectrum. [Internet]. Nice Clinical Guidelines, editor. Leicester: British Psychological Society; 2013. Available from: https://www.ncbi.nlm.nih.gov/pubmedhealth/PMH0078143/
23. Payakachat N, Tilford JM, Kovacs E, Kuhlthau K. Autism spectrum disorders: a review of measures for clinical, health services and cost-effectiveness applications. Expert Rev. Pharmacoecon. Outcomes Res. [Internet]. 2012 [cited 17 Dec 2016];12:485–503. Available from: http://www.pubmedcentral.nih.gov/articlerender.fcgi?artid=3502071&tool=pmcentrez&rendertype=abstract
24. Rogers SJ, Vismara LA. Evidence-based comprehensive treatments for early autism. J Clin Child Adolesc Psychol. 2010;37:8–38.
25. Horlin C, Falkmer M, Parsons R, Albrecht MA, Falkmer T. The cost of autism spectrum disorders. PLoS One [Internet]. 2014 [cited 27 Nov 2016];9:e106552. Available from: http://www.pubmedcentral.nih.gov/articlerender.fcgi?artid=4156354&tool=pmcentrez&rendertype=abstract
26. Allen-Meares P, MacDonald M, McGee K. Autism spectrum disorder updates – relevant information for early interventionists to consider. Front. Public Health. [Internet]. 2016 [cited 1 Dec 2016];4:236. Available from: http://www.pubmedcentral.nih.gov/articlerender.fcgi?artid=5083851&tool=pmcentrez&rendertype=abstract
27. Dawson G, Rogers S, Munson J, Smith M, Winter J, Greenson J, et al. Randomized, controlled trial of an intervention for toddlers with autism: the early start Denver Model. Pediatrics [Internet]. 2010 [cited 29 Nov 2016];125:e17–23. Available from: http://www.pubmedcentral.nih.gov/articlerender.fcgi?artid=4951085&tool=pmcentrez&rendertype=abstract
28. Chasson GS, Harris GE, Neely WJ. Cost comparison of early intensive behavioral intervention and special education for children with autism. J. Child Fam. Stud. [Internet]. 2007;16:401–13. Available from: http://dx.doi.org/10.1007/s10826-006-9094-1
29. Motiwala SS, Gupta S, Lilly MB, Ungar WJ, Coyte PC. The cost-effectiveness of expanding intensive behavioural intervention to all autistic children in Ontario: in the past year, several court cases have been brought against provincial governments to increase funding for Intensive Behavioural Intervention. Healthc. Policy [Internet]. 2006 [cited 18 Dec 2016];1:135–51. Available from: http://www.pubmedcentral.nih.gov/articlerender.fcgi?artid=2585334&tool=pmcentrez&rendertype=abstract
30. Penner M, Rayar M, Bashir N, Roberts SW, Hancock-Howard RL, Coyte PC. Cost-effectiveness analysis comparing pre-diagnosis autism spectrum disorder (ASD)-targeted intervention with Ontario's autism intervention program. J. Autism Dev. Disord. [Internet]. 2015 [cited 17 Dec 2016];45:2833–47. Available from: http://www.ncbi.nlm.nih.gov/pubmed/25936527
31. Farmer C, Thurm A, Grant P. Pharmacotherapy for the core symptoms in autistic disorder: current status of the research. Drugs [Internet]. 2013 [cited 17 Dec 2016];73:303–14. Available from: http://www.pubmedcentral.nih.gov/articlerender.fcgi?artid=3632301&tool=pmcentrez&rendertype=abstract
32. Accordino RE, Kidd C, Politte LC, Henry CA, McDougle CJ. Psychopharmacological interventions in autism spectrum disorder. Expert Opin. Pharmacother. [Internet]. 2016 [cited 27 Nov 2016];17:937–52. Available from: http://www.ncbi.nlm.nih.gov/pubmed/26891879
33. Polanczyk G, de Lima MS, Horta BL, Biederman J, Rohde LA. The worldwide prevalence of ADHD: a systematic review and metaregression analysis. Am. J. Psychiatry [Internet]. 2007 [cited 27 Nov 2016];164:942–8. Available from: http://www.ncbi.nlm.nih.gov/pubmed/17541055
34. Thomas R, Sanders S, Doust J, Beller E, Glasziou P. Prevalence of attention-deficit/hyperactivity disorder: a

systematic review and meta-analysis. Pediatrics [Internet]. 2015 [cited 18 Dec 2016];135:e994–1001. Available from: http://www.ncbi.nlm.nih.gov/pubmed/25733754
35. Küpper T, Haavik J, Drexler H, Ramos-Quiroga JA, Wermelskirchen D, Prutz C, et al. The negative impact of attention-deficit/hyperactivity disorder on occupational health in adults and adolescents. Int. Arch. Occup. Environ. Health [Internet]. 2012 [cited 18 Dec 2016];85:837–47. Available from: http://www.ncbi.nlm.nih.gov/pubmed/22752312
36. Dalsgaard S, Østergaard SD, Leckman JF, Mortensen PB, Pedersen MG. Mortality in children, adolescents, and adults with attention deficit hyperactivity disorder: a nationwide cohort study. Lancet. London [Internet]. 2015 [cited 18 Dec 2016];385:2190–6. Available from: http://www.ncbi.nlm.nih.gov/pubmed/25726514
37. Wu EQ, Hodgkins P, Ben-Hamadi R, Setyawan J, Xie J, Sikirica V, et al. Cost effectiveness of pharmacotherapies for attention-deficit hyperactivity disorder: a systematic literature review. CNS Drugs [Internet]. 2012 [cited 20 Dec 2016];26:581–600. Available from: http://www.ncbi.nlm.nih.gov/pubmed/22712698
38. Catalá-López F, Ridao M, Sanfélix Gimeno G, Peiró S. Cost-effectiveness of pharmacological treatment of attention deficit hyperactivity disorder in children and adolescents: qualitative synthesis of scientific evidence. Rev. Psiquiatr. Salud Ment. [Internet]. [cited 20 Nov 2016];6:168–77. Available from: http://www.ncbi.nlm.nih.gov/pubmed/23453596
39. Sikirica V, Haim Erder M, Xie J, Macaulay D, Diener M, Hodgkins P, et al. Cost effectiveness of guanfacine extended release as an adjunctive therapy to a stimulant compared with stimulant monotherapy for the treatment of attention-deficit hyperactivity disorder in children and adolescents. Pharmacoeconomics [Internet]. 2012 [cited 18 Dec 2016];30:e1–15. Available from: http://www.pubmedcentral.nih.gov/articlerender.fcgi?artid=3576910&tool=pmcentrez&rendertype=abstract
40. Foster EM, Jensen PS, Schlander M, Pelham WE, Hechtman L, Arnold LE, et al. Treatment for ADHD: is more complex treatment cost-effective for more complex cases? Health Serv. Res. [Internet]. 2007 [cited 18 Dec 2016];42:165–82. Available from: http://www.pubmedcentral.nih.gov/articlerender.fcgi?artid=1955245&tool=pmcentrez&rendertype=abstract
41. Gilmore A, Milne R. Methylphenidate in children with hyperactivity: review and cost-utility analysis. Pharmacoepidemiol. Drug Saf. [Internet]. [cited 18 Dec 2016];10:85–94. Available from: http://www.ncbi.nlm.nih.gov/pubmed/11499858
42. Dretzke J, Frew E, Davenport C, Barlow J, Stewart-Brown S, Sandercock J, et al. The effectiveness and cost-effectiveness of parent training/education programmes for the treatment of conduct disorder, including oppositional defiant disorder, in children. Health Technol. Assess. [Internet]. 2005 [cited 20 Nov 2016];9:iii, ix–x, 1–233. Available from: http://www.ncbi.nlm.nih.gov/pubmed/16336845
43. Foster EM, Jones DE. The high costs of aggression: public expenditures resulting from conduct disorder. Am. J. Public Health [Internet]. 2005 [cited 19 Dec 2016];95:1767–72. Available from: http://www.pubmedcentral.nih.gov/articlerender.fcgi?artid=1449434&tool=pmcentrez&rendertype=abstract
44. Foster EM, Jones D. Can a costly intervention be cost-effective?: An analysis of violence prevention. Arch. Gen. Psychiatry [Internet]. 2006 [cited 27 Nov 2016];63:1284–91. Available from: http://www.pubmedcentral.nih.gov/articlerender.fcgi?artid=2753445&tool=pmcentrez&rendertype=abstract
45. Furlong M, McGilloway S, Bywater T, Hutchings J, Smith SM, Donnelly M. Cochrane review: behavioural and cognitive-behavioural group-based parenting programmes for early-onset conduct problems in children aged 3 to 12 years (Review). Evid. Based. Child Health [Internet]. 2013 [cited 27 Nov 2016];8:318–692. Available from: http://www.ncbi.nlm.nih.gov/pubmed/23877886
46. Edwards RT, Céilleachair A, Bywater T, Hughes DA, Hutchings J. Parenting programme for parents of children at risk of developing conduct disorder: cost effectiveness analysis. BMJ [Internet]. 2007 [cited 20 Nov 2016];334:682. Available from: http://www.pubmedcentral.nih.gov/articlerender.fcgi?artid=1839236&tool=pmcentrez&rendertype=abstract
47. O'Neill D, McGilloway S, Donnelly M, Bywater T, Kelly P. A cost-effectiveness analysis of the incredible years parenting programme in reducing childhood health inequalities. Eur J Health Econ [Internet]. 2013;14:85–94. Available from: http://dx.doi.org/10.1007/s10198-011-0342-y

Part IV

Health Economics, Burden and Indirect Costs of Mental Disorders

Global Mental Health: Costs, Poverty, Violence, and Socioeconomic Determinants of Health

24

Carla Sabariego, Marta Miret, and Michaela Coenen

Abstract

Global mental health has as a goal to study mental health in countries worldwide from a broad, international perspective that considers all populations of the world and takes into account their cultural and country-specific peculiarities and complexities. This is the perspective of international public organizations such as the World Health Organization, the United Nations Secretary for Health. Sound and informative global data about mental disorders are highly important because they draw attention to the magnitude of the burden; can be used to study causes, risk factors, treatment coverage, and inequalities; and inform policies and public health actions to reduce the burden experienced by individuals and society. Reliable global data became even more important with the endorsement in September 2015 of sustainable development goals and the unprecedented inclusion of mental health and substance abuse in two of the sustainable development goal targets. Sound and reliable sources of global mental health are, however, rare. The economic and societal burdens of mental disorders are huge, estimated at US$2.5 trillion in 2010 and projected to be an astonishing US$6.0 trillion by 2030. These costs are made up of treatment expenditures and costs associated with loss of income. In addition, in 2010, 7.4% of all disability-adjusted life years worldwide were due to mental and substance use disorders. In this chapter we present and discuss relevant conceptualizations, data sources, and costs, making the link between mental disorders and well-being, poverty, violence, and socioeconomic determinants of health from a global perspective.

C. Sabariego (✉) • M. Coenen
Department of Medical Informatics, Biometry and Epidemiology-IBE, Chair for Public Health and Health Services Research, Research Unit for Biopsychosocial Health, Ludwig-Maximilians-Universität (LMU), Marchioninistr.17, Munich 81377, Germany
e-mail: Carla.Sabariego@med.uni-muenchen.de; michaela.coenen@med.lmu.de

M. Miret
Department of Psychiatry, Universidad Autónoma de Madrid, Madrid, Spain

Instituto de Salud Carlos III, Centro de Investigación Biomédica en Red de Salud Mental, CIBERSAM, Madrid, Spain

Department of Psychiatry, Hospital Universitario la Princesa, Instituto de Investigación Sanitaria Princesa (IIS-Princesa], Madrid, Spain
e-mail: marta.miret@uam.es

D. Razzouk (ed.), *Mental Health Economics*, DOI 10.1007/978-3-319-55266-8_24

Key Points Summary

- Conceptualizations of mental disorders and mental health
- Sources of global data about mental disorders
- Global economic and societal burdens of mental disorders
- Risk and protective factors for mental disorders
- Risk and protective factors for well-being
- The impact of the environment: poverty, disasters, stress, violence
- Mental health and economic well-being

24.1 Conceptualizations of Mental Disorders and Mental Health

The definition of *mental health* proposed by the World Health Organization (WHO) is "a state of well-being in which every individual realizes his or her own potential, can cope with the normal stresses of life, can work productively and fruitfully, and is able to make a contribution to her or his community."[1] This definition is very close to the WHO definition of *health*, offering a comparably aspirational goal relying on well-being.[2] This definition achieves its political mandate of offering member states an ideal they should aspire to. However, for measurement – for instance, measurement of burden, costs, or even happiness within a country and across countries – the concept first has to be operationalized,[3] and operationalization gives room to diversity because it is strongly connected with the purpose of any measurement.

Mental health has frequently been operationalized in terms of the absence or presence of health conditions (i.e., mental disorders). This is the perspective of, for instance, epidemiologists, who are very interested in learning about the prevalence and incidence of mental disorders. This is also the perspective of the Global Burden of Disease (GBD) Study, which informs and even ranks the burden attached to a range of mental disorders [1]. Defining who has or does not have a mental disorder might be challenging because it requires precise diagnoses, and mental health has been similarly operationalized as impairments in mental functions, such as attention, motivation, or the regulation of emotions. These ways of operationalizing mental health follow a rather medical tradition.

Mental health has also been frequently operationalized in terms of well-being. Here, two approaches should be differentiated: the hedonistic approach and the eudemonistic approach. The eudemonistic approach has its roots in the work of Aristotle and focuses on self-realization and on human growth and the fulfilment of one's true nature. This is the basis behind what is called "psychological well-being" [2]. The hedonistic approach is concerned with our subjective experiences of positive affect, of happiness, and is the basis of the currently growing body of work related to what is called "subjective well-being" [3]. The collection of data on both subjective and psychological well-being is widespread and is even used to measure the welfare of countries, as we will see later in this chapter.

Finally, what is meant by "global mental health"? The word *global* shifts the focus from specific countries, settings, or disease groups to the study of mental health in countries worldwide, from a broad, international perspective that considers all populations of the world and takes into account their cultural and country-specific peculiarities and complexities. This is the perspective of international public organizations (e.g., WHO, the United Nations Secretary for Health) and of private foundations (e.g., the Bill & Melinda Gates Foundation).

As this chapter is about global mental health, the WHO definition is used as a reference. It is important to keep in mind, however, that this chapter tackles the two different operationalization approaches to mental health mentioned above: the absence or presence of mental disorders or impairments in mental functions, and well-being.

[1] http://www.who.int/features/factfiles/mental_health/en/

[2] Preamble to the Constitution of the World Health Organization as adopted by the International Health Conference, New York, June19 –July 22, 1946.

[3] Definition of how a construct that is not directly measurable, for instance health, should be measured.

24.2 Sources of Global Data About Mental Disorders

Sound and informative global data about mental disorders is of huge importance: they draw attention to the magnitude of the burden; can be used to study causes, risk factors, treatment coverage, and inequalities; and inform policies and public health actions to reduce the burden experienced by individuals and society. Reliable global data became even more important with the endorsement in September 2015 of the sustainable development goals (SDGs) at the United Nations General Assembly,[4] and the unprecedented inclusion of mental health and substance abuse in two of the SDG targets of goal 3, health and well-being. Countries should, according to task 3.4,

> "By 2030, reduce by one third premature mortality from non-communicable diseases through prevention and treatment and promote mental health and well-being," and according to target 3.5, "Strengthen the prevention and treatment of substance abuse, including narcotic drug abuse and harmful use of alcohol."

This chapter presents the most current global burden data available. However, given the scarcity of (sound) data in mental health, enormous challenges associated with data collection, and methodological shortcomings of available estimates, it is important to briefly review the current, most prominent sources of global data, which underlie the important statistics and projections presented here.

To date, one of the largest efforts to directly collect and generate data from an international perspective has been the World Mental Health Survey (WMH), a project under the leadership of WHO and encompassing a large consortium of 28 countries.[5] The WMH comprises epidemiologic surveys, including general population samples, and focuses on the prevalence of, severity of, and accessibility to treatment for several mental, substance use, and behavioral disorders in all six WHO world regions [4].

[4] http://www.un.org/sustainabledevelopment/sustainable-development-goals/

[5] http://www.hcp.med.harvard.edu/wmh/

One of the challenges of collecting data on mental disorders through epidemiological surveys is the reliability of the collected information; it is barely possible to use specialized health professionals such as psychiatrists or psychologists as interviewers. The WMH is administered by lay-interviewers and overcomes the reliability issue by fully relying on the Composite International Diagnostic Interview (CIDI), developed by WHO and extensively tested for epidemiological cross-national studies [5, 6]. The WHO WMH-CIDI is a broad, completely structured interview designed to be implemented by trained lay-interviewers. The assessment using the CIDI is in line with diagnostic criteria defined by the *International Classification of Diseases, 10th Revision*, and the *Diagnostic and Statistical Manual of Mental Disorders, Fourth Edition*, and generates codes for both classifications.

The WHO WMH-CIDI can generate prevalence and severity estimates. It also measures the burden experienced in daily life and access to treatment in terms of service utilization and medication. Based on this information, the WHO WMH-CIDI also provides estimates on two very important issues in mental health: the treatment gap (i.e., the proportion of persons not receiving any treatment) and the treatment lag (i.e., the proportion of persons receiving treatment after a long delay) [7]. These estimates are broken down by severity, as this gives important information about the allocation of healthcare, discloses potentially important shortcomings of health systems, and complements information collected on burden. For instance, the WMH showed that a worryingly large proportion of severe cases remain untreated worldwide, whereas in specific countries, such as the United States, a large proportion of mild cases receive treatment [7]. This study pointed out that receiving or not receiving treatment is a matter of not only limited treatment resources but also misallocation of treatment resources because of the structural inequalities of specific health systems.

The WHO WMH has several shortcomings, which are sources of potential bias that reflect the challenge of collecting data on mental disorders [4]. As a household survey, the WHO WMH excludes from the sample specific populations, such as the homeless or people living in institutions, among whom might be found a higher prevalence of mental disorders. This might lead to an underestimation of the prevalence. Despite extensive cross-national testing of the CIDI, cultural aspects of admitting to having symptoms may be an issue as well and could explain the very low prevalence of mental disorders found in Nigeria and China [4]. Another limitation is that schizophrenia (and other nonaffective psychoses), one of the most devastating severe mental disorders, is not included in the survey because the CIDI proved to be not reliable in that case: in interviews administered by lay-interviewers, symptoms that would point to schizophrenia were dramatically overestimated [6].

Another very important source of burden data is the GBD Study.[6] The 2010 update was financed by the Bill & Melinda Gates Foundation and led by the Institute for Health Metrics and Evaluation at the University of Washington, in collaboration with WHO and three other universities. Data provided by the GBD Study, especially disability-adjusted life years (DALYs), are widely used, so it is important to keep in mind where these data come from. DALYs are estimated based on years of life lost to premature death and years of life lived in less than full health. The latter are estimated based on disability weights, which are measures for the severity of a disease, ranging from 0 (perfect health) to 1 (death). The first set of disability weights was determined in 1996 by a group of selected experts and received harsh criticism in relation to its validity. Over the years, the methodology of the GBD Study has been revised again and again, and because of the impact of the methodology on DALYs and their broad use, the 2010 GBD Study consulted philosophers, ethicists, and economists about the value choices to be incorporated into DALYs. The current disability weights are generated from a large-scale general population survey, and participants – who might have or not have any health condition – are required to make judgements about pairs of health states described in lay language [8, 9]. The disability weight of severe depression, for instance, has been estimated using the lay description, "has overwhelming, constant sadness and cannot function in daily life. The person sometimes loses touch with reality and wants to harm or kill himself (or herself)"; the weight is 0.658 (95% uncertainty interval: 0.477–0.807) and points to a high burden. The weight for profound intellectual disability, however, given the lay description "has low intelligence, cannot understand basic requests or instructions, and requires constant assistance for nearly all activities," is 0.200 (95% uncertainty interval: 0.133–0.2830), points to a low burden [9], and has been heavily criticized. WHO revised such controversial GBD weights (intellectual disability is just one of them), proposing different weights and the WHO Global Health Estimate [10].[7] For instance, the WHO weight for profound intellectual disability is 0.4440. It is important to be aware that because of such disparities and important methodological concerns, WHO did not endorse the 2010 GBD Study results and regularly publishes its own burden of disease estimates.

WHO regularly collects data about the structure and responsiveness of health systems worldwide. These kinds of data are of special concern in global mental health because of the huge treatment lag and treatment gap in the majority of countries worldwide, including high-income countries. The lack of or delay in receiving treatment is associated with a meaningful increase in burden on the individual, society, and economy. In this sense, to what extent treatment lack and gap are related to the lack (inadequacy of resources and services) or misallocation (inequity in their distribution) of health resources is very important for developing mental health policies and plans. For instance, in several countries, persons with mental disorders continue to be isolated and institutionalized in mental health hospitals, although there is plenty of evidence about the effectiveness of low-cost and low-resource treatments such as lay-interventions [11–13],

[6] http://www.healthdata.org/gbd

[7] http://www.who.int/healthinfo/global_burden_disease/en/

which could be easily implemented by shifting the tasks of available health professionals and health services.

The WHO Mental Health Atlas[8] was developed to collect, summarize, and disseminate global data, including country and out-of-pocket expenditures, on the six building blocks of the health system: governance (policies and plans), financing, care delivery, human resources, medicines, and information systems [14]. The first Mental Health Atlas report was published in 2001, and the information initially obtained was updated in 2005, 2011, and 2014. Data for the Atlas is collected through a survey: WHO headquarters and regional and country offices approach ministries of health or other relevant ministries in all countries worldwide. These designate one stakeholder as the respondent for the country. Some key findings of the 2014 report are that public expenditures on mental health are very low in low- and middle-income countries, and are still mostly allocated to inpatient care, especially mental hospitals; also, globally – even in many high-income countries – governments still spend less than 5% of their health budget on mental health, with many countries spending only up to 1%.

Further global data on the direct and indirect costs of mental disorders are rare. A study published in 2011 on the global economic burden of noncommunicable diseases [15] anticipated the economic burden of mental disorders in 2011–2030, not using direct data but by "relating the economic burden of all other [noncommunicable] diseases to their (mental disorders) associated number of DALYs. Then the burden for mental illness was projected using the relative size of the corresponding DALY numbers to all the other conditions." The global cost of mental disorders (see Chap. 25) – that is, the projected mortality rate in a population in relation to current and future economic output at the national level – estimated in the same report for 2010 was around US$2.5 trillion, with US$6.0 trillion projected for 2030. How were these values estimated? Estimates of overall global costs were partially based on data from a systematic review from 2006 [16], including studies from 1990 to 2003, and national costs reported for the United States, China, Kenya, and Australia. National cost studies published for Canada, the United Kingdom, and France were also considered. These costs from seven countries were used to estimate the global burden for the world. The report is undeniably very important and places attention on the burden of mental disorders. A look at the methodology, however, stresses the need to be aware of data sources when working with global statistics and projections, and how far projections might be from direct estimates.

24.3 Global Economic and Societal Burdens of Mental Disorders

While the global cost of mental disorders was estimated at US$2.5 trillion in 2010, the projected costs for 2030 amount to an astonishing US$6.0 trillion [15]. These costs are made up of treatment expenditures and costs associated with loss of income.

The WHO Mental Health Atlas[9] provides information on country expenditures on mental health and on the most important sources of funding (government, nongovernmental organizations, and affected individuals and their families). In 79% of 120 countries, government is ranked as the main funding body. However, 18% of countries rank private households as the main funders, and 31% rank them as the second most important source of funds, mainly through direct out-of-pocket expenditures or private health insurance fees. This is concerning because it points out that the accessibility to mental health services is strongly associated with household income, clearly disadvantaging low-income households.

The Atlas aimed to collect information on total yearly government spending in terms of inpatient and day care services, outpatient and

[8] http://www.who.int/mental_health/evidence/atlasmnh/en/

[9] http://www.who.int/mental_health/evidence/atlas/mental_health_atlas_2014/en/

primary healthcare services, social care services, and further expenditures. Over 60 countries provided some expenditure information, but only 41 reported inpatient and outpatient expenditures, and only a few reported expenditures with primary care facilities and clinics, which are very important community gatekeepers, or entrance points for mental health treatment. Keeping in mind that data on expenditures are incomplete, results point out that the median expenditure of governments per capita is US$1.53 per year in lower-middle-income countries and US$1.96 per year in upper-middle-income countries. The lion's share of these expenditures, US$1.20 per year in lower-middle-income countries and US$1.35 per year in upper-middle income countries, goes toward a kind of treatment that has proven to be often ineffective and many times even segregating, namely, mental hospitals. High-income countries report median per-capita expenditures of almost US$60, spending about 30% on mental hospitals, 30% on other inpatient and day care, and 30% on outpatient and primary care. In general, the Atlas shows that the higher the gross national income per capita, the higher the mental health expenditures. However, of 41 countries considered, only 7 allocated more than 5% of their health expenditures to mental health.

As a reference, a modeling study of the annual costs of delivering cost-effective interventions for schizophrenia, depression, epilepsy, and alcohol use disorders in sub-Saharan Africa and south Asia estimated needed expenditures to be $3–4 per capita [17], whereas global annual costs for depression treatment during 15 years of scaled-up investment were estimated to be $0.08 per person on average in low-income countries, $0.34 in lower-middle-income countries, $1.12 in upper-middle-income countries, and $3.89 in high-income countries [18].

The WHO Mental Health Atlas 2011[10] also provided figures on median expenditures on medicines (per 100,000 population) for mental and behavioral disorders. Median annual expenditures ranged from US$1,700 in low-income countries to US$17,200 in lower-middle-income countries, US$82,700 in upper-middle-income countries, to an astonishing US2,630,500 in high-income countries [19]; median expenditures by high-income countries were approximately 340 times greater than median expenditures in low- and lower-middle-income countries. When these figures are disentangled by world region, the European region has the highest median expenditures: US$2,598,300. The largest part of these expenditures goes toward antipsychotics and antidepressants. While low expenditures potentially point to a lack of treatment, huge expenditures in high-income countries, especially in Europe, raise the question of the appropriateness of such widely given prescriptions for antipsychotics and antidepressants.

Mental disorders are treatable but often have a chronic disabling characteristic; some start very early in life, such as schizophrenia, and have a meaningful negative impact on several aspects of daily life, one of which is the ability to work [20] (see Chap. 28). A large part of the economic burden of mental disorders is therefore not related to treatment, but rather to the unemployment of affected persons, as well as the reduced productivity of family caregivers and the corresponding loss of income, as stated in the WHO Report "Investing in Mental Health: Evidence for Action," published in 2013.[11] Sound and global data on the indirect costs of mental disorders are rare, but projections are available. Indirect costs represent about US$4 trillion of the global costs of mental disorders projected for 2030 [15] (see Chaps. 25, 26, 27, and 28). The total cost of illness is projected to be about US$2 trillion in 2030 in low- and middle-income countries, comprising about US$1.5 trillion in indirect costs, and total costs for high-income countries are projected to be almost double at US$4 trillion, with about US$2.5 trillion in indirect costs. The general economic burden of mental illness in terms of "value of lost output"[12] over the period

[10]http://www.who.int/mental_health/publications/mental_health_atlas_2011/en/

[11]http://apps.who.int/iris/bitstream/10665/87232/1/9789241564618_eng.pdf

[12]Projected mortality rates in a population in relation to current and future economic output at the national level.

2011–2030 has been recently estimated to be US$16.3 trillion and to surpass the estimated economic burden for diabetes (US$1.7 trillion), chronic respiratory diseases (US$4.4 trillion), and cancer (US$8.3 trillion), coming very close to the costs of cardiovascular diseases (US$15.6 trillion) [15].

Mental disorders are also globally associated with high mortality and high comorbidity [21]. A broad meta-review (i.e., a review of 20 systematic reviews) showed that all mental disorders are associated with an increased risk of mortality compared to the general population, and that several mental disorders, such as substance use and eating disorders, have comparable or even larger mortality risks than heavy smoking, leading to considerable decreases of life expectancy, ranging from 10 to 20 years lost [22]. Reasons for such high mortality are direct health consequences of the disorder, for instance, the health decrements caused by substance abuse or eating disorders; unhealthy risk behaviors, such as the high rates of heavy smoking among people with schizophrenia [23]; and a very high suicide risk, as in, for example, depression and borderline disorders, among others [22, 24]. Regarding morbidity, mental disorders increase the risk of developing communicable and noncommunicable diseases, such as cardiovascular conditions, whereas many health conditions, such as cancer and respiratory diseases, substantially increase the risk for a mental disorder, usually depression or anxiety [21].

High premature mortality rates and high comorbidity are reflected in the impressive global burden of disease attributable to mental disorders. Using data from the 2010 GBD Study, it has been estimated that in 2010, 183.9 million DALYs were due to mental and substance use disorders, representing 7.4% of all DALYs worldwide [25]. In addition, mental and substance use disorders account for 8.6 million years of life lost (YLLs), 0.5% of all YLLs worldwide, and 175.3 million years lost due to disability, 22.9% of all YLDs worldwide; mental disorders are the leading cause of years lost due to disability worldwide. Depressive disorders account for 40.5% of the DALYs attributable to mental disorders, followed by anxiety disorders (14.6%), illicit drug use disorders (10.9%), alcohol use disorders (9.6%), schizophrenia (7.4%), and bipolar disorder (7.0%) [25].

24.4 Risk and Protective Factors for Mental Disorders and Well-Being

24.4.1 Risk and Protective Factors for Mental Disorders

Information on the burden of diseases should always be complemented by information on the risk factors that might cause them. Knowledge of both burden and risk factors provide "an important input to health decision-making and planning processes" [26] (p. 2), and can provide evidence for effective interventions that might finally improve global health. Data on and knowledge of risk factors have often been fragmented and inconsistent. As diseases and disorders are mostly caused by more than one risk factor, identifying and gathering knowledge of these factors is challenging and requires a comprehensive and well-structured assessment of potentially relevant factors. In 2000, WHO used for the first time 22 global risk factors to create an universal comparative risk assessment (CRA) [27]. In 2004, these factors were complemented by another two risk factors and were allocated to the following topics [28]: (a) childhood and maternal undernutrition; (b) other nutrition-related risk factors and physical activity, (c) addictive substances, (d) sexual and reproductive health, and (e) environmental risks. Some of these risk factors are relevant to mental disorders, whereas others are not or have not yet been investigated. Although we know from this CRA that, for instance, child sexual abuse increases the risk for several mental disorders, such as depression, anxiety, drug or alcohol abuse, and for suicide [28], WHO's conceptualization of risk factors for CRA does not adequately map risk factors for mental disorders.

Another approach for the conceptualization and categorization of risk factors, as well as protective factors for mental disorders provided by WHO, relies on the definition that "risk factors are associated with an increased probability of onset, greater severity and longer duration of major health problems" [29] (p. 21), whereas "protective factors refer to conditions that improve people's resistance to risk factors and disorders" (p. 21). This conceptualization is very close to that provided by the Life Course Health Development framework, which includes determinants operating in nested genetic, biological, behavioral, social, and economic contexts [30]. Both conceptualizations distinguish between individual, family-related, social, economic, and environmental risk and protective factors, and categorize them into either generic or disease-specific risk factors. Generic risk and protective factors are defined as factors that are common across mental disorders, whereas disease-specific risk and protective factors are specific to the development of a particular disorder.

There is no doubt that several risk factors interact with each other and that their cumulative effect, either additive or multiplicative, as well as the lack of protective factors, predisposes a person to become vulnerable and finally develop a mental disorder. The WHO report "Prevention of Mental Disorders: Effective Interventions and Policy Options" provides an excellent overview of evidence-based risk and protective factors at individual and family-related level [29] (see Box 24.1).

Box 24.1 Individual and Family-Related Risk and Protective Factors for Mental Disorders [29]

Risk factors:

- Academic failure and scholastic demoralization
- Attention deficits
- Caring for chronically ill or dementia patients
- Child abuse and neglect
- Chronic insomnia
- Chronic pain
- Communication deviance
- Early pregnancies

(continued)

(continued)

- Elder abuse
- Emotional immaturity and dyscontrol
- Excessive substance use
- Exposure to aggression, violence, and trauma
- Family conflict or family disorganization
- Loneliness
- Low birth weight
- Low social class
- Medical illness
- Neurochemical imbalance
- Parental mental illness
- Parental substance abuse
- Perinatal complications
- Personal loss/bereavement
- Poor work skills and habits
- Reading disabilities
- Sensory disabilities or organic handicaps
- Social incompetence
- Stressful life events
- Substance use during pregnancy

Protective factors:

- Ability to cope with stress
- Ability to face adversity
- Adaptability
- Autonomy
- Early cognitive stimulation
- Exercise
- Feelings of security
- Feelings of mastery and control
- Good parenting
- Literacy
- Positive attachment and early bonding
- Positive parent–child interaction
- Problem-solving skills
- Prosocial behavior
- Self-esteem
- Skills for life
- Social and conflict management skills
- Socioemotional growth
- Stress management
- Social support of family and friends

Although a range of acknowledged risk and protective factors exist, it is important to stress that the knowledge of risk factors is constantly being expanded.

Regarding individual risk and protective factors, evidence from the recently published scientific literature shows, for instance, that genes [31] and dietary patterns [19, 32], just to name a few, are risk factors for depression. The interaction between risk and protective factors in depression was also disclosed in a recently published systematic review [33]. In that work, Pemberton and Fuller Tyszkiewicz [33] showed a concurrent and lagging association between poor sleep, stress, and significant life events, which act as risk factors, whereas physical activity and quality of social interactions act as protective factors.

Evidence for family-related risk factors has been recently provided by a meta-analysis of 124 studies; it showed that nonsexual maltreatment of children acts as risk factor for several mental disorders. Physical abuse was associated with depression (odds ratio [OR]: 1.54; 95% confidence interval [CI]: 1.16–2.04), anxiety disorders (OR: 1.51; 95% CI: 1.27–1.79), and substance abuse disorders (OR: 1.61; 95% CI: 1.21–2.16). Emotional abuse in childhood increased the risk for depression (OR: 3.06; 95% CI: 2.43–3.85) and anxiety disorders (OR: 3.21; 95% CI: 2.05–5.03) [34]. These results are also supported by the work of Mandelli and colleagues [35], who reported in a post hoc analysis that emotional abuse and neglect showed the strongest associations with depression when compared with other kinds of childhood trauma. Also, domestic violence increases the risk of developing depression and anxiety disorders in women [36, 37].

An overview of evidence-based risk and protective factors at social, environmental, and economic levels [29] is shown in Box 24.2.

Recent studies looking at risk factors at the environmental, societal, and economic levels confirmed that natural disasters [38] and job strain at the workplace [39] act as risk factors for depression. Migration and migration-related factors increase the risk for schizophrenia in first- and second-generation immigrants [40].

Box 24.2 Social, Environmental, and Economic Risk and Protective Factors for Mental Disorders [29]

Risk factors:

- Access to drugs and alcohol
- Displacement
- Isolation and alienation
- Lack of education, transport, housing
- Neighborhood disorganization
- Peer rejection
- Poor social circumstances
- Poor nutrition
- Poverty
- Racial injustice and discrimination
- Social disadvantage
- Unemployment
- Urbanization
- Violence and delinquency
- War
- Work stress

Protective factors:

- Empowerment
- Ethnic minority integration
- Positive interpersonal interactions
- Social participation
- Social responsibility and tolerance
- Social services
- Social support and community networks

24.4.2 Risk and Protective Factors for Well-Being

An increasing number of surveys have recently attempted to assess the level of well-being of the population and to analyze the impact of different demographic, social, personal, and health-related factors on well-being. Results from surveys around the world show that, in general, most people are quite happy and satisfied with their lives [41–43]. The evidence also suggests that the evaluative, eudaimonic, and experienced components of well-being are different constructs, although they are interrelated, and they do not necessarily have the same correlates [43].

Regarding sociodemographic factors, the results from various studies show that people with higher education and higher occupational status report more satisfaction with their lives, but these same people do not report better experienced well-being [42–44]. Women report higher life evaluation than men [42, 43], but the gender differences regarding experienced well-being are not conclusive. Some studies found a slightly higher positive affect but also more "blue affect" and more stress in women than in men [42], whereas other studies found no statistically significant differences in experienced well-being between men and women [43].

Well-being is also influenced by age, although the age distribution of well-being varies across countries. A *U*-shaped relation between evaluative well-being and age, with the nadir between ages 45 and 54 years and higher well-being in younger and older adults, has been found in high-income, English-speaking countries. In the former Soviet Union, Eastern Europe, Latin America, and sub-Saharan Africa there is a large progressive reduction in life evaluation with age [45]. In the United States there is also a *U*-shaped pattern for positive emotions, whereas negative emotions show different patterns: stress and anger steeply decline from the early 20s, worry is elevated through middle age and then declines, and sadness is essentially flat [46]. In sub-Saharan Africa, negative emotions increase slightly with age, whereas in the former Soviet Union and Easter European countries, some negative emotions such as worry also increase with age [45].

Social networks also affect well-being. Having social support is correlated with life satisfaction [47]. Married people and those living with a partner report more satisfaction with their lives, but these same people do not report better experienced well-being [42–44]. Having children is no guarantee of higher happiness. The pleasure of parenting depends on the age of the children, on the quality of the parenting couple, and on the social context, including having enough time to enjoy family life [48]. On the other hand, caring for an adult and loneliness have been reported to be strong predictors of low experienced well-being [42]. Feelings of freedom in living one's life and social support are associated with high experienced well-being [47]. Religion has a substantial influence on improving positive affect and reducing stress, but has no effect on reducing sadness or worry [42].

Health status has a strong relationship with positive affect, negative affect, and evaluative well-being, even after controlling for sociodemographic variables, the presence of a depressive episode, and cognitive functioning [43]. Chronic illnesses have also been associated with reduced experienced and eudaimonic well-being. The reductions in both experienced and eudaimonic well-being increase progressively with the number of comorbidities [45]. Headaches and smoking have also been reported to be strong predictors of low experienced well-being [42].

24.5 The Impact of the Environment: Poverty, Disasters, Stress, Violence

Natural disasters, intentional human-caused disasters, human trafficking, and violence cause new-onset psychiatric disorders, exacerbations of preexisting psychopathology, and psychological distress [49–51]. Economic recessions, and, more concretely, certain fiscal austerity and policy decisions on how to respond to the economic downturns, can also produce an increase in the prevalence of mental disorders [52–55], and these effects might be higher among the weakest and most vulnerable members of society [52]. Poverty has a negative impact on mental health. Low household income and low parental education have a stronger impact on children's and adolescents' mental health than parental unemployment or low occupational status. Children and adolescents with low socioeconomic status are two to three times more likely to have mental health problems than their peers from families with a high socioeconomic status, and are also more likely to develop comorbidities. A decrease in socioeconomic status and the persistence of low socioeconomic status over time are related to increasing mental health problems [56]. School-age homeless children are also more likely to have mental health problems than low-income housed children [57]. Adults who experience unemployment, impoverishment, debt, financial difficulties, and housing payment problems have a significantly greater risk of mental health problems, and the more debt people have, the more likely they are to have mental disorders [55].

These environmental factors also have a negative impact on well-being. Unemployment, especially in contexts where people are less accustomed to it [58], and living in an area of high deprivation [10] have a negative impact on well-being. An unhappy and violent childhood has a strong negative impact on well-being as an adult [10]. On the other hand, household income, financial satisfaction, and meeting basic needs such as food and shelter, as well as material comforts such as having electricity, are associated with life satisfaction [47]. Financial satisfaction is negatively associated with negative feelings [59]. More money does not necessarily buy more happiness, but less money is associated with emotional pain. The pain of some of life's misfortunes, including asthma, divorce, and being alone, is significantly exacerbated by poverty, but a threshold exists beyond which further increases in income are not associated with more experienced well-being [42]. The facts that income is more highly correlated with general life satisfaction than with experienced happiness, and that people with the highest incomes do not experience more positive emotions or less negative emotions than middle-income people, can be explained: the answers to global life satisfaction questions are susceptible to focusing attention on different aspects of life, and people tend to overestimate the impact of any single factor on their well-being. This phenomenon is known as the focusing illusion. On the other hand, as income increases, people's time use does not seem to shift toward the activities that matter most to their experienced well-being, such as spending time with their loved ones, avoiding pain and disease, and enjoying leisure; they also tend to be more tense [42, 44]. Contrary to popular belief, satisfaction with material aspects of life has a stronger impact on well-being in wealthier than in poorer countries. Nevertheless, post-materialist needs of autonomy, respect, and social support are essential to positive and negative feelings worldwide. This suggests that societal conditions that promote autonomy and social relations among their citizens are important in all societies as the fulfillment of such needs, not just having more money [59].

An association also exists between income and average life satisfaction in nations. Despite the high correlation, large differences in life satisfaction are seem between countries with similar incomes [47]. People living in richer nations report higher life evaluation but also experience more negative feelings [59], and they do not necessarily experience higher positive affect [60]. The same increase in personal income yields a greater increase in subjective well-being in richer nations than in poorer nations, probably because a higher value is placed on money and materialistic goods in such countries [60]. Sharp drops in growth and related increases in insecurity during economic crises negatively affect well-being [58], but more counterintuitively, large increases in income for a given country over time are not associated with increases in average subjective well-being [44], and rapid economic growth can even have negative effects as a result of concerns about inequality and changing rewards [58].

24.6 Mental Health and Economic Well-Being

Interest in national accounts of well-being has recently increased, as societies have realized that societal progress includes more than economic growth, and therefore they seek not only economic and material progress but also progress in subjective, environmental, and social well-being [47] (see Chap. 25). Even though some economists started to advocate for this change years ago, the systematic collection and use of well-being data at the population level have been slow to follow. In the 1930s the economist Simon Kuznets, who participated in the creation of the gross domestic product (GDP), warned that a nation's welfare could scarcely be inferred just from its national income and advocated for an assessment of well-being. Years later, Richard Easterlin (1974) also claimed that economic growth does not necessarily imply an increase in the happiness of the population and advocated measuring happiness in addition to economic growth. In 2009 the European Commission published a communication that acknowledged the limitations of the GDP and proposed to complement GDP with environmental and social indicators such as a comprehensive environmental index and measures of quality of life and well-being. The same year, the Commission on the Measurement of Economic Performance and Social Progress appointed by Nicolas Sarkozy, the president of the French Republic at the time, recommended shifting emphasis from measuring economic production to measuring people's well-being, and that this measurement be done at a national level [61]. Along the same lines, the World Happiness Report stated that, "

> In addition to specific measures of economic, social, and environmental performance, governments should begin the systematic measurement of happiness itself, in both its affective and evaluative dimensions" [48] (p. 8)

The United Nations, in the resolution adopted by its General Assembly on July 19, 2011, invited Member States to "pursue the elaboration of additional measures that better capture the importance of the pursuit of happiness and well-being in development with a view to guiding their public policies,", and in 2012 proclaimed March 20 the International Day of Happiness. The importance of ensuring that every person achieves a basic standard of well-being is also included in the recommendations of the High-Level Panel on the Post-2015 Development Agenda.

An attempt to address the limitations of GDP was the development of the Genuine Progress Indicator in 1995, a measure of sustainable economic well-being designed to indicate progress in people's quality of life and economic, social, and environmental well-being that was applied in Canada [62]. The British government also put the recommendations into practice and asked the Office of National Statistics to devise a new way of measuring well-being in order to start measuring progress as a country, not just by how the economy was growing, but by how the people's lives were improving [63]. In the United States, the National Academy of Sciences issued a report to provide guidance for measurement and data collection in the area of experienced well-being [64]. The constitution of Bhutan states that the happiness of the population is a public good, and that the government has the responsibility of creating an enabling environment for the pursuit of happiness [65], and the Centre for Bhutan Studies developed a Gross National Happiness Index including nine domains: psychological well-being, health, education, time use, culture, governance, community vitality, environmental diversity, and living standards [66].

Interesting cross-national initiatives also allow comparisons across countries. The Better Life Initiative, launched by the Organisation for Economic Co-operation and Development, aims to measure society's progress across 11 domains of well-being. One of the largest initiatives is the Gallup World Poll, which has collected information about well-being from at least 130 countries every year since 2006. In addition, every day it collects information about the well-being of at least 500 adults living in the United States. The Happy Planet Index from the New Economics Foundation (NEF) uses data on well-being from the Gallup World Poll, together with data on life expectancy and ecological footprint, to calculate a global measure of sustainable well-being. The NEF is calling on governments to adopt new measures of human progress that establish the goal of delivering sustainable well-being for all at the heart of the societal and economic decision-making process. Other cross-national social and health surveys that evaluate well-being are the World Values Survey, the European Social Survey, and the WHO Study on Global Ageing and Adult Health, to mention a few.

To conclude, it is important to highlight that GDP should not be the only goal of any society (see Chap. 25). Incremental gains in income among people with living standards far above just meeting basic material needs may be much less beneficial to the population than ensuring the vitality of local communities or better mental health. Subjective well-being measures should be collected widely and frequently because they will permit baseline values and trend changes to be established for subjective well-being within and across nations and communities, and will allow the consequences of subsequent events and policy changes on well-being to be assessed. The inclusion of well-being measures within surveys already being conducted for other purposes will also provide descriptions of the social and economic contexts of people's lives, and will therefore allow a more fine-grained assessment of what makes people happy [48].

Key Messages

- Global mental health is concerned not only with mental disorders but also with the study of well-being at the population level.
- Sound data on global mental health is scarce; be aware of the source and methodology behind global estimations!
- The global cost of mental disorders is huge: it was estimated at US$2.5 trillion in 2010 and projected to be US$6.0 trillion in 2030.
- The global burden is also huge: 183.9 million DALYs are due to mental and substance use disorders – 7.4% of all DALYs worldwide!
- Interest has recently increased in national accounts of well-being as a measure of societal welfare.

References

1. Whiteford HA, Ferrari AJ, Degenhardt L, Feigin V, Vos T. Global burden of mental, neurological, and substance use disorders: an analysis from the Global Burden of Disease Study 2010. In: Patel V, Chisholm D, Dua T, Laxminarayan R, Medina-Mora ME, editors. Mental, neurological, and substance use disorders: disease control priorities, vol. 4. 3rd ed. Washington, DC: The World Bank; 2016.
2. Ryff CD. Psychological well-being revisited: advances in the science and practice of eudaimonia. Psychother Psychosom. 2014;83(1):10–28.
3. Kahneman D, Diener E, Schwarz N. Well-being: the foundations of hedonic psychology. New York: Russell Sage Found; 2003.
4. Demyttenaere K, Bruffaerts R, Posada-Villa J, Gasquet I, Kovess V, Lepine JP, et al. Prevalence, severity, and unmet need for treatment of mental disorders in the World Health Organization World Mental Health Surveys. JAMA. 2004;291(21):2581–90.
5. Robins LN, Wing J, Wittchen HU, Helzer JE, Babor TF, Burke J, et al. The Composite International Diagnostic Interview: an epidemiologic instrument suitable for use in conjunction with different diagnostic systems and in different cultures. Arch Gen Psychiatry. 1988;45:1069–77.
6. Kessler RC, Ustun TB. The World Mental Health (WMH) Survey Initiative version of the World Health Organization (WHO) Composite International Diagnostic Interview (CIDI). Int J Methods Psychiatr Res. 2004;13(2):93–121.
7. Wang PS, Angermeyer M, Borges G, Bruffaerts R, Tat Chiu W, DEG G, et al. Delay and failure in treatment seeking after first onset of mental disorders in the World Health Organization's World Mental Health Survey Initiative. World Psychiatry. 2007;6(3):177–85.
8. Salomon JA. New disability weights for the global burden of disease. Bull World Health Organ. 2010;88(12):879.
9. Salomon JA, Haagsma JA, Davis A, de Noordhout CM, Polinder S, Havelaar AH, et al. Disability weights for the Global Burden of Disease 2013 study. Lancet Glob Health. 2015;3(11):e712–23.
10. Bellis MA, Hughes K, Jones A, Perkins C, McHale P. Childhood happiness and violence: a retrospective study of their impacts on adult well-being. BMJ Open. 2013;3(9):e003427.
11. Balaji M, Chatterjee S, Koschorke M, Rangaswamy T, Chavan A, Dabholkar H, et al. The development of a lay health worker delivered collaborative community based intervention for people with schizophrenia in India. BMC Health Serv Res. 2012;12:42.
12. Patel V, Weiss HA, Chowdhary N, Naik S, Pednekar S, Chatterjee S, et al. Lay health worker led intervention for depressive and anxiety disorders in India: impact on clinical and disability outcomes over 12 months. Br J Psychiatry J Ment Sci. 2011;199(6):459–66.
13. Patel V, Weiss HA, Chowdhary N, Naik S, Pednekar S, Chatterjee S, et al. Effectiveness of an intervention led by lay health counsellors for depressive and anxiety disorders in primary care in Goa, India (MANAS): a cluster randomised controlled trial. Lancet. 2010;376(9758):2086–95.
14. WHO. Monitoring the building blocks of health systems: a handbook of indicators and their measurement strategies. Geneva: World Health Organization; 2010.
15. Bloom DE, Cafiero ET, Jané-Llopis E, Abrahams-Gessel S, Bloom LR, Fathima S, et al. The global

economic burden of non-communicable diseases. Geneva: World Economic Forum; 2011.
16. Hu TW. Perspectives: an international review of the national cost estimates of mental illness, 1990–2003. J Ment Health Policy Econ. 2006;9(1):3–13.
17. Chisholm D, Saxena S. Cost effectiveness of strategies to combat neuropsychiatric conditions in sub-Saharan Africa and South East Asia: mathematical modelling study. BMJ. 2012;344:e609.
18. Chisholm D, Sweeny K, Sheehan P, Rasmussen B, Smit F, Cuijpers P, et al. Scaling-up treatment of depression and anxiety: a global return on investment analysis. Lancet Psychiatry. 2016;3(5):415–24.
19. Quirk SE, Williams LJ, O'Neil A, Pasco JA, Jacka FN, Housden S, et al. The association between diet quality, dietary patterns and depression in adults: a systematic review. BMC Psychiatry. 2013;13:175.
20. Murray CJ, Vos T, Lozano R, Naghavi M, Flaxman AD, Michaud C, et al. Disability-adjusted life years (DALYs) for 291 diseases and injuries in 21 regions, 1990–2010: a systematic analysis for the Global Burden of Disease Study 2010. Lancet. 2012;380(9859):2197–223.
21. Prince M, Patel V, Saxena S, Maj M, Maselko J, Phillips MR, et al. No health without mental health. Lancet. 2007;370(9590):859–77.
22. Chesney E, Goodwin GM, Fazel S. Risks of all-cause and suicide mortality in mental disorders: a meta-review. World Psychiatry. 2014;13(2):153–60.
23. Brown S, Inskip H, Barraclough B. Causes of the excess mortality of schizophrenia. Br J Psychiatry J Ment Sci. 2000;177:212–7.
24. Cuijpers P, Smit F. Excess mortality in depression: a meta-analysis of community studies. J Affect Disord. 2002;72(3):227–36.
25. Whiteford HA, Degenhardt L, Rehm J, Baxter AJ, Ferrari AJ, Erskine HE, et al. Global burden of disease attributable to mental and substance use disorders: findings from the Global Burden of Disease Study 2010. Lancet. 2013;382(9904):1575–86.
26. WHO. The global burden of disease: 2004 update. Geneva: World Health Organization; 2008.
27. WHO. World health report 2002. Reducing risks, promoting healthy life. Geneva: World Health Organization; 2002.
28. WHO. Global health risks: mortality and burden of disease attributable to selected major risks. Geneva: World Health Organization; 2009.
29. WHO. Prevention of mental disorders: effective interventions and policy options. Geneva: World Health Organization; Department of Mental Health and Substance Abuse in collaboration with the Prevention Research Centre of the Universities of Nijmegen and Maastricht; 2004.
30. Halfon N, Hochstein M. Life course health development: an integrated framework for developing health, policy, and research. Milbank Q. 2002;80(3):433–79. iii
31. Xia L, Yao S. The involvement of genes in adolescent depression: a systematic review. Front Behav Neurosci. 2015;9:329.
32. Rahe C, Unrath M, Berger K. Dietary patterns and the risk of depression in adults: a systematic review of observational studies. Eur J Nutr. 2014;53(4):997–1013.
33. Pemberton R, Fuller Tyszkiewicz MD. Factors contributing to depressive mood states in everyday life: a systematic review. J Affect Disord. 2016;200:103–10.
34. Norman RE, Byambaa M, De R, Butchart A, Scott J, Vos T. The long-term health consequences of child physical abuse, emotional abuse, and neglect: a systematic review and meta-analysis. PLoS Med. 2012;9(11):e1001349.
35. Mandelli L, Petrelli C, Serretti A. The role of specific early trauma in adult depression: a meta-analysis of published literature. Childhood trauma and adult depression. Eur Psychiatry. 2015;30(6):665–80.
36. Trevillion K, Oram S, Feder G, Howard LM. Experiences of domestic violence and mental disorders: a systematic review and meta-analysis. PLoS One. 2012;7(12):e51740.
37. Devries KM, Mak JY, Bacchus LJ, Child JC, Falder G, Petzold M, et al. Intimate partner violence and incident depressive symptoms and suicide attempts: a systematic review of longitudinal studies. PLoS Med. 2013;10(5):e1001439.
38. Tang B, Liu X, Liu Y, Xue C, Zhang L. A meta-analysis of risk factors for depression in adults and children after natural disasters. BMC Public Health. 2014;14:623.
39. Theorell T, Hammarstrom A, Aronsson G, Traskman Bendz L, Grape T, Hogstedt C, et al. A systematic review including meta-analysis of work environment and depressive symptoms. BMC Public Health. 2015;15:738.
40. Bourque F, van der Ven E, Malla A. A meta-analysis of the risk for psychotic disorders among first- and second-generation immigrants. Psychol Med. 2011;41(5):897–910.
41. Diener E, Diener C. Most people are happy. Psychol Sci. 1996;7(3):181–5.
42. Kahneman D, Deaton A. High income improves evaluation of life but not emotional well-being. Proc Natl Acad Sci U S A. 2010;107(38):16489–93.
43. Miret M, Caballero FF, Chatterji S, Olaya B, Tobiasz-Adamczyk B, Koskinen S, et al. Health and happiness: cross-sectional household surveys in Finland, Poland and Spain. Bull World Health Organ. 2014;92(10):716–25.
44. Kahneman D, Krueger AB, Schkade D, Schwarz N, Stone AA. Would you be happier if you were richer? A focusing illusion. Science. 2006;312(5782):1908–10.
45. Steptoe A, Deaton A, Stone AA. Subjective wellbeing, health, and ageing. Lancet. 2015;385(9968):640–8.
46. Stone AA, Schwartz JE, Broderick JE, Deaton A. A snapshot of the age distribution of psychological well-being in the United States. Proc Natl Acad Sci U S A. 2010;107(22):9985–90.
47. Diener E, Tay L. Subjective well-being and human welfare around the world as reflected in the Gallup World Poll. Int J Psychol. 2015;50(2):135–49.

48. Helliwell J, Layard R, Sachs J. World happiness report 2012: Columbia University Earth Institute; 2012.
49. Lagdon S, Armour C, Stringer M. Adult experience of mental health outcomes as a result of intimate partner violence victimisation: a systematic review. Eur J Psychotraumatol. 2014;5:1–12.
50. North CS, Pfefferbaum B. Mental health response to community disasters: a systematic review. JAMA. 2013;310(5):507–18.
51. Ottisova L, Hemmings S, Howard LM, Zimmerman C, Oram S. Prevalence and risk of violence and the mental, physical and sexual health problems associated with human trafficking: an updated systematic review. Epidemiol Psychiatr Sci. 2016;25(4):317–41.
52. Karanikolos M, Mladovsky P, Cylus J, Thomson S, Basu S, Stuckler D, et al. Financial crisis, austerity, and health in Europe. Lancet. 2013;381(9874):1323–31.
53. Salvador-Carulla L, Roca M. Mental health impact of the economic crisis in Spain. Int Psychiatry. 2013;10(4):50–65.
54. Wahlbeck K, McDaid D. Actions to alleviate the mental health impact of the economic crisis. World Psychiatry. 2012;11(3):139–45.
55. WHO. Impact of economic crises on mental health. Copenhagen: World Health Organization; Regional Office for Europe; 2011.
56. Reiss F. Socioeconomic inequalities and mental health problems in children and adolescents: a systematic review. Soc Sci Med. 2013;90:24–31.
57. Bassuk EL, Richard MK, Tsertsvadze A. The prevalence of mental illness in homeless children: a systematic review and meta-analysis. J Am Acad Child Adolesc Psychiatry. 2015;54(2):86–96. e2
58. Graham C. Happiness around the world the paradox of happy peasants and miserable millionaires. New York: Oxford University Press; 2009.
59. Ng W, Diener E. What matters to the rich and the poor? Subjective well-being, financial satisfaction, and postmaterialist needs across the world. J Pers Soc Psychol. 2014;107(2):326–38.
60. Tay L, Morrison M, Diener E. Living among the affluent: boon or bane? Psychol Sci. 2014;25(6): 1235–41.
61. Stiglitz JE, Sen A, Fitoussi JP. Report by the commission on the measurement of economic performance and social progress. 2009.
62. Anielski M. The economics of happiness: building genuine wealth. Gabriola Island: New Society Publishers; 2007.
63. Self A, Thomas J, Randall C. Measuring national well-being: life in the UK. London: ONS; 2012.
64. Council NR. Subjective well-being: measuring happiness, suffering, and other dimensions of experience. Panel on measuring subjective well-being in a policy-relevant framework. Committee on national statistics, division of behavioral and social sciences and education. Washington, DC: The National Academies Press; 2013.
65. Tobgay T, Dophu U, Torres CE, Na-Bangchang K. Health and Gross National Happiness: review of current status in Bhutan. J Multidiscip Health. 2011;4:293–8.
66. Tobgay T, Dorji T, Pelzom D, Gibbons RV. Progress and delivery of health care in Bhutan, the Land of the Thunder Dragon and Gross National Happiness. Trop Med Int Health. 2011;16(6):731–6.

Burden and Indirect Costs of Mental Disorders

25

Denise Razzouk

Abstract

The burden of mental disorders represents huge costs to society and is deleterious to economic growth. Happiness and well-being have been acknowledged as a proxy for economic growth and nation development. In this regard, mental disorders are the leading factor hindering well-being and happiness. International organizations and global policies have been warned of the need to include mental health as a priority in countries' national agendas. For this purpose, mental health and well-being were included in the United Nations Sustainable Goals for 2015–2030. Indirect costs of mental disorders are related to poverty, unemployment, productivity losses, low educational level, social exclusion and inequality, gender inequity, and violence. Depression and anxiety, schizophrenia, and mood disorders are the most burdensome mental disorders. Targeting the reduction of burden and indirect costs of mental disorders involves increasing investments in mental health and the efficiency of community mental healthcare, and also implementing cost-effective interventions. Economic evaluation should take into account broader outcomes and the indirect costs of mental disorders, because the effects of mental interventions also rely on social outcomes.

Key Points Summary

- Burden of mental disorders
- Targeting sustainable development goals: indirect costs of mental disorders
- Effects of mental health treatment on indirect costs and on reducing the burden of mental disorders

D. Razzouk (✉)
Centre of Economic Mental Health, Department of Psychiatry, Universidade Federal de Sao Paulo, Rua Borges Lagoa 570, 1° andar, São Paulo 04038-000, Brazil
e-mail: drazzouk@gmail.com

D. Razzouk (ed.), *Mental Health Economics*, DOI 10.1007/978-3-319-55266-8_25

25.1 Introduction

Almost three centuries ago, economists influenced by Jeremy Bentham were dealing with the challenge of maximizing scarce resources and enhancing the well-being and satisfaction of citizens [1] (see Chap. 1). Since 2011, the United Nations has been asking countries to estimate their citizens' happiness in order to shape the goals of global policy. In accordance to this purpose, the World Happiness Report was launched in 2013 [2], aiming to present the results of a survey in which happiness was measured as a proxy of satisfaction with life conditions, in opposition to the concept of happiness expressing hedonistic emotion used in utilitarian period.

The concept of happiness used in this report was in accordance with the Organisation for Economic Co-operation and Development (OECD) guideline [3] for measuring well-being, in which the concept is closely linked with emotional mental state, purpose and meaning of life, and evaluation of life conditions. In this report, poor mental health was reported as being the leading cause of unhappiness and strongly related to poverty.

The first report of the burden of mental disorders was from the Global Burden of Diseases study in the 1990s; since then, the economic burden of mental disorders has been increasing worldwide to a worrisome extent [4–9]. Despite innumerable claims of prioritizing mental disorders in global policy, mental health has not been present in the global agenda until recently [10]. In 2014, the OECD warned that mental illness accounted for at least 4% of countries' gross domestic products (GDPs) and that 20% of people in the workplace have a mental disorder, of which 5% account for sever mental disorders [8]. In this regard, OECD pointed out that despite some growing investments in mental health, the unmet needs still are disproportional; it used England an example, where mental illness accounted for 23% of total burden of diseases, though it received only 13% of national health budget. This scenario is still more worrisome in low- and middle income countries, where many diseases, including mental disorders, are neglected and lack investment [11]. However, a vast emerging literature has highlighted that investments in mental disorders lead to economic return and economic growth, identifying mental health as a mental capital asset for countries' development and linking it to cost-effectiveness interventions allowing its burden to be reduced [4, 6–8, 10, 12–21].

In 2015, the United Nations launched a global agenda for 2015–2030 called "Transforming Our World: The 2030 Agenda for Sustainable Development" [22]; this agenda targets investments of resources to prioritize 17 major goals, among which well-being and mental health are included for the first time. In theory, these goals encapsulate the most worthwhile targets for maximizing better lives and well-being for members of society. In this regard, promoting good mental health and well-being is a sine qua non condition to achieve at least eight of these goals: good education, good job, peace, safety and human rights, good physical health, innovation, inclusive society, and less poverty [21]. The World Health Organization recently launched the report "Health Systems, Health, Wealth and Societal Well-Being" [14], emphasizing health as a driver of economic growth; in this sense, the opportunity costs of not investing in treating mental disorders results in the societal and economic burdens they cause.

The burden of mental disorders, neurological diseases, and substance misuse together corresponds to more than 10% of total disability-adjusted life years (DALYs), of which 60% is exclusively due to mental disorders [7]. Also, they account for 28% of all years lived with disability. Among mental disorders, depression accounts for more than 40% of DALYs, followed by anxiety, drug and alcohol misuse, schizophrenia, and bipolar disorders. DALY is an indicator combining morbidity (years lived with disability) and mortality (years of life lost) (See Chap. 6) [9]. However, the growing burden of mental disorders does not exclusively affect health indicators such as mortality and morbidity [7]. On the contrary, it also causes externalities and indirect costs to society [23, 24].

The costs of mental disorders represent one-third of the total costs due to neglected diseases [25], and these costs to society were estimated to be US$2.5 trillion, based on data from the 2010

Global Burden of Diseases study [6, 26]. Almost 70% of this total cost is due to indirect or "invisible" costs [6, 26], which will reach US$6 trillion by 2030 [26, 27]. Therefore, the costs of mental disorders affect economic growth and countries' GDPs; have catastrophic economic consequences, especially in low- and middle-income countries; and mostly affect the young population [6, 26–28].

Indirect costs are related to no-health economic losses due to mental disorders. These resource losses can be at the individual, sector (enterprise), and/or national (a country's economic growth) level. While work productivity losses are the main component of indirect costs, other relevant losses must also be considered in economic evaluations [23] (Box 25.1). Despite the fact that indirect costs are a broader measure than direct costs, they are rarely measured in economic evaluation because the majority of studies take the perspective of a health provider, and for this reason, effects of mental health interventions to change these indirect impacts of mental disorders might be underestimated [29].

In this chapter I highlight indirect costs due to mental disorders (see Box 25.1) and the strategies for diminishing this economic burden, comparing them with sustainable development goals (SDGs) (Box 25.2). This chapter focuses on three major categories of burdensome disorders: anxiety and depressive disorders, schizophrenia and bipolar disorders, and dementia. Indirect costs of alcohol and drug misuse are discussed in Chap. 26, and productivity costs are discussed in detail in Chaps. 28 and 29.

Box 25.1 Indirect Costs Due to Mental Disorders

National level

Mental and human capital losses

- Early mortality (suicide)
- Violence and accidents (criminal justice)
- Greater need for social benefits (poverty, housing, early retirement, unemployment)
- Less innovation and creativity (skill quality)
- Economic growth losses

Workplace level

- Work productivity losses
- Absenteeism
- Presenteeism
- Worker replacement costs
- Earlier retirement

Individual level

- Income losses and poverty
- Poor educational attainment
- Family losses (leisure, work opportunities, income, out-of-pocket expenditures, impairment of children's development)
- Social and economic opportunity losses
- Stigma, disrespected human rights, social exclusion
- Lower life expectancy

25.2 Indirect Costs of Mental Disorders Are Targeted in the SDGs

Mental disorders cause negative economic and social externalities (Box 25.1) that are targeted by least in six SDGs (Box 25.2): (1) no poverty, (2) quality education, (3) gender equality, (4) decent work and economic growth, (5) reduced inequalities, (6) peace and justice (human rights and freedom) and (7) gender inequity. We present some data regarding indirect costs due to mental disorders that should be reduced in accordance with the six target goals listed above.

25.2.1 No Poverty

In this item are included indirect costs related to income losses, unemployment, and debts. One of the main goals of global policies is to eradicate

Box 25.2 17 Sustainable Development Goals 2015–2030 (United Nations, 2015)

1. No poverty
2. Zero hunger
3. Good health and well-being
4. Quality education
5. Gender equality
6. Clean water and sanitation
7. Affordable and clean energy
8. Decent work and economic growth
9. Industry, innovation, and infrastructure
10. Reduced inequalities
11. Sustainable cities and communities
12. Responsible consumption and production
13. Climate action
14. Life below water
15. Life on land
16. Peace, justice, and strong institutions
17. Partnerships for the goals

poverty and hunger, allowing similar opportunities for decent life and work. However, some studies have shown that income and impoverishment are associated with mental disorders [20, 30, 31]. Several factors contribute to this association, though the complexity of such association is not totally explained. The high prevalence of mental disorders among homeless people has been reported to range from 25% in EUA to 60% in Canada [32, 33]; bipolar and schizophrenia disorders predominate in these populations.

Some studies found an 11% reduction in the chance of being employed as a result of mental disorders [34, 35] (see Chaps. 27 and 28). Similarly, annual income is lower by more than 20% in people with compared with people without mental disorders, whereas among people with severe mental disorders, this rate is decreased by 75% in comparison with those without a mental disorder [36]. Unemployment rates among people with mental illness range from 30% to 52%. In England, the unemployment rate is 40% higher among people with mental disorders than among the general population [37]. Among patients with schizophrenia, however, unemployment rates in European countries range from 65% to 90%, and 4% to 38% of such people have never been employed at any stage of life [38, 39].

Unemployment is not only related to a lower chance of finding work but also to a lower chance of keeping a job after an episode of mania or depression, for instance. In Australia, one study showed that only 21% of people suffering from bipolar disorders returned to work immediately after an episode resolved, and 34% remained unable to live independently. Yet, among people with bipolar disorders, 21% had poor work adjustment and 73% were unemployed in the previous year [40]. A survey of people suffering from bipolar disorders in Chile and Argentina found that 80% faced economic difficulties as a result of their disorder, and 40% of them were unemployed [41]. The scenario of people suffering from schizophrenia is even worse. The unemployment rate among people with schizophrenia has been reported to range between 70% and 80% [38].

A survey of 8580 subjects in United Kingdom demonstrated a close association between debt and low income and mental disorders, especially among people suffering from psychosis [42]. In that study, debts were three times more prevalent among those with mental disorders than those without mental disorders. Also, those with six or more debts in the previous year were six times more likely of having a mental disorder than people with fewer debts. Another prospective study showed that lost income among people with depression was two-fold higher than among people without depression [43].

Family caregivers are also affected in terms of the costs of unemployment of a family member with mental disorder; 29% of costs associated with schizophrenia were closely related to unemployment and opportunity losses because of the length of time caring for them (opportunity costs) [44]. Similarly, in low- and middle-income countries, between 18% and 41% of caregivers of family members with dementia have decreased working time or left their work [45, 46]. An Italian study found that people suffering from dementia need, on average, 45 hrs per week of personal care provided by a caregiver, at an annual cost of informal care around U$44,736 [47].

In Brazil, a study of 150 low-income family caregivers of patients with psychosis showed that the caregivers spent more than 12% of their monthly income on caring [48].

25.2.2 Decent Work and Economic Growth

The costs of mental disorders have negative effects on countries' GDPs – by 2% and 4.4% in high-income countries [8]. Early retirement affects income taxation revenue, and an Australian study has shown that, in this sense, people with depression who retired early earned 78% less than those employed for the same job [8, 49]. Productivity losses are affected mainly by absenteeism, presenteeism, and sick leave. Compared with the number of people with physical disorders and impaired work performance, people with moderate (69%) and severe (90%) mental disorders are threefold as likely to decrease their performance (presenteeism) in the workplace [8].

The relationship between the quality of the workplace environment and mental health has a place in decreasing work-related sickness and productivity loss (see Chaps. 28 and 29). One aspect is related to a stressful and abusive workplace environment, such as one where moral and sexual harassment and violence exist. The second aspect is tasks overload, representing a key component of the emergence of mental disorders. Mental disorders are also a key component in decreasing skills and productivity in the workplace.

Among all diseases, depression is considered the most costly and disabling in terms of work impairment [19, 24, 50–52]. Depression markedly affects work performance in different ways, mainly because it impairs cognitive functions, resulting in slow reasoning, difficulty managing time, poor ability to focus on tasks, and impaired memory. Moreover, depression produce symptoms of fatigue and energy loss, and multiple somatic complains. Work absenteeism and productivity losses are more frequent and severe among people with depression than among people with other chronic diseases. Occupational impairment accounts for 60% of the total cost of depression [53]. When compared with other debilitating diseases such as rheumatoid arthritis and healthy controls, employees with depression showed worse performance in all work dimensions (time management, output tasks, mental interpersonal tasks) [54]. Similarly, when people with depression were compared with people with six other medical conditions (allergies, arthritis, asthma, back pain, headaches, and high blood pressure), depression was the only condition correlated with decreased work performance (task focus and productivity) [52].

25.2.3 Gender Equality

Women with mental disorders are particularly more affected than men regarding earnings and work impairment [34]. Mental disorders were estimated to reduce earnings by 29% among women and by 9.5% among men. Also, the effect on the chance of being employed was less among women than men [34, 36]. Moreover, women are 40% more likely than men to develop depression over their lifetime. Women are more vulnerable to mental disorders because they experience more social determinants contributing to illness (see Chaps. 24 and 27).

25.2.4 Reduce Inequality

Schizophrenia disorder is more prevalent among those having a low socioeconomic status, though other mental disorders are also prevalent [55]. Mental disorders can contribute to social exclusion as consequence of difficulties with being employed and engaging in social networks, and through stigma. Although the connections between inequality and mental disorders are complex and elusive [56], stigma and a lack of appropriate treatment are important factors for the social exclusion of people with mental disorders [31, 57, 58] (see Chap. 27).

Stigma hinders social engagement and work opportunities [57]. For instance, some people avoid offering jobs or renting apartments to people with mental disorders. Because mental disorders cause socially unacceptable behaviors in some circumstances, such as during a psychotic episode, a misconception exists that people with mental disorders are dangerous to society as a whole. On the other hand, people with mental disorders lack enough support to overcome their disabilities and perform social roles. A combination of disability and the loss of social and economic opportunities allows these people to easily progress toward lowered self-esteem and confidence, resulting in greater chances of impoverishment. Stigma and discrimination against mental illness reinforce the vicious cycle of poverty, inequity, and social exclusion (Fig. 25.1) (see Chap. 27).

25.2.5 Education Quality and Attainment

Children with mental disorders have a 17 times higher chance of being excluded from school than those without mental disorders. One survey of 2500 children and adolescents, aged 5–15 years, in the United Kingdom found that 18% of children with mental disorders were excluded from school compared with 1% of those without mental disorders. They also found that the frequency of failure in school qualification among adolescents with mental disorders were double that of adolescents without mental disorders [59].

Psychoses such as schizophrenia can also start at early ages, permanently affecting children's school performance. Studies have shown that learning difficulties and cognitive problems arise on average 4 or 5 years before the onset of schizophrenia, and these symptoms mainly start between 13 and 16 years [60]. After the onset of schizophrenia, the majority of adolescents (50–60%) [61, 62] abandons school, and a small proportion (<10%) reaches university [63]. Apart from cognitive disturbances, schizophrenia symptoms at early ages affect children's social behaviors: 44% of children have no social contact with friends [62, 64].

Fig. 25.1 Mental illness and the vicious circle of poverty

25.2.6 Human Rights and Peace

Innumerable reports of the abuse of human rights of people with mental disorders have been widely disseminated, especially during the period in which large psychiatric hospitals were the only treatment facilities available. Notwithstanding some laws addressing this topic, the human rights of people with mental disorders remain an open issue [58].

In this regard, these human rights abuses triggered mental health reform and closure of psychiatric hospitals, among other causes [65, 66]. While living in a community allows greater autonomy and, to some extent, greater protection of human rights, some data show that people with mental disorders are more vulnerable to violence, rape, and crime than the general population. The recovery model emphasizes the need to guarantee human rights for people with mental disorders [67].

People suffering violence, war, and traumatic events (disasters, fire) are at greater risk of developing mental disorders [68, 69]. The most known example of this closed relationship is posttraumatic stress disorder, which is closely related to the emergence of other mental disorders such as depression, anxiety, and psychoses, among others. Women and children are particularly more vulnerable to domestic violence, rape, and sexual abuse.

25.3 The Effect of Mental Health Interventions on Indirect Costs

The majority of studies has shown that the largest portion of costs for mental disorders is indirect costs. Treating and preventing mental disorders reduce indirect costs, as has been reported in the literature. However, the lack of cost-benefit analysis studies on mental health and the predominance of the extra-welfarist approach in health disciplines, which mainly adopt a health provider perspective and QALY outcomes, have distracted researchers on this issue. The majority of economic evaluations are focused on health-related direct costs and on insensitive methods to measure the effects of mental health interventions. While clinical trials are designed to assess the efficacy of a health intervention on a specific outcome, Health Economics addresses economic evaluation to assess the value and the worth for money of a specific effect (or benefit) to society. Similarly, health policymakers focus resource allocation according to efficacy, fairness, budget availability and impact, cost-effectiveness (sometimes!), and other factors (see Chaps. 10 and 11).

Given such a scenario, to what extent are mental health interventions cost-effective and worthwhile? Box 25.3 outlines some cost-effective mental health interventions, and previous chap-

Box 25.3 Effects of Mental Health Interventions

Reducing or achieving remission of psychiatric symptoms

Improving daily independent living skills (autonomy)

Improving work skills (e.g., supported employment)

Improving cognitive abilities, including educational interventions for autism and learning disabilities

Improving social participation

Decreasing violent and suicidal behaviors

Decreasing alcohol and drug consumption and illicit acts

Improving self-esteem and individual empowerment

Combating stigmatizing attitudes against mental disorders

Decreasing intangible suffering caused by mental disorders (for individuals and families)

Preventing and decreasing risky behaviors

Improving adherence to treatment for physical diseases

Improving child development (cognitive and emotional)

Reducing absenteeism and presenteeism in the workplace

Recovering well-being (lost because of mental disorders)

ters discuss these in depth [12, 17, 70–73]. In this sense, in Psychiatry and other mental health disciplines, the main objective is to prevent and eliminate (or alleviate) all individual and family suffering caused by mental disorders, disabilities, and social and economic externalities. Moreover, these interventions' aims are in accordance with an inclusive society, fairness, individual empowerment and freedom, human rights defense, decent life conditions, and improved health and well-being. In other words, mental health interventions address goals to maximize the welfare of individuals, families, and society. In this sense, treating a woman with puerperal depression, for instance, does not improve only depressive symptoms (efficacy); it also promotes better cognitive and emotional development for her baby and reduces mental disorders in adult life, and it prevents unemployment of the mother, income losses, and violent acts against baby. The worth of treatment in this case is for the mother (and family), for the baby, and for the society as whole.

Chisholm et al. [19] recently estimated the positive economic return to society of investing in depression treatment. If externalities and indirect costs are not included in economic evaluation, the worth of mental health interventions might be underestimated (or overestimated) , creating misleading incremental cost-effectiveness ratios (ICERs) [29] (see Chap. 5). In this regard, a review of how productivity costs measured in economic evaluations of depressive disorders affected the ICER found that 60% of total costs for depression treatment were due to productivity costs, and the inclusion of such costs in the economic evaluation affected the ICER in both directions [29].

25.4 Conclusion

A substantial body of evidence shows that mental disorders disrupt well-being, causing substantial negative externalities for society as a whole. The economic burden of mental disorders hinders development at different levels and should be targeted by global priority policies, such as those recommended by SDGs. One of the main principles of Health Economics is to maximize health and well-being, and in this regard, different aspects of mental health should be broadly measured and maximized. Similarly, the effects of mental health interventions to reduce its burden should be analyzed for all aspects of mental health and not only target clinical outcomes. Studies show evidence of the cost-effectiveness of many psychiatric and mental health treatments, but a lack of awareness of their benefits to patients and to society still exists. The costs of mental disorders overcome treatment costs.

Key Messages

- Happiness and well-being are proven to be strong components of economic development and conditions of human life.
- Mental disorders are the leading factor hindering happiness and well-being, causing a huge cost to society.
- Mental disorders are related to other non-health SDGs, as people with mental disorders are more vulnerable to experiencing poverty, discrimination, inequality, violence, low education, unemployment, and social exclusion.
- Cost-effective treatments are available to reduce the burden of mental disorders and disability, and indirect costs.
- Economic evaluations should take into account burden and the social dimensions of mental disorders when assessing the value of investments in mental health.

Reference

1. Read D. Utility theory from Jeremy Bentham to Daniel Kahneman. Working paper No: LSEOR 04–64. London: London School of Economics and Political Science; 2004. 28 Jan 2016.
2. Heliwell J, Layard R, Sachs J. The world happiness report. New York: Sustainable Development Solutions Network; 2013.

3. OECD. OECD guidelines on measuring subjective wellbeing. Paris: OECD Publishing; 2013.
4. Patel V, Chisholm D, Parikh R, Charlson FJ, Degenhardt L, Dua T, et al. Global priorities for addressing the Burden of mental, neurological, and substance use disorders. In: Patel, V et al (eds). Mental, Neurological, and Substance Use Disorders: Disease Control Priorities, Third Edition (Volume 4).Washington (DC): The International Bank for Reconstruction and Development / The World Bank, DOI:10.1596/978-1-4648-0426-7_ch1 2016.
5. Thornicroft G, Deb T, Henderson C. Community mental health care worldwide: current status and further developments. World Psychiatry. 2016;15(3):276–86.
6. Trautmann S, Rehm J, Wittchen HU. The economic costs of mental disorders: do our societies react appropriately to the burden of mental disorders? EMBO Rep. 2016;17(9):1245–9.
7. Whiteford HA, Ferrari AJ, Degenhardt L, Feigin V, Vos T. The global burden of mental, neurological and substance use disorders: an analysis from the global burden of disease study 2010. PLoS One. 2015;10(2):e0116820.
8. OECD. Making mental health count:the social and economic costs of neglecting mental health care. OECD Health Policies Studies, OECD Publishing; Paris, 2014.
9. World Health Organization. The World Health Report 2001 Mental health: new understanding, new hope. World Health Organization: Geneve; 2001.
10. Thornicroft G, Votruba N. Does the United Nations care about mental health? Lancet Psychiatry. 2016;3(7):599–600.
11. Eaton J, McCay L, Semrau M, Chatterjee S, Baingana F, Araya R, et al. Scale up of services for mental health in low-income and middle-income countries. Lancet. 2011;378(9802):1592–603.
12. Levin C, Chisholm D. Cost-effectiveness and affordability of interventions, policies, and platforms for the prevention and treatment of mental, neurological, and substance use disorders. Mental, neurological, and substance use disorders: disease control priorities, 3rd ed. Volume 4 [Internet]. The International Bank for Reconstruction and Development/The World Bank; 2016 [Cited 14 Nov 2016]. Available from: http://www.ncbi.nlm.nih.gov/pubmed/27227237. In: Patel V, Chisholm D, ua T, editors. Mental, neurological, and substance use disorders: disease control priorities, Third Edition volume 4.Washington, DC: The International Bank for Reconstruction and Development/The World Bank; 2016. p. 219–36.
13. Chong HY, Teoh SL, Wu DB, Kotirum S, Chiou CF, Chaiyakunapruk N. Global economic burden of schizophrenia: a systematic review. Neuropsychiatr Dis Treat. 2016;12:357–73.
14. WHO. The European observatory on health systems and policies. Health systems, health, wealth and societal well-being assessing the case for investing in health systems. Open University Press; Glasgow, 2015.
15. World Health Organization. Making choices in health: the WHO guide to cost-effectiveness analysis. WHO Publications. World Health Organization; Geneva, 2003.
16. Weehuizen R. Mental capital: the economic significance of mental health. University of Maastrich; Maastrich, 2008.
17. Knapp M, McDaid D, Parsonage M. Mental health promotion and mental illness prevention: the economic case. London: Department of Health, London; 2011.
18. Wong E, ollins R, Erully J. Reviewing the evidence base for mental health first aid. 2015. www.rand.org/content/dam/rand/pubs/research_reports/RR900/.../RAND_RR972.pdf. Rand Corporation; 2015.
19. Chisholm D, Sweeny K, Sheehan P, Rasmussen B, Smit F, Cuijpers P, et al. Scaling-up treatment of depression and anxiety: a global return on investment analysis. Lancet Psychiatry. 2016;3(5):415–24.
20. World Health Organization, Calouste Gulbenkian Foundation. Social determinants of mental health. Geneva: World Health Organization; 2014.
21. Razzouk D. Why should Brazil give priority to depression treatment in health resource allocation? Epidemiologia e Serviços de Saude. 2016;25(4):845–8.
22. United Nations. Transforming our world: the 2030 Agenda for sustainable development. United Nations; 2015. Report No: A/RES/70/1.
23. Knapp M. Hidden costs of mental illness. Br J Psychiatry. 2003;183:477–8.
24. Knapp M, Ilson S. Economic aspects of depression and its treatment. Curr Opin Psychiatry. 2002;15: 69–75.
25. Mihalopoulos C, Chatterton ML. Economic evaluations of interventions designed to prevent mental disorders: a systematic review. Early Interv Psychiatry. 2015;9:85–92.
26. Bloom D, Cafiero E, Jane-Llopis E, Abrahams-Gessel S, Fathima S. The global economic Burden of Non-communicable disease. World Economic Forum; Geneva, 2011.
27. McGorry P. Prevention, innovation and implementation science in mental health: the next wave of reform. Br J Psychiatry Suppl. 2013;54:s3–4.
28. Lund C, Myer L, Stein DJ, Williams DR, Flisher AJ. Mental illness and lost income among adult south Africans. Soc Psychiatry Psychiatr Epidemiol. 2013;48(5):845–51.
29. Krol M, Papenburg J, Koopmanschap M, Brouwer W. Do productivity costs matter?: the impact of including productivity costs on the incremental costs of interventions targeted at depressive disorders. PharmacoEconomics. 2011;29(7):601–19.
30. Patel V, Kleinman A. Poverty and common mental disorders in developing countries. Bull World Health Organ. 2003;81:609–15.
31. WHO. Mental health and development: targeting people with mental health conditions as a vulnerable group. Geneva: WHO; 2010.

32. Rosenheck R. Cost-effectiveness of services for mentally ill homeless people: the application of research to policy and practice. Am J Psychiatry. 2000;157(10):1563–70.
33. Bonin P, Fournier L, Lais R. Predictors of mental health service utilization by people using resources for homeless people in Canada. Psychiatr Serv. 2007;58(7):936–41.
34. Ettner S, ., Frank R, Essler R. The impact of psychiatric disorders on labour market outcomes. Ind Labor Relat Rev 1997;51:64–81.
35. Marcotte D, Wilcox-Gok V. Estimating earnings losses due to mental illness: a quantile regression approach. J Ment Health Policy Econ. 2003;6:123–34.
36. Kessler RC, Heeringa S, Lakoma MD, Petukhova M, Rupp AE, Schoenbaum M, et al. Individual and societal effects of mental disorders on earnings in the United States: results from the national comorbidity survey replication. Am J Psychiatry. 2008;165(6):703–11.
37. Dewa CS, McDaid D, Ettner SL. An international perspective on worker mental health problems: who bears the burden and how are costs addressed? Can J Psychiatr. 2007;52(6):346–56.
38. Marwaha S, Johnson S. Schizophrenia and employment – a review. Soc Psychiatry Psychiatr Epidemiol. 2004;39(5):337–49.
39. Thornicroft G, Tansella M, Becker T, Knapp M, Leese M, Schene A, et al. The personal impact of schizophrenia in Europe. Schizophr Res. 2004;69(2–3):125–32.
40. Waghorn G, Chant D, Jaeger J. Employment functioning and disability among community residents with bipolar affective disorder: results from an Australian community survey. Bipolar Disord. 2007;9(1–2):166–82.
41. Strejilevich S, Correa E. Cost and challenges of bipolar disorders: focus in South America region. J Affect Disord 2007;98:165–167.
42. Jenkins R, Bhugra D, Bebbington P, Brugha T, Farrell M, Coid J, et al. Debt, income and mental disorder in the general population. Psychol Med. 2008;38(10):1485–93.
43. Whooley MA, Kiefe CI, Chesney MA, Markovitz JH, Matthews K, Hulley SB. Depressive symptoms, unemployment, and loss of income: the CARDIA study. Arch Intern Med. 2002;162(22):2614–20.
44. Tarricone R, Gerzeli S, Montanelli R, Frattura L, Percudani M, Racagni G. Direct and indirect costs of schizophrenia in community psychiatric services in Italy. The GISIES study. Interdisciplinary study group on the economic impact of schizophrenia. Health Policy. 2000;51(1):1–18.
45. Allegri RF, Butman J, Arizaga R, Machnicki G, Serrano C, Taragano F, et al. Economic impact of dementia in developing countries: an evaluation of costs of Alzheimer-type dementia in Argentina. Int Psychogeriatr. 2007;19(4):705–18.
46. Dias A, Samuel R, Patel V, Prince M, Parameshwaran R, Krishnamoorthy ES. The impact associated with caring for a person with dementia: a report from the 10/66 dementia research Group's Indian network. Int J Geriatr Psychiatry. 2004;19(2):182–4.
47. Cavallo MC, Fattore G. The economic and social burden of Alzheimer disease on families in the Lombardy region of Italy. Alzheimer Dis Assoc Disord. 1997;11(4):184–90.
48. Barroso SM, Bandeira M, Nascimento E. Sobrecarga de familiares de pacientes psiquiátricos atendidos na rede pública. [burden in family caregivers of psychiatric patients attending public services]. Rev psiquiatr clín. 2007;34(6):270–7.
49. Schofield DJ, Shrestha RN, Percival R, Passey ME, Callander EJ, Kelly SJ. The personal and national costs of mental health conditions: impacts on income, taxes, government support payments due to lost labour force participation. BMC Psychiatry. 2011;11:72.
50. Chisholm D, Diehr P, Knapp M, Patrick D, Treglia M, Simon G. Depression status, medical comorbidity and resource costs. Evidence from an international study of major depression in primary care (LIDO). Br J Psychiatry. 2003;183:121–31.
51. Stewart WF, Ricci JA, Chee E, Hahn SR, Morganstein D. Cost of lost productive work time among US workers with depression. JAMA. 2003;289(23):3135–44.
52. Wang PS, Aguilar-Gaxiola S, Alonso J, Angermeyer MC, Borges G, Bromet EJ, et al. Use of mental health services for anxiety, mood, and substance disorders in 17 countries in the WHO world mental health surveys. Lancet. 2007;370(9590):841–50.
53. Greenberg PE, Kessler RC, Birnbaum HG, Leong SA, Berglund PA, Corey-Leslie P. The economic burden of depression in the United States: how did it change between 1990 and 2000? J Clin Psychiatry. 2003;64:1465–75.
54. Adler DA, McLaughlin TJ, Rogers WH, Chang H, Lapitsky L, Lerner D. Job performance deficits due to depression. Am J Psychiatry. 2006;163(9):1569–76.
55. Muralli V, Oyebode F. Poverty, social inequality and mental health. Adv Psychiatr Treat. 2004;10:216–24.
56. Amaddeo F, Jones J. What is the impact of socio-economic inequalities on the use of mental health services? Epidemiol Psichiatr Soc. 2007;16(1):16–9.
57. Thornicroft G, Rose D, Mehta N. Discrimination against people with mental illness: what can psychiatrists do?†. Adv Psychiatr Treat. 2010;16:53–9.
58. Wahlbeck K, McDaid D. Actions to alleviate the mental health impact of the economic crisis. World Psychiatry. 2012;11(3):139–45.
59. Meltzer H, Corbin T, Gatward R, Goodman R. Persistence, onset, risk factors and outcomes of childhood mental disorders. Available: http://www.nationalstatistics.org.uk/downloads/theme_health/PMA-ChildPersist.pdf. London: Division of the Office for National Statistics; 2003.
60. Fuller R, Nopoulos P, Arndt S, O'Leary D, Ho BC, Andreasen NC. Longitudinal assessment of premorbid cognitive functioning in patients with schizophrenia through examination of standardized scholastic test performance. Am J Psychiatry. 2002;159(7):1183–9.

61. Cannon M, Jones P, Huttunen MO, Tanskanen A, Huttunen T, Rabe-Hesketh S, et al. School performance in Finnish children and later development of schizophrenia: a population-based longitudinal study. Arch Gen Psychiatry. 1999;56(5):457–63.
62. Hollis C. Adult outcomes of child- and adolescent-onset schizophrenia: diagnostic stability and predictive validity. Am J Psychiatry. 2000;157(10):1652–9.
63. Hanssens L, LItalian G, Pugner K. Assessment of sociodemographic characteristics including employment, income and usual residence of European patients with schizophrenia: results from the star study. Eur Psychiatry. 2007;22(suppl):S101–220.
64. Jarbin H, Ott Y, von Knorring AL. Adult outcome of social function in adolescent-onset schizophrenia and affective psychosis. J Am Acad Child Adolesc Psychiatry. 2003;42(2):176–83.
65. Bolis M, PAHO/WHO. The impact of the caracas declaration on the modernization of mental health legislation in Latin America and the English-speaking Caribbean. 2002 Jul 9. Amsterdam: PAHO/WHO; 2002 p. 1–19.
66. Thornicroft G, Alem A, Antunes Dos Santos R, Barley E, Drake RE, Gregorio G, et al. WPA guidance on steps, obstacles and mistakes to avoid in the implementation of community mental health care. World Psychiatry. 2010;9(2):67–77.
67. Bonney S, Stickley T. Recovery and mental health: a review of the British literature. J Psychiatr Ment Health Nurs. 2008;15(2):140–53.
68. Cesur R, Sabia J, Tekin E. The psychological costs of war: military combat and mental health. J Health Econ. 2013;32(1):51–65.
69. World Health Organization, United Nations High Commissioner. mhGAP humanitarian intervention guide (mhGAP-HIG): clinical management of mental, neurological and substance use conditions in humanitarian emergencies. Geneva: WHO; 2015.
70. Patel V, Chisholm D, Parikh R, Charlson FJ, Degenhardt L, Dua T, et al. Addressing the burden of mental, neurological, and substance use disorders: key messages from disease control priorities, 3rd edition. Lancet. 2016;387(10028):1672–85.
71. Chisholm D, Flisher AJ, Lund C, Patel V, Saxena S, Thornicroft G, et al. Scale up services for mental disorders: a call for action. Lancet. 2007;370(9594):1241–52.
72. Chisholm D. Choosing cost-effective interventions in psychiatry: results from the CHOICE programme of the World Health Organization. World Psychiatry. 2005;4(1):37–44.
73. Chisholm D, Doran C, Shibuya K, Rehm J. Comparative cost-effectiveness of policy instruments for reducing the global burden of alcohol, tobacco and illicit drug use. Drug Alcohol Rev. 2006;25(6):553–65.

Indirect Costs and the Burden of Alcohol- and Drug-Related Problems

26

Edilaine Moraes and Paula Becker

Abstract

The aim of this chapter is to provide an overview of the economic impact of alcohol- and drug-related problems in different sectors of society, describing their indirect costs (violence, criminality, accidents, workplace, education, early exposure, social benefits, early retirement, and mortality) to society. The burden of disease is described, highlighting the importance of the indirect effects of drug abuse in its measurement. Then, the main components of indirect costs in the context of drug abuse and dependence are discussed.

Key Points Summary

- Indirect costs in alcohol- and drug-related disorders
- Burden of alcohol- and drug-related disorders
- Components of indirect costs analysis in substance-related disorders

E. Moraes (✉)
Alcohol and Other Drugs Research Unit, Universidade Federal de São Paulo (UNIAD/UNIFESP), Rua Borges Lagoa 570, 1° andar, São Paulo 04038-000, Brazil
e-mail: edilaine.moraes@mecapsico.com.br

P. Becker
Centre of Economics Mental health (CESM), Department of Psychiatry, Universidade Federal de São Paulo – Unifesp, Rua Borges Lagoa 570, 1° andar, São Paulo 04038-0001, Brazil
e-mail: pbecker259@gmail.com

26.1 Introduction

A cost analysis is structured according to the main research question and to the choice of the study perspective, which can be based on either the subjects' perspective, a payer/manager/health system perspective, or a societal perspective (see Chaps. 1 and 2). When considering the costs of substance-related disorders from a societal perspective, notice that the impact of this condition goes beyond issues of users' physical health by indirectly affecting individuals' other areas of functioning, beyond their community and families. These indirect effects carry important costs that significantly contributing to the burden of disease.

Nevertheless, one key item should be considered when discussing the definition and classification of indirect costs on health economics, especially regarding drug and alcohol abuse and dependence. Two main components of classifica-

D. Razzouk (ed.), *Mental Health Economics*, DOI 10.1007/978-3-319-55266-8_26

tion exist in indirect costs, which is defined by the study perspective and objectives. Indirect costs are usually measured using a societal perspective, mainly in cost-benefit analysis (see Chap. 4), although it can be measured in some economic evaluations such as cost-effectiveness studies (see Chap. 5).

One simple thinking exercise may help us to understand the indirect effects of alcohol- and drug-related disorders for society: think about the insecurity we feel when moving through places with a high level of criminality, or consider the significant number of short- and long-term absence from work caused by alcohol and other substance abuse or the number of workplace accidents caused by acute intoxication (see Chap. 28). We can also think about early retirements, disarranged families, contamination by infectious diseases such as HIV and hepatitis C among injection drug users, the school dropout rate among children and adolescents who start using drugs at an early age, the overload on the judiciary system when examining cases of drugs trafficking and related crimes, and the enormous number of traffic accidents and deaths. These are some examples of the indirect costs of substance-related disorders, which contribute significantly to the burden of this disease.

To get an idea of the substantial impact of indirect costs of substance-related disorders, a study of the burden of opioid poisoning conducted in the United States in 2009 estimated total costs at approximately US$20.4 billion, with indirect costs comprising 89% of the total costs [1]. In that study, the elements considered as indirect costs were productivity losses due to absenteeism and opioid-related poisoning mortality, whereas direct costs included medical costs (e.g., hospital stays, emergency visits, and medications) and nonmedical costs (e.g., transportation).

Indirect costs play a main role in economic evaluations of alcohol- and drug-related disorders, and should be identified and analyzed in studies which investigating pragmatic issues.

26.1.1 Burden of Alcohol- and Substance-Related Disorders

The burden of disease analysis is an important input in health decision-making and planning processes in that it offers information about risk factors for disease, premature death, and loss of health and disability.

The World Health Organization estimates the burden of a disease by calculating disability-adjusted life years (DALYs), years of life lost (YLLs) to premature mortality, and years lived with disability (YLDs). In 2010 mental and substance use disorders accounted for 183.9 million DALYs (95% UI (uncertainty interval) 153.5 million to 216.7 million), or 7.4% (6.2–8.6%) of all DALYs worldwide; and 8.6 million YLLs (0.5% of all YLLs) and 175.3 million YLDs (22.9% of all YLDs) worldwide [2].

From the 7.4% of DALYs attributed to mental and substance use disorders (SUDs), illicit drug use disorders accounted for 10.9% (8.9–13.2%) and alcohol use disorders, for 9.6% (7.7–11.8%) [2]. Approximately 21.5 million people aged 12 yeas or older in 2014 had an SUD in the past year, including 17.0 million people with alcohol use disorders, 7.1 million with illicit drug use disorders, and 2.6 million who had both an alcohol use and illicit drug use disorder [3].

Alcohol and drug abuse affect both the individual and society through its adverse effects on health and welfare. It has a highly significant burden worldwide, especially because of its indirect costs through absences from work by and premature deaths of users and third parties, as in car accidents, which are the ninth leading cause of death worldwide [4].

Alcohol- and drug-related disorders have an enormous burden for society mainly because of indirect costs. Thus, studies developed to provide a foundation for decision making, especially regarding allocation of public resources, should meticulously detail the components of costs included in their analysis, describing whether the economic evaluation, such as cost-effectiveness or cost-benefit, or the cost study embraces only direct or indirect costs of the disease.

26.2 Components of Indirect Costs of Alcohol- and Drug-Related Disorders

26.2.1 Traffic Accidents

Alcohol and other psychoactive substances reduce attention and concentration, and increase impulsiveness and aggressiveness, among other effects, by altering motor and sensory perception. The consumption of alcohol and other substances by drivers and pedestrians considerably increases the number of traffic accidents.

Driving after consuming these substances is the focus of significant concern worldwide, which is not limited to public authorities but is also shared with society, which suffers countless tangible and intangible losses and damages.

Approximately 25–50% of lethal traffic accidents worldwide are associated with the use of alcohol by at least one of the liable parties [5]. Overall, traffic accidents represent the tenth most frequent cause of mortality and the ninth most frequent cause of morbidity worldwide. Annually, 1.2 million deaths and 20–50 million injuries are caused by traffic accidents [6]. In Brazil, an average of 6.3 accidents occurs for every 10,000 registered vehicles. Most of the related fatalities (78.6%) occur among men, with 27% aged between 18 and 29 years [7].

A study performed in five Brazilian cities (Diadema, Belo Horizonte, Santos, Vitória, and São Paulo) found high rates (19.4%, 19.6%, 18.9%, 17.9%, and 20.0%, respectively) of drivers with blood alcohol concentrations higher than the legal limit (0.6 g/L) when the study was conducted [8]. Data from the World Health Organization indicate that 500,000 individuals are injured and 17,000 die every year in traffic accidents related to drinking and driving in the United States alone [9].

A study performed at a trauma center in the city of São Paulo showed that 28.9% of trauma victims had alcohol in their blood [10]. Another study conducted in four Brazilian cities (Brasília, Curitiba, Recife, and Salvador) found similar results: 27.2% of the victims of traffic accidents exhibited blood alcohol concentrations above 0.6 g/L [11]. Considering only the direct victims of traffic accidents, the estimated social costs resulting from the sum of material damages, medical and hospital expenses, and loss of productivity are notably high and generate a heavy socioeconomic burden [12]. However, in addition to the immediate victims, many other individuals are affected by the consequences of drinking and driving, such as the relatives of those victims. The fact that human lives are involved cannot be overlooked. In particular, the lives of the immediate and indirect victims are severely affected by traffic accidents.

In the United States, the total estimated expense incurred by victims of traffic accidents was US$230.6 billion in 2000. Of that total, 22% (US$51.1 billion) was directly related to drinking and driving [9]. In the European Union, the estimated annual (direct and indirect) expenses due to traffic accidents are greater than US$207 billion [13].

Although we are unable to directly compare estimates, we know that the costs are also considerable in developing countries. Traffic accidents associated with drinking and driving comprise 31% of nonfatal accidents in South Africa, with an estimated cost to the healthcare system of US$14 million. In Thailand, the cost of traffic accidents is as high as US$3 billion. Of that total, 30% (US$1 billion) is associated with the consumption of alcohol [9].

In 2008, a study was performed in the city of Porto Alegre, in the Brazilian state of Rio Grande do Sul, regarding the cost of traffic accidents associated with the use of alcohol. The cost of these accidents was R$31.4 million, which corresponds to 47.3% of the cost of all traffic accidents (R$66.4 million). To better understand these data, the authors distinguished between direct (23.8%) and indirect (76.2%) costs, with the former including medical expenses (6.5%) and the costs of other services, such as tow trucks to remove the vehicles, property damage, and rescue services (17.2%). The indirect costs, which included the loss of productivity due to premature death and morbidity-related disabilities, corresponded to 76.2% of the total costs [14].

The Brazilian Institute of Applied Economic Research (Instituto de Pesquisa Econômica Aplicada) analyzed the costs of accidents in urban areas and found a total cost of R$5.3 billion, or 0.4% of the gross domestic product. Of this total, 13.3% was due to medical expenses, 28.8% was due to repairing damaged vehicles, and 42.8% was related to the loss of productivity due to premature death or temporary disability of the victims [15].

Another study in Brazil evaluated the social cost of drinking and driving in the city of São Paulo and found that the annual cost of drinking and driving in this city was more than R$283 million, corresponding to 40% of all costs for traffic accidents in São Paulo in the same year [16].

As we can see, the burden of drinking and driving can be analyzed from two distinct perspectives. If a study of alcohol abuse adopts a societal perspective, all these previously mentioned costs referred could be classified as indirect costs of disease. However, if the study analyzes only the problem of drinking and driving, considering a smaller scenario and using a different perspective, such as the city's secretary of traffic and transport, the total costs involved may be classified as other kinds of direct and indirect cost categories.

26.2.2 Violence and Criminality

According to the World Health Organization [17] a high level of violence is a major public health problem. Alcohol- and drug-related disorders play a major role on these rates worldwide, and embrace, for instance, domestic violence against women, in which the aggressor usually is dependent on or an abuser of some psychoactive substance(s).

Another important fact to be considered is that the age at first use of drugs, weather legal or illegal, is correlated with the age at onset of criminality. Consequently, this risk increases when youths leaves to attend school.

Therefore, it is important to society, as well as to decision-makers, to know more about this problem and how it affects the economy and public resource allocation. Joint work by criminal, justice, and health services, with more interaction, could possibly play a larger role in reducing the indirect costs related to alcohol and substance use disorders.

In the state of Washington in the United States, the cost of substance abuse in 2012 was estimated at about US$6 billion, of which $2 billion was associated with mortality and $1 billion with crime. A total of 3224 deaths were also reported – equivalent to 7% of all deaths in that year [18].

A survey in the United States has estimated a cost of US$88.9 billion related to the application of drug laws and their effects on criminal behavior. This amount was equivalent to 62% of the annual social costs in the country. Assessing only the costs related to alcohol abuse, a cost of US$36.5 billion was estimated to be related to premature death and US$10.1 billion with crime [19].

In the city of Curitiba, Brazil, a study of the social impact of drug use using 350 participants from a rehabilitation center for drug dependence found that 20.6% of the total sample had committed some kind of criminal offense, of which 49% were related to thefts and 13% to drug trafficking. Another relevant fact was related to the practice of violence among them, which reached 26.6% (63% were verbally aggressive and 37% were physically aggressive) [20].

Based on these data, when it comes to the theme of alcohol and drug abuse, violence and criminality may be intrinsic related and must be considered in a cost analysis from a societal perspective as an indirect cost of disease because of its enormous burden to society. Data collection can be a challenge for researchers, especially in the absence of a good database regarding prevalence and incidence, in addition to the costs for the system, but should not be overlooked.

26.2.3 Social Benefits and Retirement

Alcohol- and drug-related disorders are a prevalent mental disorder in a labor context, and they affect workers' performance and security through both the use that occurs before work or during the journey to work (see Chap. 28). The effect of these substances can damage either the workers or third parties. Many of these losses entail temporary or permanent leave from work, reduced workload, relocation tasks, and others, generating a high burden for society when considering the productivity losses and the intangible costs related to workers' quality of life and lives lost.

26.2.4 Mortality

Mortality and premature mortality are the most common component of indirect costs applied in cost studies regarding alcohol- and drug-related disorders [21] because of their high incidence among addicts.

In 2010, mental and substance use disorders were directly responsible for 8.6 million YLLs (95% UI 6.5 million–12.1 million), equivalent to 232,000 deaths. Almost all of these deaths were attributable to substance use disorders (81.1% [95% UI 74.8–87.3]) [2].

It is estimated that the total mortality costs of opioid users in the United States is US$18 billion/year, with US$4.1 billion attributed to heroin and US$13.9 18 billion to prescription opioid. Oxycodone, methadone, and hydrocodone were estimated to have the highest total mortality cost: US$6.4 billion, US$4.9 billion, and US$3.2 billion, respectively [1].

It has been established that consumption of alcohol has a causal relation with several disease conditions leading to increased rates of morbidity and mortality. It is estimated that more than 2 million deaths worldwide were attributed to alcohol consumption in 2002 [22]. A literature review showed that alcohol consumption cost studies from a societal perspective have considered as indirect costs productivity loss due to premature mortality, morbidity, absenteeism, reduced activity, early retirement, and temporary disability [22].

Another literature review also found that mortality reaches higher levels than morbidity in France, Germany, Switzerland, and Scotland [23], which is impressive data considering that alcohol consumption may lead to the development of numerous chronic diseases, such as hypertension, diabetes, liver disease, psychiatric comorbidities such as depression and anxiety disorders, among others [24]. In Australia, Canada, Italy, Japan, the United Kingdom, the United States, and other countries, this scenario is inverted: morbidity reaches higher levels than mortality. Among all these losses, premature mortality plays the largest role in contributing to the total indirect costs in half of the studies found in this review.

The literature suggests that opioid- and alcohol-related disorders are the leading cause of mortality worldwide when compared with the use and abuse of other drugs. Injection drug users are at the higher risk of dying from both acute and chronic diseases and fatal overdose. Infection with human immunodeficiency virus and other blood-borne viruses transmitted through shared needles and syringes, such as hepatitis C, are the most common causes of deaths in this population [25].

26.2.5 Early Use in Childhood and Adolescence

The impact of early use of alcohol and other drugs in childhood and adolescence has been widely investigated because of its influence on the behavioral development of this population. This aspect can be considered as one of the major indirect impacts and costs of substance-related disorders. The causal association between early exposure to illicit drugs and alcohol, particularly before 15 years old, and substance disorder in adulthood is well demonstrated in the literature [26–28].

Cognitive deficits resulting from early exposure to drugs in childhood or adolescence have potentially harmful implications for subsequent academic, occupational, and social functioning extending into adulthood [27], which implies some important indirect costs in microeconomic scenarios (financial autonomy and family dynamics) and macroeconomic scenarios (a country's economy).

In general, early exposure to these substances has also been linked to risky sexual behavior and sexually transmitted diseases, low educational attainment, and crime [26], which overload public health, social, and security budgets. Regarding early exposure to alcohol consumption, age at initiation and chronic use are associated with several negative outcomes for young adults, including a high frequency of alcohol use, alcohol-related problems, aggressive behavioral, robbery, and suicidal ideation [28]. When it comes to the early use of illicit drugs such as cannabis and cocaine, both age at initiation and chronic use predict substance use disorders and mental illness in young adults [27]. In summary, early exposure to alcohol and other drugs during childhood and adolescence can lead to academic, social, and emotional problems, together with high-risk behaviors that impair adaptive psychosocial development. There is also an additional risk of developing comorbidities such as human immunodeficiency virus and hepatitis C [29] and mental disorders.

One main point that has not yet been clarified that has promoted a recent debate among researchers: some allege that early exposure to alcohol and drugs per se is not the cause of problems in adolescents' later lives because new data have shown that adolescents at risk for developing substance use disorders are not "normal" adolescents; they usually have other problems such as family and social issues [26, 30]. Armstrong and Costello [30] stated in a literature review study that 60% of youths with substance use, abuse, or dependence had a comorbid diagnosis. Conduct disorder and oppositional defiant disorder (not attention deficit/hyperactivity disorder) were the most commonly associated with substance use, abuse, or dependence, followed by depression [30].

Odgers et al. [26], in a 30-year prospective study, found that adolescents exposed early (prior to age 15) were two or three times more likely to be substance dependent, to have herpes infection, to have had an early pregnancy, and to have failed to obtain professional qualifications than adolescents not exposed early. However, the authors also found very interesting data showing that early substance exposure was not a random event: adolescents with a history of misconduct were two times more likely to be exposed to illicit substances before age 15 when compared with adolescents without a history of misconduct.

In other words, we cannot be certain of what makes a child or adolescent start using alcohol and other drugs, but we can say that early exposure brings into adulthood some important consequences that will culminate in substantial indirect costs that deserve to be considered by public policymakers in the decision-making process.

26.3 Considerations About Indirect Costs

Indirect costs are usually measured in cost analyses and burden studies or in economic evaluations such as cost-benefit analyses and in fewer studies using cot-effectiveness analysis.

The definition of an indirect cost depends on the choice of the study perspective and objectives. For instance, a cost study conducted by Jarl et al. [31] in 2007 aimed to estimate the societal costs of alcohol consumption in Sweden and considered the direct, indirect, and intangible costs involved, defining indirect costs as absence from work (short- and long-term), early retirement, mortality, and lost productivity resulting from incarceration. With the analysis of those aspects, the study could determine the range of effects of alcohol consumption in a Swedish community. One review showed that the majority of previous studies of societal costs of alcohol consumption have used a human capital approach, estimated the gross cost of alcohol consumption, and adopted a societal perspective, taking into account both direct and indirect costs in many different ways [23]. The indirect cost components described in this chapter were DALYs, YLLs to premature mortality, reduced productivity, incarceration, job loss, and the time lost by victims.

Key Messages

- Indirect costs constitute almost 90% of the total costs of substance-related disorders from a societal perspective.
- The indirect cost components usually considered in substance-related disorders are DALYs, YLLs to premature mortality, mortality, reduced productivity, incarceration, job losses, criminality, and absenteeism.

(continued)

(continued)

- Early exposure to alcohol and other drugs in childhood or adolescence negatively affects health-related and emotional and psychosocial outcomes in adulthood, and is a significant contributor to the increase in the indirect costs of substance-related disorders.
- The consumption of alcohol and drugs by drivers and pedestrians greatly increases the number of traffic accidents.
- In most cases of domestic violence, someone dependent on or abusing psychoactive substances is usually present.

References

1. Inocencio TJ, Carroll NV, Read EJ, Holdford DA, Health A. The economic burden of opioid-related poisoning in the United States. Pain Med. 2013;14:1534–47.
2. Whiteford HA, Degenhardt L, Rehm J, Baxter AJ, Ferrari AJ, Erskine HE, et al. Global burden of disease attributable to mental and substance use disorders: findings from the global burden of disease study 2010. Lancet. 2013;382(9904):1575–86.
3. Center for Behavioral Health Statistics and Quality. Behavioral health trends in the United States: results from the 2014 National survey on drug use and health [Internet]. 2015. Available from. http://www.samhsa.gov/data/sites/default/files/NSDUH-FRR1-2014/NSDUH-FRR1-2014.pdf%5Cnhttp://www.samhsa.gov/data/
4. World Health Organization. The top 10 causes of death. WHO – fact sheets on global burden of disease. World Health Organization; 2016.
5. Pinsky I, Laranjeira R. Alcohol in Brazil: recent public health aspects. Addiction. 2004;99:524–7.
6. Associação Brasileira de Medicina de Tráfego. Alcoolemia e Direção Veicular Segura. 2008.
7. DENATRAN. Anuários Estatísticos do DENATRAN [Internet]. Anuário Denatran: acidentes 2005. [Cited 15 Jul 2016]. 2005. p. 46. Available from. http://www.vias-seguras.com/os_acidentes/estatisticas/estatisticas_nacionais/estatisticas_do_denatran/anuarios_estatisticos_do_denatran
8. Oliveira LAC de, Zanelatto R, de Carvalho DG., Andreuccetti G, de Ponde J C, Leyton RPV, et al. Álcool e direção: beber ou dirigir: um guia prÁtico para educadores, profissionais da saúde e gestores de políticas públicas. Editora Fap-Unifesp; 2010. p. 128.
9. Global Road Safety Partnership. Drinking and driving: a road safety manual for decision-makers and practitioners. Geneva; 2007.
10. Gazal-Carvalho C, Carlini-Cotrim B, Silva OA, Sauaia N. Prevalência de alcoolemia em vítimas de causas externas admitidas em centro urbano de atenção ao trauma. Rev Saude Publica [Internet]. Faculdade de Saúde Pública da Universidade de São Paulo. 2002 [Cited 17 Jul 2016];36(1):47–54. Available from. http://www.scielo.br/scielo.php?script=sci_arttext&pid=S0034-89102002000100008&lng=pt&nrm=iso&tlng=pt
11. Galduróz JCF, Caetano R. Epidemiologia do uso de álcool no Brasil. Rev Bras Psiquiatr [Internet]. Associação Brasileira de Psiquiatria (ABP). 2004 [Cited 17 Jul 2016];26:3–6. Available from. http://www.scielo.br/scielo.php?script=sci_arttext&pid=S1516-44462004000500002&lng=pt&nrm=iso&tlng=pt
12. Shults RA, Eldder RW, Nichols JL, Alao MO, Carande-Kulis VG, Zaza S, Soosin DMTR. Reviews of evidence regarding interventions to reduce alcohol-impaired driving. Am J Prev Med. 2001;21(4):66–88.
13. World Health Organization. Global status report: alcohol policy [Internet]. Department of Mental Health and Substance Abuse. Geneva; 2004. Available from. http://scholar.google.com/scholar?hl=en&btnG=Search&q=intitle:Global+Status+Report+:+Alcohol+Policy#1
14. Pechansky F, Duarte P d CAV, Boni RB. Uso de bebidas alcoólicas e outras drogas nas rodovias brasileiras e outros estudos. 1st ed. Porto Alegre: Secretaria Nacional de Políticas sobre Drogas; 2010. p. 121.
15. Ipea. Impactos sociais e econômicos dos acidentes de trânsito nas aglomerações urbanas brasiliras. 1st ed. Brasília: ANTP; 2003. p. 43.
16. Moraes E, Laranjeira R. Custo Social do " beber e dirigir " na Cidade de São Paulo. São Paulo: Universidade Federal de São Paulo – UNIFESP; 2013.
17. Chalub M, Telles LEB. Alcohol, drugs and crime. Rev Bras Psiquiatr [Internet]. Associação Brasileira de Psiquiatria (ABP). 2006 [Cited 18 Jul 2016];28:s69–73. Available from. http://www.scielo.br/scielo.php?script=sci_arttext&pid=S1516-44462006000600004&lng=en&nrm=iso&tlng=en
18. Wickizer TM. State-level estimates of the economic costs of alcohol and drug abuse. J Health Care Finance [Internet]. 2013 [Cited 28 Jun 2016];39(3):71–84. Available from. http://www.ncbi.nlm.nih.gov/pubmed/23614269
19. Harwood, H. Updating Estimates of the Economic Costs of Alcohol Abuse in the United States: Estimates, Update Methods, and Data. Report prepared by The Lewin Group for the National Institute on Alcohol Abuse and Alcoholism, 2000
20. Capistrano FC, Ferreira ACZ, Maftum MA, Kalinke LP, Mantovani M. de F. Impacto social do uso abusivo de drogas para dependentes químicos registrados em printuários. Cogitare Enferm. 2013;18(3):468–74.

21. Thavorncharoensap M, Teerawattananon Y, Yothasamut J, Lertpitakpong C, Chaikledkaew U. The economic impact of alcohol consumption: a systematic review. Subst Abuse Treat Prev Policy [Internet]. 2009;4:20. Available from. http://www.pubmedcentral.nih.gov/articlerender.fcgi?artid=2791094&tool=pmcentrez&rendertype=abstract
22. Mohapatra S, Patra J, Popova S, Duhig A, Rehm J. Social cost of heavy drinking and alcohol dependence in high-income countries. Int J Public Health. 2010;55(3):149–57.
23. Thavorncharoensap M, Teerawattananon Y, Yothasamut J, Lertpitakpong C, Chaikledkaew U. The economic impact of alcohol consumption: a systematic review. Subst Abuse Treat Prev Policy. 2009;4:20.
24. Nutt DJ, Rehm J, van den Brink W, Gorwood P, Buchsbaum MS. Progress in mind: focus on alcohol use disorders, an Elsevier resource centre. Psychiatry Res [Internet]. Elsevier. 2015;226(2–3):513–4. Available from. http://dx.doi.org/10.1016/j.psychres.2015.01.013
25. Bradley M Mathers, Louisa Degenhardt, Chiara Bucello, James Lemon, Lucas Wiessing MH. Mortality among people who inject drugs: a systematic review and meta-analysis. Bull World Health Organ [Internet]. 2013;91(2):102–23. Available from. http://www.pubmedcentral.nih.gov/articlerender.fcgi?artid=3605003&tool=pmcentrez&rendertype=abstract
26. Odgers CL, Caspi A, Nagin DS, Piquero AR, Slutske WS, Milne BJ, et al. Is it important to prevent early exposure to drugs and alcohol among adolescents? Psychol Sci. 2008;19(10):1037–44.
27. Squeglia LM, Jacobus J, Tapert SF. The influence of substance use on adolescent brain development. Clin EEG Neurosci. 2009;40(1):31–8.
28. Gil AG, Wagner EF, Tubman JG. Associations between early-adolescent substance use and subsequent young-adult substance use disorders and psychiatric disorders among a multiethnic male sample in South Florida. Am J Public Health. 2004;94(9):1603–9.
29. Li J, Gilmour S, Zhang H, Koyanagi A, Shibuya K. The epidemiological impact and cost-effectiveness of HIV testing, antiretroviral treatment and harm reduction programs. AIDS [Internet]. 2012 [Cited 18 Jan 2016];26(16):2069–78. Available from. http://www.ncbi.nlm.nih.gov/pubmed/22781221
30. Armstrong TD, Costello EJ. Community studies on adolescent substance use, abuse, or dependence and psychiatric comorbidity. J Consult ClinPsychol. 2002;70:1224–39.
31. Jarl J, Johansson P, Eriksson A, Eriksson M, Gerdtham UG, Hemström Ö, et al. The societal cost of alcohol consumption: an estimation of the economic and human cost including health effects in Sweden, 2002. Eur J Health Econ. 2008;9(4):351–60.

27 The Economic Impact of Mental Health Stigma

Renee Romeo, Paul McCrone, and Graham Thornicroft

Abstract

Mental illness–related stigma has far-reaching economic effects on many life domains, including housing, religious activities, access to treatment and care, health-seeking behavior, and mortality. Well-designed and coordinated responses to these economic effects will have significant influences on the domains in an individual's life and on their family members and others. Although a paucity of economic research exists in this area to assist decision makers, the evidence base is growing. In this chapter we introduce and describe a framework within which to examine the economic effects of stigma. We also present evidence from research on the effectiveness and cost-effectiveness of interventions to combat stigma and discuss some of the gaps in our knowledge. We also include research-related recommendations, the results of which could feed into plans for commissioning services.

Key Points Summary

- Definition and models of stigma and discrimination
- Behavioral consequences of stigma
- Link between economic analysis and stigma
- Methodological and evaluative issues
- Data collection: cost of stigma and discrimination

R. Romeo (✉) • P. McCrone
King's Health Economics, Health Service and Population Research Department, Institute of Psychiatry, Psychology & Neuroscience, King's College London, Denmark Hill SE58AF, London, UK
e-mail: renee.romeo@kcl.ac.uk; paul.mcrone@kcl.ac.uk

G. Thornicroft
Centre for Global Mental Health, Health Service and Population Research Department, Institute of Psychiatry, Psychology & Neuroscience, King's College London, London, UK
e-mail: graham.thornicroft@kcl.ac.uk

D. Razzouk (ed.), *Mental Health Economics*, DOI 10.1007/978-3-319-55266-8_27

27.1 Introduction

Research on mental health–related stigma and discrimination has increased steadily in the past few decades, although until recently publications have often reported descriptive rather than intervention studies [1–9]. Earlier work also tended to focus more on public attitudes toward people with mental illness rather than to examine the direct experiences of people with these conditions [6, 10–16]

27.1.1 Definitions and Models of Stigma and Discrimination

Several theoretical approaches have been developed in this field of study, including social cognitive models [17–19] that give salience to stereotypes (negative beliefs about a group), prejudice (agreement with stereotyped beliefs and/or negative emotional reactions such as fear or anger), and discrimination (the behavioral consequences of prejudice, such as exclusion from social and economic opportunities) [20]. This approach considers self-stigma to occur when people with mental illness accept or internalize the discrediting beliefs (stereotypes) held against them, agree with these prejudiced beliefs, and lose self-esteem and self-efficacy [21–29]. This may then lead to adverse behavioral consequences, such as not applying for work [19, 30, 31] (see Chap. 30).

By comparison, sociological theories see stigma as a wider societal force affecting both the individual and society as a whole. Using labeling theory to describe how stigma is created, sociological theories are fundamentally based on the idea that the meaning of interpersonal interactions is socially constructed [10], so that stigma has been described as taking place "when elements of labelling, stereotyping, separation, status loss and discrimination co-occur in a power situation that allows the components of stigma to unfold" [11].

In this chapter we use the conceptualization developed by the National Institute for Heath and Care Excellence to assess behavior change at population, community, and individual levels – namely, to assess the knowledge, attitudinal, and behavioral outcomes of interventions intended to reduce stigma and discrimination [32]. In terms of their applicability to mental illness, these domains refer to problems of *knowledge* (ignorance/cognitive domain), problems of *attitudes* (prejudice/affective domain), and problems of *behavior* (discrimination/behavior) [6, 19, 33–336].

27.1.2 Behavioral Consequences of Stigma

The behavioral consequences of stigma (i.e., discrimination) can compound disabilities related to the primary symptoms of mental illness and may lead to disadvantages in many aspects of life, including personal relationships, education, and work [6, 37]. Such discrimination can limit life opportunities through, for example, loss of income, unemployment, and reduced access to housing or health care [10].

In addition to experiences of direct discrimination from others, people with mental illness may be disadvantaged through *structural* or *systemic discrimination*, manifested, for example, in the lesser investment of healthcare resources allocated to the care of people with mental disorders compared with those with physical illnesses [38–41]. Further, people with mental disorders also often experience unequal treatment for physical health conditions, which may contribute to excess morbidity and premature mortality [42–445].

Stigma may manifest within healthcare settings as violations of fundamental human rights [46], including the right to health [47, 48]. Poor quality of care can in turn act as an important barrier to help-seeking by people with mental illness and their family members [49, 50]. For example, people with mental disorders may delay or stop seeking [51] treatment or terminate treatment prematurely out of a fear of labeling and discrimination, or because of experiences that treatments are not effective or respectful [52].

In societies where services are scarce and support systems inadequate, families may feel forced to resort to physical measures (e.g., chaining) to restrain relatives with mental illness in the absence of any locally available or acceptable alternative [53]. Stigma and discrimination also affect family members and caregivers [54]; this has been termed "stigma by association," "affiliate stigma," or "courtesy stigma." This may lead to direct discrimination and feelings of shame and self-blame, much like the internal consequences of mental illness stigma faced by people with mental disorders [55]. In societies where the cohesion of family networks is high, the impact of stigma by association may be more severe and can include economic consequences and can affect work or marital prospects [56, 57].

Although we focus here on mental illness–related stigma, these effects can be applied to any area where attitudes and behaviors discriminate against people for any particular reason. People with tuberculosis, HIV/AIDS, epilepsy, medically unexplained illnesses, or leprosy are some specific relevant examples, as are sex workers. The aim of this chapter is to introduce and describe a framework within which to examine the economic effects of stigma with reference to research. The chapter does not intend to be an introduction to the design of economic research techniques, nor would that be needed in a book of this kind. What is required is an appreciation, on the part of individuals who undertake or use research, that stigma and discrimination have far-reaching, often hidden economic effects, and that these effects should be understood and analyzed, and the responses evaluated.

Box 27.1 Application of Neoclassical Economics to Discrimination

Wright and colleagues [59] apply a neoclassical economics model to understanding the costs of discrimination. The authors argue that individuals engage in activities to maximize their "utility" (alternatively described as "well-being"). Individuals who are prevented in any way from engaging in activities that can improve their well-being incur a "cost" because they are not able to take advantage of activities that may improve their health and well-being. For example, individuals with health or mental health complaints, who delay seeking care because of stigma, could face worse problems in the future, with potentially costly implications for services. Shrivastava et al. [60] note that stigmatizing the experiences of people with mental illness during the course of their illness and treatment influences relapse and treatment nonadherence. Although no cohort studies show direct links between stigma and future care costs, Almond et al. [61] found that individuals with schizophrenia who experienced an illness relapse had costly inpatient care admissions.

27.2 Links Between Economic Analysis and Stigma

Mental illness affects individuals at many levels, and many people with mental health problems become disadvantaged as a result of the stigma related to being labeled as mentally ill. This stigma frequently has major effects on many life domains, including marriage, parenting, housing, religious activities, access to treatment and care, health-seeking behavior, and mortality [58]. However, a number of often substantial economic consequences are often overlooked; these can arise from various sources, some of which can be placed within a neoclassical economics model (see Box 27.1).

27.2.1 Employment

Rates of employment serve as a measure of economic health in populations with a mental illness, as they provide a measure of the opportunity to maximize self-determination, choice, control, independence, and expand social connections and relationships. Factors that can explain the reasons behind the employment rates observed in this population range widely, not least of which are the negative beliefs held by employers and employees alike [62]. A survey of employment rates among people with mental health problems in Italy and the United Kingdom reported rates of 46.5% and 18.4%, respectively, for all diagnoses [63], and another study found an employment rate of 14% for people with schizophrenia [64]. An Irish survey found that one in three employers thought that people with a mental illness were less reliable than other employees, and over 50% of employers thought it was too risky to employ them [65] (see Chaps. 25 and 28).

Nevertheless, people with a mental illness are capable of working in appropriate settings and often want to work [66]. People who are employed have reported feeling socially isolated, having to cope with negative comments and being given fewer responsibilities once their illness becomes known [67, 68]. Wright et al. [59], in a study of 108 individuals with a medical or self-diagnosis of mental illness, found that over two-thirds of participants who had qualifications felt that their lack of success in employment was a result of stigma. Moreover, negative experiences at work for people with a mental illness have not only been shown to worsen mental ill health, but are known to be a risk factor for the onset of common mental health disorders, particularly if the individual has low levels of educational attainment and a low-paying job. Stansfeld and Candy [69] found that a range of factors, including, job strain, low social inputs, high psychological demands, imbalance between effort and reward, and high job insecurity, contributed to an increased risk of common mental disorders. Notably, job insecurity specifically was associated with a 33% higher risk of common mental disorders [69].

The convergence of the effects of employment and mental health stigma can be magnified further for those with a mental illness during times of economic hardship. A study across 27 European Union countries found that people with a mental illness were more vulnerable to unemployment in countries with more stigmatizing views toward mental illness [70]. This link is of considerable relevance in an uncertain economic climate, as finding a new job without appropriate support may pose a challenge.

27.2.2 Income

Evidence cited previously has shown that work-related and macroeconomic conditions have particular effects on the ability of an individual with a mental illness to work (see Chap. 28). Work plays an essential part in our lives and provides an opportunity to receive wages, yet there have been mixed findings from studies exploring associations between income and mental health needs. A systematic review of the literature using meta-analysis of studies of the relationship between socioeconomic status (such as education and income) and depression found 56 studies, with substantial heterogeneity among them [71]. Link [72] analyzed data on community and outpatient samples from the Washington Heights study investigating the relationship between having a psychiatric label and income, and found a negative relationship between psychiatric status and income after controlling for severity of illness.

A notable longitudinal, population-based study that explored temporal relationships between income and mental disorders found that lower household income was associated with an increased likelihood of mood, anxiety, and substance use disorders [73]. An earlier psychiatric epidemiological survey found contrasting evidence of a lack of an association between household income and any mood or anxiety disorder, although individuals with a low income (those in the lowest income quartile) had the most psychological distress when compared with those with higher incomes [74].

Further, when earnings of individuals who reportedly experienced mental illness stigma are compared with those of individuals without a mental illness, evidence suggests that significant wage differences exist [75]. Baldwin and Marcus [76] compared data from 1139 workers with mood, psychotic, or anxiety disorders with data from 66,341 individuals without such disorders and found that for *all* types of mental disorders examined, wages for workers with serious mental illness who reported experiencing stigma were significantly lower than wages for those with no mental illness.

There has been much debate about differences in the occurrence of mental illness in men and women. Intelligence from the World Health Organization suggests that no significant differences exist in the rates of psychiatric disorders for men and women [77]. However, sex differences have been evidenced for certain psychiatric disorders [78, 79] (see Chap. 25). Although epidemiology data from an analysis of 12 large-scale, general population studies conducted across the United Kingdom, United States, Australia, New Zealand, Chile, and South Africa did not find any statistically significant difference between sexes in schizophrenia and attention deficit/hyperactivity disorder, contrasting evidence does exist in other diagnostic areas. Approximately three in four women were more likely than men to report having recently suffered from depression, and around one in six were more likely to report an anxiety disorder [80]. Earlier research by Showalter [81] has argued that women are more likely to be diagnosed with a psychological problem as a result of behaviors that are stigmatized as mental illness.

These findings on sex differences in the occurrence of mental illness are a necessary introduction, as a recently published study provided insight into the links between, mental health, sex, and income. Platt et al. [82], in a survey of over 22,000 adults aged 30–65 years, found that where women's income was less than that of matched male counterparts, the likelihood of having depression and anxiety were significantly higher among women than men. Where women had higher incomes than men, the likelihood of having both disorders remained higher but was significantly lessened.

27.2.3 Service Use and Support

Stigma may be an important factor impeding help-seeking and acting as a barrier to recovery from mental illness. Help-seeking has been used to refer to the initiation of and engagement with care [83] provided by formal and informal services. When help is sought from formal services, individuals may be in contact with statutory primary, secondary, and tertiary health service provision or talking-therapy services. We found literature that suggests that individuals with substance use disorders may hide their misuse of substances to avoid stigma (see Chap. 26), which may result in behaviors that prevent them from seeking professional care and treatment [84, 85]. Stereotypes related to treatment services for substance use, for example, can lower the likelihood that people engage with services [86].

Following from these specific findings on substance misuse, a recent literature review of the more general effect of mental health–related stigma on help-seeking [87] provides a thorough overview of the existing literature, bringing together what is known about this relationship from both quantitative and qualitative studies. The authors of this well-conducted systematic review found that, when measuring the strength of the relationship between different types of stigma and help-seeking, internalized stigma and stigma associated with seeking or received treatment for poor mental health was always negatively associated with help-seeking.

A second notable finding by Clement et al. [87] identified population group moderators in the relationship between stigma and help-seeking. Stigma was observed to have a disproportionate effect on help-seeking among people from Asian, African American, Arabic, other minority ethnic groups, and among youth, men, those in the military, and in health-related occupations. Further, it was noted that people from ethnic minority groups have expressed experiences of stigma whereby prejudice within mental health services, when combined with public, professional, and internalized stigma of mental illness, discourages them from seeking care [88]; as a consequence, the rates of contact with mental health services are likely to be lower in these groups.

In England, for example, Keating and Robertson [89] found that the rates of contact with mental health services were lower in the Afro-Caribbean community compared with the general population. For those in the former group, the care pathway is often characterized by overrepresentation in medium- and high-security facilities [90, 91], hospital admission under a section of the Mental Health Act [92], involvement of the police and administration of medication [93], and inordinate use of Section 136/137 of the Mental Health Act [94]; they also are less likely to receive psychotherapy, psychological treatments, and alternative therapies [89].

27.2.4 Effects of Stigma on Others

Mental health stigma clearly has major economic effects on an individual's employment, income, and help-seeking behavior, which can lead to persistent social and economic disadvantages (see Chaps. 25 and 28). However, a number of often substantial economic consequences for families, who often make up informal means of support for people with mental health needs, are frequently overlooked.

The families of people who experience stigma may take time off work, give up employment, or forego leisure to provide support, or may incur out-of-pocket expenses to subsidize treatment expenses or travel to appointments. To overlook these economic effects would be serious, given that many people with mental health needs rely on their families and friends for support. At a societal level, increases in absenteeism and premature retirement as a result of mental health stigma could potentially lead to productivity loss, although this has not received attention in the literature. Further, although many economic studies provide evidence of the personal and societal costs incurred by the families and friends of those with a mental illness, no studies have estimated these costs where stigma has been reported.

27.3 Methodological and Evaluative Issues

Well-designed and well-coordinated responses to these economic effects will have significant influences on the individual's functioning, well-being, and quality of life, and might also improve the quality of life of caregiving family members and others. The challenge is that there will never be enough resources to cater to all needs or satisfy all wants. This problem of scarcity leads to difficult decisions about how best to improve opportunities and health and quality-of-life outcomes for individuals facing mental health stigma, in turn raising questions that economists are often asked to address.

Four such economic questions have relevance to discussions in mental health stigma:

- What are the costs?
- How do incurred costs compare with savings resulting from successful campaigns or interventions?
- What are the links between resources and the outcomes achieved?
- What incentives could be given to decision makers to encourage them to pursue policies or practices that are effective, efficient, and fair?

27.3.1 Cost Question

The cost question focuses on the resources used to introduce an intervention or provide treatment, care, and support. By identifying the economic effects of stigma, we can usefully translate these effects into money, the universal language of decision makers. Money is a useful metric when emphasizing the scale of the challenge and how costs are shared across sectors. Although focusing on costs is helpful, because they do not consider measures of outcome they cannot be used to evaluate the effect of anti-stigma campaigns and interventions.

27.3.2 Cost-Offset Question

The question of how the costs incurred compare with cost saved by successful campaigns or interventions is effectively a cost-offset question. Although this question ignores the outcomes of an individual experiencing mental health stigma, such as changes in functioning or quality of life, they are quite popular because they directly consider effects on other sectors and can be proxied by measures of service use. For example, for certain population groups, reduced mental health stigma could be measured by an increase in primary and community-based services use and reductions in hospital admissions. As far as we are aware, there exist to date no examples in the Economics literature of the use of cost-offset on mental health stigma.

27.3.3 Cost-Effectiveness Question

The third question – cost-effectiveness – asks about the relationships between the resources used and the outcomes achieved. For competing strategies or interventions (one of which could be doing nothing, as is most likely to be the case in anti-stigma campaigns and interventions), a cost-effectiveness analysis compares the resources used (the costs) by each strategy with health, quality of life, or other outcomes (the effectiveness). If one intervention has both lower costs and greater effectiveness than another, it will seem more attractive to decision makers, although their choice will also consider wider strategic factors. If one intervention results in greater improvements in outcome than another but only at a higher cost, then someone must decide whether those better outcomes are worth the additional money that would be spent.

Interventions can be used in various ways to combat stigma in mental health, for example, anti-stigma campaigns to raise awareness, service-based interventions designed to support people who are employed or seeking work, strategies for addressing social stigma, and training and education programs for changing stigma among medical students and professionals (e.g., psychiatrists, counselors), to name a few. A number of campaigns have been organized by international bodies and at the national level. Some examples include initiatives by the World Psychiatric Association's Global Programme Against Stigma and Discrimination. Because of Schizophrenia [95], Like Minds, Like Mine in New Zealand [96], the See Me campaign in Scotland, and the Time to Change (TTC) program in England.

In the United Kingdom, the See Me campaign and the TTC program provide economic evidence of anti-stigma campaigns. We will look at economic evidence to answer specific policy and practice questions in stigma research in the sections that follow. But first, we will describe a method that can be used to explore the additional cost incurred to obtain an extra unit of benefit from introducing an anti-stigma intervention, starting with an assessment tool that can be used to collect data to estimate costs and, in a subsequent section, the valuation of various services and supports.

27.3.4 Data Collection: The CODA Scale

The Costs of Discrimination Assessment (CODA) project, the first of its kind to develop a scale to measure the financial costs associated with stigma and discrimination, was part of a wider research program on stigma in mental health: the SAPPHIRE Research Programme (http://www.kcl.ac.uk/ioppn/depts/hspr/research/ciemh/cmh/research-projects/sapphire/index.aspx).

The approach used in CODA to develop a schedule to measure the economic effects of mental health–related stigma was based on an understanding of the literature on discrimination and the experiences of services users with mental health needs. The instrument was then further developed using other resource use schedules, such as the Client Service Receipt Inventory (CSRI) [97]. The CSRI collects information about service users' backgrounds and comprehensively gathers information about accommodation and all health-related social care and other services used; through interviews, data on service use can be collected in a way that is commensurate with accurate cost estimation (see Chap. 13).

The CSRI is a well-known and widely used resource use schedule in mental health, and this questionnaire therefore provides a useful starting point for the CODA. However, while the CODA references mental health issues in the schedule, the questions directly refer to discrimination and make it possible for respondents to take into account forms of discrimination other than those related to mental health, such as opportunity losses, which feature prominently for people who experience mental health stigma, for whom losses in welfare are a result of changes in activities.

The CODA interview schedule (http://www.kcl.ac.uk/ioppn/depts/hspr/research/ciemh/cmh/CMH-Stigma-Measures/15CODAfinal7213.pdf) was first piloted across 18 TTC projects from areas (mainly urban, but not inner city) around England. The 108 participants were all aged 18–65 years and disclosed that they had a history of treatment for mental health problems. The test-retest reliability of the CODA was assess in a subsample of 16 participants who were reinterviewed 2 weeks after the initial interview [59].

The schedule takes approximately 5 min during an interview if the interviewee is not employed, and 10 min if they are employed. Information is collected retrospectively regarding contact with formal statutory services, informal support and leisure services, and employment and income in a way that facilitates the estimation of costs. These areas are covered in five sections.

The first section of the CODA records the individual's experiences with employment, recording, for example, their current employment status; income from salary, benefits, pension, and money provided by friends and family; and experiences of stigma for those who have applied for a job and those who are in paid employment. This section establishes the effect of mental health discrimination on employment opportunities and experience in work from the perspective of individuals with mental health needs. Changes in income status (including benefits) over time may also be important, as they may reflect changes in the individual's employment status, changes to the regulations on entitlement, and changes in perceptions.

The second section of the CODA covers discrimination in financial institutions or housing. Here the individual is invited to describe their experiences with mortgage services, insurance providers, driver and vehicle licensing agencies, housing, and other financial institutions.

The third section considers receipt or avoidance of services and is one of the areas that can take up the majority of time because of the variety of services available to people with mental health needs. Also, no standard package of care is given to people who need psychiatric care, so the list of services needs to be comprehensive enough to consider likely service contacts. This section also covers help-seeking from non–health-related contacts with social workers or the police, and help from friends or family. For services that are likely to incur high costs – not only for the individual in terms of loss of welfare as a result of illness but also for services provided, such as nonelective hospital admission as a result of a crisis– attention needs to be paid to the data recorded here.

The fourth section is closely related to concerns about help-seeking from formal healthcare service providers, and considers any private healthcare purchased because of discrimination. This section asks the respondent to comment on payments made for private physical or mental healthcare.

The final section of the CODA covers participation in or avoidance of leisure activities. The assessment includes questions related to team sports, cinema or theater, art galleries or museums, gyms, pubs or restaurants, and holidays. Other social or leisure activities not covered by the activities listed could also be included here.

27.3.5 Unit Costs

Another important task in estimating the economic effects of people with stigma in mental health is costing or pricing treatments, employment, and services and supports used by clients. The principle of long-term marginal opportunity costs provides a basis on which unit costs should be applied to these effects; however ,a more practical approach is to approximate these costs, such as the short-term average revenue cost plus appropriate capital and overhead elements.

Anti-stigma interventions can vary in scope and have focused mainly on psychoeducation aimed at managing stigma and self-stigma [98–106]. Interventions such as these can require inputs from therapists and be provided in various formats (either in a group or one-on-one). The cost of an anti-stigma intervention can be obtained using a bottom-up approach whereby a detailed description of the intervention and the resources involved at every stage is provided and differentiated by location if the intervention is taking placing place across multiple sites.

The choice of a unit of measurement for each element of the intervention and the way in which they are calculated is integral to the overall costing exercise. For a paid therapist, it may be appropriate to use the cost per hour, which would then be multiplied by the time spent in each training session. For a cost per hour of therapist's time, national statistics or pricing using approaches from a national report could be used. In England, a widely used compendium "Unit Costs of Health and Social Care" can be used [107]. Curtis and Burns [107] calculate prices to approximate to the long-term marginal costs of care, including the opportunity cost of capital, and uses salary and on-costs, clerical support, relevant share of capital and maintenance of buildings and equipment, and the management of the department and other training-related expenses such as catering and stationery. Capital costs can be estimated using new-build and land requirements of an appropriate location, annuitized at a rate of 3.5% over 60 years. Statutory organizations may consider using existing facilities to host intervention sessions and events, in which case the cost for using existing facilities annuitized at the rate for capital can be used.

It is important to bear in mind that everyone allocated to the anti-stigma intervention group can be assigned the same intervention cost, regardless of whether they actually attended. Other scenarios are possible, whereby those who do not attend would be assigned an intervention cost of zero, and those who do attend would be assigned a higher cost, as the interaction with the therapist will be more intensive than if all participants attended.

The effects of increased work time on employment, either through gaining employment or having less time off work if already employed, could be costed. An appropriate wage obtained from national statistics and converted to a wage per unit of measure of the time off work (for example, per hour, per day, per week) would then be applied to value worker time.

As noted by Shearer et al. [108], the time spent by health, social care, criminal justice, or other statutory professionals can be valued by applying a cost per hour of contact with these professionals. The cost of time spent with these professionals can be obtained using information on salary; salary on-costs; capital overheads; and overhead costs to the provider for administration and management, office, training and utilities, indirect overheads such as general management, and support services such as finance and human resource departments. The annual costs would then be divided by the total number of hours worked for the year, based on the professional's conditions of service, including any entitlements for statutory leave. Appropriate adjustments would need to be made when calculating travel costs incurred in order to provide care.

We now consider economic evidence to answer specific policy and practice questions in stigma research.

27.3.6 Evidence from Health Economic Studies of Stigma and Stigma-Related Interventions

The CODA was also used to collect data from the sample used in the Mental Illness-Related Investigations on Discrimination (MIRIAD) study, which aimed to increase understanding about the nature and effects of discrimination and stigma experienced by people with mental health problems. Among the aims of the study – which were to determine the extent to which people anticipate and experience mental illness–based discrimination and whether this is affected by their diagnosis, age, sex, social background, and ethnicity; the effects of stigma and discrimination on healthcare-seeking behaviors and use of services; and people's experiences of multiple discrimination (discrimination based on mental illness and on membership in another social group that is treated unfairly) – was to determine the economic costs of mental illness–based discrimination.

To assess the economic costs of stigma, the study used a multiple regression model that took as the dependent variable the costs of all events that may be results of stigma, as measured by the CODA questionnaire, . The main independent variable was the level of stigma experienced by the individual, as measured by the Discrimination and Stigma Scale [109]. Possible confounding characteristics and clinical measures were also included.

The TTC campaign is the more recent of two anti-stigma initiatives conducted in England; it stared in 2008 and assessed related outcomes and costs. The TTC campaign is aimed at three main groups: the general population, specific groups identified by people who have experience with mental health problems, and people with mental health problems themselves [52]. The evaluation of the campaign reported mixed outcomes, although the costs for the anti-stigma campaign were small (relative to other types of public health campaigns). The TTC program brought about significant reductions in discrimination by service users and improvements in employer recognition of common mental health disorders, as well as short-term improvements in the attitudes of medical students, yet there was no improvement in knowledge or behavior among the general public or in mental health professionals' reports of discrimination. Taking into account the effects on service use and employment, an evaluation of the TTC campaign found that the economic benefits outweigh the financial costs [70]. These findings lend support to the possible positive outcomes from organized courses of action designed to reduce stigma and discrimination.

27.4 Conclusion: Knowledge Gaps and Recommendations

Despite the insights provided by the evidence on the economics of stigma and discrimination, research in this area is still at an early stage. We and our colleagues have developed a conceptual model of economic effect, but it needs further refinement. In most economic studies, if a service is used to address a particular health need, then a cost is usually attached to the service; doing so is uncontentious. With stigma, however, it is not so straightforward, because the effect may be that services are *not* used. A simple approach is to say that if a service is not used, then an economic saving exists, but this would be perverse in that an optimal situation would then be to increase stigma. Reduced services use as a result of stigma is likely to be detrimental to patients and result in a "loss" (which may manifest itself in, for example, reduced quality of life, reduced well-being, or the use of more expensive care if a relapse occurs). As such, reduced service use as a result of stigma has a "cost" that can, in theory, be represented in monetary terms. This of course makes interpretation challenging, as stigma may result in increased or decreased activity– both of which can be costed.

Similarly, stigma may result in reduced engagement in social or leisure activities. Assuming that these are valued by people, their loss again is negative and so can be viewed as a cost. What is the cost of this lost value? It may be reflected by the market price for such activities, but what about unpriced activities such as a walk through a park or spending time with friends? Further work on the measurement and valuation of such lost opportunities is required.

We referred earlier to some of the interventions designed to address stigma. A number of public campaigns have been created, and assessing their cost-effectiveness is crucial. By examining the cost-effectiveness evidence that emerged from these studies, we hope to have presented economic evidence that can be used as a tool for planning and commissioning where there is concern with the equity and efficiency of services. Undertaking research of this kind is not without difficulties, though, as controlled experiments may not be feasible. Changes may occur as a result of a campaign, but these changes may have occurred over time anyway, albeit at a much slower pace. Moreover, by presenting examples of specific policy and practice questions and the related economic evidence, we hope to have demonstrated the usefulness of economic evaluation in this context. If costing and combing cost and outcomes information is practiced more widely, it should be possible to constructively critique economic information in this area using a shared understanding of methods rather than dismissing it out of hand as "political." Many competences can be turned toward political ends by the unprincipled; the difficulty seems to arise when those skills are in the hands of only a few.

Further research into services use and the costs of discrimination, and in assessing the cost-effectiveness of anti-stigma campaigns is therefore required. No research to date has assessed the association between costs and discrimination for those who disengage from services or have been discharged from secondary care services. Further, for research to contribute to outcomes in a way more directed at service recipients, it would need to examine the pathways by which experiences of discrimination could directly affect the reduction in health services use, engagement with financial institutions, or participation in leisure activities. For this, research conducted using prospective data will be required. Such information will help decision makers at various levels formulate policy and practice questions sensibly and logically, which would then require evaluators to provide a range of answers from which decision makers can choose. It is the interplay of clinical, political, and economic priorities and economic appraisal that could provide a possible way forward.

Key Messages

- Mental illness–related stigma has far-reaching economic effects on a range of domains in an individual's life.
- Well-designed and coordinated responses to these economic effects will significantly influence an individual's functioning, well-being, and quality of life, and may also improve the quality of life of caregiving family members and others.
- A paucity of economic research exists to assist decision makers, but the evidence base is growing. Existing research lends support to the possible positive economic outcomes from interventions designed to reduce stigma and discrimination.
- Further research into pathways by which experiences of discrimination could directly affect the reduction in health services use, engagement with financial institutions, or participation in leisure activities and the cost-effectiveness of anti-stigma campaigns are required.
- Clinical and economic appraisals could assist decision makers at various levels to formulate logical and sensible policy and practice questions, which would then require evaluators to provide a range of answers from which decision makers can choose.

Acknowledgments The authors acknowledge the contributions of Claire Henderson and Elizabeth Croker in writing this chapter. GT is supported by the National Institute for Health Research (NIHR) Collaboration for Leadership in Applied Health Research and Care South London at the King's College London Foundation Trust. The views expressed are those of the author(s) and not necessarily those of the National Health Service (NHS), the NIHR, or the Department of Health. GT acknowledges financial support from the Department of Health via the NIHR Biomedical Research Centre and Dementia Unit, awarded to South London and Maudsley NHS Foundation Trust in partnership with King's College London and King's College Hospital NHS Foundation Trust. GT is supported by the European Union Seventh Framework Programme (FP7/2007–2013) Emerald project.

References

1. Goffmann E. Stigma: notes on the management of spoiled identity. Englewood Cliffs: Prentice Hall; 1963.
2. Weiss MG, Ramakrishna J. Stigma interventions and research for international health. Lancet. 2006;367(9509):536–8.
3. Sartorius N, Schulze H. Reducing the stigma of mental illness. Cambridge: Cambridge University Press; 2005.
4. Rabkin J. Public attitudes toward mental illness: a review of the literature. Schizophr Bull. 1974;10:9–33.
5. Link BG, Phelan JC, Bresnahan M, Stueve A, Pescosolido BA. Public conceptions of mental illness: labels, causes, dangerousness, and social distance. Am J Public Health. 1999;89(9):1328–33.
6. Thornicroft G. Shunned: discrimination against people with mental illness. Oxford: Oxford University Press; 2006.
7. Evans-Lacko S, Courtin E, Fiorillo A, Knapp M, Luciano M, Park A, et al. The state of the art in European research on reducing social exclusion and stigma related to mental health: a systematic mapping of the literature. Eur Psychiatry. 2014;29:381–9.
8. Mehta N, Clement S, Marcus E, Stona A-C, Bezborodovs N, Evans-Lacko S, et al. Evidence for effective interventions to reduce mental health-related stigma and discrimination in the medium and long term: systematic review. Br J Psychiatry. 2015;207(5):377–84.
9. Thornicroft G, Mehta N, Clement S, Evans-Lacko S, Doherty M, Rose D, et al. Evidence for effective interventions to reduce mental-health-related stigma and discrimination. Lancet. 2015;387:1123–32.
10. Yang L, Cho SH, Kleinman A. Stigma of mental illness. In: Patel V, editor. Mental and neurological public health: a global perspective. Amsterdam: Elsevier; 2010.
11. Link BG, Phelan JC. Conceptualising stigma. Am Sociol Rev. 2001;27:363–85.
12. Hatzenbuehler ML, Phelan JC, Link BG. Stigma as a fundamental cause of population health inequalities. Am J Public Health. 2013;103(5):813–21.

13. Raguram R, Raghu TM, Vounatsou P, Weiss MG. Schizophrenia and the cultural epidemiology of stigma in Bangalore, India. J Nerv Ment Dis. 2004;192(11):734–44.
14. Weiss MG, Jadhav S, Raguram R, Vounatsou P, Littlewood R. Psychiatric stigma across cultures: local validation in Bangalore and London. Anthropol Med. 2001;8(7):71–87.
15. Kohrt BA, Harper I. Navigating diagnoses: understanding mind-body relations, mental health, and stigma in Nepal. Cult Med Psychiatry. 2008;32(4):462–91.
16. Kohrt BA, Jordans MJ, Tol WA, Perera E, Karki R, Koirala S, et al. Social ecology of child soldiers: child, family, and community determinants of mental health, psychosocial well-being, and reintegration in Nepal. Transcult Psychiatry. 2010;47(5):727–53.
17. Corrigan P. Mental health stigma as social attribution: implications for research methods and attitude change. Clin Psychol Sci Pract. 2000;7:48–67.
18. Corrigan PW, Watson AC. Factors that explain how policy makers distribute resources to mental health services. Psychiatr Serv. 2003;54(4):501–7.
19. Corrigan P, Kleinlein P. The impact of mental illness stigma. In: Corrigan P, editor. On the stigma of mental illness: practical strategies for research and social change. Washington, DC: American Psychological Assocation; 2005.
20. Rusch N, Angermeyer MC, Corrigan PW. Mental illness stigma: concepts, consequences, and initiatives to reduce stigma. Eur Psychiatry. 2005;20(8):529–39.
21. Corrigan P, Watson A. The paradox of self-stigma and mental illness. Clin Psychol Sci Pract. 2006;9(1):35–53.
22. Fung KM, Tsang HW, Corrigan PW, Lam CS, Cheung WM. Measuring self-stigma of mental illness in China and its implications for recovery. Int J Soc Psychiatry. 2007;53(5):408–18.
23. Ritsher JB, Lucksted A, Otilingam PG, Grajales M. Hearing voices: explanations and implications. Psychiatr Rehabil J. 2004;27(3):219–27.
24. Vauth R, Kleim B, Wirtz M, Corrigan PW. Self-efficacy and empowerment as outcomes of self-stigmatizing and coping in schizophrenia. Psychiatry Res. 2007;150(1):71–80.
25. Corrigan PW, Larson J, Sells M, Niessen N, Watson AC. Will filmed presentations of education and contact diminish mental illness stigma? Community Ment Health J. 2007;43(2):171–81.
26. Yanos PT, Roe D, Markus K, Lysaker PH. Pathways between internalized stigma and outcomes related to recovery in schizophrenia spectrum disorders. Psychiatr Serv. 2008;59(12):1437–42.
27. Link BG, Phelan JC. Conceptualizing stigma. Annu Rev Sociol. 2001;27:363–85.
28. Link BG, Struening EL, Rahav M, Phelan JC, Nuttbrock L. On stigma and its consequences: evidence from a longitudinal study of men with dual diagnosis of mental illness and substance abuse. J Health Soc Behav. 1997;38:177–90.
29. Lysaker PH, Davis LW, Warman DM, Strasburger A, Beattie N. Stigma, social function and symptoms in schizophrenia and schizoaffective disorder: associations across 6 months. Psychiatry Res. 2007;149(1–3):89–95.
30. Corrigan PW, Larson JE. Stigma. In: Clinical handbook of schizophrenia. New York: Guilford Press; 2008. p. 533–40. xxi, 650 p.
31. Corrigan PW, Larson JE, Rusch N. Self-stigma and the "why try" effect: impact on life goals and evidence-based practices. World Psychiatry. 2009;8(2):75–81.
32. National Institute for Health and Clinical Excellence. Behaviour change at population, community and individual levels 2007. http://www.nice.org.uk/PH006
33. Thornicroft G, Rose D, Kassam A. Stigma: ignorance, prejudice or discrimination. Br J Psychiatry. 2007;190:192–3.
34. Clement S, Brohan E, Jeffery D, Henderson C, Hatch SL, Thornicroft G. Development and psychometric properties the barriers to access to care evaluation scale (BACE) related to people with mental ill health. BMC Psychiatry. 2012;12(1):36.
35. Dovidio JF, Major B, Crocker J. Stigma: introduction and overview. In: Heatherton TF, Kleck RE, Hebl MR, Hull JG, editors. The social psychology of stigma. New York: Guildford Press; 2000. p. 1–28.
36. Kvaale EP, Haslam N, Gottdiener WH. The 'side effects' of medicalization: a meta-analytic review of how biogenetic explanations affect stigma. Clin Psychol Rev. 2013;33(6):782–94.
37. Corrigan P. On the stigma of mental illness. Washington, DC: American Psychological Association; 2005.
38. Corrigan PW, Markowitz FE, Watson AC. Structural levels of mental illness stigma and discrimination. Schizophr Bull. 2004;30(3):481–91.
39. Corrigan PW, Watson AC, Heyrman ML, Warpinski A, Gracia G, Slopen N, et al. Structural stigma in state legislation. Psychiatr Serv. 2005;56(5):557–63.
40. Link BG, Phelan JC. On stigma and its public health implications. In: Stigma and global health: developing a research agenda. Bethesda: National Institutes of Health; 2001.
41. Corrigan PW. Target-specific stigma change: a strategy for impacting mental illness stigma. Psychiatr Rehabil J. 2004;28(2):113–21.
42. Wahlbeck K, Westman J, Nordentoft M, Gissler M, Laursen TM. Outcomes of Nordic mental health systems: life expectancy of patients with mental disorders. Br J Psychiatry. 2011;199(6):453–8.
43. Thornicroft A, Goulden R, Shefer G, Rhydderch D, Rose D, Williams P, et al. Newspaper coverage of mental illness in England 2008–2011. Br J Psychiatry Suppl. 2013;55:s64–9.
44. Thornicroft G. Physical health disparities and mental illness: the scandal of premature mortality. Br J Psychiatry. 2011;199(6):441–2.
45. Lawrence D, Hancock KJ, Kisely S. The gap in life expectancy from preventable physical illness in psychiatric patients in Western Australia: retrospective analysis of population based registers. BMJ. 2013;346:f2539.
46. Drew N, Funk M, Tang S, Lamichhane J, Chavez E, Katontoka S, et al. Human rights violations of people

with mental and psychosocial disabilities: an unresolved global crisis. Lancet. 2011;378(9803):1664–75.
47. United Nations. Convention on the rights of persons with disabilities. New York: United Nations; 2006.
48. Randall J, Thornicroft G, Burti L, Katschnig H, Lewis O, Russo J, Shaw T, Wahlbeck K, Rose D. Development of the ITHACA toolkit for monitoring human rights and general health care in psychiatric and social care institutions. Epidemiol Psychiatr Sci. 2013;22(03):241–54.
49. Brohan E, Henderson C, Wheat K, Malcolm E, Clement S, Barley EA, et al. Systematic review of beliefs, behaviours and influencing factors associated with disclosure of a mental health problem in the workplace. BMC Psychiatry. 2012;12:11.
50. Shidhaye R, Kermode M. Stigma and discrimination as a barrier to mental health service utilization in India. Int Health. 2013;5(1):6–8.
51. Clement S, Schauman O, Graham T, Maggioni F, Evans-Lacko S, Bezborodovs N, Morgan C, Rüsch N, Brown JS, Thornicroft G. What is the impact of mental health-related stigma on help-seeking? A systematic review of quantitative and qualitative studies. Psychol Med. 2015;45(1):11–27.
52. Henderson C, Thornicroft G. Evaluation of the time to change programme in England 2008–2011. Br J Psychiatry Suppl. 2013;55:s45–8.
53. Padmavati R, Thara R, Corin E. A qualitative study of religious practices by chronic mentally ill and their caregivers in South India. Int J Soc Psychiatry. 2005;51(2):139–49.
54. Angermeyer MC, Schulze B, Dietrich S. Courtesy stigma – a focus group study of relatives of schizophrenia patients. Soc Psychiatry Psychiatr Epidemiol. 2003;38(10):593–602.
55. Hinshaw S. The mark of shame. Oxford: Oxford University Press; 2007.
56. Thara R, Kamath S, Kumar S. Women with schizophrenia and broken marriages – doubly disadvantaged? Part II: family perspective. Int J Soc Psychiatry. 2003;49(3):233–40.
57. Phillips MR, Pearson V, Li F, Xu M, Yang L. Stigma and expressed emotion: a study of people with schizophrenia and their family members in China. Br J Psychiatry. 2002;181:488–93.
58. Van Brakel WH. Measuring health-related stigma – a literature review. Psychol Health Med. 2006;11(3):307–34.
59. Wright S, Henderson C, Thornicroft G, Sharac J, McCrone P. Measuring the economic costs of discrimination experienced by people with mental health problems: development of the Costs of Discrimination Assessment (CODA). Soc Psychiatry Psychiatr Epidemiol. 2015;50(5):787–95.
60. Shrivastava A, Johnston M, Bureau Y. Stigma of mental illness-1: clinical reflections. Mens Sana Monogr. 2012;10(1):70.
61. Almond S, Knapp M, Francois C, Toumi M, Brugha T. Relapse in schizophrenia: costs, clinical outcomes and quality of life. Br J Psychiatry. 2004;184(4):346–51.
62. Khalema NE, Shankar J. Perspectives on employment integration, mental illness and disability, and workplace health. Adv Public Health. 2014;20:2014.
63. McDaid, D, Knapp M, Medieros H. Employment and mental health: assessing the economic impact and the case for intervention. 2008. http://eprints.lse.ac.uk/4236/1/MHEEN_policy_briefs_5_Employment%28LSERO%29.pdf. Accessed 18 Jan 2016.
64. Marwaha S, Johnson S, Bebbington P, Stafford M, Angermeyer MC, Brugha T, Azorin JM, Kilian R, Hansen K, Toumi M. Rates and correlates of employment in people with schizophrenia in the UK, France and Germany. Br J Psychiatry. 2007;191(1):30–7.
65. NESF. National Economic and Social Forum Report on Mental Health and Social Inclusion 2007. National Economic and Social Forum: Dublin. http://files.nesc.ie/nesf_archive/nesf_research_series/nesf_rs_04.pdf. Accessed 18 Jan 2016.
66. Perkins R, Farmer, P, Litchfield P. Realising ambitions: better employment support for people with a mental health condition. London: Department for Work and Pensions. 2009. https://www.gov.uk/government/uploads/system/uploads/attachment_data/file/228818/7742.pdf. Accessed 20 Jan 2016.
67. Stuart H. Mental illness and employment discrimination. Curr Opin Psychiatry. 2006 Sep 1;19(5):522–6.
68. Schulze B, Angermeyer MC. Subjective experiences of stigma. A focus group study of schizophrenic patients, their relatives and mental health professionals. Soc Sci Med. 2003 Jan 31;56(2):299–312.
69. Stansfeld S, Candy B. Psychosocial work environment and mental health – a meta-analytic review. Scand J Work Environ Health. 2006;1:443–62.
70. Evans-Lacko S, Knapp M, McCrone P, Thornicroft G, Mojtabai R. The mental health consequences of the recession: economic hardship and employment of people with mental health problems in 27 European countries. PLoS One. 2013;8(7):e69792.
71. Lorant V, Deliège D, Eaton W, Robert A, Philippot P, Ansseau M. Socioeconomic inequalities in depression: a meta-analysis. Am J Epidemiol. 2003;157(2):98–112.
72. Link B. Mental patient status, work, and income: an examination of the effects of a psychiatric label. Am Sociol Rev. 1982;1:202–15.
73. Sareen J, Afifi TO, McMillan KA, Asmundson GJ. Relationship between household income and mental disorders: findings from a population-based longitudinal study. Arch Gen Psychiatry. 2011;68(4):419–27.
74. McMillan KA, Enns MW, Asmundson GJ, Sareen J. The association between income and distress, mental disorders, and suicidal ideation and attempts: findings from the collaborative psychiatric epidemiology surveys. J Clin Psychiatry. 2010;71(9):1–478.
75. Sharac J, Mccrone P, Clement S, Thornicroft G. The economic impact of mental health stigma and discrimination: a systematic review. Epidemiol Psichiatr Soc. 2010;19(03):223–32.
76. Baldwin ML, Marcus SC. Perceived and measured stigma among workers with serious mental illness. Psychiatr Serv. 2006;57(3):388–92.

77. World Health Organization. Gender disparities and mental health: the facts. 2016. http://www.who.int/mental_health/prevention/genderwomen/en/. Accessed 20 Jan 2016.
78. Fabrega Jr H, Mezzich J, Ulrich R, Benjamin L. Females and males in an intake psychiatric setting. Psychiatry. 1990;53(1):1–6.
79. Bebbington P, Cooper C, Minot S, et al. Suicide attempts, gender, and sexual abuse. Am J Psychiatr. 2009;166:1135–40.
80. Freeman D, Freeman J. The stressed sex: uncovering the truth about men, women, and mental health. Oxford: Oxford University Press; 2013.
81. Showalter E. The female malady: women, madness, and English culture, 1830–1980. London: Pantheon; 1985.
82. Platt J, Prins S, Bates L, Keyes K. Unequal depression for equal work? How the wage gap explains gendered disparities in mood disorders. Soc Sci Med. 2016;149:1–8.
83. Kovandžić M, Chew-Graham C, Reeve J, Edwards S, Peters S, Edge D, Aseem S, Gask L, Dowrick D. Access to primary mental health care for hard-to-reach groups: from 'silent suffering' to 'making it work'. Soc Sci Med. 2011;72:763–72.
84. Ahern J, Stuber J, Galea S. Stigma, discrimination and the health of illicit drug users. Drug Alcohol Depend. 2007;88:188–96.
85. Aromaa E, Tolvanen A, Tuulari J, Wahlbeck K. Personal stigma and use of mental health services among people with depression in a general population in Finland. BMC Psychiatry. 2011;11(1):52.
86. Keyes KM, Hatzenbuehler ML, McLaughlin KA, Link B, Olfson M, Grant BF, Hasin D. Stigma and treatment for alcohol disorders in the United States. Am J Epidemiol. 2010;172(12):1364–72.
87. Clement S, Schauman O, Graham T, Maggioni F, Evans-Lacko S, Bezborodovs N, Morgan C, Rüsch N, Brown JS, Thornicroft G. What is the impact of mental health-related stigma on help-seeking? A systematic review of quantitative and qualitative studies. Psychol Med. 2015;45(01):11–27.
88. Gary FA. Stigma: barrier to mental health care among ethnic minorities. Issues Ment Health Nurs. 2005;26(10):979–99.
89. Keating F, Robertson D. Fear, black people and mental illness: a vicious circle? Health Soc Care Community. 2004;12(5):439–47.
90. Lelliott P, Audini B, Duffett R. Survey of patients from an inner-London health authority in medium secure psychiatric care. Br J Psychiatry. 2001;178(1):62–6.
91. Bhui K. Over-representation of black people in secure psychiatric facilities. Br J Psychiatry. 2001;178(6):575.
92. Audini B, Lelliott P. Age, gender and ethnicity of those detained under part II of the Mental Health Act 1983. Br J Psychiatry. 2002;180(3):222–6.
93. Goater N, King M, Cole E, Leavey G, Johnson-Sabine E, Blizard R, Hoar A. Ethnicity and outcome of psychosis. Br J Psychiatry. 1999;175(1):34–42.
94. Churchill R, Wall S, Hotopf M, Buchanan A, Wessely S. Shaping the new mental health act: key messages from the department of health research programme. Centrally collected information: what can the data tell us. London: Department of Health; 2000.
95. Sartorius N, Schulze H. Reducing the stigma of mental illness: a report from a global association. Cambridge: Cambridge University Press; 2005.
96. Ministry of Health. MINDS OL. Like minds, like mine. 2007. https://www.likeminds.org.nz/assets/National-Plans/1plan-2007-2013.pdf. Accessed 20 Jan 2016.
97. Beecham J, Knapp M. Costing psychiatric interventions. In: Thornicroft G, editor. Measuring mental health needs. London: Gaskell; 2001.
98. Wieczynski D. Effects of a stigma management group for individuals with mental illness. Dissertation Abstracts International: Section B: the Sciences and Engineering. 61 (5-B), 2786. US: University Microfilms International; 2000.
99. Knight MT, Wykes T, Hayward P. Group treatment of perceived stigma and self-esteem in schizophrenia: a waiting list trial of efficacy. Behav Cogn Psychother. 2006;34(03):305–18.
100. Link BG, Struening EL, Neese-Todd S, Asmussen S, Phelan JC. On describing and seeking to change the experience of stigma. Psychiatric Rehabil Skills. 2002;6(2):201–31.
101. McCay E, Beanlands H, Leszcz M, Goering P, Seeman MV, Ryan K, Johnston N, Vishnevsky T. A group intervention to promote healthy self-concepts and guide recovery in first episode schizophrenia: a pilot study. Psychiatr Rehabil J. 2006;30(2):105.
102. MacInnes DL, Lewis M. The evaluation of a short group programme to reduce self-stigma in people with serious and enduring mental health problems. J Psychiatr Ment Health Nurs. 2008;15(1):59–65.
103. Fung KM, Tsang HW, Cheung WM. Randomized controlled trial of the self-stigma reduction program among individuals with schizophrenia. Psychiatry Res. 2011;189(2):208–14.
104. Lucksted A, Drapalski A, Calmes C, Forbes C, DeForge B, Boyd J. Ending self-stigma: pilot evaluation of a new intervention to reduce internalized stigma among people with mental illnesses. Psychiatr Rehabil J. 2011;35(1):51.
105. Yanos PT, Roe D, West ML, Smith SM, Lysaker PH. Group-based treatment for internalized stigma among persons with severe mental illness: findings from a randomized controlled trial. Psychol Serv. 2012;9(3):248.
106. Corrigan P, Michaels PJ, Morris S. Do the effects of antistigma programs persist over time? Findings from a meta-analysis. Psychiatric Serv. 2015;66(5):543–6.
107. Curtis L, Burns A. Unit costs of health and social care. Canterbury: University of Kent; 2015.
108. Shearer J, McCrone P, Romeo R. Economic evaluation of mental health interventions: a guide to costing approaches. Pharmaco Econ. 2016;27:1–4.
109. Brohan E, Clement S, Rose D, Sartorius N, Slade M, Thornicroft G. Development and psychometric evaluation of the discrimination and stigma scale (DISC). Psychiatry Res. 2013;208(1):33–40.

28 The Economic Impact of Mental Disorders and Mental Health Problems in the Workplace

Marcelo Pinheiro, Ivana Ivandic, and Denise Razzouk

Abstract

Work productivity is closely related to good mental health and a sustainable workplace environment. Mental disorders are among the leading causes of work losses, measured by absenteeism, presenteeism, and sick-leave rates. Depression, anxiety, and alcohol use disorders are the leading mental disorders producing financial and human capital losses. On the other hand, favorable conditions in workplace are paramount for better and healthier worker performance. Job stress, bullying, moral, sexual harassment, and violence in the workplace are factors related to poor mental health and low productivity. Burnout is another condition that depends on an individual's vulnerability and on the organization's work dynamics. Problems in work and in time organization, task structure, career development, and the relationship between the organization and workers are the main factors affecting workers' mental health and productivity. Investments in treating and preventing mental disorders save money, reduce costs, and increase productivity. Several strategies are available to promote workers' mental health in the workplace and to deliver sustainable conditions for working.

Key Points Summary

- The relationship between mental health and work productivity: mental capital, mental disorders, and indirect costs.
- The costs of depression, anxiety, and alcohol use disorders in the workplace are greater than prevention and treatment costs.
- Mental health problems in the workplace have deleterious effects related to employees' well-being and organizational

M. Pinheiro (✉)
Department of Social and Legal Sciences, Fundação Getulio Vargas, São Paulo, Brazil
e-mail: m-pinheiro@outlook.com

I. Ivandic
Institute for Public Health and Health Services Research, Department of Medical Informatics, Biometry and Epidemiology (IBE), Ludwig-Maximilians-University, Munich, Germany
e-mail: ivana.ivandic@med.uni-muenchen.de

D. Razzouk
Centre of Economic Mental Health, Department of Psychiatry, Universidade Federal de Sao Paulo, Rua Borges Lagoa 570, 1° andar, São Paulo, Brazil
e-mail: drazzouk@gmail.com

D. Razzouk (ed.), *Mental Health Economics*, DOI 10.1007/978-3-319-55266-8_28

productivity: job stress, burnout, violence, and harassment. These effects negatively affect rates of absenteeism, presenteeism, and work productivity.
- Tackling stigma is the initial step in providing a safe and supportive environment for people with mental health conditions.
- Strategies for promoting the mental health of workers are effective to reduce job stressors and psychosocial risk factors in the workplace.
- Strategies for workers with mental disorders include earlier identification of mental disorders and interventions addressed to allow sustainable and effective return to work.

28.1 The Relationship Between Mental Health and Work Productivity

In general, work productivity is related to purpose and output [1, 2]. From the beginnings of human history, working was related to survival, and output was getting food according to immediate human needs. Later, agriculture embodied the idea of having food available on a large scale and stocking it for the future. Then, the purpose was to produce for future needs or for exchanging goods to meet other needs, that is, fulfilling multiple needs simultaneously. Output has become associated with the amount of food produced or kept in stock, or even with the amount of food sold.

In the Industrial Revolution, the purpose was to produce more to get more money, capital, and power. Then, productivity was measured by the number of outputs created per hour. While machines progressively replaced human workers in multiple functions with the purpose of producing more in less time, the nature of human work has shifted to high-skill activities. In the 1950s, higher levels of education and cognition capacity were emphasized because these characteristics allowed intelligent choices, efficient management, and more innovation. Therefore, human capital has been associated with innovative knowledge, greater productivity, and nation development [1, 2].

Curiously, the term *workaholic* emerged in 1947, with the notion that spending more time at the workplace with a high level of motivation, commitment, and involvement in work activities is an efficient worker behavior pattern; nowadays, though, this concept is not supported in a positive way. Then, for a long time the idea of the longest period of time spent working would lead to the greatest productivity dominated workplace environment. However, many studies have shown that factors affecting productivity were much more complex and elusive than simply having many years of education, have a high IQ, and spending innumerable hours working.

In general, two dimensions have a great influence on the quality and the amount of output produced by work activities: the workplace environment and the individual profile [3]. The former is related to the conditions offered by employers to their employees to achieve better work performance, and to the quality of the relationship between them. The latter is related to workers' characteristics and backgrounds, ability to cope with stress, resilience, and the meaning of work to the worker.

Labor Medicine emerged as a discipline rising focused on "ergonomic" issues, and multiple theoretical models involving different disciplines addressed issues on productivity influenced by the relationship between working and stress, and reward and motivation, among other related factors. On the other hand, concepts originating from Social Psychology and other related disciplines focused on the worker's health and mental health status, including individual characteristics, resilience, and behavioral patterns influencing work productivity. Other approaches emphasized the relationship between work and individual subjectivity, that is, how work is associated with pleasure, pain, and personal development and satisfaction [4].

Undoubtedly, both approaches shed light on the importance of human capital in determining productivity. The equation between working and producing encompasses positive and negative aspects of human goals, needs, and abilities. In this sense, the economist Lock Sang-Ho introduced in 2001 the concept of mental capital in his book *Principles of Public Policy Practice* [5] . *Mental capital* refers to the ability of an individual to use all inner resources (cognitive, emotional, and behavioral) in appropriate ways to fulfill their needs and to contribute to the needs of others [6]. In other words, mental capital represents the balance of experiencing a good quality of life and being able to contribute to society.

While physical health was the central component related to better output until the agricultural era, cognitive and educational skills were crucial abilities for better outputs after the Industrial Revolution. In the Knowledge era, which emerged in the twentieth century, the perception of having good mental health became the cornerstone for efficient and competitive productivity. In this sense, a better pool of mental capital is likely to generate more knowledge, creativity, and innovation, and it is more resilient and able to overcome obstacles and contribute more to society as a whole.

28.1.1 Mental Health and Mental Capital as "Goods"

The promotion of mental health has been the cornerstone goal of policies advocating the reduction of the burden of mental disorders in the workplace and, ultimately, the enhancement of mental capital favoring nation development. From an economic perspective, the best management of resources (producing, spending, and distributing) generates better outputs; in other words, it maximizes benefits to fulfill societal needs. Equally, "maximizing" mental health leads to greater mental capital, with a greater capacity to achieve a better quality of life and to fulfill societal demands.

However, multiple factors related to the workplace environment and affecting workers' mental health are commonplace, and consequently they also affect an organization's productivity. A sustainable environment in organizations can facilitate the process of individual satisfaction and professional development, though distortions where individuals establish a relationship with workplace activities and the organization can also cause physical distress and emotional pain. External factors such as a global economic recession and increasing levels of unemployment, as well as internal organization factors such as competition and financial strain, allow greater work stress and the emergence of physical illness, psychological distress, and mental illness [7, 8].

Studies have demonstrated a growing burden of mental disorders (see Chap. 25) in the workplace, generating high indirect costs to society as a whole [9, 10]. A World Health Organization study reported a high frequency of lifetime psychiatric disorders among employees in multiple countries: the United States (48.6%), the Netherlands (40.9%), Canada (37.5%), Brazil (36.3%), Mexico (22.2%), and Turkey (12.2%) [11].

The United Nations estimates that 25% of the world's population is adversely affected in one way or another as a result of disabilities [12]. Mental disorders are among the three foremost causes of disability, together with cardiovascular disease and musculoskeletal disorders. The Organisation for Economic Co-operation and Development estimated the prevalence of moderate and severe mental disorders among industrialized working-age populations at 15% and 5%, respectively [10]. Despite the evidence of the burden of mental disorders and of preventable stressors in the workplace, many organizations have not paid much attention to preventing the negative effects of mental health problems in the workplace.

28.2 Mental Health and Mental Disorders

The nature of mental health is an issue of dispute among multiple disciplines and different theoretical viewpoints. Terms related to mental health and mental disorders cause huge misunderstandings. In the main, *mental health* refers to the level of well-being of all people, with or without mental disorders. Mental health is a global health status encompassing well-being on physical, cognitive, social, and emotional levels. It sounds like happiness, but in fact, mental health allows people to live with purpose and to assume roles according to their potential and limitations.

Mental disorders are related to pathological conditions in which people present psychiatric symptoms that lead to global mental impairment and hinder functioning at social, working, and relationship levels. It is a transitory state that also negatively affects people's mental health, but after recovering from an episode of a mental disorder, people recover their mental health, despite the residual symptoms or permanent impairment that might remain. On the other hand, people with no mental disorder can experience mental health problems in specific situations, such as living or working in stressful conditions.

Importantly, multiple strategies exist for promoting good mental health for all people and for preventing problems affecting mental health as a whole in the workplace, such as techniques for coping with stress and policies avoiding violence and harassment. On the other hand, people with mental disorders need, in addition to mental health promotion, specific treatments targeting impairments caused by psychiatric symptoms in order to be able to return to work (RTW) effectively.

28.2.1 The Hidden Costs of Mental Disorders

Mental disorders cause a huge social and economic burden in society, specifically in the workplace (see Chap. 25). They are the leading causes of absenteeism, presenteeism, sick leave, work accidents, unemployment, and early retirement. They are also responsible for employee suffering, social exclusion, and economic costs.

Therefore, mental disorders hinder productivity and the consumption of goods, and their costs ultimately correspond to 3–4% of the gross domestic product (GDP) of European countries. Similarly, the costs with absenteeism and unemployment as a result of alcohol use problems achieve 0.1% and 2.4% of the GDP, respectively, in those countries.

These indirect costs of mental disorders are much greater than the direct costs related to treatment and health system utilization. For instance, in the United Kingdom, the costs of absenteeism as a result of depression were estimated as being 23 times greater than direct costs [13]. In the United States, a study found that 62% of the costs associated with depression disorders were due to the costs of absenteeism, presenteeism, and unemployment [14]. Equally, the indirect costs of absenteeism and productivity losses due to bipolar disorders were four times greater than direct costs.

Moreover, mental disorders are related to loss of income, unemployment, disability claims, and early retirement (see Chaps. 24, 25 and 27). Mental disorders reduce the chance of being employed by 11% and annual income by more than 20%. Unemployment rates among people with mental illness range from 30% to 52%. In England, the unemployment rate is 40% higher among people with mental disorders than among the general population [15]. In Canada, one-third of disability claims were due to mental disorders, and 70% of total costs of disability benefits were addressed to people suffering from mental disorders [15]. In the United Kingdom, 39% of all claimants of the Severe Disablement allowance were due to mental disorders [16] .

28.3 The Economic Impact of Mental Disorders in the Workplace

28.3.1 Costs of Depression and Anxiety in the Workplace

Globally, the annual costs of depression and anxiety disorders are greater than $1 trillion, mainly because of productivity losses and other indirect costs [17]. Among all diseases, depression is one of the most costly and disabling in terms of work impairment [18–20]. Occupational impairment accounted for 60% of the total cost of depression in the United States [14], and the mean number of sick days among employees with depression was much higher than among those with heart diseases, diabetes, hypertension, and back pain [21]. In addition, the costs of work absenteeism among people with depression were double those among people without depression [20, 21]. Depression is the leading cause of absenteeism in the workplace in the United States, and the prevalence of depression among workers ranges between 12% and 17% [22].

Moreover, studies in European countries have shown that 50% of people suffering from depression have received long-term disability benefits, and 42% of all benefits were paid to people suffering from mental disorders [15]. In Finland, depression accounted for 50% of early retirement among middle-aged men who retired because of mental disorders [23]. In Brazil, for instance, depression is the third leading cause of sick-leave benefits and accounts for more than 60% of sick leave due to mental disorders.

Some studies have shown that treating depression can prevent these labor losses in monetary terms. A study carried by Rost et al. [24] demonstrated that the treatment of depression among workers allowed annual savings of US$1,982.00 per person by improving work productivity, and US$619.00 per person by reducing absenteeism [24]. Chisholm et al. [17] recently estimated that each dollar spent on depression and anxiety treatment would allow a return of four dollars in terms of increasing work productivity.

28.3.2 Costs of Alcoholism in the Workplace

The effect of alcohol consumption in the workplace is very costly because it affects productivity, health, and safety. The costs of absenteeism due to alcohol consumption in European countries were estimated between 0.1% and 2% of the GDP, and the costs for unemployment, between 0.4% and 2.4% of the GDP [25]. In the United Kingdom, alcohol misuse accounts for 32% of work loss costs, to one-fifth of industrial accidents [26], and to 10% of impairment reported as a result of hangovers.

28.3.3 Costs of Bipolar Disorder in the Workplace

In the United States, work absenteeism among people with bipolar disorders was reported as being three times higher than that among other employees without bipolar disorders; the annual total cost for an employer was estimated to be US$6,836.00 higher in the bipolar group compared with the group without bipolar disorder [27].

Another study showed that while physical diseases accounted for 29% of total health and productivity losses, mental disorders accounted for 47%, and among this group, bipolar and depression disorders were the most costly [28]. The annual costs for bipolar group in this study were similar to the total cost for acute myocardial infarction, whereas the costs for absenteeism in the bipolar group were similar to those of the groups with angina pectoris and trauma to the spinal cord, and were three times more costly than for severe osteoarthritis. When the costs for absenteeism were compared between mental disorders and physical diseases, the former were 10-fold higher than the latter. Another study in the Netherlands showed that the annual cost for absenteeism and loss of productivity among employees with bipolar disorder was estimated to be US$3,432.00 per employee [29].

28.4 Mental Health and Organizations

The effects of mental health problems in the workplace have serious consequences for both individuals and organizations. The most common consequences of factors affecting mental health in the workplace, according to the UK Health and Safety Executive, are described in Box 28.1.

Box 28.1Consequences of Poor Mental Health in the Workplace

- Poor decision-making
- Deterioration of planning and control of work
- Loss of motivation and engagement
- Increase in the amount of extra hours
- Postponement of deadlines
- Increase in turnover rate
- Conflicts among colleagues
- Deterioration of relationships with clients
- Intensification of disciplinary problems
- Increase in the number of accidents

28.4.1 Absenteeism

Absenteeism is an employee's recess from work and typically consists of illness-related absences and short- and long-term disability [30]. This has become a costly issue for organizations worldwide. Using the human capital approach to estimate the costs of absenteeism, cots are estimated using the number working days lost and by the organization's daily investment in the employee (e.g., wages and benefits).

According to a recent survey by PricewaterhouseCoopers, the costs of sick days to businesses in the United Kingdom is approximately US$39.5 billion a year, corresponding to employees being away from their jobs an average of 9.1 days each year because of sickness. According to the same survey, workers in the United States take at 4.9 sick days a year, whereas their counterparts in Asia Pacific take 2.2 days and workers in Western Europe take 7.3 days. The mean cost of absenteeism per employee to North American companies is around US$790.00 per year – notwithstanding productivity losses, costs of overtime, costs of training and temporarily replacing employees, and costs related to with employee turnover [31]. In the United Kingdom, these costs are also high – about US$695.00 a year per employee [32].

Costs associated with absenteeism are only one of the components of the total cost associated with productivity losses. Absenteeism costs vary depending on the job, function, organization, and country. Absenteeism has recently been suggested to be an indicator of psychosocial adjustment to work; that is, high absenteeism in the workplace is indicative of poor work adjustment.

28.4.2 Presenteeism

The concept of presenteeism emerged as a topic of discussion at the organizational setting in the mid-1980s, and was influenced by the Social Sciences and Business Administration literature worldwide. Presenteeism, or working while sick, decreases on-the-job performance because of health problems [11]. Presenteeism leads to a decrease in productivity when employees come to work but, as a consequence of poor medical conditions, they are not diligent and fully productive.

The identification and measurement of presenteeism is not a clearcut. However, the cost of presenteeism is much higher than that of absenteeism. Presenteeism costs are often measured based on the reduction of work output, number of job errors, and failure to meet company production standards [33].

Presenteeism is the second main component of productivity measurement and is beginning to garner more interest from corporate management, including medical directors [33]. Presenteeism measures the "decrease in productivity for the group of employees whose health problems have not necessarily led to absenteeism and the decrease in productivity for the disabled group before and after the absence period" [34].

Academic researchers have considered whether temporary and fixed-term employment would have an effect when examining the antecedents of presenteeism. Some authors have studied these employment statuses to determine whether a lack of job security would lead employees who do not have permanent positions to come to work more often, even while sick; however, no evidence led researchers to reconsider the job insecurity hypothesis [35]. Individuals working in certain jobs may be more prone to presenteeism, such as welfare services and teaching-related activities [36]. Besides the educational and healthcare fields, research results suggest that higher-risk jobs, which had more physical workload and stress, resulted in increased levels of presenteeism [36]. Jobs with greater workloads have been often associated with higher levels of presenteeism [37]. In such situations, presenteeism was not related to employees' perceptions of job insecurity. Instead, individuals felt they had to come to work while sick because they assumed they had a large workload, deadlines to accomplish, and often very little backup support in case they were absent from work [37].

28.4.3 Job Stress

Job stress is defined as the harmful physical and emotional response that occurs when the requirements of the job do not match the capabilities, resources, or needs of the worker. Job stress is a dynamic condition in which an employee is confronted with a demand associated with a personal, workgroup, or organizational limitation. Job stress can cause a decline in physical and mental health and can create an upsurge in rates of work-related injuries and accidents, leading to decreases in performance and productivity, and in employee well-being. The consequences of stress are now considered among the main causes of work disability. Stress can be associated with several kinds of occupations, injuring employees' health and decreasing an organization's overall performance. Stress can occur in a varied array of work situations but is often made worse when employees feel they lack support from colleagues and especially from their managers, supervisors, or leaders.

Stress is associated with three dimensions – environmental, organizational, and personal – all of which lead to physical and mental symptoms. Environmental factors include economic uncertainty, political uncertainty, and rapid technological changes, demanding employees to quickly adapt to new production methods.

Organizational factors comprise highly demanding tasks with little decision-making control by the employee, excessive workload, and relationship problems with managers and colleagues. Individual factors refer to the employee' subjectivity and ability to cope with stress, overload demand, pressure, and conflicts, and to manage difficult problems.

Some potential causes of work-related stress are overwork, a lack of clear instructions, unrealistic deadlines, a lack of decision-making over tasks, job insecurity, isolated working conditions, and surveillance. The more stressors workers experience, the greater the probability for them to become unhealthy, demotivated, less productive, and less safe at work.

Job stress is one of the most common work-related health problems in European Union countries. The Second European Survey on Working Conditions indicated that almost one in six workers (16%) reported having been a target of violence or moral and sexual harassment [30]. The majority of developed countries have adopted minimum standards for safety and health features in the workplace, but these standards focus on the physical aspects of working conditions rather than on their psychological and mental health aspects.

28.4.3.1 Categories of Psychological Stressful Experiences

Employment capability can be divided into five main categories of psychological experience that can lead to a negative effect on mental health, well-being, and work outcome [7]: relationships, work organization, task structure, time structure, and career development. Relationships are one of the most important factors affecting employees' psychological experience. They can be affected by an unsupportive culture, a poor relationship with the boss, excessive internal competition and rivalry among colleagues, sexual or moral harassment, and unsociable working hours. Work organization relates to a lack of role description, a lack of stated goals, ambiguity, or role conflict. Task structure links to the lack of control of an employee over tasks, underutilization of an employee's skills, fragmented or meaningless work, work with low social value, and inflexible and unpredictable working hours. Time structure denotes excessive amounts of Exactly, work underload, shift work, lack of variety or short work cycles, lack of control over pacing, quantities and quality, and a high level of time pressure. Finally, career development refers to the lack of a career development plan, career uncertainty, career stagnation, job insecurity and redundancy, poor or incongruous status, and poor pay.

Each of these five main categories of psychological experience can lead to a harmful set of consequences for employees, workgroups, and organizations, as shown in Box 28.2.

Box 28.2 Consequences of Stress for Employees, Workgroups, and Organizations

Concerns for employees

- Keeping the position at the company
- Decreased results of performance reviews/appraisals
- Sickness and pain, associated with fragility, decreased productivity, and higher costs

Concerns for the Organization

- Reduced productivity
- Fear that work conditions are the root of the disease
- Costs associated with healthcare
- Increased risk of lawsuits

Consequences for the workgroup

- Overworking to replace an absent colleague
- Decreased productivity
- Disbelief in the reliability of the disease

28.4.3.2 Burnout

Burnout is one of the most significant vicissitudes of professional stress. This construct was described in the 1970s by the social psychologist Cristina Maslach and the psychiatrist Herbert Freudenberger. Professional burnout is a response to chronic emotionally and interpersonally stressful situations on the job [38]. Workplace burnout affects between 19% and 30% of employees in the general working population [39]. Long-term job stress can lead to burnout in the workplace and is characterized by emotional exhaustion, feelings of cynicism and detachment from the job, and a sense of ineffectiveness and lack of accomplishment [38].

Exhaustion is the key element of burnout and the most widely reported by affected individuals, prompting behaviors of emotional and cognitive avoidance, presumably as a way to cope with work-related stressors [38]. Maslach et al. [38] point out that cynicism and detachment from the job are an attempt to create distance from others by ignoring their personal qualities, making it easier to manage their demands when they are perceived as interpersonal objects. All these factors together lead to a decrease in personal effectiveness and organizational productivity.

28.4.3.3 Workplace Bullying and Moral and Sexual Harassment

Despite the multiple definitions of the concept of workplace bullying, this phenomenon affects performance, ann organization's reputation, and employees' health, and ultimately contributes to increases in overall costs and productivity losses. Workplace bullying is defined as a form of harassment, characterized by aggressive and coercive behavior through intimidation and humiliation addressed toward a worker [40]. It affects not only individuals, but also those work colleagues who witness it.

Studies show that bullying accounts for 10–20% of overall costs due to job stress in the United Kingdom [41]. Job stress affects half a million employees, resulting in a high absenteeism rate, that is, an average of 29 days off per person because of job stress – approximately £3.7 billion.

The costs of workplace bullying include costs due to litigation and workers' compensation claims, staff turnover, absenteeism, productivity losses, early retirement, and greater use of health and psychological care by employees [40].

The frequency and costs of bullying depend on the method applied to estimate them and on the definition of bullying used, though 16.5% of employees in the United Kingdom reported an average of 7 days of work absenteeism due to bullying, equating to 33.5 million working days lost, with overall costs of £3 billion in 2007 [41]. Moreover, turnover rates due to bullying re high: approximately 25% of those employees suffering bullying leave the company, with turnover costs per employee estimated at £7750, yielding overall costs of £1.5 billion [41]. Yet, the costs of productivity losses due to bullying were calculated by reducing employee performance by 2%, and their overall costs were estimated at £9.14 billion.

Sexual harassment in the workplace is another form of a coercive and aggressive attitude with a wide range of behaviors, varying from sexist comments, to manipulative and seductive behaviors, to physical assault and rape [42]. Data from United Kingdom report sexual harassment is experienced by between 15% and 75% of employees, but these frequencies vary according to country, sample, ethnicity, age, and cultural context. In a study in the European Union, 2% of employees reported sexual harassment, 4% reported physical violence, and 8% reported bullying [42].

28.4.4 Violence and Post-traumatic Stress Disorder

Violent acts are present in a variety of conditions, such accidents, traumatic injuries, physical assaults, robbery, crimes, kidnapping, psychological torture, rape, war, terrorist attacks, and drug use. These acts can occur in the workplace environment as an isolated event or as recurring events. However, violence occurring outside the workplace environment can also affect workers' mental health and work performance. The Violent acts commonly occur among the general population. However, some data show that 10–30% of people suffering a violent episode develop a mental illness such as post-traumatic stress disorder. This disorder is highly associated with the emergence of other psychiatric disorders such as anxiety and depression.

Therefore, violent acts result in short- and long-term consequences on individual life and on organizations [42]. Individuals might be absent from work for a long period or might not RTW, remaining under welfare benefits or even going into early retirement. Yet, individuals may RTW and keep dysfunctional signs of fear, anxiety, or difficulty playing their previous work roles. In this case, costs are due to healthcare costs, decreased income, and job opportunity losses. Organizational losses and costs are due to worker turnover, absenteeism, productivity losses, healthcare costs, and insurance costs.

28.5 Mental Health Interventions in the Workplace

Several effective interventions are available to prevent mental health problems in the workplace in order to promote good mental health and well-being in a sustainable workplace environment. Moreover, specific interventions are available to treat disability due to mental disorders, enabling individuals to RTW. These interventions generate numerous benefits, including economic benefits for the individual, the employer, and society in general. Benefits at the individual level include increased commitment and job satisfaction, and improved overall health, among others. Positive aspects at the organizational level refer to staff retention, improved productivity and performance, and reduced absenteeism [43–47]. Therefore, it is worthwhile to invest in the development, implementation, and evaluation of interventions for promoting good mental health among workers.

The promotion of mental health and the prevention of mental health problems, as well as the management of mental disorders in the workplace, are addressed differently according to mental health prevention and rehabilitation level of care, as shown in Box 28.3 [48–50]. Alternatively, this set of interventions focuses on individual and/or organizational settings, as shown in Box 28.4 [51].

However, this classification is less robust when it comes to the implementation of interventions because particular approaches complement each other and sometimes overlap in practice. In addition, evidence suggests that an integrated approach to mental health promotion and prevention in the workplace, combining both individual- and organizational-level interventions, are more likely to be effective [50, 51]. Before establishing strategies to promote workers' mental health, it is important to identify individual and organizational factors affecting work performance and mental health in order to determine the set of practices feasible and effective for particular context [50] (see Table 28.1). Although interventions should be tailored to the needs of a particular workplace, LaMontagne et al. [9] suggest an integrated intervention approach that focuses on both eliminating work-related stress factors and developing positive aspects of work and workers' positive capacities in order to accomplish population-wide mental health benefits [9].

Table 28.1 Individual and organizational factors affecting work performance and mental health

Individual	Organizational
Lifecycles (pregnancy, breastfeeding, menopause, aging)	Low quality of relationship between employer and employee
Biological rhythm (sleep, feeding, light exposure, jet lag)	High workload/demand
Personality traits (resilience, vulnerability to stress)	Stressful and abusive work environment
Genetic factors for mental disorders	Lack of work policies toward career development
Substance misuse	Lack of structure and resources for appropriate work performance
Life events (death, disease, divorce, debt)	Timeline and deadline issues
Traumatic events	Lack of motivational policies
Lifestyle and quality of life	Lack of work rewards and acknowledgement

Box 28.3 Mental Health Problems Prevention and Rehabilitation Level of Care

- Primary – At this level, the main goal is to prevent mental health problems and to promote good mental health and well-being, avoiding workers' exposure to stressors and risks in the workplace by providing an optimal working environment (e.g., flexible work hours, including employees in decision-making processes).
- Secondary – At this level, the main goal is to promote or to recover mental health by focusing on managing job stressors in order to reduce the impact of stressors that have already occurred and by providing help to allow the individual to develop skills for managing these effects and, ultimately, reducing the effect of stressors (e.g., resilience and/or stress management training, time and conflict management, coping skills). Moreover, interventions are addressed to remove some workplace practices deleterious to mental health (bullying, harassment, and violence).
- Tertiary – At this level, the main goal is to treat and to support workers with mental disorders and other mental health problems, aiming to reduce the impact of the mental disorder in his/her global performance and to support and empower him or her to RTW (e.g., mental health rehabilitation care, RTW, employee assistance program).

28.5.1 Strategies for Promoting Mental Health in the Workplace

Strategies for promoting mental health in the workplace aim to prevent or reduce the occurrence of job stress related to poor mental health.

Box 28.4 Mental Health Interventions Focused on the Individual and Organizational Levels

- Individual (person): directed toward and targeting individual characteristics, in general aiming at secondary or tertiary prevention and therefore focusing on empowering employees with coping skills
- Organizational: targeting policies and practices for preventing the occurrence of job stress and other conditions that negatively influence mental health across the entire organization, predominately aiming at primary prevention strategies
- Individual and organizational interactions: targeting particular issues related to the interface between individuals and their work, and focusing on ensuring that employees can adequately carry out their tasks

Box 28.5 Strategies for Promoting Mental Health in the Workplace

- Implementing policies on mental health promotion
- Ensuring a respectful and encouraging working environment
- Promoting a healthy lifestyle (e.g., nutrition, physical activity) and work-life balance
- Ensuring employee participation in decision-making and effective two-way communication
- Appropriately managing employee workloads
- Providing resilience and/or stress management training that uses evidence-based techniques such as cognitive-behavioral therapy
- Applying various relaxation techniques
- Managing time and conflict
- Providing social support

Therefore, these strategies promote positive aspects of an individual's mental health and well-being. The International Labour Organization suggests a number of strategies based on ergonomic measures such as work organization and environment design, organizational and management development, education and training of both workers and managers, and social support, among others [52].

Primary and secondary interventions exist to minimize job stress, focusing on the individual and organizational level, as shown in Box 28.5 [53, 54].

Additional measures related to good management skills (see Box 28.6) as well as the participation of and support from the senior management are required in order to facilitate these initiatives and to tackle the challenges and barriers related to mental health [55]. In this regard, the company Great Place to Work has been coaching several enterprises to achieve benchmark practices in terms of good management skills and a sustainable work environment. It advocates nine practice areas where managers could focus on creating an environment of trust by inspiring, speaking, listening, thanking, developing, caring, hiring, celebrating, and sharing.

Other initiatives to develop standardized best practices guidelines to prevent psychosocial risk factors in the workplace were adopted by Canada, Australia, and the United Kingdom. Canada, for instance, developed a national standard guide entitled "Psychological Health and Safety in the Workplace: Prevention, Promotion and Guidance to Staged Implementation," focusing on minimizing risk, cost-effectiveness, company excellence and benchmarking, and developing a sustainable work environment [56]. Likewise, the European Union developed a tool with best practices preventing psychosocial risk factors in the workplace: the European Framework for Psychosocial Risk Management (Prima-EF) [57]. This tool addresses the prevention and monitoring of job stressors such as violence, bullying, and moral and sexual harassment.

Box 28.6 Good Practices for Management Skills

- Apply a fair and impartial management style
- Provide feedback to employees regarding their performance
- Acknowledge employees' good work
- Provide information and share knowledge weekly in meetings and daily updates
- Provide strong commitment and a supportive relationship

28.5.2 Other Approaches

28.5.2.1 Financial Advice

Before the global economic crisis, 8% of people in high-income countries were reported to have financial problems, and 9% showed signs of stress because debts and financial constraints [58]. In Brazil, for example, 63% of families reported debts in 2013. Some studies show the relationship between debts and poor mental health and a higher risk of developing mental disorders such as anxiety and depression. Some educational strategies exist for financial and debt management and can be delivered through workshops in order to reduce workers' stress related to monetary debts [59].

28.5.2.2 Mental Health Stigma and Awareness Strategies

Stigma and discrimination threaten mental health in all aspects of workers' behavior, health, and performance in the workplace (see Chap. 27). Stigma is an unfair and less favorable approach, especially toward people with mental disorders, and it has a related negative impact on their work performance [60, 61].

Anti-stigma and awareness campaigns present an initial step in promoting social inclusion and providing a safe and supportive environment for employees experiencing mental disorders [61]. However, Thornicroft [62] suggests that stigma consists of three main elements: problems of knowledge (ignorance) and attitudes (prejudice) that lead to problems of behavior (stigma). Addressing only the first two elements without changing behavior is likely to be ineffective; anti-stigma and awareness campaigns need to tackle all three domains of the problem in order to achieve positive results [61].

One of the key features in tackling stigma is providing to managers and employees the necessary skills for informed and supportive communication with colleagues who have mental health conditions. Evidence suggests Mental Health First Aid to be an effective intervention in increasing people's knowledge, decreasing negative attitudes and increasing supportive behaviors toward people with mental disorders [63–65]. Mental Health First Aid is a standardized psychoeducational program that empowers participants to approach, support, and refer individuals in distress. Participants in the training learn how to recognize signs of mental disorders and interact with the affected person. The program is not, however, a substitute for diagnostics, counseling, or therapy, but offers concrete tools to tackle prejudice and stigma and to assist and support employees with mental health disorders [64]. To promote mental health and reduce the potential for stigma, employers need to ensure processes for job design, recruitment, training, development, and appraisal [43–47].

28.6 Workplace Interventions for Persons with Mental Disorders

In addition to the previously mentioned mental health promotion strategies, two main sets of interventions are specifically addressed toward people with mental disorders: one focuses on the early recognition of the signs and symptoms of mental disorders, and the other focuses on rehabilitation strategies to RTW after long-term absenteeism.

28.6.1 Early Intervention in Mental Disorders in the Workplace

Although majority of people who develop mental disorders are able to work after receiving the appropriate care and opportunity, there is still much ignorance about mental disorders among the general public, including employers, stigma against people with these disorders, a lack of opportunities to get a job and to remain working, and a lack of knowledge on "ergonomic" measures for mental issues (see Chap. 27). It is crucial to identify the earliest signs and symptoms of mental disorders, because appropriate treatment can avoid absenteeism and sick leave and prevent further decrease in worker performance.

A set of principles, training programs, and guidelines were developed in Australia – the National Workplace Project – in order to promote awareness of the earliest signs of mental disorders and to provide a tool for the development of manager skills related to the identification of such signs, especially for depression and anxiety disorders [66].

Several cost-effective interventions exist for anxiety and depressive disorders that can be offered to workers whose performance is hindered by these disorders (see Chaps. 18–23). Psychoeducational techniques and psychosocial and cognitive-behavioral interventions added to pharmacological treatments are effective in allowing workers to recover their performance. However, an RTW might be problematic because of stigma, discrimination, and a lack of sensitivity to make some "ergonomic" adjustments.

28.6.1.1 Reasonable Accommodation and Return to Work

People with mental disorders may require particular ergonomic adjustments in the workplace in order to function effectively; this is usually referred to as "reasonable accommodation," "reasonable adjustment," or "workplace accommodation."

> Reasonable accommodation: any modification or adjustment in the workplace that allows a qualified individual with a disability to perform the essential functions of the job, such as flexible work schedules, reduced distractions or noise in the work area, working from home, and regular feedback.

People with mental disorders face high level of stigma, and for this reason they may avoid disclosing their mental illness. Job applicants in particular may be reluctant to disclose their condition out of fear of discrimination, harassment, or reduced opportunities for recruitment and career progression, which can lead to persons with mental disorders not requesting accommodation. However, they are forced to disclose it if they need to receive "reasonable accommodation." In other cases, reasonable accommodation can be provided for a person who is returning to work after absence due to a mental disorder. While many accommodations have no or low economic cost, even those accommodations that involve some expense frequently yield substantial rewards, including the economic benefits of improved productivity and performance and of the worker's satisfaction with the job.

The effect of disability caused by a mental disorder can be minimized by implementing numerous practices.

> Disability management –practices designed to minimize the disability-related effects of injuries and health conditions that arise during the course of employment.

RTW is a key part of disability management and one of the relevant components of an individual's recovery from a mental disorder. Given the multifaceted nature of disability management, concrete interventions for RTW may be delivered by different stakeholders and take place both within and outside the workplace setting. Since the workplace can play an important role in ensuring a successful return, we focus on workplace based RTW interventions for people with mental disorders.

The World Health Organization and International Labour Organization (2000) propose certain steps that can be taken by an employer, in collaboration with the employee's physician or other relevant mental health professional, to help an employee RTW after being absent due to a mental disorder:

- Informing a physician about the employee's duties on the job, before the physician makes a final decision on RTW
- Encouraging an early RTW in consultation with the individual's physician in order to prevent the employee's detachment from work and worry about losing the job because of being absent from work for treatment [7].

In addition, employers could consider a gradual RTW. Allowing part-time work for some period, flexible time, a temporary change of duties to include less stressful tasks, and other flexible arrangements can help reduce stress, leave time for additional medical counseling, and enable the worker to get back into the routine more easily.

RTW can also be embedded in employee assistance programs, employer- or group-supported programs designed to alleviate workplace issues caused by a disorder, substance use, or personal and workplace issues. It usually provides supportive, diagnostic, referral, and counseling treatment services [7, 67], which canv include on-site and telephone counseling, referral for psychological symptoms or mental health conditions, and guidance on communication in challenging situations. The general goal of the program is to have a positive effect on the employee's productivity and organizational performance [67].

Several prerequisites should be fulfilled for a successful RTW intervention. The employer and the employee should clearly agree on details of the RTW program: the duration of the accommodations, allowed day-to-day flexibilities, exact duties, and supervision [7]. The employer should take special care in communicating about the issue with the colleagues, respecting the person's wishes and taking into account confidentiality. It is relevant to treat the employee exactly the same as others in spite of the condition, unless an individual asks for specific assistance.

Key Messages

Mental disorders and poor mental health are the main factors causing absenteeism, presenteeism, and productivity losses.

- Job stress comprises workplace environmental factors (e.g., violence, harassment, bullying) and individual factors (debts, burnout, lifestyle, disease).
- Good mental health in the workplace can be achieved through various prevention and promotion strategies at the individual and organizational levels.
- Tackling stigma presents one of the initial steps in providing a safe and supportive workplace environment.
- Workers with mental disorders can be supported through provision of accommodations and RTW programs.
- To capture mental health widely and achieve the greatest effect, comprehensive mental health interventions need to be tailored and implemented.
- Cost-effectiveness interventions are available to reduce or eliminate disability due to mental disorders, to promote good mental health, to treat mental disorders, and to facilitate psychosocial rehabilitation and RTW. RTW programs present an effective way to help workers reintegrate into the work environment after an absence related to mental health.

References

1. Acemoglou D. Lectures in labour economics: the basic theory of human capital. 2011. https://economics.mit.edu/files/4689
2. Weehuizen R. Mental capital: the economic significance of mental health. Maastricht: University of Maastrich; 2008.
3. Razzouk D. Capital mental, custos indiretos e saúde mental. In: Razzouk D, Lima M, Quirino C, edi-

tors. Saúde Mental e Trabalho. 1st ed. São Paulo: CREMESP; 2016. p. 61–70.
4. Dejours C. Plaisir and souffrance dans le travail. Paris: lAOCIP; 1987.
5. Ho L-S. Principles of public policy practice. New York: Springer Sciece & Business Media; 2012.
6. The Govermment Office for Science. Foresight mental capital and wellbeing project: mental capital and wellbeing: making the most of ourselves in the 21st century final project report. London: The Government Office for Science; 2008.
7. Harnois G, Gabriel P. Mental health and work: impact, issues and good practices. Geneva: World Health Organization (WHO); 2002.
8. Warr P. Work, unemployment and mental health. Oxford: Clarendon Press; 1987. p. 1–361.
9. LaMontagne A, Martin A, Page K, Reavley N, Noblet A, Milner A. Workplace mental health: developing an integrated intervention approach. BMC Psychiatry. 2014;9(14):131.
10. OECD. OECD: sick on the job? Myths and realities about mental health and work. Mental health and work. Paris: Organisation for Economic Cooperation and Development Publishing; 2012.
11. WHO International Consortium in Psychiatric Epidemiology. Cross-national comparisons of the prevalences and correlates of mental disorders. Bull World Health Organ. 2000;78(4):413–26.
12. The Department for International Development (DFID). Disability, poverty and development. London: DFID; 2000. 7 July 2016
13. Thomas CM, Morris S. Cost of depression among adults in England in 2000. Br J Psychiatry. 2003;183:514–9.
14. Greenberg PE, Kessler RC, Birnbaum HG, Leong SA, Berglund PA, Corey-Leslie P. The economic burden of depression in the United States: how did it change between 1990 and 2000? J Clin Psychiatry. 2003;64:1465–75.
15. Dewa CS, McDaid D, Ettner SL. An international perspective on worker mental health problems: who bears the burden and how are costs addressed? Can J Psychiatr. 2007;52(6):346–56.
16. Huxley P, Thornicroft G. Social inclusion, social quality and mental illness. Br J Psychiatry. 2003;182:289–90.
17. Chisholm D, Sweeny K, Sheehan P, Rasmussen B, Smit F, Cuijpers P, et al. Scaling-up treatment of depression and anxiety: a global return on investment analysis. Lancet Psychiatry. 2016;3(5):415–24.
18. Chisholm D, Diehr P, Knapp M, Patrick D, Treglia M, Simon G. Depression status, medical comorbidity and resource costs. Evidence from an international study of major depression in primary care (LIDO). Br J Psychiatry. 2003;183:121–31.
19. Knapp M, Ilson S. Economic aspects of depression and its treatment. Curr Opin Psychiatry. 2002;15:69–75.
20. Stewart WF, Ricci JA, Chee E, Hahn SR, Morganstein D. Cost of lost productive work time among US workers with depression. JAMA. 2003;289(23):3135–44.
21. Druss BG, Rosenheck RA, Sledge WH. Health and disability costs of depressive illness in a major U.S. corporation. Am J Psychiatry. 2000;157(8):1274–8.
22. Gabriel P. Mental health in the workplace: situation analyses. Ithacha: Cornel University, International Labour Organization; 2000. 8 Dec 2013
23. Karpansalo M, Kauhanen J, Lakka TA, Manninen P, Kaplan GA, Salonen JT. Depression and early retirement: prospective population based study in middle aged men. J Epidemiol Community Health. 2005;59(1):70–4.
24. Rost KM. Improving depression treatment by integrated care. J Manag Care Pharm. 2005;11(3 Suppl):S5–8.
25. Baumberg B. The global economic burden of alcohol: a review and some suggestions. Drug Alcohol Rev. 2006;25(6):537–51.
26. Powell M. Reducing the costs of alcohol in workplace: the case of employer policies. Centre for Health Economics UoY, editor. Centre for Health Economics,University of York: Working paper 68. 2016. York.
27. Gardner HH, Kleinman NL, Brook RA, Rajagopalan K, Brizee TJ, Smeeding JE. The economic impact of bipolar disorder in an employed population from an employer perspective. J Clin Psychiatry. 2006;67(8):1209–18.
28. Goetzel RZ, Hawkins K, Ozminkowski RJ, Wang S. The health and productivity cost burden of the "top 10" physical and mental health conditions affecting six large U.S. employers in 1999. J Occup Environ Med. 2003;45(1):5–14.
29. Hakkaart-van RL, Hoeijenbos MB, Regeer EJ, ten HM, Nolen WA, Veraart CP, et al. The societal costs and quality of life of patients suffering from bipolar disorder in the Netherlands. Acta Psychiatr Scand. 2004;110(5):383–92.
30. Dobrzynska E, Rymaszewska J, Kiejna A. Needs of persons with mental disorders – definitions and literature review. Psychiatr Pol. 2008;42(4):515–24.
31. Petersen I, Lund C, Stein DJ. Optimizing mental health services in low-income and middle-income countries. Curr Opin Psychiatry. 2011;24(4):318–23.
32. Lin CL, Kopelowicz A, Chan CH, Hsiung PC. A qualitative inquiry into the Taiwanese mentally ill persons' difficulties living in the community. Arch Psychiatr Nurs. 2008;22(5):266–76.
33. Cooper C, Dewe P. Well-being – absenteeism, presenteeism, costs and challenges. Occup Med (Lond). 2008;58(8):522–4.
34. Stansfeld S, Candy B. Psychosocial work environment and mental health – a meta-analytic review. Scand J Work Environ Health. 2006;32(6):443–62.
35. Johns G. Presenteeism in the workplace: a review and research agenda. J Organ Behav. 2010;31:519–42.
36. Aronsson G, Gustafsson K, Dallner M. Sick but yet at work. An empirical study of sickness presenteeism. J Epidemiol Community Health. 2000;54:502–9.
37. Caverley N, Cunningham JB, MacGregor JN. Sickness presenteeism, sickness absenteeism,

and health following restructuring in a public service organization. J Manag Stud. 2007;44:304–19.

38. Maslach C, Schaufeli WB, Leiter MP. Job burnout. Annu Rev Psychol. 2001;52:397–422.
39. Dewa CS, Lesage A, Goering P, Craveen M. Nature and prevalence of mental illness in the workplace. Healthc Pap. 2004;5(2):12–25.
40. Kieseker R, Marchant T. Workplace bullying in Australia: a review of current conceptualisations and existing research. Aust J Manag Organ Behav. 1999;2(5):61–75.
41. Giga S, Hoel H, Lewis D. The costs of workplace bullying. Bradford: University of Bradford; 2008. p. 1–38.
42. Helge H, Sparks K, Cooper C. The cosrs of violence/stress at work and the benefits of a violence/stress-free working environment. Geneva: International Labour Organisation; 2001.
43. Boyd R, Hunt A, Ortiz R. An economic analysis of workplace interventions that promote mental well-being in the workplace. 2016. https://www.nice.org.uk/guidance/ph22/evidence/economic-analysis-of-workplace-interventions-thatpromote-mental-wellbeing-in-the-workplace-67280509
44. Knapp M, McDaid D, Parsonage M. Mental health promotion and mental illness prevention: the economic case. London: Department of Health; 2011.
45. McDaid D, Knapp M, Medeiros H, MHEEN Group. Employment and mental health: assessing the economic impact and the case for intervention. London: London School of Economics & Political Science; 2008.
46. McDaid D, Zechmeister I, Kilian R, Medeiros H, Knapp M, ennelly B, et al. Making the economic case for the promotion of mental well-being and the prevention of mental health problems. London: The MHEEN Network; 2008.
47. National Institute for Health and Care Excellence (NICE). Mental wellbeing at work: NICE Public Health Guidelines 22. London: NICE; 2009.
48. LaMontagne A, Keegel T. Reducing stress in the workplace: an evidence review: full report. 2012. https://www.vichealth.vic.gov.au/.../2012%20workplace/chw_stress_full_web_final.p. Melbourne: Victorian Health Promotion Foundation.
49. Jordan J, Gurr E, inline G. Beacons of excellence in stress prevention: Health and Safety Executive Contract Research Report RR133. Health and Safety Executive Contract Research; 2003.
50. Razzouk D. Promoção de saúde mental no trabalho. In: Razzouk D, Lima M, Quirino C, editors. Saúde Mental e Trabalho. 1st ed. São Paulo: CREMESP; 2016. p. 169–78.
51. Bergerman L, Corabian P, Harstall CE. Effectiveness of organizational interventions for the prevention of stress in the workplace. Edmonton: Institute of Health Economics (IHE); 2009.
52. International Labor Organization ILO. SOLVE: integrating health promotion into workplace OSH policies: trainer's guide In: Organization IL, editor. Geneva 2012. 2012. http://www.ilo.org/safework/info/instr/WCMS_178397/lang--en/index.htm. Geneva: ILO.
53. World Health Organization. Mental health and well-being at the workplace-protection and inclusion in challenging times. Copenhagen. 2010. www.euro.who.int/__data/assets/pdf_file/0018/124047/e94345.pdf. Copenhagen: WHO Regional Office for Europe.
54. Leka S, Cox T, Zwetsloot G. The European framework for psychosocial risk management. In: Leka S, Cox T, editors. The European framework for psychosocial risk management: PRIMA-EF. Nottingham: PRIMA-EF I-WHO Publications; 2008.
55. Solving the problem: preventing stress in the workplace. 2005. http://www.cgsst.com/stock/eng/doc115-395.pdf. Quebec: Occupational Health and Safety Management, Uniersité Laval.
56. CSA Group B. National standard of Canada: psychological health and safety in the workplace – prevention, promotion, and guidance to staged implementation. Quebec: CSA Group; 2013.
57. Institute of Work HOI. The European framework for psychosocial risk management- prima –EF30. Nottingham: WHO Publications; 2008.
58. Fearnely J. Gauging demand for free to access money advice: a discussion paper. London: Money Advice Trust; 2007.
59. Ministry of Justice United Kingdom. Twelve months latter: does the advice help? The impact of debt advice: advice agency client study. London: Ministry of Justice United Kingdom; 2007.
60. Roeloffs C, Sherbourne C, Unutzer J, Fink A, Tang L, Wells KB. Stigma and depression among primary care patients. Gen Hosp Psychiatry. 2003;25(5):311–5.
61. World Health Organization. Mental health policies and programmes in the workplace. Geneva: World Health Organization; 2005.
62. Thornicroft, G. (2006). Shunned: discrimination against people with mental illness. Geneva: Oxford.
63. Kitchener BA, Jorm AF. Mental health first aid training: review of evaluation studies. Aust N Z J Psychiatry. 2006;40(1):6–8.
64. Hadlaczky G, Hokby S, Mkrtchian A, Carli V, Wasserman D. Mental health first aid is an effective public health intervention for improving knowledge, attitudes, and behaviour: a meta-analysis. Int Rev Psychiatry. 2014;26(4):467–75.
65. Wong E, ollins R, erully J. Reviewing the evidence base for mental health first aid. 2015. www.rand.org/content/dam/rand/pubs/research_reports/RR900/.../RAND_RR972.pdf. Rand Corporation.
66. The Mentally Healthy Workplace Alliance. The beyondblue National Workplace Program (NWP). Australia Beyond Blue Ltda; 2014. https://www.headsup.org.au/training-and-resources/educational-programs/beyondblue-national-workplaceprogram
67. Attridge M, Amaral T, Bjornson T, Goplerud E, Herlihy P, McPherson TL. Selecting and strengthening employee assistance programs: a purchaser's guide. EASNA Research Notes 1. 2009.

29 Methods and Instruments for the Estimation of Production Changes in Economic Evaluations

Wolter Hassink and Bernard van den Berg

Abstract

This chapter focuses on the indirect costs of paid work that result from mental illness. It provides an overview of monetary valuation methods and approaches to measure and value production gains and losses. The methods are applied to mental illness, although they have also been applied to other diseases. As mental health and mental health care can have different effects on production, the chapter starts by explaining how to classify the consequences of mental illness for the production of firms. It follows with the definitions of different types of production. This chapter subsequently presents and discusses three major approaches to value production. It pays attention to the human capital approach, the friction costs approach, and the multiplier approach. The chapter ends with a description of survey questions and instruments to measure and value production changes in economic evaluations.

Key Points Summary

- Indirect costs: presenteeism, absenteeism
- Human capital approach
- Friction costs approach
- Multiplier approach

29.1 Background

Mental disorders and mental health problems involve a substantial economic burden. Depression and anxiety, for instance, are associated with decreased labor productivity [1, 2] (see Chap. 25). Mental disorders involve more production losses than physical health losses [3]. Effective mental care treatments might therefore lead to productivity gains in terms of preventing both job loss and fewer hours worked. It is suggested that the productivity gains related to depression outweigh the costs of effective treatment [4, 5].

Traditionally, textbooks on economic evaluations make a distinction between the direct and indirect costs of (mental) illness. Direct costs are defined as the opportunity costs of formal healthcare goods and services (see Chap. 2). Indirect

W. Hassink
Utrecht University School of Economics, Utrecht University, P.O. Box 80125, 3508 TC Utrecht, The Netherlands
e-mail: W.H.J.Hassink@uu.nl

B. van den Berg (✉)
Faculty of Economics and Business, University of Groningen, Nettelbosje 2, Groningen 9747 AE, The Netherlands
e-mail: bernard.van.den.berg@rug.nl

D. Razzouk (ed.), *Mental Health Economics*, DOI 10.1007/978-3-319-55266-8_29

costs are described as "the imputed value of foregone labour product when patients' labour services become inefficient or are withdrawn from production on account of morbidity or premature mortality" [6] (p. 253) (see Chap. 25). Indirect costs can be related to paid work, but other components of indirect costs exist, such as patient time, informal care (see Chap. 17), and unpaid work [7].

This chapter focuses on the indirect costs of paid work that result from mental illness. It provides an overview of monetary valuation methods and approaches to measure and value production gains and losses.

29.2 Losses Versus Gains

There are two perspectives on the consequences of mental illness for the production of firms. On the one hand, mental illness can involve losses of production in firms and organizations (see Chap. 28). On the other hand, mental healthcare interventions and treatments can lead to nonmedical production gains or benefits in firms and organizations.

Studies of costs of illness examine production losses related to a disease, whereas economic evaluations aim to quantify the costs and health benefits of new interventions and medical treatments. In the latter, the denominator of the ratio consists of the outcomes of an intervention, which are expressed in gains in health-related quality of life. The numerator is the monetary value of the medical costs (direct costs) of the intervention (see Chaps. 1 and 2).

Part of the impact of new treatments and medical interventions are production gains. It would be difficult to express these gains in health-related quality-of-life units and to add them to the denominator of the costs-effectiveness ratio (capturing the gains of the new intervention). To avoid adding incommensurable units to economic evaluations, these gains are expressed in monetary units and added to in the numerator of the ratio on the cost side of an economic evaluation [8]. This might explain why the majority of the economic evaluation literature seems to refer to production costs, although they are strictly speaking about production gains to society [9, 10].

In this chapter we therefore follow the convention in the majority of the literature, which uses the terms *production losses* or *production costs*. The applications are about fewer costs (production gains) that result from effective medical interventions or treatments for mental health.

29.3 Defining Labour Loss

Labour input loss is the volume component of the loss of paid labor due to mental illness. The loss of labor comprises four components.

First, mental illness may have consequences for the quality of labor input, or the work effort of an employee. While being ill, the worker may show up at work but may become less productive or even unproductive when working. Hence, production is reduced without an absence from work. This phenomenon is referred to as presenteeism [11] (see Chap. 28).

Second, mental illness may have consequences for the amount of labor performed or the number of hours spent at work. As a result of the illness, the worker may show up at work late. Furthermore, the worker may report sick to the employer, both in terms of the frequency and duration of absences [12]. Moreover, the worker may decide to work fewer hours. Alternatively, sick employees may be referred to partial sick-pay schemes in order to improve their likelihood to return to work [13]. The decision to change the input of labor to the current employer is referred to as the labor supply decision at the intensive margin [14].

Third, mental illness may have consequences for the decision to remain employed with the firm. The worker may leave the firm, and the decision to leave may be initiated by either the employee or the firm in response to the illness. There are various options. An employee may decide to resign voluntarily, or the employee may be dismissed after being diagnosed with a mental illness. Discrimination or stigma against mental illness could be a reason for dismissal of people with mental disorders (see Chap. 27). When people return from sick leave, they might lose their job because of being diagnosed with a mental disorder.

Furthermore, morbidity is possible – the employee may enroll in a disability income insurance program after a period of long-term absenteeism [15]. This is referred to as a labor supply decision at the extensive margin [14].

Fourth, mental illness may result in mortality of the employee, which apparently also leads to labor losses. For instance, excessive alcohol consumption may be responsible for about 17% of accidents in the workplace [16] (see Chap. 26).

29.4 Defining the Monetary Value of Production

The loss of paid labor due to sick leave, presenteeism, morbidity, and death of an employee may lead to reduced production by the firm by which the worker is employed. *Production* is defined as the monetized value of the number of goods and services produced by an employee in a certain period. The loss of paid labor may also lead to a change in productivity. *Productivity* is defined as the value of the output per unit of labor (for instance, per hour or per day).

It is difficult to quantify the exact value of production by an individual employee. Using firm-level information, one could calculate the firm's turnover per employee, which represents the value added per employee. However, averaging production masks the difference in production among employees. It depends on the nature of particular jobs and the employees' expertise. Production can potentially be calculated for several categories of employees [17]. Alternatively, one can take the value of goods and services produced by an individual employee; however, it is difficult to measure individual production unless people are self-employed. Various degrees of complexity exist based on an employee's occupation. A manager, for instance, may be at higher risk with respect to getting a mental illness, but it is difficult to measure how this illness might affect their production. One complication is that it is hard to disentangle the employee's own production from the goods and services produced by his or her colleagues, particularly if team production is involved [17]. Monitoring by supervisors and learning by peers are also important. It could be even more complicated if people work on projects in one team and then move to another project in another team. An option could be to consider the monetary value of piece-rate production, in which the salary fully depends on the amount produced and thereby fully captures the employee's added value. Another complication is that the output of individual employees consists of multiple dimensions, which makes it difficult to identify the various components of an individual's production [18].

To circumvent the problems of measuring production of an individual employee, one can take the gross wage of an individual employee as a proxy measure of individual production. It is based on the prediction of neoclassical theory that a wage is equal to the value of production of the marginal worker that is added to the workforce. There may, however, be a discrepancy between a worker's wage and productivity, for instance, because of their experience in the labor market [19]. This discrepancy between a worker's wage and productivity has received substantial attention in labor economics [20].

29.5 Human Capital Approach

Weisbrod [21] was one of the earliest users of the human capital approach in the context of healthcare evaluation. Historically, it is the method that has most often been used to estimate productivity costs [22]. In broad terms, the human capital approach gives a monetized value of labor loss of paid employment due to illness over an employee's lifetime, until retirement. The monetized value is calculated as the forgone earnings of the individual employee.

More specifically, the method quantifies the impact of healthcare on lost work time – whether through sick leave, presenteeism, morbidity, or death of the individual employee. Lost productivity is monetarily valued according to the gross wage of the individual employee. The loss due to absenteeism, morbidity, and death is calculated as the employee's gross daily wage multiplied by the number of work days lost (until retirement). The measure also includes the loss of labor due to presenteeism, which is calculated as a reduction in productivity due to the illness while remaining at work [23]. Note that the stream of losses in future years are discounted by a rate of 3–5% (for an explanation, see Chap. 2). It is important to acknowledge that the human capital approach has a foundation in economic theory. The rationale for this is given by Weinstein et al. [10]: "in a well-functioning labour market, productive output and the compensation to the worker are equal, because they resent the same resource" (pp. 506–507). This is one of the implications of standard neoclassical economic theory on which the approach is based. In this framework, it is assumed that individuals and firms seek to maximize their utility (for an explanation see Chaps. 1, 3, and 6) and profits, respectively, from the activities in which they are involved. From the firm's point of view, as additional employees (marginal workers) with similar skills are hired, the value of the firm's production increases, but by successively smaller amounts. It is assumed that the contribution of each additional employee to total production decreases as more workers are employed. The firm can gain by employing more workers as long as the gross wage paid by the firm is less than the marginal worker's contribution to the monetary value of the firm's production. However, the firm will reduce the number of employees if the gross wage is greater than the contribution of the marginal worker. If the firms aims to maximize its profits, it will employ workers up to the point at which the marginal contribution to production is equal to the gross wage. This reasoning forms the basis for using the gross wage as the value of lost production during absence from work in the human capital approach.

The human capital approach has some shortcomings. First, it is hard to include presenteeism in calculating the loss of labor because it requires information on the hiring of replacement workers to enhance the reduced effort of the ill worker. Second, there are difficulties in obtaining all of the information on, for instance, the employee's salary. Third, the human capital approach implicitly assumes that workers continue with paid work at the current arrangement (wage and hours worked) until they retire. For instance, as a result of the mental illness, they may have reduced output (presenteeism). Next, they may be absent, which may result in enrollment in a disability insurance program.

29.6 Friction Costs Approach

The friction cost approach was introduced by Koopmanschap and van Ineveld [24] developed as an alternative to the human capital approach. They argued that the human capital approach overestimates the true production losses: "The real production losses can be much smaller than the potential losses because sick people can often be replaced at little cost" ([24], p. 1006). Following this logic, the two key elements of the friction cost method are replacement of sick employees (and those who have died) and the costs of these replacements.

The friction cost approach focuses on a specific property of the production process inside firms, namely, that the firm decides to hire another employee to replace the absent employee. Because of the temporal decline in production, the friction costs method might result in a lower production loss than would have been estimated when applying the human capital method.

The friction cost method quantifies the future loss of production due to the loss of labor caused by the illness, until the absent worker is replaced by another worker. In other words, the production loss due to mental illness depends on the amount of time a firm needs to restore its level of production to the same level as before the employee got the illness or passed away [23–25].

The friction cost method requires three specific pieces of information [26]. First, there needs to be information on the duration of the friction period of sickness-related absenteeism. The friction period is defined as the duration of the sick leave until a substitute employee starts working. Hence, production loss is calculated as the number of hours or working days lost due to sickness-related absence or mortality, as long as the absence does not exceed the friction period. Second, the firm will create a vacancy to recruit replacements for only a fraction of the absentees. In the case of a short-term absence, it is unlikely that a replacement worker will be hired by the firm. The approach requires specific information on the costs of hiring a replacement employee. The firm incurs the costs of search and recruitment, as well as the costs of training the replacement employee. Third, the friction cost method requires information on the value of the production lost due to absence (the price component). A macroeconometric model has been recommended as a way of estimating macroeconomic consequences of work absence and disability [24]. The method requires discounting future streams of financial losses. See [26] for a further discussion of required information for the friction-cost approach, in addition to the three pieces of information discussed here.

The costs of mental illness calculated using the friction cost approach vary with the economic business cycle. During economic growth, the labor market becomes tighter, whereas during an economic recession, the labor market weakens. The costs of mental illness calculated by the friction cost approach are seemingly higher in a tight labor market, during which unemployment is low and it is harder to find suitable replacement workers. Furthermore, strong differences exist across types of workers. In particular, the duration of time needed to replace a highly educated employee is substantially longer compared with that needed to replace employees with low levels of education.

The friction cost approach has some shortcomings. First, it is hard to include presenteeism in the loss of labor because it requires information on the hiring of replacement workers because of reduced efforts by the ill worker. Sometimes employers do not replace the worker and give his or her tasks to another worker, overloading that person and avoiding additional costs. This is confirmed by a literature review that showed that when applying the friction cost method, worker effort or presenteeism is largely ignored. "All 46 studies that were reviewed included the estimation of lost time due to absence from paid working time, with only one study [27] incorporating loss from reduced productivity whilst at work (presenteeism) using the friction cost method" ([26], p. 36). This is remarkable because it is likely that some production losses costs due to mental health are related to presenteeism.

Second, to monetarily value lost output for the firm's production because of an employee's mental illness, the friction cost method does not recommend using gross wages, unlike the human capital method. However, the vast majority of studies surveyed by Kigozi et al. [26] seems to apply gross wages to monetarily value production losses. In this respect, these studies are in line with the human capital approach.

29.7 Multiplier Approach

We follow Lensberg et al. [25], who describe and debate the third approach, which they coin "multiplier approach" to determine the indirect costs of paid work. For more details see Zhang et al. [19]. The multiplier approach can be considered as a refinement of the human capital and the friction cost approach, and it is based on previous work [28–30]. This approach emphasizes that the employee often operates in a team, so there are complementarities in production among the team members. Absenteeism due to illness leads to a decline in the production of other workers who operate in the team, in addition to the loss of the absent individual's production. Other team members need to take over part of the activities of the absent employee.

The loss of production for the team relative to the loss of production by the ill employee can be formulated using a ratio. More specifically, it is a multiplier, which is defined as the ratio of the total loss of team production (the numerator) and the individual gross wage of the absentee (the denominator). A larger multiplier leads to higher indirect costs of mental health due to sickness-related absenteeism.

The multiplier depends on the following features of the production process. First, the multiplier may be large when the activities between the team members are strongly interdependent – hence there are strong complementarities. Second, the multiplier can be reduced if the production process is based on inventories, so that it mitigates a temporary decline in production caused by sickness-related absenteeism. Third, the multiplier may be dependent on the workers' morale. Absence may lead to lower morale – and lower productivity – among the colleagues within the team. Fourth, there can be time sensitivity, which means that postponed output results in a lower price or revenue of the firm [25, 29].

29.8 Examples of Survey Questions and Instruments

Which instruments are available to measure and value production, and what type of information is necessary if one wishes to include in an economic evaluation production gains due to mental illness? The answer to these questions obviously depends on the method one wishes to apply – the human capital, friction cost, or multiplier approach – as well as whether one aims to include absenteeism and presenteeism.

To apply the human capital method, the minimum required pieces of information are the number of hours worked in a paid job and the gross wage. This information is usually available in nationally representative surveys such as the British Household Panel Survey, the Survey of Health, Ageing and Retirement in Europe, and the Survey of Working Life. Table 29.1 gives examples of measuring paid work time from these national surveys.

Table 29.1 illustrates that survey and interview questions might differ slightly, although they also have similarities in that they all ask for usual work hours per week. Not surprisingly, there are more differences when asking for wages: gross wages versus net wages, period of payment, number of jobs, and salary and/or earnings from self-employment. To consistently apply the human capital approach, net wages should be adapted for taxes, which can be calculated using information from, for example, the national tax agency. Please note that when calculating productivity losses due to mortality, information on the retirement age is necessary because the indirect costs are not zero until the age of retirement (human capital approach). Retirement

Table 29.1 Examples survey questions for the human capital method

Survey	Survey question	
	Hours paid work	Gross wage
British Household Panel Survey [31]	How many hours in total do you usually work a week in your job?	How much are you usually paid? How long a period did that cover? Week Fortnight Four weeks Calendar month Year Is that before or after any deductions for tax, national insurance, union dues, and so on, or are there usually no deductions at all from your salary? Before deductions After deductions
Survey of Health, Ageing and Retirement in Europe [32]	Regardless of your basic contracted hours, how many hours a week do you usually work in this job, excluding meal breaks but including any paid or unpaid overtime?	After any taxes and contributions, what was your approximate annual income from employment in the year? Please include any additional or extra or lump sum payments, such as bonuses, 13 month, Christmas, or Summer pays If self-employed: After any taxes and contributions and after paying for any materials, equipment, or goods that you use in your work, what was your approximate annual income from self-employment for the year?
Survey of Working Life [33]	How many hours do you usually work each week including overtime in (all) your job(s)?	Before tax, what was your basic, ordinary hourly rate last week

age information likely varies among individuals. Important elements of the institutional setting are government requirements regarding the age at retirement, pension arrangements of the economic sector in which the absentee is employed, as well as private pension arrangements [22]. Questions on sickness-related absence in these surveys are usually very general. For instance, "Were you away from work last week?" and "What was the main reason for being away with a sickness-related absence?" are two of the boxes respondents could tick. Also, information on respondents' health and healthcare utilization is usually not detailed enough with respect to the consumption of health services to be able to qualify the effectiveness of medical interventions for economic evaluations. In addition, these questions are usually measured once a year, which does not allow patterns during the year to be quantified. By contrast, medical trials usually measure the effectiveness of a treatment at various points in time up to 6 month or a year. The data from national surveys have to be matched with data on the effectiveness on the medical intervention or treatment to get at the production gains (for cost-of-disease studies, one could simply link the data in the tables with the disease). More precisely, production losses due to illness must be measured alongside clinical effectiveness to be able to quantify the production gains of a medical treatment for economic evaluations. To do so, various productivity loss instruments have been developed. Lofland et al. [34] review productivity loss instruments. Some of the instruments are about general health and some are specifically developed to measure the impact of specific diseases (e.g., migraine) on production. Not all the instruments are available in the public domain, as some have been developed by pharmaceutical companies. From among the 11 instruments Lofland et al. found, they identified 6 instruments that are able to monetarily value production losses.

The oldest general health productivity instrument in the review by Lofland et al. [34] that enables the production losses to be monetarily valued is the Work Productivity and Activity Impairment Questionnaire. This instrument has also a version that is applicable to specific health domains, including mental health. It also has been translated into many languages. This instrument allows a productivity score to be calculated as the percentage time lost because of mental illness: (hours not worked due to mental illness/ [hours not worked due to mental illness + actual hours worked last week]) × 100 times the degree to which mental health affects productivity, that is, ([1 − 10/10]) × 100. (For exact details and scoring see ref. 35.) The monetary value of productivity lost as a result of mental illness is the employee's gross hourly wage times the productivity score. The Work Productivity and Activity Impairment questionnaire yields four types of scores: (1) absenteeism (work time missed); (2) presenteeism (impairment at work/reduced on-the job effectiveness); (3) work productivity lost (overall work impairment/absenteeism plus presenteeism); and (4) activity impairment [35]. It is striking that the instrument does not ask for wages. It is not uncommon in this literature to impute the wages of similar people in the general population to avoid results that are driven by randomness. As the sample size of economic evaluations is usually determined to be able to detect a statistically significant difference in medical effectiveness, there is a risk that a very rich person in the study could drive the results. To avoid this, wages of the general population who are of a similar age, sex, and education are often used. Another issue is that in a psychiatric sample there likely exists cognitive bias, especially with depressive people in terms of recall bias, which leads to an underestimation or overestimation of the true wage. Please note that Lensberg et al. [25] suggested how to consider production effects in the design of a clinical trial (see also refs. 36 and 3 [p. 27]).

Instruments to measure productivity loss can also be applied in clinical trials or observational studies developed to quantify the effectiveness of medicines or mental health interventions and treatments. When doing so, one could consider only asking about hours worked in a paid job, then comparing people receiving the intervention with people not receiving the intervention and applying the human capital method using gross wages from different sources, such as national statistics. One could, for example, take the gross wage by sex and age, and use that to monetarily value the amount of paid work gained as a result of medical treatment, then add the relevant gross wage. This has two advantages: (1) Not a lot of information has to be collected in addition to the information already collected for the study aim. (2) It avoids having random rich people in the sample, which would drive the results. It has also two disadvantages: (1) The gross wages of the general public might not be attributable to the sample. (2) The design of the trial is not based on detecting differences in worker production.

Presenteeism is only estimated for a small number of instruments [11]. They refer to the Work Productivity Short Inventory, which asks employees to estimate how many unproductive hours they spent at work during the recall period. In addition, for the friction cost method, the period in which sickness-related absenteeism is costly to the firm depends on the average duration of the vacancy (the time required to find a replacement worker). The vacancy duration differs across categories of workers, for instance, by age, sex, or education. This information can be derived from country-specific statistics. Because the vacancy duration depends on the state of the economy, it should be updated frequently. For the multiplier approach, it is important to have the ratio between the wage and the team's total production. This type of information is usually difficult to get. Zhang et al. [37] developed an instrument to apply this approach.

29.9 Discussion and Conclusion

This chapter provides an overview of methods to measure and monetarily value production changes in economic evaluations. It also briefly presented and discussed questions from general surveys and specific instruments to do so.

An important question is whether to include the effect of (mental) healthcare interventions on productivity in economic evaluations. This question has been intensively debated; see ref. 22 for an overview. A natural consequence of taking a societal perspective in economic evaluations is to include effects of productivity as long as they are not negligibly small (e.g., [23]). Because there is a substantial literature on the effects of mental health conditions on the labor market [38], it is not unlikely that the effect of mental health interventions on productivity is substantial enough to not to be ignored. For instance, in economic evaluations of treatments for depression, productivity reflected, on average, more than half of the total costs of the interventions [39].

Guidelines for economic evaluations vary with respect to recommendations for including the effects on productivity in economic evaluations. For instance, the United Kingdom recommends excluding these productivity losses and gains, whereas Sweden and the Netherlands recommend including them [25]. Part of this variation is a result of differences in the recommended perspectives: a healthcare sector perspective versus a societal perspective.

Sweden and the Netherlands both recommend adopting a societal perspective but differ with respect to the prescribed methodology to include productivity gains and losses in economic evaluations. Sweden recommends the human capital approach and the Netherlands recommends the friction cost approach. By applying costly incentive systems or costly monitoring systems, firms can reduce the costs of absenteeism [12, 40]. These strategies by firms to reduce the costs of absence seem to be ignored in the literature on valuing production changes caused by healthcare utilization, probably because it has been implicitly assumed that they are random across diseases and medical interventions. If this is not true, they should be included in measures of productivity changes. The possibility of estimating production changes for economic evaluations depends on the availability of data. In addition to differences in data availability, there is substantial variation between countries in institutions and labor markets. This variation partly reflects variation in decision makers' objectives, which should be reflected in methods and applications estimating production changes caused by changes in mental health for economic evaluations.

Key Messages

Paid worker production consists of work effort and various components of the labor supply: absenteeism and presenteeism.

- Presenteeism is the effort of a worker with health problems when at work.
- Absenteeism is the multiplication of labor supply at the extensive margin and labor supply at the intensive margin, which is the percentage of workers times the number of hours they do not work because of health problems.
- The value of production can be represented by a worker's gross wages.
- Nationally representative surveys should be complemented by specific instruments to get enough information to be able to include worker productivity in economic evaluations.

References

1. Ormel J, VonKorff M, Ustun TB, Pini S, Korten A, Oldehinkel T. Common mental disorders and disability across cultures. JAMA. 1994;272(22):1741–8.
2. Kessler RC, Barber C, Birnbaum HG, Frank RG, Greenberg PE, Rose RM, et al. Depression in the workplace: effects on short-term disability. Health Aff. 1999;18(5):163–71.
3. Huang DT. A new tool to measure the relationship between health-related quality of life and workforce productivity. PhD thesis Georgia Institute of Technology. 2008.
4. Wang PS, Patrick A, Avorn J, Azocar F, Ludman E, McCulloch J, et al. The costs and benefits of enhanced depression care to employers. Arch Gen Psychiatry. 2006;63(12):1345–53.
5. Wang PS, Beck AL, Berglund P, McKenas DK, Pronk NP, Simon GE, et al. Effects of major depression on moment-in-time work performance. Am J Psychiatr. 2014;161(10):1885–91.
6. Ernst R. Indirect costs and cost-effectiveness analysis. Value Health. 2006;9(4):253–61.
7. Brouwer WB, Koopmanschap MA, Rutten FF. Productivity costs in cost-effectiveness analysis: numerator or denominator: a further discussion. Health Econ. 1997;6(5):511–4.
8. Olsen JA, Richardson J. Production gains from health care: what should be included in cost-effectiveness analyses? Soc Sci Med. 1999;49(1):17–26.
9. Torrance GW. Measurement of health state utilities for economics appraisal: a review. J Health Econ. 1986;5(1):1–30.
10. Weinstein MC, Siegel JE, Garber AM, Lipscomb J, Luce BR, Manning WG, et al. Productivity costs, time costs and health-related quality of life: a response to the Erasmus group. Health Econ. 1997;6(5):505–10.
11. Mattke S, Balakrishnan A, Bergamo G, Newberry SJ. A review of methods to measure health-related productivity loss. Am J Manag Care. 2007;13(4):211–7.
12. Treble J, Barmby T. Worker absenteeism and sick pay. Cambridge: Cambridge University Press; 2011.
13. Markussen S, Mykletun A, Røed K. The case for presenteeism—evidence from Norway's sickness insurance program. J Public Econ. 2012;96(11–12):959–72.
14. Blundell R, Bozio A, Laroque G. Labor supply and the extensive margin. Am Econ Rev. 2011;101(3):482–6.
15. Hassink WHJ, Koning P, Zwinkels W. Employers opting out of public disability insurance: selection or incentive effects? IZA-discussion paper 9181; 2015.
16. Gutiérrec Fisac GI, Regidor E, Ronda E. Occupational accidents and alcohol consumption in Spain. Int J Epidemiol. 1992;21(6):1114–20.
17. Sauermann, J. Performance measures and worker productivity. IZA World of Labor. 2015; p. 1–11.
18. Autor D, Levy F, Murnane RJ. The skill content of recent technological change: an empirical exploration. Q J Econ. 2003;118(4):1279–331.
19. Zhang W, Bansback N, Anis AH. Measuring and valuing productivity loss due to poor health: a critical review. Soc Sci Med. 2011;72(2):185–92.
20. Lazear EP. Why is there mandatory retirement? J Polit Econ. 1979;87(6):1261–84.
21. Weisbrod B. Economics of public health. Pennsylvania: University of Pennsylvania Press; 1961.
22. Pritchard C, Sculpher M. Productivity costs: principles and practice in economic evaluation. London: OHE; 2000.
23. Berger ML, Murray JF, Xu J, Pauly M. Alternative valuations of work loss and productivity. J Occup Environ Med. 2001;43(1):18–24.
24. Koopmanschap MA, Van Ineveld BM. Towards a new approach for estimating indirect costs of disease. Soc Sci Med. 1992;34(9):1005–10.
25. Lensberg BR, Drummond MF, Danchenko N, Despiégel N, François C. Challenges in measuring and valuing productivity costs, and their relevance in mood disorders. Clinico Econ Outcomes Res. 2013;5:565–73.
26. Kigozi J, Jowett S, Lewis M, Barton P, Coast J. Estimating productivity costs using the friction cost approach in practice: a systematic review. Eur J Health Econ. 2016;17(1):31–44.
27. Smit F, Willemse G, Koopmanschap M, Onrust S, Cuijpers P, Beekman A. Cost-effectiveness of pre-

venting depression in primary care patients: randomised trial. Br J Psychiatry. 2006;188(4):330–6.
28. Coles M, Treble J. Calculating the price of worker reliability. Labour Econ. 1996;3(2):169–88.
29. Nicholson S, Pauly MV, Polsky D, Sharda C, Szrek H, Berger ML. Measuring the effects of work loss on productivity with team production. Health Econ. 2006;15(2):111–23.
30. Pauly MV, Nicholson S, Polsky D, Berger ML, Sharda C. Valuing reductions in on-the-job illness: 'presenteeism' from managerial and economic perspectives. Health Econ. 2008;17(4):469–85.
31. https://www.iser.essex.ac.uk/bhps/documentation/volb/wave1/aindresp8.html#AJSHRS.
32. http://www.share-project.org/data-access-documentation/questionnaires/questionnaire-wave-1.html
33. http://www.stats.govt.nz/browse_for_stats/income-and-work/employment_and_unemployment/survey-of-working-life.aspx
34. Lofland JH, Pizzi L, Frick KD. A review of health-related workplace productivity loss instruments. PharmacoEconomics. 2004;22(3):165–84.
35. http://www.reillyassociates.net/WPAI_Scoring.html
36. Chirban JT, Jacobs RJ, Warren J. The 36-item short form health survey (SF-36) and work productivity and the impairment (WPAI) questionnaire in panic disorder. Dis Manag Health Out. 1997;1(3):154–64.
37. Zhang W, Bansback N, Boonen A, Severens JL, Anis AH. Development of a composite questionnaire, the valuation of lost productivity, to value productivity losses: application in rheumatoid arthritis. Value Health. 2012;15(1):46–54.
38. Frijters P, Johnston D, Shields M. Mental health and labour market participation: evidence from IV panel data models. IZA Discussion Paper 4883; 2010.
39. Krol M, Papenburg J, Koopmanschap M, Brouwer W. Do productivity costs matter? The impact of including productivity costs on the incremental costs of interventions targeted at depressive disorders. Pharmaco economics. 2011;29(7):601–19.
40. Hassink WHJ, Koning P. Do financial bonuses reduce employee absenteeism? Evidence from a lottery. Ind Labor Relat Rev. 2009;62(3):327–42.

Glossary

Absenteeism an employee's recess from work, typically consisting of illness-related absences and short- and long-term disability.

Accounting costs costs directly related to the monetary costs of all inputs used for producing a good or services. Usually, the price of acquiring a product is used for accounting costs purposes.

Affect the subjective and immediate experience of emotion attached to ideas or mental representations. Affect has outward manifestations that may be classified as restricted, blunt, flat, broad, labile, appropriate, or inappropriate.

Age weights weights assigned to outcomes that are based on the age of the people included in the evaluation process.

Akaike's information criterion a statistical measure of model fit.

Analysis of variance a hypothesis testing method used when more than two comparison groups are considered.

Anhedonia loss of interest in and withdrawal from all regular and pleasurable activities. Often associated with depression.

Area under the curve (AUC) analysis a method used to calculate the marginal benefit of an intervention over a fixed time period.

Average cost-effectiveness ratio (ACER) a value that expresses the total costs of an intervention per achieved health outcome compared with a baseline situation, which in many cases would be the current situation (usual care).

Average (gross) costs the mean costs, including fixed and variable costs, consumed by a group or population. They do not take into account individual's consumption variation.

Bayesian information criterion a statistical measure of model fit.

Bootstrapping (nonparametric) a method of nonparametric assessment through random resampling with replacement from observed data.

Bottom-up approach (micro-costing) a technique based on collecting all individual data regarding resource consumption then aggregating all individual costs, summing them to achieve the total costs.

Bounded data data that are restricted to a specific range, such as non-negative cost.

Burden (disease) the social, economic, and health effects of a disease as estimated by an indicator covering the mortality and morbidity of the disease in one sole measure (e.g., disability-adjusted life year).

Burnout usually related to the workplace and characterized by emotional exhaustion, feelings of cynicism, detachment from the job, and a sense of ineffectiveness and lack of accomplishment.

Capability the things that a person is able to do or be in life; a notion arising from the work of Amartya Sen and the preferred focus of evaluation within the associated capability approach.

CAPS (Centro de Atenção Psicossocial) a community mental health service for people with moderate and severe mental disorders who need psycho-rehabilitation intervention and social inclusion promotion; called "Psychosocial Centre" in public Brazilian health system.

Categorical data discrete data that are organized in levels or categories.

D. Razzouk (ed.), *Mental Health Economics*, DOI 10.1007/978-3-319-55266-8

Censored data a type of missing data whereby the data are not collected because of incomplete follow-up.

Charge the price of a good or service.

Chi-squared test a hypothesis test used with two comparison groups and a categorical variable.

Clinical Outcomes in Routine Evaluation (CORE) measure a preference-based measure (the six-dimension CORE) or non-preference-based outcome measure (CORE-OM) used to assess the quality of life of patients with common metal health conditions.

Cognition the mental process of knowing and becoming aware; function is closely associated with judgment.

Cohort simulation model *See* Markov model.

Condition-specific measure a measure designed with a particular condition as its focus. *See* DEMQOL and DEMQOL-U as examples.

Confidence interval (CI) a frequentist statistic that describes a range within which the true value might exist.

Contingent valuation (CV) a valuation technique that can be used to assess the monetary value of commodities for use in an economic evaluation; a survey method used to obtain individuals' willingness to pay or willingness to accept an amount by asking them to consider different hypothetical situations about the intervention under investigation.

Continuous data data that can take an infinite number of values within a range.

Cost of illness a type of study focus used to identify, measure, and then aggregate the economic effects of a disorder.

Cost-benefit analysis (CBA) a technique that assesses consequences in monetary terms so that the return on investment from spending a sum of money in one program can be compared with investing that same sum in any other program, both within the health sphere and beyond, by investing these resources in, for example, public infrastructure.

Cost-consequence analysis (CCA) a technique that presents a range of outcomes measured in natural units alongside the costs of alternative programs, without defining any one outcome as primary.

Cost-effectiveness acceptability curve (CEAC) a plot of the probability of the cost-effectiveness of one or more interventions (based on the results of a probability sensitivity analysis) as a function of the highest amount individuals are willing to pay per unit of outcome set by the decision maker.

Cost-effectiveness analysis (CEA) a narrower form of opportunity cost assessment in which the assessed consequences are specific and limited to a particular field of healthcare, mostly one particular disease; a form of economic evaluation where the outcome is in natural units (such as health benefits).

Cost-minimization analysis a technique that compares the costs of different programs that lead to broadly the same result. Because there is always uncertainty around costs and around expected outcomes, in reality, the effectiveness of two programs can rarely be assumed as being equal.

Cost-utility analysis (CUA) a technique that is limited to comparisons within the health domain. Consequences are expressed in generic health units that comprise the effects of a condition on both mortality and morbidity, such as quality-adjusted life years, disability-adjusted life years, or healthy year equivalents. This is a form of economic evaluation where the outcome is "utility-weighted."

Credible interval a Bayesian confidence interval.

Disability-adjusted life year (DALY) a value estimated based on years of life lost from premature death and years of life lived in a state of less than full health. The latter is based on disability weights, a measure of the severity of a disease, ranging from 0 (perfect health) to 1 (equivalent to death), a metric of effectiveness associated with cost-utility analysis the World Health Organization.

Decision (combining) rule a method used to aggregate information about costs and benefits and feed that information into the decision-making process to produce a recommendation.

Decision-analytic model a model that combines information on the likelihood of each consequence with the values of outcomes to estimate the expected value of each alternative option.

Decision tree a graphical method of representing every consequence of a decision using branches and nodes.

Dementia Quality of Life (DEMQOL) measure a self-completed or proxy-completed (DEMQOL-Proxy) outcome measure focused on the dementia-related quality of life of patients with dementia; a condition-specific measure of health-related quality of life that aims to provide an alternative method to estimate quality-adjusted life years (QALYs) in dementia. The DEMQOL-Proxy aims to assess QALYs during later stages of dementia, when verbal ability diminishes and can only be elicited from a proxy (e.g., a caregiver). Psychometric analysis analyzed the dimensional structure and performance, and resulted in final health state classification systems for five dimensions.

Dementia Quality of Life, utility-weighted (DEMQOL-U) measure a preference-based (utility-weighted) self-completed or proxy-completed outcome measure focused on the dementia-related quality of life of patients with dementia.

Depression a mental state characterized by feelings of sadness, loneliness, despair, low self-esteem, and self-reproach; accompanying signs include psychomotor retardation or, at times, agitation, withdrawal from interpersonal contact, and vegetative symptoms, such as insomnia and anorexia. The term refers to a mood that is so characterized or a mood disorder.

Deterministic sensitivity analysis a technique used to analyze uncertainty and designed to measure the effect of varying the values of individual parameters over a preassigned range on model output.

Direct costs costs related to the consumption of healthcare resources.

Direct health costs costs closely related to healthcare and treatment, including clinical staff, medical devices, and medications.

Direct non-health costs costs supporting health treatment, such as utilities, cleaning, food, security, accommodation, criminal justice, and patient costs.

Disability weight a weight assigned to aspects of disability associated with the disability-adjusted life year. *See* Disability-adjusted life year (DALY).

Discount rate Interest rate is a concept related to the value of a benefit over time, that is, so-called time preference. Usually, people prefer getting benefit now rather than in the future; for this reason, the value of the benefit decreases over time. The costs of one good or service now are much higher than they will be within 5 or 10 years, not considering its depreciation. All future (over 1 year) costs should be discounted in economic evaluation and cost studies. It usually varies from 3% to 5%.

Discrete choice experiment (DCE) a quantitative method increasingly used in health and social care to elicit preferences from participants (caregivers, users, patients, payers, commissioners). Typically, participants are presented with a series of alternative hypothetical scenarios containing a number of variables or "attributes" (usually less than five), each of which may have a number of variations, or "levels." Participants are asked to state their preferred choice among competing scenarios (usually two or three scenarios are presented to participants at the same time); in doing so, preferences are revealed without participants explicitly being asked to state their preferred level for each attribute.

Discrete event simulation (DES) a decision-analytic model that simulates the time to progression to one of a discrete set of events.

Economic costs costs related to opportunity costs; that is, facing a choice between two alternatives, those costs of losing the forgone benefits that would be gained if another alternative was chosen.

Effect size a statistical measure of the magnitude of difference between two groups/variables.

Effectiveness how one effect is lower or similar to effects produced in controlled trials; that is, an effect occurs in real practice, within heterogeneous populations and contexts. For instance, if patients do not adhere appropriately to an antipsychotic regimen in daily life (in practice), its effects will fail.

Efficacy means that an intervention produces effects; for example, when comparing an antipsychotic with placebo, benefits from the antipsychotic must be significantly superior to those of the placebo.

Efficiency a measure of the extent to which a particular resource configuration achieves outcomes; usually considered in terms of the relationship between resource "inputs" and "outputs."

Elation a mood comprising feelings of joy, euphoria, triumph, and intense self-satisfaction or optimism; occurs in mania when not grounded in reality.

EuroQoL, five-dimension (EQ-5D) a preference-based health-related quality-of-life measure that includes five health dimensions and either three (EQ-5D-3L) or five (EQ-5D-5L) levels of severity for assessment.

Equality an objectively equal distribution of inputs or outcomes among a population.

Equity the extent to which outcomes from treatment, access to services, and payment for them are distributed fairly across a population; it refers to subjective, or moral, judgement of what is fair. In the area of healthcare this term refers to the fair or just allocation of inputs (healthcare/funding) or outputs (outcomes). This might mean that resources may be distributed unequally with the aim of creating a more equal opportunity to benefit from healthcare, regardless of age or income.

Equivalent annual annuity a value used to estimate annual capital costs, taking into account a discount factor and time horizon.

Evaluative space what we are interested in measuring in terms of outcome; should be related to primary objectives of the evaluation.

Expected preferences preferences usually elicited from among healthy people within the general public. In this case, an individual should express preference for one health state that may occur in the future or to somebody else. For instance, an individual should choose between a psychotic state or depressive state, even without any knowledge of or familiarity with the state, based only on descriptive scenarios.

Expected value of information an approach for quantifying the expected monetary value of reducing uncertainty around a decision problem by obtaining additional or better-quality information through research.

Experienced preferences the preferences of people who suffer from a particular disease or currently present active symptoms of disease, expressed according their own experience of being sick.

Externality is a consequence, resulting from service delivery or goods transaction, that affects a third part not involved in these transactions, that is, an outcome producing beneficial or deleterious effects on other people or sectors of society. A *negative externality* is an adverse consequence to one person of another person's actions in a market transaction, for instance. A *positive externality* is a benefit that indirectly affects people not involved in a market transaction.

Extra-welfarism an approach to evaluation that aims to capture more than just utility; a framework for assessing well-being associated with welfare economics that offers an extension or alternative to the framework of welfarism. Theoretically, this allows for many options in terms of both evaluation space and decision rule; in practice, within health economics, extra-welfarism is often synonymous with health maximization. Also referred to as "non-welfarism." *See* Welfarism.

Fee a payment made to a professional or public organization for advice or services.

First-order uncertainty random variability around a parameter value among individuals in a sample of data.

Fixed costs regular costs not related to consumption; they do not vary over the short term (<1 year). Examples include rent, equipment, and human resources.

Free-market competition a market that is self-regulated by supply-and-demand rules, and in which the allocation of goods and services is efficient.

Friction-costs approach a method that quantifies the future loss of production resulting from the loss of labor caused by an illness, until the absent worker is replaced by another.

Functioning the things that a person does or is in life; a notion arising from the work of Amartya Sen.

General public valuation a method of eliciting preferences from the general public rather than patients or experts.

Generalized linear model (GLM) a type of regression analysis that makes a parametric assumption about the dependent variable.

Generic measure a measure designed to include a broader assessment of a particular outcome, such as generic health-related quality of life; an example is the five-dimension EuroQoL.

Global Burden of Disease (GBD) study the name given to studies that wish to quantify health losses from diseases, injuries, and risk factors; most notably associated with the work of the World Health Organization.

Grandiosity exaggerated feelings of one's importance, power, knowledge, or identity; occurs in delusional disorder and maniac states.

Horizontal equity equal treatment of those who share similar circumstances.

Human capital approach an analysis method that give a monetized value to the loss of labor/paid employment as a result of illness over a lifetime until retirement. The monetized value is calculated as the forgone earnings of the individual employee.

Hypomania a mood abnormality with the qualitative characteristics of mania but somewhat less intense.

Incidence a statistic describing the risk of a disease occurring over a particular time period (i.e., 5000 new cases of disease A occur per year). *See* Prevalence.

Incremental cost-effectiveness plane A plot of mean incremental costs (*x*-axis) and mean incremental outcomes (*y*-axis) of an intervention versus the control treatment, generated using a probability sensitivity analysis.

Incremental cost-effectiveness ratio (ICER) a value representing the additional cost incurred per additional unit of output. An ICER gives an indication of the extra (or incremental) cost of one program for the extra effect it generates over another outcome gained; a ratio of the incremental cost of a new intervention compared with an alternative (normally usual or current care) over the incremental benefit (effectiveness) between the same two options.

Indirect costs costs related to social and economic effects, such as a decrease in workplace production, suicide, early retirement, accidents, income losses, and losses of education years. Usually, indirect costs are called "productivity costs" because the majority of studies covering indirect costs focuses on losses in productivity.

Individual-level simulation *See* Microsimulation.

Interquartile range the range of values between the 25th and 75th percentiles.

Jarque-Bera test a statistical measure model fit.

Joint production production that results from individuals performing more than one activity concurrently. If the time spent on each of these activities is quantified separately and apportioned to each activity in full, the total time spent on the activities will exceed the actual time covered. The impact is that contributions are overestimated. This issue might be dealt with by identifying a particular task as primary or by defining a new activity that covers the two jointly produced activities.

Kruskal-Wallis test a hypothesis test used for two or more comparison groups with continuous or ordinal data.

League table a method of ranking metrics of the effectiveness of interventions against each other, normally based on incremental cost-effectiveness ratios. *See* Incremental cost-effectiveness ratio (ICER).

Logistic regression a type of regression analysis used when the dependent variable is categorical.

Magnitude estimation (ME) a method that elicits preferences through inquiring about the amount of an individual's desire for one health state compared with another. In this case, individuals express their preferences for one health state, taking into account how much they consider one health state better or worse than another; the value is given by the proportion by which one health state is worse than another (e.g., 4 times worse, 10 times better).

Mania a mood state characterized by elation, agitation, hyperactivity, hypersexuality, and accelerated thought and speech (flight of ideas).

Mann-Whitney ***U*** **test** a hypothesis test used for two comparison groups with continuous or ordinal data.

Mapping a method for transforming a non-preference-based outcome measure into a preference-based measure.

Marginal cost-effectiveness ratio (MCER) a value that expresses the changes in cost and effect within one program when it is expanded in scale (e.g., an education program that is rolled out in two regions instead of one). If the size at which a program is provided is flexible, the MCER can give a useful indication of the economies of scale that can occur, which is informative in finding the optimal level of program provision.

Marginal costs the cost of one additional unit estimated based exclusively on the variable costs and takes into account cost variations among individuals.

Market failure market conditions in which the allocation of goods and services are not efficient because of the absence of perfect market competition; therefore the market is not self-regulated and it is not dependent on the rules of supply and demand.

Markov model a state transition model that assumes that the probability of an individual's progression is independent of past health states.

Maximization the aim to obtain the greatest amount of whatever outcome is of interest, within the resources available and irrespective of how outcomes are distributed among society.

Mean (arithmetic) the sum of observed values divided by the number of observations.

Median the middle observed value in a data set.

Mental capital the ability of an individual to use all inner resources (cognitive, emotional, and behavioral) in appropriate ways to fulfill his or her needs and to contribute to others; that is, it represents the balance of experiencing a good quality of life and being able to contribute to society.

Mental disorder Mental disorder is a psychiatric disorder characterized by physical and mental symptoms leading to impairment of global individual's performance, affecting all aspects of his/her social and occupational life and relationships.

Mental health problem Mental health condition refers to individual's well-being negatively affected by factors like violence, stress, work overload, grief, stigma, and other adverse conditions. Mental health conditions are not psychiatric disorders, but they may affect individual's behavior and deserve some level of care. They also constitute a risk factor for developing mental disorders.

Mental health a state of well-being in which an individual realizes his or her own potential, can cope with the normal stresses of life, can work productively and fruitfully, and is able to make a contribution to her or his community.

Micro-costing a method that involves collecting data on the frequency of an individual's consumption of services, usually directly from a patient, family, health and professionals, or from medical records. *See* Bottom-up approach.

Microsimulation a state transition model that simulates the progression of individuals, rather than the entire cohort, at predetermined time intervals.

Missing data data that contain missing values.

Mode the most common value in a data set.

Monte Carlo error variability around output values between simulated samples, generated using discrete event simulation.

Mood a pervasive and sustained feeling that is experienced internally and that, in the extreme, can markedly influence virtually all aspects of a person's behavior and perceptions of the world; distinguished from affect, the external expression of the internal feeling tone.

Multiple imputation a method for imputing missing data based on the distribution of observed data.

Opportunity costs the value of the "next best alternative use" of a resource that is not chosen and is consequently lost forever. For example, the opportunity cost of providing one treatment for depression is the loss of another treatment that could have been provided instead, at the expense of the potential benefits to patients of that other treatment.

Ordinary least squares a type of regression analysis that assumes a continuous dependent variable.

Out-of-pocket expenditure the amount a patient pays for healthcare.

Overhead administrative costs.

Parametric uncertainty *See* second-order uncertainty.

Pareto optimality a situation in which no person can be become better off without making another person worse off.

Park test a statistical measure of model fit.

Patient valuation when preferences are elicited from patients (i.e., those with a particular condition or disease).

Perfect market competition a competitive market in which supply and demand reach an equilibrium whereby there is no wastage in supply and no unmet demand. This is reached through demand, supply, prices, and profits guiding both suppliers' and buyers' decisions about investments.

Person trade-off (PTO) method a method for eliciting the social value of alternative healthcare interventions.

Perspective (of a study) the view, varying from a narrow to comprehensive, from which costs are measured on behalf of different levels of interest: individuals, public health providers, private or insurance companies, employers, governments, society.

Potential Pareto improvement a situation in which those becoming better off could theoretically compensate those becoming worse off and still be better off.

Power calculation a method for establishing an appropriate sample size to identify a statistically significant treatment effect.

Preference an umbrella term defining the choice between options when the metric can be defined as a value (certain option) or utility (uncertain option).

Preference-based measure a type of measure in which the index scoring algorithm is based on preferences elicited using techniques such as standard gamble or time trade-off.

Preference weight a weight that is elicited from a preference-based technique such as the standard gamble or time trade-off techniques. *See* Utility weights.

Presenteeism working while sick, which decreases on-the-job performance because of the presence of health problems.

Prevalence a statistic indicating how many cases of a particular condition are apparent at a particular time point (e.g., as of 2016, 50,000 people have disease A). *See* Incidence.

Probability sensitivity analysis an uncertainty analysis that measures the aggregate impact on model output of varying the values in all model parameters simultaneously by assigning probability distributions to each model parameter.

Psychosis a mental disorder in which thoughts, affective response, ability to recognize reality, and ability to communicate with and relate to others are sufficiently impaired to interfere grossly with the individual's capacity to deal with reality; the classical characteristics of psychosis are impaired reality testing, hallucinations, delusions, and illusions.

Quality-adjusted life year (QALY) a generic outcome measure that combines mortality and morbidity into a single numeric unit whereby the amount of time spent in a health state is multiplied by a weight (bounded by 0 to 1) that denotes the strength of preference for that health state; a metric of effectiveness associated with cost-utility analysis that combines both mortality and morbidity into a single summary score.

R^2 statistic a measure of the explanatory power of a model (regression analysis).

Ramsey regression equation specification error test (RESET) a statistical measure of model fit.

Recall bias the lack of accuracy in respondents' answers to a questionnaire or measure; respondents fail to report past facts because of inaccurate memory.

Recovery a comprehensive model of mental healthcare in which individuals are empowered to overcome the impact of mental disorders and to pursue well-being and a full life despite limitations.

Second-order uncertainty variability around the mean value among samples of data.

Sensitivity (responsiveness) the ability to detect a change in a person's quality of life in response to some direct or indirect effect of a change in the person's actual quality of life; this definition refers to the "sensitivity" of an outcome measure.

Shared costs costs incurred by two or more sectors or activities. For example, a nurse assistant can work in different wards in a general hospital, and when the goal is to estimate the cost of only one of the units, both of these activities should be estimated and discounted for each unit.

Skewed data data that follow a skewed distribution.

Spillover effect an increase in costs for one sector caused by a decrease in costs for another sector.

Standard costs costs extracted from public databases.

Standard deviation a measure of variation around the mean.

Standard error standard deviation of the sampling distribution of the mean.

Standard gamble (SG) a technique used to elicit preferences.

State transition model a model that represents a decision problem in terms of a set of discrete health states and the probabilities of transition between health states.

Structural uncertainty uncertainty in model results attributable to the structure and assumptions of the model.

Sufficiency the aim to obtain enough of the outcome of interest for as many people as possible, within the resources available.

t **Test** a hypothesis test used for two comparison groups.

Time horizon the time interval over which the consequences of a treatment are evaluated.

Time trade-off (TTO) a technique used to elicit preferences.

Top-down approach an approach used to measure unit costs based on average costs obtained from total costs.

Transfer payment a value amount that is considered by economists to be an income redistribution rather than a cost because they are not resources available for consumption and they are not "produced" as goods or services are; examples include social and disability benefits, work compensation payments, and taxes.

Transition probability the probability of an individual progressing into a particular pathway or state in a model.

Utility a metric of preference when the option is uncertain. (Note that *utility* has a number of definitions that also refer to it as a metric of "happiness" or "desire fulfillment, but the former is prominent in this book).

Utility weight a weight assigned to the relevant outcome of interest, mainly associated with cost-utility analysis and quality-adjusted life years; when weights are elicited using a preference-elicitation technique, these weights can also described as :preference weights." *See* Preference weight.

Value a metric of preference when the option is certain; this definition is pertinent to when describing "value" compared with "utility").

Variability *See* First-order uncertainty.

Variable costs costs that vary according to the consumption of services, for instance, food, water, disposables, clothes, electricity, telephone.

Vertical equity unequal treatment of those with unequal circumstances.

Welfare economics a branch of economics that focuses on the aggregated well-being of individuals in a society. *See* Extra-welfarism.

Welfarism an approach to evaluation that has robust foundations in neoclassical welfare economics, wherein the aim is to maximize total utility; a framework for assessing well-being associated with welfare economics.

Wilcoxon rank sum test *See* Mann-Whitney *U* test.

Willingness-to-pay threshold the highest amount a decision maker would be willing to pay for a new intervention compared with an alternative (normally usual or current care); a set central amount or range that determines the monetary incremental cost-effectiveness ratio.

Years of full (or sufficient) capability equivalent a composite measure of (sufficient) capability and well-being in life and quantity of life.

Year lost to disability (YLD) number of years living with disability; one of the estimators of disability used to determine a disability-adjusted life year.

Year of life lost (YLL) number of years lost due to premature mortality; one of the estimators of mortality used to determine a disability-adjusted life year.

Index

D. Razzouk (ed.), *Mental Health Economics*, DOI 10.1007/978-3-319-55266-8

Printed in the USA
CPSIA information can be obtained
at www.ICGtesting.com
LVHW071706190124
769282LV00007B/170